MW00526483

TRUSTS AND ESTATES

Second Edition

■ ■ ■

Jeffrey Evans Stake

Robert A. Lucas Chair and Professor of Law
Indiana University Maurer School of Law

AMERICAN CASEBOOK SERIES®

WEST
ACADEMIC
PUBLISHING

American Casebook Series is a trademark registered in the U.S. Patent and Trademark Office.

© 2020 LEG, Inc. d/b/a West Academic
© 2023 LEG, Inc. d/b/a West Academic
    444 Cedar Street, Suite 700
    St. Paul, MN 55101
    1-877-888-1330

West, West Academic Publishing, and West Academic are trademarks of West Publishing Corporation, used under license.

Printed in the United States of America

ISBN: 978-1-63659-933-5

For Janet, Christopher, Laura, Alison, Sloane, Bernadine,
Robert, Benjamin, Sara, and Jacob,
who have all done so much to make life wonderful.

PREFACE

I have written this book to help me teach a basic course in trusts and estates. It is certainly not a practitioner's guide to the law, as there are many topics and variations in the law of trusts and estates that are not mentioned herein. Relatedly, it is not a treatise or research tool, as will be evident from the paucity of citations for the ideas presented in the book. The cases are edited more lightly than they are in many casebooks (leaving intact much judicial redundancy) in the hope that students will get a better feel for the facts and for the judicial opinions in this area of law. Trusts and estates problems are often family problems, sometimes exacerbated by lawyers, and I hope that this book allows some of those dramas to come through. I have included relatively few cases in the notes on the presumption that this will keep students from thinking that it is important at this stage of their learning to memorize the widely varying laws across many jurisdictions. In the portions of the book that I have authored (which are indicated by each paragraph beginning flush left), I have raised issues of both fairness and efficiency, attempting to stimulate critical thinking about the law and its effects on society. I sincerely hope that students will enjoy thinking about the issues raised by the law of succession as much as I do.

Chapter 1 introduces the constitutional rules regarding succession with a few Supreme Court cases, moves to a basic overview of the priority of claims to decedents' assets, and ends on the broad policy question of how much of their former assets decedents should control after they die. Chapter 2 presents professional responsibility problems, identifies some bars to succession, and touches on the types of property that decedents can control. Chapter 3 discusses the default rules of intestate succession. Chapter 4 is about how to avoid those default rules by making a will. Chapter 5 sets forth will substitutes, primarily trusts (including the rights of creditors to trust assets). Chapter 6 is devoted to problems in the construction of wills and trusts, including the interpretation of language creating present and future interests. Chapter 7 ends the book with a return to the limitations on decedent control of succession, including the Rule Against Perpetuities, protection of surviving spouses, and other constraints imposed for reasons of social policy.

I thank Jon Harkness and the editors at West Academic Publishing for allowing me the time to work through various delays in my completion of the first manuscript and for their quick work in turning it and this second edition into books. My thanks go also to Kyle Langvardt for discussing pedagogical goals and helping me to find cases for this book during its early stages. David Gray provided important substantive comments and Katelyn Klingler suggested changes to the text of the first edition. Margaret Kiel-Morse carefully reviewed half of the second edition and coordinated reviewers of other parts. For their assistance, I am also grateful to Allison Coffey, James Benson, Tyler Riedinger, Daniel Schumick, Abigail Dehmlow, John Moreland, Mantas Grigorovicius, Tayler Belinske, Jason Feuerstine, Lin Ye, Rebecca Boyle, Katlyn VanDrissche, Nathan Wenk, Michael Trescone, Jesse Malone, and Cassie Fitzwater. The many remaining errors are all mine. I thank Joe Hoffmann for encouraging me, initially and repeatedly, to write this book. And I thank my wife, Janet, for her continuing patience and support.

JEFFREY EVANS STAKE

2022 08 28

ACKNOWLEDGMENTS

American Law Institute, Restatement (Third) of Property (1999, 2003, 2011); Restatement (Third) of Trusts (2003, 2007, 2012), copyright © 1999, 2003, 2007, 2011, 2012 by the American Law Institute. All rights reserved. Reprinted with permission.

National Conference of Commissioners on Uniform State Laws (NCCUSL), excerpts from the Uniform Parentage Act (2017); the Uniform Probate Code (1969, 1990, 1993, 1997, 1998, 2008, 2010, 2019); the Uniform Trust Code (2000, 2003, 2004, 2005, 2010); copyright © 1969, 1990, 1993, 1998, 2000, 2003, 2004, 2005, 2008, 2010, 2017, 2019 by NCCUSL. Reprinted by permission of NCCUSL.

Grey, Thomas C., The Hermeneutics File, 58 S. Cal. L. Rev. 211 (1985), reprinted by permission.

Friedman, Lawrence M., A History of American Law, 4th Edition (2019), reprinted by permission.

SUMMARY OF CONTENTS

TABLE OF CONTENTS

TABLE OF CASES

The principal cases are in bold type.

TABLE OF STATUTES

TRUSTS AND ESTATES
Second Edition

CHAPTER 1

INTRODUCTION TO TRUSTS AND ESTATES

■ ■ ■

A. WHAT THIS COURSE IS ABOUT

Trusts and Estates is about succession to wealth. Much of this transmission of wealth occurs by gratuitous transfer, where someone holding title to an asset creates an ownership interest in another person without receiving any assets in return. A transferor in the United States has great, though not unlimited, discretion as to whom to favor. In many cases, the transferor bestows her generosity on a spouse or descendants, but not always. Often the owner will choose to transfer assets to someone outside the family. All of these transfers of wealth fall within the scope of the law and policy examined in this course.

Many different types of transfers are possible. The ownership interest being transferred can be legal title or equitable (beneficial) title, and the underlying asset can be realty or personal property. The transferor may make a transfer that is effective during her life or a transfer that is effective at her death. Transfers at death are made according to the instructions provided by the decedent in a will ("testament") or in a will substitute such as life insurance or a trust. If the decedent does not provide adequate instructions for some assets, the decedent dies "intestate" as to those assets and the transfers are made according to default rules. Whether she makes the transfer during life or at death, and whether in law or in equity, she has many choices as to how much of an interest to transfer. She may choose to transfer all of her interest or only some of it and may choose to transfer a single interest to a single person or to create multiple interests in a number of parties. The recipient of the transfer can be any person legally capable of holding title.

In this course, you should become familiar with some of the language, concepts, processes, institutions, and functions of the law of trusts and estates, one of the primary branches growing from the majestic tree of property law. As with other areas of property law, some of the language of trusts and estates is technical and

1

unintuitive, so one goal is for you to pick up enough of this new tongue to converse with others practicing in the profession and to understand new developments in the law. Reading the materials that follow, you should nurture your capacity to analyze factual situations so that you can predict legal consequences and hone your ability to analyze legal rules so you can predict practical consequences. You should develop a skill, or sharpen your existing skill, for making arguments in modes to which courts and legislatures respond favorably. You should, in the end, have a broad overview of the many and varied rules governing trusts and estates and some of the policy choices embedded in them, in addition to knowledge of the particular rules themselves. Among the various rules, some of those that pose a heightened threat of malpractice will receive special treatment. As with all law, you will often see indeterminate standards in the law of trusts and estates. But you will also find here many rules that are clear, and a lawyer's failure to use those landmarks to guide the client around the legal pitfalls can lead to substantial professional liability.

Knowing something about trusts and estates is important for many lawyers. There are lawyers who make a living at it, others who need to be able to draw wills and trusts to keep their clients' confidence and business, and some who need to know enough to answer questions from members of their families. It might also be useful knowledge when it comes time to sit for the bar exam. Being a trusts and estates lawyer can be emotionally rewarding, as well as financially rewarding, because the trusts and estates lawyer can make people happy by helping them to provide support to others whom they care about. However, it should be kept firmly in mind that this course, however helpful, will not be sufficient to prepare you for competent practice. For example, some clients will have estates that could incur inheritance or estate tax, and successful practice will depend on substantial training in these and other advanced aspects of estate planning. In addition, the reader should also be aware that this book is not a treatise or any other sort of reference work. Not only does it omit some subject areas that a practitioner will need to know, but it also omits many of the variations in the law that can be found across the many jurisdictions making up the United States.

B. LIFE AFTER DEATH

When a person dies, she can no longer hold title to assets, and we must find a new owner for them, or put the assets back into the commons. One possibility is that the state itself succeeds to the assets. Another possibility is that the state chooses who takes next, other than itself. A third possibility, the one you probably assumed coming into this course, is that the state honors the former owner's choice of successor. In the last case, some of her assets pass through probate, and others do not.

In its narrow meaning, "probate", from a Latin word for "prove", refers to the process of proving that a will is valid. If a probate court finds a will to be valid, the will is "admitted to probate". Even when the court finds that the decedent died without a valid will, however, the term "probate" is still used to refer to the process of deciding where the decedent's assets will go next. For the probate assets, the decedent's estate serves as the transitional manager as the assets move along to the next owners, although technically the realty passes immediately to successors. The court appoints a personal representative to manage this probate estate and distribute the assets to the appropriate persons, as approved by the court. The decedent's will may appoint the personal representative, in which case that representative is usually called the "executor". If the will does not appoint an executor, then the personal representative is often called the "administrator with will annexed". Persons who take assets under the will are called "devisees". For a long time, some lawyers distinguished between realty and personalty, with the former passing by devise to devisees and the latter passing by bequest to legatees, but the term "devisees" is now often used to describe both groups. If there is no valid will, the personal representative might be called the "administrator," and recipients who take under the laws of intestate succession are called "heirs". There was a time when lawyers distinguished between realty and personalty passing by intestacy, with the former passing to heirs and the latter passing to next of kin, but the term "heirs" is now commonly used to describe both groups. A person's heirs are not determined until that person's death. *Nemo est haeres viventis.* No one is the heir of the living. The persons who would take if a person were to die are called heirs apparent.

At the death of the owners, their property may also pass outside their probate estates. Depending on the law of the jurisdiction, the methods of transferring property at death and outside of probate can include tenancy by the entirety, joint tenancy, life insurance, other payable on death contracts and accounts, and revocable trusts. When inter vivos (between the living) transfers are added to the mix, it is easy to see that a lot of property passes outside of probate.

Probate serves a number of purposes. First, and most obviously, it provides a process for making sure that the decedent's property passes to those who the decedent wished to be the next owners. Second, it provides evidence of title for those new owners. Third, it provides an opportunity for the decedent's creditors to make claims and be paid before the assets reach the hands of the decedent's beneficiaries. Psychological studies suggest that it is probably less upsetting to a potential recipient for a creditor to take an asset from the estate before the successor thinks she owns it than for the creditor to take the asset from a recipient after she thinks she owns it.

The substance and process of probate differ across jurisdictions. The basis of the probate law in most states was the common law and statutes of England, and many of those rules survive in one form or another. But all states now have statutes that have revamped inheritance law. Many of the state statutes in the past half-century have been based on some version of the Uniform Probate Code (UPC), which was first promulgated in 1969, revised in many ways in 1990, and revised again in some ways in 2008 and 2019. On many points, this course will include common law and UPC variations, but be aware that there are other variations in some states.

The exact process of probate is prescribed by statute and court rules in each jurisdiction, and there are probate practice books for each state detailing that process. You will probably look them up when it comes time to probate a will. In brief, the personal representative seeks letters testamentary or letters of administration in the decedent's domicile. The personal representative may also initiate ancillary administration in any other jurisdictions where realty was owned by the decedent; ancillary probate will be needed in the situs of the realty for that state to recognize the change in ownership and for local creditors to have notice. However, some jurisdictions require that the personal representative be a resident of the state, which could raise the costs for ancillary administration.

Under the UPC, the person asking for letters of administration chooses formal or informal probate. In a formal probate proceeding, the court supervises the personal representative at the major steps of estate administration. Informal probate dispenses with judicial supervision after the court appoints the personal representative. Informal probate also dispenses with the need to bring witnesses to prove the will was validly executed, relying solely on the personal representative's sworn statement that, to the best of the representative's knowledge, the will was validly executed. Although the person asking for letters of administration does not need to give notice before being appointed, she must give notice after appointment to those who either take under the will or will not take because of the will. Because formal proceedings are costly, in time and money, the personal representative often chooses informal probate. However, if any interested party objects to the way the personal representative is handling the estate at any time during administration, that party may file a petition for formal probate and thereby obtain the benefits of judicial review and supervision.

Creditors must make claims against the estate within a limited time; claims made too late are barred by non-claim statutes. Under the UPC, claims are barred four months after the initiation of probate and one year after the death of the decedent. The Supreme Court decided in *Tulsa Professional Collection Services, Inc. v. Pope*, 485 U.S. 478 (1988) that known and reasonably ascertainable creditors must be given actual notice before being barred by a short statute. Newspaper notice is enough for barring other creditors. Statutes barring creditors from making claims more than a year after the decedent's death have not been declared unconstitutional.

The personal representative collects and clears title to the estate's assets, settles claims by the creditors, files tax returns and pays taxes due, and distributes the estate's assets. After that, the estate may be closed. Wrapping up the estate and distributing the assets does not end the worries of the personal representative, however. Even in informal probate, the personal representative remains liable until she is discharged by the probate court or protected by a statute of limitations.

Thus, the decedent usually lives on as a financial and legal entity for at least a short time after bodily death. Yet some people desire to circumvent this short afterlife by avoiding probate. Of course, it is not the afterlife but its costs that they hope to avoid. And probate does have costs. Even if there is no litigation, probate courts charge fees, personal representatives are entitled to a commission and often must be bonded, lawyers charge for filing papers, and appraisers must be paid for their services. However, the benefits of avoiding probate should not be overestimated. Appraisers are often not needed; family members will often serve as personal representatives without pay and without bond; court costs are not huge; and avoiding probate does not obviate the need to file income, estate, and inheritance tax returns. Some costs of probate can be reduced by reducing the assets passing through probate, and the legal tools for doing so include inter vivos gifts, life insurance, transfer-on-death agreements, trusts, joint tenancies, and tenancies by the entirety. For the remaining assets, states allow summary administration for estates that are small enough. Most tangible personalty can be transferred without need for the title-clearing function of probate. (Automobiles are an exception, but many states have statutes allowing the transfer of clear title without probate proceedings.) And the representative of the estate can often collect the claims and assets of the estate by presenting to the bank an affidavit by the decedent's heirs.

C. HISTORICAL NOTES ON CONTROL OF ASSETS AFTER OWNERS DIE

Americans are so accustomed to the assumption that a decedent controls where her wealth goes after she dies that the idea is rarely challenged. The laws relating to the transfer of wealth in the United States assume that owners choose who will take next, within limits to be seen later. But owner control is required by neither the dictates of logic nor unvarying historical precedent. From the time of William the Conqueror in 1066 until the Statute of Wills in 1540, English law did not allow wills of legal interests in land. This is all the more telling when it is realized that land was the key form and source of wealth at that time. Civil law traditions in other countries similarly assumed that the decedent should not control succession to a substantial portion of her assets. Even in the United States, control of succession has been questioned. Writing from Paris in 1789, Thomas Jefferson, in a letter to James Madison, denied that control after death is a natural right:

> The question Whether one generation of men has a right to bind another, seems never to have been started either on this or our side of the water. . . . [T]hat no such obligation can be so transmitted I think very capable of proof. I set out on this ground, which I suppose to be self-evident, '*that the earth belongs in usufruct to the living*': that the dead have

neither powers nor rights over it. The portion occupied by any individual ceases to be his when himself ceases to be, & reverts to the society. If the society has formed no rules for the appropriation of it's lands in severalty, it will be taken by the first occupants. These will generally be the wife & children of the decedent. If they have formed rules of appropriation, those rules may give it to the wife and children, or to some one of them, or to the legatee of the deceased. So they may give it to his creditor. But the child, the legatee, or creditor takes it, not by any natural right, but by a law of the society of which they are members, & to which they are subject.

https://founders.archives.gov/documents/Madison/01-12-02-0248.

COMMENTARIES ON THE LAWS OF ENGLAND
William Blackstone (1766)
Excerpt from Book II, Chapter I, pages 10–13

The most universal and effectual way, of abandoning property, is by the death of the occupant; when, both the actual possession and intention of keeping possession ceasing, the property, which is founded upon such possession and intention, ought also to cease of course. For, naturally speaking, the instant a man ceases to be, he ceases to have any dominion: else, if he had a right to dispose of his acquisitions one moment beyond his life, he would also have a right to direct their disposal for a million of ages after him; which would be highly absurd and inconvenient. All property must therefore cease upon death, considering men as absolute individuals, and unconnected with civil society: for then, by the principles before established, the next immediate occupant would acquire a right in all that the deceased possessed. But as, under civilized governments which are calculated for the peace of mankind, such a constitution would be productive of endless disturbances, the universal law of almost every nation (which is a kind of secondary law of nature) has either given the dying person a power of continuing his property, by disposing of his possessions by will; or, in case he neglects to dispose of it, or is not permitted to make any disposition at all, the municipal law of the country then steps in, and declares who shall be the successor, representative, or heir of the deceased; that is, who alone shall have a right to enter upon this vacant possession, in order to avoid that confusion, which it's becoming again common would occasion. And farther, in case no testament be permitted by the law, or none be made, and no heir can be found so qualified as the law requires, still, to prevent the robust title of occupancy from again taking place, the doctrine of escheats is adopted in almost every country; whereby the sovereign of the state, and those who claim under his authority, are the ultimate heirs, and succeed to those inheritances, to which no other title can be formed.

The right of inheritance, or descent to the children and relations of the deceased, seems to have been allowed much earlier than the right of devising by testament. We are apt to conceive at first view that it has nature on it's side; yet we often mistake for nature what we find established by long and inveterate custom. It is certainly a wise and effectual, but clearly a political, establishment; since the permanent right of property, vested in the ancestor himself, was no *natural*, but merely a *civil*, right. It is true, that the transmission of one's possessions to posterity has an evident tendency to make a man a good citizen and a useful member of society: it sets the passions on the side of duty, and prompts a man to deserve well of the public, when he is sure that the reward of his services will not die with himself, but be transmitted to those with whom he is connected by the dearest and most tender affections. Yet, reasonable as this foundation of the right of inheritance may seem, it is probable that its immediate original arose not from speculations altogether so delicate and refined; and, if not from fortuitous circumstances, at least from a plainer and more simple principle. A man's children or nearest relations are usually about him on his deathbed, and are the earliest witnesses of his decease. They became therefore generally the next immediate occupants, till at length in process of time this frequent usage ripened into general law. And therefore also in the earliest ages, on failure of children, a man's servants born under his roof were allowed to be his heirs; being immediately on the spot when he died. For we find the old patriarch Abraham expressly declaring, that "since God had given him no seed, his steward Eliezer, one born in his house, was his heir."

While property continued only for life, testaments were useless and unknown; and, when it became inheritable, the inheritance was long indefeasible, and the children or heirs at law were incapable of exclusion by will. Till at length it was found, that so strict a rule of inheritance made heirs disobedient and head-strong, defrauded creditors of their just debts, and prevented many provident fathers from dividing or charging their estates as the exigence of their families required. This introduced pretty generally the right of disposing of one's property, or a part of it, by *testament*; that is, by written or oral instructions properly *witnessed* and authenticated, according to the *pleasure* of the deceased; which we therefore emphatically style his *will*. This was established in some countries much later than in others. With us in England, till modern times, a man could only dispose of one third of his movables from his wife and children: and, in general, no will was permitted of lands till the reign of Henry the eighth; and then only of a certain portion: for it was not till after the restoration that the power of devising real property became so universal as at present.

Wills therefore and testaments, rights of inheritance and successions, are all of them creatures of the civil or municipal laws, and accordingly are in all respects regulated by them; every distinct country having different ceremonies and requisites to make a testament completely valid: neither does any thing vary more than the right of inheritance under different national establishments. In England particularly, this diversity is carried to such a length, as if it had been meant to point out the power of the laws in regulating the succession to property, and how futile every claim must be, that has not it's foundation in the positive rules of the state. In personal estates the father may succeed to his children; in landed property he never can be heir, by any the remotest possibility: in general only the eldest son, in some places only the youngest, in others all the sons together, have a right to succeed to the inheritance: in real estates males are preferred to females, and the eldest male will usually exclude the rest; in the division of personal estates, the females of equal degree are admitted together with the males, and no right of primogeniture is allowed.

D. CONSTITUTIONAL RIGHTS FOR A DECEDENT TO CHOOSE A SUCCESSOR OR A SUCCESSOR TO INHERIT

Are these matters, allocation of assets after death and inheritance, matters of right or merely matters of privilege? For some time after William the Conqueror assumed the throne of England, land passed back to the overlord after death. But complete escheat to the overlord proved unsatisfactory, and it became common to transfer land with the assumption that the heir of the grantee would take next, after the overlord skimmed a portion in the form of feudal incidents. These feudal incidents can be seen as a form of estate tax, a tax paid to the overlord. This does not mean that the overlord could sell the land to someone else; the overlord's rights were subject to rights in the heir. Thus, both the heir and the overlord held rights in the land after the death of the owner. Today, of course, both escheat and payment of estate taxes are to the government rather than to human overlords. It is common to think that the land belongs to the heir subject to payment to the state, but one could flip the perspective and say that the state owns the land subject to the heir's right to redeem it by payment of a fraction of its value to the state. Either way, these taxes obviously erode the owner's control of where her assets go after she dies. How much discretion does a state have in imposing taxes on estates and inheritances? The following cases will provide some historical perspective. The reader is advised to maintain focus on the main point of the first two cases. They appear here not to show the niceties of taxation or the duties of executors, but rather to shed some light on the question of whether laws of the United States and the various States establish a right to control the disposition of assets after death.

MAGOUN V. ILLINOIS TRUST & SAVINGS BANK

Supreme Court of the United States, 1898
170 U.S. 283

* * *

This is a bill in equity filed in the circuit court of the United States in and for the Northern district of Illinois by Jessie Norton Torrence Magoun, a resident and citizen of New York, against the trust company, as executor of, and trustee under, the last will and testament of Joseph T. Torrence, deceased, and the county treasurer of Cook county, Ill., both residents and citizens of Illinois, to remove a cloud from the real estate devised by said decedent to the complainant, and to enjoin the first-named defendant from voluntarily paying, and the county treasurer from collecting or receiving, the inheritance tax, amounting to more than $5,000, alleged to be due upon the entire estate of said decedent, and for which the complainant's interest in said estate was contended by the county treasurer to be liable.

The bill set forth the will of the decedent; a description and valuation of the real estate and personal property left by him, amounting in all to $600,000 above his debts; and the demand of the county treasurer for the inheritance tax, which by the act in question is made a lien upon all of said property; the request of the complainant to the defendant trust company not to pay the same, and to contest the constitutionality of the act, to refrain from paying the same voluntarily and without protest, and to await the commencement of legal proceedings to enforce the same; the refusal of the trust company to comply with this request, and its threat and intention to pay said tax at once, voluntarily, which payment could not be recovered if said law should hereafter be declared unconstitutional.

* * *

The trust company answered, admitting the allegations of fact in the bill, but submitting the question of the constitutionality of the law to the court, and praying to be advised of its rights and duties in the premises as executor and trustee aforesaid, and as an officer of the court.

The county treasurer denied that the act was unconstitutional, and admitted the allegations respecting the estate of the deceased, the interest of the complainant therein, the lien of the inheritance tax thereon, and the demand made therefor.

* * *

McKENNA, J.

Legacy and inheritance taxes are not new in our laws. They have existed in Pennsylvania for over 60 years, and have been enacted in other States. They are not new in the laws of other countries. In Tennessee v. Alston, Judge Wilkes gave a short history of them, as follows: "Such taxes were recognized by the Roman law. They were adopted in England in 1780, and have been much extended since that date. Such taxes are now in force generally in the countries of Europe. In the United States they were enacted in Pennsylvania in 1826; Maryland, 1844; Delaware, 1869; West Virginia, 1887, and still more recently in Connecticut, New Jersey, Ohio, Maine, Massachusetts, 1891; Tennessee in 1891, chapter 25 now repealed by chapter 174, acts 1893. They were adopted in North Carolina in 1846, but repealed in 1883; were enacted in Virginia in 1844, repealed in 1855, re-enacted in 1863, and repealed in 1884." Other States have also enacted them—Minnesota, by constitutional provision.

The constitutionality of the taxes has been declared, and the principles upon which they are based explained, in *United States v. Perkins*, 163 U.S. 625, 628.

It is not necessary to review these cases, or state at length the reasoning by which they are supported. They are based on two principles: (1) An inheritance tax is not one on property, but one on the succession; (2) the right to take property by devise or descent is the creature of the law, and not a natural right—a privilege, and therefore the authority which confers it may impose conditions upon it. From these principles it is deduced that the States may tax the privilege, discriminate between relatives, and between these and strangers, and grant exemptions; and are not precluded from this power by the provisions of the respective state constitutions requiring uniformity and equality of taxation.

* * *

In *United States v. Fox*, 94 U.S. 315–321, a law of the State of New York confining devises to natural persons and corporations created under its laws was considered, and a devise of land to the United States was held void. The court said:

"The power of the state to regulate the tenure of real property within her limits, and the modes of its acquisition and transfer, and the rules of its descent, and the extent to which a testamentary disposition of it may be exercised by its owners, is undoubted. It is an established principle of law, everywhere recognized, arising from the necessity of the case, that the disposition of immovable property, whether by deed, descent, or by any other mode, is exclusively subject to the government within whose jurisdiction the property is situated. . . . Statutes of wills, as is justly observed by the court of appeals, are enabling acts, and prior to the statute of 33 Henry VIII there was no general power at common law to devise lands. The power was opposed to the feudal policy of holding lands inalienable without the consent of the lord. The English statute of wills became a part of the law of New York upon the adoption of her constitution in 1777, and, with some modification in its language, remains so at this day. Every person must therefore devise his lands in that state within the limitations of the statute, or he cannot devise them at all. His power is bounded by its conditions."

* * *

In *United States v. Perkins*, 163 U.S. 625, 628, the inheritance tax law of the State of New York was involved. Mr, Justice Brown, speaking for this court, said:

"While the laws of all civilized States recognize in every citizen the absolute right to his own earnings, and the enjoyment of his own property, and the increase thereof, during his life, except so far as the State may require him to contribute his share for public expenses, the right to dispose of his property by will has always been considered purely a creature of statute, and within legislative control. 'By the common law, as it stood in the reign of Henry II, a man's goods were to be divided into three equal parts; of which one went to his heirs or lineal descendants, another to his wife, and a third was at his own disposal; or, if he died without a wife, he might then dispose of one moiety, and the other went to his children; and so, *e converso*, if he had no children, the wife was entitled to one moiety, and he might bequeath the other; but, if he died without either wife or issue, the whole was at his own disposal. Prior to the statute of wills, enacted in the reign of Henry VIII, the right to a testamentary disposition of the property did not extend to real estate at all, and as to personal estate was limited as above stated. Although these restrictions have long since been abolished in England, and never existed in this country, except in Louisiana, the right of a widow to her dower, and to a share in the personal estate, is ordinarily secured to her by statute."

* * *

This brings us to the law in controversy. The appellant attacks both its principles and its provisions—its principles as necessarily arbitrary, and its provisions as causing discriminations and creating inequality in the burdens of taxation.

Is the act open to this criticism? The clause of the Fourteenth Amendment especially invoked is that which prohibits a State denying to any citizen the equal protection of the laws. What satisfies this equality has not been, and probably never can be, precisely defined. * * * Mr. Justice Field said in *Mobile v. Kimball* that this court is not a harbor in which can be found a refuge from illadvised, unequal, and oppressive state legislation. And he observed in another case: "It is hardly necessary to say that hardship, impolicy or injustice of state laws is not necessarily an objection to their constitutional validity."

* * *

The provisions of the statute in regard to the tax on legacies to strangers to the blood of an intestate need further comment.* * *

There are four classes created, and manifestly there is equality between the members of each class. Inequality is only found by comparing the members of one class with those of another. It is illustrated by appellant as follows: One who receives a legacy of $10,000 pays 3 per cent, or $300, thus receiving $9,700 net; while one receiving a legacy of $10,001 pays 4 per cent on the whole amount, or $400.04, thus receiving $9,600.96, or $99.04 less than the one whose legacy was actually $1 less valuable. This method is applied throughout the class.

These, however, are conceded to be extreme illustrations, and we think, therefore, that they furnish no test of the practical operation of the classification. When the legacies differ in substantial extent, if the rate increases, the benefit increases to greater degree.

* * * But neither case can be said to be contrary to the rule of equality of the Fourteenth Amendment. That rule does not require, as we have seen, exact equality of taxation. It only requires that the law imposing it shall operate on all alike, under the same circumstances. The tax is not on money; it is on the right to inherit; and hence a condition of inheritance, and it may be graded according to the value of that inheritance. The condition is not arbitrary because it is determined by that value; it is not unequal in operation because it does not levy the same percentage on every dollar; does not fail to treat "all alike under like circumstances and conditions, both in the privilege conferred and the liabilities imposed." The jurisdiction of courts is fixed by amounts. The right of appeal is. As was said at bar, the Congress of the United States has classified the right of suitors to come into the United States courts by amounts. Regarding these alone, there is the same inequality that is urged against classification of the Illinois law. All license laws and all specific taxes have in them an element of inequality, nevertheless they are universally imposed, and their legality has never been questioned. We think the classification of the Illinois law was in the power of the legislature to make, and the decree of the circuit court is

Affirmed.

———————

Magoun was about the constitutionality of a slightly irrational state law. The next case focuses instead on a federal law, deciding whether a progressive federal tax on inheritances is constitutional.

EDWIN F. KNOWLTON'S SUICIDE.

Straw Goods Manufacturer Kills Himself at His Sister's Home in West Upton, Mass.

WEST UPTON, Mass., Oct. 25.—Edwin F. Knowlton of Brooklyn, N. Y., head of the firm of William Knowlton & Sons, straw goods manufacturers of Upton, committed suicide this morning by shooting at the house of his sister, Mrs. Eben Batchelor, here. He was long a sufferer from neuralgia, and had been ill several days. This morning he shot himself in the head with a revolver, and died soon afterward.

Mr. Knowlton was a son of William Knowlton, who founded one of the best-known straw goods manufacturing houses in this country, and who was a State Senator in Massachusetts. He was born in West Upton in 1834, and, after receiving an academic education, entered his father's employ. He soon became so familiar with the business and showed such ability that his father put him in charge of a branch sales house in Montreal, and later in New York. He then became a partner in the concern and assumed the management of the purchasing, selling, and financial interests of the business. On his father's retirement he became the head of the firm. His brothers, George W., Eben J., and Daniel W. Knowlton, were his partners.

Mr. Knowlton was well known in Brooklyn, where he was a Director in the Brooklyn Trust Company, and of the Phoenix Fire Insurance Company, and a member of the Hamilton and Brooklyn Clubs. Until the marriage of their daughter, Miss Mary C. Knowlton, the Knowltons entertained on a large scale. She was married some years ago to Count Johannes Sierstorpff, and now lives in Berlin. She is Mr. Knowlton's only living child.

The New York Times
Published: October 26, 1898
Copyright © The New York Times

KNOWLTON V. MOORE

Supreme Court of the United States, 1900
178 U.S. 41

WHITE, J.

The act of Congress of June, 1898, which is usually spoken of as the war revenue act, imposes various stamp duties and other taxes. * * * To determine the issues which arise on this record it is necessary to decide whether the taxes imposed are void because repugnant to the Constitution of the United States, and, if they be valid, to ascertain and define their true import.

The controversy was thus engendered: Edwin F. Knowlton died in October, 1898, in the borough of Brooklyn, State of New York, where he was domiciled. His will was probated, and the executors named therein were duly qualified. As a preliminary to the assessment of the taxes imposed by the provisions of the statute, the collector of internal revenue demanded of the executors that they make a return showing the amount of the personal estate of the deceased, and disclosing the legatees and distributees thereof. The executors, asserting that they were not obliged to make the return because of the unconstitutionality of sections 29 and 30 of the statute, nevertheless complied, under protest. The report disclosed that the personal estate was appraised at $2,624,029.63, and afforded full information as to those entitled to take the same. The amount of the tax assessed was the sum of $42,084.67. * * *

* * *

* * * Taxes of this general character are universally deemed to relate, not to property *eo nomine*, but to its passage by will or by descent in cases of intestacy, as distinguished from taxes imposed on property, real or personal, as such, because of its ownership and possession. In other words, the public contribution which death duties exact is predicated on the passing of property as the result of death, as distinct from a tax on property disassociated from its transmission or receipt by will, or as the result of intestacy. Such taxes so considered were known to the Roman law and the ancient law of the continent of Europe, Smith's Wealth of Nations, London ed. of 1811, vol. 3, p. 311. Continuing the rule of the ancient French law, at the present day in France inheritance and legacy taxes are enforced, being collectible as stamp duties. * * *

* * *

In the colonies of Great Britain death duties, as a general rule, obtain. Some of the statutes are modeled upon those of the mother country, and levy taxes on legacies, etc., passing, measured by their value and on the estate proper. Others, again, have merely the estate tax without the legacy tax. * * *

* * *

As early as 1797 Congress imposed a legacy tax. * * * In this act, as in the English legacy duty statute of 1780 and supplementary statutes, the mode of collection provided was by stamp duties laid on the receipts evidencing the payment of the legacies or distributive shares in personal property, and the amount was, like the English legacy tax, charged upon the legacies and not upon the residue of the personal estate.

* * *

Once more, quite recently, the subject was considered in *Magoun v. Illinois Trust & Savings Bank*, 170 U.S. 283. * * * In the course of its opinion the court, speaking through Mr. Justice McKenna, after briefly adverting to the history of inheritance and legacy taxes in other countries, referred to their adoption in many of the States of the Union as follows:

* * *

"It is not necessary to review these cases or state at length the reasoning by which they are supported. They are based on two principles: 1. An inheritance tax is not one on property, but one on the succession. 2. The right to take property by devise or descent is the creature of the law, and not a natural right—a privilege, and therefore the authority which confers it may impose conditions upon it. From these principles it is deduced that the States may tax the privilege, discriminate between relatives, and between these and strangers, and grant exemptions; and are not precluded from this power by the provisions of the respective state constitutions requiring uniformity and equality of taxation."

Thus, looking over the whole field, and considering death duties in the order in which we have reviewed them,—that is, in the Roman and ancient law, in that of modern France, Germany and other continental countries, in England and those of her colonies where such laws have been enacted, in the legislation of the United States and the several States of the Union, the following appears: Although different modes of assessing such duties prevail, and although they have different accidental names, such as probate duties, stamp duties, taxes on the transaction, or the act of passing of an estate or a succession, legacy taxes, estate taxes, or privilege taxes, nevertheless tax laws of this nature in all countries rest in their essence upon the principle that death is the generating source from which the particular taxing power takes its being, and that it is the power to transmit, or the transmission from the dead to the living, on which such taxes are more immediately rested.

Having ascertained the nature of death duties, the first question which arises is this: Can the Congress of the United States levy a tax of that character? * * * The act of 1797, which ordained legacy taxes, was adopted at a time when the founders of our government and framers of our Constitution were actively participating in public affairs, thus giving a practical construction to the Constitution which they had helped to establish. Even the then members of the Congress who had not been delegates to the convention which framed the Constitution must have had a keen appreciation of the influences which had shaped the Constitution and the restrictions which it embodied, since all questions which related to the Constitution and its adoption must have been, at that early date, vividly impressed on their minds. It would, under these conditions, be indeed surprising if a tax should have been levied without question upon objects deemed to be beyond the grasp of Congress because exclusively within state authority. It is, moreover, worthy of remark that similar taxes have at other periods and for a considerable time been enforced; and, although their constitutionality was assailed on other grounds held unsound by this court, the question of the want of authority of Congress to levy a tax on inheritances and legacies was never urged against the acts in question. * * *

* * *

The contention is that because the statute exempts legacies and distributive shares in personal property below $10,000, because it classifies the rate of tax according to the relationship or absence of the relationship of the taker to the deceased, and provides for a rate progressing by the amount of the legacy or share, therefore the tax is repugnant to that portion of the first clause of section 8 of article 1 of the Constitution, which provides that "duties, imposts, and excises shall be uniform throughout the United States."

* * *

The necessities which gave birth to the Constitution, the controversies which preceded its formation, and the conflicts of opinion which were settled by its adoption, may properly be taken into view for the purpose of tracing to its source any particular provision of the Constitution, in order thereby to be enabled to correctly interpret its meaning.

The paralysis which the Articles of Confederation produced upon the Continental Congress because of the want of power in that body to enforce necessary taxation to sustain the government needs no more than statement. And the proceedings of the Congress during the confederation afford abundant evidence of the constant effort which was made to overcome this situation by attempts to obtain authority from the States for Congress to levy the taxes deemed by it essential, and thus relieve it from the embarrassment occasioned by the fact that all demands for revenue depended for fulfilment wholly upon the action of the respective States. Despite the constant agitation as to the subject and the abundant discussions which took place in relation to it during the period of the confederation, in the whole of the proceedings not a word can be found which can give rise to even the suggestion that there was then any thought of restraining the taxing power with reference to the intrinsic operation of a tax upon individuals. * * *

The proceedings of the Continental Congress also make it clear that the words "uniform throughout the United States," which were afterwards inserted in the Constitution of the United States, had, prior to its adoption, been frequently used, and always with reference purely to a geographical uniformity and as synonymous with the expression "to operate generally throughout the United States." * * *

* * *

We add that those who opposed the ratification of the Constitution clearly understood that the uniformity clause as to taxation imported but a geographical uniformity, and made that fact a distinct ground of complaint. * * *

* * *

Lastly, it is urged that the progressive rate feature of the statute is so repugnant to fundamental principles of equality and justice that the law should be held to be void, even although it transgresses no express limitation in the Constitution. Without intimating any opinion as to the existence of a right in the courts to exercise the power which is thus invoked, it is apparent that the argument as to the enormity of the tax is without merit. It was disposed of in *Magoun v. Illinois Trust & Savings Bank.*

The review which we have made exhibits the fact that taxes imposed with reference to the ability of the person upon whom the burden is placed to bear the same have been levied from the foundation of the government. So, also, some authoritative thinkers, and a number of economic writers, contend that a progressive tax is more just and equal than a proportional one. In the absence of constitutional limitation, the question whether it is or is not is legislative and not judicial. The grave consequences which it is asserted must arise in the future if the right to levy a progressive tax be recognized involves in its ultimate aspect the mere assertion that free and representative government is a failure, and that the grossest abuses of power are foreshadowed unless the courts usurp a purely legislative function. If a case should ever arise, where an arbitrary and confiscatory exaction is imposed bearing the guise of a progressive or any other form of tax, it will be time enough to consider whether the judicial power can afford a remedy by applying inherent and fundamental principles for the protection of the individual, even though there be no express authority in the Constitution to do so. That the law which we have construed affords no ground for the contention that the tax imposed is arbitrary and confiscatory is obvious.

It follows from the foregoing opinion that the court below erred in denying all relief, and that it should have held the plaintiff entitled to recover so much of the tax as resulted from taxing legacies not exceeding $10,000, and from increasing the tax rate with reference to the whole amount of the personal estate of the deceased from which the legacies or distributive shares were derived. For these reasons

> *The judgment below must be reversed, and the case be remanded, with instructions that further proceedings be had according to law and in conformity with this opinion, and it is so ordered.*

Compare the approach taken by the Supreme Court in the two cases above to the Supreme Court's analysis in the next case below.

HODEL V. IRVING

Supreme Court of the United States, 1987
481 U.S. 704

O'CONNOR, J.

The question presented is whether the original version of the "escheat" provision of the Indian Land Consolidation Act of 1983 effected a "taking" of appellees' decedents' property without just compensation.

I

Towards the end of the 19th century, Congress enacted a series of land Acts which divided the communal reservations of Indian tribes into individual allotments for Indians and unallotted lands for non-Indian settlement. This legislation seems to have been in part animated by a desire to force Indians to abandon their nomadic ways in order to "speed the Indians' assimilation into American society," and in part a result of pressure to free new lands for further white settlement. Two years after the enactment of the General Allotment Act of 1887, Congress adopted a specific statute authorizing the division of the Great Reservation of the Sioux Nation into separate reservations and the allotment of specific tracts of reservation land to individual Indians, conditioned on the consent of three-fourths of the adult male Sioux. Under the Act, each male Sioux head of household took 320 acres of land and most other individuals 160 acres. In order to protect the allottees from the improvident disposition of their lands to white settlers, the Sioux allotment statute provided that the allotted lands were to be held in trust by the United States. Until 1910, the lands of deceased allottees passed to their heirs "according to the laws of the State or Territory" where the land was located, and after 1910, allottees were permitted to dispose of their interests by will in accordance with regulations promulgated by the Secretary of the Interior. Those regulations generally served to protect Indian ownership of the allotted lands.

The policy of allotment of Indian lands quickly proved disastrous for the Indians. Cash generated by land sales to whites was quickly dissipated, and the Indians, rather than farming the land themselves, evolved into petty landlords, leasing their allotted lands to white ranchers and farmers and living off the meager rentals. The failure of the allotment program became even clearer as successive generations came to hold the allotted lands. Thus 40-, 80-, and 160-acre parcels became splintered into multiple undivided interests in land, with some parcels having hundreds, and many parcels having dozens, of owners. Because the land was held in trust and often could not be alienated or partitioned, the fractionation problem grew and grew over time.

A 1928 report commissioned by the Congress found the situation administratively unworkable and economically wasteful. Good, potentially productive, land was allowed to lie fallow, amidst great poverty, because of the difficulties of managing property held in this manner. In discussing the Indian Reorganization Act of 1934, Representative Howard said:

> "It is in the case of the inherited allotments, however, that the administrative costs become incredible. . . . On allotted reservations, numerous cases exist where the shares of each individual heir from lease money may be 1 cent a month. Or one heir may own minute fractional shares in 30 or 40 different allotments. The cost of leasing, bookkeeping, and distributing the proceeds in many cases far exceeds the total income. The Indians and the Indian Service personnel are thus trapped in a meaningless system of minute partition in which all thought of the possible use of land to satisfy human needs is lost in a mathematical haze of bookkeeping."

In 1934, in response to arguments such as these, the Congress acknowledged the failure of its policy and ended further allotment of Indian lands.

But the end of future allotment by itself could not prevent the further compounding of the existing problem caused by the passage of time. Ownership continued to fragment as succeeding generations came to hold the property, since, in the order of things, each property owner was apt to have more than one heir. In 1960, both the House and the Senate undertook comprehensive studies of the problem. These studies indicated that one-half of the approximately 12 million acres of allotted trust lands were held in fractionated ownership, with over 3 million acres held by more than six heirs to a parcel. Further hearings were held in 1966, but not until the Indian Land Consolidation Act of 1983 did the Congress take action to ameliorate the problem of fractionated ownership of Indian lands.

Section 207 of the Indian Land Consolidation Act—the escheat provision at issue in this case—provided:

"No undivided fractional interest in any tract of trust or restricted land within a tribe's reservation or otherwise subjected to a tribe's jurisdiction shall descendent [sic] by intestacy or devise but shall escheat to that tribe if such interest represents 2 per centum or less of the total acreage in such tract and has earned to its owner less than $100 in the preceding year before it is due to escheat."

Congress made no provision for the payment of compensation to the owners of the interests covered by § 207. The statute was signed into law on January 12, 1983, and became effective immediately.

The three appellees—Mary Irving, Patrick Pumpkin Seed, and Eileen Bissonette—are enrolled members of the Oglala Sioux Tribe. They are, or represent, heirs or devisees of members of the Tribe who died in March, April, and June 1983. Eileen Bissonette's decedent, Mary Poor Bear-Little Hoop Cross, purported to will all her property, including property subject to § 207, to her five minor children in whose name Bissonette claims the property. Chester Irving, Charles Leroy Pumpkin Seed, and Edgar Pumpkin Seed all died intestate. At the time of their deaths, the four decedents owned 41 fractional interests subject to the provisions of § 207. The Irving estate lost two interests whose value together was approximately $100; the Bureau of Indian Affairs placed total values of approximately $2,700 on the 26 escheatable interests in the Cross estate and $1,816 on the 13 escheatable interests in the Pumpkin Seed estates. But for § 207, this property would have passed, in the ordinary course, to appellees or those they represent.

Appellees filed suit in the United States District Court for the District of South Dakota, claiming that § 207 resulted in a taking of property without just compensation in violation of the Fifth Amendment. The District Court concluded that the statute was constitutional. It held that appellees had no vested interest in the property of the decedents prior to their deaths and that Congress had plenary authority to abolish the power of testamentary disposition of Indian property and to alter the rules of intestate succession.

The Court of Appeals for the Eighth Circuit reversed. Although it agreed that appellees had no vested rights in the decedents' property, it concluded that their decedents had a right, derived from the original Sioux allotment statute, to control disposition of their property at death. The Court of Appeals held that appellees had standing to invoke that right and that the taking of that right without compensation to decedents' estates violated the Fifth Amendment.[1]

* * *

III

The Congress, acting pursuant to its broad authority to regulate the descent and devise of Indian trust lands, enacted § 207 as a means of ameliorating, over time, the problem of extreme fractionation of certain Indian lands. By forbidding the passing on at death of small, undivided interests in Indian lands, Congress hoped that future generations of Indians would be able to make more productive use of the Indians' ancestral lands. We agree with the Government that encouraging the consolidation of Indian lands is a public purpose of high order. The fractionation problem on Indian reservations is extraordinary and may call for dramatic action to encourage consolidation. The Sisseton-Wahpeton Sioux Tribe, appearing as *amicus curiae* in support of the Secretary of the Interior, is a quintessential victim of fractionation. Forty-acre tracts on the Sisseton-Wahpeton Lake Traverse Reservation, leasing for about $1,000 annually, are commonly subdivided into hundreds of undivided interests, many of which generate only pennies a year in rent. The average tract has 196 owners and the average owner undivided interests in 14 tracts. The administrative headache this represents can be fathomed by examining Tract 1305, dubbed "one of the most fractionated parcels of land in the world." Tract 1305 is 40 acres and produces $1,080 in income annually. It is valued at $8,000. It has 439 owners, one-third of whom receive less than $.05 in annual rent and two-thirds of whom receive less than $1. The largest interest holder receives $82.85 annually. The common denominator used to compute fractional interests in the property is 3,394,923,840,000. The smallest heir receives $.01 every 177 years. If the tract were sold (assuming the 439 owners could agree) for its estimated $8,000 value, he would be entitled to $.000418. The administrative costs of handling this tract are estimated by the Bureau of Indian Affairs at $17,560 annually.

---

[1] The Court of Appeals, without explanation, went on to "declare" that not only the original version of § 207, but also the amended version not before it, 25 U.S.C. § 2206, unconstitutionally took property without compensation. Since none of the property which escheated in this case did so pursuant to the amended version of the statute, this "declaration" is, at best, dicta. We express no opinion on the constitutionality of § 207 as amended.

This Court has held that the Government has considerable latitude in regulating property rights in ways that may adversely affect the owners. The framework for examining the question whether a regulation of property amounts to a taking requiring just compensation is firmly established and has been regularly and recently reaffirmed. As THE CHIEF JUSTICE has written:

> "[T]his Court has generally 'been unable to develop any "set formula" for determining when "justice and fairness" require that economic injuries caused by public action be compensated by the government, rather than remain disproportionately concentrated on a few persons.' Rather, it has examined the 'taking' question by engaging in essentially ad hoc, factual inquiries that have identified several factors—such as the economic impact of the regulation, its interference with reasonable investment backed expectations, and the character of the governmental action—that have particular significance." *Kaiser Aetna v. United States*, 444 U.S., at 175.

There is no question that the relative economic impact of § 207 upon the owners of these property rights can be substantial. Section 207 provides for the escheat of small undivided property interests that are unproductive during the year preceding the owner's death. Even if we accept the Government's assertion that the income generated by such parcels may be properly thought of as *de minimis,* their value may not be. While the Irving estate lost two interests whose value together was only approximately $100, the Bureau of Indian Affairs placed total values of approximately $2,700 and $1,816 on the escheatable interests in the Cross and Pumpkin Seed estates. These are not trivial sums. There are suggestions in the legislative history regarding the 1984 amendments to § 207 that the failure to "look back" more than one year at the income generated by the property had caused the escheat of potentially valuable timber and mineral interests. Of course, the whole of appellees' decedents' property interests were not taken by § 207. Appellees' decedents retained full beneficial use of the property during their lifetimes as well as the right to convey it *inter vivos*. There is no question, however, that the right to pass on valuable property to one's heirs is itself a valuable right. Depending on the age of the owner, much or most of the value of the parcel may inhere in this "remainder" interest. See 26 CFR § 20.2031–7(f) (Table A) (1986) (value of remainder interest when life tenant is age 65 is approximately 32% of the whole).

The extent to which any of appellees' decedents had "investment-backed expectations" in passing on the property is dubious. Though it is conceivable that some of these interests were purchased with the expectation that the owners might pass on the remainder to their heirs at death, the property has been held in trust for the Indians for 100 years and is overwhelmingly acquired by gift, descent, or devise. Because of the highly fractionated ownership, the property is generally held for lease rather than improved and used by the owners. None of the appellees here can point to any specific investment-backed expectations beyond the fact that their ancestors agreed to accept allotment only after ceding to the United States large parts of the original Great Sioux Reservation.

Also weighing weakly in favor of the statute is the fact that there is something of an "average reciprocity of advantage," to the extent that owners of escheatable interests maintain a nexus to the Tribe. Consolidation of Indian lands in the Tribe benefits the members of the Tribe. All members do not own escheatable interests, nor do all owners belong to the Tribe. Nevertheless, there is substantial overlap between the two groups. The owners of escheatable interests often benefit from the escheat of others' fractional interests. Moreover, the whole benefit gained is greater than the sum of the burdens imposed since consolidated lands are more productive than fractionated lands.

If we were to stop our analysis at this point, we might well find § 207 constitutional. But the character of the Government regulation here is extraordinary. In *Kaiser Aetna v. United States*, 444 U.S., at 176, we emphasized that the regulation destroyed "one of the most essential sticks in the bundle of rights that are commonly characterized as property—the right to exclude others." Similarly, the regulation here amounts to virtually the abrogation of the right to pass on a certain type of property—the small undivided interest— to one's heirs. In one form or another, the right to pass on property— to one's family in particular—has been part of the Anglo-American legal system since feudal times. The fact that it may be possible for the owners of these interests to effectively control disposition upon death through complex *inter vivos* transactions such as revocable trusts is simply not an adequate substitute for the rights taken, given the nature of the property. Even the United States concedes that total abrogation of the right to pass property is unprecedented and likely unconstitutional. Moreover, this statute effectively abolishes both descent and devise of these property interests even when the passing of the property to the heir might result in consolidation of property—as for instance when the heir already owns another undivided interest in the property.[2] Since the escheatable interests are not, as the United States argues, necessarily *de minimis,* nor, as it also argues, does the availability of *inter vivos* transfer obviate the need for descent and devise, a *total* abrogation of these rights cannot be upheld. But cf. *Andrus v. Allard,* 440 U.S. 51 (1979) (upholding abrogation of the right to sell endangered eagles' parts as necessary to environmental protection regulatory scheme).

In holding that complete abolition of both the descent and devise of a particular class of property may be a taking, we reaffirm the continuing vitality of the long line of cases recognizing the States', and where appropriate, the United States', broad authority to adjust the rules governing the descent and devise of property without implicating the guarantees of the Just Compensation Clause. The difference in this case is the fact that both descent and devise are completely abolished; indeed they are abolished even in circumstances when the governmental purpose sought to be advanced, consolidation of ownership of Indian lands, does not conflict with the further descent of the property.

There is little doubt that the extreme fractionation of Indian lands is a serious public problem. It may well be appropriate for the United States to ameliorate fractionation by means of regulating the descent and devise of Indian lands. Surely it is permissible for the United States to prevent the owners of such interests from further subdividing them among future heirs on pain of escheat. It may be appropriate to minimize further compounding of the problem by abolishing the descent of such interests by rules of intestacy, thereby forcing the owners to formally designate an heir to prevent escheat to the Tribe. What is certainly not appropriate is to take the

---

[2] JUSTICE STEVENS argues that weighing in the balance the fact that § 207 takes the right to pass property even when descent or devise results in consolidation of Indian lands amounts to an unprecedented importation of overbreadth analysis into our Fifth Amendment jurisprudence. The basis for this argument is his assertion that none of appellees' decedents actually attempted to pass the property in a way that might have resulted in consolidation. But the fact of the matter remains that before § 207 was enacted appellees' decedents had the power to pass on their property at death to those who already owned an interest in the subject property. This right too was abrogated by § 207; each of the appellees' decedents lost this stick in their bundles of property rights upon the enactment of § 207. It is entirely proper to note the extent of the rights taken from appellees' decedents in assessing whether the statute passes constitutional muster under the *Penn Central* balancing test. This is neither overbreadth analysis nor novel. * * *

extraordinary step of abolishing both descent and devise of these property interests even when the passing of the property to the heir might result in consolidation of property. Accordingly, we find that this regulation, in the words of Justice Holmes, "goes too far." *Pennsylvania Coal Co. v. Mahon*, 260 U.S., at 415. The judgment of the Court of Appeals is

Affirmed.

JUSTICE BRENNAN, with whom JUSTICE MARSHALL and JUSTICE BLACKMUN join, concurring.

* * *

JUSTICE STEVENS, with whom JUSTICE WHITE joins, concurring in the judgment.

* * *

I

* * *

* * * [T]he Bureau of Indian Affairs of the Department of the Interior issued a memorandum * * *

The memorandum then explained how Indian landowners who wanted their heirs or devisees, rather than the tribe, to acquire their fractional interests could avoid the impact of § 207. It outlined three ways by which the owner of a fractional interest of less than two percent of a tract could enlarge that interest to more than two percent.[6]

* * *

'Tis better to give than to receive.'

Did the heirs apparent have a constitutional right to receive, or did the ancestors have a right to give? Congress in the twentieth century

---

[6] The memorandum stated: "To assure the effectiveness of a will or heirship succession under state law, any Indian owner within the above category (if he or she is concerned that the tribe rather than his or her heirs or devisees will take these interests) may purchase additional interests from coowners pursuant to 25 CFR 151.7 and thereby increase his/her ownership interest to more than two percent. Another alternative is for such an owner to convey his/her interest to coowners or relatives pursuant to 25 CFR 152.25 and reserve a life estate, thus retaining the benefits of the interest while assuring its continued individual, rather than tribal, ownership. A third alternative, if feasible, is to partition the tract in such a way as to enlarge the owner's interest in a portion of said tract.

"Indians falling within the above category and who are presently occupying, or in any other way using, the tract in question should especially be advised of the aforementioned alternatives."

realized that Congress in the nineteenth century had made a mistake in passing a statute that individualized ownership of tribal lands. After the bundles of sticks became scattered splinters, Congress tried to correct the earlier error by bringing some small individual interests back into tribal ownership without paying for them or making the tribe pay for them, but the Supreme Court said that the attempt was unconstitutional. Does it make sense to require compensation when the administrative costs of compensating are greater than the amount of compensation?

The Fifth Amendment "Takings Clause" says, "nor shall private property be taken for public use, without just compensation." As you learned in your property course, takings law is complicated. A court will find a taking per se if the government has deprived an owner of a fundamental attribute of property. Even if the government has not deprived the owner of a fundamental attribute (an essential stick in the bundle of sticks), a court can find a taking in fact on the basis of three factors: the economic impact on the claimant, the extent of interference with distinct investment-backed expectations, and the character of the governmental action. *See Penn Central Transportation Co. v. City of New York*, 404 U.S. 104 (1978).

What was the basis of the Court's decision? The Court said, "[s]ince the escheatable interests are not, as the United States argues, necessarily *de minimis*, nor, as it also argues, does the availability of *inter vivos* transfer obviate the need for descent and devise, a total abrogation of these rights cannot be upheld." If the statute abrogated an essential right, then it would not matter if the value was *de minimis*. Additionally, by saying, "[i]n holding that complete abolition of both the descent and devise of a particular class of property *may* be a taking . . ." (italics added), the Court indicated that it was not automatically a taking. Moreover, the Court discussed the "investment-backed expectations" of the owners, which it would not need to do if it were establishing a *per se* taking. And finally, in subsequent decisions, the Court has not listed transfer by descent and devise as a fundamental attribute.

Chester Irving could have accomplished a transfer of property at death with a trust, such as "I transfer all my rights in land to a revocable trust, for the benefit of myself for life and then to Mary Irving." Critics have said that the Court did not pay enough attention to that practical alternative. Trusts need not be complicated, and they have fewer formal requirements than wills.

The *Hodel* Court emphasized that "both descent and devise are completely abolished". But it is possible that either one could be completely abolished without violating the constitution. The *Hodel* Court itself said, "It may be appropriate to minimize further compounding of the problem by abolishing the descent of such interests by rules of intestacy." And the Court in an earlier case, *Irving Trust Co. v. Day*, 314 U.S. 556, 562 (1942), said, "[n]othing in the Federal Constitution forbids . . . abolish[ing] the power of testamentary disposition." So, neither descent nor devise is an essential right, but abolishing both is constitutionally risky.

How can we reconcile *Hodel* with *Magoun v. Illinois Trust* and *Knowlton v. Moore*? First, the statute in *Hodel* deprived the owner of rights to transmit rather than depriving successors of rights to receive. Second, the older cases involved the taxing power. Perhaps the government should have styled the program in *Hodel* as a tax. *Cf., National Federation of Independent Business v. Sebelius*, 567 U.S. 519 (2012) (upholding the incentive involved in the Affordable Care Act as a tax). Third, the older cases were not takings cases. However, in *Knowlton v. Moore*, the Court implied that the Takings Clause would not be applicable when it said, "If a case should ever arise, where an arbitrary and confiscatory exaction is imposed bearing the guise of a progressive or any other form of tax, it will be time enough to consider whether the judicial power can afford a remedy by applying inherent and fundamental principles for the protection of the individual, even though there be *no express authority in the Constitution* to do so. That the law which we have construed affords no ground for the contention that the tax imposed is arbitrary and confiscatory is obvious." (Emphasis added.)

During the *Hodel* litigation, Congress amended the statute to give the decedent power to devise to other owners of the land, but not to non-owners. Did that make the statute constitutional? In *Babbitt v. Youpee*, 519 U.S. 234 (1997), the Court found that the reform failed to make the statute constitutional because the group of permissible transferees might not include descendants. The Court thus established that an owner has a right not just to transmit by devise or descent to *someone*, but to transmit to *relatives*, as it had signaled in *Hodel*. In 2004, Congress tried again, passing the American Indian Probate Reform Act, which supplanted state law for American Indian reservations. As amended by that Act, § 207 provides that trust land may be devised to any descendant, another owner of the same parcel, the Indian tribe, or any Indian. If there is no will, a surviving spouse gets a life estate in trust land. There are special rules for small fractional interests. (The law also allows tribes to supplant the new federal scheme with their own probate rules.)

Another example of the disaster that can come from the devolution of property by intestate succession is what has happened to "heirs property" (or "heirs' property"). As you have seen, when an owner dies without a will, the owner's property devolves to heirs by intestate succession rather than to devisees by testate succession. If there is more than one heir, they hold as tenants in common. If those owners die with multiple heirs and without a will, the land is further divided into smaller shares in the next generation. At this point, a new problem can arise, one not seen in *Hodel*. Each of the tenants in common has the power to sell a share in the land to anyone. An outsider can buy an interest and, no matter how small the interest, can force a partition of the land. Given the difficulties of a partition in kind, a court will often order a partition by sale. At the auction, many of the family members will lack access to the resources needed to bid up the price, and the outsider may end up buying the rest of the land for a bargain bid. This process has been especially devastating to Black American ownership of farmland because of both a high frequency of intestacy and reduced access to the capital needed to outbid better-heeled bidders. The result has been that many Black families have lost their homes and sources of employment, contributing to the gap in wealth between White and Black Americans.

Twenty-one states have reduced this heirs-property problem by enacting the Uniform Partition of Heirs Property Act. The Act requires the land being partitioned to be appraised. The owners not wishing to sell can buy out the owner who petitioned for partition at the proportionate value of that appraisal. If no owner buys out the petitioner, the land will be partitioned in kind unless that would work great prejudice to all the owners. If the land is partitioned by sale, it cannot be sold below the appraised value.

These heirs-property problems are not limited to Black Americans, although they have been hit especially hard. Another problem with heirs property arose after Hurricane Katrina when owners could not prove their titles well enough to qualify for grants to rebuild their homes.

E. PRIORITY OF CLAIMS TO ASSETS AFTER AN OWNER'S DEATH

There are at least three options for what to do with assets after the death of the owner. One is for the government to own the assets, which we call escheat. A second is for the government to specify which private parties take next. A third is for the government to enforce the decedent's choices as to which private parties take next. In theory, there is a fourth option, which is to declare the assets available to all, held in a commons or subject to first occupation, but that would occasion "confusion" in the words of Blackstone. Americans have, through the law, chosen to combine all of the first three above.

The next sections of this subchapter set out very briefly the priority of claims to the assets held by decedents before their death. Before describing this succession to assets, perhaps it should be noted that the death of one owner does not ordinarily terminate the interests of other owners. If X and Y own an asset together, Y's death usually does not terminate X's interest. An exception to this is that some interests do terminate with the death of another person. For example, when A and B hold as long as both are alive, the death of one deprives both of their interests. We will get to such interests under the heading of present and future interests, much later in the book.

1. SECURED CREDITORS

Just as the death of one co-owner does not usually deprive other co-owners of their interests, the death of an owner does not deprive secured creditors of their security interests in the property pledged to them as security for the debt. Secured creditors have priority to their collateral. Expenses for burial and estate administration may also come off the top of the decedent's estate.

2. FAMILY

The law declares that the first claimants to the assets that formerly belonged to the decedent are private parties, private parties specified by the government rather than the decedent. The law favors two groups in this way, family and creditors. First, ahead of unsecured creditors, in the states following the Uniform Probate Code (UPC), three rules protect the surviving spouse and family of a decedent domiciled in the state. The homestead allowance in UPC

§ 2–402 offers $22,500 to the surviving spouse. (Regarding domestic partnerships and similar relationships, the UPC advises states to "add appropriate language" to references to "spouse" or "marriage".) If there is no surviving spouse, minor and dependent children share the homestead allowance. The protection of exempt property in UPC § 2–403 provides $15,000 worth of property to the surviving spouse. If there is no surviving spouse, children share the exempt property. The homestead allowance and exempt property may change with the cost of living under UPC § 1–109. The family allowance in UPC § 2–404 provides a reasonable allowance from the estate during estate administration to the surviving spouse and dependent children. Under UPC § 2–405, the personal representative may pay the family allowance in a lump sum up to $27,000. Under UPC § 2–213, all of these rights can be waived. Unless provided otherwise, these amounts are not chargeable against shares passing under the decedent's will.

3. UNSECURED CREDITORS

The second group of private parties favored by the law is unsecured creditors. Unsecured creditors of the decedent take after family members take their homestead and family allowances and exempt property. Under "non-claim" statutes, creditors have a limited amount of time to make their claims against the estate. *See, e.g.,* UPC §§ 3–801, 3–803.

These family and creditor groups have a right to a portion of the decedent's former assets in spite of the intent of the decedent. In other words, they take before the will or rules of intestate succession are applied.

4. GOVERNMENTS, VIA TAXES

The claims next in priority are those of the governments themselves, reminding us of a feudal lord's right to a "relief" payment from the heir. These claims come in the form of taxes, of two different types. Estate taxes are imposed by the Federal Government and about a dozen state governments and the District of Columbia. Estate taxes allocate to the government a portion of the assets formerly belonging to the decedent, with that portion being determined in part by the net value of those assets. Inheritance taxes, which are imposed by about a half dozen states, are calculated on each inheritance separately. Inheritance taxes often vary according to the recipient, with exemptions for surviving spouses and sometimes children. The federal estate tax and most state estate and inheritance taxes apply only to estates that are above certain thresholds. In theory, one might say that these taxes take priority over the claims of the family. However, as a practical matter, the exclusions of at least $1,000,000 under the estate taxes and the exemptions of spouses under the inheritance taxes have the effect of giving higher priority to the small claims of the family under the homestead allowance, personal property exemption, and family allowance.

5. SURVIVING SPOUSES

After taxes, the surviving spouse has additional rights against the estate in the form of community property in some states and in the form of the spousal elective share (sometimes called the forced share) in non-community-property states. These rights will be given a closer look later in this book.

6. ALLOCATIONS BY THE DECEDENT

Laws in all states provide that a decedent may allocate any assets remaining after the family, the creditors, the state, and the spouse have been paid. A competent decedent can exercise that power by executing a will or trust. However, even for this portion of the assets, the law places some limits on the decedent's choices. A good portion of this course will be spent on the rules governing wills and trusts.

7. DEFAULT RULES

And finally, if there are assets remaining after the allocations above, all states provide default rules for allocating those residual assets. These default rules could be viewed as an allocation by the government because the rules are written by legislatures. But an allocation pursuant to the default rules could also be viewed as an allocation by the decedent because the decedent has the power to override the statutes of intestate succession. We will examine these default rules before we reach the rules on wills and trusts, which are better understood as intended deviations from the rules of intestacy, which apply if an owner takes no action.

F. POLICY REGARDING THE EXTENT OF DECEDENT CONTROL OVER SUCCESSION

The *Knowlton* Court said that the policy choices relating to death taxation were up to the legislature. What choices should the legislature make? When an owner dies, should the next taker of the property be determined by reference to unavoidable rules of law or by reference to the intent of the former owner? Can you think of arguments for determining succession by reference only to fixed rules of law? Why do we currently let owners decide where any assets go next? Is it because doing so efficiently allocates assets, because it results in good incentives, because it is administratively inexpensive, because it is demanded by justice, because people would lose respect for the law if it were otherwise, or for some other reason? Which assets and how much of them should be allocated by the former owner?

1. CONTROL OF ASSETS WITH POTENTIALLY HIGH IDIOSYNCRATIC VALUE

(a) Moveable Personalty

At the moment of death, many decedents own many items of moveable personal property. Some of these items, such as those with sentimental worth, have a much higher subjective value to one person than to anyone else. A granddaughter might treasure her grandmother's engagement ring simply because it was her grandma's and get far more utility from owning it than would be indicated by its market value. If personalty were allocated to the state upon death, an auction could be used to attempt to find the person who values it most highly, but the administrative costs might overwhelm the subjective value the auction is intended to protect. In addition, an auction is not always won by the person who gets the most utility from the asset. If the person for whom the item has the highest subjective value is relatively short of funds, the auction could misallocate the item. There are two limitations that might come into play. One, the liquidity constraint, is that the person with the highest reservation price might not be able to bid that price because she cannot scare up the money in time. The other, the declining marginal utility of wealth, is that the person who gets more utility from the thing might also value money more highly. A billionaire might not care too much about the grandmother's ring, but if he wants it at all, he might outbid the granddaughter for it, even if the ring would generate more utility in the granddaughter's hands. Society could achieve even greater utility by auctioning the ring to the billionaire and giving the proceeds to the granddaughter, but that result could also be achieved by allocating the ring to the granddaughter and allowing the granddaughter to auction it to the billionaire. To achieve either result, the initial allocation (whether the ring or the proceeds) must be made to the granddaughter.

There is an additional, practical problem with assigning moveable personalty to the state after the death of the former owner. If that were the law, unethical friends and relatives close to the decedent might simply steal the decedent's property before the government showed up to make its claim. The same can happen, of course, when those assets pass under a will to anyone who is not near the assets at the time of death, but the problem is worse when the next owner is the government for a couple of reasons. First, opportunities for theft are greater. Immediately after death, the government is not present to guard the assets against thieves and, later, unlike most devisees or intestate successors, the government has no knowledge of what personalty the decedent had before death and would have a hard time discovering the theft. Sending guards to protect the state's assets immediately after death does not seem like a good idea. Second, if the law says the former owner's property goes to the government, a lot of the people that do have an opportunity to steal will have a greater incentive to steal than they would have if they thought the law might allocate some of the property to them. Assigning the decedent's moveable personalty to his next of kin or legatees reduces both the opportunities and incentives for theft.

For these reasons, the law ought to grant to the decedent control of subsequent ownership of all of the tangible personalty that the typical decedent would own at her death. This rule requires some limit, for if there were none, those approaching death might convert all of their assets into tangible personalty. A simple exclusion of some value should suffice to limit the opportunities and incentives for theft of tangible personalty in all but a few cases. What should that value be?

(b) Homes, Family Farms, Family Businesses

A similar case could be made for some homes, farms, and businesses, all of which can have a subjective value to the family, especially a surviving spouse and children. The case is not as strong, however, because it is much less common for a survivor to hang on to a house for sentimental reasons than to hang on to a grandmother's wedding ring. There is an additional reason for keeping the assets in the family. It could be the case that the surviving family members, practiced in operating the assets, might manage them more efficiently than anyone else. In such cases, it might be a good idea to allocate homes, family farms, and small businesses to the surviving relatives.

Of course, doing this would require a much larger exclusion from estate tax than the exclusion needed to preserve the sentimental value of tangible personalty. Indeed, this argument has been used to support the idea of eliminating the estate tax entirely, and bills have been introduced in Congress to do so. As a result, some time ago, the Congressional Budget Office (CBO) studied the issue, attempting to determine how many family farms and businesses would be forced to sell off assets to pay estate taxes under various assumptions. It found that, in the year 2000, if taxes had been 55% on the estate above a $3,500,000 exclusion, there would have been 94 family businesses and 65 family farms that owed estate taxes. Of these, only 41 businesses and 13 farms would have lacked sufficient liquid assets to pay that tax, requiring the sale of some of the business or farm.[1] The CBO study shows that the estate tax does make it difficult for some families to continue with the historical operation of their businesses and farms, but the number of such cases is small enough to raise doubts as to any substantial impact on the productivity of the nation.

2. CONTROL OF ASSETS WITH TYPICALLY LOW IDIOSYNCRATIC VALUE

It seems clear that there ought to be some threshold below which an estate stays in private hands, passing either under the direction of the decedent or automatically to heirs. What to do with assets above an initial exclusion is a more difficult policy question. And it is an important question because essentially all of the nation's assets will be freed from their owners within a century or less. As above, the benefits of decedent control must be weighed against the benefits of state control, but for most assets exceeding an excluded amount, we need not worry about protecting subjective value. If idiosyncratic value is not a concern, how much control ought the law to grant to decedents? Beyond the exclusion, should decedents control 0%, 100%, or something in between?

---

[1] Note that sometimes a portion of a family farm can be sold without much harm to the remainder from the severance. Often family farms include pastures and crop lands that are not contiguous with the remainder of the farm, and those parcels could often be sold to others without impeding the operation of the remaining farm. In addition, a business or farm need not be sold when a loan could be obtained to pay the taxes. Indeed, the government itself could lend the cash for the taxes to the farmers and business owners to spread the burden over any number of years by paying interest at the government's prevailing borrowing rate on the unpaid portion of the tax.

Before we address this question and related issues, one thing ought to be noted. If the government imposes a tax on assets at death, it will need to impose some kind of tax on transfers during life to prevent owners from avoiding the tax at death by making transfers just before death. Because of the relatively easy substitution of inter vivos gifts for testamentary gifts, all gifts should be treated in a unified manner.

The question for now is, when a person dies, and after we allocate a portion of that person's personalty as she wished, how should society divide up the remaining assets held by the decedent the moment before death? In particular, how much should be owned by the government and how much by individuals chosen by the decedent? As we saw above, one way to frame this issue is to ask how much tax the estate should pay. But framing the question this way begs the question by assuming the decedent still owns the assets and the state is imposing a tax upon her. The opposite view is that the government owns all of the assets and grants to the former owner the privilege of controlling where some of them go next. The goal here is to start with a conceptually clean slate that assumes neither of the above and then to decide how the decedent's estate (above the exclusion) should be divided. What considerations should enter into the determination of that division of the estate? Should the division between the state and individual successors depend on the degree of taxation imposed on the assets when they were earned? Should the division depend on the size of the whole estate, or should it depend on the size of the portions taken by successors?

(a) Fairness

An argument sometimes heard is that it is fair for the decedent to control assets after death because the assets are his stuff. Put the other way around, it is unfair or immoral for the government to take property away from the dead former owner.[2] Both versions of this argument fail to recognize that the whole issue being discussed here is, who is the next owner of the property the decedent used to own. To say that property is taken from the decedent is to assume it is the decedent's property, which assumes the answer to the question we are asking.

---

[2] To tax assets after death, "is immoral because it empowers the state to seize private property without just compensation." Charles Kadlec, Why the Death Tax is the Dumb Tax, http://www.forbes.com/sites/charleskadlec/2012/07/30/why-the-death-tax-is-the-dumb-tax/2/.

A less tautological argument for giving decedents some control relates to the relationship between older and younger generations. As a matter of fairness, children might owe some emotional support to their parents and other caretakers, who have often given them much. Giving the older generation control of some wealth after death creates an incentive for the younger generation to pay them back by giving them some attention before they die. Other cultures have norms that help the elderly, but in ours, something more concrete might be needed. By allowing decedents some control over ownership after they die, the law gives them a lever for prying generosity out of the younger generation. If this is the theory, how much control do we need to give the older generation in order for the younger generation to repay them fairly? Would an exclusion of $1,000,000 or $5,000,000 be enough in most cases?

Speaking of just deserts, what is the justice in allowing inheritance? Some of those who inherit great wealth have done nothing to deserve an inheritance far greater than average. They are getting something for nothing, a windfall. Some would say that they are unjustly enriched. On the other side of the flipped coin, many of those who inherit nothing have done nothing to justify giving them a smaller initial endowment than that given the average member of society. These differences in inheritance cascade down through the generations.

The germ of another argument for allocating a portion of estates to society can be found in a famous article by Walter Blum and Harry Kalven, The Uneasy Case for Progressive Taxation, 19 U. Chi. L. Rev. 428 (1951–1952). The article analogizes the rewards offered by our free-market economic system to the rewards offered to contestants in a race. Some contestants in our free-market "race" are rewarded with riches for winning the race. Those who lose the race are punished with poverty. Such a system appears fair because the outcome depends on the performance of each runner. But does it? The fact is that the contestants do not start the race the same distance from the finish line. Some line up a step or more ahead, with the advantages that come from being well-nourished, or from attending good schools, or from being hired by family members, or from being able to access capital from parents or grandparents. Studying families that moved from one county to another, economists Raj Chetty and Nathaniel Hendren found that the longer a child lives in a poor neighborhood, the less that child earns later in life. See Justin Wolfers, Why the New Research on Mobility

Matters, N.Y. Times, May 4, 2015, http://nyti.ms/1DO7qqd. For a child in a family at the 25th percentile of national income, every year that child spends in Baltimore City reduces that child's later earnings by 0.86 percent, for a total loss of about one-sixth for a child who spends all his childhood in that county. By contrast, growing up in DuPage County, Illinois, would grant a child an earnings advantage of 0.76 percent per year, for an income gain of almost one-sixth compared to the national average.

There is nothing wrong with people helping whomever they wish to help and nothing wrong with people taking the help offered, as far as the rules of the game allow it. But it is the rules of the game that we are discussing. Should we allow these advantages to change the free-market race as much as they do? Would we allow children of Olympic gold medalists to start their races ahead of the children of others as a reward for having won the races they did? This argument is not that the disparity between winning and losing races is too large, a point to be discussed below, but that some contestants do not get a fair start. Estate taxation has the potential to reduce the lead gained from inheritance by providing capital for food, housing, and education for poor children, moving their starting line a little closer to that for children in the middle class.

Another fairness argument relates to the disparity between outcomes, the distribution of wealth across the population. John Rawls suggested that we might determine a just distribution by imagining what distribution we would choose if we did not know which role we would play in the socio-economic hierarchy. Of course, not all people would choose the same distribution because we differ in many ways, including our attitudes toward incentives to work and our aversion to risk. Nevertheless, it is interesting to see what sort of distribution people consider to be optimal. Michael Norton and Dan Ariely asked people in the United States to choose an ideal distribution of wealth for the country. Of the three choices allowed, the actual wealth distribution in the United States garnered less than ten percent of the choices, while distributions with more equality were preferred by most of those surveyed. The rules for allocating the property of decedents play a role in the distribution of assets across society. At present, most of the federal estate tax falls upon the top 1% of the holders of wealth in the U.S. Therefore, if there were no estate tax, the disparity between poor and rich would likely increase. Should the median voter's preferred distribution be adopted as a target for the distribution of American wealth? Should we put the question of the ideal distribution to a referendum?

A different sort of fairness argument focuses on the source of wealth. It might be said that labor creates wealth, so it is fair to reward labor. Likewise, capital creates wealth, so it is fair to reward capital, too. And part of the reward can be the ability to control who takes next. If that is true for capital, it is true for both kinds of capital, public as well as private. On this theory, society, too, is entitled to its reward for providing capital. If taxes on income to an individual during life are inadequate to justly reward society for contributing capital to the generation of that wealth, society is entitled to a return on its capital at the death of the owner. Of course, the heir will also pay income taxes, so the idea is not that society is being cashed out as an owner. The point here is to recognize that the income stream from taxes during life might not be as high as the income stream that can be justly allocated to the capital provided by society.

How much of the income is due to society's capital contribution? Most wealth today comes from activities that would be impossible without substantial social infrastructure, including physical and intellectual capital. We see far because we stand on the shoulders of giants. But let us not forget that giants stand on the shoulders of ordinary people. From those who imagined to those who implemented, countless souls have built institutions that enable the creation of great wealth. How far would we have progressed and how rich would any of us be without the widely distributed invention of language? Without societies, including their linguistic, legal, social, and economic networks, people with good ideas and great industriousness would not get far. The most productive people would achieve more than anyone else, but their rewards would be small. What would Paul McCartney, Steve Jobs, Carl Lewis, Taylor Lautner, or Thomas Kinkade have earned if they were born in an earlier era? Are they more talented than Johann Sebastian Bach, Johannes Gutenberg, Jesse Owens, Edwin Booth, or Vincent Van Gogh? Social, economic, and legal institutions today create opportunities for hard work and creativity to generate wealth reserved in the past for kings. The queen bee may pride herself on her awesome productivity, but she'd be nowhere without a hive. It is often noted that the inventor would be nothing without the factory worker's efforts and the state's grant of monopoly, but the point here is broader than that. It is the multiplicative power of networks that levers individual effort into global movement. How much credit goes to the hand on the lever, and how much to the many who made the lever and the fulcrum? Given a society's contribution to the creation of wealth, how much of that wealth ought society to claim upon a person's death?

A related question is whether society's contribution should be viewed as different depending on the way in which wealth is developed. Some people save their wages, compensation paid for their labor and talents. Some people save profits from their capital, property that is more profitable because it is protected by the state. Some people save the gains from activities protected by the state from competition. Doctors, for example, earn more income because laws protect them from competition from others who would sell competing (albeit usually inferior) services at lower prices. Authors earn more income because the state protects them from those who would copy their writings. Those who have marketable persona are protected against the use of their image without their consent. In such cases, both personal effort and the law are directly responsible for some of the individual's wealth. Should the role of the state in producing income during life matter to the taxation of savings at death?

The division of assets at death could be designed to reflect the relative contributions of the decedent and the capital provided by society less the returns to capital already granted to society. To put it in terms of taxes, the estate tax could approximate the difference between the income due to society's capital and the income tax paid before death. Would it be fair, on that theory or another, for estate taxes to be higher on estates that were amassed from capital, as opposed to labor, because income from capital is taxed at lower rates than income from wages? Some gains are never taxed under the income tax. Suppose that a person buys a sports team for $3,000,000,000 and later dies. If, just after his death, his estate sells his interest for $5,000,000,000, his $2,000,000,000 in gains would avoid income taxation. Should the estate tax be higher for income that escapes the income tax? Would that be practical?

One last argument might be that we simply think or feel that it is just and fair for children to inherit whatever belonged to their parents, be it infinite or infinitesimal. It is possible that people would harbor this intuition even if the law were to say that assets belong to the state after the death of the owner. In 1918, the Soviet Union entirely abolished inheritance, but that law was repealed in short order, perhaps in part because it offended a sense of justice. How far does this sense of fairness extend, in terms of wealth and in terms of generations? Is the first million dollars the same as the 500th? Consider a second generation who inherited all of their wealth, adding nothing of their own. When they die, should all of their assets go to the third generation? Should they be given as much control of their assets after death as those who made the money by their labor? Should taxation be the same or should they be taxed more because they did not earn their money? Should the answer depend on how much the first generation was taxed at death? And what about the third generation?

(b) Efficiency

In addition to fairness, policy discussions in this course will often consider the goal of efficiency. One easy argument for giving people some control of their assets after they die is that doing so makes them happy while they are alive. Perhaps it even fosters a sense of responsibility for society to say to people that it will honor their intent in allocating assets after they die.

On the other hand, there are arguments for allocating some control to the state. One argument starts with the idea of public goods. Public goods are goods that have both of two characteristics: they are non-rivalrous and non-excludable. A good that is non-rivalrous (or non-preclusive) is one that can be consumed (enjoyed) by one person without interfering with consumption by another. When I enjoy the security provided by nuclear deterrence, or the illumination from streetlights, or the benefits of good laws, or clean air, or flood control, it does not preclude you from enjoying them as well. This is not to say that such goods are all good. Nuclear weapons have their dark side, and streetlights add to light pollution and use energy. But, up to a point, enjoyment by one does not preclude enjoyment by another. A good that is non-excludable is one that when supplied to one person becomes available to all, or at least all within a region. Again, once the government protects your classmates from darkness, flooding, or foreign attack, that protection is similarly available to you. Many benefits of good government, and in a democracy the benefits of good voting, are widely distributed. There is no practical way to provide the benefit to one without providing it to others. Usually, the free market will not supply an efficient level of public goods because there is little profit in providing something that, once it is bought by one person, will be available to others who did not pay for it. In short, we need governments to provide public goods.

To provide public goods, the government needs a source of capital. Assuming the government is not going to make money by selling goods or services, or liquidating public assets, or stealing from outsiders, the capital must come from its citizens. But which citizens? If we needed one dollar of public goods, should we take the dollar from a billionaire or from you? It would probably cause less pain to take it from the billionaire. At some point, however, the next dollar will cause more pain to the billionaire than to you. As a matter of minimizing the pain of providing public goods, there comes a time when we need to shift from billionaires to other sources. But that is not the only consideration. If we were to tax you only after first reducing the wealth of wealthier people to something near your level, we would undermine incentives for those others to be productive. On the other hand, as suggested above, failing to reward public capital appropriately might also be inefficient. Efficient taxation, whether via income taxes or estate and gift taxes, involves a balancing of those and other concerns.

Those are not the only components of the efficiency analysis. We must also take into account the happiness generated by letting owners continue to control the disposition of their wealth after they die. It makes me happy to know that the state will honor my request that my assets go to the persons named in my will. This might be particularly important in the case of goods to which I have a sentimental attachment. But the point applies as well to goods with no idiosyncratic value. It makes me feel good now to know that my children will have support if I die. We care about nearly all sources of subjective well-being,[3] and one important source is the enjoyment from knowing one controls where assets are flowing.

The benefits of decedent control also include the good incentives it creates and the bad incentives it avoids. One benefit of decedent control over the disposition of property after death is the incentive to continue being productive. If decedents have too little control of assets above the exclusion, they might reduce their productivity while alive. One counterpoint to this is that gifts reduce the incentives for the recipients to be productive during their lives. Since gratuitous transfers usually shift assets from older to younger people, the reduction in beneficiaries' incentives for productivity might outweigh transferors' incentives to remain productive.

---

[3]   One source of enjoyment that we do not count on the benefit side of a cost-benefit analysis is gain from another person's pain, schadenfreude.

If the law gives decedents too little control of assets after they die, people might go beyond reducing their productivity to actually destroying their assets while they are alive rather than leaving them to the government. In other words, increasing escheat to the state might lead to increased consumption of wealth. We do not want people to push their Cadillacs over cliffs just to spite the government. While most rich Americans (those with assets above the exclusion) would not be so spiteful, some might be, and their spite could result in erasures of societal wealth.

Some people argue against taxing estates by claiming that it interferes with capital formation. Taking capital from the private sector will probably reduce capital investment by the private sector. But that is only half of the picture. Taxing reduces private capital formation, but failing to tax interferes with state capital formation in the form of roads, buildings, health, and education. Some opponents of taxation argue that individuals trying to make money will invest capital better than government officials who do not have that profit incentive to stimulate their efforts. But how many people would carry the argument so far as to say that we should invest no capital in roads, police cars, national defense, or, say, courts? Even if we assume the government is substantially less efficient at management of resources, at some point government formation of capital is more important than additional private formation. Where the next dollar of capital would generate the most societal wealth is an empirical question, one that cannot be solved by pure theory.

In addition to the tradeoff between public and private capital formation, there is a tradeoff between types of taxation, as well as between taxes and deficits. If taxing estates raises revenue, that revenue could be used to form public capital, reduce other taxes, reduce the deficit, or a combination of the three. The discussion of the relative efficiency of various taxes is beyond the scope of this book but would need to be included in any comprehensive discussion of the efficiency of taxing estates.

(c) Promotion of Families

It has been suggested that the law promotes families by allowing decedents to control their wealth and distribute it within the family. Families are a key dimension of our social network and are worth fostering. Assuming that is a goal, however, is there any empirical evidence that inheritance helps more than hurts family structure? Are richer families more cohesive than poorer families? If wealth increases family cohesion, does it do so infinitely, or is there a point at which allocation of wealth to the government might do more for families than allocation to families of high wealth? Does the ability of the decedent to send assets out of the family increase family cohesion? Both in litigated disputes and in disputes that never get to court, the willingness of the law to follow a decedent's instructions could end up dividing families rather than bringing them together. As you read the cases in this book, ask yourself whether the families involved would have ended up stronger if the state had allocated the decedent's assets directly, or had even kept control of the decedent's assets itself, rather than attempting to defer to the choices made by the decedent.

(d) Democracy

Especially since political campaigns have become expensive and the Supreme Court has decided that giving money is speech, vast disparities in money have led to vast disparities in political power. Candidates, including those who are already legislators, executives, and even judges, cannot afford to ignore the interests of those who contribute heavily to their campaigns. Conversely, reducing disparities in wealth might reduce disparities in political influence, increasing the level of democracy. In addition, Paul Krugman has suggested that wealth disparities are related to partisanship in politics. Our government might function in a less partisan way if wealth divisions were not so extreme.

CHAPTER 2

PRELIMINARY ISSUES

■ ■ ■

A. LAWYERING PROBLEMS ARISING FROM WEALTH TRANSFERS

Lawyers sometimes put themselves in precarious positions when they draft wills and trusts. Indeed, trusts and estates practice is one of the top practices when it comes to ethics complaints. This chapter will take a brief look at a couple of the problems that can arise. Some problems are conflicts of interest that the lawyer fails to anticipate, as we will take up in a bit. Other problems are created when the lawyer makes a mistake in drafting, as you will see in a number of cases later in the book.

1. DUTIES TO INTENDED BENEFICIARIES

Clearly, a lawyer is liable to the client if the lawyer injures the client by malpractice. But what about others, persons who are not clients but who are persons the client might have intended to benefit from the lawyer's work? To whom is the lawyer liable when she commits malpractice? To whom should she be liable?

PARKS V. FINK
Court of Appeals of Washington, Division 1, 2013
293 P.3d 1275

LAU, J.

In this attorney negligence case, nonclient Terry Parks alleges that attorney Janyce Fink owed him a duty of care to promptly execute the will naming him as a prospective beneficiary. To impose a duty in this case would severely compromise the attorney's duty of undivided loyalty to the client and impose an untenable burden on the attorney-client relationship. We therefore hold that an attorney owes no duty of care to a prospective beneficiary to have a will executed promptly.

FACTS

Testator John J. Balko suffered from terminal cancer. He signed a will prepared by attorney Alan Montgomery in the presence of two witnesses and a notary public on November 9, 2005, leaving specific gifts to John Rich and Victoria Doyle and the residue of the estate to "Betty Rich" and Craig Eckland in equal shares. It is undisputed that the name "Betty Rich" was a clerical error and Balko meant "Betty Parks," his aunt.

Attorney Janyce Fink performed various legal services for Balko from 2001 until Balko's death in 2007. She met with Balko—who was hospitalized for cancer treatment—in March 2006 to discuss the "Betty Rich" error in the 2005 will. At Balko's direction, Fink drafted a new will correcting this error. Fink stated this was "essentially a 'blank' Will for [Balko] to fill in because [Fink] was concerned about the error in his 2005 Will and the fact that he was preparing to have a stem cell transplant. . . ." The draft will left Balko's estate to "Betty Parks" and contained several blanks requiring Balko's attention. Fink brought the will to Balko in the hospital on the evening of April 26, 2006. Balko reviewed the document and either he or Fink handwrote into one of the blanks: "If Betty Parks does not survive me, I give the residue of my estate as follows: *Terry Parks (son of Betty Parks)*." (Emphasis indicates handwriting in the blank space). Balko also filled in several other blanks, initialed each handwritten insertion, and signed and dated all of the signature blocks.

Fink testified that she did not know why Balko signed the draft will.[3] She claimed she "didn't bring it to him with the idea that this was going to be the evening that he ultimately signed this document." She stated that she "brought [the new will] to him to take and review, fill out, thinking that either the next day or the day after, he would actually sign it in front of two witnesses and have a notary available." She brought no witnesses to the April 26 meeting because she did not intend to conduct a formal signing ceremony that day. In her answer to Parks's interrogatories, Fink stated, "There was no intention to execute a final Will at that time—I knew full well that there were no notaries who could attest to the witnesses' signatures in the hospital in the evening." Fink stated her "intent

---

[3] Fink hired Watson Blair, an active practitioner in the area of trusts and estates, as an expert to comment on duty and standard of care for lawyers relating to preparation and execution of wills. Blair testified in his declaration, "It is not uncommon to have clients fill in blanks on a document and then write their name in the signature block (as another blank) and then give the document to the attorney to be retyped."

was for [Balko] to fill out the 'blank' Will then give the document back to [her] to type up a clean version for him to sign at a later date and in front of two witnesses and the notary." Fink stated she brought the document to Balko "for him to look at, to write anything in there if he wanted [her] to take it back and redraft it."

Fink testified that she advised Balko on April 26 that the new will was invalid until he had it witnessed and notarized. Fink testified that she "very plainly explained to [Balko] that, without two witnesses watching him sign his Will, and then expressly attest to said signing, the document was not any good and would not serve to distribute his assets upon his death." Fink left that day "knowing that [Balko] was very clear that the 2006 Draft Will was not valid" and Fink "understood that [Balko] did not want to do further work on the Will until 'he was feeling better.'"

Fink testified that she took the signed draft with her to her office for safekeeping and kept it in an envelope stamped "original." She testified she regularly stored documents for Balko because he did not want to keep documents in the hospital. Fink testified that on several occasions after April 26, she advised Balko that he should formally sign the will in front of witnesses and a notary, but Balko repeatedly refused, grew agitated, and claimed he wanted to wait until he was feeling better. Fink testified that she wrote and hand delivered three letters to Balko—in September 2006, January 2007, and March 2007—explaining each time that he should have the new will witnessed and notarized if he wanted to revoke the 2005 will. She also stated that she brought other blank wills to Balko after April 2006—at least once with a notary present—but Balko "wouldn't do it. He wanted to wait until he felt better."

Alan Montgomery's declaration testimony indicates that he discussed the 2005 will with Balko in September 2006. According to Montgomery,

[Balko] said the name 'Betty Rich' in the 2005 Will was wrong, that it should have been Betty Parks, and that Betty Parks had already died leaving Craig Eckland as the main beneficiary under that will. [Balko] said that "Terry" will be his main heir instead of Craig Eckland, and needed to change his will but wanted to think about it more before doing so.

Montgomery never discussed the April 2006 draft will with Balko and had "no knowledge about what [Balko] might have understood about its validity or how it affected the 2005 Will."

Parks disputes these facts. He submitted two declarations by Balko's girl friend, Victoria Doyle. In the first declaration, Doyle stated that because Betty Parks's health was fragile, Balko "wanted Betty Parks' son and his cousin, Terry Parks, to take Betty Parks's place in case something happened to her." Doyle claimed Balko "never wavered or changed his mind on that." Doyle stated that in April 2006, Balko came back to his hotel one day "feeling very relieved because he had just signed and finalized a new will Ms. Fink had prepared and brought to him at the hospital." Doyle claimed Balko assured her that all wills and legal papers were taken care of and were stored at Fink's office. Doyle claimed that when Balko's health worsened, Fink "began panicking about the fact that [Balko] might never wake up from his coma." Doyle claimed that around the time Balko died, Fink suggested that Doyle and Parks sign the 2006 will and then "find" the will.

In her second declaration, Doyle testified that in early 2006, she and Balko learned that Betty Parks was terminally ill. Doyle stated that shortly after learning this, Balko told her he was going to add Terry Parks to his will in case Betty predeceased him. Doyle stated that in April 2006, Balko told her he "was relieved because his will was signed and everything was in order."

Parks also submitted declarations by his wife, Elizabeth, and Betty Parks's live-in caretaker, Lisa Kane. Elizabeth stated that in July 2007, Parks called her and told her that "Mr. Balko's lawyer, Ms. Janyce Fink, had just told him he was the main beneficiary in Mr. Balko's will." Kane testified that she knew "without a shadow of a doubt that Mr. Balko wanted his money to go first to Betty Parks after his death, but if she passed away before Mr. Balko, Mr. Balko wanted his money to go to Mr. Terry Parks, who could use the money for the missing children charity."

In Parks's responses to Fink's first set of interrogatories, he claimed that on July 10, 2007, Fink "told [him] in private that Mr. Balko's will was in order and that [he] was the main beneficiary." He also claimed that on July 11, Fink "told [him] that she and [he] would be co-executors or co-personal representatives for Mr. Balko's estate." According to Parks, Fink told him they "needed to find the notarized and witnessed 2006 will" and Fink "said that she gave Mr.

Balko the 2006 will that was signed but not witnessed to have it witnessed and notarized." Parks claimed that on July 12, doctors told them they should consider taking Mr. Balko off life support and Fink "asked whether [they] could get the doctors to make Mr. Balko 'lucid' so that we can get the will signed and witnessed." Parks also claimed that on July 14, after the decision to take Mr. Balko off life support, Fink spoke with him in private and "suggested that she would leave the unwitnessed 2006 will in Mr. Balko's hotel room, and Laurie Doyle and [he] could sign as witnesses on the 2006 will and 'find' the 2006 will before our scheduled dinner the next day. . . ." Parks also claimed Fink asked him to sign an agreement to hire a lawyer to represent Fink and Parks and hopefully get "the 2006 will probated in court even though it was not witnessed or notarized." A copy of this purported agreement appears in the record but is not signed or initialed by any of the parties. The agreement states only that Dussault Law Group will serve as attorney for Fink and Parks "with regard to Probate of the Estate of [Balko]." A letter from Fink to Dussault also appears in the record. In that letter, Fink acknowledged signing the attorney-client fee agreement and stated that she and Parks were going to Balko's safe deposit box to inventory its contents.

Regarding Parks's allegations regarding her conduct around the time Balko died, Fink stated that because of Balko's history of "having gone independently to Al Montgomery to have the 2005 Will prepared, [she] was not 100% certain that [she] knew what all he had done in regards to Wills. . . ." After Balko died, Fink wanted to find out if he had formalized another will before his death, so she asked Parks and Doyle to "keep an eye out for documents that were notarized and/or witnessed, and, later, mentioned to them [she] was interested in finding documents dated April 2006." Fink stated that she and Parks hired a lawyer to advise them on gathering Balko's original paperwork. She stated she told Parks about the April 2006 draft will only after they both consulted with the lawyer. She claimed she urged Parks to continue looking through Balko's belongings because she "was wondering if, without telling [her], [Balko] had executed a valid Will after April 2006."

Balko lived for more than a year after he filled in the blanks on the April 2006 will. He died in July 2007 without ever having it witnessed or notarized. The November 2005 will—which made no provision for Parks—was admitted to probate and fully administered over Parks's objection. Parks filed a malpractice lawsuit against

Fink and Fink Law Group PLLC alleging that Fink's legal representation of Balko "gave rise to a duty of reasonable care to Balko as her client as well as to Parks as the intended primary beneficiary under [Balko's] will" and that Fink breached this duty.[6] Fink moved for summary judgment dismissal, arguing that because Parks was never her client, she owed him no duty of care.

The trial court granted Fink's motion and dismissed Parks's legal malpractice claim on lack of standing grounds. In its oral ruling—later incorporated into its written ruling—the court decided on policy grounds that to expose an attorney to liability to a nonclient potential beneficiary when a signed will has not been witnessed or notarized "burden[s] the [legal] profession with untenable conflicts of interest." Parks appeals.

ANALYSIS

* * *

Evidentiary Issues

Parks contends that the dead man's statute prevents the admission of Fink's "self-serving testimony"—contained in her declarations, interrogatory answers, and deposition testimony concerning her interactions with Balko—such that summary judgment was inappropriate. The dead man's statute provides:

> No person offered as a witness shall be excluded from giving evidence by reason of his or her interest in the event of the action, as a party thereto or otherwise, but such interest may be shown to affect his or her credibility: PROVIDED, HOWEVER, That in an action or proceeding where the adverse party sues or defends as executor, administrator or legal representative of any deceased person, or as deriving right or title by, through or from any deceased person, or as the guardian or limited guardian of the estate or person of any incompetent or disabled person, or of any minor under the age of fourteen years, then a party in interest or to the record, shall not be admitted to testify in his or her own behalf as to any transaction had by him or her with, or any statement made to him or her, or in his or her presence, by

---

[6] In her amended answer, Fink alleged counterclaims, including civil assault and outrage. She claimed Parks threatened, intimidated, and terrorized her on several occasions, including sending her a letter containing death threats and insults. The court dismissed the assault counterclaim but concluded the outrage counterclaim survived summary judgment. The court severed the outrage counterclaim from Parks's legal malpractice claim. The counterclaim is not at issue in this appeal.

any such deceased, incompetent or disabled person, or by any such minor under the age of fourteen years: PROVIDED FURTHER, That this exclusion shall not apply to parties of record who sue or defend in a representative or fiduciary capacity, and have no other or further interest in the action.

We review the admissibility of evidence in summary judgment proceedings de novo.

The purpose of the dead man's statute is to prevent interested parties from giving self-serving testimony regarding conversations and transactions with the deceased because the dead cannot respond to unfavorable testimony. By its terms, the statute only applies when an adverse party sues or defends as a representative or successor of the deceased person.

Here, Parks, the plaintiff, sued in his own capacity as a third party beneficiary of Fink's representation of Balko. He is asserting claims on his own behalf, not on behalf of Balko's estate. The dead man's statute does not apply.

Duty

Lawyer's Duty to Nonclient

Parks contends that Fink owed him a duty to properly execute the will by having it witnessed either at the time Balko signed it in April 2006 or in the following 15 months before Balko's death in July 2007.[8]

The elements for a legal malpractice claim are:

(1) The existence of an attorney-client relationship which gives rise to a duty of care on the part of the attorney to the client; (2) an act or omission by the attorney in breach of the duty of care; (3) damage to the client; and (4) proximate causation between the attorney's breach of the duty and the damage incurred.

The duty issue here turns on a single question of law—whether Fink owed nonclient Parks a duty of care to ensure that the decedent executed his will promptly. The existence of a duty is a question of

---

[8]   In defining the duty he alleges Fink owed him, Parks claims that Fink "fail[ed] to have the 2006 Will *properly* executed *when the execution actually occurred* on April 26, 2006." He claims this case is about "improper execution at the time of execution" and argues the duty here was "to have [the] will executed *properly* at the time of will signing or execution." In essence, his argument is that Fink should have executed the will on the day Balko signed it or during the ensuing 15 months before Balko's death. In either case, his argument depends on the proposition that Fink had a duty to promptly execute the will after Balko signed it.

law. The general rule is that only an attorney's client may bring an action for attorney malpractice. "But an attorney may owe a nonclient a duty even in the absence of this privity."

In *Trask,* our Supreme Court adopted a multifactor balancing test to determine whether an attorney owes a duty to a nonclient:

(1) The extent to which the transaction was intended to benefit the [nonclient] plaintiff;

(2) The foreseeability of harm to the plaintiff;

(3) The degree of certainty that the plaintiff suffered injury;

(4) The closeness of the connection between the defendant's conduct and the injury;

(5) The policy of preventing future harm; and

(6) The extent to which the profession would be unduly burdened by a finding of liability.

The analysis of these factors necessarily involves an individualized factual determination in each case.

At issue in this case are factors five and six noted above. Because material issues of fact exist on whether Parks was an intended beneficiary, we assume, without deciding, that Parks was an intended beneficiary under Balko's will. As such, factor one is not before us and factors two, three, and four are unchallenged on appeal.

In this case, our examination of factors five and six requires us to consider the policy conflict between the prevention of future harm to attorney malpractice victims and the burden imposed on the legal profession by imposing liability. For the reasons discussed below, we join the majority of courts confronting this issue in holding that an attorney owes no duty of care to an intended will beneficiary to have the will executed promptly.

To support his duty claim, Parks relies on several non-Washington cases in which the courts imposed a duty. None of those cases control because they are factually and legally distinguishable from the present case. Most of the cases Parks cites involve drafting errors. None involve the critical duty issue here—whether a duty is owed to an intended beneficiary where the attorney fails to ensure the decedent executes the will promptly. For example, *Biakanja v. Irving,* 49 Cal.2d 647 (1958), involved a nonattorney notary public who prepared a will that contained no witness signatures. The court imposed a duty in favor of the plaintiff, a potential beneficiary under the invalid will. Because *Biakanja* involved negligence by a nonattorney, the court necessarily omitted any discussion about whether imposition of a duty on a negligent attorney results in a burden on the legal profession.

Similarly, in *Licata v. Spector*, 26 Conn.Supp. 378 (1966), the court never addressed the critical question at issue here—the burden a duty of care would impose on the legal profession. *Licata* involved an attorney who drafted a will that failed to provide for the required number of witnesses, resulting in the will's invalidity.

By contrast, Fink relies on case authority that declines to extend an attorney's duty to timely execute a will involving a nonclient beneficiary. The rationales in these cases are all identical—the potential conflict of interest such a duty would create for an attorney.

In *Radovich v. Locke-Paddon*, 35 Cal.App.4th 946 (1995), the decedent's estate plan provided for trust income to her husband and sister. The decedent met with attorney Locke-Paddon to discuss a new will under which her husband would receive all of the trust income. Locke-Paddon delivered a rough draft of the new will to the decedent for review. The decedent told Locke-Paddon she intended to confer with her sister before finalizing the new will. The decedent died without formalizing the will. The court distinguished *Biakanja*, *Lucas*, and *Heyer*, noted above, on grounds that the decedent had signed the will in those cases:

> The case before us differs from *Biakanja*, *Lucas* and *Heyer* in one significant respect: the decedent never signed the will Locke-Paddon drafted. While the crux of *Biakanja*, *Lucas* and *Heyer* was that a will the decedent *had signed* had been rendered wholly or partially ineffective, at least as to the beneficiaries, by the negligence of the person who had prepared the will, the crux of Radovich's claim is that a will potentially beneficial to him had never become effective because, assertedly due to Locke-Paddon's negligence, the decedent *had not signed* it.

The court noted, "[T]his is not as strong a case for an inference of commitment to the potential beneficiary. . . ." The court reasoned:

> [B]oth practical and policy reasons [exist] for requiring more evidence of commitment than is furnished by a direction to prepare a will containing specified provisions. From a

practical standpoint, common experience teaches that potential testators may change their minds more than once after the first meeting. Although a potential testator may also change his or her mind *after* a will is signed, we perceive significantly stronger support for an inference of commitment in a signature on testamentary documents than in a preliminary direction to prepare such documents for signature. From a policy standpoint, we must be sensitive to the potential for misunderstanding and the difficulties of proof inherent in the fact that disputes such as these will not arise until the decedent—the only person who can say what he or she intended—has died. Thus we must as a policy matter insist on the clearest manifestation of commitment the circumstances will permit.

The court also explained that imposition of liability under the circumstances could compromise an attorney's duty of undivided loyalty to his or her client and create an incentive to exert pressure on the client to execute estate planning documents summarily.[12]

Radovich found the rationale in *Krawczyk v. Stingle*, 208 Conn. 239 (1988), persuasive. There, the decedent met with his attorney to arrange for disposition of his estate. The decedent directed the attorney to prepare two trust documents intended to benefit the plaintiffs and avoid probate. Several delays ensued, and by the time the attorney completed the documents, the decedent was too ill to see her. The decedent died without signing the documents. The nonclient plaintiffs argued that when the attorney learned approximately 24 hours before the decedent died that he had suffered a heart attack and was gravely ill, she

> should have inquired whether the decedent was in any condition to sign the documents and whether it was possible for her to come to the hospital to have him execute them; and . . . she should either have brought hand-written documents to the hospital for the decedent's signature or

---

[12] In *Chang v. Lederman*, 172 Cal.App.4th 67, 81 (2009), the court recognized the factual distinction between *Radovich* and *Osornio*:

The *Osornio* court emphasized this difference between the failed bequest in the case before it and the frustration of the potential beneficiary's expectations in *Radovich*: "In that instance, there was no plain expression of the testator's intention to benefit the plaintiff. . . . In contrast, here we have a clear expression of [the testator's] intention that Osornio be her sole beneficiary under the signed 2001 Will." That is, to hold an attorney owed a duty of care not only to his or her testator client but also to an intended beneficiary, the testator's intent must be "*expressed* and *formalized* in [a] signed will." (*Ibid.*)

alternatively have prepared a simple will that she could have presented to him for his immediate signature.

The *Krawczyk* court acknowledged cases from other jurisdictions—including *Lucas* and *Licata* noted above—recognizing a cause of action in favor of intended beneficiaries against attorneys who fail to draft a will in conformity with a testator's wishes or fail to supervise the proper execution of a will. The court stated, "The question before us is whether such liability should be further expanded to encompass negligent delay in completing and furnishing estate planning documents for execution by the client." It noted, "Determining when attorneys should be liable to parties with whom they are not in privity is a question of public policy." The court held that imposing liability to nonclients for negligent delay in the execution of estate planning documents would undermine a lawyer's duty of undivided loyalty to the client. It reasoned:

> Imposition of liability would create an incentive for an attorney to exert pressure on a client to complete and execute estate planning documents summarily. Fear of liability to potential third party beneficiaries would contravene the attorney's primary responsibility to ensure that the proposed estate plan effectuates the client's wishes and that the client understands the available options and the legal and practical implications of whatever course of action is ultimately chosen.

In *Sisson v. Jankowski*, 148 N.H. 503 (2002), the court reached a similar conclusion. There, the disgruntled brother of a deceased testator sued the decedent's lawyer for malpractice based on the following facts: The decedent hired Jankowski to prepare his will. According to the plaintiff, the decedent wanted to leave his entire estate to the plaintiff and disinherit another estranged brother. Jankowski prepared a will, mailed it to the decedent for his review, and visited the decedent in his nursing home for a formal will signing. The decedent wanted changes made, so Jankowski left without obtaining signatures. Jankowski returned three days later with a revised will but concluded that the decedent was not competent to sign at that time. Jankowski made no additional effort to determine whether the decedent regained sufficient testamentary capacity to execute his will, and the decedent died intestate. Rather than passing entirely to the plaintiff, the estate was divided between the plaintiff, the estranged brother, and the children of a third deceased brother.

The court formulated the dispositive issue:

> Whether . . . an attorney's negligent failure to arrange for his or her client's timely execution of a will and/or an attorney's failure to provide reasonable professional advice with respect to the client's testamentary options . . . gives rise to a viable common law claim against that attorney by an intended beneficiary of the unexecuted will.

It found no doubt that the decedent intended the plaintiff to inherit the entire estate. For purposes of determining the duty question, the court assumed negligence by Jankowski for not returning to obtain signatures. The court then addressed whether a putative heir had standing to sue the decedent's lawyer. The court held Jankowski owed the plaintiff no duty of care:

> After weighing the policy considerations the parties identify, we conclude that the potential for conflict between the interests of a prospective beneficiary and a testator militates against recognizing a duty of care. "It is the potential for conflict that is determinative, not the existence of an actual conflict." Whereas a testator and the beneficiary of a will have a mutual interest in ensuring that an attorney drafts the will non-negligently, a prospective beneficiary may be interested in the will's prompt execution, while the testator or testatrix may be interested in having sufficient time to consider and understand his or her estate planning options. As the Massachusetts Supreme Judicial Court recognized:
>
> > Confronting a last will and testament can produce complex psychological demands on a client that may require considerable periods of reflection. An attorney frequently prepares multiple drafts of a will before the client is reconciled to the result. The most simple distributive provisions may be the most difficult for the client to accept.
>
> > Creating a duty, even under the unfortunate circumstances of this case, could compromise the attorney's duty of undivided loyalty to the client and impose an untenable burden upon the attorney-client relationship. To avoid potential liability, attorneys might be forced to pressure their clients to execute their wills summarily,

without sufficiently reflecting upon their estate planning options.

The court "join[ed] the majority of courts that have considered this issue and [held] that an attorney does not owe a duty of care to a prospective will beneficiary to have the will executed promptly."

In *Hall v. Kalfayan*, 190 Cal.App.4th 927 (2010), the court addressed a prospective beneficiary's legal malpractice claim against the attorney who drafted the will but failed to execute it before the testator died. The court discussed *Biakanja*, *Lucas*, and *Heyer* and noted:

> In these cases, the testamentary instrument had been executed; the question was whether the will or trust had been negligently prepared so as to frustrate the testator's intent. *But in cases where a potential beneficiary seeks to recover for negligence where the will or trust has not been executed, courts have refused to extend liability.*"

The court reviewed those cases and concluded:

> We agree with the *Radovich* and *Chang* courts that there is a need for a clear delineation of an attorney's duty to nonclients. The essence of the claim in the case before this court is that Kalfayan failed to complete the new estate plan for Ms. Turner and have it executed on her behalf by her conservator before her death, thereby depriving Hall of his share of her estate. In the absence of an executed (and in this instance, approved) testamentary document naming Hall as a beneficiary, Hall is only a potential beneficiary. Kalfayan's duty was to the conservatorship on behalf of Ms. Turner; he did not owe Hall a duty of care with respect to the preparation of an estate plan for Ms. Turner.

> This conclusion is particularly appropriate in this case, where Ms. Turner herself had not expressed a desire to have a new will prepared and had only limited conversation with Kalfayan about the disposition of her estate. In addition, there is no certainty that the court would have approved the petition for substituted judgment. We also observe that extending Kalfayan's duty to potential beneficiaries of Ms. Turner's estate would expose him to liability to her niece, whose share of the estate would have been reduced. This is precisely the type of unreasonable burden on an attorney

that militates against expanding duty to potential beneficiaries.

As a matter of law, Hall cannot establish duty, a necessary element for his claim for professional negligence. The trial court properly granted summary judgment on this basis.

Finally, in *Rydde v. Morris*, 381 S.C. 643 (2009), the South Carolina Supreme Court found *Krawczyk* and *Sisson* persuasive and declined to extend an attorney's duty to nonclient prospective beneficiaries where the attorney negligently failed to draft and finalize a will before the testator died. In *Rydde*, the testator hired an attorney to prepare her estate plan one month before she died. The testator gave the attorney a completed estate planning questionnaire. Five days later, the attorney delivered to the testator a portion of the requested estate planning documents. The documents did not include a will and were not finalized before the testator died. The individuals identified in the questionnaire as prospective beneficiaries sued the attorney for malpractice. The court dismissed the complaint based on a Civil Rule 12(b)(6) motion, reasoning in part:

> Our decision today not to impose a duty on an attorney in favor of a prospective beneficiary for alleged negligent failure to draft a will follows the law in other jurisdictions. *We find persuasive the reasoning of decisions from New Hampshire, Connecticut, and Florida. We reference these three jurisdictions, for these states recognize generally that an attorney owes a duty to a non-client intended beneficiary of an executed will where it is shown that the testator's intent has been defeated or diminished by negligence on the part of the attorney, resulting in loss to the beneficiary. Having relaxed the traditional privity requirement in legal malpractice claims, these states nevertheless draw the line and refuse for compelling policy reasons to permit a malpractice claim by a non-client for negligent failure to draft a will.*

The court concluded, "The imposition of a duty on an attorney to a prospective beneficiary of a nonexistent will would wreak havoc on the attorney's ethical duty of undivided loyalty to the client and force an impermissible wedge in the attorney-client relationship."

While we have assumed without deciding that Parks was an intended beneficiary, the *Trask* court stated that if the transaction was not intended to benefit the plaintiff, no further inquiry need be made. But the court went on to say:

> The multifactor balancing test also requires that we evaluate public policy before finding a duty to a third party. The policy considerations against finding a duty to a nonclient are the strongest where doing so would detract from the attorney's ethical obligations to the client. This occurs where a duty to a nonclient creates a risk of divided loyalties because of a conflicting interest or of a breach of confidence.

Trask, 123 Wash.2d at 844. After weighing policy considerations, we conclude that *Radovich, Krawczyk, Sisson, Hall,* and *Rydde* are dispositive of the duty question here. These jurisdictions decline to impose a duty of care where the alleged negligence concerns the failure to have a will executed promptly even if by doing so, an intended beneficiary is denied a remedy. In this case, the undisputed evidence shows that Fink brought the draft will to the hospital to discuss and review its contents with Balko. There is no record evidence that Fink knew before she presented the draft to Balko at the hospital that he intended to designate Parks as a beneficiary or to formally execute the will in the presence of witnesses and a notary public. Nor is there any dispute that Balko told Montgomery five months *after* signing the draft that Parks would be his main heir and the will needed to be changed but he wanted to think about it more before doing so. And it is undisputed that during the 15 months since he signed the draft will until his death, Balko never had it formally executed. Under these circumstances,

> [i]mposition of liability would create an incentive for an attorney to exert pressure on a client to complete and execute estate planning documents summarily. Fear of liability to potential third party beneficiaries would contravene the attorney's primary responsibility to ensure that the proposed estate plan effectuates the client's wishes and that the client understands the available options and the legal and practical implications of whatever course of action is ultimately chosen.

Krawczyk.

We also agree with the concerns expressed in *Sisson:*

Whereas a testator and the beneficiary of a will have a mutual interest in ensuring that an attorney drafts the will non-negligently, a prospective beneficiary may be interested in the will's prompt execution, while the testator or testatrix may be interested in having sufficient time to consider and understand his or her estate planning options. . . .

. . . .

. . . . *To avoid potential liability, attorneys might be forced to pressure their clients to execute their wills summarily, without sufficiently reflecting upon their estate planning options.*

Sisson (emphasis added).

Washington ethics rules are clear that " '[t]he standards of the legal profession require undeviating fidelity of the lawyer to his client. No exceptions can be tolerated.' " The same policy concerns underlying *Sisson, Radovich*, and *Krawczyk* apply here. Imposing a duty on Fink creates an irreconcilable conflict of interest involving a simultaneous duty owed to both Balko and Parks.

Parks argues that absent a duty, he lacks a legal remedy against Fink.[13] Imposing a duty even under these circumstances could diminish the attorney's duty of undivided loyalty to the client and impose an untenable burden on the attorney-client relationship. On balance, we conclude that the risk of interfering with the attorney's duty of undivided loyalty to the client exceeds the risk of harm to the prospective beneficiary. For the reasons discussed above, we join the majority of courts that have considered the issue and hold that an attorney owes no duty of care to a prospective will beneficiary to have the will executed promptly.

---

[13] The *Radovich* and *Sisson* courts rejected a similar "lack of remedy" argument. The *Radovich* court reasoned:

[O]bviously the notion that liability can legitimately be imposed to deter carelessness cannot be applied arbitrarily or in a vacuum. Just as it would not do to award damages to a randomly selected bystander simply to bring home a message that the defendant and others like him or her should not be careless, so it would not do to make such an award, even to a rationally selected plaintiff, if in the circumstances the objective of deterrence is outweighed by countervailing policy considerations.

Similarly, the *Sisson* court concluded that the potential for conflict of interest between a prospective beneficiary and a testator militates against imposing a duty of care even though some plaintiffs will be left without a remedy. ("Creating a duty, even under the unfortunate circumstances of this case, could compromise the attorney's duty of undivided loyalty to the client and impose an untenable burden upon the attorney-client relationship.").

CONCLUSION

For the reasons discussed above, we affirm the trial court.

———————

According to the common-law rule, a lawyer is not liable to third party beneficiaries because the lawyer has no duty to those persons. There is no duty because there is no privity. The client is in privity of contract with the lawyer, but the beneficiary is not. There is a substantial modern trend that has changed this rule, making lawyers liable to third party beneficiaries for malpractice relating to wills in some cases. But even in jurisdictions following the modern trend, lawyers are not always liable to intended third party beneficiaries. Courts are rightly concerned about conflicts of interest between the client and the beneficiaries. For example, they do not want to create a duty that would create an incentive for lawyers to put pressure on clients.

The modern approach includes exceptions under which the lawyer is not liable to third party beneficiaries. There are a few different variations regarding these exceptions. Variation 1: There is no duty to third parties to get the client to execute the will. Variation 2: There is no duty to third parties when the will was not executed. Variation 3: There is no duty to third parties when a balancing of factors indicates otherwise.

As a matter of policy, what are the benefits of the first variation, as compared to the third? The first might generate less litigation because it is clearer, more determinate. It is relatively easy for a court to determine whether a plaintiff is claiming that the lawyer had a duty to get the will executed. Consider the following example.

> Example 2.01: A lawyer prepares a will for the client, which the lawyer sends by email to the client. The client tells the lawyer that it says exactly what the client wants. The client gets sick and enters the hospital. On his death bed, the client repeatedly emails and calls the lawyer, imploring the lawyer to bring the will to him to be executed. The lawyer fails to do so and the client dies. The intended beneficiary sues the lawyer for malpractice. If the common-law privity requirement is applied, the beneficiary has no standing. Under the modern variations, the results vary.

What is the result in Example 2.01 if the first variation of the modern rule is applied? Does the first variation generate a just result in that example? Could the balancing rule used in *Parks* be used to come to a different decision in Example 2.01? Is the balancing rule more likely to reach a just result?

Consider the following variation on the modern rule: Variation 4: The duty to the intended third party beneficiaries is exactly the same as the duty to the client. If the lawyer would be liable to the client for breach of duty and the breach harms a beneficiary, then the lawyer is liable to the beneficiary. Would this avoid potential conflicts of interest? Would Variation 4 increase the incentives for the lawyer to satisfy his duty to the client? In what ways would this rule harm clients? Would this rule reach a just result in Example 2.01 above? Would this modern rule plus exception generate more litigation than the common law? Would this rule generate more litigation than Variation 1 of the modern rule? As in much of the law, many of the policy questions in this course pit litigation against injustice, efficiency against justice. We can reach more just results if we are willing to pay for the litigation needed to get there. What is the proper balance between litigation and injustice?

Another question raised by the multifactor test in *Parks v. Fink* is whether burdens on the legal profession should matter. Why should they? Two things happen when lawyer liability increases. Some of the increased cost is borne by lawyers; they get poorer. Do we care about reduced income for lawyers? Some of the increased cost is borne by clients; they pay more. Are the costs to the clients justified? They will get better services. Some will pay and be happy. Some will pay and not get enough additional value to be worth the increased cost. Some will not pay for higher value services when they would have paid for lower value services, and they are clearly worse off.

The reputation of lawyers should improve if they make fewer mistakes. Do we care about the reputation of lawyers? Does society work better or worse when lawyers are distrusted? Should lawyers want to be liable? In 1999, a Tennessee lawyer was shot and killed by an intended beneficiary who lost $100,000 because the lawyer, who was a former probate judge, used the words "all monies" instead of "all residue". The murderer also shot the life insurance agent who was trying to sell the lawyer life insurance at the time of the shooting.

2. CONFLICTS OF CLIENTS' INTERESTS

A. v. B.

Supreme Court of New Jersey, 1999
726 A.2d 924

POLLOCK, J.

This appeal presents the issue whether a law firm may disclose confidential information of one co-client to another co-client. Specifically, in this paternity action, the mother's former law firm, which contemporaneously represented the father and his wife in planning their estates, seeks to disclose to the wife the existence of the father's illegitimate child.

A law firm, Hill Wallack (described variously as "the law firm" or "the firm"), jointly represented the husband and wife in drafting wills in which they devised their respective estates to each other. The devises created the possibility that the other spouse's issue, whether legitimate or illegitimate, ultimately would acquire the decedent's property.

Unbeknown to Hill Wallack and the wife, the husband recently had fathered an illegitimate child. Before the execution of the wills, the child's mother retained Hill Wallack to institute this paternity action against the husband. Because of a clerical error, the firm's computer check did not reveal the conflict of interest inherent in its representation of the mother against the husband. On learning of the conflict, the firm withdrew from representation of the mother in the paternity action. Now, the firm wishes to disclose to the wife the fact that the husband has an illegitimate child. To prevent Hill Wallack from making that disclosure, the husband joined the firm as a third-party defendant in the paternity action.

In the Family Part, the husband, represented by new counsel, Fox, Rothschild, O'Brien & Frankel ("Fox Rothschild"), requested restraints against Hill Wallack to prevent the firm from disclosing to his wife the existence of the child. The Family Part denied the requested restraints. The Appellate Division reversed and remanded "for the entry of an order imposing preliminary restraints and for further consideration."

Hill Wallack then filed motions in this Court seeking leave to appeal, to present oral argument, and to accelerate the appeal. Pursuant to *Rule* 2:8–3(a), we grant the motion for leave to appeal, accelerate the appeal, reverse the judgment of the Appellate Division and remand the matter to the Family Part. Hill Wallack's motion for oral argument is denied.

I.

Although the record is both informal and attenuated, the parties agree substantially on the relevant facts. Because the Family Part has sealed the record, we refer to the parties without identifying them by their proper names. So viewed, the record supports the following factual statement.

In October 1997, the husband and wife retained Hill Wallack, a firm of approximately sixty lawyers, to assist them with planning their estates. On the commencement of the joint representation, the husband and wife each signed a letter captioned "Waiver of Conflict of Interest." In explaining the possible conflicts of interest, the letter recited that the effect of a testamentary transfer by one spouse to the other would permit the transferee to dispose of the property as he or she desired. The firm's letter also explained that information provided by one spouse could become available to the other. Although the letter did not contain an express waiver of the confidentiality of any such information, each spouse consented to and waived any conflicts arising from the firm's joint representation.

Unfortunately, the clerk who opened the firm's estate planning file misspelled the clients' surname. The misspelled name was entered in the computer program that the firm uses to discover possible conflicts of interest. The firm then prepared reciprocal wills and related documents with the names of the husband and wife correctly spelled.

In January 1998, before the husband and wife executed the estate planning documents, the mother coincidentally retained Hill Wallack to pursue a paternity claim against the husband. This time, when making its computer search for conflicts of interest, Hill Wallack spelled the husband's name correctly. Accordingly, the computer search did not reveal the existence of the firm's joint representation of the husband and wife. As a result, the estate planning department did not know that the family law department had instituted a paternity action for the mother. Similarly, the family law department did not know that the estate planning department was preparing estate plans for the husband and wife.

A lawyer from the firm's family law department wrote to the husband about the mother's paternity claim. The husband neither objected to the firm's representation of the mother nor alerted the firm to the conflict of interest. Instead, he retained Fox Rothschild to represent him in the paternity action. After initially denying paternity, he agreed to voluntary DNA testing, which revealed that he is the father. Negotiations over child support failed, and the mother instituted the present action.

After the mother filed the paternity action, the husband and wife executed their wills at the Hill Wallack office. The parties agree that in their wills, the husband and wife leave their respective residuary estates to each other. If the other spouse does not survive, the contingent beneficiaries are the testator's issue. The wife's will leaves her residuary estate to her husband, creating the possibility that her property ultimately may pass to his issue. Under *N.J.S.A.* 3B:1-2;:3-48, the term "issue" includes both legitimate and illegitimate children. When the wife executed her will, therefore, she did not know that the husband's illegitimate child ultimately may inherit her property.

The conflict of interest surfaced when Fox Rothschild, in response to Hill Wallack's request for disclosure of the husband's assets, informed the firm that it already possessed the requested information. Hill Wallack promptly informed the mother that it unknowingly was representing both the husband and the wife in an unrelated matter.

Hill Wallack immediately withdrew from representing the mother in the paternity action. It also instructed the estate planning department not to disclose any information about the husband's assets to the member of the firm who had been representing the mother. The firm then wrote to the husband stating that it believed it had an ethical obligation to disclose to the wife the existence, but not the identity, of his illegitimate child. Additionally, the firm stated that it was obligated to inform the wife "that her current estate plan may devise a portion of her assets through her spouse to that child." The firm suggested that the husband so inform his wife and stated that if he did not do so, it would. Because of the restraints imposed by the Appellate Division, however, the firm has not disclosed the information to the wife.

II.

This appeal concerns the conflict between two fundamental obligations of lawyers: the duty of confidentiality, *Rules of Professional Conduct (RPC)* 1.6(a), and the duty to inform clients of material facts, *RPC* 1.4(b). The conflict arises from a law firm's joint representation of two clients whose interests initially were, but no longer are, compatible.

Crucial to the attorney-client relationship is the attorney's obligation not to reveal confidential information learned in the course of representation. Thus, *RPC* 1.6(a) states that "[a] lawyer shall not reveal information relating to representation of a client unless the client consents after consultation, except for disclosures that are impliedly authorized in order to carry out the representation." Generally, "the principle of attorney-client confidentiality imposes a sacred trust on the attorney not to disclose the client's confidential communication." *State v. Land*, 73 N.J. 24, 30 (1977).

A lawyer's obligation to communicate to one client all information needed to make an informed decision qualifies the firm's duty to maintain the confidentiality of a co-client's information. *RPC* 1.4(b), which reflects a lawyer's duty to keep clients informed, requires that "[a] lawyer shall explain a matter to the extent reasonably necessary to permit the client to make informed decisions regarding the representation." In limited situations, moreover, an attorney is permitted or required to disclose confidential information. Hill Wallack argues that *RPC* 1.6 mandates, or at least permits, the firm to disclose to the wife the existence of the husband's illegitimate child. *RPC* 1.6(b) requires that a lawyer disclose "information relating to representation of a client" to the proper authorities if the lawyer "reasonably believes" that such disclosure is necessary to prevent the client "from committing a criminal, illegal or fraudulent act that the lawyer reasonably believes is likely to result in death or substantial bodily harm or substantial injury to the financial interest or property of another." *RPC* 1.6(b)(1). Despite Hill Wallack's claim that *RPC* 1.6(b) applies, the facts do not justify mandatory disclosure. The possible inheritance of the wife's estate by the husband's illegitimate child is too remote to constitute "substantial injury to the financial interest or property of another" within the meaning of *RPC* 1.6(b).

By comparison, in limited circumstances *RPC* 1.6(c) permits a lawyer to disclose a confidential communication. *RPC* 1.6(c) permits, but does not require, a lawyer to reveal confidential information to the extent the lawyer reasonably believes necessary "to rectify the consequences of a client's criminal, illegal or fraudulent act in furtherance of which the lawyer's services had been used." *RPC* 1.6(c)(1). Although *RPC* 1.6(c) does not define a "fraudulent act," the term takes on meaning from our construction of the word "fraud," found in the analogous "crime or fraud" exception to the attorney-client privilege. *See N.J.R.E.* 504(2)(a) (excepting from attorney-client privilege "a communication in the course of legal service sought or obtained in the aid of the commission of a crime or fraud"); Kevin H. Michels, *New Jersey Attorney Ethics* ("While the RPCs no longer incorporate the attorney-client privilege into the definition of confidential information, prior constructions of the fraud exception may be relevant in interpreting the exceptions to confidentiality contained in *RPC* 1.6(b) and (c) . . . .") (internal citation omitted). When construing the "crime or fraud" exception to the attorney-client privilege, "our courts have generally given the term 'fraud' an expansive reading."

We likewise construe broadly the term "fraudulent act" within the meaning of *RPC* 1.6(c). So construed, the husband's deliberate omission of the existence of his illegitimate child constitutes a fraud on his wife. When discussing their respective estates with the firm, the husband and wife reasonably could expect that each would disclose information material to the distribution of their estates, including the existence of children who are contingent residuary beneficiaries. The husband breached that duty. Under the reciprocal wills, the existence of the husband's illegitimate child could affect the distribution of the wife's estate, if she predeceased him. Additionally, the husband's child support payments and other financial responsibilities owed to the illegitimate child could deplete that part of his estate that otherwise would pass to his wife.

From another perspective, it would be "fundamentally unfair" for the husband to reap the "joint planning advantages of access to information and certainty of outcome," while denying those same advantages to his wife. In effect, the husband has used the law firm's services to defraud his wife in the preparation of her estate.

* * *

Under *RPC* 1.6, the facts support disclosure to the wife. The law firm did not learn of the husband's illegitimate child in a confidential communication from him. Indeed, he concealed that information from both his wife and the firm. The law firm learned about the husband's child through its representation of the mother in her paternity action against the husband. Accordingly, the husband's expectation of nondisclosure of the information may be less than if he had communicated the information to the firm in confidence.

In addition, the husband and wife signed letters captioned "Waiver of Conflict of Interest." These letters acknowledge that information provided by one client could become available to the other. The letters, however, stop short of explicitly authorizing the firm to disclose one spouse's confidential information to the other. Even in the absence of any such explicit authorization, the spirit of the letters supports the firm's decision to disclose to the wife the existence of the husband's illegitimate child.

Neither our research nor that of counsel has revealed a dispositive judicial decision from this or any other jurisdiction on the issue of disclosure of confidential information about one client to a co-client. Persuasive secondary authority, however, supports the conclusion that the firm may disclose to the wife the existence of the husband's child.

The forthcoming *Restatement (Third) of The Law Governing Lawyers* § 112 comment *l* ("the *Restatement*") suggests, for example, that if the attorney and the co-clients have reached a prior, explicit agreement concerning the sharing of confidential information, that agreement controls whether the attorney should disclose the confidential information of one co-client to another. ("Co-clients . . . may explicitly agree to share information" and "can also explicitly agree that the lawyer is not to share certain information . . . with one or more other co-clients. A lawyer must honor such agreements."); *see also Report of the ABA Special Study Committee on Professional Responsibility: Comments and Recommendations on the Lawyer's Duties in Representing Husband and Wife* ("Although legally and ethically there is no need for a prior discussion and agreement with the couple about the mode of representation, discussion and agreement are the better practice. The agreement may cover . . . the duty to keep or disclose confidences."); American College of Trust and Estate Counsel, *ACTEC Commentaries on the Model Rules of Professional Conduct* ("When the lawyer is first consulted by the multiple potential clients the lawyer should review with them the terms upon which the lawyer will undertake the representation, including the extent to which information will be shared among them.").

As the preceding authorities suggest, an attorney, on commencing joint representation of co-clients, should agree explicitly with the clients on the sharing of confidential information. In such a "disclosure agreement," the co-clients can agree that any confidential information concerning one co-client, whether obtained from a co-client himself or herself or from another source, will be shared with the other co-client. Similarly, the co-clients can agree that unilateral confidences or other confidential information will be kept confidential by the attorney. Such a prior agreement will clarify the expectations of the clients and the lawyer and diminish the need for future litigation.

In the absence of an agreement to share confidential information with co-clients, the *Restatement* reposes the resolution of the lawyer's competing duties within the lawyer's discretion:

> [T]he lawyer, after consideration of all relevant circumstances, has the . . . discretion to inform the affected co-client of the specific communication if, in the lawyer's reasonable judgment, the immediacy and magnitude of the risk to the affected co-client outweigh the interest of the communicating client in continued secrecy.

Additionally, the *Restatement* advises that the lawyer, when withdrawing from representation of the co-clients, may inform the affected co-client that the attorney has learned of information adversely affecting that client's interests that the communicating co-client refuses to permit the lawyer to disclose.

In the context of estate planning, the *Restatement* also suggests that a lawyer's disclosure of confidential information communicated by one spouse is appropriate only if the other spouse's failure to learn of the information would be materially detrimental to that other spouse or frustrate the spouse's intended testamentary arrangement. The *Restatement* provides two analogous illustrations in which a lawyer has been jointly retained by a husband and wife to prepare reciprocal wills. The first illustration states:

> Lawyer has been retained by Husband and Wife to prepare wills pursuant to an arrangement under which each spouse agrees to leave most of their property to the other. Shortly

after the wills are executed, Husband (unknown to Wife) asks Lawyer to prepare an inter vivos trust for an illegitimate child whose existence Husband has kept secret from Wife for many years and about whom Husband had not previously informed Lawyer. Husband states that Wife would be distraught at learning of Husband's infidelity and of Husband's years of silence and that disclosure of the information could destroy their marriage. Husband directs Lawyer not to inform Wife. The inter vivos trust that Husband proposes to create would not materially affect Wife's own estate plan or her expected receipt of property under Husband's will, because Husband proposes to use property designated in Husband's will for a personally favored charity. In view of the lack of material effect on Wife, Lawyer may assist Husband to establish and fund the inter vivos trust and refrain from disclosing Husband's information to Wife.

In authorizing non-disclosure, the *Restatement* explains that an attorney should refrain from disclosing the existence of the illegitimate child to the wife because the trust "would not materially affect Wife's own estate plan or her expected receipt of property under Husband's will."

The other illustration states:

Same facts as [the prior Illustration], except that Husband's proposed inter vivos trust would significantly deplete Husband's estate, to Wife's material detriment and in frustration of the Spouses' intended testamentary arrangements. If Husband will neither inform Wife nor permit Lawyer to do so, Lawyer must withdraw from representing both Husband and Wife. In the light of all relevant circumstances, Lawyer may exercise discretion whether to inform Wife either that circumstances, which Lawyer has been asked not to reveal, indicate that she should revoke her recent will or to inform Wife of some or all the details of the information that Husband has recently provided so that Wife may protect her interests. Alternatively, Lawyer may inform Wife only that Lawyer is withdrawing because Husband will not permit disclosure of information that Lawyer has learned from Husband.

Because the money placed in the trust would be deducted from the portion of the husband's estate left to his wife, the *Restatement* concludes that the lawyer may exercise discretion to inform the wife of the husband's plans.

An earlier draft of the *Restatement* described the attorney's obligation to disclose the confidential information to the co-client as mandatory. When reviewing the draft, however, the governing body of the American Law Institute, the Council, modified the obligation to leave disclosure within the attorney's discretion.

Similarly, the American College of Trust and Estate Counsel (ACTEC) also favors a discretionary rule. It recommends that the "lawyer should have a reasonable degree of discretion in determining how to respond to any particular case." The ACTEC suggests that the lawyer first attempt to convince the client to inform the co-client. When urging the client to disclose the information, the lawyer should remind the client of the implicit understanding that all information will be shared by both clients. The lawyer also should explain to the client the potential legal consequences of non-disclosure, including invalidation of the wills. Furthermore, the lawyer may mention that failure to communicate the information could subject the lawyer to a malpractice claim or disciplinary action.

The ACTEC reasons that if unsuccessful in persuading the client to disclose the information, the lawyer should consider several factors in deciding whether to reveal the confidential information to the co-client, including: (1) duties of impartiality and loyalty to the clients; (2) any express or implied agreement among the lawyer and the joint clients that information communicated by either client to the lawyer regarding the subject of the representation would be shared with the other client; (3) the reasonable expectations of the clients; and (4) the nature of the confidence and the harm that may result if the confidence is, or is not, disclosed.

The Section of Real Property, Probate and Trust Law of the American Bar Association, in a report prepared by its Special Study Committee on Professional Responsibility, reached a similar conclusion:

> Faced with any adverse confidence, the lawyer must act as a fiduciary toward joint clients. The lawyer must balance the potential for material harm to the confiding spouse caused

by disclosure against the potential for material harm to the other spouse caused by a failure to disclose.

The report stresses that the resolution of the balancing test should center on the expectations of the clients. In general, "the available ruling authority . . . points toward the conclusion that a lawyer is not required to disclose an adverse confidence to the other spouse." At the same time, the report acknowledges, as did the *Restatement,* that the available ruling authority is "scant and offers little analytical guidance."

The Professional Ethics Committees of New York and Florida, however, have concluded that disclosure to a co-client is prohibited.

The New York opinion addressed the following situation:

A and B formed a partnership and employed Lawyer L to represent them in connection with the partnership affairs. Subsequently, B, in a conversation with Lawyer L, advised Lawyer L that he was actively breaching the partnership agreement. B preceded this statement to Lawyer L with the statement that he proposed to tell Lawyer L something "in confidence." Lawyer L did not respond to that statement and did not understand that B intended to make a statement that would be of importance to A but that was to be kept confidential from A. Lawyer L had not, prior thereto, advised A or B that he could not receive from one communications regarding the subject of the joint representation that would be confidential from the other. B has subsequently declined to tell A what he has told Lawyer L.

In that situation, the New York Ethics Committee concluded that the lawyer may not disclose to the co-client the communicating client's statement. The Committee based its conclusion on the absence of prior consent by the clients to the sharing of all confidential communications and the fact that the client "specifically in advance designated his communication as confidential, and the lawyer did not demur."

The Florida Ethics Committee addressed a similar situation:

Lawyer has represented Husband and Wife for many years in a range of personal matters, including estate planning. Husband and Wife have substantial individual assets, and they also own substantial jointly-held property. Recently,

Lawyer prepared new updated wills that Husband and Wife signed. Like their previous wills, their new wills primarily benefit the survivor of them for his or her life, with beneficial disposition at the death of the survivor being made equally to their children.

* * *

Several months after the execution of the new wills, Husband confers separately with Lawyer. Husband reveals to Lawyer that he has just executed a codicil prepared by another law firm) that makes substantial beneficial disposition to a woman with whom Husband has been having an extra-marital relationship.

Reasoning that the lawyer's duty of confidentiality takes precedence over the duty to communicate all relevant information to a client, the Florida Ethics Committee concluded that the lawyer did not have discretion to reveal the information. In support of that conclusion, the Florida committee reasoned that joint clients do not necessarily expect that everything relating to the joint representation communicated by one co-client will be shared with the other co-client.

In several material respects, however, the present appeal differs from the hypothetical cases considered by the New York and Florida committees. Most significantly, the New York and Florida disciplinary rules, unlike *RPC* 1.6, do not except disclosure needed "to rectify the consequences of a client's ... fraudulent act in the furtherance of which the lawyer's services had been used." *RPC* 1.6(c). *But see New York Code of Professional Responsibility* DR 4–101; *Florida Rules of Professional Conduct* 4–1.6. Second, Hill Wallack learned of the husband's paternity from a third party, not from the husband himself. Thus, the husband did not communicate anything to the law firm with the expectation that the communication would be kept confidential. Finally, the husband and wife, unlike the co-clients considered by the New York and Florida Committees, signed an agreement suggesting their intent to share all information with each other.

Because Hill Wallack wishes to make the disclosure, we need not reach the issue whether the lawyer's obligation to disclose is discretionary or mandatory. In conclusion, Hill Wallack may inform the wife of the existence of the husband's illegitimate child.

Finally, authorizing the disclosure of the existence, but not the identity, of the child will not contravene *N.J.S.A.* 9:17–42, which provides:

> All papers and records and any information pertaining to an action or proceeding held under [the New Jersey Parentage Act] which may reveal the identity of any party in an action, other than the final judgment or the birth certificate, whether part of the permanent record of the court or of a file with the State registrar of vital statistics or elsewhere, are confidential and are subject to inspection only upon consent of the court and all parties to the action who are still living, or in exceptional cases only upon an order of the court for compelling reason clearly and convincingly shown.

The law firm learned of the husband's paternity of the child through the mother's disclosure before the institution of the paternity suit. It does not seek to disclose the identity of the mother or the child. Given the wife's need for the information and the law firm's right to disclose it, the disclosure of the child's existence to the wife constitutes an exceptional case with "compelling reason clearly and convincingly shown."

The judgment of the Appellate Division is reversed and the matter is remanded to the Family Part.

After the case is decided, should Hill Wallack disclose? There are at least two frameworks Hill Wallack could use in making that determination. One is to determine whether disclosure would be in the best interest of the client. Another is to determine how the client would answer if asked.

What are the problems with reciprocal wills? What more should Hill Wallack have done to protect itself? Some states require lawyers to obtain engagement letters. The American College of Trusts and Estates Counsel (ACTEC) has drafted recommended language for such engagement letters, and that recommended language states that the clients authorize the lawyer to disclose information related to the representation.

The court gives some useful advice about what a lawyer should do to prevent this sort of situation from arising, distinguishing between waiving conflicts and waiving confidentiality. But is the court convincing when it says that the "possible inheritance of the wife's estate by the husband's illegitimate child is too remote to constitute 'substantial injury to the financial interest or property of another' within the meaning of RPC 1.6(b)"? How remote is that chance? What would have to happen for the child to inherit?

B. LIMITATIONS IMPOSED ON RECIPIENTS

1. STATUS

(a) Enslaved People and Noncitizens

Slavery was one of the original sins of the United States. It divided the states at the time the nation was founded and continued to divide the nation up through the Civil War. Because enslaved people were considered to be property of their owners, it was hard to conceive of the enslaved themselves holding property. How could property own property? And because they could not hold property, they could not inherit property. Thus, the status of being enslaved was a bar to inheritance in some states. The abolition of slavery eliminated that status-based bar to succession.

Under the English common law, an alien could not acquire land by descent, and statutes against ownership of realty by noncitizens have appeared in the United States. In 1913, California passed an "Alien Land Law" barring land ownership by "aliens ineligible to citizenship". It was amended in 1920, 1923, and 1927, making it enforceable by escheat and prosecution for criminal conspiracy. Following California, more than a dozen states enacted restrictions on ownership of land by noncitizens. UPC § 2–111 rejects that approach by providing that "[n]o individual is disqualified to take as an heir because the individual or an individual through whom the individual claims is or has been an alien." However, one should distinguish between nonresidency, noncitizenship, and the combination of the two. In *Estate of Constan*, 384 A.2d 495 (1978), the Supreme Court of New Hampshire upheld a decree of distribution that excluded the "nonresident alien heirs" who resided in Communist Poland. After noting that there was no treaty on point, the court said, "Real estate vests in the heirs at the time of death, and because the nonresident heirs could not inherit, they have no interest in the proceeds of the sale of the real estate. Their exclusion from the distribution of those funds is proper." The Polish relatives did not challenge the constitutionality of their exclusion from the class of heirs.

(b) Minors

Minors, persons who have not reached the age of majority, may own property. Despite parents having a great deal of control over their minor children, they do not own them or their property. But devolution of property to minors does present practical problems. Minors often lack the mental ability to manage property well. A few different legal mechanisms are used to overcome this problem. Guardians of the property, conservators, custodians, and trustees have the power to manage property owned by minors. (Uniform Trust Code (UTC) § 103 uses "guardian" to refer to a person who makes personal decisions and "conservator" to refer to one who administers an estate of a minor.) Guardians and conservators are supervised by courts, whereas custodians and trustees are mostly free from judicial supervision. The powers of the first three, but not the trustees, terminate automatically when the owner reaches the age of majority. For assets of substantial value, the trust is usually the preferred tool of management.

2. RELEASE OR ASSIGNMENT OF AN EXPECTANCY

There are a number of actions that can bar a person from inheriting. One action that might prevent a person from inheriting is transferring the inheritance, the "expectancy", before the decedent dies. According to the common law, such a purported transfer of an expectancy has no legal effect because the person expecting to be an heir or devisee has no rights in the decedent's property before the decedent's death. An expectancy is not property. That said, it is possible for a court to enforce a purported transfer of an expectancy in order to achieve fairness in a given case. For example, a mother gives her son money as consideration for the inheritance he would take upon her death, and he acknowledges that her gift satisfies his share of her estate. To enforce the transfer of an expectancy, a court might require the transfer to be made for fair consideration and to be acknowledged by the transferor. If the purported transfer is to the person from whom the expectancy is expected, as in the example just given, it is called a release. If the purported transfer is made to a third party rather than the decedent, it is called an assignment.

3. DISCLAIMER

A competent person is not required to accept any gift, whether the gift was made inter vivos or at death under a will or intestate succession. If a donor is alive, the donee can refuse to accept the inter vivos gift. If the donor has died, the UPC allows the donee to refuse the gift by disclaiming it. Traditionally, the word "disclaimer" was used to refer to a rejection of a devise by a devisee and "renunciation" referred to the rejection of an inheritance by an heir, but UPC § 2–1105 uses "disclaimer" in both situations.

Under the UPC, disclaimers prevent the gift from passing to the disclaimant. UPC § 2–1106 accomplishes this result by creating a fiction that the disclaimant died before the time of distribution of the disclaimed interest, which is the time the interest would have taken effect in possession or enjoyment.

> Example 2.02: O dies intestate, survived by two children, A and B, and no other relatives. A disclaims. Because of the disclaimer, A's disclaimed interest passes as if A died before O; the result is that all of O's assets pass to B. The assets do not pass through A's estate to B; they pass directly from O, or O's estate, to B.

We will examine the operation of disclaimers in more detail during the discussion of intestate succession.

For reasons indicated below, it might be important for a donee to disclaim. However, many donees do not know about this possibility, so it is up to lawyers to tell them about it. Indeed, it can be malpractice for a lawyer to fail to advise a client about the possibility of disclaiming. It might also be malpractice for a lawyer to fail to file notice of disclaimer in a timely fashion. Keep in mind that the federal deadline, which allows only nine months, might be shorter than the state disclaimer requirement. Don't commit malpractice; it is a career-shortening move ("CSM").

(a) Why Might Someone Disclaim?

Why would a person not want to receive a gift from a decedent? You can imagine many reasons, but one common reason is to avoid estate or gift taxes on the asset at the time of the *disclaimant's* death.

> Example 2.03: Grandma dies leaving her assets by will to Mom. Mom has plenty of resources and does not want the assets from Grandma. If she accepts the devise, Mom is wealthy enough that she will have to pay gift taxes if she gives the assets away during life or estate taxes if she gives them to Daughter when she dies. Mom can disclaim her devise, allowing it to pass to Daughter without passing through Mom's estate. (However, in some states following

the common-law rule for renunciations, this might not work to avoid gift taxes. Under the common law, if Grandma dies without a will, the assets pass to Mom automatically. She can renounce, passing the assets to Daughter, but that renunciation is treated as a gift from Mom to Daughter.)

(b) Effect on Creditors

Another reason that a disclaimant might want to avoid receiving assets is that the disclaimant has creditors who would take the assets, preventing the assets from ever reaching the disclaimant's relatives. In most states, a debtor's disclaimer is not fraud on the disclaimant's creditors, and the creditors cannot reach the disclaimed assets. However, a debtor in bankruptcy cannot keep assets from creditors by disclaiming. In addition, the right to disclaim may be waived, and voluntary creditors should get such waivers if they are counting on inherited assets to be available when they make their claims against disclaimants. Moreover, some creditors are special in that they may reach the debtor's assets without obtaining a waiver in advance. Consider the following case.

DRYE V. UNITED STATES

Supreme Court of the United States, 1999
528 U.S. 49

GINSBURG, J.

This case concerns the respective provinces of state and federal law in determining what is property for purposes of federal tax lien legislation. At the time of his mother's death, petitioner Rohn F. Drye, Jr., was insolvent and owed the Federal Government some $325,000 on unpaid tax assessments for which notices of federal tax liens had been filed. His mother died intestate, leaving an estate with a total value of approximately $233,000 to which he was sole heir. After the passage of several months, Drye disclaimed his interest in his mother's estate, which then passed by operation of state law to his daughter. This case presents the question whether Drye's interest as heir to his mother's estate constituted "property" or a "righ[t] to property" to which the federal tax liens attached under 26 U.S.C. § 6321 despite Drye's exercise of the prerogative state law accorded him to disclaim the interest retroactively.

We hold that the disclaimer did not defeat the federal tax liens. The Internal Revenue Code's prescriptions are most sensibly read to look to state law for delineation of the taxpayer's rights or interests, but to leave to federal law the determination whether those rights or interests constitute "property" or "rights to property" within the meaning of § 6321. "[O]nce it has been determined that state law creates sufficient interests in the [taxpayer] to satisfy the requirements of [the federal tax lien provision], state law is inoperative to prevent the attachment of liens created by federal statutes in favor of the United States." *United States v. Bess*, 357 U.S. 51, 56–57 (1958).

I

A

The relevant facts are not in dispute. On August 3, 1994, Irma Deliah Drye died intestate, leaving an estate worth approximately $233,000, of which $158,000 was personalty and $75,000 was realty located in Pulaski County, Arkansas. Petitioner Rohn F. Drye, Jr., her son, was sole heir to the estate under Arkansas law. On the date of his mother's death, Drye was insolvent and owed the Government approximately $325,000, representing assessments for tax deficiencies in years 1988, 1989, and 1990. The Internal Revenue Service (IRS or Service) had made assessments against Drye in November 1990 and May 1991 and had valid tax liens against all of Drye's "property and rights to property" pursuant to 26 U.S.C. § 6321.

Drye petitioned the Pulaski County Probate Court for appointment as administrator of his mother's estate and was so appointed on August 17, 1994. Almost six months later, on February 4, 1995, Drye filed in the Probate Court and land records of Pulaski County a written disclaimer of all interests in his mother's estate. Two days later, Drye resigned as administrator of the estate.

Under Arkansas law, an heir may disavow his inheritance by filing a written disclaimer no later than nine months after the death of the decedent. The disclaimer creates the legal fiction that the disclaimant predeceased the decedent; consequently, the disclaimant's share of the estate passes to the person next in line to receive that share. The disavowing heir's creditors, Arkansas law provides, may not reach property thus disclaimed. In the case at hand, Drye's disclaimer caused the estate to pass to his daughter, Theresa Drye, who succeeded her father as administrator and promptly established the Drye Family 1995 Trust (Trust).

On March 10, 1995, the Probate Court declared valid Drye's disclaimer of all interest in his mother's estate and accordingly ordered final distribution of the estate to Theresa Drye. Theresa Drye then used the estate's proceeds to fund the Trust, of which she and, during their lifetimes, her parents are the beneficiaries. Under the Trust's terms, distributions are at the discretion of the trustee, Drye's counsel Daniel M. Traylor, and may be made only for the health, maintenance, and support of the beneficiaries. The Trust is spendthrift, and under state law, its assets are therefore shielded from creditors seeking to satisfy the debts of the Trust's beneficiaries.

Also in 1995, the IRS and Drye began negotiations regarding Drye's tax liabilities. During the course of the negotiations, Drye revealed to the Service his beneficial interest in the Trust. Thereafter, on April 11, 1996, the IRS filed with the Pulaski County Circuit Clerk and Recorder a notice of federal tax lien against the Trust as Drye's nominee. The Service also served a notice of levy on accounts held in the Trust's name by an investment bank and notified the Trust of the levy.

B

On May 1, 1996, invoking 26 U.S.C. § 7426(a)(1), the Trust filed a wrongful levy action against the United States in the United States District Court for the Eastern District of Arkansas. The Government counterclaimed against the Trust, the trustee, and the trust beneficiaries, seeking to reduce to judgment the tax assessments against Drye, confirm its right to seize the Trust's assets in collection of those debts, foreclose on its liens, and sell the Trust property. On cross-motions for summary judgment, the District Court ruled in the Government's favor.

The United States Court of Appeals for the Eighth Circuit affirmed the District Court's judgment. The Court of Appeals understood our precedents to convey that "state law determines whether a given set of circumstances creates a right or interest; federal law then dictates whether that right or interest constitutes 'property' or the 'right to property' under § 6321."

We granted certiorari to resolve a conflict between the Eighth Circuit's holding and decisions of the Fifth and Ninth Circuits. We now affirm.

II

Under the relevant provisions of the Internal Revenue Code, to satisfy a tax deficiency, the Government may impose a lien on any "property" or "rights to property" belonging to the taxpayer. Section 6321 provides: "If any person liable to pay any tax neglects or refuses to pay the same after demand, the amount . . . shall be a lien in favor of the United States upon all property and rights to property, whether real or personal, belonging to such person." A complementary provision, § 6331(a), states:

> "If any person liable to pay any tax neglects or refuses to pay the same within 10 days after notice and demand, it shall be lawful for the Secretary to collect such tax . . . by levy upon all property and rights to property (except such property as is exempt under section 6334) belonging to such person or on which there is a lien provided in this chapter for the payment of such tax."

The language in §§ 6321 and 6331(a), this Court has observed, "is broad and reveals on its face that Congress meant to reach every interest in property that a taxpayer might have." *United States v. National Bank of Commerce*, 472 U.S. 713, 719–720 (1985) (citing 4 B. Bittker, Federal Taxation of Income, Estates and Gifts); see also *Glass City Bank v. United States*, 26 U.S. 265, 267 (1945) ("Stronger language could hardly have been selected to reveal a purpose to assure the collection of taxes."). When Congress so broadly uses the term "property," we recognize, as we did in the context of the gift tax, that the Legislature aims to reach " 'every species of right or interest protected by law and having an exchangeable value.' "

Section 6334(a) of the Code is corroborative. That provision lists property exempt from levy. The list includes 13 categories of items; among the enumerated exemptions are certain items necessary to clothe and care for one's family, unemployment compensation, and workers' compensation benefits. The enumeration contained in § 6334(a), Congress directed, is exclusive: "Notwithstanding any other law of the United States . . ., no property or rights to property shall be exempt from levy other than the property specifically made exempt by subsection (a)." Inheritances or devises disclaimed under state law are not included in § 6334(a)'s catalog of property exempt from levy. See *Bess*, 357 U.S., at 57 ("The fact that . . . Congress provided specific exemptions from distraint is evidence that Congress did not intend to recognize further exemptions which would prevent attachment of [federal tax] liens[.]"); *United States v. Mitchell*, 403 U.S. 190, 205 (1971) ("Th[e] language [of § 6334] is specific and it is clear and there is no room in it for automatic exemption of property that happens to be exempt from state levy under state law."). The absence of any recognition of disclaimers in §§ 6321, 6322, 6331(a), and 6334(a) and (c), the relevant tax collection provisions, contrasts with § 2518(a) of the Code, which renders qualifying state-law disclaimers "with respect to any interest in property" effective for federal wealth-transfer tax purposes and for those purposes only.

Drye nevertheless refers to cases indicating that state law is the proper guide to the critical determination whether his interest in his mother's estate constituted "property" or "rights to property" under § 6321. His position draws support from two recent appellate opinions: *Leggett v. United States*, 120 F.3d 592, 597 (C.A.5 1997) ("Section 6321 adopts the state's definition of property interest."); and *Mapes v. United States*, 15 F.3d 138, 140 (C.A.9 1994) ("For the answer to th[e] question [whether taxpayer had the requisite interest in property], we must look to state law, not federal law."). Although our decisions in point have not been phrased so meticulously as to preclude Drye's argument, we are satisfied that the Code and interpretive case law place under federal, not state, control the ultimate issue whether a taxpayer has a beneficial interest in any property subject to levy for unpaid federal taxes.

III

As restated in *National Bank of Commerce*: "The question whether a state-law right constitutes 'property' or 'rights to property' is a matter of federal law." We look initially to state law to determine what rights the taxpayer has in the property the Government seeks to reach, then to federal law to determine whether the taxpayer's state-delineated rights qualify as "property" or "rights to property" within the compass of the federal tax lien legislation. Cf. *Morgan v. Commissioner*, 309 U.S. 78, 80 (1940) ("State law creates legal interests and rights. The federal revenue acts designate what interests or rights, so created, shall be taxed.").

In line with this division of competence, we held that a taxpayer's right under state law to withdraw the whole of the proceeds from a joint bank account constitutes "property" or the "righ[t] to property" subject to levy for unpaid federal taxes, although state law would not allow ordinary creditors similarly to deplete the account. And we earlier held that a taxpayer's right under a life insurance policy to compel his insurer to pay him the cash surrender value qualifies as "property" or a "righ[t] to property" subject to attachment for unpaid federal taxes, although state law shielded the cash surrender value from creditors' liens. By contrast, we also concluded, again as a matter of federal law, that no federal tax lien could attach to policy proceeds unavailable to the insured in his lifetime. ("It would be anomalous to view as 'property' subject to lien proceeds never within the insured's reach to enjoy.").

Just as "exempt status under state law does not bind the federal collector," so federal tax law "is not struck blind by a disclaimer". Thus, in *Mitchell*, the Court held that, although a wife's renunciation of a marital interest was treated as retroactive under state law, that state-law disclaimer did not determine the wife's liability for federal tax on her share of the community income realized before the renunciation. See 403 U.S., at 204 (right to renounce does not indicate that taxpayer never had a right to property).

IV

The Eighth Circuit, with fidelity to the relevant Code provisions and our case law, determined first what rights state law accorded Drye in his mother's estate. It is beyond debate, the Court of Appeals observed, that under Arkansas law Drye had, at his mother's death, a valuable, transferable, legally protected right to the property at issue. * * * (although Code does not define "property" or "rights to property," appellate courts read those terms to encompass "state-law rights or interests that have pecuniary value and are transferable"). The court noted, for example, that a prospective heir may effectively assign his expectancy in an estate under Arkansas law, and the assignment will be enforced when the expectancy ripens into a present estate.

Drye emphasizes his undoubted right under Arkansas law to disclaim the inheritance, a right that is indeed personal and not marketable. But Arkansas law primarily gave Drye a right of considerable value—the right either to inherit or to channel the inheritance to a close family member (the next lineal descendant). That right simply cannot be written off as a mere "personal right . . . to accept or reject [a] gift."

In pressing the analogy to a rejected gift, Drye overlooks this crucial distinction. A donee who declines an inter vivos gift generally restores the status quo ante, leaving the donor to do with the gift what she will. The disclaiming heir or devisee, in contrast, does not restore the status quo, for the decedent cannot be revived. Thus the heir inevitably exercises dominion over the property. He determines who will receive the property—himself if he does not disclaim, a known other if he does. This power to channel the estate's assets warrants the conclusion that Drye held "property" or a "righ[t] to property" subject to the Government's liens.

* * *

In sum, in determining whether a federal taxpayer's state-law rights constitute "property" or "rights to property," "[t]he important consideration is the breadth of the control the [taxpayer] could exercise over the property." Drye had the unqualified right to receive the entire value of his mother's estate (less administrative expenses), see *National Bank of Commerce*, 472 U.S., at 725 (confirming that unqualified "right to receive property is itself a property right" subject to the tax collector's levy), or to channel that value to his daughter. The control rein he held under state law, we hold, rendered the inheritance "property" or "rights to property" belonging to him within the meaning of § 6321, and hence subject to the federal tax liens that sparked this controversy.

For the reasons stated, the judgment of the Court of Appeals for the Eighth Circuit is

Affirmed.

Drye treats the IRS better than other creditors are treated. From the perspective of bearing losses, is the IRS more or less able to bear losses than an ordinary creditor? What is the rationale for the Court's decision? If you were the lawyer, how could you have structured the instruments to avoid the Commissioner's claims?

(c) Effect on Medicaid Eligibility

Medicaid helps people who are poor or disabled with their medical expenses. Should a person be allowed to qualify for Medicaid if he has impoverished himself by disclaiming assets? What is the impact of allowing people to do so? As a lawyer, you should be very careful in this area of law. First, the rules are complex and the disclaimant might fail to qualify for Medicaid when the disclaimant wanted to retain eligibility. Second, it might be possible for a lawyer to commit a crime by advising a client to do this.

4. ADULTERY AND DESERTION, ABUSE, REFUSAL TO SUPPORT

MATTER OF ESTATE OF PHELPS

Court of Appeals of Indiana, 2020
152 N.E.3d 1

MATHIAS, J.

* * *

Facts and Procedural History

Kara, Hailey, and Colby are the children of the decedent Thomas with his first wife. Kara, born in December 1992, is the oldest child. A second daughter, Hailey, was born in August 1996, and a son, Colby, was born in August 2004. All three children had a close relationship with their father. Kara had just received a degree in business management at the time of her father's death. She worked for her father's sanitation company, Sanitation Solutions, after graduation and lived with him until his death. Hailey was attending college at the time of her father's death. Thomas supported Hailey while she was in college by paying for her health insurance, car insurance, cell phone bill, and other college expenses. Colby was eleven years old at the time of his father's death. Although Colby did not live with Thomas at the time of Thomas's death, Thomas paid child support and health insurance premiums for Colby.

Erica was married to another man from 2003 until her divorce in 2012. Erica had two minor children from this prior marriage. Following Erica's divorce, Thomas asked her to work for his business, Sanitation Solutions. In the summer of 2012, Thomas petitioned to dissolve his marriage with his first wife, and he and Erica began to live together.

Thomas and Erica were married in October 2013, and had one daughter together, who was born in June 2014. Prior to their marriage, Thomas and Erica entered into a prenuptial agreement that provided in pertinent part:

> Except as herein provided, in the event that the marriage of Tom and Erica is terminated other than by the death of one of them, or in the event of a *legal separation*, Erica agrees to waive and does hereby waive all rights to Tom's Property
>
> . . . .

Thomas and Erica separated in August 2014, at which time Erica left the marital home to live with her parents. On February 17, 2015, Erica filed a petition to dissolve her marriage with Thomas. Although Erica and Thomas still saw each other periodically, and engaged in sexual intercourse at least once, Erica also became romantically involved with another man. After the separation, Erica became pregnant with this man's child.

On October 19, 2015, Thomas was killed when he was struck by a vehicle while standing on the side of the road next to one of his sanitation trucks. Thomas died intestate. On November 2, 2015, Julie Maloy ("Maloy") was appointed as personal representative of Thomas's estate. On November 20, 2015, Maloy was appointed as special administratrix for the purposes of commencing a wrongful death action. Maloy filed a wrongful death suit that was ultimately settled.

On August 20, 2019, the trial court held a hearing regarding the apportionment of the wrongful death proceeds and the payment of estate administration fees. On September 13, 2019, the trial court entered findings of fact and conclusions of law, determining in relevant part that: (1) Erica was "living in a state of adultery" and therefore not entitled to one-half of Thomas's net probate estate under the intestacy statutes;[1] (2) Erica was entitled to a share of the proceeds of the wrongful death claim because such proceeds were not part of Thomas's estate and because, under the terms of the prenuptial agreement, she and Thomas were not legally separated at the time of Thomas's death; and (3) Erica was entitled to one-half of the net proceeds of the wrongful death claim, with Thomas's four children each entitled to a one-eighth share. The Phelps Children now appeal.

Standard of Review

On appeal, the Phelps Children argue that the trial court erred in construing and applying the general wrongful death statute and the intestacy statutes. The construction of statutes is a matter of law that we review de novo.

I. The Wrongful Death Statute

The Phelps Children first claim that the trial court erred by concluding that Erica was entitled to receive a share of the net

---

[1] See Ind. Code § 29—1—2—14 ("If either a husband or wife shall have left the other and shall be living at the time of his or her death in adultery, he or she as the case may be shall take no part of the estate or trust of the deceased husband or wife").

proceeds of the wrongful death action. With regard to damages, the general wrongful death statute provides in relevant part:

> That part of the damages which is recovered for reasonable medical, hospital, funeral and burial expense shall inure to the exclusive benefit of the decedent's estate for the payment thereof. **The remainder of the damages, if any, shall, subject to the provisions of this article, inure to the exclusive benefit of the widow or widower, as the case may be, and to the dependent children, if any, or dependent next of kin, to be distributed in the same manner as the personal property of the deceased.** . . .

Ind. Code § 34–23–1–1 (emphasis added). The Phelps Children contend that the emphasized portion of the statute is ambiguous. We disagree.

The wrongful death statute first provides that the portion of damages recovered for medical, hospital, funeral, and burial expenses inure to the exclusive benefit of the decedent's estate for the payment of such expenses. It then provides that any remainder of damages shall inure to the "exclusive benefit of the *widow* . . . and to the dependent children . . . to be distributed in the same manner as the personal property of the deceased." *Id.* (emphasis added). It is clear from this language that Erica, who is Thomas's widow, and Thomas's "dependent children" are entitled to share in the remainder of the proceeds of the wrongful death action, less the amount recovered for medical, hospital, funeral, and burial expenses, in the same manner as they would Thomas's personal property. We find nothing unclear or ambiguous about this portion of the wrongful death statute.

* * *

II. Erica's Share of the Proceeds

The Phelps Children argue that the trial court abused its discretion by awarding Erica one-half of the remainder of the proceeds of the wrongful death action. Again, we disagree. As noted above, the wrongful death statute clearly and unambiguously provides that Erica, as Thomas's widow, and Thomas's dependent children are entitled to share in the remainder of the proceeds "in the same manner as the personal property of [Thomas]." I.C. § 34–23–1–1. Thomas died intestate. The relevant portion of Indiana's intestacy statutes, Indiana Code section 29–1–2–1, provides:

(a) The estate of a person dying intestate shall descend and be distributed as provided in this section.

(b) Except as otherwise provided in subsection (c), the surviving spouse shall receive the following share:

(1) One-half (½) of the net estate if the intestate is survived by at least one (1) child or by the issue of at least one (1) deceased child . . . .

Ind. Code § 29–1–2–1 (emphasis added).

Based on the plain language of this section, Erica, as the surviving spouse, would generally be entitled to receive one-half of the net estate, including personal property, because Thomas was survived by at least one child. The plain language of the wrongful death statute, in conjunction with the plain language of the intestacy statute, supports the trial court's conclusion that Erica is entitled to a one-half share of the net proceeds of the wrongful death action in the same manner as she would be entitled to Thomas's personal property.

The Phelps Children insist that this is incorrect. They claim that Erica should not receive one-half of the net proceeds of the wrongful death action because Indiana Code section 29–1–2–14, part of the intestacy statutes, provides that "[i]f either a husband or wife shall have left the other and shall be living at the time of his or her death in adultery, he or she as the case may be shall take no part of the estate or trust of the deceased husband or wife."[5] Since the wrongful death statute provides that the widow is entitled to a share of the net proceeds of the wrongful death action "in the same manner as the personal property of the deceased," and since Erica is not entitled to a share of Thomas's intestate estate due to the fact that she had left Thomas and was living in a state of adultery, the Children argue that Erica is therefore not entitled to any share of the net proceeds

---

[5] Erica argues in her Appellee's Brief that she did not leave Thomas or live in adultery. But the trial court found otherwise, and there was ample evidence to support the trial court's finding. Erica testified that she "left the [marital] house," and that she and Thomas "did not live together after filing for divorce." She further testified that she had sexual intercourse with another man, with whom she later had a child, on a regular basis after the dissolution action was filed and before Thomas died. Still, Erica claims that she was not "living in adultery" because she was living with her parents, not her paramour. But the adultery statute does not require that the decedent's spouse to live with his or her paramour before its provisions are applicable; it simply requires that the decedent's spouse be "living in adultery." Adultery is defined as "Consensual sexual intercourse between a married person and a person other than the spouse." American Heritage Dictionary online. The trial court did not clearly err by determining that the adultery statute applied to Erica, who left the marital residence and had voluntary sexual intercourse with someone other than Thomas while still legally married to Thomas.

of the wrongful death action. Although this argument has some facial appeal, it ultimately cannot stand.

The "adultery" section of the intestacy code provides that a spouse who has left the decedent and is living in a state of adultery at the time of the decedent's death shall take "no part of the *estate* or trust" of the decedent. I.C. § 29–1–2–14 (emphasis added). But it has long been held that the proceeds from a wrongful death action are not part of the decedent's *estate*. *See Goldman v. Cha*, 704 N.E.2d 157, 158 (Ind. Ct. App. 1999) ("Wrongful death proceeds do not become part of the decedent's estate and are not subject to claims of creditors of the decedent.").

In *Bruck*, we held that wrongful death proceeds did not become part of the intestate estate but instead "pass through *intestate distribution*." 632 N.E.2d at 748 (emphasis added). In other words, wrongful death proceeds are not part of the decedent's estate but are distributed in the same manner as if they were part of the intestate estate. And the adultery statute acts to bar an adulterous spouse only from taking part of the decedent's *estate*, which does not include the proceeds of a wrongful death claim.

We therefore conclude that, even though Erica may not be entitled to share in Thomas's estate, the wrongful death proceeds are not part of Thomas's estate. Such proceeds, even though not part of the decedent's estate, are to be *distributed* as set forth in the intestacy distribution statute, which provides that the widow of the intestate shall receive one-half of the estate if the intestate is survived by at least one child. Erica is therefore, as the trial court concluded, entitled to one half of the net proceeds of the wrongful death action.

The Phelps Children claim that it is unjust for Erica to receive half of the net proceeds of the wrongful death action. To do so, they observe that Indiana's child wrongful death statute—as compared to the adult wrongful death statute at issue here—specifically excludes the distribution of damages recovered in a wrongful death action to a "parent or grandparent who abandoned [the] deceased child while the child was alive[.]" Ind. Code § 34–23–2–1(i)(3). And they note that the adultery provision of the intestate probate code prohibits Erica, as the adulterous spouse, from receiving a portion of the intestate estate. The Phelps Children then pose the question, "If the wrongful death statutes for the death of a child, consider the existence of abandonment, and the probate codes address it, why wouldn't the criteria for the adult wrongful death distribution include a similar analysis?" This is not a question for a court, but for a legislative body. For whatever reason, the general wrongful death statute simply does not include similar language regarding abandoning spouses. Indeed, the absence of such abandonment language from the general wrongful death statute is all the more telling given the presence of such language in the child wrongful death statute. We will not read into the statute a provision the legislature clearly did not include. The Phelps Children's arguments that the result of this case is unjust or inequitable are inapposite given what we consider to be the plain language of the statutes at issue.

Conclusion

The trial court did not err by concluding that the wrongful death statute unambiguously provides that the net proceeds of the wrongful death statute inure to the exclusive benefit of Thomas's widow, Erica, and his dependent children, to be distributed in the same manner as Thomas's personal property. And under the intestacy statutes, Erica is entitled to one-half of such property as Thomas's widow. Although the adultery section of the intestacy code may deprive Erica of the right to receive distributions from Thomas's estate, the wrongful death proceeds are not part of Thomas's estate. Therefore, the trial court properly determined that Erica is entitled to one-half of the net proceeds of the wrongful death settlement, and we affirm the judgment of the trial court.

Affirmed.

The court said that the statute is not ambiguous. Did the court read the statute the way you would read the statute? Is the result what the decedent would have wanted? (Does it matter what the decedent would have wanted?) Is the court's reading what the legislators would have wanted? Should the statute have said, "to be distributed in the same manner as the personal property of the deceased including all provisions of the laws of intestacy that affect the distribution of the personal property of the decedent"?

In some states, adultery or desertion is a bar to inheritance. Similarly, in some states, a person who abused the decedent cannot inherit from the decedent. And, under UPC § 2–114, a parent cannot inherit from a child if there is clear and convincing evidence that the parent's parental rights could have been terminated for lack of support before the child died.

5. HOMICIDE

Since lack of support can prevent inheritance, it should come as no surprise that statutes often prevent murderers from inheriting from their victims. If there is no statutory provision preventing murderers from gaining an interest, should courts allow them to take?

(a) Constructive Trust

PRESTON V. CHABOT
Supreme Court of Vermont, 1980
412 A.2d 930

LARROW, J.

This is an appeal from a declaratory judgment order entered in Caledonia Superior Court which, in order to prevent Edward Chabot, Jr., from profiting by his crime, imposed a constructive trust upon defendants, Shirley Chabot and Edwin W. Free, Jr., of an undivided one-half interest in certain real property for the benefit of plaintiffs, children of Edward Chabot, Jr.'s first marriage.

Edward Chabot, Jr., and Norma Chabot were married on January 22, 1938, and subsequently, by virtue of two deeds, took title as tenants by the entirety to certain real estate located in Hardwick, Vermont. On November 15, 1965, Edward Chabot, Jr., shot his wife and was charged with murder. He pleaded guilty to second degree murder and was sentenced to the state penitentiary. Norma Chabot died intestate and her probate estate consisted entirely of personal property; no real property was listed in the inventory or final account.

After his release from prison in 1969, Edward Chabot, Jr., married Shirley Chabot and later, by straw deed, purportedly conveyed the Hardwick property to himself and Shirley Chabot as tenants by the entirety. He also on that same day, December 10, 1975, executed a will which left his entire estate, real and personal, to Shirley Chabot with the exception of small cash bequests to each of his children and grandchildren. Edward Chabot, Jr., died on December 29, 1975, survived by Shirley Chabot, children and grandchildren. Plaintiffs, though aware of their father's remarriage, did not learn of the December 10, 1975, deed and will until after his death.

A declaratory judgment action, seeking a constructive trust for the benefit of plaintiffs over the Hardwick property, was commenced on January 10, 1976. By agreement of the parties, an evidentiary hearing was waived, and the case submitted upon an agreed statement of facts and memoranda of law.

Defendants appeal, the trial court having found for plaintiffs, and assign as error the court's findings that: (1) this action was not barred by laches; and (2) in order to prevent Edward Chabot, Jr., from profiting by his crime, a constructive trust be imposed upon defendants of an undivided one-half interest in the subject property.

We deal first with the issue of laches. Laches is an affirmative equitable defense, and the burden is on the party relying on it. Laches involves prejudice to the adverse party, actual or implied, resulting from plaintiffs' delay in asserting their rights. It does not, however, arise from delay alone, but from delay that disadvantages another. Furthermore, a trial court's determination on the issue of laches is a matter of much discretion which will not be overturned unless clearly shown to be wrong.

Although more than eleven years elapsed between the murder of Norma Chabot and the institution of this action, there was no showing below that this delay in any way prejudiced the defendants. No evidence whatsoever was introduced as to defendant Edwin Free, Jr., who is a party to this action only by virtue of being executor of Edward Chabot, Jr.'s estate. Nor did evidence below indicate that defendant Shirley Chabot was prejudiced; her only change in status during this period was marrying Edward Chabot, Jr., and, two weeks before his death, receiving a deed purporting to make her a tenant by the entirety in the Hardwick property. Defendants have not shown how they are worse off by the trial court's imposition of a constructive trust now, than had it been imposed immediately after Shirley Chabot's marriage in 1970 to Edward Chabot, Jr. In both instances, Shirley Chabot would receive one-half of her late husband's interest in the subject property; defendants have not demonstrated prejudice.

Defendants' claim that if plaintiffs had taken legal action earlier and prevailed, Edward Chabot, Jr., would have made "other suitable arrangements" for Shirley Chabot is without merit. The evidence below is to the contrary. He willed Shirley Chabot substantially everything he owned, and even if he knew during his lifetime of this lawsuit, he could not have acted differently; there was nothing more to leave her.

In their second claim, defendants contend the trial court erred in holding that plaintiffs, Edward Chabot, III, and Evelyn Preston, owned legal title to an undivided one-half interest in the property. We disagree.

There was at the time of Norma Chabot's death in 1965 no Vermont statutory provision governing the descent and distribution of property from a decedent to the slayer of that decedent. But cf. 14 V.S.A. § 551(6) (statutory provision added in 1972 which caused a person convicted of intentionally and unlawfully killing another person to forfeit his share of that person's estate). This Court had, however, adopted the common law principle that one should not profit from his wrong. *In re Estate of Mahoney*, 126 Vt. 31, 34 (1966). This principle was not extended to every case where a killer acquired the victim's property as a result of the killing. Instead, the Court reasoned that the slayer should not be permitted to improve his position by the killing, but should not be compelled to lose property that he had a vested interest in had there been no killing.

Based on *Mahoney*, defendants argue that Edward Chabot, Jr., received at his wife's death the entire property, forfeiting nothing. They contend Edward Chabot, Jr., did not profit from his killing as he already, as a tenant by the entirety with his slain wife, Norma Chabot, owned the whole property, and should not forfeit this vested right in the whole.

Tenants by the entirety are, as defendants claim, viewed as *each* being vested, under a legal fiction, with title to the whole; there being no moieties. Additionally, during their joint lifetimes, neither has a share that can be disposed of without the other joining.

While Edward Chabot, Jr., had a vested right in the subject property, defendants' claim that he did not profit from this killing, if he received the entire property, is frivolous. A legal fiction, that each tenant by the entirety owns the whole, cannot obscure the fact that before Norma Chabot's murder, Edward Chabot, Jr., as a tenant by the entirety, had to share the profits of the property and, moreover, his right to sole and complete ownership was contingent upon surviving his wife. Whereas, after, and because of, this murder Edward Chabot, Jr., became the sole owner of the Hardwick property, no longer sharing the profits, nor fearing the loss of his interest.

As the trial court correctly indicates, it would be unconscionable for Edward Chabot, Jr., after murdering his wife and cotenant by the entirety, to retain the entire interest in the property and then pass title to his second wife as a successor tenant by the entirety. A husband who murders his wife should not be better off propertywise merely because he holds property by the entireties rather than some other way. Therefore, to avoid this unconscionable result, the trial court imposed a constructive trust on one-half of the subject property for benefit of plaintiffs.

The trial court found, and we think correctly, that the most equitable and appropriate method of distribution for resolving the instant case is one which recognizes that the estate was severed by the unlawful killing, and that the Hardwick property held by Edward, Jr., and Norma Chabot as tenants by entirety vested in Edward, Jr., when he survived Norma, but his estate is required to hold one-half of the property in constructive trust for Norma's heirs, the plaintiffs. The trial court analogized the present situation to a divorce, which under Vermont law destroys the tenancy by the entirety and creates by operation of law a tenancy in common among the parties. This position has been taken by other jurisdictions to prevent the "unconscionable mode" of acquiring full legal title by the husband's survival of his murdered wife. *Pannone v. McLaughlin*, 37 Md.App. 395, 405 (1977); *Barnett v. Couey*, 224 Mo.App. 913, 915 (1930). See also *National City Bank v. Bledsoe*, 237 Ind. 130 (1957); *Budwit v. Herr*, 339 Mich. 265 (1954).

This result works no forfeiture to defendants as they receive what Edward Chabot, Jr., was entitled to. Nor, however, do defendants profit, as they are prevented from acquiring any additional benefits from the murder of Norma Chabot. Despite the theory of ownership of the whole by tenants by the entirety, which defendants espouse, we think it is incorrect to suggest that the interest of a surviving husband is the same as his interest prior to his wife's death. Death severed the tenancy by the entirety and created a tenancy in common between the parties, the deceased's, Norma Chabot's, share being held in constructive trust for benefit of her heirs, the plaintiffs.

A constructive trust is a tool often used by courts to prevent unjust enrichment. It is a "formula through which the conscience of equity finds expression," and is, under these facts, a most appropriate vehicle. See *In re Estate of Mahoney*. The trial court's imposition of a constructive trust was proper, and the judgment below is affirmed.

Judgment affirmed.

BILLINGS, J., dissenting.

I cannot agree with the majority's reasoning or disposition of this case. The court below erred in construing the decision of this Court in *In re Estate of Mahoney*, 126 Vt. 31 (1966) and the law of tenancies by the entirety.

In the case of *Town of Corinth v. Emery*, 63 Vt. 505, 506–07 (1891), this Court set forth the common law of tenancies by the entirety as follows:

> This estate, created by conveyance to husband and wife, is a peculiar one. The interest of the grantees is not joint, nor in common. The parties do not hold moieties, but take as one person, taking as a corporation would take; they have but one title; each is seized of the whole and each owns the whole. If one dies the estate continues in the survivor, the same as if one of several corporators dies. It does not descend upon the death of either, but the longest liver, being already seized of the entire estate, is the owner of it. One tenant by entirety cannot sever the tenancy by deed, as a joint tenant can, for neither can alien so as to bind the other. . . . Divorce *vinculo* does not destroy the estate, and the *jus accrescendi* takes effect, upon the death of the one first dying.

Except insofar as absolute divorce is now deemed to transform the tenancy into one in common, these principles remain the law today. At the death of the first spouse the entire estate continues in the survivor.

It has been the law of this state, even before women acceded to their full beneficial life interests in the tenancy, that the husband "cannot do any act to the prejudice of the ulterior rights of the wife." The "ulterior rights" of the spouse include legal ownership of the whole estate from the date of acquisition. This principle is not changed by the recognition of the wife's separate lifetime interests which were formerly submerged in the husband's marital rights over his wife's property.

Since the enactment of the married women's property acts, this Court has made it clear that during the lifetime of both spouses each has a "separate estate" in the entirety. This "separate estate" consists of the powers of management and control, and the right to enjoy the rents, profits and income from the land.

Despite these changes in the lifetime benefits of the tenancy, this Court has declined to allow one spouse alone the power to encumber the estate by the entirety. Moreover, where both spouses do join in an agreement respecting the property, both are bound to its consequences and cannot for their separate benefits treat the estate as divided. No act of one spouse can alter the legal title which each holds in the whole estate. On the death of the first spouse, the survivor continues in his legal interest in the entirety as he had from the time of its vesting in the marital unit, irrespective of any attempt by the other spouse to alien or encumber the estate. There is, however, change in the survivor's estate, but it is equitable. His interest is no longer subject to the "ulterior rights" or "separate estate" of his spouse.

The rulings of this Court with respect to the character of the legal estate after divorce do not alter this result. In fact, this Court reaffirmed its interpretation of the legal estate in the very case in which it held that, upon divorce, the estate by the entirety is transformed into one in common. There the Court distinguished the effect on the estate of divorce from that of death as follows:

> [T]he continued existence of the estate would seem naturally and necessarily to depend upon the continued legal unity of the two persons to whom the conveyance was made. The survivor takes the whole in case of death, because that event has terminated the marriage and the consequent unity of person. An absolute divorce terminates the marriage and unity of person just as completely as does death itself, only instead of one as in the case of death there are in the case of divorce two survivors of the marriage, and there are from the time of such divorce two living persons in whom the title still remains.

Thus, it is only because there is a termination of the unity of the jural entity by judicial act *and* two surviving persons to accede to its interests that the law transforms the estate of tenancy by the entirety into one in common. A death of one spouse remains the only way in which a sole surviving spouse can enjoy independent legal powers and rights in the estate held of the marriage.

It is apparent, therefore, that each tenant by the entirety owns the whole legal estate from its original acquisition, that one spouse cannot alter the legal estate of either spouse in the entirety, and that at the death of the first, the surviving spouse acquires no new legal rights, but continues in his interest in the entirety. Nevertheless, upon the death of the first spouse, the survivor does acquire the benefits of an estate free from the separate lifetime interest and "ulterior rights" of the other spouse. This Court is now called upon to apply these principles to the rights of a murdering cotenant by the entirety in light of *In re Estate of Mahoney, supra.*

In *Mahoney* the probate estate of one spouse was held to have passed to the slayer spouse pursuant to 14 V.S.A. § 551. (This was prior to the enactment of subsection (6) in 1972.) The Court recognized, however, that equity would impose a constructive trust upon the property passing, under which the slayer would be obliged to transfer legal and equitable title to the decedent's heirs. In arriving at this conclusion, the Court rejected two alternative approaches to the problem of the slaying heir. The first of these would have permitted the slayer to obtain all legal and equitable title passing to him by operation of law without the interposition of any equitable consideration that but for the slaying the slayer would not have been so benefited. The second approach rejected by this Court would have equity prevent legal title from passing to the slayer at all.

The approach adopted by the Court was summarized as follows:

> The legal title passes to the slayer but equity holds him to be a constructive trustee for the heirs or next of kin of the decedent. This disposition of the question presented avoids a judicial engrafting on the statutory laws of descent and distribution, for title passes to the slayer. But because of the unconscionable mode by which the property is acquired by the slayer, equity treats him as a constructive trustee and compels him to convey the property to the heirs or next of kin of the deceased.

The Court adopted this view because through it "logic received its tribute, by holding that legal title passed," but equity was also done by denying the legal title holder the benefits of that passing. Put another way, "[the] principle . . . is that the slayer should not be permitted to improve his position by the killing, but should not be compelled to surrender property to which he would have been entitled if there had been no killing."

The Restatement of Restitution § 188 (1937) applies this principle to the situation before the Court, in which there has been a murder of a cotenant. It is stated as follows:

> Where two persons have an interest in property and the interest of one of them is enlarged by his murder of the other, to the extent to which it is enlarged he holds it upon a constructive trust for the estate of the other.

Comment b for this section states that with respect to joint tenants "if one of them murders the other, the murderer takes by survivorship the whole legal interest in the property, but he can be compelled to hold the entire interest upon a constructive trust for the estate of his co-tenant, except that he is entitled to one-half of the income for life. . . . The same rule is applicable to husband and wife holding as tenants by the entireties . . . ." This position also has the support of G. Bogert, Law of Trusts and Trustees and V A. Scott, Law of Trusts (lists five alternative solutions, but endorses the Restatement approach with respect to joint tenancies in reasoning equally applicable to tenancies by the entirety).

There are also a significant number of well reasoned decisions in other jurisdictions adopting this view, preeminent of which is *Bryant v. Bryant*. There the court stated that "[as] a question of common law the homicide does not prevent the legal title from passing to the criminal . . ., but equity, acting in personam, compels the wrongdoer who has acquired the res to hold it as a constructive trustee of the person wronged . . . ." Recognizing that while the legal estate by the entirety continued solely in the surviving spouse by operation of law, but that equity acts in personam to prevent unjust enrichment, the court imposed a constructive trust on the entire estate subject to the surviving husband's life interest in the whole income from the property. (North Carolina still permitted a husband a usufruct on his wife's property.) Massachusetts also appears to have adopted this rule. Similarly, stating that although the entire legal title rests in the slayer, equity imposes a constructive trust on the whole excepting one-half of the rents, profits and income for the slayer's life for the benefit of the victim's heirs, Oregon has adopted the Restatement approach.

In *Colton v. Wade*, 32 Del.Ch. 122 (1951), it was held that the surviving slayer spouse held legal title as constructive trustee in favor of the decedent on the entire estate subject to a life interest of the slayer in the commuted value of one-half the net income for his life expectancy. That life interest was "required to prevent infringement of vested rights." There is support for this view in New York, see *In re Hawkins' Estate*, 213 N.Y.S.2d 188, 191 (Sur.Ct. 1961), and New Jersey, see *Neiman v. Hurff*, 11 N.J. 55, 62 (1952); *Whitney v. Lott*, 134 N.J.Eq. 586, 591 (1944) (murder and suicide).

In the case at bar the Restatement rule is consistent with Vermont law. The rule recognizes that at common law each tenant by the entirety owns the whole legal interest from the date of original acquisition and does not acquire *legal* interest upon the death of the first spouse to die. At the same time, the rule acknowledges that the surviving tenant by the entirety accedes to beneficial interests upon the death of his spouse. Moreover, the rule does not require that this Court give the felonious act any legal significance, but rather permits equity to impose a constructive trust because "the legal title to property is obtained by a person in violation, express or implied, of some duty owed to the one who is equitably entitled, and . . . the property thus obtained is held in hostility to his beneficial rights of ownership."

Most importantly, this rule is fully consistent with the principle enunciated in *In re Estate of Mahoney, supra*, requiring that the slayer not be permitted to improve his position by killing, but not be compelled to surrender that to which he would otherwise be entitled. It follows *Mahoney* in recognizing that legal title in the whole is vested in the slayer and cannot be denied him, but strips the slayer of the beneficial enjoyment of accession to all lifetime rents, profits and income and the power of unilateral alienation. It restores to the heirs of the decedent spouse the "ulterior rights" of the spouse which the slayer prejudiced by his felony because equity irrebuttably presumes that the slain spouse would have outlived the slayer. The rule permits the slayer to retain one-half the value of the rents, profits and income of the property for his lifetime, since he would have enjoyed these in any event, but deprives him of any other benefit.

* * *

In light of our cases and the strength of cases supporting the Restatement position, we should adopt the rule of the Restatement of Restitution § 188 as it applies to tenancies by the entirety. The slayer and his successor in interest should be deemed to have obtained legal title to the entirety, but be held a constructive trustee for the entire estate, subject to the slayer's right to the value of the rents, profits and income of one-half the estate for the slayer's lifetime. The order below should be reversed and the case remanded for disposition not inconsistent with this opinion.

I am authorized to state that HILL, J., joins in this opinion.

———————————

Consider the majority and dissenting opinions. Both say killers should not profit from their wrong. Which of the approaches allows a killer to profit from killing?

Notice that courts have sometimes felt compelled to deviate from the statute by imposing a constructive trust on the assets held by the slayer. At the time of the *Mahoney* case, cited in *Preston*, the statute provided that the spouse inherits from the decedent, with no exception for a spouse who killed the decedent. The *Mahoney* court held that a constructive trust could be imposed upon the assets held by the killer, Charlotte Mahoney. The practical result of the constructive trust differed completely from what would have been reached under the statute. The *Mahoney* court said that its approach "avoids a judicial engrafting on the statutory laws of descent and distribution." Does it matter whether the court engrafts an exception on the statute or creates a constructive trust to reach the same result as it would by engrafting? Should the *Mahoney* court have enforced the statute, so the killer would take, or allow the imposition of a constructive trust, so the killer would not take from the decedent? In 1971, after Edward murdered Norma, the Vermont legislature amended § 551 of the statute by adding the following subsection to prevent slayers from inheriting from their victims.

> (6) Notwithstanding the foregoing rules or provisions otherwise made in any case where a person is entitled to inherit, including a devisee or legatee under the last will of a decedent, such person's share in the decedent's estate shall be forfeited and shall pass to the remaining heirs of the decedent if such person stands convicted * * * of intentionally and unlawfully killing the decedent.

14 V.S.A. § 551(6) (1974). That amendment effectively endorsed the result in *Mahoney* but did not deal with situations like that in

Preston because a surviving tenant by the entirety (or joint tenant) takes by right of survivorship rather than by inheriting from the decedent.

Are courts being activist courts when they reach results different from what statutes specify? Have courts been activist for a long time? Would the activities of courts be clearer to the public if courts were still divided into law and equity? Why don't legislatures prevent these deviations from the statutes they write?

(b) Statutory Bar

UPC § 2–803 generally prevents killers from profiting by killing, obtaining this result by treating killers as having disclaimed their intestate share and by revoking dispositions in instruments (including wills and trusts) executed by the decedent. How would the UPC treat the facts of *Preston*? UPC § 2–803(c)(2) "severs the interests of the decedent and killer in property held by them at the time of the killing as joint tenants with the right of survivorship [or as community property with the right of survivorship], transforming the interests of the decedent and killer into equal tenancies in common." On its face, that does not seem to apply to the facts of *Preston* because that case involved a tenancy by the entirety, not a joint tenancy. However, UPC § 1–201(25) says that "joint tenants with the right of survivorship" "includes co-owners of property held under circumstances that entitle one or more to the whole of the property on the death of the other or others," in effect defining joint tenancy to include tenancy by the entirety. So, § 2–803(c)(2) would apply, and the interests of the killer and decedent would be transformed into tenancies in common.

> Problem 2.04: K and D are tenants by the entirety in Blackacre. K is on his deathbed and asks healthy D to bring him a gun to shoot himself. K then shoots D instead. D is intestate, survived by K and H. (H is D's closest blood relative under the UPC.) How much of Blackacre does H take under the UPC? Is that a fair result? § 2–803(f) states that a "wrongful acquisition of property or interest by a killer not covered by this section must be treated in accordance with the principle that a killer cannot profit from the killer's wrong." Does that subsection allow a court to reduce the one-half share going to K under § 2-803(c)(2)?

(c) Scope of the Bar

The UPC bar applies to an individual who feloniously and intentionally kills the decedent. A conviction of felonious and intentional killing is conclusive, and the killer is barred. Killers who were never tried and even killers who were tried but not convicted can still be barred, and they are barred if they would be found criminally accountable under a preponderance of evidence standard for killing feloniously and intentionally.

Should the bar apply to those who assist the decedent in suicide?

> Question 2.05: H says, day after day, "Just shoot me." W gets a gun and holds it for H while H pulls the trigger. H's will says, "all to W." Should W inherit?

Should the killer's children be barred?

> Question 2.06: D marries W1. They divorce. W2 has children, not by D. Later, W2 marries D. D executes a will devising "60% to W2, and if she predeceases him to her children." W2 hires a hitman who kills D. Should W2's children take?

C. PROPERTY SUBJECT TO TRANSFER

1. POSTHUMOUSLY ACQUIRED RIGHTS

A decedent's estate carries on some of the decedent's legal life after her death. It is possible for the estate to acquire rights that would have been the decedent's rights had the decedent survived. For example, Jacob might grant a bonus to his employee, Ruth, after Ruth dies. Or Mary's will might make a gift "to Ruth or her estate" after Ruth has died. In these cases, the assets pass to Ruth's estate and pass from her estate to someone else. One question is whether the law chooses the next taker or allows Ruth's will to pass these assets that did not belong to Ruth during life. In *In re Estate of Braman*, 258 A.2d 492 (Penn. 1969) the court held that Ruth's will did not pass the assets; they followed intestate succession instead. Today, UPC § 2–602 takes the opposite position, allowing Ruth's will to pass the after-acquired property.

SHAW FAMILY ARCHIVES LTD. v. CMG WORLDWIDE, INC.

United States District Court for the Southern District of New York, 2007
486 F.Supp. 2d 309

McMahon, J.

On March 23, 2005, Plaintiffs Marilyn Monroe, LLC ("MMLLC") and CMG Worldwide, Inc. ("CMG") filed a complaint against the Shaw Family Archives and Bradford Licensing Associates ("the SFA parties"), in the United States District Court for the Southern District of Indiana, thereby setting in motion a tortuous series of events leading up to the instant cross-motions for summary judgment. In its Second Amended Complaint pursuant to the Indiana action, MMLLC alleges, among other things, that SFA and Bradford have violated Marilyn Monroe's right of publicity by using her name, image and likeness for commercial purposes without consent in violation of Indiana's Right of Publicity Act and that MMLLC has suffered damages as a result of that alleged violation of Ms. Monroe's right of publicity ("Count II"). On March 22, 27 and 28, 2005, MMLLC and CMG also filed three related actions in the Southern District of Indiana against other photographers and their agents concerning these same intellectual property rights.

* * *

Factual Background

* * *

Marilyn Monroe, perhaps the most famous American sex symbol of the twentieth century, died testate on August 5, 1962. Her will, which did not expressly bequeath a right of publicity, contained the following residuary clause:

> SIXTH: All the rest, residue and remainder of my estate, both real and personal of whatsoever nature and whatsoever situate, of which I shall die seized or possessed or to which I shall be in any way entitled, or over which I shall possess any power of appointment by Will at the time of my death, including any lapsed legacies, I give, devise and bequeath as follows:
>
> (a) To MAY REIS the sum of $ 40,000 or 25% of the total remainder of my estate, whichever shall be the lesser.
>
> (b) To DR. MARIANNE KRIS 25% of the balance thereof, to be used by her as set forth in ARTICLE FIFTH (d) of this my Last Will and Testament.

(c) To LEE STRASBERG the entire remaining balance.

The will also named Aaron Frosch, Ms. Monroe's New York-based attorney, as the executor. It was subject to primary probate in New York County Surrogate's Court.

In 1968, six years after probate of the Monroe Estate had commenced, Lee Strasberg married Anna Strasberg. Lee Strasberg died in 1982, leaving his wife Anna Strasberg as the sole beneficiary under his will. Upon the death of Mr. Frosch in 1989, the New York Surrogate's Court appointed Anna Strasberg as Administratrix, c.t.a., of the Monroe Estate. The Monroe Estate remained open until June 19, 2001, on which date the Surrogate's Court authorized the Administratrix to close the estate and transfer the residuary assets to MMLLC, a Delaware company formed by Ms. Strasberg to hold and manage the intellectual property assets of the residuary beneficiaries of Marilyn Monroe's will.

SFA is a limited liability company organized under New York law with its primary place of business in New York. Its principals are the three children of the late photographer Sam Shaw. Among the photographs owned by SFA and comprising the Shaw Collection is a series of photographs of Marilyn Monroe, including many "canonical" Marilyn images. The copyrights to the Marilyn photographs are purportedly owned by Sam Shaw's daughters, Edith Marcus and Meta Stevens.

This dispute arises out of (1) the alleged sale of a T-shirt at a Target retail store in Indianapolis, Indiana on September 6, 2006, which bore a picture of Marilyn Monroe and the inscription of the "Shaw Family Archives" on the inside neck label and tag, and (2) the alleged maintenance of a website by SFA and Bradford through which customers could purchase licenses for the use of Ms. Monroe's picture, image and likeness on various commercial products. MMLLC asserts that it is the successor-in-interest to the postmortem right of publicity that was devised through the residuary clause of Ms. Monroe's will, and that the commercial use of Ms. Monroe's picture, image, and likeness by SFA and Bradford without MMLLC's consent violates its rights under Indiana's 1994 Right of Publicity Act. This statute, passed over three decades after Ms. Monroe's death, by a state with which she had (as far as the court is aware) absolutely no contact during her life, creates a descendible and freely transferable right of publicity that survives for 100 years after a personality's death. The statute purports to apply to an act or event that occurs within Indiana, regardless of a personality's domicile, residence, or citizenship.

* * *

Discussion

In their cross-motion for summary judgment, the SFA parties argue, *inter alia,* that even if a postmortem right of publicity in Marilyn Monroe's name, likeness and persona exists, MMLLC and CMG cannot demonstrate that they are the owners of that right because only property actually owned by a testator at the time of her death can be devised by will. Since neither New York nor California (the only possible domiciles of Ms. Monroe at the time of her death)— nor for that matter, Indiana—recognized descendible postmortem publicity rights at the time of Ms. Monroe's death in 1962, she could not transfer any such rights through her will, and MMLLC cannot be a successor-in-interest to them. Moreover, the SFA parties contend, neither the California nor the Indiana right of publicity statutes allow for the transfer of the publicity rights they recognize through the wills of personalities who were already deceased at the time of their enactment. The court agrees.

1. *Ms. Monroe did not have the testamentary capacity to devise property rights she did not own at the time of her death.*

MMLLC argues that its ownership interest in Ms. Monroe's postmortem right of publicity—assuming *arguendo* that such a right exists—stems from Ms. Monroe's valid devise of this right to Lee Strasberg through the residuary clause in her will. The court concludes—regardless of Ms. Monroe's domicile at the time of her death, and regardless of any rights purportedly conferred after her death by the Indiana Right of Publicity Act or by Cal. Civil Code § 3344.1—Ms. Monroe could not devise by will a property right she did not own at the time of her death in 1962.

Descendible postmortem publicity rights were not recognized, in New York, California, or Indiana at the time of Ms. Monroe's death in 1962. To this day, New York law does not recognize any common law right of publicity and limits its statutory publicity rights to living persons. California recognized descendible publicity rights when it passed its postmortem right of publicity statute in 1984, 22 years after Ms. Monroe's death. Prior to that time, a common law right of publicity existed, but it was not freely transferable or descendible. Indiana first recognized a descendible, postmortem right of publicity in 1994, when it passed the Indiana Right of Publicity Act. Prior to that time, rights of publicity were inalienable in Indiana, since they could only be vindicated through a personal tort action for invasion of privacy.

Thus, at the time of her death in 1962 Ms. Monroe did not have any postmortem right of publicity under the law of any relevant state. As a result, any publicity rights she enjoyed during her lifetime were extinguished at her death by operation of law.

Nevertheless, MMLLC argues that her will should be construed as devising postmortem publicity rights that were later conferred on Ms. Monroe by statute. Such a construction is untenable.

Indiana follows the majority rule that the law of the domicile of the testator at his or her death applies to all questions of a will's construction. *White v. United States*, 511 F.Supp. 570 (S.D.Ind.1981). There are disputed issues of fact concerning whether Ms. Monroe was domiciled in New York or California at the time of her death. (There is absolutely no doubt that she was not domiciled in Indiana.) However, it is not necessary to resolve the question of domicile because neither New York nor California—the only two states in which Ms. Monroe could conceivably have been domiciled—permitted a testator to dispose by will of property she does not own at the time of her death.

It is well-settled that, under New York law, "A disposition by the testator of all his property passes all of the property he was entitled to dispose of *at the time of his death.*" The corollary principle recognized by the courts is that property not owned by the testator at the time of his death is not subject to disposition by will. *See also In re Estate of Gernon*, 35 Misc.2d 12 (1962) ("In the absence of a contrary intent the will must be interpreted as applying to all property owned by [the testator] *at the date of his death*") (emphasis added).

MMLLC—which clearly derived any interest in Monroe's post-mortem right of publicity through her will (via the legatees)—tries to distinguish *Gernon* by arguing that a testator's "contrary intent" can overcome the prohibition on passing property not owned by the testator at the time of his death. The argument is unpersuasive. The "contrary intent" contemplated by *Gernon* and the cases cited therein is an intent to devise only the property owned by the testator at the time of the will's execution rather than at the time of death. The legislative history of EPTL § 3–3.1 makes clear that it was enacted to codify the rule that a will is deemed pass all of the property the testator owns at the time of his death, rather than only the property owned at the time when the will was executed. Thus, when the *Gernon* court and others refer to "after-acquired" property, the term signifies property acquired after the execution of the will and before the testator's death—not property acquired after the testator's death. Nothing in EPTL § 3–3.1 or *Gernon* stands for the proposition that any intent on the part of the testator can overcome his testamentary incapacity to devise property he does not own at the time of his death.

California law does not differ from New York's. Section 21105 of the California Probate Code provides that, with inapplicable exceptions, "A will passes all property *the testator owns at death, including property acquired after execution of the will.*" (emphasis added). In *In re Buzza's Estate*, the court held that a testator/wife could not devise an inter vivos trust that terminated by operation of law when her husband predeceased her. 194 Cal.App.2d 598, 601 (1961) The *Buzza* court explained the probate rule as follows:

> It is settled law that a will is construed as applying to and disposing of the estate in its condition at the time of death. A testator may dispose only of such property as is subject to his testamentary power, and the testator is presumed to know the law. In interpreting a will, a court should view the will in a manner which will reveal the intent of the testator as disclosed by the language in the will and, if possible, effectuate the intent. This does not mean, however, that a testator may validly dispose of non-existent property.

See also *McKay v. Lauriston*, 204 Cal. 557, 569–70 (1928) (holding that wife could not devise an interest in community property that terminated and became her husband's upon her death).

MMLLC cites various provisions of the EPTL and the California Probate Code and asks this court to draw the inference that property not owned by Ms. Monroe at the time of her death can nonetheless pass through the residuary clause in her will. However, those provisions do not speak to the precise question presented—whether Ms. Monroe had the testamentary capacity to devise a right she did not own at the time of her death. Faced with the unequivocal language of the provisions and cases that are precisely on point, the court is unpersuaded by MMLLC's endeavor to reason from attenuated analogies.

Nor does § 2–602 of the Uniform Probate Code, which states that a will may pass "property acquired by the estate after the testator's death," have anything to do with the present case, because neither New York nor California is among the 18 states that have adopted the Uniform Probate Code in whole or even in part. This court has not found, nor has MMLLC cited, any provision in either the New York or the California probate laws that codifies § 2–602.

MMLLC's reliance on the case of *In re Hite*, 700 S.W.2d 713, 717 (Tex.App.1985) for the proposition that a residuary clause may dispose of property "that the testator may have overlooked, property that lacked particular definition or property that the testatrix did not know that she was entitled to at the time the will was executed" is equally unavailing. First, the case is a Texas case and Texas law has nothing to do with the matter before the court. Second, Ms. Monroe's purported postmortem right of publicity does not fit into any of the categories mentioned by the *Hite* court. Ms. Monroe could not have overlooked a right that did not come into being (assuming she was domiciled in California) until 22 years after her death. The property right that she allegedly devised through the residuary clause did not "lack particular definition"—it did not exist. Nor, for identical reasons, is this a case where the testatrix was entitled to certain property at the time her will was executed (or at the time of her death) but was unaware of her entitlement.

Third, *In re Hite* reaffirmed, rather than undermined, the rule that only property owned at death can be devised by will. In *In re Hite*, the court refused to alter the disposition of property as between two beneficiaries under a will in light of events that occurred after the testatrix's death. In her will, the testatrix devised to her husband an undivided one-half interest in "all oil and gas royalties to which I may be entitled" from leases on land, with the remainder passing to her son. At the time of her death, the testatrix owned a fee mineral estate that had no operating leases on it. The court was called upon to determine whether royalties from an oil and gas lease on that fee mineral estate that was executed after the testatrix's death passed to the husband (as royalties to which the testatrix "may be entitled") or to the son (who took the land on which the lease was executed under the residuary clause of the will).

The court held that the execution of a new lease after the death of the testatrix created a royalty interest for the benefit of the son, not for the benefit of the testatrix herself, so the son was entitled to the royalties from the lease executed after her death. The court explained the rationale as follows:

> It is well established that a will speaks of the testator's estate as of the time of the testator's death, and it is the estate of the testator then possessed that passes according to the terms of the will. It has been said that there is no shorter interval of time from when a testator dies and his estate passes to the devisees under his will. Title to an estate vests immediately in the devisees at the very moment of the testator's death, though title to the estate is subject to administration. Here, at the time of the testatrix' death, she owned an undivided interest in a fee mineral estate which was not burdened with any royalty interests. This fee mineral estate was devised to appellee (her son) in the residuary clause of her will.

Thus, far from holding that property in which the testatrix held no ownership interest at the time of her death could pass through the residuary clause of her will, the *In re Hite* court reaffirmed that a will speaks of the testator's estate at the time of her death, and that rights that vested in devisees under a will at the moment of the testator's death cannot be altered by events occurring thereafter.

Even if, as MMLLC implies, there has been some recent shift away from the unequivocal rule that only property owned by the testator at the time of death can be passed by will (as evidenced by § 2–602 of the Uniform Probate Code), it does not help MMLLC's cause. "Testamentary disposition . . . is controlled by the law in effect *as of the date of death.*" *Dep't of Health Services v. Fontes*, 169 Cal.App.3d 301, 305 (1985) (emphasis added). There is no question— based on the case law recited above—that at the time of Ms. Monroe's death in 1962, neither New York nor California permitted a testator to dispose by will of property she did not own at the time of her death. Any argument that the residuary clause of Ms. Monroe's will could devise a postmortem right of publicity is thus doubly doomed because the law in effect at the time of Ms. Monroe's death did not recognize descendible postmortem publicity rights and did not allow for distribution under a will of property not owned by the testator at the time of her death.

2. *Ms. Monroe did not "intend" to devise any rights she may have acquired under the Indiana of [sic] California right of publicity statute through the residuary clause of her will.*

MMLLC argues that Marilyn Monroe intended to bequeath a postmortem right of publicity to her testamentary legatees. The argument is unpersuasive. Adhering to the well-settled principles of probate law discussed above does no violence to Ms. Monroe's testamentary intent, the touchstone in construing her will under both New York and California law. MMLLC makes much of Ms. Monroe's purported intent to include in her residuary estate all property "to which [she] shall be in any way entitled." In the absence of any other evidence concerning Ms. Monroe's intent, this boilerplate language is much too slender a reed on which to hang a devise of postmortem publicity rights that did not come into being until 22 years after her death.

First, the language Ms. Monroe used does not reveal any actual intent to devise property she did not own at the time of her death, much less an intent to devise a postmortem right of publicity whose existence Ms. Monroe could not have contemplated. The entire residuary clause reads as follows:

> All the rest, residue and remainder of my estate, both real and personal of whatsoever nature and whatsoever situate, of which I shall die seized or possessed or to which I shall be in any way entitled, or over which I shall possess any power of appointment by Will at the time of my death, including any lapsed legacies, I give, devise and bequeath as follows:

MMLLC improperly construes the "to which I shall in any way be entitled" phrase independently of the limitation that precedes it within the same clause. Because there is no comma separating the phrases "of which I shall die seized or possessed" and "to which I shall be in any way entitled," they are part of a single term or clause and must be construed together. The limitation "of which I shall die" thus applies to every verb that follows it in the clause, including the verb "entitled." This reading is bolstered by Ms. Monroe's disposition in the very next clause of property over which she "shall possess any power of appointment by Will at the time of [her] death." The "to which I shall in any way be entitled" language is thus book-ended by phrases in which Ms. Monroe explicitly recognizes that her powers of testamentary disposition are limited to property she owns at the time of her death. This court cannot take this common phrase out of its context and attribute to it the preternatural foresight that MMLLC suggests.

Second, a testator is presumed, as a matter of law, to know that he cannot dispose of property over which he has no testamentary power, including property he does not own at the time of his death.

Even if the language Ms. Monroe employed clearly demonstrated her intent to devise property she had no capacity to devise, the effect would be to render the disposition invalid, because she had no legal right to dispose of property that did not exist at the time of her death. In *In re Van Winkle's Will*, the New York Surrogate's Court stated the rule unequivocally: "Under no circumstances, in, the absence of a valid power, can any amount of testamentary intent produce the effect of subjecting property not owned by a testator at the date of his death to any disposition whatever." 86 N.Y.S.2d at 600.

Finally, MMLLC's argument that refusing to allow property that did not exist at the time of Ms. Monroe's death to pass through the residuary clause of her will improperly favors intestacy without any countervailing considerations borders on the absurd. The countervailing consideration that MMLLC refuses to recognize is Ms. Monroe's legal incapacity to devise what she did not own.

3. *Neither the California nor the Indiana postmortem right of publicity statutes allows for testamentary disposition of the rights it recognizes by celebrities already deceased at the time of its enactment.*

Finally, MMLLC's case is doomed because both the California and Indiana postmortem right of publicity statutes recognize that an individual cannot pass by will a statutory property right that she did not possess at the time of her death. California's Civ. Code § 3344.1(b)–(d) provides that, if no transfer of a personality's postmortem right of publicity has occurred before the personality's death, either "by contract or by means of a trust or testamentary documents," then the rights vest in certain statutorily specified heirs. Since a testamentary transfer has no effect until the testator's death, such a transfer could not be effectuated "before death" for purposes of the California statute. Thus, any rights bestowed by § 3344.1 on a personality already deceased at the time of its enactment could not be transferred by will (which is how the purported property right came to MMLLC from the Administratrix at the time the Monroe Estate wound up). It would vest instead in the persons provided for by statute.

The Indiana statute likewise provides that if a personality has not transferred her right of publicity by "contract," license," "gift," "trust," or "testamentary document," the right will "vest" in those individuals entitled to her property through the "[o]peration of the laws of intestate succession applicable to the state administering the estate and property of the intestate deceased personality, regardless of whether the state recognizes the property rights set forth under this chapter." Ms. Monroe's legatees under her will are not her statutory heirs for intestacy purposes.

Thus, even if a postmortem right of publicity in Marilyn Monroe's persona could have been created after her death, neither of the statutes that arguably bestowed that right allows for it to be transferred through the will of a "personality" who, like Ms. Monroe, was already deceased at the time of the statute's enactment. To the extent that other courts, including *Joplin Enterprises v. Allen*, 795 F.Supp. 349 (W.D.Wash.1992) and *Miller v. Glenn Miller Productions*, 318 F.Supp.2d 923 (C.D.Cal.2004), assumed without explicitly deciding that California's right of publicity statute allows for the disposition of the rights it recognizes through wills of personalities already deceased at the time of its enactment, and that such disposition is permissible under the applicable probate principles, this court respectfully disagrees.

Having determined that any postmortem right of publicity in Marilyn Monroe could not have passed to MMLLC's predecessors-in-interest through the residuary clause in her will, the court need not consider the SFA parties' alternative arguments.

Conclusion

MMLLC's motion for summary judgment on Count II of its Second Amended Complaint is denied, and SFA's cross-motion for summary judgment on the same Count is granted.

This constitutes the decision and order of the Court.

―――――――――

A legislature may create new rights to be held by individuals who are already dead. The opinion in *Shaw* focuses on whether the rights in persona that came into being later were transferred under the law of wills that existed at the time of Marilyn Monroe's death and holds that those laws did not allow the transfer of rights not yet in existence. The court is right to examine that issue, for if the law of wills at that time allowed transfer of subsequently created rights, Marilyn's will would have governed their disposition. But that is not the only possible legal ground on which Marilyn might have transferred her personality rights by her will. It is within the power of a legislature to create a new right that did not exist in the past, to attribute that new right to persons who died in the past, and to make that new right subject to allocation by wills of those persons who died in the past. But the court found that the California statute did not do that; it did not allow a dead personality to pass the newly created rights by the will of the dead personality. What did that statute say?

At the time of the case, the California Civil Code read as follows:

(a)(1)   Any person who uses a deceased personality's name, voice, signature, photograph, or likeness, in any manner, on or in products, merchandise, or goods, or for purposes of advertising or selling, or soliciting purchases of, products, merchandise, goods, or services, without prior consent from the person or persons specified in subdivision (c), shall be liable for any damages sustained by the person or persons injured as a result thereof. * * *

(b) The rights recognized under this section are property rights, freely transferable, in whole or in part, by contract or by means of trust or testamentary documents, whether the transfer occurs before the death of the deceased personality, by the deceased personality or his or her transferees, or, after the death of the deceased personality, by the person or persons in whom the rights vest under this section or the transferees of that person or persons.

* * *

(e) If any deceased personality does not transfer his or her rights under this section by contract, or by means of a trust or testamentary document, and there are no surviving persons as described in subdivision (d), then the rights set forth in subdivision (a) shall terminate.

* * *

(g) No action shall be brought under this section by reason of any use of a deceased personality's name, voice, signature, photograph, or likeness occurring after the expiration of 50 years from the death of the deceased personality.

* * *

Can subsection (b) above reasonably be read as follows?

> [These] rights . . . are property rights, freely transferable . . . by means of trust or testamentary documents . . . .

In other words, did the legislature intend the words after "documents" to limit the modes of transfer, or just give examples of possibilities? Should the legislature have said, "including but not limited to"? The court took the position that the words "before the death of the deceased personality" limit the preceding words of free transferability. Applying that limit, the court said, "Since a testamentary transfer has no effect until the testator's death, such a transfer could not be effectuated 'before death' for purposes of the California statute." The court is technically correct in saying that a transfer by will takes effect at the instant of death, not before or after. But, if one takes that position, would it ever be possible for "testamentary documents" of the personality to transfer the personality's rights? Does it seem likely that the legislature meant to create rights in a personality that could not be transferred by the will of the personality, but could be transferred by wills of other persons? Does subsection (e), above, help to answer that question?

It did not take the California legislature long to respond. In 2007, the legislature amended the statute by adding the following:

> * * * The rights recognized under this section shall be deemed to have existed at the time of death of any deceased personality who died prior to January 1, 1985, and, except as provided in subdivision (o), shall vest in the persons entitled to these property rights under the testamentary instrument of the deceased personality effective as of the date of his or her death. In the absence of an express transfer in a testamentary instrument of the deceased personality's rights in his or her name, voice, signature, photograph, or likeness, a provision in the testamentary instrument that provides for the disposition of the residue of the deceased personality's assets shall be effective to transfer the rights recognized under this section in accordance with the terms of that provision.

What does that tell you about the *Shaw* court's reading of the earlier version of the statute? Do you think the legislature would have preferred the court to allow the personality to transfer her rights by will or to preclude such transfers by applying the technical rule that a will is effective at the moment of death and not before or after?

Another new type of right is the right to control one's avatar on social and gaming media. Assuming those rights are not already transferred before death, are there reasons they should not pass in the decedent's estate? Should the rights terminate rather than pass by intestate succession?

2. PERSONA AND PUBLICITY

Shaw shows that persona and rights to publicity can be subject to transfer by will. What else might be transferred by will?

3. HUMAN DNA

(a) Enslaved People (Not Anymore, Obviously and Thankfully)

Enslaved people were once considered to be property and as such could pass at death by descent or devise. It was also legally possible sometimes for an owner to transfer ownership of enslaved persons to themselves. We now know that ownership of persons is morally abhorrent.

(b) Minors

Persons under the age of majority are not property. And they have the capacity to own property. However, they do not have the capacity to manage their property or even themselves. For that reason, they need someone to make decisions for them. Wills of parents or current guardians can suggest the next guardian of the minor, and this is one reason that people execute wills. However, a court has the power to ignore those instructions and choose someone else to be the guardian of the minor. Indeed, this is consistent with the idea that human beings are not property. They are not owned by their parents, and their parents do not have the right to control who takes custody of them next.

(c) Unexecuted DNA Instructions (Gametes and Zygotes)

ESTATE OF KIEVERNAGEL

Court of Appeal, Third District, California, 2008
166 Cal.App.4th 1024

MORRISON, J.

In this case we must decide whether a widow has the right to use her late husband's frozen sperm to attempt to conceive a child where her late husband signed an agreement with the company storing the frozen sperm providing that the frozen sperm was to be discarded upon his death. We conclude that in determining the disposition of gametic material, to which no other party has contributed and thus another party's right to procreational autonomy is not implicated, the intent of the donor must control. In this judgment roll appeal, the widow cannot challenge the probate court's finding that the decedent's intent was to have his frozen sperm discarded upon his death. Accordingly, we affirm the decision denying distribution of the frozen sperm to the widow.

FACTUAL AND PROCEDURAL BACKGROUND

Joseph and Iris Kievernagel were married for 10 years prior to Joseph's death. They contracted with the Northern California Fertility Medical Center, Inc., to perform in vitro fertilization (IVF) to allow Iris to conceive. The fertility center operated a sperm cryopreservation storage program under which sperm was collected and stored at temperatures as low as -196 degrees centigrade. The frozen sperm could then be thawed and used for insemination. The center required Joseph to store a sperm sample under this program in case his live sperm could not used on the day of insemination.

As part of the sperm cryopreservation storage program, the center required an IVF Back-Up Sperm Storage and Consent Agreement (the Agreement). Iris completed the Agreement and Joseph signed it. The Agreement provided that the sperm sample was Joseph's sole and separate property and he retained all authority to control its disposition. The Agreement provided for two options for the disposition of the sperm sample upon death or incapacitation: donate the sperm to his wife or discard the sperm sample. The box indicating the sperm sample was to be discarded was checked and Joseph initialed it. The Agreement also provided the sperm sample was to be discarded upon divorce. Iris signed, acknowledging the sperm sample was Joseph's sole and separate property.

Joseph died in a helicopter crash in July 2005.

Iris was appointed administrator of Joseph's estate. She petitioned under Probate Code section 11623 for a preliminary distribution of an "asset of no financial value" but "of immense sentimental value to the widow." The item she sought was a vial of Joseph's frozen sperm. The fertility center would not release it without a court order.

Joseph's parents, as interested parties, objected to the preliminary distribution. They contended it was contrary to Joseph's express wishes, as set forth in the Agreement, that upon his death, his sperm sample was to be discarded. The Agreement comported with their understanding that their son did not wish to father a child posthumously.

After an evidentiary hearing, the probate court issued a tentative decision. The court found the following undisputed evidence. Joseph and Iris "loved each other deeply and completely." Joseph was opposed to having children, but agreed to the fertility procedures due to Iris's strong desire for children. The couple's dispute over having children led them to marriage counseling. According to the marriage counselor, Joseph believed Iris would divorce him if he did not agree to have children and a divorce would devastate him. The Agreement provided the sperm sample was to be discarded upon Joseph's death. This option was selected instead of the option to donate the sperm sample to Iris. Iris completed the Agreement, making the selections. Joseph signed it.

The probate court found the key issue was the intent of the decedent regarding use of his sperm. The court's analysis was based on *Hecht v. Superior Court* (1993), 16 Cal.App.4th 836, a case involving a dispute over disposition of frozen sperm, and *Davis v. Davis* (Tenn.1992) 842 S.W.2d 588, involving a dispute over disposition of frozen preembryos. The court found the Agreement evidenced the intent of both Iris and Joseph that the sperm be discarded upon his death. There was no evidence they ever discussed changing the provisions of the Agreement.

Iris objected to the tentative decision. She questioned the court's analysis of intent. She argued her testimony that Joseph did not even read the Agreement was admissible evidence with probative value. Finally, she asserted Joseph's intent was that she have his child.

The court denied the request for clarification of its analysis. It found Iris failed to prove the Agreement did not express Joseph's intent. By a preponderance of the evidence, the court found Joseph's intent was to stop the fertility process upon his death by discarding his frozen sperm.

The petition for distribution of the sperm sample was denied.

DISCUSSION

In making its decision, the court below found "little to no guiding precedent," but found some guidance in the *Hecht* and *Davis* cases. Iris contends the court erred in applying *Hecht* and argues that its requirement of an "unequivocable" intent provides an unworkable standard. Iris further contends the surviving spouse has a right to procreate that should be considered and the balancing test set forth in *Davis* should be applied. In applying the balancing test, the surviving spouse's interest prevails.

We begin our analysis by discussing the *Hecht* and *Davis* cases. We then conclude the probate court properly determined that the disposition of the frozen sperm is governed by the intent of the deceased donor and that the *Davis* balancing test is inappropriate in these circumstances.

In *Hecht,* William Kane deposited 15 vials of his sperm in an account at a sperm bank and then took his own life. The storage agreement provided that upon Kane's death, the sperm bank was to continue to store the specimens upon request of the executor of Kane's estate or to release the specimens to the executor. Kane's will named his girlfriend, Deborah Hecht, as executor. The will also bequeathed the sperm specimens stored at the sperm bank to Hecht for her to become impregnated, if she wished. Kane wrote a letter to his children about family memories and why he was committing suicide. It was addressed to his two children from a previous marriage, but included the possibility that he could have posthumous children by Hecht.

Kane's will was admitted into probate and a special administrator appointed. Kane's children contested the will. The parties attempted to settle the dispute, entering into two settlement agreements. The first was a tentative agreement that did not specifically mention the sperm. The second agreement sought to assign the estate's interest in the sperm to Hecht. In proceedings to settle the estate, the administrator, at the request of the children, petitioned for instructions to order the sperm destroyed on public policy grounds, or for an order of a preliminary distribution of either 100 or 80 percent of the sperm to the children on alternate theories of entitlement. The probate court ordered the sperm destroyed and Hecht petitioned the appellate court for a writ of mandate or prohibition to vacate the order.

The appellate court first determined that the frozen sperm fell within the broad definition of property in Probate Code section 62, so the probate court had jurisdiction over it. The court began with the acknowledgment that the law on property rights in the human body was unsettled. It looked to ethical standards in the IVF field. The American Fertility Society took the position that gametes and concepti are the property of the donors and donors had the right to decide their disposition. The court also found the *Davis* case informative. Relying on *Davis,* the court concluded the decedent's interest in the frozen sperm vials "occupies 'an interim category that entitles them to special respect because of their potential for human life.' " At the time of his death, Kane "had an interest, in the nature of ownership, to the extent that he had decisionmaking authority as to the use of his sperm for reproduction."

The *Hecht* court then turned to whether the probate court's order to destroy the sperm could be upheld. It found the decision could not be upheld on the basis of the will or the parties' settlement agreement because neither permitted destruction of all the sperm. It found no public policy against insemination of an unmarried woman. Finally, the court found no public policy against postmortem artificial insemination. The court noted it was premature to address the issue of family integrity urged by the children and speculative whether any child conceived by Hecht using Kane's sperm would be a burden to society. The appellate court found the order for destruction of the sperm was an abuse of discretion.

In discussing the public policy concerns of postmortem artificial insemination, the *Hecht* court discussed a French case, *Parpalaix v. CECOS,* as described in Shapiro & Sonnenblick, *The Widow and the Sperm: The Law of Post-Mortem Insemination* (1986) 1 J. Law & Health 229. Alain Parpalaix, a 24-year-old suffering from testicular cancer, made a deposit of sperm at CECOS, with no instructions for its future use. At the time, Alain was living with his girlfriend; he married her two days before his death. She then requested the sperm deposit. When CECOS denied the request, the widow, joined by her in-laws, went to court. Their complaint sounded in contract; they claimed they were owners of the sperm as Alain's natural heirs and CECOS had broken the contract of bailment by refusing the return the sperm. The widow's attorney also argued she had a moral right to the sperm. The French court noted the difficulties under French law governing inheritance rights and illegitimacy posed by children born post-mortem, but offered no solutions.

The French court refused to apply contract principles to the case. It also refused to consider the sperm as an indivisible body part; "it described sperm as 'the seed of life . . . tied to the fundamental liberty of a human being to conceive or not to conceive.' " The fate of the sperm was to be decided by the person from whom it was drawn; the sole issue was that of intent. "The court had to decide not only whether Alain Parpalaix had intended his widow to be artificially inseminated with his sperm, but also whether that intent was 'unequivocable.' " From the testimony of Alain's wife and parents, the French court found Alain intended to make his wife the mother of his child.

Relying on this description of the French case, the *Hecht* court appears to have accepted the rule that the sperm donor's intent controls in disposition of his frozen sperm after his death. The *Hecht* court did not have to actually decide that question because, as it made clear repeatedly, it was not deciding the issue of intent or the actual disposition of the frozen sperm; factual issues remained to be resolved. For purposes of determining whether the probate court order to destroy the sperm could be upheld, the *Hecht* court assumed "that decedent intended to allow Hecht to use his sperm for posthumous artificial insemination [.]"

The *Davis* case arose in a divorce action after the parties agreed on all the terms of dissolution except one. They could not agree on the disposition of seven cryogenically-preserved preembryos stored by a fertility clinic that had assisted the Davises with IVF. The court found the preembryos were neither persons nor property, but held an intermediate position, entitled to greater respect than property but not accorded the respect of persons. "We conclude that preembryos are not, strictly speaking, either 'persons' or 'property,' but occupy an interim category that entitles them to special respect because of their potential for human life." The Davises did not have a true property interest in the preembryos, but "they do have an interest in the nature of ownership, to the extent that they have decision-making authority concerning disposition of the preembryos, within the scope of policy set by law."

The *Davis* court held that an agreement regarding disposition of untransferred preembryos in the event of contingencies (such as death or divorce) should be presumed valid and enforceable. "This conclusion is in keeping with the proposition that the progenitors, having provided the gametic material giving rise to the preembryos, retain decision-making authority as to their disposition."

The Davises had not made such an agreement, so the court was required to resolve the dispute. "[W]e hold that disputes involving the disposition of preembryos produced by *in vitro* fertilization should be resolved, first, by looking to the preferences of the progenitors. If their wishes cannot be ascertained, or if there is dispute, then their prior agreement concerning disposition should be carried out. If no prior agreement exists, then the relative interests of the parties in using or not using the preembryos must be weighed. Ordinarily, the party wishing to avoid procreation should prevail, assuming that the other party has a reasonable possibility of achieving parenthood by means other than use of the preembryos in question."

We agree with the *Hecht* court that gametic material, with its potential to produce life, is a unique type of property and thus not governed by the general laws relating to gifts or personal property or transfer of personal property upon death.[1] We also agree that Joseph, as the person who provided the gametic material, had at his death an interest, in the nature of ownership, to the extent he had decisionmaking authority as to the use of the gametic material for reproduction. Accordingly, in determining the disposition of Joseph's frozen sperm, the trial court properly relied on Joseph's intent as to its use after his death.

Using the intent of the donor to determine the disposition of gametic material upon the donor's death is consistent California law in this area. Probate Code section 249.5 addresses the property rights of a child of a decedent conceived and born after the death of the decedent. Such a child is deemed to have been born within the decedent's lifetime, if, among other things, it is proved by clear and convincing evidence that the decedent specified in writing "that his

---

[1] In this regard, we note the gametic material at issue here is distinguishable from the preembryos at issue in *Davis*. It is further removed from potential life because Joseph's sperm could not produce life until joined with an egg. We express no opinion as to the proper resolution of a dispute regarding disposition of preembryos.

or her genetic material shall be used for the posthumous conception of a child." (Prob.Code, § 249.5, subd. (a).) Under the Uniform Anatomical Gift Act, a person has the right to make, amend, revoke, or refuse to make a donation of any part of his body to take effect after his death. (Health & Saf.Code, §§ 7150.20–7150.30.) This law suggests that when the issue is postmortem reproduction using gametic material from a deceased donor, the decedent's intent as to such use should control.

The probate court found Joseph intended that his frozen sperm be discarded upon his death. Iris faults the court for relying on the Agreement and contract law to find Joseph's intent. Iris cannot attack the court's finding. The record on appeal does not contain a transcript of the hearing. * * *

Iris contends *Hecht* requires a finding of the decedent's "unequivocable" intent. She argues both that the probate court failed to follow *Hecht* on this point and that the "unequivocable" intent test is unworkable. Unequivocal intent is not the test set forth in *Hecht*. Although the term is used by the *Hecht* court in quoting the *Parpalaix* case, it nowhere else in the opinion refers to an unequivocal intent. Rather, the court speaks only of the "decedent's actual intention" or the "decedent's intent." The probate court found by a preponderance of evidence that it was Joseph's intent that his sperm be discarded upon his death. That finding was sufficient.

Iris argues intent is difficult to determine because those undergoing IVF face great emotional and psychological turmoil, circumstances change, and their intent may change over time. (See, e.g., *Roman v. Roman* (Tex.Ct.App.2006) 193 S.W.3d 40 [upholding agreement to discard frozen embryos upon divorce despite woman's desire to use embryo]; *A.Z. v. B.Z.* (Mass. 2000) 431 Mass. 150 [declining to enforce agreement to give preembryos to wife upon divorce over husband's objection]; *Kass v. Kass* (N.Y.S. 1997) 663 N.Y.S.2d 581 [enforcing informed consent agreement to permit IVF program to retain cryopreserved pre-zygotes for approved research despite woman's change of heart].) Further, those undergoing IVF may not consider the possibility of their premature death. That may be and we can only encourage those undergoing IVF to fully consider all its ramifications and plan for all contingencies. (See Health & Saf.Code, § 1644.7 [form for establishing donor's intent as to use of genetic material for conception after death].) We need not consider what disposition is appropriate where the donor's intent cannot be determined because in this case the court was able to determine Joseph's intent.

Finally, Iris contends the probate court's decision ignores the fundamental right of the donee spouse to procreate. She contends the balancing test of *Davis* should be employed. The *Hecht* court indicated the *Davis* balancing test would be pertinent if the trier of fact determined the decedent's intent was contrary to Hecht's intent to bear his child. Iris further contends that since procreative rights are based on the right to privacy, and that right ends at death, in balancing the relative interests, hers prevails.

We disagree that the *Davis* balancing test applies in this situation. The *Davis* court noted, "the right of procreational autonomy is composed of two rights of equal significance—the right to procreate and the right to avoid procreation." Although the court recognized the impact of the IVF procedure was more severe on women, considering the joys of desired parenthood or the anguish of unwanted parenthood, it found the Davises "must be seen as entirely equivalent gamete-providers." The right of procreative autonomy "dictates that decisional authority rests in the gamete-providers alone, at least to the extent that their decisions have an impact upon their individual reproductive status."

In this case, there is only one gamete-provider. The material at issue is Joseph's sperm, not a preembryo. Only Joseph had "an interest, in the nature of ownership, to the extent that he had decisionmaking authority as to the use of his sperm for reproduction." The disposition of Joseph's frozen sperm does not implicate Iris's right to procreative autonomy. That would be so only if she could show that she could become pregnant only with Joseph's sperm.

DISPOSITION

The judgment is affirmed.

According to *Hecht*, frozen sperm are an asset that can be transferred at death via a writing authorizing release to a designated person. In *Kievernagel* the frozen sperm did not pass by intestate succession. In both *Hecht* and *Kievernagel*, women who had lost their partners wished to have children using sperm from those deceased partners. In both cases, relatives of the deceased wished to prevent those children from being conceived. Why were the results different?

What should the default rule be if the decedent's intent is unclear? Why should it matter that the decedent wanted the asset destroyed when living people value the asset enough to litigate over it? What should the result have been if the sperm had already been used to fertilize Iris's eggs? The asset was protected in one case and destroyed in the other. We return to destruction of assets at the end of the book. These cases did not raise the question of whether the children born from gametes of the deceased would qualify as children of the deceased. That question arises in the next chapter.

What about other body parts? In the past, governments controlled bodies after death. It was a health problem. Families now exercise substantial control. Should a person be able to transfer them by will? Should they pass by intestacy?

Should the disposal of bodies be more regulated than it is today? The environmental impact of body disposal varies by the method of disposal. Standard economic analysis suggests that methods creating negative externalities should be taxed, or subsidies should be given for beneficial methods of disposal. "Green burial" might become an issue in the future. Perhaps people should be encouraged to plan for disposal of their bodies, rather than leaving it up to their relatives to decide such questions in their time of grief.

CHAPTER 3

THE DEFAULT RULES THAT APPLY WHEN THE DECEDENT FAILS TO DETERMINE WHO TAKES NEXT

■ ■ ■

A. THE PREFERENCE FOR RELATIVES IN INTESTATE SUCCESSION

1. CUSTOM

COMMENTARIES ON THE LAWS OF ENGLAND
William Blackstone (1766)
Excerpt from Book II, Chapter I, pages 11–12

The right of inheritance, or descent to the children and relations of the deceased, seems to have been allowed much earlier than the right of devising by testament. We are apt to conceive at first view that it has nature on it's side; yet we often mistake for nature what we find established by long and inveterate custom. It is certainly a wise and effectual, but clearly a political, establishment; since the permanent right of property, vested in the ancestor himself, was no *natural*, but merely a *civil*, right. It is true, that the transmission of one's possessions to posterity has an evident tendency to make a man a good citizen and a useful member of society: it sets the passions on the side of duty, and prompts a man to deserve well of the public, when he is sure that the reward of his services will not die with himself, but be transmitted to those with whom he is connected by the dearest and most tender affections. Yet, reasonable as this foundation of the right of inheritance may seem, it is probable that its immediate original arose not from speculations altogether so delicate and refined; and, if not from fortuitous circumstances, at least from a plainer and more simple principle. A man's children or nearest relations are usually about him on his death-bed, and are the earliest witnesses of his decease. They became therefore generally the next immediate occupants, till at length in process of time this frequent usage ripened into general law. And therefore also in the earliest ages, on failure of children, a man's servants born under his roof were allowed to be his heirs; being immediately on the spot when he died. For we find the old patriarch Abraham expressly declaring, that "since God had given him no seed, his steward Eliezer, one born in his house, was his heir."

———————————

Blackstone seems to say that inheritance by children probably arose more from the "plainer and more simple principle" that they are around at death and became the next immediate occupants rather than from the law's attempt to honor the decedent's "dearest and most tender affections." It is entirely possible, of course, that both were involved. Where do tender affections come from?

2.   BIOLOGY (HAMILTON, INCLUSIVE FITNESS)

Why do people so frequently have such tender affections for their children? This was biologically explained decades ago by William D. Hamilton, who coined the idea of inclusive fitness. This idea, which looks at reproduction from the gene's point of view, is that a gene is more likely to survive through millennia and be more pervasive in the population if it inclines its phenotype to help other bodies that contain the same gene. To use Richard Dawkins's expression, genes are selfish. In this context, selfishness means a gene helping itself by helping the body it is in and helping copies of itself in other bodies. Of course, each offspring of a decedent bears half of the decedent's genes. So, from a gene's point of view, each of its body's offspring has a 50% chance of containing a copy of itself. (Because of genetic defects, errors in copying, and so forth, the chances are somewhat smaller than one half.) The gene's body's siblings also have a 50% chance of containing a copy of the gene. Offspring of a decedent's siblings have a 25% chance of carrying one of the decedent's genes. A gene maximizes the number of copies of itself in future generations by maximizing its body's offspring equivalent, in other words, by promoting its relatives in proportion to their relatedness. Therefore, it is evolutionarily adaptive for parents to favor their children and other blood relatives. Genes in the past that inclined their bodies in that direction tend to be more common in the world today.

Reciprocal altruism is another inclination that can lead to increased genetic fitness, and hence can be common in a population. Those who were inclined toward reciprocity and signaled that inclination were helped more by others. The result of such helping and sharing is often that both parties have more success in survival and reproduction.

The basic point here is that these inclinations toward inclusive fitness and reciprocal altruism could be embedded deeply, emotionally, genetically, in our brains.

Keep in mind, however, that this explanation of reality is no justification of it. Knowing how the world operates does not tell us how it should operate. We cannot derive what ought to be done from what we know is natural to do. Is is is; is is not ought. Description and explanation of behavior are not justifications of behavior. Who we can expect decedents to support and who they should support as a matter of morality are two separate questions.

3.   THE VALUE OF CLEAR RULES

Although one of the goals of the rules of intestacy is to do what the decedent would have wanted done, there are times when other social goals are more important. Sometimes the specific results that were desired by the decedent are themselves undesirable from a societal point of view. Other times it is important to avoid spending too much lawyer time, fact-finder time, and potential beneficiary time in the process of trying to determine and accomplish what the decedent would have wanted. When the decedents did not execute a will, we could hold hearings to determine what the decedent wanted done next. But why should society expend resources in an attempt to determine what the decedent wanted when the decedent did not think it was worth fewer resources to execute a will that would obviate the need for hearings?

It is obvious that it is inefficient to waste a lot of beneficiary time, but it should also be clear that it is inefficient to waste lawyer time, and paying lawyers for their time does not make it any less wasted. Sure, it is good for people to have jobs, but lawyers are talented people, and it would be better to put their skills to work actually doing something valuable than to perform make-work. A simple example illustrates the point. We could pass a rule that no person's assets will pass to private beneficiaries unless that testator hires a lawyer to cast stones in the ocean and hires a lawyer to gather the stones together. That rule would create lots of jobs for lawyers and shift assets to them, but from a societal point of view it would waste human time and effort. The reason we know that the effort would be wasted is that the market tells us so; people rarely pay lawyers or anyone else to throw stones in the ocean.

A question that repeats itself throughout the law is whether the extra time that will be spent by lawyers and others resolving an issue of fact will be justified by the extra justice that is reached as a consequence. Clear rules based on easily determined facts can often reach results at a low cost. Does a less determinate rule add enough justice to be worth its higher cost? With regard to intestate succession, it would be possible to hold hearings to determine what the decedent wanted. But lawmakers for centuries have come to the judgment that the extra justice (if any) would not be worth the time spent on that task. As a result, the laws of intestate succession are, for the most part, reasonably determinate and do not often call for litigation to determine the distribution of the assets.

B. THE TECHNICAL RULES OF INTESTATE SUCCESSION

If a decedent dies without a will, the assets that once belonged to the decedent pass in part to successors defined by statutes. These state laws vary widely and some of the variations will be noted as we reach each topic. A good starting point for understanding the laws of intestate succession is the Uniform Probate Code, many provisions of which have been adopted in many states. But do not get the impression that probate law is uniform across the states. Even the body promoting the Uniform Probate Code, the Commission on Uniform Laws, counts the number of states that have adopted the UPC at less than half, and many of those have deviated from the UPC in some particulars at the time of adoption. Moreover, the time of adoption matters, as the UPC itself has changed in important ways over the decades, with major revisions in 1989, 1990, 2008, and 2019 after the initial promulgation in 1969. Obviously, practice in the area of trusts and estates requires knowledge of the specific law of the state, which might or might not conform to the UPC. Nevertheless, we will start with the words of the UPC.

UPC § 2–101

SECTION 2–101. INTESTATE ESTATE.

(a) Any part of a decedent's estate not effectively disposed of by will passes by intestate succession to the decedent's heirs as prescribed in this [code], except as modified by the decedent's will.

(b) A decedent by will may expressly exclude or limit the right of an individual or class to succeed to property of the decedent passing by intestate succession. If that individual or a member of that class survives the decedent, the share of the decedent's intestate estate to which that individual or class would have succeeded passes as if that individual or each member of that class had disclaimed the intestate share.

***

1.   THE SURVIVING SPOUSE'S SHARE

As we have seen, the rules of intestate succession apply after the decedent's estate has been reduced by provisions for families, claims of creditors, governmental taxes, and any devises by will. From the remaining estate, the spouse of the decedent is first in line to take.

UPC §§ 2–102 AND 2–102A

SECTION 2–102. SHARE OF SPOUSE.

The intestate share of a decedent's surviving spouse is:

(1) the entire intestate estate if:

(A) no descendant or parent of the decedent survives the decedent; or

(B) all of the decedent's surviving descendants are also descendants of the surviving spouse and there is no other descendant of the surviving spouse who survives the decedent;

(2) the first [$300,000], plus three-fourths of any balance of the intestate estate, if no descendant of the decedent survives the decedent, but a parent of the decedent survives the decedent;

(3) the first [$225,000], plus one-half of any balance of the intestate estate, if all of the decedent's surviving descendants are also descendants of the surviving spouse and the surviving spouse has one or more surviving descendants who are not descendants of the decedent;

(4) the first [$150,000], plus one-half of any balance of the intestate estate, if one or more of the decedent's surviving descendants are not descendants of the surviving spouse.

[ALTERNATIVE PROVISION FOR COMMUNITY PROPERTY STATES]

[SECTION 2–102A. SHARE OF SPOUSE.

(a) The intestate share of a decedent's surviving spouse in separate property is:

(1) the entire intestate estate if:

(A) no descendant or parent of the decedent survives the decedent; or

(B) all of the decedent's surviving descendants are also descendants of the surviving spouse and there is no other descendant of the surviving spouse who survives the decedent;

(2) the first [$300,000], plus three-fourths of any balance of the intestate estate, if no descendant of the decedent survives the decedent, but a parent of the decedent survives the decedent;

(3) the first [$225,000], plus one-half of any balance of the intestate estate, if all of the decedent's surviving descendants are also descendants of the surviving spouse and the surviving spouse has one or more surviving descendants who are not descendants of the decedent;

(4) the first [$150,000], plus one-half of any balance of the intestate estate, if one or more of the decedent's surviving descendants are not descendants of the surviving spouse.

(b) the one-half of community property belonging to the decedent passes to the [surviving spouse] as the intestate share.]

In all states, non-community-property and community-property states, the UPC grants all of the decedent's intestate estate to the surviving spouse in some situations. There is no limit on the surviving spouse's share unless the decedent is survived by a parent or a stepchild of the decedent or the decedent's spouse. Which provision applies if the decedent and surviving spouse had a child together and each separately had a child before they married?

Why would the UPC limit the surviving spouse's share when there is a stepchild? Statistically, stepparents treat stepchildren worse than their own children in a number of ways. Kermyt Anderson and his colleagues studied 615 men in Albuquerque, New Mexico. They found that stepfathers treated genetic children better than stepchildren on five measures of support: odds of attending college (61% versus 39%), odds of receiving financial support for college (75% versus 52%), financial expenditures on children of age 0–17 ($2,570 versus $1,861), financial expenditures on children of age 18–24 ($4,293 versus $1,828), and time of involvement (20.1 hours per week versus 16.2). More disturbingly, a different study of Canadian children found that a young child's chances of suffering child abuse are multiplied by about 100 when there are one parent and one stepparent in the house compared to two genetic parents.

There are evolutionary reasons this might be the case, despite social norms and criminal laws to the contrary. Stepchildren have no special genetic relationship to their stepparents. As a result, stepchildren are less likely to be within the scope of their stepparents' most tender affections and natural generosity.

UPC § 2–102(3) and § 2–102(4) are both built on the assumption that parents are less inclined to support their stepchildren than their children. But that does not mean that § 2–102(3) and § 2–102(4) are equally justified. One potential justification for § 2–102(3) is that the decedent would not want to support a stepchild. Section 2–102(3) allocates assets to the common children of the decedent and spouse and allocates nothing to the decedent's stepchildren. Without § 2–102(3), the spouse might inherit the decedent's entire estate and use it to support all of the children equally. By contrast, the justification for § 2–102(4) in one subset of its cases is that the decedent would want to reduce the opportunity for unequal treatment of the decedent's children. When the decedent has no stepchildren, § 2–102(4) allocates some of the decedent's estate directly to the decedent's children, with the surviving spouse's children and stepchildren receiving equal portions. In the other subset of cases, the justification for § 2–102(4) is a combination of the two justifications above. In those cases, § 2–102(4) provides equal shares to all of the decedent's children, but not to the decedent's stepchildren. Are those two rationales equally attractive as a matter of social policy?

> Problem 3.01: S has a child, A, by mate X. When A is two years old, O and S marry. They have children, B and C. When A is 11, O dies leaving an intestate estate of $425,000 (after allowances and creditors). Under the UPC, S does not take all of the estate; B and C take some assets directly. How much does each take? Is that what the decedent would

want? Is that socially desirable? Does it matter whether A lived with O and S? Should it make a difference if X is still supporting A? Should it make a difference if, instead, A is now 50 years old, or if A was an adult when O and S married, or if A disapproved of S's marriage to O?

2. THE SHARE REMAINING AFTER THE SURVIVING SPOUSE'S SHARE

UPC §§ 2–103, 2–105, AND 2–106

SECTION 2–103. SHARE OF HEIRS OTHER THAN SURVIVING SPOUSE.

(a) [Definitions.] In this section:

(1) "Deceased parent", "deceased grandparent", or "deceased spouse" means a parent, grandparent, or spouse who either predeceased the decedent or is deemed under this [article] to have predeceased the decedent.

(2) "Surviving spouse", "surviving descendant", "surviving parent", or "surviving grandparent" means a spouse, descendant, parent, or grandparent who neither predeceased the decedent nor is deemed under this [article] to have predeceased the decedent.

(b) [Heirs Other Than Surviving Spouse.] Any part of the intestate estate not passing under Section 2–102 to the decedent's surviving spouse passes to the decedent's descendants or parents as provided in subsections (c) and (d). If there is no surviving spouse, the entire intestate estate passes to the decedent's descendants, parents, or other heirs as provided in subsections (c) through (j).

(c) [Surviving Descendant.] If a decedent is survived by one or more descendants, any part of the intestate estate not passing to the surviving spouse passes by representation to the decedent's surviving descendants.

(d) [Surviving Parent.] If a decedent is not survived by a descendant but is survived by one or more parents, any part of the intestate estate not passing to the surviving spouse is distributed as follows:

(1) The intestate estate or part is divided into as many equal shares as there are:

(A) surviving parents; and

(B) deceased parents with one or more surviving descendants, if any, as determined under subsection (e).

(2) One share passes to each surviving parent.

(3) The balance of the intestate estate or part, if any, passes by representation to the surviving descendants of the decedent's deceased parents, as determined under subsection (e).

(e) [When Parent Survives: Computation of Shares of Surviving Descendants of Deceased Parent.] The following rules apply under subsection (d) to determine whether a deceased parent of the decedent is treated as having a surviving descendant:

(1) If all the surviving descendants of one or more deceased parents also are descendants of one or more surviving parents and none of those surviving parents has any other surviving descendant, those descendants are deemed to have predeceased the decedent.

(2) If two or more deceased parents have the same surviving descendants and none of those deceased parents has any other surviving descendant, those deceased parents are deemed to be one deceased parent with surviving descendants.

(f) [Surviving Descendant of Deceased Parent.] If a decedent is not survived by a descendant or parent but is survived by one or more descendants of a parent, the intestate estate passes by representation to the surviving descendants of the decedent's deceased parents.

(g) [Surviving Grandparent.] If a decedent is not survived by a descendant, parent, or descendant of a parent but is survived by one or more grandparents, the intestate estate is distributed as follows:

(1) The intestate estate is divided into as many equal shares as there are:

(A) surviving grandparents; and

(B) deceased grandparents with one or more surviving descendants, if any, as determined under subsection (h).

(2) One share passes to each surviving grandparent.

(3) The balance of the intestate estate, if any, passes by representation to the surviving descendants of the decedent's deceased grandparents, as determined under subsection (h).

(h) [When Grandparent Survives: Computation of Shares of Surviving Descendants of Deceased Grandparent.] The following rules apply under subsection (g) to determine whether a deceased grandparent of the decedent is treated as having a surviving descendant:

(1) If all the surviving descendants of one or more deceased grandparents also are descendants of one or more surviving grandparents and none of those surviving grandparents has any other surviving descendant, those descendants are deemed to have predeceased the decedent.

(2) If two or more deceased grandparents have the same surviving descendants and none of those deceased grandparents has any other surviving descendant, those deceased grandparents are deemed to be one deceased grandparent with surviving descendants.

(i) [Surviving Descendant of Deceased Grandparent.] If a decedent is not survived by a descendant, parent, descendant of a parent, or grandparent but is survived by one or more descendants of a grandparent, the intestate estate passes by representation to the surviving descendants of the decedent's deceased grandparents.

(j) [Surviving Descendant of Deceased Spouse.] If a decedent is not survived by a descendant, parent, descendant of a parent, grandparent, or descendant of a grandparent but is survived by one or more descendants of one or more deceased spouses, the intestate estate passes by representation to the surviving descendants of the deceased spouse or spouses.

SECTION 2–105. NO TAKER. If there is no taker under the provisions of this [article], the intestate estate passes to the state.

SECTION 2–106. REPRESENTATION.

(a) [Definitions.] In this section:

(1) "Deceased descendant", "deceased parent", "deceased grandparent", or "deceased spouse" means a descendant, parent, grandparent, or spouse who either predeceased the decedent or is deemed under this [article] to have predeceased the decedent.

(2) "Surviving descendant" means a descendant who neither predeceased the decedent nor is deemed under this [article] to have predeceased the decedent.

(b) [Decedent's Descendants.] If, under Section 2–103(c), all or part of a decedent's intestate estate passes by representation to the decedent's surviving descendants, the estate or part is divided into as many equal shares as there are (i) surviving descendants in the generation nearest to the decedent which contains one or more surviving descendants and (ii) deceased descendants in the same generation who left surviving descendants, if any. Each surviving descendant in the nearest generation is allocated one share. The remaining shares, if any, are combined and then divided in the same manner among the surviving descendants of the deceased descendants as if the surviving descendants who were allocated a share and their surviving descendants had predeceased the decedent.

(c) [Descendants of Parent When Parent Survives.] If a decedent is survived by one or more parents and, under Section 2–103(d) and (e) , the balance of the decedent's intestate estate or part passes by representation to the surviving descendants of one or more of the decedent's deceased parents, the balance passes to those descendants as if they were the decedent's surviving descendants under subsection (b).

(d) [Descendants of Parent When No Parent Survives.] If a decedent is not survived by a parent and, under Section 2–103(f), the decedent's intestate estate passes by representation to the surviving descendants of one or more of the decedent's deceased parents, the intestate estate passes to those descendants as if they were the decedent's surviving descendants under subsection (b).

(e) [Descendants of Grandparent When Grandparent Survives.] If a decedent is survived by one or more grandparents and, under Section 2–103(g) and (h), the balance of the decedent's intestate estate passes by representation to the surviving descendants of one or more of the decedent's deceased grandparents, the balance passes to those descendants as if they were the decedent's surviving descendants under subsection (b).

(f) [Descendants of Grandparent When No Grandparent Survives.] If a decedent is not survived by a grandparent and, under Section 2–103(i), the decedent's intestate estate passes by representation to the surviving descendants of one or more of the decedent's deceased grandparents, the intestate estate passes to those descendants as if they were the decedent's surviving descendants under subsection (b).

(g) [Descendants of Deceased Spouse.] If a decedent is survived by descendants of one or more deceased spouses and, under Section 2–103(j), the decedent's intestate estate passes by representation to the surviving descendants of one or more of the decedent's deceased spouses, the intestate estate passes to those descendants as if they were the decedent's surviving descendants under subsection (b).

(a) Descendants

After the spouse's share has been determined, next come the decedent's descendants. If a decedent's children are alive, they take after the spouse, and they take equally. If one of the decedent's children predeceases the decedent, that child's share either passes down to that child's offspring or, if there are no living offspring of that predeceased child, then to the other children. If more than one of the decedent's children predeceased the decedent and they left surviving descendants, then there are a few different ways to divide up the descendants' part of the estate. Three phrases have been used to name different approaches: *per stirpes*, *per capita with representation* (with two variations), and *per capita at each generation*.

> Problem 3.02: A dies, leaving descendants as indicated in the diagram. (Those described as "dead" predeceased A.) What portion of A's estate does each person in the diagram take under each of the four approaches described below?

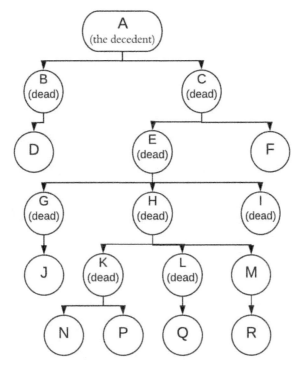

Diagram 3.02

(i) Per Stirpes

Per stirpes means by the stocks. To determine the distribution according to "English per stirpes", start at the generation of the decedent's children (B and C above), dividing the estate by the number of them that either survive or leave descendants surviving them. Each part then passes to the surviving child or through the predeceased child to the child's children in the same manner. Pretty simple. However, be aware that a few courts have interpreted "per stirpes" to mean modified per stirpes, described below.

(ii) Per Capita with Representation

Per capita with representation was the approach taken in the 1969 version of the UPC and is still the law in many states. Ignoring generations where no one is alive, find the oldest generation of the decedent's descendants in which there is still at least one member alive at the time of the decedent's death (the D, E, F generation above). Divide the estate by the number of descendants in that root generation that are either alive or have living descendants (three).

Each living descendant in that root generation (D and F) takes his or her portion, and the portions of those already deceased descendants in that generation (E) pass to their descendants.

There are two variations of per capita with representation. One variation might be called "modified per stirpes", "modern per stirpes", or "per capita with per stirpes representation", the portion passing to the deceased members of the root generation (E) passes down per stirpes. The other variation can be found in the 1969 UPC. Under that UPC approach, the portion passing to the deceased members of the root generation (E) passes to the descendants of the deceased members in the same manner as if each of them were the decedent.

(iii) Per Capita at Each Generation

Per capita at each generation is the approach perhaps preferred by most clients, and it is the system adopted by the 1990 UPC and maintained in the 2019 UPC. It is sometimes described with the phrase "equally near, equally dear". Start, as just above, by finding the oldest generation in which someone is alive and dividing by the number of living descendants in that root generation plus the number of predeceased descendants in that root generation who left living descendants. Again, as above, each living member of that generation takes an equal share. But next comes the change from the older UPC, which is accomplished by redefining "representation". Instead of passing the share of a predeceased member to his or her descendants, collect the portions of all predeceased members of a generation together and drop those collected shares as a bundle down to all the descendants of those predeceased members in the generation, to be divided equally by the survivors in that generation. All descendants in the same generation who take something at all will take the same amount. (Those whose living parent took a portion of the estate do not take anything, of course.)

Note that these systems have different evolutionary effects. Per stirpes gives the same portion to each of the lines of descendants of the decedent. The other approaches can give more assets to genes that have reproduced more often, which might be something that pleases decedents. But is it in the interests of society to give more assets to more reproductive human genes?

(iv) The Effect of a Disclaimer

When we studied disclaimers above, we noted that the UPC essentially treats the disclaimant as a person who predeceased the decedent. But, under the UPC, unlike per stirpes, *when* some person dies can make a difference to the portion taken by that person's relatives. Consider the following problems.

> Problem 3.03 basic facts: A has two children, B and C. B has one child, D. C has four minor children, E, F, G, and H. A has $80,000. (Each person described as "dead" predeceased A.) The jurisdiction follows the UPC. (Each problem below has its own additional facts.)

> Problem 3.03a: A dies. Who takes what?

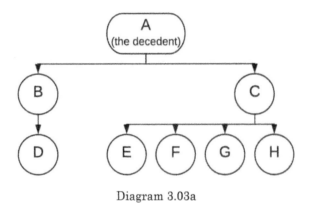

Diagram 3.03a

> Problem 3.03b: B and C die. A dies. Who takes what? (Maybe you can already see problems that are coming.)

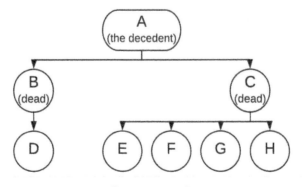

Diagram 3.03b

Problem 3.03c: C dies. A dies. Who takes what?

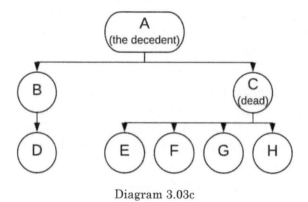

Diagram 3.03c

Problem 3.03d: B dies. A dies. Who takes what?

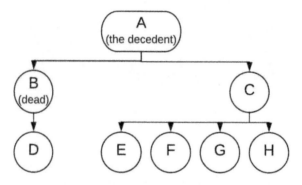

Diagram 3.03d

Problem 3.03e: (same family tree as in 3.03d above) B dies. A dies. C disclaims. Who takes what? If the law were simply to treat C as dying before A, then both C and B would predecease A and the result would be like that in Problem 3.03b, which is different from the result in Problem 3.03d. In many states, C can reduce D's portion by disclaiming. Should C be able to reduce D's portion by disclaiming? Does the UPC prevent that?

UPC § 2-1106

SECTION 2–1106. DISCLAIMER OF INTEREST IN PROPERTY.

(b) Except for a disclaimer governed by Section 2–1107 or 2–1108, the following rules apply to a disclaimer of an interest in property:

* * *

(3) If the instrument does not contain a provision described in paragraph (2), the following rules apply:

(A) If the disclaimant is not an individual, the disclaimed interest passes as if the disclaimant did not exist.

(B) If the disclaimant is an individual, except as otherwise provided in subparagraphs (C) and (D), the disclaimed interest passes as if the disclaimant had died immediately before the time of distribution.

(C) If by law or under the instrument, the descendants of the disclaimant would share in the disclaimed interest by any method of representation had the disclaimant died before the time of distribution, the disclaimed interest passes only to the descendants of the disclaimant who survive the time of distribution.

* * *

Problem 3.03f: (same family tree as in 3.03c above) C dies. A dies. B disclaims. Who takes what? If we were to treat B as dying before A, then both C and B would predecease A, and the result would be like that in Problem 3.03b. In many states, B's disclaimer would increase the portion for C's children. If B does not disclaim, B takes half and can pass that half to D. Should B be faced with reducing D's portion by disclaiming instead of taking from A and then making a gift to D? How does the UPC prevent that?

(b) Ancestors and Collaterals

Under the UPC, if there are no descendants surviving the decedent, the parents of the decedent or their descendants take all of the estate not taken by the spouse. If all of the parents are alive, they take equal shares, unless a parent is barred under UPC § 2–114 because parental rights were terminated or could have been terminated. Why does UPC § 2–103 prefer grandchildren of the decedent to parents of the decedent, who are more closely related?

Under the 2019 UPC, if a parent of the intestate has died leaving surviving descendants, the portion not taken by surviving parents may pass by representation to the surviving descendants of the decedent's predeceased parent. For blended families, the 2019 UPC represents a substantial change from the pre-2019 UPC, which does not pass assets to the children of the predeceased parent if the other parent survives. However, under 2019 UPC § 2–103(e), if the surviving descendants of a predeceased parent are the same as the surviving descendants of a surviving parent, those descendants are deemed to have predeceased the decedent.

If there are no surviving parents or issue of parents, the decedent's estate passes to the grandparents or their descendants. Under the UPC, the descendants of deceased grandparents would take by representation. However, as with parents, if the descendants of a deceased grandparent are exactly the same as the descendants of a surviving grandparent, those descendants are deemed to have predeceased the decedent.

(i) Parentelic System; UPC

The UPC is a parentelic system. It gives priority to the parents of the decedent and all of their descendants before turning to the next closest line, the grandparents and their descendants. The UPC stops with the second line of collaterals, not looking for great-grandparents or their descendants. Indeed, UPC § 2–115(4) defines "relative" as "a grandparent or a descendant of a grandparent."

(ii) Degree of Relationship System

Under the degree of relationship system followed in some states, unlike the UPC, if there are no surviving issue and a parent has died, that parent's share of the estate passes to the closest blood relatives on that side of the family. The number of parent-child steps to the decedent are counted for each claimant, and the claimant with the lowest number of steps is the closest relative and takes the deceased parent's share of the estate. For example, to get from the decedent to her second cousin, it is three steps up to her great-grandparent and then three steps down to her second cousin, for a total of six steps. To get from the decedent to her cousin's great-grandchild, it is two steps up to her grandparent and then five steps down to that great-grandchild (two steps to the cousin and three more to her great-grandchild), for a total of seven steps. So, the second cousin is closer than the great-grandchild of the cousin, and the second cousin would take under a degree of relationship system.

(c) Whole and Half Blood

The 2019 revision of UPC § 2–107 deletes the references to whole and half blood. That section now provides that "[a]n heir inherits without regard to how many common ancestors in the same generation the heir shares with the decedent."

(d) Laughing Heirs

Sometimes persons who take under the laws of descent and distribution are so distantly related that they did not even know the decedent. These relatives who take from someone they did not know are sometimes called "laughing heirs". Why does the law allow distant relatives to inherit? Perhaps the presumption is that the decedent would prefer them to the government. However, the choice between distant relatives and the government is not so simple from a societal point of view. One cost of allowing laughing heirs to take is that this expands the group of persons with a claim to the estate, which can dramatically increase the costs of administering the estate. This can happen when there is no will, obviously, as the court must look for increasingly distant relatives until it finds some. In some cases, thousands of persons have made claims to the estate of an intestate decedent, generating litigation taking years to resolve. Moreover, allowing distant relatives to take can also increase the costs of administering estates of some decedents who have wills, because heirs have standing to challenge the will. Hence, somewhat ironically, testate decedents might be better off if the law did not recognize too many intestate successors. The UPC avoids some of these costs of administration by limiting heirs to those persons who are grandparents and their descendants, the second line of collaterals. Again, we see a potential tension between efficiency and justice. It probably saves litigation costs to reduce the potential claimants, but doing so might exclude a person the decedent would have wanted to take some of the estate. Keeping in mind that this is only a default rule that can be avoided by executing a will or trust, what is the most distant line of collaterals that should be allowed to take under the law of intestate succession?

(e) Stepchildren (and Their Issue)

Under the law in the past, stepchildren of the decedent were the stepchildren of the law. They did not take. UPC § 2–103(j) changes that rule, allowing descendants of the decedent's deceased spouses to take by intestate succession if there are no relatives.

> Question 3.04: In 2000, O, F, and M are born, all into different families. In 2020, F and M have a child, A. In 2060, when A is 40 and M is 60, M marries O. In 2063, M dies, devising her estate to A. In 2095, when A is 75 and O is 95, O dies leaving $1,000,000 and no close relatives and no will. The state takes under the old UPC, but A takes under the current UPC. Who should take in that situation? Under the current UPC, after M and F are dead, A can inherit from O but O cannot inherit from A. Does that lack of symmetry make sense?

3. CHILDREN

Some children have achieved the age of majority, and some have not. Being a minor does not prevent a person from inheriting property. However, minors cannot legally manage their property, so there are various legal tools for doing that. An ancient practice was for a guardian to take control of a ward's lands. In theory, guardianship of the property was subject to judicial oversight. A conservator of property has more flexibility and less oversight than a guardian. A custodian holds property for the benefit of a minor under terms set out by state statutes, often based on the Uniform Transfers to Minors Act (UTMA) or Uniform Gifts to Minors Act (UGMA). And, finally, a trustee holds property, the res of a trust, for the benefit of another person, the beneficiary. The trustee can be given a large degree of discretion, but the trustee must exercise that discretion consistently with the trustee's fiduciary duty to act for the benefit of the beneficiary or beneficiaries of the trust.

The next question is who qualifies as someone's child in the context of intestate succession. The large majority of cases are easy. But, sometimes, whether a person takes as someone's child is not easy to resolve.

HALL V. HALL

Supreme Court of Appeals of West Virginia, 2018
818 S.E.2d 838

DAVIS, J.

* * *

I.

FACTUAL AND PROCEDURAL HISTORY

The following facts are not disputed. Petitioner, Michaelin Brooke Hall ("Michaelin"), is the only child born of a marriage between Kathy Hall French and Michael Eugene Hall ("Michael Hall"). At some point during the marriage, the Department of Health and Human Services filed an abuse and neglect petition against Michael Hall alleging that he abused Michaelin.[1] Thereafter, he voluntarily relinquished his parental rights with respect to Michaelin in April 2008. The circuit court acknowledged Michael Hall's voluntary relinquishment of his parental rights and entered an order legally terminating the same. As a further result of the proceedings, Kathy Hall French and Michael Hall divorced in July 2008. Michael Hall never remarried and apparently fathered no other children. He died intestate on April 3, 2011.

On February 26, 2016, Kathy Hall French, as mother and next friend of Michaelin, filed the instant action in the Circuit Court of Mercer County claiming that Michaelin is the rightful heir to the estate of the decedent, Michael Hall. The defendants named in the complaint are Lona Sue Hall, Robert E. Hall, Loretta Hall (aka Loretta Jenkins), and Samantha Hazelwood (collectively "the Defendants").[3] Robert E. Hall, Loretta Hall, and Samantha Hazelwood each filed, *pro se*, a handwritten answer to the complaint. On January 5, 2017, Kathy Hall French filed a motion for summary judgment. Thereafter, on January 11, 2017, an amended complaint was filed removing Kathy French Hall as plaintiff and naming Michaelin, who had reached the age of majority, as plaintiff. The

---

[1]   Michael Hall also was criminally charged for his abuse of Michaelin and sentenced to a lengthy term of incarceration. The appendix record submitted in connection with this appeal does not contain any documents from the abuse and neglect or criminal proceedings. However, the circuit court's order observes that "[t]he records of the companion juvenile abuse and criminal cases referenced herein are replete with evidence of the abuse [Michaelin] suffered while in the care of [Michael Hall]."

[3]   It appears that defendants Lona Sue Hall and Robert E. Hall are the parents of the decedent Michael Hall, Loretta Hall (aka Loretta Jenkins) is the decedent's sister, and Samantha Hazelwood is the decedent's niece. Lona Sue Hall was appointed administratrix of Michael Hall's estate.

Defendants timely filed a joint response to the motion for summary judgment along with their own motion for summary judgment. The circuit court heard arguments on the motions and, by order entered on April 13, 2017, granted summary judgment to the Defendants. This appeal followed.

* * *

III.

DISCUSSION

Michaelin assigns error to the circuit court's award of summary judgment to the Defendants, which was based upon its conclusion that a child may not inherit from a parent who died intestate after his parental rights to said child were legally terminated. Michaelin encourages this Court to rely on the West Virginia Child Welfare Act, found at W. Va. Code § 49–1–101 *et seq.*, along with precedent of this Court that allows a parent's obligation to support a child to continue beyond the termination of parental rights, to reverse the circuit court's ruling on this novel issue.

Respondents Lona Sue Hall and Robert E. Hall ("the Halls") contend that the circuit court's order was correct insofar as the West Virginia descent and distribution statutes do not permit the child of a parent whose parental rights have been terminated to share in the parent's intestate estate. The Halls recognize that continuing financial support following termination pursuant to the Child Welfare Act is a right belonging to the child and is in the child's best interest. They point out, however, that the laws of intestate succession are designed to meet a different goal, *i.e.*, to distribute real and personal property in accordance with what a decedent would have done in a will. *See King v. Riffee*, 172 W. Va. 586, 589 (1983) ("Our laws concerning intestate succession are designed to effect the orderly distribution of property for decedents who lacked either the foresight or the diligence to make wills. The purpose of these statutes, then, is to provide a distribution of real and personal property that approximates what decedents would have done if they had made a will.").

* * *

[T]he Court in *Ryan B.* observed that

> case law from this Court as well as courts around the country have held that an obligation of support is owed to a child by both of his parents until such time as the child is

placed in the permanent legal custody of another guardian/parent/obligor, such as in adoption. As this Court has frequently emphasized, the best interest of the child is the polar star by which all matters affecting children must be guided. This Court has previously stated that child support obligations are not only responsibilities parents owe to their children, *they are also rights which belong to children. "Child support is a right which belongs to the child." Allowing a parent who voluntarily relinquishes his/her parental rights to avoid this right that belongs to the child goes against the overall goal of the child welfare statutory scheme and is in opposition to our well established case law.*

In re Ryan B., 224 W. Va. at 467 (footnotes omitted; bold emphasis added). Although *Ryan B.* involved a voluntary relinquishment, as does the instant matter, the Court made clear that "[t]he issue presently before us is applicable to both voluntary and involuntary relinquishments."

Insofar as this Court has made clear that the termination of parental rights does not extinguish certain rights belonging to the child, such as the right to child support, it would seem to follow, based upon the same rationale focusing on the best interests of the child, that it also would be in a child's best interest to inherit from a terminated parent who dies intestate. Indeed, numerous states have adopted legislation allowing a child to retain the right to inherit from a parent whose parental rights have been terminated.[6] Unfortunately, West Virginia is not among those states that have enacted specific legislation on this topic. Furthermore, because Michaelin seeks her share of her biological father's intestate estate in accordance with West Virginia statutory provisions pertaining to descent and distribution, we may not rely solely on the Child Welfare Act. Instead, it is necessary to examine the descent and distribution provisions of the West Virginia Code.

Pursuant to W. Va. Code § 42–1–3a (1992) (Repl. Vol. 2014),

[a]ny part of the intestate estate not passing to the decedent's surviving spouse under section three [§ 42–1–3] of this article, or the entire intestate estate if there is no

---

[6]   [In this footnote, the court cited to statutes in more than a dozen other states. Ed.]

surviving spouse, passes in the following order to the individuals designated below who survive the decedent:

(a) To the decedent's descendants by representation;

(Emphasis added). Michael Hall had not remarried following his divorce from Michaelin's mother. Therefore, according to W. Va. Code § 42–1–3a, his entire estate passes to his surviving *descendants*. In other words, in order for Michael Hall's intestate estate to pass to Michaelin, she must be his descendant.

The term "descendant" is expressly defined in chapter forty-two of the code: " 'Descendant' of an individual means all of his or her descendants of all generations, *with the relationship of parent and child at each generation being determined by the definition of child and parent contained in this code.*" (emphasis added). According to the language used in this statute, the question of whether Michaelin is a descendant of Michael Hall is "determined by the definition of *child and parent* contained in this code."

Looking first to the term "child," we observe that it is not defined in chapter forty-two of the West Virginia Code. Oddly, though, W. Va. Code § 42–1–1(5) does not refer to the definition of "child" located in a particular chapter or article of the code. Rather, it refers to "the definition . . . contained in *this code.*" W. Va. Code § 42–1–1(5) (emphasis added). Thus, the absence of a definition of "child" within the provisions relating to descent and distribution would seem to indicate that a definition found elsewhere in the code might be applied. Although the term "child" is defined in numerous places throughout the West Virginia Code, none of those definitions appear to be applicable in the context of descent and distribution insofar as they primarily refer to a child who has yet to reach the age of majority or who is subject to some other form of dependency. *See, e.g.,* * * * W. Va. Code § 48–12–101(6) (2007) (Repl. Vol. 2015) (providing that " '[c]hild' means a child to whom a duty of child support is owed" in domestic relations statute for purposes of medical support enforcement); W. Va. Code § 48–16–102(1) (2015) (Repl. Vol. 2015) (defining "child" as "an individual, whether over or under the age of majority, who is or is alleged to be owed a duty of support by the individual's parent or who is or is alleged to be the beneficiary of a support order directed to the parent" in West Virginia Uniform Interstate Family Support Act); * * * W. Va. Code § 48–31–102(3) (2017) (Supp. 2017) (defining "child" for purposes of Uniform Deployed Parents Custody and Visitation Act as "(A) An unemancipated individual who has not attained eighteen years of age; or (B) An adult son or daughter by birth or adoption, or under law of this state other than this article, who is the subject of a court order concerning custodial responsibility"); * * *.

While the absence of a clear definition of the term "child" is troublesome, W. Va. Code § 42–1–1(5) specifies that, for the purpose of identifying descendants, "the relationship of parent and child" is "determined by the definition of child *and* parent contained in this code." (Emphasis added). Use of the conjunctive "and" in this provision directs that consideration be given to the definition of both "child" and "parent" in determining the relationship of parent and child. Because both definitions must be met, we next consider the term "parent." If a parent whose parental rights have been terminated does not come within the definition of "parent" as set out in the descent and distribution statutes, then this issue may be resolved even in the absence of a clear definition of the term child.

The term "parent," as defined within the descent and distribution statutes, "includes any person entitled to take, or who would be entitled to take if the child died without a will, as a parent under this code by intestate succession from the child whose relationship is in question and excludes any person who is only a stepparent, foster parent or grandparent." W. Va. Code § 42–1–1(26) (emphasis added). Under the plain language of this provision, then, a "parent" for purposes of intestate succession is one who would be entitled to take if the child died without a will. A parent whose rights have been terminated does not meet this definition. Termination of parental rights terminates all rights of the parent. Because, the relationship of a terminated parent with his or her child is utterly severed by virtue of W. Va. Code § 49–4–604(b)(6), a parent whose parental rights have been terminated would not be entitled to take from the subject child and, therefore, does not meet the definition of "parent" set out in W. Va. Code § 42–1–1(26).[8] As one court has aptly observed, "[e]quity, morality, and common sense dictate that

---

[8]   The laws allowing for termination of parental rights have existed in West Virginia since at least 1941. Therefore, we may presume that the Legislature knew of this provision in 1992 when it revised the laws pertaining to intestate succession and included the above-quoted definition of the term "parent." See Syl. pt. 5, *Dale v. Painter*, 234 W. Va. 343 (2014) ("A statute should be so read and applied as to make it accord with the spirit, purposes and objects of the general system of law of which it is intended to form a part; it being presumed that the legislators who drafted and passed it were familiar with all existing law, applicable to the subject matter, whether constitutional, statutory or common, and intended the statute to harmonize completely with the same and aid in the effectuation of the general purpose and design thereof, if its terms are consistent therewith.").

physically or sexually abusive parents have no right of inheritance by intestacy." New Jersey Div. of Youth & Family Servs. v. M.W., 398 N.J. Super. 266 (App. Div. 2007).

Insofar as the identity of "descendants" who may take an intestate share of an estate is dependant upon the existence of a relationship that includes both a "parent" and a "child," and a terminated parent fails to meet the definition of "parent" with respect to the subject child, the child is not a "descendant" of that biological parent. *See* W. Va. Code § 42–1–1(5) (" 'Descendant' of an individual means all of his or her descendants of all generations, *with the relationship of parent and child at each generation being determined by the definition of child and parent contained in this code.*" (emphasis added)). Accordingly, we now expressly hold that a child may not inherit under W. Va. Code § 42–1–3a(a) from a biological parent who dies intestate after his or her parental rights to said child have been either voluntarily relinquished or involuntarily terminated.

Applying the foregoing holding to the instant matter, we must affirm the circuit court's correct determination that Michaelin may not inherit from her father's intestate estate. While we are sympathetic to Michaelin's circumstances, the decisions of this Court must be guided by the law and not our sympathies. We firmly believe our holding is the best representation of Legislative intent based upon the relevant statutes. Any change in this law must be enacted by the Legislature, as that is the proper body to address policy considerations and resolve the myriad of questions associated with such a change in the law. Such considerations simply are not proper undertakings for courts. "It is not the province of the courts to make or supervise legislation, and a statute may not, under the guise of interpretation, be modified, revised, amended, distorted, remodeled or rewritten . . . ." *State v. General Daniel Morgan Post No. 548, Veterans of Foreign Wars*, 144 W. Va. 137, 145 (1959). In other words,

> [t]his Court does not sit as a superlegislature, commissioned to pass upon the political, social, economic or scientific merits of statutes pertaining to proper subjects of legislation. It is the duty of the Legislature to consider facts, establish policy, and embody that policy in legislation. It is the duty of this Court to enforce legislation unless it runs afoul of the State or Federal *Constitutions*.

Syl. pt. 2, *Huffman v. Goals Coal Co.*, 223 W.Va. 724 (2009).

IV.

CONCLUSION

For the reasons explained herein, we affirm the April 13, 2017, order of the Circuit Court of Mercer County granting summary judgment to the defendants.

Affirmed.

WORKMAN, C.J., dissenting, joined by KETCHUM, J.

Without question, Michaelin Brooke Hall is entitled to inherit the estate of her biological father, the decedent, Michael Eugene Hall. As explained below, Michaelin's right to inherit flows from her relationship as his biological child in accordance with our intestacy statutes. Even though *his* parental rights were legally terminated, *her* rights as his child and descendant remain intact. By creating new law extinguishing that valuable right, the majority fails to apply the plain language of the statute and ignores compelling precedent. Because this disturbing decision piles even more hardship on this child whose life was already severely damaged by parental abuse and neglect, I vehemently dissent.

Our analysis begins with the general premise that "[a]ny part of a decedent's estate not effectively disposed of by will passes by intestate succession to the decedent's heirs as prescribed in this code[.]" W.Va. Code § 42–1–2(a) (2014). We then turn to the pertinent statute, West Virginia Code § 42–1–3a (2014), which provides, in relevant part:

Any part of the intestate estate not passing to the decedent's surviving spouse under section three [§ 42–1–3] of this article, or the entire intestate estate if there is no surviving spouse, passes in the following order to the individuals designated below who survive the decedent:

(a) To the decedent's descendants by representation;

(b) If there is no surviving descendant, to the decedent's parents equally if both survive, or to the surviving parent[.]

Under the plain language of this statute, Michaelin—the decedent's only child and surviving descendant—inherits his entire estate because he left no surviving spouse. Case closed.

The majority's convoluted path to the contrary conclusion fails to respect the most basic of all canons of statutory interpretation: statutes mean what they plainly say.[1] In its tortured analysis, the majority reasons that the impediments to Michaelin's inheritance are the statutory definitions of "descendant," West Virginia Code § 42–1–1(5) (2014), and "parent," *Id.* § 42–1–1(26). Essentially, the majority reasons that after his parental rights were terminated, Mr. Hall would not meet the definition of "parent" for purposes of the descent and distribution statutes. The majority then abruptly leaps to the unsupported conclusion that their parent-child relationship was "utterly severed" to such a degree that Michaelin no longer remained Mr. Hall's "descendant."

The majority is half right: the decedent, Mr. Hall, would not meet the definition of "parent" for purposes of the descent and distribution statutes. All this means, however, is that *he* would not be entitled to inherit from Michaelin *if* she predeceased him. However, that hypothetical question is not before us. Although our statutes do not specifically address that issue, I agree with the majority that Mr. Hall lost those rights after he voluntarily relinquished all his parental rights as a result of his abuse of this child.[2]

Nevertheless, it makes little sense to construe West Virginia Code § 42–1–3a as creating a per se statutory barrier to the reverse—Michaelin's ability to inherit from Mr. Hall. The central flaw in the majority's reasoning is that it assumes the rights flowing from the parent-child relationship are reciprocal here when under the instant circumstances, they are not.

Significantly, the majority fails to acknowledge that the pertinent statutes which control the distribution of the decedent's estate were modeled upon the 1990 Revised Uniform Probate Code ("RUPC"). In fact, West Virginia was the first state to enact the intestacy provisions of the RUPC. West Virginia Code § 42–1–3a

---

[1] "As Chief Justice Marshall said more than a century and a half ago: [T]he intention of the legislature is to be collected from the words they employ. Where there is no ambiguity in the words there is no room for construction." Watt v. Alaska, 451 U.S. 259, 285–86 (1981) (Stewart, J., dissenting) (quotation marks and citation omitted).

[2] See W.Va. Code § 49–4–604(6) (2015) (providing court shall terminate parental *rights* of abusing parent).

"A majority of [ ] states have adopted a statutory exception to the mandatory succession by intestacy statutes applicable to children to extinguish the inheritance rights of 'bad parents.'" Most "are directed to parental abandonment and non-support, although several preclude inheritance by a parent who has been convicted of crimes against the child including physical abuse, sexual abuse, and endangering the child's welfare."

tracks the same language as the RUPC, as well as the Uniform Probate Code ("UPC"), 8 U.L.A. 91 (2010), when dealing with intestate distribution of an estate which does not pass to a surviving spouse. Therefore, references to the RUPC/UPC are important in order to facilitate an understanding of the statutes at issue in the case before us.

In comparison to the provision of West Virginia law dealing with intestacy inheritance, the UPC has the same definition of "descendant" and "parent." " 'Descendant' of an individual means all of his [or her] descendants of all generations, with the relationship of parent and child at each generation being determined by the definition of child and parent contained in this [code]." UPC § 1–201(9) and W.Va. Code § 42–1–1(5). " 'Parent' includes any person entitled to take, or who would be entitled to take if the child died without a will, as a parent under this [code] by intestate succession from the child whose relationship is in question and excludes any person who is only a stepparent, foster parent, or grandparent." UPC § 1–201(32) and W.Va. Code § 42–1–1(26).

In contrast, however, West Virginia Code Chapter 42 contains no definition of "child" when the UPC does define the term. The UPC provides that: " 'Child' includes an individual entitled to take as a child under this [code] by intestate succession from the parent whose relationship is involved and excludes a person who is only a stepchild, a foster child, a grandchild, or any more remote descendant." It is not disputed that Michaelin is Mr. Hall's biological daughter. Therefore, she plainly meets this definition of child.

Notably, the UPC does not extinguish the right of the *child* to inherit from his or her biological parent following a parental termination proceeding, but it does extinguish the *parent's* right to inherit from his or her child in this context. Thus, the UPC teaches that there is unilateral extinguishment of intestacy rights in these matters under the same definition of "descendant." Yet, the majority wholly ignores the UPC's express endorsement of the more sensible result here. Also, among states that have statutes explicitly addressing the effect of the parental termination order on the child's inheritance rights, there is often no reciprocity of rights; some expressly bar the parent's right to inherit after termination, but also expressly retain the child's right to inherit (until the child is adopted).

Consistent with the UPC, West Virginia statutes dealing with descent and distribution contain no language purporting to divest a child's right of inheritance under these facts. Therefore, the termination of Mr. Hall's parental rights in no way negates the fact that Michaelin is his child, descendant, and sole beneficiary under West Virginia Code § 42–1–3a. One would have thought it too obvious to mention that this Court is duty bound to apply the statute, not amend it.

The disinheritance of children of terminated parents is not only inconsistent with the plain language of the statute, it runs counter to the broader scheme of intestate succession. "In the American legal system, inheritance rights are almost invariably based on the parent-child relationship—children inherit from their biological mothers and fathers." Brown, *Disinheriting the "Legal Orphan": Inheritance Rights of Children After Termination of Parental Rights*, 70 Mo. L. Rev. at 126. There are exceptions to this rule; for instance, adopted children inherit from their adoptive parents, not their biological parents. However, there is simply no "rationale for extinguishing the right of children to inherit from their terminated biological parents [in this context]."

Moreover, the majority's central premise—that Michaelin lost her statutory rights to inherit from her biological father through intestate succession when *his* parental rights were terminated because of *his* child abuse—does not square with our case law and the sound public policies that underlie our child welfare system. The primary goal of a child abuse and neglect proceeding is to further the welfare of the child. And this Court has made it abundantly clear that parental termination proceedings do not extinguish certain rights enjoyed by a child, e.g., the loss of statutory rights is not reciprocal in this context. In *In re: Ryan B.*, 224 W.Va. 461 (2009), we held that a parent whose parental rights have been terminated must typically continue paying child support, so long as such payments are in the child's best interest. *See also* Syl. Pt. 7, *In re: Stephen Tyler R.*, 213 W.Va. 725 (2003) ("Pursuant to the plain language of W.Va. Code § 49–6–5(a)(6) (1998) (Repl.Vol. 2001), a circuit court may enter a dispositional order in an abuse and neglect case that simultaneously terminates a parent's parental rights while also requiring said parent to continue paying child support for the child(ren) subject thereto.").

Under this precedent, Michaelin's rights under our intestacy statutes remain intact following the parental termination proceeding until extinguished for some other reason, such as adoption. There is simply no plausible basis for inferring that the Legislature intended to disinherit the child in this equation. The gaping hole in the majority opinion is its failure to answer the crucial question upon which all else depends: Where is the statutory support for this exception to the clear statutory command? That question is unanswered because there is none. Consequently, the majority's adoption of such exception here amounts to a blatant judicial override of the statute. However, this Court is not at liberty to read into a statute that which simply is not there.

* * *

The majority decision, no matter how much it says otherwise, ultimately crafts a judge-made exception to the general rule regarding intestate succession plainly set forth in West Virginia Code § 42–1–3a. But not one of the cases on which the majority relies supports the extraordinary premise that courts can create out of whole cloth such an exclusion.

Accordingly, this Court should have applied the clear language of West Virginia Code § 42–1–3a and the foundational principles of *In re: Ryan B.* to recognize Michaelin's statutory right to inherit from Mr. Hall through intestate succession continued after his parental termination proceeding. The majority's decision is wrong, wrong, wrong, both from a legal and human perspective.

Because there is nothing legally right or just about this decision, I respectfully dissent. I am authorized to state that Justice Ketchum joins this dissent.

———————————

What would Michael have wanted? Does the majority or the dissent have the better argument as a matter of justice? Does the majority or the dissent have the better argument as a matter of statutory construction? The 2019 revisions to the UPC add a new subsection, § 2–114(c), to repudiate the holding in *Hall v. Hall*.

(a) Adoptees

(i) Legal Adoptees

Legal adoption can move a person from one family to another. This is sometimes called "a fresh start". As of 2019, UPC §§ 2–115 and 2–118 also recognize "de facto" parents in addition to adoptive parents.

These situations sometimes raise questions as to whether there is a parent-child relationship for purposes of inheritance.

UPC §§ 2–118 AND 2–119

SECTION 2–118. PARENT-CHILD RELATIONSHIP ESTABLISHED THROUGH ADOPTION OR DE FACTO PARENTAGE.

(a) [Parent-Child Relationship Established Through Adoption.] A parent-child relationship exists between an adoptee and the adoptee's adoptive parent.

(b) [Parent-Child Relationship Established Through De Facto Parentage.] A parent-child relationship exists between an individual and the individual's de facto parent.

SECTION 2–119. EFFECT OF ADOPTION; EFFECT OF DE FACTO PARENTAGE.

(a) [Definitions.] In this section:

(1) "Parent before the adjudication" means an individual who is a parent of a child:

(A) immediately before another individual is adjudicated a de facto parent of the child; or

(B) immediately before dying, or being deemed under this [article] to have died, and before another individual is adjudicated a de facto parent of the child.

(2) "Parent before the adoption" means an individual who is a parent of a child:

(A) immediately before another individual adopts the child; or

(B) immediately before dying, or being deemed under this [article] to have died, and before another individual adopts the child.

(b) [Effect of Adoption on Parent Before the Adoption.] A parent-child relationship does not exist between an adoptee and an individual who was the adoptee's parent before the adoption unless:

(1) otherwise provided by [court order or] law other than this [code]; or

(2) the adoption:

(A) was by the spouse of a parent before the adoption;

(B) was by a relative or the spouse or surviving spouse of a relative of a parent before the adoption; or

(C) occurred after the death of a parent before the adoption.

(c) [Effect of De Facto Parentage on Parent Before the Adjudication.] Except as otherwise provided by a court order [under Uniform Parentage Act (2017) Section 613], an adjudication that an individual is a child of a de facto parent does not affect a parent-child relationship between the child and an individual who was the child's parent before the adjudication.

———————

For the following problems, assume the UPC is in effect.

Problem 3.05: Genetic mother, GM, and genetic father, GF, have a child, C. A court adjudicates that C is a child of de facto parent, DP. DP dies. Can C inherit from DP? GM dies. Can C inherit from GM? GM's mother, GGM, dies. Can C inherit from GGM through GM?

Problem 3.06: Genetic mother, GM, and genetic father, GF, have a child, C. They allow their child to be adopted by adoptive father, AF. AF dies. Can C inherit from AF? GF dies. Can C inherit from GF? C dies. Can GM inherit from C?

Problem 3.07: Genetic mother, GM, and genetic father, GF, have a child, C. GF dies. C is adopted by adoptive mother, AM. C dies. Can GM inherit from C?

HALL V. VALLANDINGHAM

Court of Special Appeals of Maryland, 1988
540 A.2d 1162

GILBERT, C.J.

Adoption did not exist under the common law of England, although it was in use "[a]mong the ancient peoples of Greece, Rome, Egypt and Babylonia." The primary purpose for adoption was, and still is, inheritance rights, particularly in "France, Greece, Spain and most of Latin America." Since adoption was not a part of the common law, it owes its existence in this State, and indeed in this nation, to statutory enactments.

The first two general adoption statutes were passed in Texas and Vermont in 1850. Maryland first enacted an Adoption Statute in Laws 1892, Ch. 244, and that law has continued in existence, in various forms, until the present time. The current statute, § 5–308 provides, in pertinent part:

"(b) [A]fter a decree of adoption is entered:

(1) the individual adopted:

(i) is the child of the petitioner for all intents and purposes; and

(ii) is entitled to all the rights and privileges of and is subject to all the obligations of a child born to the petitioner in wedlock;

(2) each living natural parent of the individual adopted is:

(i) relieved of all parental duties and obligations to the individual adopted; and

(ii) divested of all parental rights as to the individual adopted; and

(3) *all rights of inheritance between the individual adopted and the natural relations shall be governed by the Estates and Trusts Article.*" (Emphasis supplied.)

The applicable section of the Md.Estates and Trusts Code Ann., § 1–207(a), provides:

"An adopted child shall be treated as a natural child of his adopted parent or parents. On adoption, a child no longer shall be considered a child of either natural parent, except that upon adoption by the spouse of a natural parent, the child shall be considered the child of that natural parent."

With that "thumbnail" history of adoption and the current statutes firmly in mind, we turn our attention to the matter *sub judice.*

Earl J. Vallandingham died in 1956, survived by his widow, Elizabeth, and their four children. Two years later, Elizabeth married Jim Walter Killgore, who adopted the children.

In 1983, twenty-five years after the adoption of Earl's children by Killgore, Earl's brother, William Jr., died childless, unmarried, and intestate. His sole heirs were his surviving brothers and sisters and the children of brothers and sisters who predeceased him.

Joseph W. Vallandingham, the decedent's twin brother, was appointed Personal Representative of the estate. After the Inventory and First Accounting were filed, the four natural children of Earl J. Vallandingham noted exceptions, alleging that they were entitled to the distributive share of their natural uncle's estate that their natural father would have received had he survived William.

The Orphan's Court transmitted the issue to the Circuit Court for St. Mary's County. That tribunal determined that the four natural children of Earl, because of their adoption by their adoptive father, Jim Walter Killgore, were not entitled to inherit from William M. Vallandingham Jr.

Patently unwilling to accept that judgment which effectively disinherited them, the children have journeyed here where they posit to us:

> "Did the trial court err in construing Maryland's current law regarding natural inheritance by adopted persons so as to deny the Appellants the right to inherit through their natural paternal uncle, when said Appellants were adopted as minors by their stepfather after the death of their natural father and the remarriage of their natural mother?"

When the four natural children of Earl J. Vallandingham were adopted in 1958 by Jim Killgore, then Md.Ann.Code art. 16, § 78(b) clearly provided that adopted children retained the right to inherit from their natural parents and relatives. That right of inheritance was removed by the Legislature in 1963 when it declared: "Upon entry of a decree of adoption, the adopted child shall lose all rights of inheritance from its parents and from their natural collateral or lineal relatives." Subsequently, the Legislature in 1969 enacted what is the current, above-quoted language of Est. & Trusts Art. § 1–207(a).

The appellants contend that since the explicit language of the 1963 Act proscribing dual inheritance by adoptees was not retained in the present law, § 1–207(a) implicitly permits adoptees to inherit from natural relatives, as well as the adoptive parents.

The right to receive property by devise or descent is not a natural right but a privilege granted by the State. Every State possesses the power to regulate the manner or term by which property within its dominion may be transmitted by will or inheritance and to prescribe who shall or shall not be capable of receiving that property. A State may deny the privilege altogether or may impose whatever restrictions or conditions upon the grant it deems appropriate.

Family Law Art. § 5–308(b)(1)(ii) entitles an adopted person to all the rights and privileges of a natural child insofar as the adoptive parents are concerned, but adoption does not confer upon the adopted child *more* rights and privileges than those possessed by a natural child. To construe Est. & Trusts Art. § 1–207(a) so as to allow dual inheritance would bestow upon an adopted child a superior status. That status was removed in Laws 1963, Ch. 174 which, as we have said, expressly disallowed the dual inheritance capability of adopted children by providing that "the adopted child shall lose all rights of inheritance from its parents and from their natural collateral or lineal relatives." We think that the current statute, § 1–207(a), did not alter the substance of the 1963 act which eliminated dual inheritance. Rather, § 1–207(a) merely "streamlined" the wording while retaining the meaning.

Family Law Art. § 5–308 plainly mandates that adoption be considered a "rebirth" into a completely different relationship. Once a child is adopted, the rights of both the natural parents and relatives are terminated. Est. & Trusts Art. § 1–207(a) and Family Law Art. § 5–308 emphasize the clean-cut severance from the natural bloodline. Because an adopted child has no right to inherit *from* the estate of a natural parent who dies intestate, it follows that the same child may not inherit *through* the natural parent by way of representation. What may not be done directly most assuredly may not be done indirectly. The elimination of dual inheritance in 1963 clearly established that policy, and the current language of § 1–207(a) simply reflects the continuation of that policy.

We hold that because § 1–207(a) eliminates the adopted child's right to inherit from the natural parent it concomitantly abrogated the right to inherit through the natural parent by way of representation.

"The Legislature giveth, and the Legislature taketh away."

JUDGMENT AFFIRMED.

COSTS TO BE PAID BY APPELLANTS.

Are you convinced as a matter of logic? The court says, "Because an adopted child has no right to inherit *from* the estate of a natural parent who dies intestate, it follows that the same child may not inherit *through* the natural parent by way of representation. What may not be done directly most assuredly may not be done indirectly." Could these children have inherited directly from their father, Earl, at the time of his death?

Are you convinced as a matter of policy? Are children who lose a father so lucky that the law, as a matter of fairness, needs to prevent them from inheriting from two sets of paternal relatives? If their natural uncle, William, had died just before Jim adopted them, the children could have inherited from their uncle. Would Jim have adopted them if Jim knew that his adoption would cut off their inheritance from their uncle? Is it a good idea to create a disincentive to adoption in these situations by cutting off inheritance?

On the same facts, what would happen under the UPC?

IN RE ESTATE OF GALLEGOS

Colorado Court of Appeals, Division V, 2021
499 P.3d 1058

GROVE, J.

In this probate case, appellants Shennae Finan, formerly known as Shennae Jaramillo, and Corpus A. Gallegos Ranches, LLLP, appeal the district court's ruling that appellee Patricia Vialpando is an heir of Joseph Celestino Gallegos, who died intestate. Applying section 15–11–119(3), C.R.S. 2020, we conclude that, for the purpose of intestate succession, the parent-child relationship between Gallegos and Vialpando was not terminated when Vialpando was adopted in 1991. Therefore, we affirm.

I.   Background

Gallegos died in December 2016. He had two biological children: Vialpando and Finan. Vialpando was born in 1990 and was adopted by her maternal grandparents in 1991. However, she maintained a relationship with Gallegos throughout his life and he named her as the beneficiary of his savings and retirement accounts. Finan, who was born in 1989 and who otherwise had no relationship with Gallegos, learned that Gallegos was her father nearly two years after his death. Both biological daughters now seek a share of his estate, and Finan's heirship is not in dispute.

Gallegos died without a spouse or a will, meaning that his children are entitled to inherit the estate's assets in equal shares.

See § 15–11–103(2), C.R.S. 2020. The district court named Vialpando his sole heir and appointed her as personal representative for his estate. Once Finan learned that Gallegos was her biological father, however, she moved to modify the court's determination of heirship. Finan's motion claimed that she was Gallegos's sole heir because Vialpando's adoption cut off Vialpando's relationship with Gallegos for the purpose of intestate succession. Gallegos Ranches, a family partnership owned by the late Gallegos and his two brothers, joined Finan's argument.

The district court ruled that both Vialpando and Finan are heirs to Gallegos's estate. Although Vialpando was adopted by her maternal grandparents—thereby terminating her parent-child relationship with Gallegos—the court concluded that a 2010 amendment to the Probate Code, which allowed children adopted by relatives to inherit from their genetic parents, revived that relationship for the purpose of intestate succession. Finan and Gallegos Ranches now jointly appeal, contending that the district court erred by applying the amended Probate Code provision because it was passed nearly twenty years after Vialpando's adoption was finalized.

* * *

III. Children's Code

Under the Children's Code, a final decree of adoption divests the biological parents "of all legal rights and obligations with respect to the child." § 19–5–211(2), C.R.S. 2020. Relatedly, a "child's status as an heir at law . . . shall cease only upon a final decree of adoption." § 19–3–608(1), C.R.S. 2020. Under these provisions, as things stood in 1991, once Vialpando was adopted (by anyone), any right to inherit property via Colorado's laws of intestate succession was terminated along with the parent-child relationship.

IV. Probate Code

In 2010, the General Assembly amended Colorado's intestate succession laws. As relevant here, those amendments included a provision allowing children who are adopted by relatives of either genetic parent to inherit from a genetic parent who dies without a will.

> A parent-child relationship exists between both genetic parents and an individual who is adopted by a relative of a genetic parent, or by the spouse or surviving spouse of a

relative of a genetic parent, but only for the purpose of the right of the adoptee or a descendant of the adoptee to inherit from or through either genetic parent.

§ 15–11–119(3). This language was in effect in 2016 at the time of Gallegos's death.

V. Analysis

The sole question before us is whether the 2010 amendment applies to Vialpando. We hold that it does and as a result conclude that Vialpando is Gallegos's heir.

Appellants contend that upon Vialpando's adoption in 1991, Gallegos was permanently divested of "all legal rights and obligations with respect to" Vialpando, and the parent-child relationship was forever terminated. Because of the finality of the adoption decree and the corresponding provisions of the Children's Code, which specify that "a child's status as an heir at law" ceases upon a final decree of adoption, § 19–3–608(1), appellants assert that the 2010 amendment to the Probate Code had no effect on Vialpando's status as an heir.[1] Because no parent-child relationship existed in 2010, appellants contend, there was no parent-child relationship to revive, even for the limited purpose of intestate succession. We disagree.

A. Conflict of Laws

Probate courts must consider the adoption and inheritance laws in effect at the time of adoption, but the right of adopted children to inherit is determined by the inheritance laws in effect when the intestate died. The Probate Code in effect at the time of Gallegos's death provided that a parent-child relationship existed between "both genetic parents and an individual who is adopted by a relative of a genetic parent . . . *but only* for the purpose of the right of the adoptee or a descendant of the adoptee to inherit from . . . either genetic parent." § 15–11–119(3) (emphasis added). The statute does not clarify whether it is intended to have only prospective effect, but because Vialpando was adopted by her maternal grandparents, it applies unless the adoption irreversibly severed the parent-child relationship between Vialpando and Gallegos for all purposes.

---

[1]   Notably, appellants do not distinguish between an heir and an heir apparent. It is settled law that heirs can only be determined after a decedent's death. Prior to his death, a decedent's relative can only be an heir apparent — someone with a mere expectation of inheriting in the future. It is upon the decedent's death that the legal title to estate property vests instantly in his heirs at law.

Nothing in Vialpando's adoption records addressed the effect of the adoption on Vialpando's status as Gallegos's heir. However, under the Children's Code, Vialpando's "status as an heir at law" ceased "upon a final decree of adoption." § 19–3–608(1). This provision conflicts with the 2010 amendment to the Probate Code. Simply put, if section 15–11–119(3) controls, Vialpando became Gallegos's heir upon his death. On the other hand, if adoption irrevocably severed Vialpando's relationship with Gallegos for all purposes, then she did not. To resolve this conflict, we apply principles of statutory construction to determine which provision controls.

B. Principles of Statutory Construction

The overriding goal of statutory construction is to effectuate the legislature's intent. We interpret the statute within the context of its broader scheme to give consistent, harmonious, and sensible effect to all its parts. When we conclude, as we do here, that two applicable provisions are irreconcilable, we look to both specificity and recency to resolve the conflict.

First, the more specific statute prevails over the more general one. § 2–4–205, C.R.S. 2020 (explaining that if a conflict between a special provision and a general provision is irreconcilable, "the special . . . provision prevails as an exception to the general provision"). "Interpreting a specific provision as prevailing over a general one still allows for both provisions to exist," *People v. Cooper*, 27 P.3d 348, 355 (Colo. 2001), an approach that is consistent with the goal of giving full and sensible effect to the entire statutory scheme, *see Smith v. Colo. Motor Vehicle Dealer Bd.*, 200 P.3d 1115, 1118 (Colo. App. 2008).

Second, the more recent statute prevails over the older one. This is true even if the General Assembly did not clearly intend the more recent statute to supplant an existing statute. We assume the legislature is aware of its enactments, and, therefore, we conclude that by passing an irreconcilable statute at a later date, it "intended to alter the prior statute."

Applying these principles here, we conclude that because the probate statute is both more specific and more recent, it prevails over the conflicting provisions of the Children's Code.

At the outset, we recognize that the conflict between section 15–11–119(3) and section 19–3–608(1) is quite limited. It only applies to children who have been adopted by certain relatives of their biological parents; section 19–3–608(1) continues to apply to nonrelative adoptions. Because we aim to give full and sensible effect to the entire statutory scheme, we interpret section 15–11–119(3) as carving out a limited exception to the general rule outlined in section 19–3–608(1).

The timing of section 15–11–119(3)'s passage lends support to our conclusion that the General Assembly intended to alter the scope of section 19–3–608. To be sure, we assume that the legislature is familiar with its previous enactments. But it is also clear that the amendment to the Probate Code would not make sense unless the General Assembly understood the general rule established in the Children's Code. Therefore, we are confident that the legislature "intended to alter" the Children's Code when it passed the more recent amendment to the Probate Code.

* * *

VI. Conclusion

The judgment is affirmed.

Would the legislature have wanted its changes to apply to children adopted before the date of enactment? If one goal of the rules of intestate succession is to approximate what decedents would have wanted, what would decedents in Joseph's position want?

(ii) Contracts to Adopt and Equitable Adoption

Sometimes a child lives with a person who plays the role of a parent without going through the formalities of a legal adoption. How do the rules of intestacy apply in those situations?

> Problem 3.08: Genetic mother, GM, and genetic father, GF, have a child, C. They sign a contract to allow C to be adopted by adoptive father, AF. C goes to live with AF. AF dies without having legally adopted C. Does the following case suggest a theory on which can C inherit from or through AF?

O'NEAL V. WILKES

Supreme Court of Georgia, 1994
439 S.E.2d 490

FLETCHER, J.

In this virtual adoption action, a jury found that appellant Hattie O'Neal had been virtually adopted by the decedent, Roswell Cook. On post-trial motions, the court granted a judgment notwithstanding the verdict to appellee Firmon Wilkes, as administrator of Cook's estate, on the ground that the paternal aunt who allegedly entered into the adoption contract with Cook had no legal authority to do so. We have reviewed the record and conclude that the court correctly determined that there was no valid contract to adopt.

O'Neal was born out of wedlock in 1949 and raised by her mother, Bessie Broughton, until her mother's death in 1957. At no time did O'Neal's biological father recognize O'Neal as his daughter, take any action to legitimize her, or provide support to her or her mother. O'Neal testified that she first met her biological father in 1970.

For four years after her mother's death, O'Neal lived in New York City with her maternal aunt, Ethel Campbell. In 1961, Ms. Campbell brought O'Neal to Savannah, Georgia, and surrendered physical custody of O'Neal to a woman identified only as Louise who was known to want a daughter. Shortly thereafter, Louise determined she could not care for O'Neal and took her to the Savannah home of Estelle Page, the sister of O'Neal's biological father. After a short time with Page, Roswell Cook and his wife came to Savannah from their Riceboro, Georgia home to pick up O'Neal. Page testified that she had heard that the Cooks wanted a daughter and after telling them about O'Neal, they came for her.

Although O'Neal was never statutorily adopted by Cook, he raised her and provided for her education and she resided with him until her marriage in 1975. While she never took the last name of Cook, he referred to her as his daughter and, later, identified her children as his grandchildren.

In November 1991, Cook died intestate. The appellee, Firmon Wilkes, was appointed as administrator of Cook's estate and refused to recognize O'Neal's asserted interest in the estate. In December 1991, O'Neal filed a petition in equity asking the court to declare a virtual adoption, thereby entitling her to the estate property she would have inherited if she were Cook's statutorily adopted child.

1.   The first essential of a contract for adoption is that it be made between persons competent to contract for the disposition of the child. A successful plaintiff must also prove:

> Some showing of an agreement between the natural and adoptive parents, performance by the natural parents of the child in giving up custody, performance by the child by living in the home of the adoptive parents, partial performance by the foster parents in taking the child into the home and treating [it] as their child, and . . . the intestacy of the foster parent.

The only issue on this appeal is whether the court correctly determined that Page was without authority to contract for O'Neal's adoption.

2.   O'Neal argues that Page, a paternal aunt with physical custody of her, had authority to contract for her adoption and, even if she was without such authority, any person with the legal right to contract for the adoption, be they O'Neal's biological father or maternal aunts or uncles, ratified the adoption contract by failing to object.

As a preliminary matter, we agree with O'Neal that although her biological father was living at the time the adoption contract was allegedly entered into, his consent to the contract was not necessary as he never recognized or legitimized her or provided for her support in any manner. See *Williams*, 239 Ga. 276 (mother alone may contract for adoption where the father has lost parental control or abandoned the child); § 74–203 (only mother of child born out of wedlock may exercise parental power over the child unless legitimized by the father); see also § 19–8–10 (parent not entitled to notice of petition of adoption where parent has abandoned the child). What is less clear are the rights and obligations acquired by Page by virtue of her physical custody of O'Neal after her mother's death.

3.   The Georgia Code defines a "legal custodian" as a person to whom legal custody has been given by court order and who has the right to physical custody of the child and to determine the nature of the care and treatment of the child and the duty to provide for the care, protection, training, and education and the physical, mental, and moral welfare of the child. A legal custodian does not have the

right to consent to the adoption of a child, as this right is specifically retained by one with greater rights over the child, a child's parent or guardian.

O'Neal concedes that, after her mother's death, no guardianship petition was filed by her relatives. Nor is there any evidence that any person petitioned to be appointed as her legal custodian. Accordingly, the obligation to care and provide for O'Neal, undertaken first by Campbell, and later by Page, was not a legal obligation but a familial obligation resulting in a custodial relationship properly characterized as something less than that of a legal custodian. Such a relationship carried with it no authority to contract for O'Neal's adoption. While we sympathize with O'Neal's plight, we conclude that Page had no authority to enter into the adoption contract with Cook and the contract, therefore, was invalid.

4.   Because O'Neal's relatives did not have the legal authority to enter into a contract for her adoption, their alleged ratification of the adoption contract was of no legal effect and the court did not err in granting a judgment notwithstanding the verdict in favor of the appellee. See *Foster v. Cheek*, 212 Ga. 821 (1957) (adoption contract made between persons not competent to contract for child's adoption specifically enforceable where the parent with parental power over the child acquiesced in and ratified the adoption contract).

Judgment affirmed.

SEARS-COLLINS, J., dissenting.

I disagree with the majority's holding that O'Neal's claim for equitable adoption is defeated by the fact that her paternal aunt was not a person designated by law as one having the authority to consent to O'Neal's adoption.

1.   In *Crawford v. Wilson*, 139 Ga. 654, 658 (1913), the doctrine of equitable or virtual adoption was recognized for the first time in Georgia. Relying on the equitable principle that "equity considers that done which ought to have been done," we held that an agreement to adopt a child, so as to constitute the child an heir at law on the death of the person adopting, performed on the part of the child, is enforceable upon the death of the person adopting the child as to property which is undisposed of by will. We held that although the death of the adopting parents precluded a literal enforcement of the contract, equity would "enforce the contract by decreeing that the child is entitled to the fruits of a legal adoption." In *Crawford*,

we noted that the full performance of the agreement by the child was sufficient to overcome an objection that the agreement was unenforceable because it violated the statute of frauds. We further held that

> [w]here one takes an infant into his home upon a promise to adopt such as his own child, and the child performs all the duties growing out of the substituted relationship of parent and child, rendering years of service, companionship, and obedience to the foster parent, upon the faith that such foster parent stands in loco parentis, and that upon his death the child will sustain the legal relationship to his estate of a natural child, there is equitable reason that the child may appeal to a court of equity to consummate, so far as it may be possible, the foster parent's omission of duty in the matter of formal adoption.

Although the majority correctly states the current rule in Georgia that a contract to adopt may not be specifically enforced unless the contract was entered by a person with the legal authority to consent to the adoption of the child, *Crawford* did not expressly establish such a requirement, and I think the cases cited by the majority that have established this requirement are in error.

Instead, I would hold that where a child has fully performed the alleged contract over the course of many years or a lifetime and can sufficiently establish the existence of the contract to adopt, equity should enforce the contract over the objection of the adopting parents' heirs that the contract is unenforceable because the person who consented to the adoption did not have the legal authority to do so. Several reasons support this conclusion.

First, in such cases, the adopting parents and probably their heirs know of the defect in the contract and yet voice no objection to the contract while the child fully performs the contract and the adopting parents reap the benefits thereof. Under these circumstances, to hold that the contract is unenforceable after the child has performed is to permit a virtual fraud upon the child and should not be countenanced in equity. Equity does not permit such action with regard to contracts that are initially unenforceable because they violate the statute of frauds, but instead recognizes that the full performance of the contract negates its initial unenforceability and renders it enforceable in equity.

Moreover, the purpose of requiring consent by a person with the legal authority to consent to an adoption, where such a person exists, is to protect that person, the child, and the adopting parents. However, as equitable adoption cases do not arise until the death of the adopting parents, the interests of the person with the consent to adopt and of the adopting parents are not in jeopardy. On the other hand, the interests of the child are unfairly and inequitably harmed by insisting upon the requirement that a person with the consent to adopt had to have been a party to the contract. That this legal requirement is held against the child is particularly inequitable because the child, the course of whose life is forever changed by such contracts, was unable to act to insure the validity of the contract when the contract was made.

Furthermore, where there is no person with the legal authority to consent to the adoption, such as in the present case, the only reason to insist that a person be appointed the child's legal guardian before agreeing to the contract to adopt would be for the protection of the child. Yet, by insisting upon this requirement after the adopting parents' deaths, this Court is harming the very person that the requirement would protect.

For all the foregoing reasons, equity ought to intervene on the child's behalf in these types of cases, and require the performance of the contract if it is sufficiently proven. In this case, I would thus not rule against O'Neal's claim for specific performance solely on the ground that her paternal aunt did not have the authority to consent to the adoption.

2. Moreover, basing the doctrine of equitable adoption in contract theory has come under heavy criticism, for numerous reasons. For instance, as we acknowledged in *Wilson*, supra, 139 Ga. at 659, the contract to adopt is not being specifically enforced as the adopting parents are dead; for equitable reasons we are merely placing the child in a position that he or she would have been in if he or she had been adopted. Moreover, it is problematic whether these contracts are capable of being enforced in all respects during the child's infancy. Furthermore, because part of the consideration for these contracts is the child's performance thereunder, the child is not merely a third-party beneficiary of a contract between the adults involved but is a party thereto. Yet, a child is usually too young to know of or understand the contract, and it is thus difficult to find a meeting of the minds between the child and the adopting parents and the child's acceptance of the contract. I agree with these

criticisms and would abandon the contract basis for equitable adoption in favor of the more flexible and equitable theory advanced by the foregoing authorities. That theory focuses not on the fiction of whether there has been a contract to adopt but on the relationship between the adopting parents and the child and in particular whether the adopting parents have led the child to believe that he or she is a legally adopted member of their family.

3. Because the majority fails to honor the maxim that "[e]quity considers that done which ought to be done," § 23–1–8, and follows a rule that fails to protect a person with superior equities, I dissent.

I am authorized to state that JUSTICE HUNSTEIN concurs in the result reached by this dissent.

———————————

The majority said, "A legal custodian does not have the right to consent to the adoption of a child, as this right is specifically retained by one with greater rights over the child, a child's parent or guardian." Does that statement support its decision when the child has no parent or guardian with "greater rights" than the aunt who was caring for her? The decedent, Cook, referred to O'Neal as his daughter and later identified her children as his grandchildren. Do you think he would have wanted her to inherit from him? Is it fair that she did not? For hundreds of years, courts of equity have reached results that would not have obtained at law. You have already seen one example of this, where the court imposed a constructive trust to prevent a slayer from inheriting from the victim. The majority in this case applied the rules of law regarding adoption and determined that the aunt had no "legal" authority to contract for adoption. However, O'Neal's original claim was a "petition in equity". One issue, then, is which rules of law should apply when the court sits in equity. As a matter of fairness, should the court have ignored some of the legal rules for adoption and held that "equity considers that done which ought to have been done"? Did the posture of the case allow the court to do that? The majority opinion says, "The only issue on this appeal is whether the court correctly determined that Page was without authority to contract for O'Neal's adoption."

DeHart v. DeHart

Supreme Court of Illinois, 2013
986 N.E.2d 85

THOMAS, J.

Plaintiff, James Thomas DeHart, filed a six-count, second-amended complaint against Blanca DeHart, in her individual capacity and as executor of the estate of Donald M. DeHart (Donald), deceased, contesting Donald's will dated December 4, 2006, and raising claims of lack of testamentary capacity, undue influence, fraudulent inducement, tortious interference with economic expectancy, contract for adoption and equitable adoption. The circuit court of Will County dismissed with prejudice all of plaintiff's counts. The circuit court also denied plaintiff's motion to compel the deposition of William J. Peters, the attorney who drafted the disputed will. Plaintiff appealed, and the appellate court reversed the dismissal of all six counts and reversed the denial of the motion to compel the deposition of attorney Peters. The appellate court's decision was unanimous on all matters, except on the contract-for-adoption count, in which case one justice dissented, finding that there were insufficient factual allegations to support a cause of action for that claim. This court subsequently allowed defendant's petition for leave to appeal.

BACKGROUND

The following facts were alleged in plaintiff's second amended complaint and are set forth in the appellate court's opinion. During Donald's lifetime and for more than 60 years, he held plaintiff out to both individuals and institutions as his biological son. In May 2003, Donald made arrangements for his own funeral and listed plaintiff as his son. Donald listed plaintiff's children and grandchildren as his own grandchildren and great-grandchildren. In addition to telling members of the community over the years that plaintiff was his son, Donald provided plaintiff with a birth certificate that listed Donald as plaintiff's natural father. Throughout their lifetimes, Donald and plaintiff used the purported birth certificate, to conduct the affairs of life (until the year 2000), using it to enroll plaintiff in grade school and high school and using it to convey to those requesting proof of identity that plaintiff was Donald's son.

In 2000, however, plaintiff attempted to use the birth certificate to obtain a passport, and the United States passport office would not accept it as a record of plaintiff's birth, instead requiring him to produce a certified (raised stamp) copy of his birth certificate. Plaintiff obtained the certified copy from the Cook County Office of Vital Statistics and learned that it was identical in most respects, except it listed his name as James Thomas Staley, Jr. and his father's name as James Thomas Staley, Sr., and did not mention "DeHart" after his mother's maiden name. Both birth certificates listed plaintiff's birth date as May 23, 1944.

Plaintiff then confronted Donald with the information contained on the certified copy of the newly obtained birth certificate. In response, Donald said that plaintiff's mother, Virginia, married Staley, plaintiff's biological father, after she became pregnant out of wedlock in 1943. Donald also told plaintiff that he adopted plaintiff in 1946 when plaintiff was two years old, but he had agreed with Virginia to keep the adoption a secret for the good of plaintiff and the family. As part of this agreement, Donald and Virginia agreed to celebrate their wedding anniversary, but never discuss how many years they had been married. Donald also explained in no uncertain terms that he had hired a lawyer in Homewood, Illinois, to handle the adoption so that "it was all legal."

There is no legal documentation of an adoption in the record. Plaintiff's mother, Virginia, died in April 2001. She was suffering from early onset dementia at the time plaintiff learned of the information on the certified birth certificate. James Staley, Sr., abandoned plaintiff and Virginia when plaintiff was two years old and has had no contact with plaintiff in the ensuing six decades.

Even after plaintiff confronted Donald in 2000 about the birth certificates, Donald continued to represent and describe plaintiff as his son. In May 2003, Donald made funeral arrangements listing plaintiff as his son. In the spring of 2005, Donald, plaintiff and plaintiff's wife and children took a family vacation—with Donald assuming the bulk of the costs and expenses. Donald also executed a will that was prepared prior to December 2006 that provided bequests for plaintiff, plaintiff's children and Donald's church. This prior will was prepared by the law firm of Krusemark and Krusemark in Frankfort, Illinois, and plaintiff alleges that the original is in the exclusive control of defendant who is either preventing it from surfacing or has destroyed it.

Donald met defendant while she was working at a jewelry counter at a Tinley Park Sam's Club in the spring of 2005. The two were married on December 5, 2005; at that time, Donald was 83 years old and defendant was 54 years old. Donald invited plaintiff to the wedding and reception. But the complaint does not mention whether plaintiff attended the wedding.

The complaint alleges that on December 4, 2006—the day before Donald's and defendant's first wedding anniversary—Donald signed the contested will in the office of attorney William J. Peters. At that time, Donald was 84 years old. The will states, "I am married to Blanca DeHart. I have no children." The complaint further alleges that Donald demonstrated he was of unsound mind and memory when he signed the will and could not remember plaintiff—now 61 years old—whom Donald had held out to all the world as his son for nearly 60 years.

The complaint further alleges that in the months between the wedding of defendant and Donald and the execution of the contested will, defendant developed and maintained a position of trust and confidence, amounting to a fiduciary relationship with Donald. Despite the fact that she had only been married to Donald a short time and he had amassed his wealth over 84 years of his life, she became joint tenants with Donald on real estate, bank accounts and brokerage accounts worth millions of dollars. She also obtained a power of attorney to act on Donald's behalf, and exercised significant control over Donald's real estate dealings, including the sale of the family farm.

The complaint also alleges that defendant made several misrepresentations to Donald concerning plaintiff and his character, each of which was told to Donald shortly before the execution of the will on December 4, 2006. In particular, defendant lied to Donald by telling him that plaintiff was not his son and by not telling Donald that plaintiff and other family members had called him on the telephone and had sent cards and letters, as well as intercepting and destroying those cards and letters. Defendant's lies were made in order to improperly force and persuade Donald to alter his will by providing exclusively for her, as opposed to plaintiff, who would otherwise inherit as next of kin or, alternatively, as specifically stated in Donald's prior will. Donald, succumbing to defendant's influence, executed the will on December 4, 2006, stating that he had "no children," when in fact he did. The complaint alleges that under all of these circumstances, the will was the product of defendant's influence and therefore not the last will of Donald.

Donald died in February 2007, a couple of months after executing the will in question on December 4, 2006. After Donald's death, defendant filed that will in the circuit court of Will County. Plaintiff's second amended complaint challenges that will on the grounds of testator incapacity (count I) and as the product of undue influence by defendant (count II). The complaint also alleges that defendant fraudulently induced Donald into executing the new will (count III), and it seeks to set aside the purported will and compel distribution of the estate under the prior will or pursuant to law or equity based on intentional interference with testamentary expectancy (count IV). Finally, the complaint alleges that Donald entered into a contract to adopt plaintiff (count V), and that in any event, an equitable adoption occurred under the circumstances and that Donald's estate is therefore estopped from denying plaintiff as an heir at law (count VI). Additionally, plaintiff sought to compel the deposition testimony of William J. Peters, the attorney who prepared the December 2006 will, and defendant objected on the basis of attorney-client privilege.

In July 2009, defendant moved to dismiss the second amended complaint pursuant to section 2–615 of the Code of Civil Procedure (Code), arguing that the complaint failed to allege sufficient facts to state a cause of action. The circuit court dismissed with prejudice all of plaintiff's counts and denied his motion to compel the deposition of attorney Peters.

Plaintiff appealed. The appellate court unanimously reversed the dismissal of counts I through IV and count VI, along with the denial of the motion to compel the deposition testimony of attorney Peters. A majority of the court also reversed the dismissal of count V. With respect to that count, Justice Schmidt dissented, believing that the complaint failed to identify the parties to the contract to adopt and whether the agreement was oral or written, and therefore plaintiff failed to allege a valid cause of action on that count. Although the appellate court unanimously concluded that dismissal of the equitable adoption count must be reversed, Justice McDade wrote separately to emphasize her belief that whether a claim for equitable adoption can be recognized in this state should ultimately be resolved by the Illinois Supreme Court.

Defendant filed a petition for leave to appeal, which we granted.

ANALYSIS

* * *

IV. Contract to Adopt

We next address the count of plaintiff's complaint alleging that a contract for adoption existed and plaintiff should therefore be considered an heir of Donald's estate under Illinois case law. Defendant argues that for this theory to be established there must be proof that a contract for adoption was entered into between the foster parent and the child's natural parents or some individual or institution standing *in loco parentis,* and the natural parents must "give up" custody. Defendant maintains that plaintiff's complaint is deficient because it does not allege who the parties to the agreement were. Plaintiff in turn relies upon this court's decision in *Monahan v. Monahan,* 14 Ill.2d 449 (1958), to contend that sufficient facts were alleged to state a cause of action. We agree with plaintiff.

In *Monahan,* the plaintiff's natural mother boarded her son with the Monahans when he was two years old. The plaintiff's natural father abandoned him a year later and was never seen again. The plaintiff's mother continued to pay board for another four years, but then apparently gave up the plaintiff to the Monahans and consented to his adoption. This was shown by notations that Mrs. Monahan had made to papers found among her personal effects after her death. The Monahans then raised the boy as their own, had him baptized as Edward Francis Monahan, and consulted an attorney about adoption when he was seven years old. The adoption never took place, however, because the Monahans mistakenly believed that they needed the natural's father's consent to proceed and were unable to locate him. The Monahans entered the plaintiff into school as their adopted son, continuously referred to him as their son and themselves as "mom and dad," and many of their relatives were under the impression that the plaintiff was adopted.

This court in *Monahan* found that a contract to adopt did exist. In so doing, this court reconciled its earlier decision in *Weiss v. Beck,* 1 Ill.2d 420 (1953), stating that there, the court merely determined that the evidence presented failed to give rise to a "clear, positive indication that the agreement to adopt ever existed, but left reasonable doubt, and harmonized as readily with the intention to provide a good home as with an intent to adopt." The *Monahan* court continued, stating that "[c]ertainly a contract to adopt, as any other fact, may be proved by circumstantial evidence, provided that evidence meets the requisite tests of sufficiency." *Monahan* then found that the evidence of a contract as well as the intention to adopt the plaintiff is "clear and convincing" based on the following evidence. The family relationship of parents and son clearly existed, neighbors and relatives believed the plaintiff had been adopted, and the plaintiff conducted himself as a dutiful child. Moreover, the Monahans indicated to others that the plaintiff's natural mother "gave" the plaintiff to them to adopt and this was confirmed by written notations, along with their abortive attempts at legal adoption.

We find that *Monahan* compels the result that sufficient facts were pled in the present case to allege a claim for a contract to adopt. In *Monahan,* the court found that the contract-for-adoption claim was proven by "clear and convincing" evidence at trial. Here, plaintiff is not required to prove his case at the pleading stage by clear and convincing evidence. Instead, he needed only to allege sufficient facts to support his conclusion that a contract to adopt existed.

Defendant incorrectly argues that Donald failed to allege the identity of the parties to the contract for adoption. The instant appellate court correctly found that the well-pled facts, viewed in the light most favorable to plaintiff, sufficiently inferred that a contract to adopt existed between Donald and plaintiff's mother Virginia and that plaintiff was a third-party beneficiary of that contract. In that regard, plaintiff's complaint specifically alleges that Donald "had agreed with Virginia to keep the adoption a secret for the good of [plaintiff] and the family." And "[a]s part of this agreement, the two agreed to celebrate their wedding anniversary, but never discuss how many years they had been married." We believe that implicit in the agreement to "keep the adoption a secret" is an agreement between Virginia and Donald that Donald adopt plaintiff.

In an adoption where a spouse adopts the natural child of his or her spouse, it is not necessary that the spouse giving up the child for adoption to the other spouse actually give up his parental rights. In such a case, an agreement for adoption exists even though the natural parent is not giving up all—or even any of—his parental rights. At any rate, it can be readily inferred from the allegations of plaintiff's complaint that Virginia in agreeing to allow Donald to adopt plaintiff conferred the full benefits of fatherhood upon him and relinquished some of her control of the child to plaintiff. We also think it obvious that mutual consideration exists for such an agreement, and defendant has not supported her claim that consideration is lacking with any relevant citation to Illinois authority. Further support for the claim that a contract for adoption existed is the well-pled fact that Donald had hired an attorney in Homewood to complete the adoption and that Donald believed it had actually been completed, telling plaintiff that it was "all legal."

Defendant is also mistaken in her assertion that plaintiff cannot proceed on a contract to adopt theory in this case where there is no evidence that plaintiff's natural father (who abandoned plaintiff) was a party to an agreement with Donald for an adoption. We find no merit to defendant's contention that a party who has permanently abandoned a child need be a party to the contract to adopt that is being enforced for inheritance purposes. The natural father in *Monahan* also abandoned the plaintiff in that case when he was a small child and there was no evidence that he ever consented to adoption, but this fact did not preclude the plaintiff from prevailing in that case. In sum, we conclude that the appellate court correctly determined that the circuit court erred in dismissing plaintiff's adoption contract claim.

V. Equitable Adoption

As an alternative to his contract for adoption theory, plaintiff relies upon the theory of equitable adoption. Plaintiff suggests that even in the absence of an expressed or implied contract to adopt, a finding of an equitable adoption would nonetheless be proper in a case where there is clear and convincing evidence of a foster parent's intent to adopt and treat the child as one's adopted or natural child. Defendant, on the other hand, argues that any recognition of equitable adoption should be limited to situations where a contract to adopt exists and the natural parent gives up his or her child.

We note that the concept of "equitable adoption" is somewhat murky because many states seem to equate the theory of equitable adoption with a contract-to-adopt theory. In these states, it is clear that where the doctrine of "equitable adoption" is recognized, the most important prerequisite to its application is proof that a contract of adoption was entered into between the foster parents and the natural parents or someone standing *in loco parentis*. These jurisdictions apply estoppel or quasi-contract considerations where there has been clear proof of a contract, expressed or implied, reliance upon the parent-child relationship, and performance of obligations under the *de facto* relationship. This makes so-called equitable adoption, as recognized in many states, essentially indiscernible from the Illinois cases involving a failure to follow the statute for adoption that have proceeded on a contract theory.

A few states, however, have refused to apply a steadfast requirement that an expressed or implied contract to adopt exists before finding that an equitable adoption has occurred. See, *e.g.*, *Estate of Ford v. Ford,* 82 P.3d 747, 754 (Cal. 2004); *Wheeling Dollar Savings & Trust Co. v. Singer,* 250 S.E.2d 369, 373–74 (W.Va. 1978). In *Wheeling,* the Supreme Court of West Virginia declined to take the view that an expressed or implied contract to adopt was absolutely necessary to establish that an equitable adoption had taken place where a person has "stood from an age of tender years in a position *exactly* equivalent to a formally adopted child." (Emphasis added.) The court stated that while the existence of an expressed or implied contract of adoption is "very convincing evidence, an implied contract of adoption is an unnecessary fiction created by courts as a protection from fraudulent claims." The court held that "if a claimant can, by clear, cogent and convincing evidence, prove sufficient facts to convince the trier of fact that his status is identical to that of a formally adopted child, except only for the absence of a formal order of adoption, a finding of an equitable adoption is proper without proof of an adoption contract." The court noted that circumstances that tend to show the existence of an equitable adoption include the following: the benefits of love and affection accruing to the adopting party; the performances of services by the child; the surrender of ties by the natural parent; the society, companionship and filial obedience of the child; an invalid or ineffectual adoption proceeding; reliance by the adopted person upon the existence of his adopted status; the representation to all the world that the child is a natural or adopted child; and the rearing of the child from an age of tender years by the adopting parents.

In *Ford,* the California Supreme Court also concluded that an equitable adoption claimant need not prove all of the elements of an enforceable contract to recover. *Ford,* however, employed a stricter approach than the one adopted by the West Virginia Supreme Court in *Wheeling. Ford* held that to prove an equitable adoption, a claimant "must demonstrate the existence of some direct expression, on the decedent's part, of an intent to adopt the claimant." The court found that this intent may be shown by an unperformed agreement or promise to adopt, but that it also may be shown by "proof of other acts or statements directly showing that the decedent intended the child to be, or to be treated as, a legally adopted child, such as an invalid or unconsummated attempt to adopt, the decedent's statement of his or her intent to adopt, the child, or the decedent's representation to the claimant or to the community at large that the claimant was the decedent's natural or legally adopted child." *Ford* also held that along with a statement or act by the decedent evincing an unequivocal intent to adopt, the claimant must also show "the decedent acted consistently with that intent by forming with the claimant a close and enduring familial relationship." In other words, there must be objective conduct indicating mutual recognition of a parent-child relationship to such an extent that in equity and good conscience an adoption should be deemed to have taken place. *Ford* strongly cautioned, however, that it would not recognize estoppel arising merely from a familial relationship between the decedent and the claimant without any direct expression by the decedent of an intent to adopt the child or to have him treated as a legally adopted child.

Applying the above-mentioned principles along with a "clear and convincing" burden of proof, *Ford* examined all of the evidence presented in the case before it and concluded that an equitable adoption had not been proven even though the claimant had a close and enduring familial relationship with the decedent, Mr. Ford. The court noted that there was no evidence that the Fords ever made an attempt to adopt the claimant and they never held him out to the world as their natural or adopted son, nor represented to him that he was their child, even though the claimant called them "Mom" and "Dad." It was also noted that Mrs. Ford's single statement to a family friend that she wanted to adopt claimant, but was under the impression that she could not do so while he was still in the home, was deemed insufficient evidence that Mr. Ford intended claimant to be adopted.

Although no Illinois court has expressly recognized the concept of equitable adoption as it is presented here, no Illinois court has expressly rejected it either. We do find, however, that the underpinnings to pave the way for its recognition can be found in this court's earlier decisions of *Monahan* and *Weiss*. Both cases were brought purely under a contract-to-adopt theory, and there was no argument presented by the parties that this court should recognize equitable adoption in any form. Both decisions, however, addressed arguments that a contract to adopt could be proven by circumstantial evidence, and in the course of addressing that argument, both courts cited approvingly to the Eight Circuit Court of Appeals decision in *Roberts v. Roberts,* 223 F. 775 (8th Cir.1915), which, even though it did not expressly address equitable adoption, seemed to ultimately rest its outcome on principles of equity.

In *Roberts,* there was no evidence of a contract to adopt, but plaintiff nonetheless proceeded under a contract-to-adopt theory. The evidence did show that the foster parents took the plaintiff into their home at a young age, they gave her their own surname, and they baptized her using that surname. Thereafter, they treated her as their natural child. It was not until plaintiff was an adult that she was ever permitted to know that her foster parents were not her natural parents. This fact was then only revealed to the plaintiff by her foster mother on her deathbed. There was also evidence that the foster parents had stated, both orally and in writing, that they had adopted plaintiff. The court inferred from the circumstances that an agreement for adoption "must have existed" even though there was no direct evidence of it and all the parties that would have known about it were deceased.

We note that despite the constraints of being a contract-to-adopt case, *Roberts* seems to rest more on equitable principles of fairness and intent rather than the ordinary rules of contract law. In that regard, it found applicable language from a Missouri Supreme Court case, which stated in part as follows:

> " 'The life of that whole family in reference to this child, from the time she was first taken into it until the death of Mr. Lynn, would have to be construed to be a deception and a fraud, if we would give to it the effect that respondents claim for it. * * * Like a bud that has been cut from its natural stem and grafted into a foreign tree, she grew into the family and became a part of its very life. Everything that adoption contemplates was accomplished.' "

Again, both *Weiss* and *Monahan* cited *Roberts* with approval, albeit to support the notion that a contract to adopt can be shown by circumstantial evidence, with *Weiss* discussing it at length. We find that *Roberts* supports the position that in Illinois an equitable adoption theory should be recognized under the right circumstances even in the absence of a statutory adoption or a contract for adoption.

The question remaining is under what circumstances should an equitable adoption theory be recognized. We believe that the California Supreme Court struck the proper balance in *Ford,* and therefore adopt its holding here. We do not believe it sufficient merely to prove that a familial relationship existed between the decedent and the plaintiff. Nor do we deem it sufficient to show, as *Wheeling* held, that the plaintiff merely demonstrate that from an age of tender years, he held a position exactly equivalent to a statutorily adopted child. Rather, we hold that a plaintiff bringing an equitable adoption claim must prove an intent to adopt along the lines described in *Ford* and, additionally, must show that the decedent acted consistently with that intent by forming with the plaintiff a close and enduring familial relationship.

We note that *Ford* found that it could be possible to prove intent by showing that the decedent represented to the plaintiff and the community at large that the plaintiff was the decedent's "*natural* or legally adopted child." (Emphasis added.) Our holding is couched in terms of an "intent to adopt" and the allegations of the complaint in the present case have certainly alleged that much. But we envision a case where, like *Roberts* and similar to the present case, a decedent had held out the plaintiff his whole life as his or her natural child, never even letting it be known throughout the childhood of the plaintiff that the child was not the natural offspring of the deceased. We believe that in such cases there is every bit as much equitable justification for finding an equitable adoption as in cases where the plaintiff was merely incorrectly held out as the legally adopted child. We believe that to not recognize an equitable adoption in such cases would work a "deception and a fraud" and would be contrary to the decedent's intent to treat and continuously hold out the plaintiff as his or her natural child.

Defendant argues that recognizing the theory of equitable adoption in the absence of a contract to adopt will have detrimental, unintended consequences. She contends that a person who does not take any affirmative action to become a parent—whether through birth, adoption or contract to adopt—but who is nonetheless kind and compassionate to a child, should not be deemed to confer legal rights to that person as an heir.

We believe that all of these concerns are allayed by the limited nature of our holding—only in those cases where there is sufficient, objective evidence of an intent to adopt (or fraudulently or mistakenly holding out as a natural child on a continual basis), supported by a close enduring familial relationship, will an equitable adoption be recognized. The narrow nature of our holding forecloses claims against the estate of *any* foster parent or stepparent who merely treats a foster or stepchild lovingly and on an equal basis with his or her natural or legally adopted children.

Finally, we consider the quantum of evidence needed to prove an equitable adoption claim. Most courts to have considered the issue require clear and convincing evidence to prove an equitable adoption. We note that in the context of proving a contract-to-adopt claim, this court has found that the existence of a contract must be "clear and conclusive of the existence and terms of the contract, leaving no room for reasonable doubt." *Monahan,* 14 Ill.2d at 452, 153. The court will "weigh the evidence scrupulously and with caution." Moreover, the evidence must be "strong and compelling [and not] readily harmonizable with any other theory" such as with the mere intention to provide a good home as opposed to the intent to adopt. There are a number of valid reasons to apply an analogous, but similarly demanding, standard of proof to equitable adoption claims.

First, and foremost, equitable adoption cases in the inheritance context deal with deceased persons who can no longer testify as to their intent. When the lips of a deceased person who is alleged to have intended an adoption are sealed by death, proof of the facts necessary to invoke principles of equity should be clear, unequivocal and convincing. See *Cavanaugh v. Davis,* 235 S.W.2d 972, 978 (Tex. 1951). Second, if too lax a standard were created it could create a danger that a person could not take in a child in need without having a *de facto* adoption perpetrated upon him after his death. *Ford,* at 754–55. "[I]f the evidentiary burden is lowered too far, 'then couples, childless or not, will be reluctant to take into their homes orphan children, and for the welfare of such children, as well as for other reasons, the rule should be kept and observed. No one, after he or she has passed on, should be adjudged to have adopted a child unless the evidence is clear, cogent, and convincing.' "

Accordingly, we find that a plaintiff must prove an equitable adoption claim to recover against an estate by clear and convincing evidence. Moreover, the decedent's intent to adopt and form a close and enduring familial relationship must be clear and conclusive. And it must not be just as readily harmonizable with the mere intention to provide a good home, but must instead indicate a clear intent to adopt or to continuously represent to the plaintiff and the world at large that the plaintiff was the decedent's natural child.

In sum, we affirm the result of the appellate court in finding that plaintiff could proceed on count VI of his complaint under an equitable adoption theory and that plaintiff has alleged sufficient facts to avoid dismissal under section 2–615 of the Code. We note, however, that the appellate court's analysis appears to have rested on the belief that, as is the case in many states, an agreement for adoption must always be alleged to support an equitable adoption theory. Accordingly, we affirm the result reached by the appellate court on count VI, but reject its reasoning requiring proof of a contract.

* * *

CONCLUSION

For the reasons set forth above, we conclude that plaintiff's second amended complaint alleged sufficient facts to state a cause of action for lack of testamentary capacity, undue influence, contract for adoption and equitable adoption. We further find that dismissal of the two tort claims at this point was premature. The appellate court therefore properly reversed the circuit court's dismissal of each of the six counts of the second amended complaint. We further conclude that the appellate court properly reversed the circuit court's denial of plaintiff's motion to compel the deposition of attorney Peters. Accordingly, we affirm the judgment of the appellate court in its entirety, which remanded the cause to the circuit court of Will County for further proceedings.

Appellate court judgment affirmed.

———————

What did Donald want to happen to his estate? Donald had executed an earlier will in favor of James (Jim), Jim's children, and Donald's church. Donald had always held Jim out to be his son and, in his prepaid funeral arrangements, Donald had listed Jim's children and grandchildren as his grandchildren and great-grandchildren. The family did not want Jim to know that he had been adopted, or not quite adopted, because that could have led to the fact that Jim was conceived out of wedlock. Although Jim's parents celebrated their anniversary, they never said how long they had been married. The adoption was kept a secret for Jim's benefit (although one wonders whether this litigation might have been avoided if they had told him earlier in life). Oddly enough, Jim's wife was told on the eve of their marriage that Jim had been adopted and was told to keep it a secret.

When Jim was in his fifties, while trying to obtain a passport, Jim discovered that the birth certificate he had relied upon was not authentic. After the Illinois Supreme Court issued its decision and with the potential for lengthy litigation ahead on the issues of capacity, undue influence, a less than clear adoption, and the prospect of a dwindling estate, the parties settled the case. In addition to sharing in Donald's estate, the court's decision gave Jim DeHart the comfort of knowing that his name would forever be connected prominently in the law with the only man he had ever known as a father. (Personal communication between the author and Thomas Paris, attorney for Jim DeHart.)

(iii) Strangers to the Adoption

A "stranger" to an adoption is a person who is not the adopting parent and not the adopted child. The law of intestate succession is sometimes confronted with the question of whether an adopted child is considered to be a child for purposes of inheritance from a stranger to the adoption.

> Problem 3.09a: S and B are siblings. N is their nephew by a deceased sister. The parents of S and B are dead. B executes a will which gives everything to F. B secretly adopts F as a daughter, even though F is an adult. B dies. Can S challenge just B's will?

> Problem 3.09b: (continuing the facts above) S does not challenge B's will. S dies intestate, leaving $1,000,000 and never knowing that F is B's adopted child. Does F inherit from S under the UPC? Is that a just result?

Should UPC § 2–118 be amended by adding a new subsection along the lines of the following proposal?

> (c) [Decedent Not Parent.] If a decedent is not a parent of an individual, the individual is not considered the child of the parent unless:

>> (1) the parent, a relative of the parent, or the spouse or surviving spouse of the parent or of a relative of the parent performed functions customarily performed by a parent before the individual reached [18] years of age;

>> (2) the parent intended to perform functions under paragraph (1) but was prevented from doing so by death

or another reason, if the intent is proved by clear and convincing evidence; or

    (3) the adoptive parent notified the decedent of the adoption and the decedent acknowledged receipt of the notice.

The model for subsections (1) and (2) above is UPC § 2–705(d), which applies to wills; subsection (3) is not a part of UPC § 2–705.

(b) Children Born out of Wedlock

The potential cruelty of the law is well illustrated by its former treatment of children born out of wedlock. They were *filius nullius*, the children of no one, and therefore they inherited from no one. The law of intestacy is less heartless now. In some states, the laws of intestacy refer to family law to determine how a child can establish paternity or maternity. Other states have adopted the UPC approach, which says that the marital status of the parents does not matter. The 2019 amendments to the UPC track § 202 of the Uniform Parentage Act (2017).

UPC § 2–117

    SECTION 2–117. NO DISTINCTION BASED ON MARITAL STATUS OF PARENT. A parent-child relationship extends equally to every child and parent, regardless of the marital status of the parent.

(c) Children Resulting from Modern Medicine, Including Posthumously Conceived

ASTRUE V. CAPATO EX REL. B.N.C.
Supreme Court of the United States, 2012
566 U.S. 541

GINSBURG, J.

Karen and Robert Capato married in 1999. Robert died of cancer less than three years later. With the help of in vitro fertilization, Karen gave birth to twins 18 months after her husband's death. Karen's application for Social Security survivors benefits for the twins, which the Social Security Administration (SSA) denied, prompted this litigation. The technology that made the twins' conception and birth possible, it is safe to say, was not contemplated by Congress when the relevant provisions of the Social Security Act (Act) originated (1939) or were amended to read as they now do (1965).

Karen Capato, respondent here, relies on the Act's initial definition of "child" in 42 U.S.C. § 416(e): " '[C]hild' means . . . the child or legally adopted child of an [insured] individual." Robert was an insured individual, and the twins, it is uncontested, are the biological children of Karen and Robert. That satisfies the Act's terms, and no further inquiry is in order, Karen maintains. The SSA, however, identifies subsequent provisions, §§ 416(h)(2) and (h)(3)(C), as critical, and reads them to entitle biological children to benefits only if they qualify for inheritance from the decedent under state intestacy law, or satisfy one of the statutory alternatives to that requirement.

We conclude that the SSA's reading is better attuned to the statute's text and its design to benefit primarily those supported by the deceased wage earner in his or her lifetime. And even if the SSA's longstanding interpretation is not the only reasonable one, it is at least a permissible construction that garners the Court's respect under *Chevron U.S.A. Inc.* v. *Natural Resources Defense Council, Inc.*, 467 U.S. 837, 104 S.Ct. 2778, 81 L.Ed.2d 694 (1984).

I

Karen Capato married Robert Capato in May 1999. Shortly thereafter, Robert was diagnosed with esophageal cancer and was told that the chemotherapy he required might render him sterile. Because the couple wanted children, Robert, before undergoing chemotherapy, deposited his semen in a sperm bank, where it was frozen and stored. Despite Robert's aggressive treatment regime, Karen conceived naturally and gave birth to a son in August 2001. The Capatos, however, wanted their son to have a sibling.

Robert's health deteriorated in late 2001, and he died in Florida, where he and Karen then resided, in March 2002. His will, executed in Florida, named as beneficiaries the son born of his marriage to Karen and two children from a previous marriage. The will made no provision for children conceived after Robert's death, although the Capatos had told their lawyer they wanted future offspring to be placed on a par with existing children. Shortly after Robert's death, Karen began in vitro fertilization using her husband's frozen sperm.

She conceived in January 2003 and gave birth to twins in September 2003, 18 months after Robert's death.

Karen Capato claimed survivors insurance benefits on behalf of the twins. The SSA denied her application, and the U.S. District Court for the District of New Jersey affirmed the agency's decision. In accord with the SSA's construction of the statute, the District Court determined that the twins would qualify for benefits only if, as § 416(h)(2)(A) specifies, they could inherit from the deceased wage earner under state intestacy law. Robert Capato died domiciled in Florida, the court found. Under that State's law, the court noted, a child born posthumously may inherit through intestate succession only if conceived during the decedent's lifetime.

The Court of Appeals for the Third Circuit reversed. Under § 416(e), the appellate court concluded, "the undisputed biological children of a deceased wage earner and his widow" qualify for survivors benefits without regard to state intestacy law. Courts of Appeals have divided on the statutory interpretation question this case presents.

II

Congress amended the Social Security Act in 1939 to provide a monthly benefit for designated surviving family members of a deceased insured wage earner. "Child's insurance benefits" are among the Act's family-protective measures. An applicant qualifies for such benefits if she meets the Act's definition of "child," is unmarried, is below specified age limits (18 or 19) or is under a disability which began prior to age 22, and was dependent on the insured at the time of the insured's death. § 402(d)(1).

To resolve this case, we must decide whether the Capato twins rank as "child[ren]" under the Act's definitional provisions. Section 402(d) provides that "[e]very child (as defined in section 416(e) of this title)" of a deceased insured individual "shall be entitled to a child's insurance benefit." Section 416(e), in turn, states: "The term 'child' means (1) the child or legally adopted child of an individual, (2) a stepchild [under certain circumstances], and (3) . . . the grandchild or stepgrandchild of an individual or his spouse [who meets certain conditions]."

The word "child," we note, appears twice in § 416(e)'s opening sentence: initially in the prefatory phrase, "[t]he term 'child' means . . .," and, immediately thereafter, in subsection (e)(1) ("child or legally adopted child"), delineating the first of three beneficiary categories. Unlike §§ 416(e)(2) and (e)(3), which specify the circumstances under which stepchildren and grandchildren qualify for benefits, § 416(e)(1) lacks any elaboration. Compare § 416(e)(1) (referring simply to "the child . . . of an individual") with, *e.g.*, § 416(e)(2) (applicant must have been a stepchild for at least nine months before the insured individual's death).

A subsequent definitional provision further addresses the term "child." Under the heading "Determination of family status," § 416(h)(2)(A) provides: "In determining whether an applicant is the child or parent of [an] insured individual for purposes of this subchapter, the Commissioner of Social Security shall apply [the intestacy law of the insured individual's domiciliary State]."

An applicant for child benefits who does not meet § 416(h)(2)(A)'s intestacy-law criterion may nonetheless qualify for benefits under one of several other criteria the Act prescribes. First, an applicant who "is a son or daughter" of an insured individual, but is not determined to be a "child" under the intestacy-law provision, nevertheless ranks as a "child" if the insured and the other parent went through a marriage ceremony that would have been valid but for certain legal impediments. Further, an applicant is deemed a "child" if, before death, the insured acknowledged in writing that the applicant is his or her son or daughter, or if the insured had been decreed by a court to be the father or mother of the applicant, or had been ordered to pay child support. In addition, an applicant may gain "child" status upon proof that the insured individual was the applicant's parent and "was living with or contributing to the support of the applicant" when the insured individual died.

The SSA has interpreted these provisions in regulations adopted through notice-and-comment rulemaking. The regulations state that an applicant may be entitled to benefits "as a natural child, legally adopted child, stepchild, grandchild, stepgrandchild, or equitably adopted child." Defining "[w]ho is the insured's natural child," § 404.355, the regulations closely track 42 U.S.C. §§ 416(h)(2) and (h)(3). They state that an applicant may qualify for insurance benefits as a "natural child" by meeting any of four conditions: (1) The applicant "could inherit the insured's personal property as his or her natural child under State inheritance laws"; (2) the applicant is "the insured's natural child and [his or her parents] went through a ceremony which would have resulted in a valid marriage between them except for a legal impediment"; (3) before death, the insured acknowledged in writing his or her parentage of the applicant, was decreed by a court to be the applicant's parent, or was ordered by a court to contribute to the applicant's support; or (4) other evidence shows that the insured is the applicant's "natural father or mother" and was either living with, or contributing to the support of, the applicant.

As the SSA reads the statute, 42 U.S.C. § 416(h) governs the meaning of "child" in § 416(e)(1). In other words, § 416(h) is a gateway through which all applicants for insurance benefits as a "child" must pass.

III

Karen Capato argues, and the Third Circuit held, that § 416(h), far from supplying the governing law, is irrelevant in this case. Instead, the Court of Appeals determined, § 416(e) alone is dispositive of the controversy. Under § 416(e), "child" means "child of an [insured] individual," and the Capato twins, the Third Circuit observed, clearly fit that definition: They are undeniably the children of Robert Capato, the insured wage earner, and his widow, Karen Capato. Section 416(h) comes into play, the court reasoned, only when "a claimant's status as a deceased wage-earner's child is in doubt." That limitation, the court suggested, is evident from § 416(h)'s caption: "Determination of family status." Here, "there is no family status to determine," the court said, so § 416(h) has no role to play.

In short, while the SSA regards § 416(h) as completing § 416(e)'s sparse definition of "child," the Third Circuit considered each subsection to control different situations: § 416(h) governs when a child's family status needs to be determined; § 416(e), when it does not. When is there no need to determine a child's family status? The answer that the Third Circuit found plain: whenever the claimant is "the biological child of a married couple."

We point out, first, some conspicuous flaws in the Third Circuit's and respondent Karen Capato's reading of the Act's provisions, and then explain why we find the SSA's interpretation persuasive.

A

Nothing in § 416(e)'s tautological definition (" 'child' means . . . the child . . . of an individual") suggests that Congress understood the word "child" to refer only to the children of married parents. The dictionary definitions offered by respondent are not so confined. See

Webster's New International Dictionary (defining "child" as, *inter alia*, "[i]n *Law*, legitimate offspring; also, sometimes, esp. in wills, an adopted child, or an illegitimate offspring, or any direct descendant, as a grandchild, as the intention may appear"); Merriam-Webster's Collegiate Dictionary ("child" means "son or daughter," or "descendant"). See also Restatement (Third) of Property § 2.5(1) (1998) ("[a]n individual is the child of his or her genetic parents," and that may be so "whether or not [the parents] are married to each other"). Moreover, elsewhere in the Act, Congress expressly limited the category of children covered to offspring of a marital union. See § 402(d)(3)(A) (referring to the "legitimate . . . child" of an individual). Other contemporaneous statutes similarly differentiate child of a marriage ("legitimate child") from the unmodified term "child."

Nor does § 416(e) indicate that Congress intended "biological" parentage to be prerequisite to "child" status under that provision. As the SSA points out, "[i]n 1939, there was no such thing as a scientifically proven biological relationship between a child and a father, which is . . . part of the reason that the word 'biological' appears nowhere in the Act." Notably, a biological parent is not necessarily a child's parent under law. Ordinarily, "a parent-child relationship does not exist between an adoptee and the adoptee's genetic parents." Uniform Probate Code § 2–119(a). Moreover, laws directly addressing use of today's assisted reproduction technology do not make biological parentage a universally determinative criterion.

We note, in addition, that marriage does not ever and always make the parentage of a child certain, nor does the absence of marriage necessarily mean that a child's parentage is uncertain. An unmarried couple can agree that a child is theirs, while the parentage of a child born during a marriage may be uncertain.

Finally, it is far from obvious that Karen Capato's proposed definition—"biological child of married parents,"—would cover the posthumously conceived Capato twins. Under Florida law, a marriage ends upon the death of a spouse. If that law applies, rather than a court-declared preemptive federal law, the Capato twins, conceived *after* the death of their father, would not qualify as "marital" children.

B

Resisting the importation of words not found in § 416(e)—"child" means "the biological child of married parents," Brief for Respondent 9—the SSA finds a key textual cue in § 416(h)(2)(A)'s opening instruction: "In determining whether an applicant is the child . . . of [an] insured individual *for purposes of this subchapter*," the Commissioner shall apply state intestacy law. Respondent notes the absence of any cross-reference in § 416(e) to § 416(h). She overlooks, however, that § 416(h) provides the crucial link. The "subchapter" to which § 416(h) refers is Subchapter II of the Act, which spans §§ 401 through 434. Section 416(h)'s reference to "this subchapter" thus includes both §§ 402(d) and 416(e). Having explicitly complemented § 416(e) by the definitional provisions contained in § 416(h), Congress had no need to place a redundant cross-reference in § 416(e).

The original version of today's § 416(h) was similarly drafted. It provided that, "[i]n determining whether an applicant is the . . . child . . . of [an] insured individual *for purposes of sections 401–409* of this title, the Board shall apply [state intestacy law]."

Reference to state law to determine an applicant's status as a "child" is anything but anomalous. Quite the opposite. The Act commonly refers to state law on matters of family status. For example, the Act initially defines "wife" as "the wife of an [insured] individual," if certain conditions are satisfied. Like § 416(e), § 416(b) is, at least in part, tautological (" 'wife' means the [insured's] wife"). One must read on, although there is no express cross-reference, to § 416(h) (rules on "[d]etermination of family status") to complete the definition. Section 416(h)(1)(A) directs that, *"for purposes of this subchapter,"* the law of the insured's domicile determines whether "[the] applicant and [the] insured individual were validly married," and if they were not, whether the applicant would nevertheless have "the same status" as a wife under the State's intestacy law. (Emphasis added.) The Act similarly defines the terms "widow," "husband," and "widower."

Indeed, as originally enacted, a single provision mandated the use of state intestacy law for "determining whether an applicant is the wife, widow, child, or parent of [an] insured individual." All wife, widow, child, and parent applicants thus had to satisfy the same criterion. To be sure, children born during their parents' marriage would have readily qualified under the 1939 formulation because of their eligibility to inherit under state law. But requiring all "child" applicants to qualify under state intestacy law installed a simple test, one that ensured benefits for persons plainly within the legislators' contemplation, while avoiding congressional entanglement in the traditional state-law realm of family relations.

Just as the Act generally refers to state law to determine whether an applicant qualifies as a wife, widow, husband, widower, child or parent, so in several sections, the Act sets duration-of-relationship limitations. Time limits also qualify the statutes of several States that accord inheritance rights to posthumously conceived children. No time constraints attend the Third Circuit's ruling in this case, under which the biological child of married parents is eligible for survivors benefits, no matter the length of time between the father's death and the child's conception and birth.

The paths to receipt of benefits laid out in the Act and regulations, we must not forget, proceed from Congress' perception of the core purpose of the legislation. The aim was not to create a program "generally benefiting needy persons"; it was, more particularly, to "provide . . . dependent members of [a wage earner's] family with protection against the hardship occasioned by [the] loss of [the insured's] earnings." We have recognized that "where state intestacy law provides that a child may take personal property from a father's estate, it may reasonably be thought that the child will more likely be dependent during the parent's life and at his death." Reliance on state intestacy law to determine who is a "child" thus serves the Act's driving objective. True, the intestacy criterion yields benefits to some children outside the Act's central concern. Intestacy laws in a number of States, as just noted, do provide for inheritance by posthumously conceived children, and under federal law, a child conceived shortly before her father's death may be eligible for benefits even though she never actually received her father's support. It was nonetheless Congress' prerogative to legislate for the generality of cases. It did so here by employing eligibility to inherit under state intestacy law as a workable substitute for burdensome case-by-case determinations whether the child was, in fact, dependent on her father's earnings.

Respondent argues that on the SSA's reading, natural children alone must pass through a § 416(h) gateway. Adopted children, stepchildren, grandchildren, and step-grandchildren, it is true, are defined in § 416(e), and are not further defined in § 416(h). Respondent overlooks, however, that although not touched by

§ 416(h), beneficiaries described in §§ 416(e)(2) and (e)(3) must meet *other* statutorily prescribed criteria. In short, the Act and regulations set *different* eligibility requirements for adopted children, stepchildren, grandchildren, and step-grandchildren, but it hardly follows that applicants in those categories are treated more advantageously than are children who must meet a § 416(h) criterion.

The SSA's construction of the Act, respondent charges, raises serious constitutional concerns under the equal protection component of the Due Process Clause. She alleges: "Under the government's interpretation . . ., posthumously conceived children are treated as an inferior subset of natural children who are ineligible for government benefits simply because of their date of birth and method of conception."

Even the Courts of Appeals that have accepted the reading of the Act respondent advances have rejected this argument. We have applied an intermediate level of scrutiny to laws "burden[ing] illegitimate children for the sake of punishing the illicit relations of their parents, because 'visiting this condemnation on the head of an infant is illogical and unjust.'" No showing has been made that posthumously conceived children share the characteristics that prompted our skepticism of classifications disadvantaging children of unwed parents. We therefore need not decide whether heightened scrutiny would be appropriate were that the case.

Under rational-basis review, the regime Congress adopted easily passes inspection. As the Ninth Circuit held, that regime is "reasonably related to the government's twin interests in [reserving] benefits [for] those children who have lost a parent's support, and in using reasonable presumptions to minimize the administrative burden of proving dependency on a case-by-case basis."

IV

As we have explained, § 416(e)(1)'s statement, "[t]he term 'child' means . . . the child . . . of an individual," is a definition of scant utility without aid from neighboring provisions. That aid is supplied by § 416(h)(2)(A), which completes the definition of "child" "for purposes of th[e] subchapter" that includes § 416(e)(1). Under the completed definition, which the SSA employs, § 416(h)(2)(A) refers to state law to determine the status of a posthumously conceived child. The SSA's interpretation of the relevant provisions, adhered to without deviation for many decades, is at least reasonable; the agency's reading is therefore entitled to this Court's deference under *Chevron*, 467 U.S. 837.

Chevron deference is appropriate "when it appears that Congress delegated authority to the agency generally to make rules carrying the force of law, and that the agency interpretation claiming deference was promulgated in the exercise of that authority." Here, as already noted, the SSA's longstanding interpretation is set forth in regulations published after notice-and-comment rulemaking. Congress gave the Commissioner authority to promulgate rules "necessary or appropriate to carry out" the Commissioner's functions and the relevant statutory provisions. The Commissioner's regulations are neither "arbitrary or capricious in substance, [n]or manifestly contrary to the statute." They thus warrant the Court's approbation.

V

Tragic circumstances—Robert Capato's death before he and his wife could raise a family—gave rise to this case. But the law Congress enacted calls for resolution of Karen Capato's application for child's insurance benefits by reference to state intestacy law. We cannot replace that reference by creating a uniform federal rule the statute's text scarcely supports.

* * *

For the reasons stated, the judgment of the Court of Appeals for the Third Circuit is reversed, and the case is remanded for further proceedings consistent with this opinion.

It is so ordered.

As you can see from *Astrue v. Capato*, differences across states in the law of intestate succession can lead to differences across states in federal Social Security benefits for children. About one-third of the states have responded to *Capato* by passing legislation allowing posthumously conceived children to inherit, with those rules in some cases depending on whether the parent consented and how soon the child was born after the parent's death. A few states have adopted 2008 UPC § 2–120, which provides a set of requirements for a posthumously conceived child to inherit from a parent. The 2019 UPC jettisons those rules, with § 2–120 now providing that the parentage of an individual conceived by assisted reproduction and not born to a surrogate is determined under the Uniform Parentage Act (2017) Article 7 except for § 708(b)(2).

UPA § 708

SECTION 708. PARENTAL STATUS OF DECEASED INDIVIDUAL.

(a) If an individual who intends to be a parent of a child conceived by assisted reproduction dies during the period between the transfer of a gamete or embryo and the birth of the child, the individual's death does not preclude the establishment of the individual's parentage of the child if the individual otherwise would be a parent of the child under this [act].

(b) If an individual who consented in a record to assisted reproduction by a woman who agreed to give birth to a child dies before a transfer of gametes or embryos, the deceased individual is a parent of a child conceived by the assisted reproduction only if:

(1) either:

(A) the individual consented in a record that if assisted reproduction were to occur after the death of the individual, the individual would be a parent of the child; or

(B) the individual's intent to be a parent of a child conceived by assisted reproduction after the individual's death is established by clear-and-convincing evidence; and

(2) either:

(A) the embryo is in utero not later than [36] months after the individual's death; or

(B) the child is born not later than [45] months after the individual's death.

For situations involving an individual conceived by assisted reproduction and born to a gestational or genetic surrogate, the 2019 revision to UPC § 2–121 similarly incorporates the Uniform Parentage Act (other than § 810(b)(2) and § 817(b)(2)). The provisions of the Uniform Parentage Act deemed inappropriate for incorporation into the UPC are those which deny the existence of a parent-child relationship if an individual born as a result of a posthumous pregnancy fails to satisfy certain time limits. Note, however, that under UPC § 2–104(b)(3), infra, an individual resulting from assisted reproduction can take from a decedent by intestate succession only if the embryo was in utero within 36 months of the decedent's death or the individual was born within 45 months of the decedent's death.

> Problem 3.10: GF is a parent of F. F marries M. F is facing death. F and M decide they would like to have a child and F preserves gametes for that purpose. F states in a record that F wishes to be the parent of any child born from F's gametes even if the child is conceived after F dies. F consents in a record to assisted reproduction by M, who agrees to give birth to a child. F dies. Four years later, M combines M's gametes with F's gametes to have a child, C. GF dies. Can C inherit from F? Can C inherit from GF?

Should Social Security benefits be the same in all states? If they are not the same, does that create unfairness? Does that create incentives for states to change their laws of intestacy so that their citizens qualify for benefits? Is the concern for closing estates a concern when it comes to Social Security benefits?

Why was the Social Security insurance system created? During the depression, the private sector had failed to provide income security to huge numbers of people. Companies large and small had failed entirely or failed to live up to their obligations to provide pensions. Requiring employers to provide coverage through private insurers was dangerous when the survival of large insurance companies could not be assumed. *See* David A. Moss, WHEN ALL ELSE FAILS, p. 181. Signing in 1935, President Roosevelt said,

> "We can never insure one hundred percent of the population against one hundred percent of the hazards and vicissitudes of life, but we have tried to frame a law which will give some measure of protection to the average citizen and to his family against the loss of a job and against poverty-ridden old age."

How close to failing is the Social Security system? Current projections are that the system will become insolvent sometime around 2034. What does insolvency mean in this context? Many Americans think that Social Security will be unable to pay any benefits and that young workers today will receive nothing when they are old. But they are wrong. A 2021 projection under intermediate assumptions is that Social Security will continue to be able to pay 74% of scheduled benefits for 60 years even after the trust fund is depleted in 2034. *See* The 2021 ANNUAL REPORT OF THE BOARD OF TRUSTEES OF THE FEDERAL OLD-AGE AND SURVIVORS INSURANCE AND FEDERAL DISABILITY INSURANCE TRUST FUNDS (Figure II.D2).

4. NEARLY SIMULTANEOUS DEATHS

Various problems arise when people die at about the same time. One of the problems in some cases is determining who died first. The events in the following cases are disturbing. However, these are the kinds of events that the law in some states requires the court to consider in making its legal determinations of property succession.

MATTER OF CAMPBELL'S ESTATE
Court of Appeals of Oregon, 1982
641 P.2d 610

BUTTLER, P.J.

Defendants appeal from the decree of the circuit court determining that Albert Earl Campbell and Roberta Marvine Campbell, husband and wife, died simultaneously in a boating accident at Hyatt Lake on September 22, 1979, and directing distribution of their jointly held property and life insurance proceeds pursuant to the Uniform Simultaneous Death Act. Both parties died intestate. Mr. Campbell was survived by three sisters and a brother, and Mrs. Campbell was survived by the defendants: a daughter and a son from a prior marriage. The sole issue is whether there is "sufficient evidence" under the Act to establish that one of the Campbells survived the other. Plaintiff contends that there is not; defendant contends that there is. We review de novo and affirm.

On September 22, 1979, Mr. and Mrs. Campbell were out in a small boat on Hyatt Lake near Ashland. Between 2:30 and 3 p.m., the boat capsized near the middle of the lake approximately 250 to 300 yards from the western shoreline. No one saw the capsizing or either of the Campbells alive in the water. The deputy sheriff called to the scene testified that before his arrival at the lake at about 5 o'clock the Campbells' boat had been pulled ashore and numerous people were searching the lake for the Campbells. He began a ground search along the shoreline; however, the Campbells were not located before nightfall, and all efforts were temporarily abandoned.

The next morning at approximately 10:30 a.m. the body of Mrs. Campbell was found 25 yards from the western shoreline. She was clothed in pants, a shirt and jacket and shoes; the glasses which she normally wore were not found. During the ensuing three days, various items from the Campbells' boat were found on the western shoreline and also in the southern area of the lake. On September 26, 1979, the body of Mr. Campbell was located west of the area where the boat was believed to have capsized. His body was clad in heavy denim pants, boots, a coat, sweater and a shirt; his glasses were in place.

The evidence indicates that Mrs. Campbell, 61, although mildly obese, was in better health, generally, than her husband. Mr. Campbell, 59, had suffered a heart attack several years earlier and immediately prior to his death was suffering from emphysema, and his physical activities had become somewhat curtailed in the past few years. It was undisputed that Mrs. Campbell could swim; however, there was a conflict in the testimony as to Mr. Campbell's swimming ability.[1]

An autopsy was performed on each of the Campbells. The two pathologists who performed the autopsies testified. Dr. Tinsley, who examined Mr. Campbell's body, stated that the cause of death was compatible with drowning. Although Dr. Tinsley noted that the autopsy revealed some arteriosclerotic disease affecting the coronary arteries and the septum of the heart, he testified that there was no evidence of a stroke or coronary accident. A blood alcohol test measured Mr. Campbell's blood alcohol content as .21 at the time of the death. Dr. Tinsley could not determine accurately the time of Mr. Campbell's death. He reviewed Mrs. Campbell's autopsy report, but was unable to form an opinion as to the sequence of the Campbells' deaths.

Dr. Newland, who performed Mrs. Campbell's autopsy, testified that the cause of her death was asphyxiation by drowning. Hyperinflation, hyperemia and edema of the lungs, all commonly associated with drowning, were present. Further, the autopsy indicated hardened cerebral and coronary arteries and severe hardening of the arteries in the aorta and its main branches. The extremities evidenced small multiple contusions. No test for blood alcohol content was taken. On the basis of his findings, Dr. Newland could not determine the time of Mrs. Campbell's death. After

---

[1]   Mr. Campbell's brother and brother-in-law testified that Mr. Campbell could swim quite well in his youth. Other friends and relatives, however, testified that either Mr. Campbell had never been seen swimming or that he had stated that he did not know how to swim. No one had seen Mr. Campbell swim since before World War II.

comparing the two autopsy reports, Dr. Newland further testified that any opinion as to which of them died first would be speculative.

Dr. Weldon Walker, an internist specializing in cardiovascular disease, testified as an expert witness for defendants. He expressed the opinion that, based on the physical conditions of the Campbells, their respective swimming ability, the location of the bodies when found,[2] the autopsy findings and other testimony adduced at trial,[3] it was "highly probable" that Mrs. Campbell had survived Mr. Campbell. He reasoned that the findings of hyperinflation, hyperemia and edema in Mrs. Campbell's lungs, coupled with the contusions on her extremities, indicated a violent death struggle. Similar findings were not made in Mr. Campbell's autopsy. In Dr. Walker's opinion, the absence of signs of a struggle, together with Mr. Campbell's past coronary disease, which increased the risk of sudden death from any sudden stress, indicated to him either that Mr. Campbell did not have the capacity to struggle upon entering the water or that he experienced cardiac arrhythmia[4] when the boat capsized. In either event, in the doctor's opinion, he died immediately.

ORS 112.595[5] of the Uniform Simultaneous Death Act provides:

"(1) Where there is no sufficient evidence that two joint tenants or tenants by the entirety have died otherwise than simultaneously the property so held shall be distributed one-half as if one had survived and one-half as if the other had survived. If there are more than two joint tenants and all of them have so died the property thus distributed shall

---

[2]   Mrs. Campbell was found in water approximately six feet deep, while Mr. Campbell was found in water approximately 12 feet deep.

[3]   Defendants attach great significance to the fact that Mrs. Campbell's glasses, normally attached around her neck on a chain, were not found with her body, whereas Mr. Campbell's glasses, not attached by a chain, were still in place when his body was found. From this defendants conclude that Mrs. Campbell lost her glasses in a strenuous death struggle and, thus, survived Mr. Campbell, whose glasses remained intact as he passively sank to his death. That argument, however, does not consider the possibility that Mrs. Campbell fought vigorously for her life and drowned before Mr. Campbell entered the water.

[4]   Cardiac arrhythmia is a disturbance in the heart beat which could be fatal, yet be undetectable in an autopsy.

[5]   Besides property held in joint tenancy, Mr. Campbell was insured under two life policies which named his wife as beneficiary. ORS 112.615 provides:

"Where the insured and the beneficiary in a policy of life or accident insurance have died and there is no sufficient evidence that they have died otherwise than simultaneously the proceeds of the policy shall be distributed as if the insured had survived the beneficiary, except if the policy or any interest therein is community property of the insured and his spouse, and there is no alternative beneficiary except the estate or personal representatives of the insured, the proceeds of such interest shall be distributed as community property under ORS 112.605."

be in the proportion that one bears to the whole number of joint tenants.

"(2) The term 'joint tenants' includes owners of property held under circumstances which entitled one or more to the whole of the property on the death of the other or others."

Under that statute, there is neither a presumption of survivorship nor a presumption of simultaneous death. The statute becomes applicable when two or more persons have died under circumstances where there is insufficient evidence that one of them outlived the other. The burden of proof is on the party whose claim depends upon survivorship.

Here, defendants have the burden of proof. They make a reasonable argument, based on circumstantial evidence aided by an expert's opinion, that Mrs. Campbell survived her husband. They contend that, in addition to Mrs. Campbell's being in better health than Mr. Campbell, evidence of her having struggled and doubt as to Mr. Campbell's ability to swim, the fact that Mrs. Campbell's body surfaced three days before that of Mr. Campbell, and was found close to shore in shallow, warm water,[6] supports the inference that Mrs. Campbell attempted to swim ashore after Mr. Campbell expired in the water. On the basis of that inference, they contend Mrs. Campbell outlived her husband. Although circumstantial evidence may be sufficient to establish survivorship, the evidence supporting the inference we are asked to draw is in conflict,[7] permitting several

---

[6] Defendants' expert witness testified that two bodies entering the water at the same time and submersing at the same time would surface at approximately the same place and time, because the temperature of the water affects the rate at which gaseous diffusion occurs. Based on this theory, defendants argue that Mrs. Campbell's body surfaced three days earlier than that of Mr. Campbell, because she succumbed in shallower, warmer water.

[7] Contrary to defendants' expert witness, the two pathologists did not think it was significant that Mrs. Campbell was found three days earlier than Mr. Campbell. Rather, they testified that any number of variables could account for the bodies surfacing at different times, including the Campbells' relative body weights, clothing (Mr. Campbell had on heavier clothing) and water currents. All of the experts agreed that a female is likely to surface before a male, because of the greater fat content normally found in the female body. The testimony also indicated that there were different currents in the lake which could account for the different location of the Campbells' bodies when found. That factor apparently accounted for the different location of the various items from the Campbells' boat retrieved from the lake.

Similarly, the expert testimony was in conflict as to the significance of the hyperinflation, hyperemia and edema found in Mrs. Campbell's lungs and absence of those findings in Mr. Campbell's lungs. Defendants' expert concluded that the findings supported a violent death struggle for Mrs. Campbell and a passive submission for Mr. Campbell. Dr. Tinsley, however, testified that the edema found in Mrs. Campbell could have been caused by heart failure or the arterial embalming process which occurred prior to the autopsy. Dr. Newland testified that the hyperemia and edema were nonspecific findings commonly associated with drownings. Neither pathologist felt that those findings supported the conclusion that Mrs. Campbell survived Mr.

different inferences. All we can say is that defendants' contention that Mrs. Campbell attempted to swim ashore after Mr. Campbell's death is a plausible explanation; however, there are numerous scenarios, equally plausible, of the events, some of which would result in Mr. Campbell's having survived Mrs. Campbell.

We may not speculate as to which scenario is the most probable.[8] As the court stated in In re Estate of Cruson, supra:

> "In trying to determine whether one survived the other, we cannot engage in conjecture or guesswork. We cannot balance probability against probability. Survivorship is a question of fact which must be proved by evidence. * * *".

We conclude that defendants have not sustained their burden of proving that Mrs. Campbell survived her husband. Any other conclusion would be speculation or conjecture.[9] Accordingly, the decree of the circuit court is affirmed.

Affirmed.

A goal of the Uniform Simultaneous Death Act (USDA) was to reduce litigation. It is reasonable to assume that there would be fewer cases litigated on the question of whether there was substantial evidence of who died first than cases litigated on the question of who died first. Nevertheless, the USDA did not totally eliminate litigation regarding the order of deaths, as *Campbell* shows.

In addition to the problem of determining facts, there are two other problems that arise when two people die at nearly the same time. One is that the assets of the first to die might pass to the second to

---

Campbell. Additionally, we find no significance in the alcohol content found in Mr. Campbell's blood; a similar test was not conducted on Mrs. Campbell.

[8]   It is just as plausible that Mrs. Campbell fell into the water and Mr. Campbell capsized the boat in an effort to save her, but only after she had drowned; or that Mr. Campbell, realizing his physical limitations, might have held onto the side of the capsized boat and remained there until after Mrs. Campbell drowned and his arms grew too weary to continue; or Mr. Campbell might have become disoriented after the boat capsized and begun swimming in another direction, drowning after Mrs. Campbell, his body drifting to the location where it was recovered. As plaintiff notes, "(T)he possibilities are truly endless."

[9]   Defendants, relying on *Azvedo v. Benevolent Soc. of Cal.*, 125 Cal.App.2d Supp. 894 (1954), contend that unless the evidence supports the conclusion that decedents expired at the same instant, the Uniform Simultaneous Death Act does not apply and the court must determine which one survived the other, no matter how difficult the task. Such a literal interpretation of the Act would render it almost useless, and it has not been adopted by the Oregon court, or by the majority of courts. Rather, it has been construed to mean that if it cannot be determined by "sufficient evidence" which decedent died first, the Act becomes applicable.

die and go through two estate administrations. The other problem is that the law might not reach the result that a decedent would have intended.

JANUS V. TARASEWITZ

Appellate Court of Illinois, First District, First Division, 1985
482 N.E.2d 418

O'CONNOR, J.

This non-jury declaratory judgment action arose out of the death of a husband and wife, Stanley and Theresa Janus, who died after ingesting Tylenol capsules which had been laced with cyanide by an unknown perpetrator prior to its sale in stores. Stanley Janus was pronounced dead shortly after he was admitted to the hospital. However, Theresa Janus was placed on life support systems for almost two days before being pronounced dead. Claiming that there was no sufficient evidence that Theresa Janus survived her husband, plaintiff Alojza Janus, Stanley's mother, brought this action for the proceeds of Stanley's $100,000 life insurance policy which named Theresa as the primary beneficiary and plaintiff as the contingent beneficiary. Defendant Metropolitan Life Insurance Company paid the proceeds to defendant Jan Tarasewicz, Theresa's father and the administrator of her estate. The trial court found sufficient evidence that Theresa survived Stanley Janus. We affirm.

The facts of this case are particularly poignant and complex. Stanley and Theresa Janus had recently returned from their honeymoon when, on the evening of September 29, 1982, they gathered with other family members to mourn the death of Stanley's brother, Adam Janus, who had died earlier that day from what was later determined to be cyanide-laced Tylenol capsules. While the family was at Adam's home, Stanley and Theresa Janus unknowingly took some of the contaminated Tylenol. Soon afterwards, Stanley collapsed on the kitchen floor.

Theresa was still standing when Diane O'Sullivan, a registered nurse and a neighbor of Adam Janus, was called to the scene. Stanley's pulse was weak so she began cardiopulmonary resuscitation (CPR) on him. Within minutes, Theresa Janus began having seizures. After parmedic teams began arriving, Ms. O'Sullivan went into the living room to assist with Theresa. While she was working on Theresa, Ms. O'Sullivan could hear Stanley's "heavy and labored breathing." She believed that both Stanley and

Theresa died before they were taken to the ambulance, but she could not tell who died first.

Ronald Mahon, a paramedic for the Arlington Heights Fire Department, arrived at approximately 5:45 p.m. He saw Theresa faint and go into a seizure. Her pupils did not respond to light but she was breathing on her own during the time that he worked on her. Mahon also assisted with Stanley, giving him drugs to stimulate heart contractions. Mahon later prepared the paramedic's report on Stanley. One entry in the report shows that at 18:00 hours Stanley had "zero blood pressure, zero pulse, and zero respiration." However, Mahon stated that the times in the report were merely approximations. He was able to say that Stanley was in the ambulance en route to the hospital when his vital signs disappeared.

When paramedic Robert Lockhart arrived at 5:55 p.m., both victims were unconscious with non-reactive pupils. Theresa's seizures had ceased but she was in a decerebrate posture in which her arms and legs were rigidly extended and her arms were rotated inward toward her body, thus, indicating severe neurological dysfunction. At that time, she was breathing only four or five times a minute and, shortly thereafter, she stopped breathing on her own altogether. Lockhart intubated them both by placing tubes down their tracheae to keep their air passages open. Prior to being taken to the ambulance, they were put on "ambu-bags" which is a form of artificial respiration whereby the paramedic respirates the patient by squeezing a bag. Neither Stanley nor Theresa showed any signs of being able to breathe on their own while they were being transported to Northwest Community Hospital in Arlington Heights, Illinois. However, Lockhart stated that when Theresa was turned over to the hospital personnel, she had a palpable pulse and blood pressure.

The medical director of the intensive care unit at the hospital, Dr. Thomas Kim, examined them when they arrived in the emergency room at approximately 6:30 p.m. Stanley had no blood pressure or pulse. An electrocardiogram detected electrical activity in Stanley Janus' heart but there was no synchronization between his heart's electrical activity and its pumping activity. A temporary pacemaker was inserted in an unsuccessful attempt to resuscitate him. Because he never developed spontaneous blood pressure, pulse or signs of respiration, Stanley Janus was pronounced dead at 8:15 p.m. on September 29, 1982.

Like Stanley, Theresa Janus showed no visible vital signs when she was admitted to the emergency room. However, hospital personnel were able to get her heart beating on its own again, so they did not insert a pacemaker. They were also able to establish a measurable, though unsatisfactory, blood pressure. Theresa was taken off the "ambu-bag" and put on a mechanical respirator. In Dr. Kim's opinion, Theresa was in a deep coma with "very unstable vital signs" when she was moved to the intensive care unit at 9:30 p.m. on September 29, 1982.

While Theresa was in the intensive care unit, numerous entries in her hospital records indicated that she had fixed and dialated pupils. However, one entry made at 2:32 a.m. on September 30, 1982, indicated that a nurse apparently detected a minimal reaction to light in Theresa's right pupil but not in her left pupil.

On September 30, 1982, various tests were performed in order to assess Theresa's brain function. These tests included an electroencephalogram (EEG) to measure electrical activity in her brain and a cerebral blood flow test to determine whether there was any blood circulating in her brain. In addition, Theresa exhibited no gag or cord reflexes, no response to pain or other external stimuli. As a result of these tests, Theresa Janus was diagnosed as having sustained total brain death, her life support systems then were terminated, and she was pronounced dead at 1:15 p.m. on October 1, 1982.

Death certificates were issued for Stanley and Theresa Janus more than three weeks later by a medical examiner's physician who never examined them. The certificates listed Stanley Janus' date of death as September 29, 1982, and Theresa Janus' date of death as October 1, 1982. Concluding that Theresa survived Stanley, the Metropolitan Life Insurance Company paid the proceeds of Stanley's life insurance policy to the administrator of Theresa's estate.

On January 6, 1983, plaintiff brought the instant declaratory judgment action against the insurance company and the administrators of Stanley and Theresa's estates, claiming the proceeds of the insurance policy as the contingent beneficiary of the policy. Also, the administrator of Stanley's estate filed a counterclaim against Theresa's estate seeking a declaration as to the disposition of the assets of Stanley's estate.

During the trial, the court heard the testimony of Ms. O'Sullivan, the paramedics, and Dr. Kim. There was also testimony that, while Theresa was in the intensive care unit, members of Theresa's family requested that termination of her life support system be delayed until the arrival of her brother who was serving in the military. However, Theresa's family denied making such a request.

In addition, Dr. Kenneth Vatz, a neurologist on the hospital staff, was called as an expert witness by plaintiff. Although he never actually examined Theresa, he had originally read her EEG as part of hospital routine. Without having seen her other hospital records, his initial evaluation of her EEG was that it showed some minimal electrical activity of living brain cells in the frontal portion of Theresa's brain. After reading her records and reviewing the EEG, however, he stated that the electrical activity measured by the EEG was "very likely" the result of interference from surrounding equipment in the intensive care unit. He concluded that Theresa was brain dead at the time of her admission to the hospital but he could not give an opinion as to who died first.

The trial court also heard an evidence deposition of Dr. Joseph George Hanley, a neurosurgeon who testified as an expert witness on behalf of the defendants. Based on his examination of their records, Dr. Hanley concluded that Stanley Janus died on September 29, 1982. He further concluded that Theresa Janus did not die until her vital signs disappeared on October 1, 1982. His conclusion that she did not die prior to that time was based on: (1) the observations by hospital personnel that Theresa Janus had spontaneous pulse and blood pressure which did not have to be artificially maintained; (2) the instance when Theresa Janus' right pupil allegedly reacted to light; and (3) Theresa's EEG which showed some brain function and which, in his opinion, could not have resulted from outside interference.

At the conclusion of the trial, the court held that the evidence was sufficient to show that Theresa survived Stanley, but the court was not prepared to say by how long she survived him. Plaintiff and the administrator of Stanley's estate appeal. In essence, their main contention is that there is not sufficient evidence to prove that both victims did not suffer brain death prior to their arrival at the hospital on September 29, 1982.

Dual standards for determining when legal death occurs in Illinois were set forth in the case of *In Re Haymer* (1983). There, the court determined that a comatose child attached to a mechanical life support system was legally dead on the date he was medically determined to have sustained total brain death, rather than on the date that his heart stopped functioning. The court stated that in most instances death could be determined in accordance with the common law standard which is based upon the irreversibly cessation of circulatory and respiratory functions. If these functions are artificially maintained, a brain death standard of death could be used if a person has sustained irreversible cessation of total brain function. In a footnote, the court stated that widely accepted characteristics of brain death include: (1) unreceptivity and unresponsivity to intensely painful stimuli; (2) no spontaneous movement or breathing for at least one hour; (3) no blinking, no swallowing, and fixed and dilated pupils; (4) flat EEG's taken twice with at least a 24-hour intervening period; and (5) absence of drug intoxication or hyperthermia. . . . see Report of the Ad. Hoc Committee of the Harvard Medical School to Examine the Definition of Brain Death: A Definition of Irreversible Coma, 205 J.A.M.A. 337 (1968); see also Report of the Medical Consultants on the Diagnosis of Death to the President's Commission for the Study of Ethical Problems in Medicine and Biomedical and Behavioral Research, 246 J.A.M.A. 2184 (proposing other criteria.) However, the court refused to establish criteria for determining brain death because it noted that the advent of new research and technologies would continue to change the tests used for determining cessation of brain function. Instead, the court merely required that the diagnosis of death under either standard must be made in accordance with "the usual and customary standards of medical practice."

Even though *Haymer* was decided after the deaths of Stanley and Theresa, we find that the trial court properly applied the *Haymer* standards under the general rule that a civil case is governed by the law as it exists when judgment is rendered, not when the facts underlying the case occur. The application of *Haymer* is not unfair since the treating physicians made brain death diagnoses at the time of the deaths, and the parties presented evidence at trial regarding brain death.

Regardless of which standard of death is applied, survivorship is a fact which must be proven by a preponderance of the evidence by the party whose claim depends on survivorship. The operative provisions of the Illinois version of the Uniform Simultaneous Death Act provides in pertinent part:

"If the title to property or its devolution depends upon the priority of death and there is no sufficient evidence that the persons have died otherwise than simultaneously and there is no other provision in the will, trust agreement, deed, contract of insurance or other governing instrument for distribution of the property different from the provisions of this Section:

(a) The property of each person shall be disposed of as if he had survived.

* * * * * *

(d) If the insured and the beneficiary of a policy of life or accident insurance have so died, the proceeds of the policy shall be distributed as if the insured had survived the beneficiary."

Ill.Rev.Stat.1981, ch. 110 ½, par. 3–1.

In cases where the question of survivorship is determined by the testimony of lay witnesses, the burden of sufficient evidence may be met by evidence of a positive sign of life in one body and the absence of any such sign in the other. In cases such as the instant case where the death process is monitored by medical professionals, their testimony as to "the usual and customary standards of medical practice" will be highly relevant when considering what constitutes a positive sign of life and what constitutes a criteria for determining death. Although the use of sophisticated medical technology can also make it difficult to determine when death occurs, the context of this case does not require a determination as to the exact moment at which the decedents died. Rather, the trial court's task was to determine whether or not there was sufficient evidence that Theresa Janus survived her husband. Our task on review of this factually disputed case is to determine whether the trial court's finding was against the manifest weight of the evidence. We hold that it was not.

In the case at bar, both victims arrived at the hospital with artifical respirators and no obvious vital signs. There is no dispute among the treating physicians and expert witnesses that Stanley Janus died in both a cardiopulmonary sense and a brain death sense when his vital signs disappeared en route to the hospital and were never reestablished. He was pronounced dead at 8:15 p.m. on September 29, 1982, only after intensive procedures such as electro-shock, medication, and the insertion of a pacemaker failed to resuscitate him.

In contrast, these intensive procedures were not necessary with Theresa Janus because hospital personnel were able to reestablish a spontaneous blood pressure and pulse which did not have to be artificially maintained by a pacemaker or medication. Once spontaneous circulation was restored in the emergency room, Theresa was put on a mechanical respirator and transferred to the intensive care unit. Clearly, efforts to preserve Theresa Janus' life continued after more intensive efforts on Stanley's behalf had failed.

It is argued that the significance of Theresa Janus' cardiopulmonary functions, as a sign of life, was rendered ambiguous by the use of artificial respiration. In particular, reliance is placed upon expert testimony that a person can be brain dead and still have a spontaneous pulse and blood pressure which is indirectly maintained by artificial respiration. The fact remains, however, that Dr. Kim, an intensive care specialist who treated Theresa, testified that her condition in the emergency room did not warrant a diagnosis of brain death. In his opinion, Theresa Janus did not suffer irreversible brain death until much later, when extensive treatment failed to preserve her brain function and vital signs. This diagnosis was confirmed by a consulting neurologist after a battery of tests were performed to assess her brain function. Dr. Kim denied that these examinations were made merely to see if brain death had already occurred. At trial, only Dr. Vatz disagreed with their finding, but even he admitted that the diagnosis and tests performed on Theresa Janus were in keeping with the usual and customary standards of medical practice.

There was also other evidence presented at trial which indicated that Theresa Janus was not brain dead on September 29, 1982. Theresa's EEG, taken on September 30, 1982, was not flat but rather it showed some delta waves of extremely low amplitude. Dr. Hanley concluded that Theresa's EEG taken on September 30 exhibited brain activity. Dr. Vatz disagreed. Since the trier of fact determines the credibility of expert witnesses and the weight to be given to their testimony, the trial court in this case could have reasonably given greater weight to Dr. Hanley's opinion than to Dr. Vatz'. In addition, there is evidence that Theresa's pupil reacted to light on one occasion. It is argued that this evidence merely represents the subjective impression of a hospital staff member which is not corroborated by any other instance where Theresa's pupils reacted to light. However, this argument goes to the weight of this evidence and not to its admissibility. While these additional pieces of neurological data were by no means conclusive, they were competent evidence which tended to support the trial court's finding, and which also tended to disprove the contention that these tests merely verified that brain death had already taken place.

In support of the contention that Theresa Janus did not survive Stanley Janus, evidence was presented which showed that only Theresa Janus suffered seizures and exhibited a decerebrate posture shortly after ingesting the poisoned Tylenol. However, evidence that persons with these symptoms tend to die very quickly does not prove that Theresa Janus did not in fact survive Stanley Janus. Moreover, the evidence introduced is similar in nature to medical presumptions of survivorship based on decedents' health or physical condition which are considered too speculative to prove or disprove survivorship. Similarly, we find no support for the allegation that the hospital kept Theresa Janus on a mechanical respirator because her family requested that termination of her life support systems be delayed until the arrival of her brother, particularly since members of Theresa's family denied making such a request.

In conclusion, we believe that the record clearly established that the treating physicians' diagnoses of death with respect to Stanley and Theresa Janus were made in accordance with "the usual and customary standards of medical practice." Stanley Janus was diagnosed as having sustained irreversible cessation of circulatory and respiratory functions on September 29, 1982. These same physicians concluded that Theresa Janus' condition on that date did not warrant a diagnosis of death and, therefore, they continued their efforts to preserve her life. Their conclusion that Theresa Janus did not die until October 1, 1982, was based on various factors including the restoration of certain of her vital signs as well as other neurological evidence. The trial court found that these facts and circumstances constituted sufficient evidence that Theresa Janus survived her husband. It was not necessary to determine the exact moment at which Theresa died or by how long she survived him, and the trial court properly declined to do so. Viewing the record in its entirety, we cannot say that the trial court's finding of sufficient evidence of Theresa's survivorship was against the manifest weight of the evidence.

Because of our disposition of this case, we need not and do not consider whether the date of death listed on the victims' death certificates should be considered "facts" which constitute prima facie evidence of the date of their deaths.

Accordingly, there being sufficient evidence that Theresa Janus survived Stanley Janus, the judgment of the circuit court of Cook County is affirmed.

Affirmed.

How do the UPC sections below address the problems presented in the cases above?

UPC § 2–104

SECTION 2–104. REQUIREMENT OF SURVIVAL BY 120 HOURS; GESTATIONAL PERIOD; PREGNANCY AFTER DECEDENT'S DEATH.

(a) [Definitions.] In this section:

(1) "Assisted reproduction" means a method of causing pregnancy other than sexual intercourse.

(2) "Gestational period" means the time between the start of a pregnancy and birth.

(b) [Requirement of Survival by 120 Hours; Gestational Period; Pregnancy After Decedent's Death.] For purposes of intestate succession, homestead allowance, and exempt property, and except as otherwise provided in subsection (c), the following rules apply:

(1) An individual born before a decedent's death who fails to survive the decedent by 120 hours is deemed to have predeceased the decedent. If it is not established by clear and convincing evidence that an individual born before the decedent's death survived the decedent by 120 hours, it is deemed that the individual failed to survive for the required period.

(2) If the decedent dies during a gestational period that results in the birth of an individual who lives at least 120 hours after birth, that individual is deemed to be living at the decedent's death. If it is not established by clear and convincing evidence that the individual lived 120 hours after birth, it is deemed that the individual failed to survive for the required period.

(3) If the decedent dies before the start of a pregnancy by assisted reproduction resulting in the birth of an individual who

lives at least 120 hours after birth, that individual is deemed to be living at the decedent's death if [the decedent's personal representative, not later than [6] months after the decedent's death, received notice or had actual knowledge of an intent to use genetic material in the assisted reproduction and]:

> (A) the embryo was in utero not later than [36] months after the decedent's death; or

> (B) the individual was born not later than [45] months after the decedent's death.

(c) [Section Inapplicable if Estate Would Pass to State.] This section does not apply if its application would cause the estate to pass to the state under Section 2–105.

UPC § 2–702

SECTION 2–702. REQUIREMENT OF SURVIVAL BY 120 HOURS.

(a) [Requirement of Survival by 120 Hours Under Probate Code.] For the purposes of this [code], except as provided in subsection (d), an individual who is not established by clear and convincing evidence to have survived an event, including the death of another individual, by 120 hours is deemed to have predeceased the event.

(b) [Requirement of Survival by 120 Hours under Governing Instrument.] Except as provided in subsection (d), for purposes of a provision of a governing instrument that relates to an individual surviving an event, including the death of another individual, an individual who is not established by clear and convincing evidence to have survived the event, by 120 hours is deemed to have predeceased the event.

(c) [Co-owners With Right of Survivorship; Requirement of Survival by 120 Hours.] Except as provided in subsection (d), if (i) it is not established by clear and convincing evidence that one of two co-owners with right of survivorship survived the other co-owner by 120 hours, one-half of the property passes as if one had survived by 120 hours and one-half as if the other had survived by 120 hours and (ii) there are more than two co-owners and it is not established by clear and convincing evidence that at least one of them survived the others by 120 hours, the property passes in the proportion that one bears to the whole number of co-owners. For the purposes of this subsection, "co-owners with right of survivorship" includes joint tenants, tenants by the entireties, and other co-owners of property or accounts held under circumstances that entitles one or more to the whole of the property or account on the death of the other or others.

(d) [Exceptions.] Survival by 120 hours is not required if:

(1) the governing instrument contains language dealing explicitly with simultaneous deaths or deaths in a common disaster and that language is operable under the facts of the case;

(2) the governing instrument expressly indicates that an individual is not required to survive an event, including the death of another individual, by any specified period or expressly requires the individual to survive the event by a specified period; but survival of the event or the specified period must be established by clear and convincing evidence;

(3) the imposition of a 120-hour requirement of survival would cause a nonvested property interest or a power of appointment to fail to qualify for validity under Section 2–901(a)(1), (b)(1), or (c)(1) or to become invalid under Section 2–901(a)(2), (b)(2), or (c)(2); but survival must be established by clear and convincing evidence; or

(4) the application of a 120-hour requirement of survival to multiple governing instruments would result in an unintended failure or duplication of a disposition; but survival must be established by clear and convincing evidence.

* * *

Would the UPC have resolved the issues in *Campbell* and *Janus* without litigation? Would the UPC have reached the right results as a matter of the probable intent of the decedents?

How long should survivors be required to survive the decedent in order to succeed to assets of the decedent? A shorter period of required survival increases the amount of litigation, a longer one decreases it. But the downside of a long survival period is that those who do survive long enough must wait out that period before taking from the estate. Notice that that UPC § 2–104 establishes a 120-hour survival requirement for the homestead allowance and exempt property and also for intestate succession. It makes sense for the survival period to be short for purposes of the homestead allowance and exempt property because the family might need the assets immediately and there is no need for the personal representative to wait for creditors' claims before making those distributions. But the bulk of large estates passes by intestate succession only after the creditors are paid. With regard to the assets to which creditors have priority, should the period of survival required for succession be tied to the time allowed for creditors to make their claims?

> Question 3.11: S1 and S2 are married. S1's parent is M. S2's parent is F. S1 dies leaving substantial assets. Then S2 dies. How long should S2 be required to survive S1 in order to take from S1's estate?

Note that UPC § 2–104 does not apply if the result would be an escheat to the state. The effect of that provision could be to send assets to the decedent's in-laws instead of the state. Is that what would be desired by most people who die intestate?

Similarly, UPC § 2–702 establishes a 120-hour period of survival for wills and other governing instruments, although that can be changed in the instrument.

> Question 3.12: R and D are siblings in their thirties. R's will says to give R's assets to D if D is alive and otherwise to the Republican party. D's will says to give D's assets to R if R is alive and otherwise to the Democratic party. D dies 6 days after R. Under the UPC, all of their assets go to the Democratic party. Is that what R would want?

Wills often have survival requirements of substantially more than five days, perhaps 30 or 60 days. If you were writing your own will, would you require your beneficiaries to survive you by more than five days to take from your estate? What time period would you choose? Should the time period be different for different successors? For some clients, having control of the survival period could be a benefit of executing a will.

5. NEGATIVE WILLS

Can the laws of intestate succession be overridden by a will that does not give away assets but merely says someone shall not take? Under the common law, such "negative wills" were not honored. The UPC and modern trend have changed that, allowing them to be effective.

> Example 3.13: O dies, leaving a will which says, "My homestead and personalty all go to my children, Benjamin, Sara, and Jacob. I intend my son, Jeff, to take nothing." (Benjamin, Sara, Jacob, and Jeff are O's only heirs.) O leaves a homestead, personalty, and a retirement lot in Florida. O is survived by Jeff, Benjamin, Sara, and Jacob. Clearly, Benjamin, Sara, and Jacob take the personalty and the homestead. Does Jeff take a portion of the retirement lot? Under the common law and the 1969 UPC, yes, because the law of intestate succession would apply to the assets not devised by the will. However, in 1990 the UPC changed the result in this case, allowing the negative will to prevent Jeff from taking. Jeff would take nothing under the UPC. *See* UPC § 2–101, above.

6. ADVANCEMENTS

An advancement is an inter vivos gift that is counted as a part of an inheritance. If a gift is an advancement, then that amount is counted as having been received by the heir from the decedent's estate at the time that estate is distributed. If an inter vivos gift is not an advancement, then it is ignored at the time the estate is distributed.

(a) Hotchpot

Hotchpot is the name for the process of calculating portions when there is an advancement.

> Example 3.14: During life, O gives one child, A, $100,000. O dies leaving two children, A and B, and a probate estate of $300,000 after allowances and creditors' claims. If the gift is not an advancement, A keeps that $100,000 and also gets $150,000 from the estate. If the gift is an advancement, it is brought into "hotchpot" and added to the probate estate before distribution. The total hotchpot estate is $400,000, which is divided between A and B, $200,000 each. A already has the $100,000 advancement, so A gets $100,000 from the estate and B gets the other $200,000 from the estate.

A person given an advancement has a choice: 1) hotchpot or 2) keep the advancement and disclaim any interest in the estate.

Problem 3.15: O dies intestate, leaving $50,000, and is survived by 3 children, A, B, and C. With writings to show O's intent, A had been given $34,000 as an advancement and B had been given $6,000 as an advancement. If B chooses hotchpot, what do A, B, and C end up with?

Problem 3.16: Assume the same facts as Problem 3.15 except that B stays out of hotchpot and disclaims his interest in O's estate. What does A get?

Example 3.17: Assume the same facts as Problem 3.15 except that before O dies, B dies leaving two children, X and Y. How much do they take under the UPC, assuming A disclaims? If and only if O's contemporaneous writing indicates O's intent that the gift to B be taken into account against X and Y, then the $6,000 gift to B is brought into hotchpot and charged against the shares of X and Y, who take $11,000 each. If O's contemporaneous writings do not indicate such intent, under the UPC, we ignore the intended advancement to B. In that case, there is $50,000 in the estate, with X and Y splitting B's share, $12,500 each.

(b) Identifying an Advancement

Whether an inter vivos gift will be considered part of an inheritance as an advancement has varied across space and time. There are a number of points on which the doctrine can differ. 1) For an inter vivos gift to be an advancement, does the recipient of the lifetime gift have to turn out to be an heir? Under UPC § 2–109(c), no. If the decedent's contemporaneous writing says so, a gift during life to a recipient that dies before the decedent might be counted against someone else, as in the example above. 2) For an inter vivos gift to be an advancement, does the recipient have to be an heir apparent at the time of the gift? In states following the UPC, no. A gift might be an advancement even if it was made to a person who would not have been an heir if the decedent had died at the time of the gift. In other states, a gift can be an advancement only if the recipient was an heir apparent at the time of the gift. 3) Is the advancements doctrine limited to gifts to the decedent's children or descendants? Under the UPC, no. 4) For the advancements doctrine to apply, must the decedent die wholly intestate? Under the common law, yes; but under the UPC, no, the doctrine can apply in cases of partial intestacy. On these points, the UPC has expanded the advancements doctrine somewhat.

It has always been the case that a decedent can choose whether an inter vivos gift is an advancement or not. But in many cases, decedents do not make their intent clear, and the law applies a presumption. This presumption as to whether the gift is indeed an advancement and how the presumption can be overcome have changed over time. The 1670 English Statute of Distribution and the common law following it presumed rebuttably that the gift was an advancement. That presumption was rebutted if the preponderance of the evidence indicated that the donor did not consider the gift to be an advancement. UPC § 2–109, like the law in most states today, adopts the opposite presumption: the gift was not an advancement. Moreover, under the UPC, the presumption is hard to rebut. The UPC says that the gift was not an advancement unless there is a writing to indicate otherwise. As a result, the advancements doctrine applies much less often under the UPC than under the common law. By changing the default and making it hard to overcome the default, the UPC has greatly narrowed the doctrine of advancements.

UPC § 2–109

SECTION 2–109. ADVANCEMENTS.

(a) If an individual dies intestate as to all or a portion of the estate, property the decedent gave during the decedent's lifetime to an individual who, at the decedent's death, is an heir is treated as an advancement against the heir's intestate share only if (i) the decedent declared in a contemporaneous writing or the heir acknowledged in writing that the gift is an advancement, or (ii) the decedent's contemporaneous writing or the heir's written acknowledgment otherwise indicates that the gift is to be taken into account in computing the division and distribution of the decedent's intestate estate.

(b) For purposes of subsection (a), property advanced is valued as of the time the heir came into possession or enjoyment of the property or as of the time of the decedent's death, whichever first occurs.

(c) If the recipient of the property fails to survive the decedent, the property is not taken into account in computing the division and distribution of the decedent's intestate estate, unless the decedent's contemporaneous writing provides otherwise.

(c) Advancements Policy

The common-law default rule was that an inter vivos gift was an advancement. Under the UPC, a gift is not an advancement unless the intention is indicated in a writing.

> Question 3.18: O has two children, H1 and H2. Before three witnesses, O hands H1 a check for $1,000,000, and says, "This gift is an advancement of your intestate share." Later, O dies leaving an estate of $1,000,000. What is the just result?

Suppose that a decedent has not specified whether a gift should be an advancement. Should the default rule reflect the preference of society or the preference of the decedent? Because the advancements doctrine is merely a default rule, one that applies when the decedent has not executed a will, it raises the question of whether the law should do what society thinks is just or try to mimic what the decedent might have wanted. Suppose a parent has favored one child during life. At death, the law could leave that favoritism in place and divide up the estate equally, or it could apply the advancements doctrine, as the common law assumed, and equalize the parental support at death. One example of systematically unequal support might be favoritism for oldest or youngest children.

Another example is favoritism on the basis of the sex of the child. The Trivers-Willard hypothesis, from biology, says that rich parents might favor male offspring and poor parents might favor female offspring. There is some support for this from studies of non-human animals. And there is a study of human fathers that supports the hypothesis. That study found that an increase in fathers' occupational status produces a greater educational increase for sons than for daughters. If the Trivers-Willard hypothesis is true for humans, it means that more support and wealth might be given to males than to females. If rich humans systematically favor male children, should the law do a little bit to equalize support by applying the advancements doctrine more often, as the common law did? Notice that the advancements doctrine does nothing if there has been no favoritism; it operates only to reduce favoritism. And, of course, it can be overridden entirely by the execution of a will. If the decedent has not specified what to do, should the law be written to do what we think is just?

CHAPTER 4

AVOIDING THE DEFAULT RULES WITH A WILL

■ ■ ■

A. REQUIREMENTS FOR A VALID WILL

We have seen the default rules that apply when a person fails to execute an instrument that qualifies for admission to probate. One way to avoid the default rules of intestate succession is to die without property, in other words, to consume or give it away during life. One downside of that approach is that the donor might give away or consume property she will need before she dies. Another reason donors avoid giving away and consuming all their assets before death is that they worry that doing so would reduce the attention potential donees will pay to them. Whatever the reasons, many donors wait until death to give away most of their real and intangible property. Later we will talk about inter vivos trusts, which a person can use to make gifts that are not effective until death. This chapter examines the will as a method of transferring assets at death.

Lawmakers have decided that, in many cases, the decedents should control where some of the assets that were theirs during life will go after they die. What the decedent wanted matters even though the decedent is not with us. Two opposing concerns arise when we attempt to follow the intent of the decedent. On one hand, we want to deny probate to those instructions that the decedent did not want us to follow. On the other hand, we want to admit to probate those instructions that the decedent did want us to follow. This is a conflict between false positives and false negatives. A false positive is to honor (admit to probate) an instrument that the decedent did not want to be her will. A false negative is to ignore (deny probate to) an instrument that the decedent wanted to serve as her will. Often, an attempt to reduce one problem will increase the other. Making it easier to admit instruments to probate decreases false negatives but increases false positives. Making it harder to probate instruments increases false negatives but decreases false positives.

But the intent of the decedent should not be the sole consideration in designing probate law. It would be wasteful to spend $10,000 of society's resources in the process of deciding who should take $1,000. The efficiency of the fact-finding process is important. In addition to the costs of decision making, we should consider unwanted behaviors. Rules vary with regard to the opportunities they create for people to gain from actions that harm others, such as fraud or even murder. Sometimes, a probate rule can reduce those opportunities. So, while the government has determined to pay a great deal of attention to the intent of the decedent, it has also imposed rules that strike some balance between following that intent, keeping administrative costs low, and avoiding opportunities and incentives for unwanted behaviors.

A will is legally effective only if it qualifies for admission to probate. We turn presently to the rules that determine which instruments qualify for probate. One way of looking at these rules is as procedural limitations on dead hand control; certain steps must be followed for a person to avoid intestacy. Specific substantive limitations on the dead hand come later in this book.

Before we get to those rules, though, it might be helpful to note a few terms often found in wills. By means of a will, a testator gives property to people or entities that survive him. In language used more commonly in the past, the testator bequeaths personalty to legatees and devises realty to devisees. The UPC has simplified this language, using the words "devise" and "devisee" in the contexts of both personalty and realty. A drafter may use the simple words "I give" in a will, to replace both "I bequeath" and "I devise".

One clause that should appear in a well-drafted will is a designation of the executor of the estate, also sometimes called the personal representative. The executor has a duty to wrap up the estate, following the provisions of the will, within the rules of law. However, lawyers should make it clear to testators that executors have a lot of practical power and the testator should choose someone trustworthy. For example, an executor might legally sell assets when it would be better to distribute them to someone in the family. For another example, it is possible for an executor to illegally spend estate funds and it might be difficult for the survivors to obtain repayment of those funds. Testators should be aware of this possibility before deciding to avoid the bonding expense by waiving the default requirement that the executor be bonded.

One important reason for writing a will, for some people, is to request that a certain person take custody of the decedent's minor children after the death of the decedent. When a will includes custody instructions, however, the lawyer should advise the client that courts do not always honor such provisions. Notwithstanding the attitudes of some parents, children are not property, and it is sometimes the duty of the court to override the will in order to serve the best interests of the child. On this issue, the behavior of courts varies widely across states, and it is often not easy to predict how much a court will defer to the judgment of the deceased parents as expressed in testamentary documents. To put it another way, the question of a child's custody after the death of her parents is one that is decided more by the rules of family law than by the rules of wills.

The rise of social media has created another reason for executing a will. Social media might in some instances include copyrights, but even testators who hold no copyrights might desire to specify who will manage their social media after their death.

Now that we have seen a few of the reasons a person might wish to execute a will, we will turn to the basic legal requirements for an instrument to be admitted to probate as a will.

1. INTENT (OR ANIMUS TESTANDI)

We enforce wills on the assumption that they tell us what the decedent wanted to happen after death. For that reason, the law of wills says that a document can be admitted to probate only if the decedent intended it to be her will. If the court knows the decedent did not intend for the document to be given effect as her will, the document will usually not be admitted to probate even if all formalities of execution have been observed. If a portion of a document was not intended to be the will of the decedent, the courts will refuse to admit to probate at least that portion, perhaps more. This intent element is not the same as a requirement that the decedent have expressed intent for the document to be her will, which is also required, albeit perhaps with less strictness. The intent requirement looks to the subjective state of being of the decedent, requiring that the decedent actually wanted a court to carry out the instructions in the document after she died.

In *Fleming v. Morrison*, 72 N.E. 499 (Mass. 1904), Mary Fleming applied to probate the will of Francis Butterfield, which left all his property to her. Sidney Goodrich had drafted the will for Butterfield.

Butterfield signed it and Goodrich signed it as a witness. As they parted, Butterfield told Goodrich that the will 'was a fake, made for a purpose,' which was to induce Fleming to let him sleep with her. Later, Butterfield told two other persons that the instrument was his will and they signed it as witnesses. The lower court issued a judgment sustaining a probate decree allowing the will. But the appellate court reversed, agreeing with the contestants' contention that "the proponent of the will has failed to prove the necessary animus testandi." The court held that, when the testator's signature is acknowledged in the presence of three witnesses separately, the animus testandi must exist when it is acknowledged before each of the necessary three witnesses. Because Butterfield had the requisite intent only before the last two of the three necessary witnesses, the will was not valid.

In *In re Siemers' Estate*, 261 P. 298 (Cal. 1927), the court found that there was meager but sufficient evidence for the trial court to find that

> "the decedent did not at the time of its signing intend that said writing should take effect as his last will, but that he executed the same simply for the purpose of bringing to an end the importuning of Catherine Raftery that he make a will in her favor. . . Proof that the contestant Catherine Raftery was endeavoring to secure decedent's property, and that the latter was bothered and annoyed by her actions in this respect, followed by the further proof that he executed a will in her favor, which he gave to her, but in a few days thereafter he executed another will in many, if not in all, respects inconsistent with the former will, which latter will he left in his safe deposit box, sufficiently justified the trial court in believing that decedent did not intend that the first of said writings should be or remain his last will and testament. In our opinion, the finding in question was justified by the evidence."

However, in *Matter of Estate of Duemeland*, 528 N.W.2d 369 (N.D. 1995), a challenge on the basis of lack of testamentary intent did not prevail. The court refused to admit evidence that the decedent was "merely bluffing". The court wrote,

> "It is abundantly clear that Lorin intended to draft this instrument. Additionally, it is clear that he intended to sign it. To these actions our law attaches consequences. It is,

therefore, irrelevant whether Lorin harbored some secret intention that his actions would have no effect on the disposition of his estate. The consequence of drafting and executing an unambiguous will is that it will have legal effect upon your death. A contrary holding would leave every will open to attack as to the testator's alleged "real" intent, and would deprive testators of any certainty as to the eventual disposition of their estates."

The testamentary intent requirement applied by most courts reduces the chances of admitting to probate a document not intended to be a will. On the other hand, it increases the chances of denying probate to a document intended to be a will and, as *Duemeland* points out, increases uncertainty for that reason. Along with that uncertainty, of course, come increased costs of both litigation and steps taken to avoid litigation. As a matter of policy, should testamentary intent be a requirement when there is a properly executed formal will? If subjective intent is not a requirement, what should be done in cases of mistake in the execution?

(a) No Mistake in the Execution

Mistakes happen. Sometimes a person signs a document not realizing it is a will or not realizing it contains provisions that were not intended to be part of the will. Those are cases of mistake in the execution. The decedents did not know what they were signing. In such cases, intent is missing and the court can deny probate to the document or deny probate to a portion of the document on the ground that the document or portion was not intended to be given testamentary effect.

Another kind of mistake in the execution occurs when the testator signs a will that is missing something the testator thought was part of the will. In those situations, the court will admit the will to probate provided that the testator had an animus testandi, an intent that the instrument be her will. The court cannot, however, add the omitted clause into the will, as that would give testamentary effect to words that were not executed in compliance with the formalities demanded by the Wills Acts, which we will explore later.

Mistake in the inducement is different from mistake in the execution. A mistake in the inducement occurs when the testator makes a mistake about some extrinsic fact, outside the will, and signs the will because of that mistake. Thinking her best friend has died, the testator might sign a will giving all her assets to her second cousin instead of her best friend. In those cases, the decedent did know what she was signing and had the intent that it be her will. If the other requirements are met, that document will be admitted to probate, even though the testator would have not signed it but for the mistake about her friend's death. And if the will is admitted to probate, the traditional rule is that it is not reformed to make a gift to the best friend because doing so would give effect to words not executed in compliance with the statutory formalities.

(b) No Coercion, No Duress

An act of coercion substitutes the intent of the coercing agent for the intent of the decedent and thereby prevents the court from finding the requisite intent. If a court knows that someone coerced the decedent into signing the document, it will be denied probate.

> Example 4.01: X threatens to unplug O's respirator unless O signs a document. O sees that the document is titled "O's will" and that it gives all her property to X. O is fully aware of the document's contents and O does not want X to get her assets, but to avoid physical harm, O signs the document. X leaves with the document. Later that day, O dies. X presents the document for probate. If the court knows these facts, the court will refuse probate to the document on the ground that X coerced O to sign the document.

The presence of coercion prevents the court from coming to the required conclusion that O wanted the instructions in the document to be followed after her death.

There are at least two rationales for this requirement of no coercion. First, it serves the interests of justice. We do not want to give the decedent's assets to someone the decedent did not want to benefit, and the victim of coercion is unlikely to want to make a gift to the coercer. Second, denying probate avoids creating an incentive for coercion. Denying probate when the decedent was coerced reduces the opportunities for gain from acts of coercion, acts which create fear in those being coerced.

(c) No Undue Influence

Undue influence involves less pressure than the force or threats that can constitute coercion. Nevertheless, the effect of undue influence is the same. Undue influence nullifies the presumption of intent that usually accompanies the signing of a document; it gives us reason to believe that the decedent would not have wanted to make the gifts desired by the undue influencer. An act need not be illegal in order to be undue influence. Mental pressure that leads a decedent to sign a document that does not express her wishes could constitute undue influence. It is sometimes said that undue influence is psychological domination that leads to a loss of free agency. But free agency is an ambiguous concept, as different parts of the brain may have different inclinations.

The Restatement (Third) of Property (Wills and Other Donative Transfers) § 8.3(b) says, "A donative transfer is procured by undue influence if the wrongdoer exerted such influence over the donor that it overcame the donor's free will and caused the donor to make a donative transfer that the donor would not otherwise have made." Would the Restatement (Third) find undue influence in the following situation?

> Question 4.02: O is old, lonely, and has a great fear of being alone. O properly executes a will leaving all his property to his alma mater. X comes along and befriends O, who comes to depend on X's visits and companionship. During their talks, O learns that X has few assets and X learns that O has many. X continues the friendly behavior and, influenced by X's friendly behavior, O executes a new will making X the devisee of all his property. Should O's will be admitted to probate? X's behavior did cause O to make a donative transfer to X that O would not have otherwise made. Did X overcome O's free will? It seems that X changed O's "free will" from an intent to give to his alma mater to an intent to give to X. Did X exert influence? Does it depend on whether X hoped that being friendly would motivate O to change O's will? One might say that X is not a "wrongdoer," but wrongdoing is what the Restatement is attempting to define. Perhaps you are starting to get a feel for one of the reasons why there are so many cases alleging undue influence; it is not well defined.

There are a few considerations that might help to clarify what the law means by undue influence. First, ask whether X's behavior is the kind of behavior that we want to discourage. Is it making O less comfortable or increasing his happiness? Second, focus on intent, recalling the distinction between intending the results expressed in the document and intending to execute the document. When O signs the new will, does O want the provisions of the will to be followed? Or, does O sign the will in spite of his wishes that its provisions not be honored? Third, consider a temporal dimension. Does O sign the will because he likes what X has done in the past or because he fears what X will do in the future?

Does your view of the correct result change if part of X's motive was to get O to make a new will? Should X's motive matter to the analysis?

> Question 4.03: Assume the same facts as above, but add the following: Before O executed the new will, X said to O, "I will not be coming to visit you anymore unless you sign that new will." Should O's will be admitted to probate?

Partly because the law is unclear and partly because the facts are often unclear, the line between acceptable influence and undue influence is a fuzzy one and, as a result, there are many cases alleging this as a ground for denying probate.

A number of courts have suggested elements or factors for applying the "loss of free agency" test. Those elements or factors include:

> 1) Unnaturalness of result. Did the testator make gifts to the natural objects of her bounty? Did the testator make gifts to persons who were not natural objects?

> 2) Opportunity. Did the person who is alleged to have exercised undue influence have an opportunity to do so?

> 3) Motive to influence. Did the alleged influencer have a motive to exercise undue influence?

> 4) Susceptibility. Was the testator susceptible to psychological domination?

Establishing all four of the above will sometimes create a rebuttable presumption of undue influence. If a court treats these four as elements, then all must be shown. But if a court treats them as factors, then undue influence can be found even if not all of them are established by the contestant (or objectant). In addition to the loss-of-free-agency approach, there are other approaches that courts might take to identify undue influence, including ones that focus specifically on whether the influencer engaged in unethical or improper conduct. In all, the doctrine of undue influence is quite indeterminate, causing society to bear the burden of costly litigation. To get an idea of the potential cost of litigation brought on by allegations of undue influence, *see* UNDUE INFLUENCE: THE EPIC BATTLE FOR THE JOHNSON & JOHNSON FORTUNE by David Margolick, a story of the fight between the children and third wife of J. Seward Johnson. However, keep in mind that, as always, these costs of disputes might be worth paying in order to achieve justice.

(i) Shifting the Burden of Proof for a Confidential Relationship

Ordinarily, the burden of proof is on the contestant to show undue influence. However, sometimes a court will shift the burden and require the proponent of the will to rebut a presumption of undue influence. In some jurisdictions, the contestant can shift the burden to the proponent by showing three things: 1) that the testator placed confidence in the influencer, i.e., that there was a confidential relationship between them; 2) that the influencer received the bulk of the estate; and 3) that the testator's intellect was weak. Other courts shift the burden of proof to the proponent if the contestant can show a confidential relationship plus suspicious circumstances. Confidential relationships include those where the influencer is a fiduciary (including a lawyer), a trusted advisor, and a caregiver upon whom the testator is dependent.

MUELLER V. WELLS
Supreme Court of Washington, En. Banc., 2016
367 P.3d 580

YU, J.

This case involves a will contest and whether the will proponents presented sufficient evidence to rebut a presumption of undue influence. The trial court invalidated the will at issue, finding that it was the product of undue influence. The trial court's factual findings were not challenged on appeal, but the Court of Appeals reversed and remanded for a new trial, holding that the trial court failed to make findings of direct evidence to support its conclusion of undue influence, relying solely on the presumption of undue influence to invalidate the will.

The proper inquiry here is whether the trial court's unchallenged findings of fact support its conclusions of law. The Court of Appeals erred by reweighing evidence that sufficiently supported the trial court's conclusions. We reverse the Court of

Appeals and reinstate the trial court's judgment invalidating the will as a product of undue influence.

FACTUAL AND PROCEDURAL HISTORY

The following summary of facts is based on the trial court's extensive and detailed findings of fact and conclusions of law. Eva Johanna Rova Barnes was born on July 17, 1916, in Bellingham, Washington. She died at her home in Poulsbo, Washington, on June 27, 2011, just a few weeks before her 95th birthday. Barnes' will was admitted to probate on July 1, 2011. Respondent Michelle Wells was appointed personal representative with nonintervention powers but was later removed by the court and replaced by her husband, Dennis Wells. Barnes' estate includes an acreage of land located on Rova Road that was homesteaded by her parents. The property contains her residence and a rental property in which the petitioners (the Rovas)[1] shared a one-half interest. Barnes' probated will completely disinherited the Rovas in favor of Wells and her husband. Wells became acquainted with Barnes as Barnes' rural mail carrier, and the two became friends after Barnes' husband and daughter passed away. After Barnes suffered a fall in her home, Wells became her caretaker.

The Rovas challenged the validity of Barnes' will for lack of testamentary capacity and undue influence by Wells. After a five-day bench trial, the trial court issued 83 findings of fact and 23 conclusions of law, finding that while Barnes had testamentary capacity when she executed the will in contest, the will was invalid as a result of Wells' undue influence. The trial court found that Barnes' increasing dependence on Wells coincided with Barnes' estrangement from her family and that Wells made numerous false statements that "fanned the flame" of Barnes' unfounded anger and mistrust of the Rovas. Wells became the only person close to Barnes on a consistent basis, eventually replacing Barnes' niece as her attorney-in-fact and assuming the role of caretaker after Barnes fell in her home. Isolated from her family and friends, physically and mentally impaired,[2] and totally dependent on Wells, it is indisputable that Barnes was highly vulnerable to undue influence.

---

[1]   Petitioners Vicki Rova Mueller, Karen Bow, Marsha Rova, and John Rova are Barnes' nieces and nephew from her brother Victor. Following the death of Barnes' husband and daughter, the Rovas were Barnes' closest remaining family.

[2]   Barnes was never diagnosed with dementia, but her physician Dr. Kina began noting " 'mild cognitive impairment' " in his medical reports as early as 2009. His observations throughout Barnes' treatment reflected her "gradual mental deterioration." After Barnes suffered a second fall in 2011, which preceded her death a month later, Dr. Kina observed that Barnes' cognitive

Throughout her relationship with Barnes, Wells and her husband were struggling financially.[4] After Wells became more involved in her life, Barnes began writing checks to Wells and Wells' family members for various services and expenses. Just days before Barnes passed away, Wells paid her own mortgage with a check issued from Barnes' personal bank account. Barnes was in or close to being in a coma when Wells wrote this check. The check posted on the same day that Barnes passed away.

On appeal, Wells did not challenge the trial court's findings of fact but assigned error to the conclusions that the Rovas had established a presumption of undue influence that Wells failed to rebut, and that Barnes' will was invalid because it was a product of Wells' undue influence. In an unpublished opinion, the Court of Appeals reversed and remanded for a new trial, holding that Wells had sufficiently rebutted the presumption of undue influence. The Court of Appeals also found that the trial court did not make any findings of fact of " 'positive evidence,' " but had "wholly relied on the presumption" to find that there was undue influence sufficient to invalidate the will.

* * *

ANALYSIS

The right to testamentary disposition of one's property is a fundamental right protected by law. *Dean v. Jordan*, 194 Wash. 661, 668 (1938). A will that is executed according to all legal formalities is presumed valid. Nevertheless, a will executed by a person with testamentary capacity may be invalidated if "undue influence" existed at the time of the testamentary act. "Undue influence" that is sufficient to void a will must be "something more than mere influence but, rather, influence 'which, at the time of the testamentary act, controlled the volition of the testator, interfered with his free will, and prevented an exercise of his judgment and choice.' "

The applicable legal framework for determining whether a will is the result of undue influence was established in our seminal case *Dean*. For nearly eight decades, *Dean* has remained the governing

---

impairment was " '[p]robably early Alzheimer's dementia.' " While the trial court did not find clear and convincing evidence that Barnes lacked testamentary capacity when she signed the 2011 will, the facts establish that Barnes' progressive cognitive impairment and susceptibility to undue influence coincided with Wells' increasing involvement in her life.

⁴   The court found it relevant to include that Wells was convicted of third degree theft during this time period.

case on undue influence, and it continues to be controlling precedent. The present case does not require us to disturb settled law. The trial court properly invalidated the will in contest for undue influence under the *Dean* framework.

A. Establishing the Presumption of Undue Influence

When challenging the validity of a will, the will contestant bears the burden of proving the will's illegality by "clear, cogent, and convincing" evidence.[5] Circumstantial evidence may be used to establish suspicious facts that raise a presumption of undue influence. If the presumption is raised, the will proponent must produce evidence to rebut the presumption. The absence of rebuttal evidence may be sufficient to set aside a will, but the contestant retains the ultimate burden of proof.

The court in *Dean* identified certain suspicious facts and circumstances that could raise a presumption of undue influence:

> The most important of such facts are (1) that the beneficiary occupied a fiduciary or confidential relation to the testator; (2) that the beneficiary actively participated in the preparation or procurement of the will; and (3) that the beneficiary received an unusually or unnaturally large part of the estate. Added to these may be other considerations, such as the age or condition of health and mental vigor of the testator, the nature or degree of relationship between the testator and the beneficiary, the opportunity for exerting an undue influence, and the naturalness or unnaturalness of the will.

Whether the existence of the so-called *Dean* factors raises a presumption of undue influence is a highly fact-specific determination that requires careful scrutiny of the totality of the circumstances.

The trial court properly held that the facts raised a presumption of undue influence based on the presence of all the *Dean* factors and other considerations. We reaffirm the *Dean* factors and find that the undisputed facts in this case substantially support the trial court's conclusion of undue influence.

---

[5] "[C]lear, cogent, and convincing" evidence is a quantum of proof that is more than a preponderance of the evidence, but less than what is needed to establish proof beyond a reasonable doubt.

1. Opportunity—existence of a fiduciary or confidential relationship

The first *Dean* factor establishes that a confidential or fiduciary relationship may give rise to a presumption of undue influence. The crux of these relationships is a level of trust that leads the testator to believe that the beneficiary is acting in his or her best interests, creating an opportunity for the beneficiary to exert undue influence.

The trial court's findings of fact were sufficient to meet this *Dean* factor. A fiduciary relationship inheres in the role of attorney-in-fact and it is undisputed that Wells was Barnes' attorney-in-fact at the time the will in contest was signed. Wells exercised her power of attorney by signing checks on behalf of Barnes. These facts are sufficient to find that a fiduciary relationship existed.

2. Causation—active participation in procurement of the will

The second *Dean* factor requires that the beneficiary's actions bring about or affect the testamentary instrument. In this case, although Wells was not present in the room when Barnes signed the will, she was Barnes' sole means of transportation and drove Barnes to the series of meetings that led to the execution of the new will.[6]

While the mere act of driving Barnes to the meeting with her attorney is not sufficient in and of itself to satisfy this *Dean* factor, the new will was executed on the heels of what appeared to be Wells' systematic manipulation of Barnes. Wells alienated Barnes from her family by making numerous false statements that "fanned the flame" of Barnes' unfounded anger towards the Rovas. Wells suggested that the Rovas had deliberately destroyed Barnes' address book—an irreplaceable item of great sentimental value to Barnes—when John Rova helped Wells unclutter Barnes' home, which had been declared unsafe due to Barnes' hoarding tendencies. She also accused John of trying to "throw Ms. Barnes under the bus" and stated that the Rovas wanted to put Barnes in a nursing home—untrue statements that "acted to further poison" Barnes' relationship with the Rovas. Wells also falsely told the rental property tenants that the Rovas were "greedy villains" who intended to evict them in order to sell the land, develop the property, and

---

[6] Barnes had actually attempted to execute the new will two days prior. When Barnes could not remember one of her niece's names, her attorney asked her to return on another day. Immediately before the meeting in which Barnes executed her new will, Wells took Barnes to see Dr. Kina and requested that he "prescribe a medication to help Ms. Barnes with her memory problems." The trial court did not draw any conclusions directly from these facts, but they certainly support the conclusion that Wells participated in procurement of the will.

become millionaires. Wells further isolated Barnes by changing her long distance calling plan, making it difficult for family and friends to reach her by phone.

When viewed in the context of these actions, driving Barnes to the meeting in which she executed a new will can be reasonably seen as the last act in Wells' campaign to influence Barnes. These findings support the conclusion that the will would not have come into being but for Wells' activities and influence on Barnes.

3.   Result—unusually or unnaturally large bequest

Under the third *Dean* factor, the effect of undue influence must manifest in the testamentary instrument in an "unnatural" or "unusual" way. "Unusualness" or "unnaturalness" can be measured by comparison to the decedent's previous testamentary instruments.

The trial court found that Barnes' new will was a "radical departure" from her prior wills. Both of Barnes' prior wills included the Rovas: first as alternate beneficiaries, then as primary beneficiaries following the death of Barnes' husband and daughter. The will in contest completely disinherited the Rovas in favor of Wells and her husband as the sole beneficiaries. Wells and her husband were never named as beneficiaries in Barnes' prior wills, yet they received the entirety of Barnes' estate in the new will, leaving nothing to the prior beneficiaries. These facts are sufficient to support the conclusion that the Wells received an unusually and unnaturally large bequest.

4.   Other considerations

In addition to the three main factors, *Dean* enumerates other considerations that could weigh in favor of finding undue influence. These considerations speak to the testator's vulnerability to undue influence due to mental or physical infirmity and the nature of the relationship with the beneficiary.

The trial court properly concluded that all of the " 'other considerations' " enumerated by the *Dean* court were present. Barnes was elderly—nearly 95 when the will was executed—and "extremely vulnerable to undue influence due to physical limitations, [and] some degree of cognitive impairment." Barnes was dependent on Wells as her caregiver, and Wells' constant presence created ample opportunity to exert undue influence over Barnes.

The trial court cited the unnaturalness of the will as a "critical factor" in its decision. A will is unnatural "when it is contrary to what the testator, from his known views, feelings, and intentions would have been expected to make." The bequest to the Wells was "unnatural" in that they were not natural objects of Barnes' bounty: Wells was 51 years younger than Barnes, she and her husband were unrelated to Barnes, and Wells became consistently involved with Barnes only in the last few years of Barnes' life. In contrast, the Rovas are Barnes' closest living relatives and direct lineal descendants of the property's homesteaders. They grew up near Barnes and spent a significant amount of time on the property. Up until the last few years of her life, the Rovas shared a close family relationship with Barnes, celebrating her 90th birthday together and including her in important family events, like the wedding of Karen Bow's daughter. Under these circumstances, the trial court stated that it "cannot conceive of Ms. Barnes disinheriting the [Rovas] and making this absolutely radical and unnatural change to her prior wills unless she was subjected to undue influence that the evidence suggests she was vulnerable to."

The trial court's conclusion that all the *Dean* factors and other considerations were present is sufficiently supported by its findings of fact.

B.   Effect of the Presumption of Undue Influence

If the facts raise a presumption of undue influence, the burden of production shifts to the will proponent, who must then rebut the presumption with evidence sufficient to "balance the scales and restore the equilibrium of evidence touching the validity of the will." However, the will contestant retains the ultimate burden of proving undue influence by "clear, cogent, and convincing" evidence.

1.   *Wells failed to rebut the presumption of undue influence*

The trial court properly found that the evidence presented by Wells was insufficient to overcome the presumption of undue influence in light of the totality of the evidence presented. The Court of Appeals correctly stated that the scope of review is "limited to whether the unchallenged findings of fact support the conclusions of law." However, the court reversed based on its own reweighing of the evidence in favor of an alternative theory for upholding the will— that "[t]he trial court's unchallenged findings of fact contain more than sufficient evidence that Barnes changed her will for a valid reason, unaffected by undue influence: that she had grown apart from, was suspicious of, and disliked the Rovas."

This was error—the appellate court's role is to review findings supporting the conclusions the trial court did reach, not to look for evidence supporting an alternate conclusion the court could have reached. Wells does not challenge any of the trial court's findings or offer any evidence disputing the presence of the *Dean* factors, but selectively restates the trial court's findings to support her alternative theory for Barnes' will. While Wells' story may be persuasive in isolation, we must defer to the weight given to all the evidence by the trial court and its credibility assessment that the facts Wells points to do not balance the scales against the overwhelming evidence of undue influence.

2. *The Rovas met their burden of proving undue influence by clear, cogent, and convincing evidence*

Whether or not the presumption of undue influence is established or rebutted, the will contestant bears the ultimate burden of proving the will's illegality by "clear, cogent, and convincing" evidence. We have long recognized that circumstantial evidence alone can be sufficient to support a finding of undue influence. However, a will contestant cannot rely solely on the weight of the presumption to invalidate a will and "mere suspicion of undue influence is not enough". Rather, the contestant must establish undue influence by producing direct or circumstantial "positive evidence."[7]

Here, the trial court properly found that the evidence met the clear, cogent, and convincing standard in order to find undue influence. The trial court did not delineate which evidence went to any particular proposition, but we have never held that evidence of the presumption could not also be considered as direct or circumstantial evidence of actual undue influence. As the taking of testimony unfolds at trial, the trial court must consider the evidence as a whole, regardless of which party offers it. The trial court's extensive findings of fact established an unrebutted presumption of undue influence based on the *Dean* factors, supported by further positive evidence of Wells' systematic influence over Barnes and

---

[7] Neither *Dean* nor its progeny are clear on what constitutes "positive evidence." However, to the extent that the Court of Appeals reversed because there was no direct (as opposed to circumstantial) evidence of undue influence, this was error. Our case law has long recognized that "[f]rom the very nature of things, undue influence can rarely be proved by direct evidence" and the "surrounding circumstances" are "competent sources for the guidance of the courts" when deciding will contests.

active efforts to isolate and alienate Barnes from the Rovas.[8] Taken together, the findings are easily sufficient to establish undue influence.

The Rovas met their burden and, under the appropriate standard of review, the trial court's conclusions are sustainable. We reverse the Court of Appeals and reinstate the trial court's judgment.

C. Attorney Fees

The Rovas request reasonable attorney fees pursuant to RCW 11.96A.150. Under RCW 11.96A.150(1), we have the discretionary authority to award reasonable attorney fees "to any party: (a) [f]rom any party to the proceedings; (b) from the assets of the estate or trust involved in the proceedings; or (c) from any nonprobate asset that is the subject of the proceedings."

The Rovas properly requested attorney fees in accordance with RAP 18.1(b). We grant the request for fees pursuant to RCW 11.96A.150(1) and order that the fees be paid by respondents Michelle and Dennis Wells.

CONCLUSION

The Court of Appeals exceeded the proper function of appellate review in these types of cases. We reaffirm the *Dean* factors and reiterate that the substantial evidence standard of review applies on appeal. Applying this precedent to the case before us, we reverse the Court of Appeals and reinstate the trial court's conclusion that Eva Johanna Rova Barnes' will is invalid due to undue influence exercised by Michelle Wells.

(ii) When Drafters or Lawyers Are Beneficiaries

Often it is the case that the alleged agent of undue influence is the person who drafted the will. There are many opportunities for a scrivener to exercise undue influence over the testator, in addition to the possibility of outright fraud in drafting the will. The *Los Angeles Times* reported that James D. Gunderson attracted elderly clients from a retirement community and wrote himself millions of

---

[8] It is unclear what further evidence would be necessary, short of Wells dictating the terms of the will or forcing Barnes to execute the testamentary instrument against her volition. If this is the quality of evidence required to invalidate a will, it would be nearly impossible to prove, wholly undermining the purpose and function of the presumption of undue influence doctrine.

dollars' worth of gifts in their wills and trusts. A court concluded that one will that he drafted for a 98-year-old resident of Leisure World improperly included a gift to himself of stock valued at $3.5 million out of the man's $18-million estate.

Lawyers are experts, and clients hope to be able to trust their experts. Some clients are trusting or unable to read their wills, with the result that they execute their wills on the basis of what the drafter has said about the contents of the will rather than their own reading of it. Does it raise a presumption of undue influence when a lawyer receives a gift in a will he drafted? Courts following the traditional rule do not presume undue influence. But the modern and now majority rule is that it raises a presumption of undue influence when a lawyer writes himself into a client's will. Does it raise a presumption of undue influence when a lawyer receives a gift in a will he did not draft? Most courts would say no, *but see In re Will of Moses*, 227 So. 2d 829 (Miss. 1969).

What does it take to rebut a presumption of undue influence? Some states require independent legal advice. Many states allow the presumption of undue influence to be rebutted only if there is clear and convincing evidence that there was no undue influence or that the alleged wrongdoer behaved fairly. In *Matlock v. Simpson*, 902 S.W.2d 384 (Tenn. 1995), the lawyer, Paul Simpson, prepared wills for his client, Lonnie Matlock, in 1986, 1987, 1988, and 1989, before Matlock died in 1990. Before 1989, his wills left all his assets to his children. The wills in 1989 left most of his estate to Simpson, the lawyer. The confidential relationship followed by a benefit to Simpson created a rebuttable presumption of undue influence. The court held that the presumption could be overcome only by clear and convincing evidence of the fairness of the transaction. In *Clarkson v. Whitaker*, 657 N.E.2d 139 (Ind. Ct. App. 1995), the court upheld a finding that a will was void for undue influence because the lawyer, C. Jack Clarkson, had prepared the will and was a beneficiary under the will. The court said,

> "When an attorney drafts a will that includes a bequest or provides a benefit to the attorney or one of his family members, the will is presumed to be void for undue influence or fraud. To overcome this burden, the attorney must prove the transaction was fair. He must then rebut the presumption of undue influence and fraud by clear and unequivocal proof."

(iii) Other Ways to Deal with Undue Influence, in Addition to Denial of Probate

Denying probate to the will is not the only way to deal with undue influence. Another possibility is to invalidate gifts to people who have or might have exercised undue influence. Such rules focus on certain groups of persons, usually those with special opportunities to exercise undue influence and who would not also be expected to be objects of the decedent's beneficence. For example, after the Gunderson exposé, the California legislature enacted a law invalidating specified gifts to the lawyer that drafted the instrument containing the gift. The current version deems a substantial gift to the drafter or the drafter's close relatives to be the product of fraud or undue influence, with exceptions for drafters sufficiently related to the transferor and gifts certified by an independent attorney not to be the product of fraud or undue influence. Cal. Probate Code Sections 21380, 21382, 21384 (2020). Is this a helpful addition to the law? Will it invalidate some gifts that the testator wanted to make? Will it invalidate some gifts that were the result of undue influence?

Another approach is to make the drafting of a gift to oneself a violation of the rules of professional conduct. In *Lawyer Disciplinary Board v. Ball*, 633 S.E.2d 241 (W. Va. 2006), the court annulled John Patrick Ball's license to practice law for "charging excessive fees, drafting self-aggrandizing wills and assisting a client to enrich his children." The court was unimpressed with the lawyer's claim that he did not know that was a violation of the Rules of Professional Conduct. The court wrote, "It has been appropriately observed that 'although lawyers who have drafted a bequest to themselves often claim lack of knowledge of the ethics prohibition, ignorance is no defense to a disciplinary charge.' . . .We find Mr. Ball's position to be insulting to the integrity of the Rules and to this Court." Id. at 250. Try to avoid drafting gifts that will get your name in a casebook.

(d) No Fraud

Courts provide remedies for fraud in many different contexts, of which probate is merely one. It is sometimes said that fraud is a misrepresentation made with intent to deceive and purpose to influence that causes a change in behavior. Cases of fraud can be subdivided in the same way that we subdivided mistakes.

(i) Fraud in the Execution

Fraud in the execution occurs when someone gets a decedent to sign a document by telling him that the document is something other than a will. In such cases, it is plain that the decedent did not have the intent to execute that document as a will, and it is not admitted to probate. In other words, if a court finds that an instrument was procured by fraud in the execution, it may refuse probate to the instrument.

> Example 4.04: O's friend F says to O "Please sign here as a witness to my will" while presenting a document that is actually written as the will of O. The probate court can deny probate to that document on the ground that O did not have the requisite intent for the document to be O's will.

There are other instances of fraud in the execution where denial of probate is not an adequate remedy. Other remedies appear below.

(ii) Fraud in the Inducement

Fraud in the inducement can be found when the decedent was intentionally told something that is false, something that induced her to sign a will that makes a different disposition than she would have otherwise desired. Fraud in the inducement changes the testator's testamentary goals. These situations are different from fraud in the execution. When there is fraud in the inducement, the decedent intended that the provisions of the will be given effect. However, that intent was based on misrepresentations. One might say that the intent was conditional on false beliefs that were generated by the fraud.

Some early cases of fraud in the inducement involved a promise that the devisee would use the devise in some way that was desired by the testator. But a finding of fraud may be based on other sorts of false statements such as statements designed to make the decedent mistrust someone who would otherwise be a natural object of the decedent's bounty.

PUCKETT V. KRIDA

Court of Appeals of Tennessee, 1994
1994 WL 475863

LEWIS, J.

OPINION

* * *

In a will contest, the proponent of the will has the initial burden of proving due execution of the will and its *prima facie* validity. The burden of proof then shifts to the contestant to prove facts necessary to void the will. The law does not presume fraud or undue influence, and generally the contestant who alleges fraud or undue influence must prove them. The execution of a will brought about as the result of fraud or undue influence is void. To invalidate a will, the undue influence must destroy the free agency of the testator to the extent that the will is in reality that of another. "[F]raud upon a testator consists of making that which is false appear to him to be true, and so effecting his will." Fraud may be present without undue influence and undue influence need not include fraud. "Fraud is a trick, artifice, or management which induces a person to dispose of his property or to do some act contrary to his wishes or in such a way as he would not do but for such fraud."

"The two grounds of undue influence and fraud are closely related, but in the case of fraud the free agency of the testator remains, but he is misled into doing that which he otherwise would not have done." To set aside a will on the basis of fraud, "the fraud must be of the active, tortious, deceitful kind and not of the constructive or resultant nature."

* * *

Generally, it is difficult to invalidate a will on the basis of undue influence and/or fraud, because direct evidence rarely exists. "Without direct evidence, a contestant must establish the existence of more than one suspicious circumstance. . . . Proof of a confidential relationship alone will not support a finding of undue influence."

Once the existence of a confidential relationship and suspicious circumstances are proven, undue influence or fraud is presumed. A confidential relationship will be found to exist when there is proof that one of the parties was in a "position to exercise dominion, control, or influence over the other." At least one Tennessee case has held that a confidential relationship between parties arises through the use of an unrestricted power of attorney. Furthermore, the relationship of nurse and invalid is a confidential relationship.

Once the presumption of undue influence or fraud arises, the presumption may be rebutted by proof of the fairness of the transaction established by a preponderance of the evidence.

* * *

In the instant case, the evidence shows that at the time the defendants were employed, the deceased loved her family and was very close to them. She was frugal and conservative, but entrusted the management of her financial affairs to her niece, Jean Law. The evidence is that Mrs. Law carefully managed these finances and promised to keep the deceased out of a nursing home, making every effort to do so. She never reimbursed herself for any of her expenses.

Subsequent to the defendants' employment, the deceased began to believe that Jean Law wanted to put her in a nursing home and that Ms. Law had misappropriated funds. The evidence shows that neither of these beliefs were true. The evidence further shows that these false beliefs originated with the defendants who systematically separated the deceased from her family and friends and isolated her from all those individuals with whom she had previously dealt, personally and professionally. All of this was done in order to perpetuate the fraud.

Defendants, either individually or collectively, made false statements to the deceased and concealed facts from her. The deceased was led to believe that her family wasted her money. When the defendants arrived in the deceased's life, her greatest fear was going to a nursing home. The evidence shows that these defendants suddenly began to exert control over the deceased by listening in on her telephone conversations and by deluding her into believing that her family intended to place her in a nursing home. Once this fear was planted, defendants fostered and nurtured it until the deceased firmly opposed those formerly most dear to her. The deceased was told by the defendants that her niece was wasting or misappropriating funds and was reimbursing herself for airline expenses and to rent fancy cars. Defendants told the deceased that her niece was wasting money and that the deceased would be left penniless. The defendants offered no proof to refute these statements, and the trial court found that Jean Law, the deceased's niece, kept meticulous records. When the defendants accepted employment to provide around-the-clock care for the deceased, they entered into a fiduciary or confidential relationship with her, and the defendant Krida assumed additional fiduciary obligations under the unrestricted power of attorney she obtained.

"Since frauds are generally secret [they] have to be tracked by the footprints, marks, and signs made by the perpetrators and discovered by the light of the attending facts and circumstances."

By limiting information available to the deceased and by concealing their acts from the critical examination of those whom the deceased had previously known and trusted, the defendants isolated the deceased and controlled access to her. The defendants terminated the deceased's former legal and financial relationships and arranged new ones. They made her neighbors feel unwelcome and threatened her family with legal action. They replaced her long-time tenant with a family member of one of the defendants. Furthermore, the defendants made detrimental decisions regarding the sale of the deceased's real property, to avoid contact with a realtor who had previously handled the deceased's affairs.

The dealings with the deceased's money by the defendants was irregular and unusual. Defendant's offered no suitable explanation at trial to account for any of the cash funds that the deceased received while the defendant Krida managed the financial affairs.

* * *

The judgment of the trial court is affirmed in all respects, and the cause is remanded to the trial court for implementation of its judgment and any further necessary proceedings. Costs on appeal are taxed to the respondent/appellant, Laverne Krida.

In addition to a false statement, the contestant alleging fraud must show that the person making the false statement intended to deceive the decedent and had the purpose to influence the decedent's legacy. This intent requirement helps to distinguish fraud from mistake on the part of the person making the misstatement. There would be no reason to care about the misstatement if it did not cause some change in the decedent's behavior, which is the fourth element. This change in behavior might be the making of a will or a devise in a will or the failure to make a will or a devise, or the revocation of an instrument or the failure to revoke one. The misstatement made with purpose to influence and the change in behavior must be connected together through the element of causation. Causation can be a difficult element both because the legal standard is unclear and because the facts are ambiguous. Perhaps fraud is not as indeterminate a doctrine as undue influence, but it is indeterminate enough to generate costly litigation, and fraud is alleged along with undue influence in many cases.

MCDANIEL V. MCDANIEL
Supreme Court of Georgia, 2011
707 S.E.2d 60

NAHMIAS, J.

In this probate case, the propounder filed a petition for probate in solemn form to have a 2007 will declared the testator's last will and testament. The caveator challenged the will on the grounds of lack of testamentary capacity, undue influence, and fraud. A jury found that the 2007 will was the product of undue influence and fraud, and the probate court entered judgment on the verdict. In Case No. S10A1497, the propounder appeals, contending that the probate court erred in denying his motion for directed verdict on undue influence and fraud and, in the alternative, that a new trial is required due to erroneous evidentiary rulings. In Case No. S10X1498, the caveator files a defensive cross-appeal, asserting error in the exclusion of testimony by a doctor who treated the decedent and two instances of alleged instructional error. For the reasons that follow, we affirm the probate court's judgment denying admission of the 2007 will to probate; the cross-appeal is therefore moot.

1. Viewed in the light most favorable to the verdict, the facts are as follows. Mary Agnes Royster McDaniel (Ms. McDaniel) was married to Luther Lee "Mutt" McDaniel (the testator) for over 60 years, until her death at age 87 on December 10, 2006. The testator died two-and-a-half years later on June 24, 2009, at the age of 92. The McDaniels had two sons, Charles Lee McDaniel (the caveator) and Jerry Clyde McDaniel, Sr. (the propounder), both of whom are married. Prior to the events that gave rise to this litigation, the family apparently got along well.

In 2002, the testator and his wife, who were then in their 80's, executed wills prepared by their attorney, James Clyde Morris, Jr., leaving everything to the surviving spouse, and if there was no surviving spouse, to their two sons equally. Ms. McDaniel suffered from Alzheimer's-related dementia and other ailments, and by 2006, the testator could no longer care for her on his own. The caveator moved in with his parents in January 2006, and for the first part of that year, the propounder and his wife stayed with the elder McDaniels some weekends to alleviate the burden on the caveator. They continued to visit regularly after that time. Over the course of 2006, the elder McDaniels added the caveator's name to all their bank accounts so that he could manage their financial affairs for them.

Ms. McDaniel exhibited some common signs of dementia. For example, she was often confused, occasionally paranoid, and had trouble remembering where she put things. She would ask the caveator to take her silver and jewelry and put them someplace safe. The caveator would store them in his safe-deposit box at the bank, and when his mother asked for them a month or so later, he would bring them back until his mother asked him to take them away again. The caveator also held the receipt for a mink stole that his mother had stored at a facility in Athens. When she could still ride in a car, the caveator would drive his mother to Athens to retrieve the stole whenever she wanted it. However, when she could no longer ride in a car, she asked him to take the mink stole to the storage facility, which he did, and he held onto the receipt, which was in his name.

Toward the end of 2006, the testator also exhibited signs of confusion and declining mental status. Shortly before his wife of 60 years died, the testator got into his truck and turned on the windshield wipers but could not recall how to turn them off. The testator also had difficulty sleeping and trouble differentiating between night and day and remembering what day of the week it was. After his wife died, the testator's confusion worsened.

When the testator's wife died on December 10, 2006, the propounder and his wife strongly encouraged the caveator and his wife to take a much-needed vacation to Florida. The caveator was concerned about leaving his father alone, but the propounder and his wife assured him that they would stay with the testator to keep him company. The plan was that the caveator and his wife would leave for Florida on December 29 and stay there for a week or so before returning. Before leaving, the caveator drove his father to several banks to remove Ms. McDaniel's name from joint accounts worth several hundred thousand dollars, and on Tuesday, December 26, 2006, the caveator drove the testator to attorney Morris's office to inquire about the process for probating Ms. McDaniel's will. They scheduled a meeting for that Friday, December 29, 2006, with Morris, the testator, the propounder, the caveator, and their wives.

On Thursday, December 28, 2006, the caveator went to Regions Bank and closed an account worth approximately $32,000 that had been held jointly in his and his mother's names, transferring the funds into a new account in his name only. It was important to Ms. McDaniel to provide for her funeral and that of her husband before she died. To that end, she had told the caveator to use the $32,000 account to pay for the two funerals and to keep whatever was left.

At the meeting on December 29, Morris informed the testator and the caveator that they should not have removed Ms. McDaniel's name from the joint bank accounts. The propounder asked why the accounts were all in the testator and the caveator's names and suggested that the testator's name be removed from them and that his name be added along with the caveator's. The caveator took that to mean that the propounder did not think their father should have any further say-so in his financial affairs, and the caveator said that things should be left the way they were. The issue was not resolved at that meeting, which appeared to end amicably. The caveator and his wife dropped the testator off at his home on the way out of town for their Florida vacation, and the propounder and his wife came over later that evening to stay with the testator.

Unbeknownst to the caveator, the propounder and his wife now believed that the caveator had stolen from the testator the roughly $600,000 they estimated was held in the joint bank accounts by having his name added to the accounts. They went through the testator's drawers, found his bank statements, and convinced the testator that the caveator had stolen all his money, that he was now "broke," and that the caveator and his wife had moved to Florida and were not coming back. The testator was confused and distraught, and he repeated these claims to other relatives, as did the propounder.

The propounder also told his father that he would help fix everything, and when the banks opened on January 2, 2007, the propounder and his wife drove the testator to the banks, where the testator removed the caveator's name from all the joint accounts. The propounder called attorney Morris's office and set a meeting to change the testator's will for January 4, and he also changed the locks on the testator's house. The caveator and his wife remained in Florida.

At the January 4 meeting, the propounder asked Morris to draft a new will for his father that left the propounder everything and disinherited his older brother completely. Morris refused to take instructions from the propounder because the propounder was not his client. The propounder got mad, argued with Morris, and threatened to take the testator to another attorney to make the changes. The dispute subsided, and Morris took the testator into another room, where the testator told him to draw up a new will leaving everything to the propounder. The testator told Morris that the caveator "has gotten all the money from me he's going to get." Morris asked the testator if he wanted to leave anything to his grandchildren through the caveator, and the testator said to draft the will to leave his granddaughter 10% of his estate and his grandson 1%, with the rest to the propounder and nothing to the caveator.

The next day, the propounder and his wife brought the testator back to Morris's office, where the testator executed the new will. He also executed a durable power of attorney authorizing the propounder to take full control of his financial affairs. The propounder's wife told Morris that Ms. McDaniel's jewelry and other items were missing, and the testator instructed Morris to get a restraining order to keep the caveator from coming back to his father's house.

When the caveator got back from Florida a few days later, he called the propounder to ask what was going on, but the propounder refused to speak with him and told him that he needed to call Morris. The caveator called Morris and arranged a meeting for January 9, 2007. At the meeting, Morris handed the caveator a letter saying that the testator did not want the caveator to come on his property again until after the probate of his mother's estate was completed due to "some questionable actions and/or statements which have been made by yourself over the last several months prior to and immediately after your mother's death." The letter threatened the caveator with "judicial restraint" if he failed to respect his father's wishes. Morris again told the caveator that he had no right to close out the $32,000 account and put it in his name and asked him to return his mother's jewelry and the mink stole.

After the meeting, the caveator's wife called Morris's office and left a message saying that she and her husband never meant to take any money or cause any problems, that they were just trying to do what they thought Ms. McDaniel wanted them to do with the

$32,000 account, and that they would return everything that was being requested. Two days later, the caveator took a check to Morris's office for all the money taken from the joint account he had with his mother and returned his mother's jewelry and the claim ticket for the mink stole.

The caveator did not see his father for the next six months while the probate of his mother's estate was pending. When he was allowed to visit his father again, he did so. His father did not recognize him at first, but when the caveator told him who he was, his father was glad to see him. The caveator never discussed with his father the changes to the will, but at one point, the testator made reference to it, saying that "it was just a bad situation." Around this time, the propounder began using the testator's power of attorney to convert the testator's property into the names of the propounder and the testator jointly, giving himself survivorship rights on real estate, bank accounts, certificates of deposit, and mutual funds.

The propounder and his wife moved the testator into the basement of their new home in December 2007, where he lived until his death on June 24, 2009. The caveator was not allowed to visit his father without first making an appointment with the propounder, and the propounder told the caveator that he was recording the visits. The propounder also attempted to make the caveator "sign in" on a register whenever he visited.

After the testator's death, the propounder filed a petition to probate the 2007 will in solemn form, and the caveator filed a caveat. The parties presented their case to a jury, and the probate court denied the propounder's motion for a directed verdict sustaining the 2007 will. The jury found that the 2007 will was not valid and should be denied probate on the grounds of undue influence and fraud, and the probate court entered judgment on the verdict. The propounder appealed, and the caveator filed a defensive cross-appeal.

2.   The sole question in a proceeding to probate a will in solemn form is " 'whether the paper propounded is, or is not, the last will and testament of the deceased.' " The result turns on three issues: (1) whether the document was properly executed; (2) whether the testator had the mental capacity to execute a will; and (3) whether the document was the result of undue influence, fraud, duress, or mistake. The caveator conceded due execution of the will, and the jury found in favor of the propounder on the issue of testamentary capacity. The propounder contends that the probate court erred in

denying his motion for directed verdict on undue influence and fraud.

(a) Undue Influence: The standards we apply in reviewing a jury's finding of undue influence in the execution of a will are well established.

> "Undue influence 'may take many forms and may operate through diverse channels.' " There is no requirement that the undue influence be directly attributable to the propounder or to a single beneficiary. Although evidence which merely shows an opportunity to influence is not itself sufficient, a "caveat based upon the ground of undue influence may be supported by a wide range of evidence, as such influence can seldom be shown except by circumstantial evidence."

Absent legal error on the part of the probate court, a jury's finding of undue influence will be affirmed "if there is any evidence to support the trier of fact's determination."

As shown by the detailed recitation in Division 1 of the evidence presented at trial, the jury in this case was clearly authorized to find that the 2007 will was the result of undue influence. When the testator could no longer care for his sick wife of over 60 years, the caveator moved in with them and provided the care his mother and father needed with little help from the propounder. After Ms. McDaniel died, the propounder and his wife encouraged the caveator and his wife to leave the state for a vacation and in their absence poisoned the testator's mind against the caveator, telling him falsely that the caveator had stolen all his money, that he was now broke, and that the caveator had abandoned him and would not return. The propounder and his wife also participated in the preparation of the 2007 will.

Furthermore, acting under the influence of the propounder and his wife, the testator secured a restraining order that prevented the caveator from seeing him for six months after the caveator returned from Florida, and the propounder made sure that the caveator was never left alone with their father again. Although the jury found that the testator had sufficient testamentary capacity, he was elderly and showing signs of declining mental acuity before the 2007 will was executed, and his symptoms had increased after his wife passed just a few weeks earlier.

Finally, the 2007 will radically changed the distribution of the estate envisioned by the testator's 2002 will, which would have divided the estate equally between the testator's two grown sons, to a scheme awarding 89% of the estate to the propounder and nothing to the caveator. We therefore conclude that evidence regarding "the circumstances and surroundings of the testator and his associations" authorized the jury's finding that the 2007 will was the product of undue influence.

(b) Fraud: There was also sufficient evidence to support the jury's finding that the will was procured by fraud. The evidence showed that after the propounder and his wife encouraged the caveator and his wife to go on vacation in Florida, they embarked on a campaign to convince the testator that the caveator had stolen all his money, left him broke, and abandoned him by moving to Florida. These were misrepresentations, but they worked; the testator changed his will to disinherit the caveator completely. As a result of these misrepresentations, the propounder went into the meeting with the attorney who drafted the 2007 will intending to leave his entire estate to the propounder, and he would have done so were it not for the attorney's suggestion that he leave something to the caveator's children, who were the testator's grandchildren. Accordingly, we conclude that the evidence supports the jury's finding that the 2007 will was procured through "misrepresentation" and "fraudulent practices upon the testator's fears, affections, or sympathies." OCGA § 53–4–12.

3. The propounder's remaining enumerations of error challenge various evidentiary rulings by the probate court, which we review for abuse of discretion.

* * *

(d) The propounder argues that the probate court abused its discretion by admitting, in contravention of a pretrial ruling, the caveator's testimony that he stayed continuously with his mother until she died, that he slept on the couch while caring for her, and that the propounder stayed with her only four to six times, while barring the propounder's witnesses from testifying in rebuttal that the caveator's care of their mother was sub-par and contributed to the testator's decision to disinherit him. The probate court did not preclude all testimony involving who provided what care for the testator or his wife. Rather, the court ruled as follows:

> I don't have a problem with parties presenting evidence that different family members provided care for both parents, each son, other family members, but [I] don't want to get into the argument of somebody was a bad caretaker versus another party, somebody didn't spend enough time with a family member.

Evidence regarding whether, when, and for how long the caveator took care of his mother demonstrated how odd it was that the caveator's father suddenly wanted him off the premises and out of the will entirely, and the propounder stated at the outset that he did not object to such testimony and confirmed this position during the trial. Thus, the court allowed the admission of relevant evidence and excluded testimony that it thought would get the trial off course and focus the jurors' attention on matters too far removed from the issues to be decided. We cannot say this was an abuse of discretion.

* * *

4.   The evidence supports the jury's findings of undue influence and fraud, and the probate court's evidentiary rulings were not an abuse of discretion. Having ruled in favor of the caveator on the propounder's appeal, we need not address the issues raised in the caveator's cross-appeal, which is now moot.

Judgment affirmed in Case No. S10A1497. Appeal dismissed in Case No. S10X1498.

(iii) Other Remedies for Fraud

Denial of probate to instruments procured by fraud is not always an appropriate or adequate remedy. Other remedies are sometimes needed, and one classic is the equitable remedy of a constructive trust. As was said in *Latham v. Father Divine*, 85 N.E.2d 168 (N.Y. 1949), "a constructive trust is merely 'the formula through which the conscience of equity finds expression' . . .". A court applying this remedy determines who would have received the property if there had been no fraud and orders that the person who did receive the property holds it in constructive trust for those who should have received it. Interestingly, the court may impose a constructive trust on a person who did not commit any wrong if that person is unjustly enriched by the wrong of another. For example, in *Pope v. Garrett*, 211 S.W.2d 559 (Tex. 1948), the court ordered that the intestate successors held in constructive trust for persons who were named as beneficiaries under an unexecuted will. When a court declares a constructive trust, the constructive trustee holds legal title for the constructive beneficiary, the person who should have taken the property in the first place. But this constructive trust is not much like an ordinary trust in that the constructive trustee has little power over the property and must transfer it to the constructive beneficiary, who is effectively the owner as soon as the constructive trust is declared. The constructive trust remedy leads to some doctrinal inconsistency. Courts have created constructive trusts in favor of persons named in wills that were not executed because of fraud. That appears to be inconsistent with the rule (to be discussed in the next section) that an instrument that has not been properly executed may not be admitted to probate or given testamentary effect.

Another cause of action that might be brought in these cases of fraud is one for tortious interference with an expectancy.

SCHILLING V. HERRERA

District Court of Appeal of Florida, Third District, 2007
952 So.2d 1231

ROTHENBERG, J.

The plaintiff, Edward A. Schilling ("Mr. Schilling"), appeals from an order granting the defendant Maria Herrera's ("Ms. Herrera") motion to dismiss the amended complaint with prejudice based on the trial court's finding that the amended complaint fails to state a cause of action and that Mr. Schilling is barred from filing to action because he failed to exhaust his probate, remedies. We disagree as to both findings and, therefore, reverse and remand for further proceedings.

PROCEDURAL HISTORY

Mr. Schilling, the decedent's brother, sued Ms. Herrera, the decedent's caretaker, for intentional interference with an expectancy of inheritance. Ms. Herrera moved to dismiss the complaint, arguing that Mr. Schilling failed to state a cause of action and that he was barred from filing his claim because he failed to exhaust his probate remedies. The trial court granted the motion to dismiss without prejudice.

Thereafter, Mr. Schilling filed an amended complaint asserting the same cause of action against Ms. Herrera. The amended complaint alleges that in December 1996, Mignonne Helen Schilling (the decedent) executed her Last Will and Testament, naming her brother and only heir-at-law, Mr. Schilling, as her personal representative and sole beneficiary, and in May 1997, she executed a Durable Power of Attorney, naming Mr. Schilling as her attorney-in-fact.

In December 1999, the decedent was diagnosed with renal disease, resulting in several hospitalizations. During this period, Mr. Schilling, who resides in New Jersey, traveled to Florida to assist the decedent. In January 2000, the decedent executed a Power of Attorney for Health Care, naming Mr. Schilling as her attorney-in-fact for health care decisions.

On January 12, 2001, when the decedent was once again hospitalized, Mr. Schilling traveled to Florida to make arrangements for the decedent's care. After being released from the hospital, the decedent was admitted to a rehabilitation hospital, then to a health care center, and then to the Clairidge House for rehabilitation. While at the Clairidge House, Ms. Herrera became involved in the decedent's care, and when the decedent was discharged from the Clairidge House on December 16, 2001, Ms. Herrera notified Mr. Schilling.

After being discharged from the Clairidge House, the decedent returned to her apartment, and Ms. Herrera began to care for her on an "occasional, as needed basis." In 2003, when the decedent's condition worsened and she was in need of additional care, Ms. Herrera converted her garage into a bedroom, and the decedent moved in. The decedent paid Ms. Herrera rent and for her services as caregiver.

When Mr. Schilling spoke to Ms. Herrera over the phone, Ms. Herrera complained that she was not getting paid enough to take care of the decedent, and on April 10, 2003, Mr. Schilling sent Ms. Herrera money. While living in the converted garage, the decedent became completely dependent on Ms. Herrera. In September 2003, without Mr. Schilling's knowledge, Ms. Herrera convinced the decedent to prepare and execute a new Power of Attorney, naming Ms. Herrera as attorney-in-fact, and to execute a new Last Will and Testament naming Ms. Herrera as personal representative and sole beneficiary of the decedent's estate.

Mr. Schilling visited the decedent in March of 2004. On August 6, 2004, the decedent died at Ms. Herrera's home.

On August 24, 2004, Ms. Herrera filed her Petition for Administration. On December 2, 2004, following the expiration of the creditor's period, Ms. Herrera petitioned for discharge of probate. On December 6, 2004, after the expiration of the creditor's period and after Ms. Herrera had petitioned the probate court for discharge of probate, Ms. Herrera notified Mr. Schilling for the first time that the decedent, his sister, had passed away on August 6, 2004. Shortly thereafter, in late December 2004, the Final Order of Discharge was entered by the probate court. Mr. Schilling alleges that prior to being notified of his sister's death on December 6, 2004, he attempted to contact the decedent through Ms. Herrera, but Ms. Herrera did not return his calls until the conclusion of probate proceedings and did not inform him of his sister's death, thereby depriving him of both the knowledge of the decedent's death and the opportunity of contesting the probate proceedings. Mr. Schilling further alleges that prior to the decedent's death, Ms. Herrera regularly did not immediately return his phone calls, and that Ms. Herrera's "intentional silence was part of a calculated scheme to prevent [Mr.] Schilling from contesting the Estate of Decedent, and was intended to induce [Mr.] Schilling to refrain from acting in his interests to contest the probate proceedings in a timely fashion, as [Mr.] Schilling was used to long delays in contact with [Ms.] Herrera, and did not suspect that the delay was intended to fraudulently induce [Mr.] Schilling to refrain from acting on his own behalf." Finally, Mr. Schilling alleges that he expected to inherit the decedent's estate because he was the decedent's only heir-at-law and because he was named as the sole beneficiary in the 1996 will; Ms. Herrera's fraudulent actions prevented him from receiving the decedent's estate, which he was entitled to; and but for Ms. Herrera's action of procuring the will naming her as sole beneficiary, he would have received the benefit of the estate.

After Mr. Schilling filed his amended complaint, Ms. Herrera filed a renewed motion to dismiss, arguing the same issues that she had raised in her previous motion to dismiss. The trial court granted the motion to dismiss with prejudice, finding that Ms. Herrera had no duty to notify Mr. Schilling of the decedent's death as Mr. Schilling did not hire Ms. Herrera to care for the decedent, and therefore, there was "no special relationship giving rise to a proactive responsibility to provide information. . . ." The trial court also found that Mr. Schilling was barred from filing a claim for intentional interference with an expectancy of inheritance because he failed to exhaust his probate remedies.

LEGAL ANALYSIS

A trial court's ruling on a motion to dismiss for failure to state a cause of action is an issue of law, and therefore, our standard of review is *de novo*. This court "must accept the facts alleged in a complaint as true when reviewing an order that determines the sufficiency of the complaint."

To state a cause of action for intentional interference with an expectancy of inheritance, the complaint must allege the following elements: (1) the existence of an expectancy; (2) intentional interference with the expectancy through tortious conduct; (3) causation; and (4) damages. *Claveloux v. Bacotti*, 778 So.2d 399, 400 (Fla. 2d DCA 2001)(citing *Whalen v. Prosser*, 719 So.2d 2, 5 (Fla. 2d DCA 1998)). The court in *Whalen* clearly explained that the purpose behind this tort is to protect the testator, not the beneficiary:

> Interference with an expectancy is an unusual tort because the beneficiary is authorized to sue to recover damages primarily to protect the testator's interest rather than the disappointed beneficiary's expectations. The fraud, duress, undue influence, or other independent tortious conduct required for this tort is directed at the testator. The beneficiary is not directly defrauded or unduly influenced; the testator is. Thus, the common law court has created this cause of action not primarily to protect the beneficiary's inchoate rights, but to protect the deceased testator's former right to dispose of property freely and without improper interference. In a sense, the beneficiary's action is derivative of the testator's rights.

Whalen, 719 So.2d at 6.

In the instant case, the trial court's ruling was based on the fact that the amended complaint fails to allege that Ms. Herrera breached a legal duty owed to Mr. Schilling. However, as the *Claveloux* court noted, there are four elements for a cause of action for intentional interference with an expectancy of inheritance, and breach of a legal duty is not one of the elements. This is consistent with the *Whalen* court's explanation that the "fraud, duress, undue influence, or other independent tortious conduct required for this tort is directed at the testator. The beneficiary is not directly defrauded or unduly influenced; the testator is." (emphasis added). We, therefore, review the amended complaint to determine if it sufficiently pleads a cause of action for intentional interference with an expectancy of inheritance.

In essence, the amended complaint alleges that Mr. Schilling was named as the sole beneficiary in the decedent's last will and testament; that based on this last will and testament, he expected to inherit the decedent's estate upon her death; that Ms. Herrera intentionally interfered with his expectancy of inheritance by "convincing" the decedent, while she was ill and completely dependent on Ms. Herrera, to execute a new last will and testament naming Ms. Herrera as the sole beneficiary; and that Ms. Herrera's "fraudulent actions" and "undue influence" prevented Mr. Schilling from inheriting the decedent's estate. Based on these well-pled allegations, we conclude that the amended complaint states a cause of action for intentional interference with an expectancy of inheritance. Therefore, the trial court erred, as a matter of law, in dismissing the amended complaint on that basis.

Mr. Schilling also contends that the trial court erred in finding that he was barred from filing a claim for intentional interference with an expectancy of inheritance as he failed to exhaust his probate remedies. We agree.

In finding that Mr. Schilling was barred from filing his action for intentional interference with an expectancy of inheritance, the trial court relied on *DeWitt v. Duce*, 408 So.2d 216 (Fla.1981). In *DeWitt,* the testator's will was admitted to probate after his death. Thereafter, the plaintiffs filed a petition for revocation of probate of the testator's will, but voluntarily dismissed the petition, choosing to take under the will instead of challenging the will in probate court. More than two years later, the plaintiffs filed their claim for intentional interference with an inheritance, arguing that the defendants exercised undue influence over the testator at a time when he lacked testamentary capacity, causing the testator to execute the probated will, which was less favorable to the plaintiffs and more favorable to the defendants than the testator's previous will. The trial court dismissed the action, finding that pursuant to section 733.103(2), Florida Statutes (1977), the plaintiffs were foreclosed from proving the facts necessary to establish a cause of action for intentional interference with an expectancy of inheritance. Section 733.103(2), Florida Statutes (1977), provides as follows:

In any collateral action or proceeding relating to devised property, the probate of a will in Florida shall be conclusive of its due execution; that it was executed by a competent testator, free of fraud, duress, mistake, and undue influence; and of the fact that the will was unrevoked on the testator's death.

The decision was appealed to a federal district court, and the federal court determined it would be better for the Florida Supreme Court to decide the issue, certifying the following question to the Florida Supreme Court:

> Does Florida law, statutory or otherwise, preclude plaintiffs from proving the essential elements of their claim for tortious interference with an inheritance where the alleged wrongfully procured will has been probated in a Florida court and plaintiffs had notice of the probate proceeding and an opportunity to contest the validity of the will therein but chose not to do so?

DeWitt, 408 So.2d at 216–17.

In answering the certified question in the affirmative, the Florida Supreme Court stated that "[t]he rule is that if adequate relief is available in a probate proceeding, then that remedy must be exhausted before a tortious interference claim may be pursued." The Court, however, stated that an exception to this general rule is that "[i]f the defendant's fraud is not discovered until after probate, plaintiff is allowed to bring a later action for damages since relief in probate was impossible." The Court also noted that "[c]ases which allow the action for tortious interference with a testamentary expectancy are predicated on the inadequacy of probate remedies. . . ." In conclusion, the Florida Supreme Court held:

> In sum, we find that [plaintiffs] had an adequate remedy in probate with a fair opportunity to pursue it. Because they lacked assiduity in failing to avail themselves of this remedy, we interpret section 733.103(2) as barring [plaintiffs] from a subsequent action in tort for wrongful interference with a testamentary expectancy, and accordingly answer the certified question in the affirmative.

Therefore, the Court's holding that the plaintiffs were barred from pursuing their claim for intentional interference with an expectancy of inheritance, was based on the fact that the plaintiffs had an adequate remedy in probate; the plaintiffs had a fair opportunity to pursue their remedy; and the plaintiffs' failure to pursue their remedy was due to their lack of diligence.

We find that *DeWitt* is factually distinguishable, and therefore inapplicable. A review of the amended complaint reflects that Mr. Schilling has alleged two separate frauds. The first alleged fraud stems from Ms. Herrera's undue influence over the deceased in procuring the will, whereas the second alleged fraud stems from Ms. Herrera's actions in preventing Mr. Schilling from contesting the will in probate court. We acknowledge that pursuant to *DeWitt*, if only the first type of fraud was involved, Mr. Schilling's collateral attack of the will would be barred. However, language contained in *DeWitt* clearly indicates that a subsequent action for intentional interference with an expectancy of inheritance may be permitted where "the circumstances surrounding the tortious conduct effectively preclude adequate relief in the probate court."

This issue was later addressed by the Fourth District in *Ebeling v. Voltz*, 454 So.2d 783 (Fla. 4th DCA 1984). In *Ebeling*, the plaintiffs filed an action against the defendant for intentional interference with an expectancy of inheritance, alleging that, although they knew of the probate proceeding, they did not contest the will in probate court because the defendant made fraudulent statements inducing them not to contest the will. The trial court granted the defendant's motion to dismiss, finding that pursuant to section 733.103, Florida Statutes (1983) , the plaintiffs were barred from attacking the will. The Fourth District reversed, finding that "[e]xtrinsic fraud, or in other words, fraud alleged in the prevention of the will contest, as opposed to in the making of the will, would appear to be the type of circumstance that would preclude relief in the probate court." The court noted that the fraud alleged in the complaint prevented the plaintiffs from pursuing the incapacity claim in the probate court, and therefore, the action "falls into the category of cases that *DeWitt* considers outside the purview of Section 733.103(2), Florida Statutes."

In the instant case, we must accept the facts alleged by Mr. Schilling as true. He alleges in the amended complaint that when the decedent began to live in Ms. Herrera's home, pursuant to powers of attorney executed by the decedent, Mr. Schilling was the decedent's attorney-in-fact; throughout the decedent's numerous illnesses, Mr. Schilling made decisions regarding the decedent's care; Mr. Schilling traveled to Miami on numerous occasions to visit the decedent, whose condition progressively worsened; Mr. Schilling stayed in contact with Ms. Herrera while the decedent was living in her home; Mr. Schilling relied on Ms. Herrera to obtain information regarding the decedent; Mr. Schilling sent money to Ms. Herrera to pay for the decedent's care; after the decedent passed away, Mr. Schilling called Ms. Herrera numerous times, but she would not return his calls; and Ms. Herrera did not inform Mr. Schilling of his sister's death until after she petitioned for discharge of probate. As the facts in the amended complaint sufficiently allege that Mr. Schilling was prevented from contesting the will in the probate court due to Ms. Herrera's fraudulent conduct, we find that the trial court erred in finding that Mr. Schilling's claim for intentional interference with an expectancy of inheritance was barred.[2]

Accordingly, we reverse the order dismissing Mr. Schilling's amended complaint, and remand for further proceedings.

———————

Ordinarily, the plaintiff in a case alleging intentional interference with an expectancy needs to show 1) the existence of an expectancy under intestate succession or a previous will, 2) intent to interfere with that expectancy through tortious conduct, 3) the conduct caused interference, and 4) damages. The tortious conduct could be fraud, undue influence, duress, or some other tort.

Schilling provides another example of the tension between justice and efficiency. Without this new tort, Ms. Herrera is not liable to Mr. Schilling. With this new tort, we have additional litigation. Is the added justice worth the cost in human resources? Should courts adopt this new tort?

WELLIN V. WELLIN

United States District Court, D. South Carolina, Charleston Division, 2015
135 F.Supp.3d 502

NORTON, J.

This matter is before the court on defendant Wendy Wellin's ("Wendy") motion to dismiss ten of the eleven claims asserted against her by plaintiffs Peter J. Wellin ("Peter"), Cynthia Wellin Plum ("Cynthia"), and Marjorie Wellin King ("Marjorie"). For the

---

[2] Ms. Herrera argues that although she did not inform Mr. Schilling of the decedent's death until after she petitioned for discharge of probate, there was no fraud as Mr. Schilling learned of the decedent's death prior to the entry of the Final Order of Discharge. We find that this argument lacks merit.

reasons set forth below, the court grants in part and denies in part Wendy's motion to dismiss.

I. BACKGROUND

On October 20, 2014, Keith Wellin's ("Keith") three adult children—Peter, Cynthia, and Marjorie (collectively, "the Wellin children"), individually and as co-trustees and beneficiaries of the Wellin 2009 Irrevocable Trust—filed a complaint against Wendy, individually and as trustee of the Keith S. Wellin Florida Revocable Living Trust u/a/d December 11, 2001. The complaint alleges that

> [t]hrough her prolonged and consistent pattern of mistreatment toward the children and Keith, Wendy defamed the children to Keith and others, unduly influenced and coerced Keith with respect to his finances and estate planning, isolated Keith from his children, grandchildren, and other relatives, instilled in Keith anger, distrust, and hatred toward his three children, and, ultimately, enriched herself and her family at the expense of the children and Keith's other lineal descendants.

Wendy, to whom Keith was married for almost twelve years before his death on September 14, 2014, was Keith's fourth wife. The Wellin children, who collectively have eight children, assert that both they and their children maintained a "close, loving relationship" with Keith until 2013. At the time of his marriage to Wendy, Keith's net worth exceeded $150 million.

On November 12, 2002, shortly before their marriage, Keith and Wendy entered into a prenuptial agreement. The prenuptial agreement "[sought] to protect [the Wellin children's] interests in [Keith's] estate by having this Agreement in full force and effect." The prenuptial agreement identified Keith's assets at the time of his marriage as "Keith's Separate Property" and provided that Wendy "waive[d] any claim to whatsoever to [Keith's] Separate Property . . . that she may now have or hereinafter acquire as Keith's Wife." The prenuptial agreement provided that Wendy would receive $7.6 million in the event Keith predeceased Wendy and they were still married, and further provided that should Keith become infirm or mentally incapacitated, Wendy would not take actions to limit the Wellin children's access to Keith.

In 2001, Keith, with the assistance of attorney Tom Farace ("Farace"), created the Keith S. Wellin Florida Revocable Living

Trust ("the Revocable Trust"), which was the primary instrument that provided for distribution of Keith's assets upon his death. Under the terms of the Revocable Trust, Keith was the trustee, Peter was the successor trustee, and Cynthia was the backup successor trustee. Over the course of his marriage to Wendy and prior to 2013, Keith revised the Revocable Trust on multiple occasions, increasing the fixed amount Wendy would receive upon his death from $7.6 million to $25 million. At all times prior to 2013, Keith's estate planning documents were structured so that Wendy would receive a fixed amount, and the Wellin children would receive the bulk of Keith's residuary estate, an amount significantly greater than the amount left to Wendy.

In 2003, Keith set aside approximately 900 shares of Berkshire Hathaway stock for the benefit of the Wellin children. Acting on the advice of Farace, Keith placed these shares in a family limited partnership (the "LP"). Keith retained a 98.9% limited partnership interest in the LP, but the LP was controlled by the Wellin children. The purpose of this transaction was to reduce Keith's tax liability and protect his assets for the Wellin children. Between 2003 and 2009, Keith's estate planning documents provided that when Keith died, the Wellin children would receive his 98.9% interest in the LP. In 2009, Farace advised Keith to enter into a [sic] another transaction, whereby Keith would create an intentionally defective grantor trust, the Wellin Family 2009 Irrevocable Trust (the "Irrevocable Trust"), naming the Wellin children as beneficiaries, and transfer his 98.9% interest in the LP to the Irrevocable Trust in exchange for a promissory note. Farace clearly communicated with Keith about the advantages and disadvantages of this transaction. Before and after the 2003 and 2009 transactions, Keith's estate planning documents provided that the Wellin children would receive the value of the Berkshire Hathaway shares, while Wendy would receive a fixed amount as provided in the Revocable Trust.

Beginning in 2011, Keith's health began to deteriorate, which increased his dependence on Wendy and caregivers controlled by Wendy to provide for his health and safety. Around July 29, 2011, Keith, acting as trustee of the Revocable Trust, divided a UBS account which held the majority of the Revocable Trust's liquid assets into two separate accounts. Keith then executed a power of attorney appointing Wendy as his attorney-in-fact with respect to one such account, UBS Account number XXX-4378.

In the spring of 2013, Keith's mental capacity began to decline. During this time period, Keith terminated Farace and other long-time advisors and retained new attorneys and advisors, including attorneys selected by Wendy. The new attorneys requested that the Wellin children prepay the promissory note held by the Irrevocable Trust so that Keith could transfer the $25 million bequest to Wendy, as set out in the Revocable Trust, prior to his death. In the spring or summer of 2013, Keith transferred $4.5 million to Wendy, which she used to purchase a home in Sullivan's Island, South Carolina. Around the same time, he transferred $25 million to Wendy. These transfers were the product of Wendy "manipulating, coercing or unduly influencing Keith." Also in the spring or summer of 2013, Keith failed to consummate the sale of a property in Friendship, Maine to Marjorie, even though he had previously expressed excitement about the sale.

In July 2013, Keith filed a lawsuit, Wellin v. Wellin ("Wellin I") against the Wellin children. Around the same time, Keith revoked powers of attorney granted to Peter and Cynthia, removed Peter as successor trustee of the Revocable Trust, and removed Cynthia as backup successor trustee of the Revocable Trust, and installed Wendy into these positions. In the months following the initiation of litigation, Keith's new lawyers drafted one or more revised versions of the Revocable Trust that eliminated or significantly reduced Keith's bequests to the Wellin children and increased his bequests to Wendy and her children.

In November 2013, Keith and his new attorneys attempted to "turn off" grantor status on the Irrevocable Trust, which would have caused the Irrevocable Trust to incur over $40 million in tax liability, and attempted to execute a "swap" transaction that would have significantly reduced the assets of the Irrevocable Trust. If effective, these actions would have shifted tens of millions of dollars that would have been received by Keith's children and grandchildren to Wendy and her children. In November 2013, Keith purported to hire a new trust protector of the Irrevocable Trust to bring a separate lawsuit, *McDevitt v. Wellin* ("McDevitt") against the Wellin children, in their capacity as trustees of the Irrevocable Trust.

The Wellin children allege that "Keith's uncharacteristic and bizarre behavior" was the result of "certain lies, fraudulent misrepresentations, undue influence, coercion, and isolation" by Wendy designed to interfere with the Wellin children's inheritance and enrich herself. The Wellin children allege that Wendy's actions to interfere with the relationship between Keith and his children include: (1) preventing the Wellin children from visiting Keith; (2) refusing to answer calls from the Wellin children and failing to inform Keith when they called; (3) insisting that she be present for all visits between Keith and the Wellin children; (4) telling Keith and others lies about the Wellin children; and (5) initiating and controlling the litigation brought by Keith against the Wellin children. The Wellin children further allege that Wendy has taken steps to influence Keith with respect to his finances and estate planning, including: (1) "coaching" Keith regarding what he should say to lawyers, health care providers, friends, and others regarding the facts of the lawsuits; (2) meeting with Keith's lawyers outside his presence and instructing them on Keith's intentions with respect to the litigation; (3) disseminating communications on behalf of Keith not consistent with his actual or expressed intentions; (4) coercing Keith to terminate Farace and other long-time advisors; (5) coercing Keith to change his will, the Revocable Trust, and other estate planning documents to provide more for Wendy and less for the Wellin children; (6) signing documents on Keith's behalf without his informed consent; and (7) making distributions from Keith's accounts over which Wendy served as Keith's power of attorney that were inconsistent with Keith's best interests.

The Wellin children bring the following causes of action against Wendy individually: (1) defamation; (2) intentional interference with inheritance; (3) intentional interference with prospective contractual relations/prospective economic advantage; (4) breach of fiduciary duty; (5) breach of prenuptial agreement related to the Wellin children's access to Keith; (6) breach of prenuptial agreement related to Wendy's control of Keith's separate property; (7) breach of contract accompanied by a fraudulent act; (8) constructive trust; (9) barratry; and (10) negligence per se. The Wellin children also seek a declaratory judgment against Wendy in her official capacity declaring that "all purported amendments to the Revocable Trust after the Tenth Amendment to and Restatement of the Revocable Trust, dated August 30, 2011 . . . were and are ineffective, invalid, ultra vires, and void."

On December 3, 2014, Wendy, in her individual capacity, moved to dismiss ten of the eleven claims for failure to state a claim. The Wellin children responded to this motion on January 12, 2014. Following a hearing on February 5, 2015, the Wellin children filed a supplemental response on February 13, 2015. Wendy replied to this response on February 23, 2015. This motion has been fully briefed and it is ripe for the court's review.

* * *

III. DISCUSSION

Pursuant to Federal Rule of Civil Procedure 12(b)(6), Wendy individually moves the court to dismiss the following claims against her: (1) intentional interference with inheritance; (2) intentional interference with prospective contractual relations/prospective economic advantage; (3) breach of fiduciary duty; (4) breach of prenuptial agreement—interfering with the Wellin children's access to Keith; (5) breach of prenuptial agreement—exercising control over Keith's separate property; (6) breach of contract accompanied by a fraudulent act; (7) constructive trust; (8) barratry; and (9) negligent per se. The court will address each claim in turn.

A.   Count II—Intentional Interference with Inheritance

Wendy first argues that the Wellin children's claim for intentional interference with inheritance should be dismissed because it is not a recognized cause of action under South Carolina law. It is true that South Carolina has not adopted the tort of international interference with inheritance. *See Douglass ex rel. Louthian v. Boyce*, 542 S.E.2d 715, 717 (2001) ("We have not adopted the tort of intentional interference with inheritance."); *Meehan v. Meehan*, 2006 WL 7285712, at *3 n. 3 (S.C.Ct.App. Feb. 10, 2006) ("South Carolina has yet to recognize intentional interference with inheritance rights as a valid cause of action."); *see also Malloy v. Thompson*, 762 S.E.2d 690, 692 (2014) ("[T]his opinion must not be understood as either adopting or rejecting the tort of intentional interference with inheritance.").

However, this does not end the court's inquiry. Rather, "[w]here there is no case law from the forum state which is directly on point, the district court attempts to do as the state court would do if confronted with the same fact pattern." *Roe v. Doe*, 28 F.3d 404, 407 (4th Cir.1994); *see also Twin City Fire Ins. Co. v. Ben Arnold-Sunbelt Beverage Co. of S.C.*, 433 F.3d 365, 369 (4th Cir.2005) ("If the Supreme Court of South Carolina has spoken neither directly nor indirectly on the particular issue before us, we are called upon to predict how that court would rule if presented with the issue.") "In deciding how the courts of South Carolina would rule, this court is authorized to consider all available legal sources, including restatements of the law, treatises, law review commentaries, decisions from other jurisdictions whose doctrinal approach is substantially the same, and the 'majority rule.' " *TC X, Inc. v. Commonwealth Land Title Ins. Co.*, 928 F.Supp. 618, 623 (D.S.C.1995); *see also Twin City Fire*, 433 F.3d at 369 (holding that in predicting state law, courts may "consider lower court opinions in South Carolina, the teachings of treatises, and the practices of other states."). The court may also consider "well considered dicta," *Private Mortg. Inv. Servs., Inc. v. Hotel & Club Assocs, Inc.*, 296 F.3d 308, 312 (4th Cir.2002), and "recent pronouncements of general rules or policies by the state's highest court." *Wells v. Liddy*, 186 F.3d 505, 528 (4th Cir.1999).

The court will consider the aforementioned available sources in turn to determine what the South Carolina Supreme Court would do if confronted with the instant fact pattern.

1. South Carolina Supreme Court *Dicta*

The South Carolina Supreme Court's most illuminating treatment of intentional interference with inheritance comes in *Douglass ex rel. Louthian v. Boyce*. In *Douglass*, a seventeen-year-old boy was killed in an automobile accident and the plaintiff alleged that he was the decedent's son. 542 S.E.2d at 716. After the decedent's parents settled a wrongful death action, the plaintiff brought an action against the parents, alleging that he was entitled to recover in the wrongful death action. The plaintiff later amended his complaint to assert a claim for intentional interference with inheritance rights against the parents' attorneys. The court held that it did not need to decide whether to recognize a cause of action for intentional interference with inheritance because the attorneys were immune from liability to third persons arising from their professional activities. However, in a footnote discussing intentional interference with inheritance, the South Carolina Supreme Court stated:

> We have adopted the closely analogous tort of intentional interference with prospective contractual relations. Most jurisdictions adopting the tort of intentional interference with inheritance have required the plaintiff to prove the following elements: (1) the existence of an expectancy (2) an intentional interference with that expectancy through tortious conduct (3) a reasonable certainty that the

expectancy would have been realized but for the interference and (4) damages.

This discussion, though brief, is instructive. First, the court noted that South Carolina has adopted the "closely analogous" tort of intentional interference with prospective contractual relations. Specifically, in *Crandall*, the South Carolina Supreme Court "join[ed] the vast majority of [its] sister jurisdictions in recognizing" the tort of intentional interference with prospective contractual relations. In both *Crandall* and *Douglass*, the South Carolina Supreme Court cited decisions from the Oregon Supreme Court. Specifically, the *Douglass* court cited the Oregon Supreme Court decision, *Allen v. Hall*, 328 Or. 276 (1999), for the proposition that the tort of intentional interference with prospective contractual relations is analogous to the tort of intentional interference with inheritance.

In *Allen*, the Oregon Supreme Court held that "intentional interference with a prospective inheritance may be actionable under a reasonable extension of the well-established tort known as intentional interference with economic relations." The *Allen* court pointed to "the very close analogy that exists between an expectancy of inheritance and those other interests to which this court already has extended the protections of the tort of intentional interference with prospective economic advantage," noting that "[a]lthough an expectancy of inheritance is, by definition, purely prospective, so are many of the commercial interests that have been associated with and are protected by the tort." he same analogy can be drawn in South Carolina, where courts have also recognized that the tort of intentional interference with prospective contractual relations protects purely prospective interests, such as a plaintiff's "reasonable expectation of benefits."

Moreover, after citing *Allen*, the *Douglass* court listed the elements of intentional interference with inheritance, citing multiple state courts that have adopted the tort and the Restatement (Second) of Torts section articulating the trot. Notably the court did not cite any authority rejecting the application of the tort.

The court finds that the foregoing case law strongly suggests that the South Carolina Supreme Court would adopt the tort of intentional interference with inheritance.

2. Majority Rule

Restatement (Second) of Torts § 774B, cited by the South Carolina Supreme Court in *Douglass*, states that "[a] substantial majority of the cases now grant recovery in tort for intentionally and tortiously interfering with the expectation of an inheritance or gift." Restatement (Second) of Torts § 774B reporter's note (1979); *see also Marshall v. Marshall*, 547 U.S. 293, 296 (2006) (recognizing intentional interference with inheritance as a "widely recognized tort").

Here, Wendy argues that there is no true majority, as only twenty-five states have adopted the tort of intentional interference with inheritance. While different observers have reached difference conclusions as to the specific number of states that have adopted the tort, what is clear is that "a majority of courts that have considered the tort have approved it." Nita Ledford, Note—Intentional Interference with Inheritance, 30 Real Prop. Prob. & Tr. J. 325, 352 (1995) *see also* John C.P. Goldberg & Robert H. Sitkoff, Torts and Estates: Remedying Wrongful Interference with Inheritance, 65 Stan. L.Rev. 335, 362 (2013) (recognizing that while appellate courts in twenty states have recognized the tort, "these numbers understate courts' receptiveness to the tort," and noting that only three states have rejected it). Thus, even if a formal majority of states has not adopted the tort, the court finds it significant that the great majority of courts that have reached the issue have adopted it.

Wendy also argues that the court must consider differences in the character, origin, and elements of each state's version of the tort when assessing the strength of the majority position. Unsurprisingly, although states have adopted different formulations of the tort, the court is not convinced that the differences are significant enough to undermine the clear trend toward the tort's adoption. The core elements recognized in *Douglass* are analogous to formulations used in other states, which sometimes require "a causal effect between the interference and the harm" rather than a "reasonable certainty that the expectancy would have been realized," or an "improper means or [an] improper purpose" rather than "tortious conduct."

As noted above, the South Carolina Supreme Court has "join[ed] the vast majority of [its] sister jurisdictions in recognizing" the tort of intentional interference with prospective contractual relations. There is no apparent reason why South Carolina would not join the majority of state courts in recognizing the closely analogous tort of intentional interference with inheritance. Thus, to the extent this court must consider the "majority position" as a factor in its analysis, this factor clearly weighs in favor of the tort's adoption.

3. Treatises

Section § 74B of the Restatement (Second) of Torts ("the Restatement") defines the tort of intentional interference with inheritance as: "One who by fraud, duress or other tortious means intentionally prevents another from receiving from a third person an inheritance or gift that he would otherwise have received is subject to liability to the other for loss of the inheritance or gift." This tort "represents an extension to a type of noncontractual relation of the principle found in the liability for intentional interference with prospective contracts."

The South Carolina Supreme Court's reliance on the Restatement supports recognizing the tort of intentional interference with inheritance. For example, in *Crandall*, the South Carolina Supreme Court cited the Restatement in recognizing intentional interference with prospective contractual relations. Additionally, South Carolina courts have frequently looked to the Restatement when interpreting other areas of South Carolina law.

Besides the Restatement, other treatises have also recognized the tort of intentional interference with inheritance. *See* Dan B. Dobbs et al., The Law of Torts § 642 (2d ed.) ("Most courts addressing the issue have recognized a cause of action against defendants who prevent the plaintiff from receiving an inheritance or gift she would otherwise have received, provided the defendant uses undue influence, duress, or tortious means such as fraud or murder."); W. Page Keeton et al., Prosser and Keeton on the Law of Torts § 130 (5th ed.1984) (noting that courts permit the tort with sufficient evidence of "a high degree of probability that the testator would have made or changed a bequest"). Notably, the South Carolina Supreme Court has cited to both Dobbs and Keeton in analyzing intentional interference with prospective contractual relations.

The tort treatises' general acceptance of the tort of intentional inference with inheritance and the South Carolina Supreme Court's historical reliance on these same treatises suggests that the court would follow them in adopting this tort.

4. Recent Pronouncements of General Rules or Policies

Finally, the South Carolina Supreme Court has recently recognized that the interests of intended beneficiaries of wills and trusts are entitled to protection under South Carolina law and has expanded an existing tort to provide a remedy for negligent harm to intended beneficiaries.[8] In *Fabian v. Lindsay*, the South Carolina Supreme Court recognized, for the first time, a cause of action in both tort and contract "by a third party beneficiary of an existing will or estate planning document against a lawyer whose drafting error defeats or diminishes the client's intent." In *Fabian*, the plaintiff brought an action for professional negligence and breach of contract against her late uncle's lawyer, alleging that the lawyer's drafting error in her uncle's trust resulted in her being disinherited. Notably, while the dissent would not have recognized a breach of contract claim under the circumstances, the court unanimously agreed that the tort claim should be recognized.

In doing so, the court adopted a "balancing of factors test" previously articulated by the Supreme Court of California in *Lucas v. Hamm*:

> [T]he determination [of] whether in a specific case the defendant will be held liable to a third person not in privity is a matter of policy and involves the balancing of various factors, among which are the extent to which the transaction was intended to affect the plaintiff, the foreseeability of harm to him, the degree of certainty that the plaintiff suffered injury, the closeness of the connection between the defendant's conduct and the injury, and the policy of preventing future harm.

(quoting *Lucas v. Hamm*, 56 Cal.2d 583 (1961)). The court noted that the *Lucas* court, in applying these factors, reasoned that

> one of the main purposes which the transaction between defendant and the testator intended to accomplish was to provide for the transfer of property to plaintiffs; the damage to plaintiffs in the event of invalidity of the bequest was clearly foreseeable; it became certain, upon the death of the

---

[8]   This factor presents another notable similarity to the Oregon Supreme Court's decision in *Allen*, where the court observed that "prospects of inheritance long have been recognized as interests that are worthy of common-law protection." *Allen*, 974 P.2d at 202 (permitting an intended beneficiary of a will to sue an attorney who failed to include a gift in the testator's will).

testator without change of the will, that plaintiffs would have received the intended benefits but for the asserted negligence of defendant; and if persons such as plaintiffs are not permitted to recover for the loss resulting from negligence of the draftsman, no one would be able to do so, and the policy of prevent[ing] future harm would be impaired.

(quoting *Lucas*).

Here, many of these same factors mentioned in *Fabian* weigh in favor of recognizing a claim for intentional interference with inheritance. First, damage to the Wellin children is foreseeable. Second, it would become certain upon the Keith's death that, but for the interference with inheritance, the Wellin children would have received the intended benefits. Finally, recognizing the tort will prevent future harm by holding interferers accountable for their actions. As noted by the Wellin children, because intentional interference with inheritance deals with intentional action, it would seem even more deserving of liability than the conduct at issue in *Fabian*, which was merely negligent.

Based on past well-considered dicta, the majority rule, treatises, and recent pronouncements of general rules or policies by the state's highest court, the court predicts that the South Carolina Supreme Court would recognize the tort of intentional interference with inheritance.[10] Although Wendy argues that the numerous differences in the variety of elements, prerequisites, and standards used by courts to enforce this tort make this issue more appropriate for certification to the South Carolina Supreme Court, certification should only be used when available state law is "clearly insufficient." *Roe v. Doe*, 28 F.3d 404, 407 (4th Cir.1994).

The court does not find the available state law insufficient in this case. The elements set forth in *Douglass* are very similar to the elements required by other courts that have adopted the tort. *See Douglass*, 542 S.E.2d 715, 717 n. 4 ("(1) the existence of an expectancy (2) an intentional interference with that expectancy through tortious conduct (3) a reasonable certainty that the expectancy would have been realized but for the interference and (4)

---

[10] The court also notes that the reporter's comments to South Carolina Code assume that a claim for intentional interference with inheritance exists under South Carolina law. S.C.Code § 62–7–604 reporter's cmt. (providing a claim for intentional interference with inheritance is not subject to the statute of limitations in that section and referring the Restatement (Second) of Torts § 774B for the law on such a claim).

damages.").[11] These elements are also conceptually consistent with the elements required by the Oregon Supreme Court in *Allen*. *See Allen*, 974 P.2d at 202("(1) the existence of a [prospective inheritance]; (2) intentional interference with that relationship or advantage; (3) by a third party; (4) accomplished through improper means or for an improper purpose; (5) a causal effect between the interference and the harm to the relationship or prospective advantage; and (6) damages."). Courts have also found these elements to be consistent with Section § 774B of the Restatement (Second) of Torts. *See Morrill*, 712 A.2d at 1041 (stating "[w]e have adopted the Restatement formulation of the tort" and listing elements consistent with those found in *Douglass*). The policy motivations underlying the South Carolina Supreme Court's recent decision in *Fabian* also weigh in favor of the tort's adoption. Thus, it is appears likely that the South Carolina Supreme Court would adopt the tort of intentional interference with inheritance, and in doing so, the court would require plaintiffs to prove the elements set forth in *Douglass*.

5. Availability of Remedy at Probate

Wendy also contends that the court must predict whether the South Carolina Supreme Court would restrict the tort to cases where the plaintiff has no adequate remedy at probate. Though it is a somewhat closer question, the court finds that the South Carolina Supreme Court would likely adopt this prerequisite. Numerous states, including three of the states cited in *Douglass*, have restricted the tort in some way based on the availability of a remedy in probate. This approach is consistent with the goal of protecting beneficiaries who would otherwise be left without a remedy, which has been a significant justification for the expansion of tort liability to protect inheritance expectancies in many jurisdictions, including South Carolina.

Moreover, without this restriction, the tort would conflict with South Carolina's legislative preference for adjudicating estate-related claims in probate court as evidenced by S.C. Code Ann. § 62–1–302, which grants probate courts "exclusive original jurisdiction

---

[11] *Compare Morrill v. Morrill*, 712 A.2d 1039, 1041–42 (Me.1998) ("(1) the existence of an expectancy of inheritance; (2) an intentional interference by a defendant through tortious conduct, such as fraud, duress, or undue influence; (3) a reasonable certainty that the expectancy of inheritance would have been realized but for the defendant's interference; and (4) damage resulting from that interference.").

over all subject matter related to . . . estates of decedents."[13] *See Minton v. Sackett*, 671 N.E.2d 160, 162 (Ind.Ct.App.1996) ("A majority of the states which have adopted the tort . . . have achieved [ ] a balance [between the competing goals of providing a remedy to injured parties and honoring the strictures of our probate code] by prohibiting a tort action to be brought where the remedy of a will contest is available and would provide the injured party with adequate relief."). In light of these considerations, the court finds that South Carolina courts would not permit plaintiffs to bring a cause of action for intentional interference with inheritance where an adequate remedy exists at probate.

6. Conclusion

Applying these elements to the case at hand, the court finds that the Wellin children have sufficiently pleaded a plausible claim for intentional interference with inheritance. As an initial matter, it is clear that at least a portion of the damages sought in the Wellin children's complaint, particularly the damages arising from wrongful inter vivos transfers, could not be recovered through probate remedies. Turning to the elements of the tort of intentional interference with inheritance, the Wellin children have sufficiently pleaded: (1) a valid expectancy that they would inherit the vast majority of their father's estate, based on Keith's consistent, long-standing estate plan prior to 2013; (2) that Wendy intentionally interfered with that expectancy through tortious conduct, in the form of fraudulent misrepresentations, defamatory statements, and undue influence; (3) that, but for Wendy's conduct, there is a reasonable certainty that the expectancy would have been realized, based on the timing and nature of the alleged tortious conduct; and (4) damages, in the form of lost devises and bequests that would otherwise have been distributed to the Wellin children through Keith's will, Revocable Trust, and IRA Designation form. Notably, Wendy does not argue that the Wellin children have failed to plead any of these elements. Therefore, the court denies Wendy's motion to dismiss the claim for intentional interference with inheritance claim.

* * *

---

[13] The probate exception to federal diversity jurisdiction reinforces the importance of this conflict. Without the abovementioned restriction, many disputes that might otherwise be forced into probate proceedings, and thus, outside the scope of federal diversity jurisdiction, would be able to circumvent not only probate court, but state court altogether.

C. Count IV—Breach of Fiduciary Duty

The Wellin children's claim for breach of fiduciary duty alleges that Wendy, acting pursuant to her power of attorney as trustee of the Revocable Trust with respect to UBS Account number XXX-4378, breached her duty to the trust beneficiary through a series of wrongful purchases and distributions. Wendy argues that the Wellin children's claim for breach of fiduciary duty should be dismissed because Wendy's power of attorney did not create a fiduciary relationship between herself and the Wellin children, as the Wellin children were not vested beneficiaries of the Revocable Trust at the time the alleged breaches occurred.

* * *

The Wellin children note that under Florida law, a vested beneficiary may sue a trustee for breach of a duty owed to a settlor/beneficiary that occurred during the settlor/beneficiary's lifetime, which subsequently affects the interest of the vested beneficiary. The Wellin children argue that this rule should extend to Wendy's breach of her fiduciary duties to Keith. Specifically, they argue that as the power of attorney for the Revocable Trust, Wendy had a duty to act in the best interests of Keith, the settlor/beneficiary of the Revocable trust. Wendy argues that her fiduciary duty under the power of attorney was only to Keith, and the Wellin children are not entitled to bring a claim on his behalf. Thus, as an initial matter, the court must decide the threshold question of whether Florida law would allow a vested beneficiary to bring claims for a breach of a fiduciary duty owed to the settlor/beneficiary against persons other than trustees. This analysis seeks to determine whether Florida law would allow the Wellin children to step into Keith's shoes and utilize a claim that would otherwise belong only to him.

Florida courts have not discussed the nature of a vested beneficiary's right to bring claims against a trustee for the breach of a fiduciary duty owed to the settlor/beneficiary. The Wellin children rely on *Brundage v. Bank of Am.*, in which the court indicated that beneficiaries are allowed to bring such claims because they are harmed by the trustee's conduct:

> [O]nce the interest of the contingent beneficiary vests upon the death of the settlor, the beneficiary may sue for breach of a duty that the trustee owed to the settlor/beneficiary which was breached during the lifetime of the settlor and subsequently affects the interest of the vested beneficiary.

> *Smith v. Bank of Clearwater* illustrates this principle. In *Smith* the court held that a contingent remainderman of a trust, whose interest vested with the death of the lifetime beneficiary, had standing to sue for mismanagement of trust assets during the lifetime of the income beneficiary, because such mismanagement diminished the value of the trust assets to which the remainderman was entitled. The trustee owed the lifetime beneficiary the duty to properly manage the assets of the trust, and a breach of that duty could be enforced by the remainderman.

Brundage v. Bank of Am., 996 So.2d 877, 882 (Fla.Dist.Ct.App.2008) (emphasis added). *Siegel v. Novak*, cited approvingly in *Brundage*, applied the same principle under New York law, stating that preventing beneficiaries from bringing such claims would violate the court's "sense of justice." The *Siegel* court explained that "a trustee should not be able to violate its fiduciary duty and authorize withdrawals contrary to the provisions of the trust, and yet escape responsibility because the settlor did not discover the transgressions during her lifetime." This rationale would certainly extend to claims alleging breaches of other fiduciary duties owed to the settlor, especially where, as here, the fiduciary duty at issue gave the defendant the power to act as a trustee. Therefore, because the Wellin children have sufficiently pleaded facts establishing that they are vested beneficiaries of the Revocable Trust and were harmed by Wendy's breach of her fiduciary duties, the court finds that they may bring a cause of action based on such a breach.

Having established that the Wellin children may assert such a claim, the court turns to the question of whether the Wellin children have pleaded facts showing that Wendy actually breached her fiduciary duty as Keith's power of attorney. New York law provides that a power of attorney owes fiduciary duties to the principal "[t]o act according to any instructions from the principal or, where there are no instructions, in the best interest of the principal," and that one "may be subject to liability for conduct or omissions which violate any fiduciary duty."

In this case, where the power of attorney placed Wendy in the position of trustee of the Revocable Trust, the fiduciary duties Wendy owed pursuant to this power encompassed the trustee's duty to act in the best interests of the settlor/lifetime beneficiary and comply with the provisions of the Revocable Trust. The complaint states that Wendy breached this duty by wrongfully transferring trust assets and spending funds in excess of the amount customarily spent by the trustee to maintain Keith and Wendy's lifestyle. The court finds that these allegations support a plausible claim against Wendy for breach of fiduciary duty and denies Wendy's motion to dismiss this claim.

* * *

E.   Count VIII—Constructive Trust

Wendy next argues that the Wellin children's cause of action for constructive trust should be dismissed because the accusations contained in the complaint are conclusory.

"An action to declare a constructive trust is in equity, and a reviewing court may find facts in accordance with its own view of the evidence." "A constructive trust will arise whenever the circumstances under which property was acquired make it inequitable that it should be retained by the one holding legal title." Constructive trusts result from "fraud, bad faith, abuse of confidence, or violation of a fiduciary duty which gives rise to an obligation in equity to make restitution" and "is resorted to by equity to vindicate right and justice or frustrate fraud." "Fraud is an essential element, although it need not be actual fraud."

As detailed in the background discussion above, the Wellin children have identified specific misconduct by Wendy, including allegedly false statements that Wendy made to Keith. Therefore, the court finds that the Wellin children have pleaded sufficient facts to survive Wendy's motion to dismiss their constructive trust claim.

* * *

III. CONCLUSION

For the foregoing reasons, the court **DENIES** Wendy's motion to dismiss the Wellin children's claims for intentional interference with inheritance, breach of fiduciary duty, breach of the prenuptial agreement related to the Wellin children's access to Keith, breach of the prenuptial agreement related to Wendy's control of Keith's separate property, breach of contract accompanied by a fraudulent act, constructive trust, barratry, and negligence per se. The court **GRANTS** Wendy's motion to dismiss the Wellin children's claim for intentional interference with prospective contractual relations/prospective economic advantage, to the extent that claim is based on the Wendy's interference with the Wellin children's expectation that they would receive certain bequests under Keith's estate planning documents. However, this claim may proceed to the extent it arises from Marjorie's anticipated purchase of the Friendship, Maine property.

AND IT IS SO ORDERED.

It is interesting that the *Wellin* court does not categorize any of its lengthy opinion as a discussion of the policy questions implicated by an adoption of the tort of intentional interference with an expectancy. Perhaps that is to be expected given that the court is trying to predict what the Supreme Court of South Carolina would do. Still, it might not have been out of place for the court to say that it would predict the state court to favor justice over the increased costs of litigation.

(e) Multiple Wills and Codicils

Sometimes, a testator has executed more than one instrument that is admissible to probate. To the extent it is possible, the various wills are read together, but often the wills are inconsistent. If so, the priority is given on the basis of time, with more recent wills overriding earlier wills, to the extent they are inconsistent, on the obvious grounds that 1) wills are revocable and giving priority to earlier documents would interfere with that revocability and 2) later wills are more likely to express the intent of the decedent at the time of her death.

A codicil is an instrument that is intended to modify or amend an existing will. The requirements for a codicil are the same as for a will. Indeed, the UPC simply calls a codicil a "will". To be effective, a codicil requires intent in the same way that a will requires intent. Since a codicil requires intent, the question arises whether a valid codicil can supply the intent for a previously executed instrument that lacked intent at the time it was executed. The answer is that the law in some states allows intent to be supplied later, from the codicil, under the doctrine of republication by codicil.

> Example 4.05: In 1995, O executes an instrument titled "Will of 1995", meeting all requirements except intent. In 1996, O executes "1996 Codicil to Will of 1995", meeting all requirements for admission of a will to probate, including intent. O dies. A court applying the doctrine of republication by codicil can admit to probate both the 1996 Codicil and the

Will of 1995. The intent missing from the Will of 1995 when it was executed is supplied at the execution of the 1996 Codicil. (Capacity missing at the time of the earlier will might likewise be supplied under the doctrine.)

Under the doctrine of republication by codicil, the execution of a codicil also has the effect of updating a previously executed will to the codicil's date of execution.

Because a codicil is more recent than the will it amends, inconsistencies are resolved in favor of the codicil.

Example 4.06: In 2005, O properly executes a will titled "Last Will and Testament" which says, "I give to X my car and to my children, X and Y, the residue of my estate." In 2008, O properly executes a document which says, "at my death, by this document, I give my car to Z." O dies in 2009. The 2008 document is a codicil. The 2008 codicil does not expressly revoke the 2005 will; and it revokes the 2005 will by inconsistency only to the extent that the two documents conflict, which is regarding the gift of the car to X. Z gets O's car and X and Y split the rest of O's estate.

If a subsequent will includes a residuary devise disposing of all remaining assets but does not expressly revoke a prior will, a question may arise as to whether the subsequent will revokes the prior will entirely or is merely a codicil, leaving some of the prior will effective. A lawyer should make this explicit in the subsequent will by stating expressly that prior wills are revoked, if that is what is intended. In the absence of such a revoking clause, the law has varied in result. The common law took the position that the residuary clause in the subsequent will did not revoke by inconsistency any specific or general gifts in the prior will. UPC § 2–507 goes the other way, declaring that a will with a residuary clause that disposes of the decedent's entire estate presumptively revokes prior wills. However, if the subsequent will does not dispose of all assets, it is viewed, by both the UPC and the common law, as a codicil to the earlier will, allowing the earlier will to dispose of assets not devised in the later will.

(f) No-Contest Clauses

As we have seen, probate challenges based on undue influence or fraud are common and costly. The costs of the challenges fall on the public (which pays for the tribunals), the parties to other litigation (who experience delays in the resolution of their cases), the contestants, and the beneficiaries of the estates (which pay to defend against the challenge). It is understandable that testators will wish to save their estate the costs of these challenges, even though the challenge is, ostensibly, one designed to determine the true intent of the testator. One way for testators to reduce the expected cost of such challenges is to include a "no-contest" clause in the will.

A no-contest clause, or *in terrorem* clause, provides that an unsuccessful challenger to the probate of the will receives nothing (or perhaps a reduced devise). Although a successful contestant will not be harmed by the clause, the clause enhances the negative consequences of losing a challenge, and thus increases the disincentive to contest the probate of the will. In cases of successful deterrence, the devisees are spared a pointless delay, and everyone saves substantial litigation expenses. On the other hand, of course, such clauses also discourage valid challenges for undue influence or lack of capacity. Thus, no-contest clauses increase the chances of false positives, where instruments or provisions that do not reflect the intent of the decedent are admitted to probate. If a wrongdoer wishes to increase the chances of getting an unintended instrument or clause admitted to probate, that wrongdoer might include in the will a no-contest clause to reduce the chances of a challenge. And if no-contest clauses reduce challenges, wrongdoers are more likely to prey upon those who are in positions of weakness. This is obviously harmful to those who succumb to undue influence or fraud, but it can also be stressful even for those who succeed in resisting the pressures exerted by the wrongdoers.

Given these tradeoffs, it is not surprising that states vary in their friendliness toward no-contest clauses. The UPC approach to these clauses is to enforce them unless there is probable cause for the contest; some states enforce them for some challenges and not others; and Florida does not enforce them at all. How should the increased possibility of false positives and attempts to influence be weighed against increased costs of litigation and delay? Is the testator in a good position to balance the chances of false positives against the costs of litigation? What is the best policy regarding the enforcement of no-contest clauses, to enforce them or not? Should persons worried about being a victim of fraud be able to opt out of no-contest clauses for their future wills? Should a state set up a registry that would allow such private ordering? To what extent should the law allow forum building, construction of a legal regime to suit the preferences of a testator?

When you draft a will for a domiciliary of a state that honors no-contest clauses, should you include a no-contest clause? In some situations, they make sense. If the will treats heirs or close family members substantially unequally, the disfavored relatives might be likely to challenge the will and a no-contest clause might save assets, or even save the will. However, the clause will work only if the disfavored relatives (or others who would take under a previous will) are given something substantial enough to deter them. A testator might chafe at the thought of giving these people anything at all.

The scope of a no-contest clause should be tailored to the situation. Broadly drafted no-contest clauses prohibit challenges to any provision in the will. Such a clause could be triggered by a challenge to the appointment of the designated executor. After the death of the testator, however, the beneficiaries might have good reasons for opposing the named executor. Similarly, beneficiaries might have good reasons to challenge the appointment of a trustee. In *Capobianco v. Dischino*, 98 Mass.App.Ct. 1101 (2020), a trust beneficiary triggered a no-contest clause by attempting to remove trustees. He lost his beneficial interest in the trust. You should point out to your client that the effect of the *in terrorem* clause might be to disinherit a beneficiary who made a well-founded, though ultimately unsuccessful, challenge. Also consider whether a revocable inter vivos trust might reduce the chances of a challenge without risking disinheritance of the objects of the client's beneficence. We will study trusts later in this book.

(g) Motivational Clauses

Wills often include a testator's reasons for the dispositions in the will. These statements can be helpful to the executor in arguing to claimants or to a court that the testator had good reasons for making gifts to some beneficiaries and for choosing not to make gifts to other persons. However, a drafter should be very careful when including such clauses and it is important to make sure that the statements are not false. First, false statements a testator publishes in a will could form the basis of a libel suit, leading to the ironic result that the words added in an attempt to avoid litigation over the estate became the basis for litigation. Second, false statements might provide evidence of lack of capacity, which is a separate basis on which a court can deny a will's admission to probate.

2. CAPACITY

As seen above, for an instrument to be admitted to probate as a will, it must have been intended to be the decedent's will. But intent is not the only requirement relating to the mental state or condition of the decedent. For the decedent's intent to matter, the decedent had to have capacity to execute a will. With some exceptions in some jurisdictions,[1] the law does not care about the decedent's intent if he was not thinking well enough, or if he was not old enough.

UPC § 2–501

SECTION 2–501. WHO MAY MAKE WILL. An individual 18 or more years of age who is of sound mind may make a will.

Why should minors with sound minds be excluded from the class of persons able to make a will? Would litigation over the capacity of minors or possible undue influence outweigh the vindication of their interests dignity and autonomy? At one time, English law allowed females of the age of 12 and males of the age of 14 to make wills. At other times, the age was even lower. Should minors be able to make wills of their social media assets even if not their ordinary financial assets?

Whether a person is old enough is usually not hard to determine, but whether a person had a sound mind is the source of much litigation. The phrasing of the test for mental capacity varies across states. Sometimes, mental capacity is divided into two forms, general and specific, with different tests for each, and potentially different consequences for an absence of capacity.

(a) General Mental Capacity

For a will to be admitted to probate, the testator must have had general testamentary capacity at the time it was executed. If the

---

[1] Indiana allows a person under 18 to make a will if she is in the military:

IC 29–1–5–1 Sound mind; age; armed forces

Sec. 1.   Any person of sound mind who is eighteen (18) years of age or older, or who is younger and a member of the armed forces, or of the merchant marine of the United States, or its allies, may make a will. (Formerly: Acts 1953, c.112, s.501; Acts 1971, P.L.404, SEC.1.)"

Why should the law extend capacity to minors in the military? Should loggers and fishers be allowed to make wills too? They have high death rates.

testator did not have general testamentary capacity, the court will deny probate to the entire will. To find that a person had general capacity, the courts often require that the testator be capable of knowing and understanding 1) the nature and extent of her property, 2) the natural objects of her bounty, and 3) the dispositions made and not made by the will. Sometimes courts also require that the testator be capable of forming an orderly plan of disposition. Note what is generally not required. The testator need not know exactly what her property is; she need only be capable of knowing what it is. The testator may be unaware of the death or birth of the natural objects of her bounty, that is to say, her close relatives and friends. The testator need not give her property to those natural objects, but she must be capable of knowing who they are and that she is not providing for them. In many states, the threshold for testamentary capacity is lower than the threshold for contractual capacity or the capacity for making an inter vivos gift. This higher bar for gifts inter vivos might be justified on the ground that the state has an interest in preventing people from impoverishing their later living selves, but that interest dies with them. The respect that lawmakers accord to the intent of decedents is further indicated by the fact that being a felon or alien is no bar to making a valid will. In a majority of jurisdictions, capacity is initially presumed and the burden of proof is on the contestant to show that the testator did not have capacity at the time of execution.

Lack of capacity to execute a will cannot be overcome by execution of a durable power of attorney. Although an agent holding a durable power of attorney can act for the principal after the principal becomes incapacitated, the agent cannot make, amend, or revoke a principal's will.

What can happen if the decedent lacks capacity?

IN RE DISCIPLINARY ACTION AGAINST KUHN

Supreme Court of North Dakota, 2010
785 N.W.2d 195

PER CURIAM.

* * *

I.

* * * In 2005, Kuhn wrote a will for Jake Leno. In that will, Jake Leno devised his condominium to his daughter, Kathleen McKinley.

In 2006, McKinley filed a petition for appointment of a guardian/ conservator for Jake Leno. The district court appointed Guardian and Protective Services, Inc. ("GAPS") as Jake Leno's temporary guardian/conservator. The district court also appointed a physician, guardian ad litem, and visitor to meet with Jake Leno and report back to the district court.

* * *

At the hearing on the guardianship/conservatorship petition, Kuhn represented Jake Leno's sons, Ronald Leno and Randy Leno. Ronald Leno and Randy Leno testified they were willing to serve as Jake Leno's guardians/conservators. Jake Leno testified he did not think he needed a guardian/conservator. The district court found Jake Leno "has a current medical diagnosis of Parkinson's disease with adult onset diabetes and exhibits short term memory loss." The district court concluded Jake Leno was incapacitated and appointed GAPS full guardian and conservator, with full control over his place of residence, legal matters, financial matters, and medical treatment.

In 2007, an unidentified person contacted Kuhn's office and told Kuhn's receptionist Jake Leno wanted his will changed. Kuhn testified at the disciplinary hearing that he thought an employee of GAPS had contacted his office to change the will. However, Kuhn acknowledged he did not contact GAPS to verify whether one of its employees had called his office. Kuhn learned later one of Jake Leno's caregivers had contacted his office. After speaking with Jake Leno, Kuhn drafted a new will that gave all of Jake Leno's property, including the condominium, to the three children equally, instead of devising the condominium solely to McKinley.

Kuhn testified that at the time he wrote the will he "knew [Jake Leno] had been declared incompetent" and "there was allegations that he had dementia of the Alzheimer's type." Kuhn took two of his employees to Jake Leno's apartment to act as witnesses as Jake Leno executed the new will. Kuhn testified at the disciplinary hearing regarding his state of mind:

> I was a little uneasy because he was in—under a judicial order that said he was incompetent. So I questioned him, I questioned his caregiver to ask her if he's—how he's doing. And she said, "Oh, he's fine. He knows what's going on, and, Jake, he knows." And I questioned him in front of the witnesses—in front of the two witnesses about the will. Told

him exactly what—what he was doing. And said, "Now, are you sure this is what you want to do? This is what's going to happen." And he said, "Yes." So, I mean, my impression that day was that he was fine.

* * *

In 2009, counsel for the Disciplinary Board filed a petition alleging Kuhn had violated N.D.R. Prof. Conduct 1.2(a), Scope of Representation and Allocation of Authority Between Client and Lawyer; 1.4(a)(2) and (b), Communication; 1.7(a) and (c), Conflict of Interest; and 1.14, Client With Limited Capacity, by his actions regarding Jake Leno's guardianship/conservatorship hearing and second will. * * *

The allegations in the Petition for Discipline of misconduct assert a violation of N.D.R. Prof. Conduct 1.14, Comment 5

> which provides that if the client has an appointed representative, the lawyer should ordinarily look to the representative for decisions on behalf of the client, in that Kuhn prepared a new will for Jake Leno without having first looked to Guardian & Protective Services, Inc., as the court-appointed guardian and conservator of Jake Leno, for decision-making authority to make a new will.

* * * The hearing panel also concluded Kuhn violated N.D.R. Prof. Conduct 1.14, Client With Limited Capacity, when he "prepared a new will for Jake without communicating with or securing decision-making authority from GAPS, the court-appointed guardian and conservator with full authority over Jake's legal matters."* * *

* * *

II.

* * *

B.

Rule 1.14 of the North Dakota Rules of Professional Conduct states, in pertinent part:

> (a) When a client's capacity to make adequately considered decisions in connection with a representation is limited, whether because of minority, mental impairment, or for some other reason, the lawyer shall, as far as

reasonably possible, maintain a normal client-lawyer relationship with the client.

(b) When the lawyer reasonably believes that the client has limited capacity, is at risk of substantial physical, financial, or other harm unless action is taken, and the client cannot adequately act in the client's own interest, the lawyer may take reasonably necessary protective action, including consulting with individuals or entities that have the ability to take action to protect the client and, in appropriate cases, seeking the appointment of a guardian ad litem, conservator, or guardian.

Comment 5 of the rule states, "If the client has an appointed representative, the lawyer should ordinarily look to the representative for decisions on behalf of the client. The lawyer should be cognizant of the extent of the powers and duties conferred upon the client's appointed representative." * * *

Kuhn argues he did not violate Rule 1.14 because he was abiding by his client's wishes. Kuhn cites Comment 3 of Rule 1.14:

The fact that a client is a minor or has limited capacity does not diminish the lawyer's obligation to treat the client with attention and respect. Even if the person has an appointed representative, the lawyer should as far as possible accord the represented person the status of client, particularly in maintaining communication.* * *

Kuhn argues he was fulfilling his duty to give Jake Leno attention and respect when he drafted the new will.

* * *

* * * Counsel for the Disciplinary Board cites North Dakota Ethics Opinion No. 09–03. [In that opinion, the] ethics committee cited favorably the Massachusetts Supreme Court's opinion in Guardianship of Hocker. The Massachusetts Supreme Court stated:

When a person is adjudicated incompetent . . . the necessary effect . . . is that the ward is in law . . . incapable of taking care of himself, as to all the world. The permanent guardian stands in the place of the ward in making decisions about the ward's well-being, and the guardian is held to high standards of fidelity in exercising this authority for the ward's benefit. To be sure, an adjudication of incompetency . . . does not obviate the need for a guardian or judge to consult a ward's feelings or opinions on a matter concerning his care. It does not make the ward any less worthy of dignity or respect in the eyes of the law than a competent person. It does not deprive the ward of fundamental liberty interests. But the rights and interests of one adjudicated to be incompetent must of necessity and for the benefit or advantage of the ward, often be vindicated in a manner different from that of the mentally competent.

* * *

The record shows Kuhn knew Jake Leno had been declared incapacitated and GAPS had been named his guardian with full authority over his legal matters. Kuhn was present at the guardianship hearing. He reviewed all the documents indicating Jake Leno suffered from Parkinson's disease and short-term memory loss. He concedes it was his responsibility to communicate with Jake Leno's guardian. He failed to meet this responsibility, however. Kuhn's understandable desire to give his client attention and respect does not overcome Jake Leno's incapacity to make legal decisions on his own behalf. Kuhn did not look to Jake Leno's appointed representative, as required by N.D.R. Prof. Conduct 1.14, comment 5. Kuhn persisted in executing a will that was invalid because of Jake Leno's incapacity. Furthermore, we do not ignore the fact the second will drafted by Kuhn benefitted Ronald Leno and Randy Leno, Kuhn's clients at the guardianship/conservatorship hearing. Clear and convincing evidence indicates Kuhn violated N.D.R. Prof. Conduct 1.14.

* * *

III

On the basis of the record, we * * * accept the hearing panel's finding that Kuhn clearly and convincingly violated N.D.R Prof. Conduct 1.14, Client With Limited Capacity. We order Kuhn be suspended from the practice of law for ninety days, effective August 1, 2010, and that he pay the costs of the disciplinary proceeding in the amount of $2,654.07.

The warning of *Kuhn* is clear. You could be suspended from practice if you draft a will for a person who you know is not competent. Was that the right result? The court focused on one comment in the state's rules of professional conduct: "If the client has an appointed representative, the lawyer should ordinarily look to the representative for decisions on behalf of the client. The lawyer should be cognizant of the extent of the powers and duties conferred upon the client's appointed representative." However, there is some tension within the rules. Another comment to North Dakota's rules of professional conduct said, "Even if the person has an appointed representative, the lawyer should as far as possible accord the represented person the status of client, . . ."

In many states, a guardian or conservator cannot execute a valid will for the ward. The UPC has changed its position on whether a conservator may make a will for a protected person. 1990 UPC § 5–407(b)(3) did not allow it. But 2019 UPC § 5–411(a)(7) does allow it if authorized by a court and notice is given to interested persons. For this purpose, the UPC endorses a substituted judgment approach, which looks primarily to the decision the protected person would have made.

Facts that raise questions about client capacity put the lawyer in a difficult position. The lawyer must worry about whether the client has capacity to execute a will and must also worry about whether the client is being subjected to undue influence. In Admonition No. 22-09, the Massachusetts Board of Bar Overseers admonished a lawyer for telling the client's daughter about the client's request to give the proceeds from the sale of her home to a charity rather than to a trust for her daughter and then her granddaughters' education. The lawyer had revealed confidential information and had failed to consult with the client about speaking with her daughter. In addition to taking great pains not to reveal any confidential information, the lawyer should have spent more time discussing the proposed changes with the client. Lawyers in doubt about their client's capacity can consult the ABA's ASSESSMENT OF OLDER ADULTS WITH DIMINISHED CAPACITIES: A HANDBOOK FOR LAWYERS, now in its second edition. It offers advice to lawyers in many contexts, including questions for assessing the capacity of a client.

What is general testamentary capacity?

SHEPHERD V. JONES

Court of Appeals of Arkansas, Division II, 2015
461 S.W.3d 351

GLOVER, J.

John H. Jones died in hospice care at the age of sixty-six on July 17, 2011. Two days before his death, he executed a power of attorney and last will and testament. The will bequeathed John's personal and household effects to his half-sister, appellant Marcia Jane "Janey" Shepherd; $5,000 each to siblings James Taylor Jones (appellee), Elizabeth Allison, and Virginia Crawford; $15,000 each to siblings Eugene Jones and James E. Jones, Jr.; $5,000 to St. Luke's Methodist Church; and left the remainder of his estate to Janey and to Madge Helm, a friend, in equal shares. The value of John's estate totaled over $415,000, including more than $118,000 in savings bonds and over $114,000 from two joint accounts he had held with his aunt, Eula Ruth Harrison, who predeceased him by four days.

On July 21, 2011, Arvest Trust Company (Arvest) petitioned to probate John's will and for appointment to administer John's estate. An order admitting the will to probate and appointing Arvest as personal representative of the estate was filed on July 22, 2011. A notice of contest of John's will was filed by James Taylor Jones on October 28, 2011. After a hearing on the matter, the Pulaski County Circuit Court found that John's will should be denied admission to probate. The trial court set aside and vacated that part of the July 22, 2011 order admitting the will to probate, finding that the will was not properly executed by John, that John lacked testamentary capacity at the time his will was executed, and that the will was procured by undue influence by Madge Helm and Janey Shepherd. The trial court further found that a confidential relationship existed between John, Madge, and Janey. Janey now appeals, arguing that the trial court erred in finding that the will was not properly executed, that John did not have the testamentary capacity to execute the will, and that the will was procured by undue influence by Madge and Janey. We affirm.

* * *

Testamentary Capacity & Undue Influence

Janey contends that the trial court erred in finding that John did not have the testamentary capacity to execute his will and in finding that the will was a product of undue influence. The questions of mental competency and undue influence are so closely related and interwoven that we consider them together. In a case where the mind of the testator is strong and alert, the facts constituting undue influence would be required to be far stronger than a case in which the mind of the testator was impaired, such as by disease or advancing age. Testamentary capacity means that the testator must be able to retain in his mind, without prompting, the extent and condition of his property, to comprehend to whom he is giving it, and relations of those entitled to his bounty. The relevant inquiry is not the mental capacity of the testator before or after a challenged will is signed, but rather the level of capacity at the time the will was signed. Undue influence is defined as "not the legitimate influence which springs from natural affection, but the malign influence which results from fear, coercion, or any other cause that deprives the testator of his free agency in the disposition of his property." Undue influence may be inferred from the facts and circumstances of a case, and cases involving questions of undue influence will frequently depend on a determination of witness credibility.

With regard to testamentary capacity * * *, the trial court found as follows:

* * *

31. Decedent, at the time of the making and execution of the proffered will, lacked the requisite testamentary capacity to make and execute a valid will. Decedent was in hospice care, severely ill, and regularly medicated on morphine when attorney Holzwarth contacted him, unsolicited, regarding making a will. Madge Helm described to attorney Holzwarth how Decedent's property should be devised in the will, and attorney Holzwarth followed those instructions. Helm, attorney Holzwarth, and Marcia Jane Shepherd did not tell Decedent that Eula Ruth Harrison had already died, even though all three were aware at the time the proffered will was executed that Harrison was dead. None of these individuals, and notably Holzwarth—the attorney who was drafting the will and who owed a fiduciary duty to Decedent—told Decedent about the effect Harrison's death would have on his own estate. The three individuals did not simply fail to tell Decedent he was in hospice care or that his aunt had already died. They all made conscious decisions to withhold this information from him. Decedent was unable to speak and could barely communicate with those around him,

if at all. He was wholly unable to sign his own name without substantial assistance. Attorney Holzwarth had to prompt from Decedent information regarding his property. It is clear that Decedent lacked the ability, at the time of the making and execution of the proffered will, to retain in his memory, without prompting, the nature and extent of his property or to comprehend how he was disposing of his property.

* * *

With respect to John's testamentary capacity, Janey's argument attacks the credibility determinations made by the trial court. Janey argues that James Taylor Jones offered "no credible evaluation" of John at the time of the execution of the will and "therefore failed to meet his burden on this issue." However, this ignores Larry Jones's testimony that John was not conscious and was unaware of what was happening at the time of the execution of the will; that John did not respond to attorney Holzwarth when she asked if he wanted to sign his will; that John did not say anything to Larry when Larry asked if he wanted to sign the will; and that John could not take an active part in signing his name to the will. According to Larry, John was unable to retain in his mind, without prompting, the extent and condition of his property or to comprehend to whom he was giving it. Furthermore, John was never told that Eula Ruth had passed away and that the joint accounts he held with her now belonged solely to him and would be part of his estate, nor was there any evidence that John had any idea of the value of his savings bonds; in fact, Janey's own testimony indicated that she did not know if John even knew the extent of his property, thus bolstering the fact that John was unaware of the extent of his estate. On this evidence, we cannot say that the trial court's finding that John did not have the testamentary capacity to execute his will is clearly erroneous.

* * *

Affirmed.

What was the evidence that the testator did not have the capacity to know the nature and extent of his property? Should it matter that the testator did not know about some of his property?

IN RE ESTATE OF MCINTYRE

Tennessee Court of Appeals, 2000
2000 WL 33191354

LILLARD, J.

* * *

This is a tragic case involving the contest of a holographic will. On April 28, 1996, fifty-six-year-old W.O. McIntyre ("McIntyre") committed suicide. He was survived by his wife of eighteen years, Jane McIntyre ("Mrs.McIntyre"), and two grown children from a previous marriage, daughter Teresa Burns ("Teresa") and son Stacey Keith McIntyre ("Keith"). Prior to his death, McIntyre was in a state of extreme depression, stemming in part from his relatively recent diagnosis of diabetes, and the resulting fear that his health would worsen and leave him a burden to his family.

Prior to McIntyre's death, he wrote three handwritten suicides notes. The notes, dated March 3, March 13, and April 27, 1996, were entitled "W. O. McIntyre Last Wishes Will and Notes." In them, McIntyre expressed his wish that everything he owned go to his widow, with the exception of a $25,000 bequest each to his son and daughter. Mrs. McIntyre offered the notes to the probate court as her husband's holographic will.

* * *

Mrs. McIntyre testified that her husband had been diagnosed with diabetes a couple of years before his death, and that the diagnosis upset him considerably. Although his diabetes could be controlled by pills, McIntyre worried about eventually becoming an invalid. Mrs. McIntyre testified that in the six months or so preceding her husband's suicide, his behavior changed remarkably. She said that he began to sleep a lot during the day, spend less time with his family, and was not as physically active as he previously had been.

Mrs. McIntyre testified that on March 1, 1996, McIntyre came home early from his job as a river boat captain because he was so depressed that he felt incapable of captaining the boat. At his employer's insistence, McIntyre talked to a counselor, Linda Laney ("Laney"), about his depression. He met with Laney twice, on March 7, 1996, and again on March 8, 1996. On March 13, 1996, Mrs. McIntyre met with Laney and told her that she was afraid to leave her husband alone, for fear that he would commit suicide. Laney recommended that McIntyre be hospitalized for treatment of his depression, and she scheduled an "intervention" for the next morning, March 14. On the morning of the intervention, Mrs. McIntyre found McIntyre's second suicide note, dated March 13, 1996. McIntyre was hospitalized later that day.

Shortly after he was released from the hospital, McIntyre returned to work. He had requested, and received, a demotion from captain to pilot. However, on Friday, April 26, he again left the boat early to return home. Mrs. McIntyre testified that McIntyre committed suicide on Sunday, April 28, while she was away from home. When she came home that day, she found the last suicide note, dated Saturday, April 27. In her testimony, Mrs. McIntyre expressed her opinion that McIntyre, although clearly depressed, was of sound mind when he wrote the three suicide notes.

* * *

[T]he Proponents moved the court to find that due execution of the will had been proven, and that, consequently, the burden of proof shifted to Contestants to show that McIntyre lacked testamentary capacity when he executed the will. The Contestants argued that the burden to prove testamentary capacity remained on the will's Proponents because of "suspicious circumstances" surrounding the execution of the will, namely that it consisted solely of the testator's suicide notes. The trial court ruled that the Proponents had satisfied their burden of proving due execution of the will, and that the burden then shifted to the children to show that their father lacked testamentary capacity at the time he executed the will.

The Contestants then presented testimony regarding McIntyre's testamentary capacity. McIntyre's grown children, Teresa Burns and Keith McIntyre, indicated that McIntyre had been a vibrant, energetic man, but that his personality dramatically changed in the six months prior to his death. Teresa testified that, in the six months prior to his suicide, McIntyre was frequently unclean, unshaven and sloppily dressed, and that she often found him asleep in the middle of the day. Referring to McIntyre's hospitalization for depression, Teresa testified that her father probably tried to "fake his way out" by pretending his mental state had improved. Keith testified that, after McIntyre was released from the hospital, he was uncharacteristically emotional and physically affectionate. Both Teresa and Keith acknowledged that McIntyre continued to appear aware of what he owned and continued to know close family members and friends. Keith acknowledged that his father and stepmother had a good relationship. However, Teresa maintained that McIntyre was not of sound mind when he wrote the suicide notes that served as his will.

Linda Laney testified about her counseling with McIntyre. She said that she saw McIntyre twice, several days before he was hospitalized. She testified that, although McIntyre was "deeply depressed," he was oriented as to time and place, recognized Laney, and knew who his wife, children and other family members were.

Paul King, M.D. ("Dr. King") testified by deposition that he treated McIntyre during his hospitalization. He diagnosed McIntyre as suffering from "major depression without psychotic features." Dr. King said that McIntyre's belief that his diabetes was "terrible" was an "irrational feeling" but not a delusion. He testified that the suicide notes were the result of McIntyre's "irrational feelings" about his diabetes, combined with "rational thinking" about his family and the manner in which he wanted his estate divided. Dr. King stated that McIntyre remained oriented as to time, place and person, did not become out of touch with reality, and showed no signs of being psychotic.

Another psychiatrist, Catherine Morton Greene, M.D. ("Dr. Greene") testified about McIntyre's mental state after reviewing his medical records, Linda Laney's records, and the suicide notes. Dr. Greene felt that McIntyre was having "irrational thoughts and feelings" when he wrote the suicide notes. Dr. Greene said that McIntyre's feelings of hopelessness about his rather mild case of diabetes demonstrated that he was, to a degree, "out of touch with reality." She opined that the fact that McIntyre committed suicide demonstrated that he was not thinking rationally.

After deliberation, the jury found that McIntyre had been of sound and disposing mind and had sufficient mental capacity to make the will. Consequently, on March 30, 1998, the trial court entered an order finding that the holographic will "was valid in all respects," and confirming its previous probate. In response, Contestants filed a motion for a new trial. The trial court denied the motion on June 30, 1998. The Contestants now appeal the decision of the trial court.

On appeal, the Contestants argue that the trial court erred in refusing to place the burden of proving testamentary capacity on the will's Proponents, due to the "suspicious circumstances" surrounding the death of the decedent. They contend there was no material evidence supporting the jury's verdict that the decedent possessed a sound and disposing mind at the time he executed the will. * * *

The Contestants first argue that the trial court erred by ruling that the burden was upon the Contestants to prove that McIntyre lacked testamentary capacity. They assert that McIntyre's will is suspect because it consists of suicide notes written while in a deep depression and under the influence of a delusional belief about his diabetes. They argue that these facts amount to "suspicious circumstances" surrounding the execution of McIntyre's will, and that consequently the burden to prove testamentary capacity remained on the will's proponents.

The trial court's ruling on the burden of proof in a will contest case is a conclusion of law, which we review *de novo,* with no presumption of correctness attached to the trial court's conclusion of law. A holographic will is one that is written in the testator's own hand. To be prima facie valid, "the signature and all its material provisions must be in the handwriting of the testator and his handwriting must be proved by two (2) witnesses." In this case, the testimony was undisputed that the suicide notes were entirely in the handwriting of McIntyre and were signed by him.

Ordinarily, once due execution of a will has been proven, the burden shifts to the will's contestants to prove that the will is invalid due to fraud, lack of testamentary capacity, or undue influence. This Court has stated:

> In a will contest the initial burden is upon the proponent of the will to show its prima facie validity and this is a question for the determination of the court. Upon the proponent's satisfactorily showing prima facie validity, the burden shifts to the contestant and, generally, the burden is upon the contestant to show facts relied upon to void the will.

A testator is presumed to have the capacity to execute a will. If the testator has previously been adjudicated insane, the burden to show testamentary capacity fall upon the will's proponents; in all other cases, the burden shifts to the will's contestants to show that the testator lacked testamentary capacity.

However, where "suspicious circumstances" are shown to have surrounded the execution of the will, that is, circumstances which raise doubts as to whether the testator understood the significance of his actions, the proponents have the burden of coming forward with evidence that the testator had the capacity to execute the will:

> The rules of burden of proof with regard to testamentary capacity are substantially similar to those with regard to undue influence. Ordinarily, there exists a presumption of testamentary capacity once the prima facie validity of the will is shown, but the existence of suspicious circumstances, once shown by the contestant, shifts the burden to the proponent to come forward with evidence that capacity existed, whereupon the issues go to the jury.

The burden to show the existence of suspicious circumstances is always on the contestant in a will contest case.

In this case, Contestants argue that McIntyre's delusional belief about the severity of his diabetes, the resulting suicide, and the fact that his will consists of suicide notes, amounted to suspicious circumstances which placed the burden upon Proponents to produce evidence of McIntyre's capacity. * * *

   * * *

In *Curry v. Bridges*, 325 S.W.2d 87 (Tenn.Ct.App.1959), the testator committed suicide shortly after execution of the will, and was found to have testamentary capacity. In *Curry,* the testator executed a will in which he established a trust in favor of Union University in Jackson, Tennessee. Forty-seven days later, he committed suicide by tightly sealing himself into a hand-made box in which he had rigged fire extinguishers to slowly release carbon dioxide gas. In the will contest case filed by the testator's relatives, the trial court granted a directed verdict to the will's proponents. This decision was appealed. After considering the circumstances, the Court of Appeals found that the testator "was fully capacitated at the time he made his will to understand what he was doing, to whom he wanted bequests and devises made, and the way and manner in which he wanted the trust administered." It concluded that "the deliberation with which he went about the preparation of the way that he would take his life makes it clear and unmistakable that he knew the result of his act and knew what he wanted to do," and that "he died just like he wanted to die, aloof and alone." Thus McIntyre's suicide, in and of itself, does not necessarily demonstrate lack of testamentary capacity. *See also In re Estate of Bonjean*, 413 N.E.2d 205, 208 (Ill.App.Ct.1980) ("The act of suicide, or attempted suicide, is not, per se, proof of insanity or insane delusions").

The Contestants contend, however, that even if McIntyre was generally competent, he suffered from an "insane delusion" regarding the severity of his diabetes, and that this delusion motivated his suicide and the creation of his will. A person is said to suffer from an insane delusion " 'when he conceives something extravagant or unreasonable to exist which has no existence except in his own abnormal imagination, but having once conceived the thing or conditioned [sic] to exist, it is impossible to reason him out of it.' *See also In re Estate of Breeden*, 992 P.2d 1167, 1170 (Colo.2000) (defining insane delusion as " 'persistent belief in that which has no existence in fact, and which is adhered to against all the evidence' ") (quoting *In re Cole's Estate*, 226 P.143, 145 (Colo.1924)); *In re Estate of Diaz*, 524 S.E.2d 219, 221 (Ga.1999) (insane delusion is "a delusion having no foundation in fact and that springs from a diseased condition of mind"); *In re Estate of Weil*, 518 P.2d 995, 999 (Ariz.Ct.App.1974) (insane delusion is " 'the conception of a disordered mind which imagines facts to exist of which there is no evidence and the belief in which is adhered to against all evidence and argument to the contrary' ") (quoting *Estate of Cook*, 159 P.2d 797, 802 (Ariz.1945)). The will of a testator found to suffer from an insane delusion will not be held invalid, however, unless it is shown that his delusion materially affected the terms and provisions of his will.

At trial, both psychiatrists agreed that McIntyre's persistent belief about the severity of his diabetes was "irrational"; one labeled it a delusion, the other would not. Regardless, there was no evidence that McIntyre's belief about his diabetes materially affected the terms of his will. Rather, the contestants argue that it motivated the creation of the will. Under these circumstances, we find no error in the trial court's refusal to shift the burden of showing testamentary capacity from the will's Contestants to the Proponents.

The Contestants also argue that there was no material evidence to support the verdict of the jury. They assert that no reasonable jury could conclude that McIntyre was of sound mind at the time that he wrote the suicide notes.

    * * *

A testator is deemed to have testamentary capacity if, at the time that he executes his will, he is able to know and understand the significance of his action. Generally, all that is required to show testamentary capacity is that the testator was aware of the property which he was disposing of and the manner in which it would be distributed, knew the natural objects of his bounty, and understood the significance of his disposition. "The testator must have an intelligent consciousness of the nature and effect of the act, a knowledge of the property possessed and an understanding of the disposition to be made." *Estate of Elam*, 738 S.W.2d at 171. A strong presumption exists that the testator possessed the requisite capacity to know and understand his actions at the time he executed his will. "Inquiry must center on the decedent's mental condition at the time of execution of the will, and a contestant must introduce strong evidence to establish a lack of testamentary capacity at the time of the execution of the will."

In this case, even those witnesses who expressed the belief that McIntyre had not been of sound mind at the time he wrote the suicide notes acknowledged that McIntyre always knew his family. In the notes, McIntyre listed his various accounts in detail, by name, account number, and latest account balance. He gave Mrs. McIntyre detailed instructions on the location of his savings bonds and the office of a person with whom he had placed some investments. Virtually every close family member and friend was mentioned by name. Moreover, he explained the reason for leaving the bulk of his estate to his wife, writing that she had been "a dear and understanding partner in life," and she was the one who would be "affected and hurt the most" and would "need it all." "While proof of the reason for making a disposition is not necessary, it is nevertheless relevant to show the testator knew the force and consequences of his act." Clearly there was substantial evidence that McIntyre was aware of the property of which he was disposing and the manner in which it would be distributed, the natural objects of his bounty, that he understood the nature and effect of his act.

* * *

The decision of the trial court is affirmed. Costs are assessed against the Appellants, Teresa Burns and Stacey Keith McIntyre, and their surety for which execution may issue, if necessary.

(b) Specific Mental Capacity, Insane Delusion

In addition to general testamentary capacity, a decedent must have had specific capacity with regard to persons and assets. As with general capacity, the testator must have specific capacity at one point in time, the moment of executing the will. If a testator lacks specific capacity with regard to a provision of a will, the court will deny probate to that provision or to the entire will. Put another way, a provision of a will may be denied probate if it was the product of an insane delusion. There are two basic steps to the analysis. First, did the testator have an insane delusion? Second, did it materially affect a dispositive provision in the will?

LEVIN V. LEVIN
District Court of Appeal of Florida, Fourth District, 2011
60 So.3d 1116

LEVINE, J.

Appellant, Gail Levin, challenges the will and trust executed on May 22, 2008, by the decedent, Shirley Sunshine Levin. Appellant challenges the execution on several grounds, but we find only one issue is of merit. We affirm the finding of the trial court in determining that there was no presumption of undue influence in the execution of the will and trust. We also find that the trial court did not err by denying appellant's motion for continuance and by excluding the testimony of her expert witness. We reverse only for the trial court to determine from the record, or after an evidentiary hearing, whether the decedent suffered from an "insane delusion" at the time of the execution of the will and trust.

* * *

Finally, Gail claims that the will and trust were based upon an "insane delusion." The law states that "[w]here there is an insane delusion in regard to one who is the object of the testator's bounty, which causes him to make a will he would not have made but for that delusion, the will cannot be sustained." "An insane delusion is a 'spontaneous conception and acceptance as a fact, of that which has no real existence adhered to against all evidence and reason.' "

In the present case, the mother persisted in the belief that Gail had visited her only once in about ten years. The mother told William and the attorney who prepared the will and trust that she had not seen Gail anywhere from ten to eleven years ago.[1] The mother sent Gail an email complaining that Gail had been to see her only once in

---

[1]   In the taped execution of the will and trust documents, the mother again repeated to the attorney that she had not "seen my daughter but one time in seven years."

eleven years. Gail replied and disputed in detail the mother's contention.

In the record, there was evidence that the mother and Gail had seen each other multiple times within the seven-year period preceding the execution of the testamentary documents.[2] The trial court did not address the evidence of visitations between the mother and Gail or that the evidence appeared to contradict the many assertions by the mother that Gail had not visited her in seven to eleven years. Thus, the trial court never decided whether this contradiction in evidence rose to the level of "insane delusion" and whether this incorrect statement repeated by the mother was linked to reducing the bequest to Gail from the 1987 will to the amount given to her in the disputed will and trust. We therefore reverse on this issue for the trial court to make findings on this issue either after reviewing the record or, in its discretion, after an evidentiary hearing.

In summary, we reverse and remand with directions for the trial court to decide whether the mother suffered from an insane delusion at the time she executed the will and trust that caused her to make a will that she "would not have made but for that delusion." We affirm on all other grounds.

Affirmed in part, reversed in part, and remanded.

What is an insane delusion? First, what is a delusion? Consider the American Psychiatric Association's definition in the DIAGNOSTIC AND STATISTICAL MANUAL OF MENTAL DISORDERS, 5th Edition, DSM-5 (2013), published by American Psychiatric Association Publishing.

> Delusion: "A false belief based on incorrect inference about external reality that is firmly held despite what almost everyone else believes and despite what constitutes incontrovertible and obvious proof or evidence to the contrary. The belief is not ordinarily accepted by other members of the person's culture or subculture (i.e., it is not an article of religious faith). When a false belief involves a value judgment, it is regarded as a delusion only when the judgment is so extreme as to defy credibility. . . ." (DSM-5 "Glossary of Technical Terms" Appendix p. 819).

---

[2] The record denotes that Gail and her mother saw each other in February 2001, August 2002, January 2003, September 2003, January 2004, January 2005, and March 2007.

Usually, a delusion requires a false belief, a belief that is inconsistent with reality. However, some beliefs are hard to prove true or false. How high should the standard be for proof of falsity? How convinced should a court be that the belief was false? Or, should a court avoid that issue by making truth irrelevant? At least if the propounder can show the belief was more likely to be true than false, it would make little sense to deny probate to a document that was based on such a true belief. But not all false beliefs are delusions; some are mistakes. What distinguishes a delusion from a mistake? A delusion is a false belief held despite conflicting evidence or reason. By contrast, a mistaken belief is amenable to correction by evidence or logic.

> Example 4.07: O believes his son, S, is dead. O executes a will giving everything to his daughter, D. O dies. S shows up at the funeral, decidedly not dead. Can O's will be admitted to probate? Yes; this is a sane mistake, which does not undermine O's specific capacity. We can admit the will to probate. However, if people kept telling O that his son was alive and offering evidence of that fact, then a court could find that he held a delusion.

If an insane delusion requires a belief that is false, what is the delusion in the following case?

IN RE STRITTMATER'S ESTATE
Court of Errors and Appeals of New Jersey, 1947
53 A.2d 205

Appeal from Prerogative Court.

Proceeding in the matter of the estate of Louisa F. Strittmater, deceased. From a decree of the Essex County Orphans' Court admitting Strittmater's to probate the will of the deceased, the contestants appealed to the Prerogative Court, claiming that deceased was insane. From a decree of the Prerogative Court setting aside the probate, the proponents appeal.

Decree affirmed.

The opinion of the Vice Ordinary Bigelow. follows:

This is an appeal from a decree of the Essex County Orphans' Court admitting to probate the will of Louisa F. Strittmater. Appellants challenge the decree on the ground that testatrix was insane.

The only medical witness was Dr. Sarah D. Smalley, a general practitioner who was Miss Strittmater's physician all her adult life. In her opinion, decedent suffered from paranoia of the Bleuler type of split personality. The factual evidence justifies the conclusion. But I regret not having had the benefit of an analysis of the data by a specialist in diseases of the brain.

The deceased never married. Born in 1896, she lived with her parents until their death about 1928, and seems to have had a normal childhood. She was devoted to both her parents and they to her. Her admiration and love of her parents persisted after their death to 1934, at least. Yet four years later she wrote: 'My father was a corrupt, vicious, and unintelligent savage, a typical specimen of the majority of his sex. Blast his wormstinking carcass and his whole damn breed.' And in 1943, she inscribed on a photograph of her mother 'That Moronic she-devil that was my mother.'

Numerous memoranda and comments written by decedent on the margins of books constitute the chief evidence of her mental condition. Most of them are dated in 1935, when she was 40 years old. But there are enough in later years to indicate no change in her condition. The Master who heard the case in the court below, found that the proofs demonstrated 'incontrovertably her morbid aversion to men' and 'feminism to a neurotic extreme.' This characterization seems to me not strong enough. She regarded men as a class with an insane hatred. She looked forward to the day when women would bear children without the aid of men, and all males would be put to death at birth. Decedent's inward life, disclosed by what she wrote, found an occasional outlet such as the incident of the smashing of the clock, the killing of the pet kitten, vile language, etc. On the other hand,—and I suppose this is the split personality,—Miss Strittmater, in her dealings with her lawyer, Mr. Semel, over a period of several years, and with her bank, to cite only two examples, was entirely reasonable and normal.

Decedent, in 1925, became a member of the New Jersey branch of the National Women's Party. From 1939 to 1941, and perhaps later, she worked as a volunteer one day a week in the New York office, filing papers, etc. During this period, she spoke of leaving her estate to the Party. On October 31, 1944, she executed her last will, carrying this intention into effect. A month later, December 6, she died. Her only relatives were some cousins of whom she saw very little during the last few years of her life.

The question is whether Miss Strittmater's will is the product of her insanity. Her disease seems to have become well developed by 1936. In August of that year she wrote, 'It remains for feministic organizations like the National Women's Party, to make exposure of women's "protectors" and "lovers" for what their vicious and contemptible selves are.' She had been a member of the Women's Party for eleven years at that time, but the evidence does not show that she had taken great interest in it. I think it was her paranoic condition, especially her insane delusions about the male, that led her to leave her estate to the National Women's Party. The result is that the probate should be set aside.

PER CURIAM.

The decree under review will be affirmed for the reasons stated in the opinion of Vice Ordinary Bigelow.

What sorts of unconventional views or preferences are evidence of a lack of capacity? Should evidence of lack of capacity be limited to beliefs that are very likely to be factually false? Courts often use the phrase "insane delusion". Does the word "insane" add anything to the word "delusion"? Consider the following case.

DOUGHERTY V. RUBENSTEIN
Court of Special Appeals of Maryland, 2007
914 A.2d 184

EYLER, J.

The "insane delusion rule" of testamentary capacity came into being almost 200 years ago, as the invention of British jurists in *Dew v. Clark,* 162 Eng. Rep. 410 (Prerog.1826). The rule was devised to cover a gap in the existing law, which held that "idiots and persons of non-sane memory" could not make wills, *see* 34 & 35 Hen. 7, ch. 5 (1534), but accepted as valid the will of a testator "who knew the natural objects of his or her bounty, the nature and extent of his or her property, and could make a 'rational' plan for disposition, but who nonetheless was as crazy as a March hare[.]"

In the *Dew* case, a father insisted that his grown daughter, who by all accounts was a well-behaved, sweet, and docile person, was the devil incarnate. The father's wife had died in childbirth, and so as a young child the daughter was raised for the most part away from the father, by nannies and in boarding schools. The father's peculiar thinking about her first manifested itself when, in response to a letter reporting that the child was suffering "chilblains" that were "gross," the father went on a tirade, sending letter after letter insisting that the child was "gross" in every way.

By the time his daughter was 8 or 9 years old, the father spoke of her only as wicked, having vices not possible of a girl that young, depraved in spirit, vile, of unequaled depravity, deceitful, and violent in temper. He told others that she was a child of the devil and a "special property of Satan." When the child came to live with him, he treated her as a servant and physically tortured her.

In 1818, the father made a will that disinherited his daughter. Three years later, he was the subject of a writ *"de lunatico inquirendo"* and was declared by a court of chancery to be of unsound mind. He died later that year.

In a caveat proceeding by the daughter, the evidence showed that the daughter was known by all for her good disposition and that the father had boasted to others that he lavished his daughter with love and material items, when the exact opposite was true. The probate court found that, although in 1818, when the will was made, the father's behavior was usual in all respects, except toward his daughter, his warped thinking about her was a delusion that "did and could only proceed from, and be founded in, insanity." The court further found that the father's "partial insanity" or "monomania"— insanity about a particular subject—about the evil nature of his daughter had caused him to disinherit her. On that basis, the court held that the father had been without testamentary capacity when he made his will, and set the will aside.

Within a few years of the decision in *Dew v. Clark,* the insane delusion rule made its way into will contest cases in the United States, first appearing in the Maryland law of estates and trusts in *Townshend v. Townshend,* 7 Gill. 10 (1848).[2] Since then, appellate opinions about the insane delusion rule have been a rarity in this

---

[2] The *Townshend* case is a startling example of the changes in American society and law in the past 200 years. There, a testator slave-owner made a will in which he freed his slaves and bequeathed all of his property to them. When he died, his relatives brought a caveat proceeding, seeking to have the will set aside. The evidence disclosed, prophetically, that the testator had claimed to have spoken "face to face" with God, who directed him how to dispose of his property "for the safety of his soul." The relatives argued that the testator was laboring under an insane delusion that God wanted him to free his slaves and give them his property, and that that delusion produced the will. A jury in the caveat proceeding found in favor of the caveators. The Court of Appeals reversed on evidentiary issues and remanded the matter for further proceedings.

state—with seven squarely addressing the issue, the last of which was published by the Court of Appeals in 1973.

In the case before us, James J. Dougherty, IV ("Jay"), the appellant, invoked the insane delusion rule before the Circuit Court for Harford County, sitting as the Orphans' Court, in an effort to set aside the June 9, 1998 Will of his father, James J. Dougherty, III ("James"), the decedent, which disinherited him. Jay is James's only child. According to Jay, James's Will was the product of an insane delusion that Jay had stolen his money. The Will named James's sister, Janet C. Rubenstein, the appellee, personal representative ("PR") of James's estate and bequeathed virtually all of James's assets to Rubenstein and his two other sisters, Elizabeth J. Hippchen and Dorothy D. Schisler. The estate was comprised mainly of James's house, valued at about $200,000.

* * *

The evidence, viewed in a light most favorable to the verdict, showed the following. James and Jay had a rocky father-son relationship over the years. When Jay was a teenager, James divorced Jay's mother. That led to a four-year estrangement between the two, beginning in 1986, when Jay was 18 years old. In 1990, at the urging of a friend, Jay reinitiated contact with his father. The two were close for the next seven years. During that time, Jay talked to James by telephone daily and visited him regularly.

On October 26, 1990, James executed a Last Will and Testament that appointed Rubenstein as PR and left his estate to Jay.

* * *

On March 20, 1996, James executed a Power of Attorney appointing Jay as his attorney-in-fact. On January 11, 1997, James designated Jay as the primary beneficiary of his life insurance policy.

The chain of events most immediately relevant to the issue on appeal began on December 9, 1997, when James suffered a minor stroke and was admitted to Fallston General Hospital. He was diagnosed with congestive heart failure and dilated cardiomyopathy (an enlarged heart caused by alcohol abuse). During the hospitalization, James often was disoriented and confused and had trouble expressing himself and understanding what was being said to him. He was rarely oriented to where he was or what day or time it was.

* * *

Dr. Freilich recommended that James be placed in a nursing home. Jay and his wife Christy decided instead to place him in the Cantler's Personal Care Home ("Cantler Home"), which the doctors referred to as a boarding home. James adamantly objected, insisting that he be returned to his own house to live.

On January 5, 1998, James was discharged from Harford Memorial and was transported to the Cantler Home. There, he was assigned a small private bedroom with access to a common area and to a bathroom that he shared with three other residents. The other residents of the Cantler Home were considerably older than James, who was 52.

By all accounts, James was miserable at the Cantler Home. He complained incessantly to his sisters, his mother, his friends, and Jay and Christy about being there. He told his sisters that he did not have access to the telephone because it was located in a locked area of the home. When Richard Hodges, an old friend, visited James at the Cantler Home, the first thing James said was that he wanted help to "get out." James told him that the owners of the home kept the residents locked downstairs, even for meals. James said he had asked Jay and Christy to "get me out of here," but they would not, because they wanted "to keep me here."

James's sisters and his mother visited him at the Cantler Home and were disturbed by the conditions they saw. James was in a small area sitting on a hard chair. The first thing he said when they walked in was, "Get me out of here before I go crazy like the rest of them." One of the sisters sat on a chair not realizing it was covered with urine from another boarder.

Every other day, Jay tried to visit James at the Cantler Home. James "wanted nothing to do with [him]," however, because James was angry that Jay had placed him in the home instead of letting him move back to his own house. About a week after James moved into the Cantler Home, Jay and Christy left for an annual five-day ski trip with Christy's family. While they were away, Rubenstein removed James from the Cantler Home and returned him to his house.

When Jay and Christy returned from their trip, they learned that James was back at home. They went to see him. Jay had started handling his father's financial affairs when James was admitted to the hospital, and therefore was in possession of all of James's financial records. Jay and Christy brought the financial records with them because James "needed to take [them] back over." James lashed out at Jay, accusing him of stealing his money and saying that, to James, Jay "didn't exist." Jay tried to show James the financial records, to prove that nothing had been stolen, but James would not look at the records or listen to what Jay had to say.

Over the next few weeks, Jay tried to reason with James, but James ignored him. He insisted that Jay had stolen money from him. James told Jay, "As far as I'm concerned, you are dead." That was the last time the two saw each other.

* * *

From 1998 until his death in 2004, James lived alone. There was much conflicting testimony about his mental state during those years. * * *

James complained to almost all of his friends and family members that Jay had stolen his money. * * *

* * *

James also continued to complain to many of his friends and family members that Jay had put him in the Cantler Home against his wishes. He described the Cantler Home as a prison. He believed that Jay had sent him there to live permanently.

James died on October 29, 2004, never having reconciled with his son. * * *

* * *

DISCUSSION

The sole issue for decision in this appeal is whether the trial judge erred in concluding that the Will was not the product of an insane delusion on the part of the testator.

Jay argues that the court committed legal error by requiring proof not only that James was suffering from an insane delusion that produced the Will, but also that the delusion was caused by a mental illness. He further argues that the evidence adduced at trial compelled a factual finding that, when James made his Will on June 9, 1998, he was experiencing an insane delusion that he (Jay) had stolen his money; and that the Will was a product of that insane delusion. That being so, the court was obligated to set the Will aside.

Rubenstein counters that the orphans' court properly rejected Dr. Freilich's opinion that James had been suffering from dementia; and the evidence supported the judge's finding that, on June 9, 1998, James was competent to execute the Will. Alternatively, Rubenstein asserts that, even if the orphans' court erred in finding that James's mistaken belief was *not* an insane delusion, that error was harmless, because the court also found that James's decision to disinherit Jay was based in part upon a true belief: that Jay had placed him in the Cantler Home against his wishes.

* * *

A testator's "insane delusion," also called "monomania," is in the law a type of unsoundness of mind that will invalidate his will, for lack of capacity, if the delusion produced the disposition made in the will. The testator's delusion must have been *insane* and his will must have been a consequence of the insane delusion, however. *Benjamin v. Woodring*, 268 Md. 593, 601 (1973). *See also Sellers v. Qualls*, 206 Md. 58, 66 (1954) (holding that testatrix's delusion that her sister tried to poison her, even if insane, did not control the making of her will and therefore will would not be set aside on that basis); *Brown v. Fidelity Trust Co.*, 126 Md. 175, 182–83 (1915) (holding that even if grantor of trust was operating under an insane delusion when she disposed of certain property, the trust would not be set aside because there was no evidence that the trust resulted from the delusion).

The Court of Appeals has said that an "insane delusion" is "a belief in things impossible, or a belief in things possible, but so improbable under the surrounding circumstances, that no man of sound mind could give them credence." *Johnson, supra*, 105 Md. at 85–86, 65 A. 918. It also has defined the term to mean "a false belief for which there is no reasonable foundation . . . concerning which [the testator's] mind is not open to permanent correction through argument or evidence." *Doyle v. Rody*, 180 Md. 471, 479 (1942). Eccentricity, peculiar beliefs (such as in spiritualism or healing powers), and hostility or aversion to one relative or another are not, standing alone, insane delusions. *See Brown v. Ward*, 53 Md. 376 (1880) (testatrix who spoke to spirits, believed they could heal diseases, did not believe in the Bible, and despised some of her relatives was not suffering from an insane delusion when she made her will).

"Insane delusion" or "monomania" insanity is not a general defect of the mind. It is an insanity directed to something specific, that is, a particular person or thing. A testator can be laboring under the influence of an insane delusion while otherwise acting and appearing competent.

Before analyzing the issues raised by Jay on appeal, it will be helpful to review the two Maryland appellate cases in which a decision to set aside a will on the ground of insane delusion testamentary incapacity has been affirmed, and the one Maryland case in which a "directed verdict" in favor of a caveatee was reversed, upon a determination that the evidence adduced by the caveator was legally sufficient to make the insane delusion issue one of fact.

In *Johnson v. Johnson*, 105 Md. 81 (1907), the evidence showed that the testator and his wife married in 1898, and then had two children. The testator already had four children from a prior marriage. Until the wife's second pregnancy, the couple and their child lived happily and the testator showed pride in his family and fondness for them. Suddenly, and for no apparent reason, the husband started abusing the wife and accusing her of being unfaithful. He insisted that their child and the unborn baby were not his. After the second child was born, he denied paternity of both children and treated his wife and the children with such harshness, hostility, and aversion that the wife was forced to leave the home. The evidence showed that there was no rational basis whatsoever for the testator's obsessive belief about his wife and children.

In late 1904, the testator made a will that left nothing to his wife and two youngest children; his entire estate was bequeathed to his four oldest children from his first marriage. The testator died eight months later, in August 1905. The wife challenged the will on the ground that the testator was laboring under the insane delusion that his two youngest children had been fathered by someone else. The parties agreed that the will was the product of this false belief. Their dispute centered upon whether the false belief was an insane delusion.

The Court held that a testator's hostility or aversion toward a particular close family member (or members) is not alone sufficient to prove insanity; however, such an aversion that is without cause and is founded upon a delusion may be. In deciding that the evidence supported a finding that the testator's delusion was insane, the Court relied upon *Bell v. Lee*, 28 Grant, Ch. R.U.C. 50 (1883), in which the Chancery Court of Upper Canada held that "a fixed and unalterable conviction on the part of the testator that his child was illegitimate was evidence of an insane delusion, when it appeared that there was not a scintilla of evidence to support such a belief." In *Bell,* the court, quoting Sir James Hannen in *Boughton v. Knight,* L.R. 3 Prob. & Div., 64, explained:

> "It is unfortunately not a thing unknown to parents, and in justice to women I am bound to say that it is more frequently the case with fathers than mothers, that they take unduly harsh views of the character of their children, some especially. That is not unknown. But there is a limit, beyond which one feels that it ceases to be a question of harsh, unreasonable judgment and character, and that the repulsion which a parent exhibits towards one or more of his children must proceed from some mental defect in himself. It is so contrary to the whole current of human nature that a man should not only form a harsh judgment of his children, but that he should put that into practice so as to do them injury, or deprive them of advantages which most men desire above all things to confer upon their children. I say there is a point at which such repulsion and aversion are in themselves evidence of unsoundness in mind."

Johnson, supra, 105 Md. at 87–88, 65 A. 918.

The *Johnson* Court found that the testator had been suffering from an insane delusion, adopting the view of the New York Court of Appeals, in *Am. Seamen's Friend Soc'y v. Hopper*, 33 N.Y. 619, 624 (1865):

> "If a person persistently believes supposed facts, which have no real existence except in his perverted imagination, and against all evidence and probability, and conducts himself, however logically, upon the assumption of their existence, he is, so far as they are concerned, under a morbid delusion; and delusion in that sense is insanity. Such a person is essentially mad or insane on those subjects, although on other subjects he may reason, act and speak like a sensible man."

Johnson, supra, 105 Md. at 88.

Doyle v. Rody, 180 Md. 471 (1942), concerned a trust bank account established by a grantor shortly before his death. The grantor had a wife, a brother, and nephews and nieces. He had been separated from his wife for two years, during which he lived in a boarding house. In late 1939, at the age of 68, he was briefly hospitalized and was diagnosed with senility and hardening of the arteries. Two days after being discharged from the hospital, he went to Westminster to visit his brother.

A few days later, the grantor walked into a police station in Baltimore City, in a dazed and confused state, claiming that he had been robbed. He was carrying with him some medicines, $26.47 in cash, a bankbook showing an account with a balance of $11,000, and a piece of paper bearing his niece's address. The police contacted the niece, who with her husband retrieved the grantor from the station house and kept him at their house for the night, giving him food and drink.

The next day, the niece helped the grantor get organized and took him to his boarding house, where he wanted to be. When they arrived, he became insistent that his clothes had been taken away, when they had not. The niece called a doctor for assistance, but before help arrived the grantor ran away. He managed to return to his brother's house in Westminster. There, he insisted that his niece and her husband had "ganged up against [him]" and had held him at their house against his will. He became obsessed with the thought that his niece and her husband had conspired to injure him and to rob him of his money. There was no basis in fact for this belief; on the contrary, the niece had treated the grantor kindly.

The brother in Westminster took the grantor to the bank and had him transfer his $11,000 into a new trust account, in both of their names, the balance to be paid at the death of either to the survivor. About a month later, the grantor died. The administrator of his estate brought suit, seeking a declaration that the trust account funds belonged to the estate and not to the brother. The chancellor found upon the evidence that, when the grantor established the trust account, he was operating under the insane delusion that his niece had stolen money from him; and the trust account benefitting the brother upon the grantor's death was the product of that delusion. The Court of Appeals affirmed the decree, remarking:

> Th[is] case falls within the definition of an insane delusion:
> a false belief, for which there is no reasonable foundation,
> and which would be incredible under similar circumstances
> to the same person if he were of sound mind, and concerning

which his mind is not open to permanent correction through argument or evidence.

Id. at 479. The Court observed that the grantor's false belief that he had been robbed, which prompted his visit to the police station, became misdirected, for no reason, toward his niece and her husband, the only family members who actually had helped him. The Court drew a distinction between "eccentricities or peculiarities of behavior[,]" which are not sufficient in and of themselves "to constitute mental incapacity[,]" and a "delusion, which was calculated to pervert [a testator's] judgment and control his will in respect to the disposition of his estate." When the latter is the case, "the court should hold that [the testator] did not possess testamentary capacity, although he may have been rational and sane on other subjects. . . . It has been specifically held by this court that violent dislike for one's near relatives, when founded upon an insane delusion, may be proof of his insanity."

In the most recent Maryland case addressing the insane delusion rule, the Court of Appeals reversed a "directed verdict" granted in favor of the caveatee in a will contest case. The Court held that the evidence adduced by the caveator at trial had been legally sufficient to make it a question of fact whether the testator was under the influence of an insane delusion when he made a will disinheriting his wife. In *Benjamin v. Woodring*, 268 Md. 593 (1973), the testator made his will about a month before he died from an overdose of prescription medication. In a handwritten note penned about five weeks before he died, the testator ranted about his wife's infidelity during and before their marriage and said that he would leave her nothing after his death, as punishment.

The testator never spoke of this with his wife directly. Instead, his manner toward her suddenly changed; he became withdrawn during the six months prior to his death. There also was evidence that the testator confided in a friend his belief that his wife had been unfaithful. The friend testified that he tried to persuade the testator that there was no truth to his belief, to no avail. There was no evidence whatsoever that the testator's wife ever had been unfaithful to him. The testator's false belief in his wife's infidelity was a preoccupation that seemed to have entered the testator's mind out of the blue, with no basis in fact.

The Court held that the testator's letter, the friend's testimony, and the evidence that there was no truth to the testator's belief about his wife constituted legally sufficient evidence to support a finding that the testator was laboring under an insane delusion that resulted in the disposition in his will; therefore, the issue of testamentary capacity should have been submitted to the trier of fact for decision.

The insane delusions in these three cases share common features. All were negative false beliefs about the character of a particular close relative of the testator that were not connected to any reality or true experience, existing only in the testator's (or grantor's) mind. Even an illogical thought process or generalization could not link the negative false belief to some true fact about the subject of the delusion. Not only was there no evidence in any of the cases that the subject of the delusion had done whatever it was the testator was convinced he or she had done; there also was no evidence that the subject of the delusion had done *anything* negative toward the testator (or any one else) that could account, even irrationally, for the testator's wrath. The delusions did not suggest mistake, unreasonableness, confusion, stubbornness, poor judgment, denial, or willfulness; they only could be explained by a deranged mind.

Mindful of the above, we return to the case at bar. Jay's first argument is strictly legal. He maintains that the trial court erred by adding an element to the insane delusion rule and then basing its finding that there was not an insane delusion upon the absence of proof of that element. Specifically, he complains that the trial court not only required proof that James's delusion was insane and that it resulted in the disinheritance, but also that the delusion was caused by a mental disease. He argues that the controlling cases hold that proof that the testator was suffering from an insane delusion gives rise to a reasonable inference that he was mentally ill; and therefore the existence of a mental disease need not be separately proven.

We do not read the trial judge's references, in his ruling, to a "mental disease" as injecting an additional element of proof into the insane delusion rule. The judge framed the question before him as whether James's "false belief" that Jay had stolen from him was "the product of a mental disease[,]" and ultimately found that the evidence did not show that James's "delusion or incorrect belief was the product of a mental disease[.]" It is clear that the judge was using "mental disease" and "insanity" interchangeably, and that his references showed his understanding that it is not sufficient that the testator have held a false belief or a delusion; it also is necessary that the false belief or delusion was insane, i.e., the product of a mental disease. Indeed, in one state in which the courts have continued to use the somewhat antiquated medical label "monomania" to mean an insane delusion, the supreme court observed: "Monomania is *a mental disease* which leaves the sufferer sane generally but insane on a particular subject or class of subjects." The court in the case at bar did not add an element to the insane delusion rule, and therefore did not commit legal error.

Jay next argues that the application of the insane delusion rule to the evidence adduced at trial compelled a finding that James disinherited him due to an insane delusion that Jay had stolen his money. Jay points out that there was no evidence that he had stolen James's money (or that any of James's money had been stolen), as the parties stipulated, and therefore James's belief plainly was false; that no amount of reasoning could get James to change his mind about his false belief, and James's mind was not open to being changed, even by records that would have shown conclusively that no money was missing; that the false belief arose soon after a hospitalization during which James was unable to understand what was being said to him or to communicate and was disoriented; that while James's functional abilities improved over time, after he was discharged from the Cantler Home, he could not overcome the false belief that Jay had stolen his money; and all of the evidence, and especially that of Mr. Siebert, a disinterested person, showed that James left nothing to Jay in his Will because he was convinced that Jay already had all of his money.

Beginning with the last point, we note that the orphans' court indeed found that James's false belief that Jay had stolen from him had caused James to disinherit Jay. The court observed that James also was angry with Jay for moving him into the Cantler Home but that "that was not a false belief"; and that, if the false belief (about stealing money) was an insane delusion "then it's going to invalidate the Will. If it is not, then the Will stands, given the other findings I made." So, the court in fact found, as Jay argues it was compelled to find, that the delusion about his having stolen money prompted James to disinherit him.

We disagree, however, that the law of insane delusions compelled a finding by the orphans' court that James's delusion that Jay stole his money was an *insane* delusion. To be sure, James's delusion shared many of the characteristics of the insane delusions in the *Johnson, Doyle,* and *Benjamin* cases. James and Jay were close relatives, and Jay would be expected to have been the object of James's bounty. James came suddenly to believe that Jay had harmed him by stealing his money, when there was no evidence to support that belief, and he refused to hear the evidence that would refute it. James's false belief did not subside, but became central to his thinking about Jay, causing hostility and aversion.

This case is factually distinguishable from the three cases discussed at length above, however. In those cases, there simply was no explanation, whether or not rational, for the testator's sudden false belief, and therefore the delusion only could have come from within the testator's own mind. In this case, the delusion entered James's mind when he was a resident, not by choice, of the Cantler Home, which for him was a terrible experience that he blamed completely upon Jay. As James saw it, he was confined to a home similar to a nursing home, without privacy or access to a telephone, in the company of residents who were enfeebled by old age, and with no hope of being let out. The witnesses who testified about having visited James in the Cantler Home confirmed that the accommodations were insufficient for him and that he felt like he had been imprisoned—and that he was of the view that Jay had failed him by forcing him in and by not coming to his aid to get out.

From the time he arrived at the Cantler Home forward, James was convinced that Jay had betrayed him by not letting him go home instead. James's delusion that Jay also had betrayed him by stealing his money was a generalization, albeit not a logical one, drawn from his true belief that Jay had been the decision-maker who had kept him in the Cantler Home until his sisters rescued him. In essence, this is what the trial judge found from the evidence: that James's delusion was an outgrowth of a stubborn conviction that Jay had "done something wrong" by "imprisoning" him at the Cantler Home. Although it was false, and it prompted James to disinherit Jay, it was not an inexplicable delusion that only could have come into being as the product of an insane mind.

The facts as found by the orphans' court did not compel a finding that James was suffering from an insane delusion, under the law of testamentary capacity. The court's finding that James was suffering from a delusion that Jay had stolen his money, but that the delusion was not an insane delusion, was a reasonable interpretation of the evidence. Accordingly, we shall not disturb it on appeal.

JUDGMENT AFFIRMED. COSTS TO BE PAID BY THE APPELLANT.

James falsely believed that Jay had stolen his money. Was that a delusion? Could James's belief have been dislodged by evidence or reason? Why did the will survive the insane delusion challenge?

Notice that the insane delusion rule started with *Dew v. Clark*, an English decision that deviated from a statute that had been on the books for hundreds of years. Was that court wrong to deny probate to the will of the father who thought his daughter was "gross" and a child of the devil and a "special property of Satan"? Should the court have applied the statute, probating the will and disinheriting the daughter, and waited for the legislature to cure what the court viewed as a defect in the statute? Does the adoption of the rule by many courts, or the failure of legislatures to eliminate the doctrine, mean anything about the legitimacy of the decision in *Dew*? As a matter of policy, how ought the benefits of an insane delusion rule be balanced against the potential harms from such a rule (such as those seen in the *Townshend* case, overturning the decedent's grant of freedom and property to his enslaved people)?

To deny probate to a will or a provision in a will based on an insane delusion, courts require that the insane delusion materially affect a dispositive provision of the will. There are two approaches to this requirement. The majority, "but-for", test asks whether the dispositive provision must have been the result of the delusion. *See Levin v. Levin*, supra. The minority test asks whether the dispositive provision might have been the result of the delusion. Which test was implicitly applied in *Strittmater's Estate*, supra? Which is the better rule? Should a provision in a will be stricken if it might have been caused by something other than the delusion? How sure should a court be about the influence of the delusion before denying probate?

Perhaps one way to reduce the chances of a capacity contest in a few jurisdictions is by taking advantage of ante-mortem probate, living probate. In these jurisdictions, the will can be probated before the death of the testator, and challenges based on lack of capacity or undue influence can be resolved while the testator is available for examination.

(c) Why Require Capacity?

Why does the law require that the testators have a sound mind for their wills to be admitted to probate? We could probably reduce the public costs of estate administration if there were no such requirement because it is not easy to determine without a trial whether a person who is now dead had a sound mind at some point in the past. For the litigation on this element to be justified, it must serve an important purpose.

Through the years, various purposes have been suggested. One is that it protects families. It is often the case that denying probate for lack of capacity will result in intestacy and, hence, in assets flowing to the decedent's family instead of others outside the family. In that sense, members of the decedent's family are protected when the decedent lacked capacity. However, because estates bear a portion of the costs of litigation on the issue of capacity and because estates often flow to family members, family members bear some costs of the capacity requirement. Notice that these litigation costs might be borne by relatives of both those who are judicially determined to have capacity and those who lack capacity. It is unclear whether the costs of litigation borne by families exceed the benefits transferred to families by the capacity requirement. Moreover, financial effects make up only a part of the costs borne by families. Families can be riven by fights regarding capacity; and family harmony is not necessarily advanced by receiving wealth. The net effects on families as families are not easy to determine. Finally, it should be asked, why should the family be protected? Are family members more deserving than others who would have taken under the will of the person lacking capacity?

A related argument for the capacity requirement is that it tends to support people who are old by keeping assets in the family. It is not clear whether this is true. While invalidating wills often does have the effect of keeping assets in the family, the capacity requirement makes it harder for some people who need care to attract support from others. The greater the requirement of capacity, the fewer elderly persons that have the power to change the distribution of their assets. Without power to dispose by will, they have less ability to reward those who help and support them. On the other hand, perhaps relatives will give the elderly more care when they know that they will inherit. The capacity requirement changes the incentives of both family members and others.

Another purpose of the capacity requirement is to reduce exploitation of persons lacking capacity. If cunning predators know that wills of those with reduced capacity will not be effective, they have less incentive to prey upon them. Whether this change in behavior turns out to be a benefit to the testators depends on what activities are curtailed. Clearly, despite the undue influence doctrine, some predators prey upon those with diminished capacity by subjecting them to impositions and abusive treatment. Other predators attempt to gain favor by friendly behaviors. The incentives for both sorts of behavior are reduced by the capacity requirement. Overall, though, it may make sense to offer some protection to those lacking capacity beyond the protection available from the undue influence doctrine.

It could be argued that the capacity requirement enhances the legitimacy of the law. Wealth allocations by persons without capacity could be arbitrary (both unfair and inefficient), and honoring them could undermine legal institutions, which should be rational rather than arbitrary and capricious. This is an empirical question. Would the law lose legitimacy if it enforced wills without regard to mental capacity? If the capacity requirement does enhance the legitimacy of the state, is it fair to accomplish that result by taking away rights from people who lack capacity?

Perhaps the capacity requirement can be justified on a cost-benefit analysis. It seems likely that those who lack capacity will in some cases allocate resources poorly, as compared to the allocations in their previous wills or under the laws of intestate succession. In other words, there would be an efficiency loss from following their instructions and the capacity requirement avoids that loss. In addition, people who lack general capacity are often unaware that the law will not follow the instructions in their wills, either because they are not aware of the law or because they are not aware that they lack capacity. *See Kuhn*, supra. As a result, the capacity requirement does not upset those who lack capacity. If these are both true, the balance tips in favor of refusing to probate the wills of people who have insufficient capacity.

Professor Radin wrote, "In fact, the concepts of sanity and personhood are intertwined: At some point we question whether the insane person is a person at all." Margaret J. Radin, Property and Personhood, 34 Stan. L. Rev. 957, 969 (1982). Does that explain our refusal to honor the wills of insane persons? It is true that we would not honor the wills of non-human animals. And, as a descriptive matter, she might be right that some people question whether an insane person is a person. But that does not serve as a normative reason for refusing to allow an insane person to execute an effective will. That normative leap might risk the dangers of considering insane people not to be persons for other purposes.

Ulysses, as instructed by Circe, said,

> "Therefore, take me and bind me to the crosspiece half way up the mast; bind me as I stand upright, with a bond so fast that I cannot possibly break away, and lash the rope's ends to the mast itself. If I beg and pray you to set me free, then bind me more tightly still."

HOMER, THE ODYSSEY, Book XII. Ulysses tells his crew to bind him so that he cannot heed the song of the Sirens, which if he follows will lead to his death. When he gives his orders, he knows that his future self might try to do something disastrous. The capacity requirement can be seen as serving the same purpose as a Ulysses pact, providing testators assurance that their irrational future selves will not undo their careful plans. Until they lose capacity, testators are happier knowing they cannot change dispositive course during a period of insanity. However, sometimes, those who have lost capacity will be less happy knowing they are unable to change their wills. In such cases, the capacity requirement trades away some happiness after incapacitation in return for increased security and happiness before that point in time. Consider this for yourself. Suppose that you are sane now and have written a will (or are happy with intestate succession), and suppose that you know you will lose capacity in the future, and suppose that after losing capacity you will write a new will. Do you want the law to follow those new instructions? If the answer is no, the capacity requirement should increase your sense of security about your testamentary plans. But if your answer is yes, then the capacity requirement probably reduces your net happiness because you know that your later self, if irrational, will be ignored by the law.

Could private ordering improve the law? Could we make both groups happy by changing the limiting rule into a default rule? A will executed by a testator with capacity could include a clause that says, "Do not apply a capacity requirement to my future wills." In order to have the desired effect, subsequent wills would need to avoid revoking that provision of the will. What should be done for people who never have capacity and thus lack the ability to opt out? For their sake, should the default rule be that capacity is not required?

3.   FORMAL WILLS

Formal wills are wills that are witnessed or notarized. In the United States, they are the recommended form of will. The requirements of signature and attestation are known as "formalities", and they help to achieve a variety of goals.

(a) Functions of Formalities

Consider the following excerpt from *In re Groffman,* [1969] 1 W.L.R. 733, [1969] 2 All E.R. 108, 1969 WL 26902 (Probate, Divorce, & Admiralty Division, High Court of Justice, England, 1968).

> "I am perfectly satisfied that the document was intended by the deceased to be executed as his will and that its contents represent his testamentary intentions.
>
> * * *
>
> As must appear from the fact that I have been satisfied that the document does represent the testamentary intentions of the deceased, I would very gladly find in its favour; but I am bound to apply the statute, which has been enacted by Parliament for good reason.
>
> * * *
>
> In the end, therefore, although I would gladly accede to the arguments for the plaintiffs if I could consistently with my judicial duty, in my view there was no acknowledgment or signature by the testator in the presence of two or more witnesses present at the same time; and I am bound to pronounce against this will."

Id. at 735. 737, 739. For admission to probate, it is not enough that an instrument be intended to be a will by a person with capacity. The instrument must also have been executed in compliance with certain formalities, which are the subject of the following materials. *Groffman* ought to give you pause, if only for a moment. Assuming we want to allow people to determine who takes some of their property after they die, why would we ignore that determination? Why would the law require that formalities be observed in addition to requiring that intent be shown? If a probate court thinks the decedent probably intended the document to be her will, why not follow the document's instructions? One answer, of course, is that we want to reduce incentives and opportunities for unwanted behaviors such as fraud and overreaching. Another answer is that we want to minimize the cost of errors with regard to the intent of the decedent.

As noted earlier, errors can be divided into two types: false negatives and false positives. A false negative is a denial of probate to a document that was intended to be the will of the decedent. A false positive is an admission of probate to an instrument that the decedent did not in fact intend to be effective. A key function of the formalities is to reduce the costs of false-positive errors by reducing the frequency of those errors.

The formalities reduce the cost of false positives in at least two ways. The formalities directly reduce false positives by keeping out of probate documents that courts erroneously would have admitted to probate if intent and capacity had been the only tests. The decedent might have signed a will while her hand was steady, thinking she would take it to friends or family for witnessing when she determined finally that she wanted it to be effective, but never actually resolved to make it effective. Without the witnessing formalities, a court might find erroneously that she did intend it to be effective. Courts do not always determine facts correctly and in some of those cases a formality could save the day. This is sometimes called the evidentiary function.

It might be assumed that to achieve a reduction in false positives, formalities must increase the frequency of false-negative errors. While this is possible, it is not certain. The less stringent the formalities, the fewer steps a testator must take to get a will admitted to probate. If a document costs little time and money to create, the testator will likely treat it more casually, taking fewer precautions to keep it safe and fewer steps to make sure it is found and identified as his will after his death. In such situations, it is possible that the survivors will either not find the will or not identify it as an important document, with the result that the document fails to be presented for probate. The formalities increase the chances it will be offered for probate, by making the document more costly, by making it look more official, and by getting it into more hands. It is possible that, as the degree of formality increases from zero, the number of false negatives initially decreases before eventually increasing. This might be included within the evidentiary function of formalities.

Another function of formalities is the protective function. The formalities can reduce false negatives by denying probate to documents that have been procured by undue influence or fraud. For example, a father asks his son to bring business documents for him to sign. The son includes a document that the father did not request. That document gives the bulk of his estate to the son and little to the daughter, when the decedent had wanted equal treatment. The decedent signs it and dies a few days later. The son presents the document for probate and convinces the court that the document was intended to be a will, but the court denies probate because it was not properly witnessed. (Notice that the court might well write the opinion in a way that suggests the situation is one resulting in a false negative rather than a true negative.)

Likely more often, formalities discourage wrongdoers from even trying to get unintended documents into probate. Having heard of the witness requirement, the son in the example above might give up on the idea of bringing his father the wrong document for execution or give up on the idea of presenting it for probate. If the formalities reduce fraud and undue influence, the idea of committing some malefaction may be less likely to spread to susceptible brains. Without the witness requirement, not only might the son succeed in his efforts to get the bulk of his father's estate, but others might hear of that success and make similar efforts of their own. Reducing the frequency of attempts to defraud and unduly influence testators has a couple of other consequences. One is that, by protecting those who are trusting from those who are untrustworthy, formalities might increase the sense of trust in society, which may correlate to subjective well-being. Another consequence is that reducing attempted malefactions could reduce the discomfort that such attempts generate, even when they are unsuccessful.

The cost of errors includes both the frequency of errors and the magnitude of those errors. If there is a tradeoff of false positives for false negatives, which errors are worse? As indicated in the example above, some of the false positives avoided by the formalities arise in situations involving someone's attempt to get a greater portion of an estate than the decedent intended to give. The result of such a false positive would be to give assets to a wrongdoer. On the other hand, the false negative either results in the probate of a previous will or intestacy, either of which less often involves transfer of property to someone who has engaged in a scheme to obtain more than his share of the estate. False negatives result in transfers to the wrong person, but rarely persons who have taken wrongful steps to interfere with the intent of the decedent. Which one is further from the intent of the decedent and more annoying to the decedent, a false positive or a false negative? In criminal law, we assume false positives (convictions of innocents) are worse than false negatives (acquittals of criminals). If costs and benefits are similar in the context of probate, we should be willing to suffer a number of false negatives to prevent a false positive.

Another way to compare false positives to false negatives is to ask what a testator must do to avoid them. If a lawyer or client is concerned about the possibility that someone will get a false document admitted to probate, what can he do? One possibility is to execute a new will every few weeks. That new testament will displace the previous, false will, if such a will shows up. That is, however, a fairly bothersome way to reduce the risk. On the other hand, what can the lawyer and client do if they are worried that the court will refuse probate to an intended will? They can take extra steps to make sure that all formalities are observed and to show that the decedent intended the document to be a will. If the false-negative problem is easier for lawyers to prevent, the law should set the balance in favor of fewer false positives and more false negatives.

Unfortunately, even if we could calculate an ideal ratio of false positives to false negatives, reported cases do not allow us to determine whether a set of formalities has hit the target ratio. The problem is that false positives and false negatives are not equally likely to be identified in the opinions written by courts; there is a bias in the reported data. There are cases such as *Groffman* in which the courts say that the document in question was intended to be the will of the decedent, but that it cannot be probated because this or that formal step was missed. This is as it should be; we do want courts to warn testators that they must observe the formalities, and nothing warns better than a case denying probate.

On the other hand, courts rarely report false positives. The intent requirement discussed above usually prevents a court from admitting to probate a document that was not intended to be the decedent's will. (But not always. In *Matter of Estate of Duemeland*, 528 N.W.2d 369 (N.D. 1995), the court refused to admit evidence that the decedent was "merely bluffing" on the ground that allowing such evidence would leave every will open to attack and deprive testators of certainty of disposition.) But the fact that courts rarely report admitting documents to probate that were not intended to be wills should not lull us into thinking that it never happens. Given how much money can be gained by convincing a court to probate a document, it seems indubitable that it does happen.

Because the false positives are often hidden from view and the false negatives are announced, the data set of reported cases is biased and we are left, as a matter of balancing the concerns, with speculating about the costs and benefits of imposing additional safeguards. Moreover, even if it were true that there are no false positives today, that fact would not imply that there would be no false positives if we eliminated the formalities. The formalities have contributed to that happy result. We should ask whether a given formality is difficult to observe and, on the other hand, whether there are opportunities for fraud if that formal step is not required. In any case, the mere existence of false negatives does not justify a conclusion that the law needs reforming. They are the price we pay to lower the frequency of false positives and attempted malfeasance.

Reducing the costs of false positives and incentives for malfeasance are not the only benefits of formalities. They can impress upon the testator the importance of the document, inducing caution and deliberation and making him more likely a thoughtful and grave man. It will not surprise you to hear that this has been called the ritual or cautionary function.

The requirement of observing formalities can also lead, some would say drive, clients to lawyers, who can help plan for contingencies. The presumption here is that well-considered dispositive provisions will either save the costs of subsequent revisions or will result in greater utility to those remaining after the decedent's death than the recipients would enjoy if the decedent spent less time and money planning the dispositions. This is the channeling function.

Another benefit of observing formalities is that testators learn that it is not easy to execute a new will. That increases their confidence that the will they are executing will indeed be effective and will not be supplanted by an ill-considered will made hastily or under pressure in the future, perhaps after they are senile. Let's call this the assurance function.

Perhaps too little attention has been given to the value of formalities in reducing the cost of determining whether to admit documents to probate. Although it could take a lawyer and client a few hours to observe the formalities, it takes many more lawyer and client hours to litigate the issue of whether an instrument was intended to be the will of the decedent. It is much cheaper to prevent the dispute than to resolve it. That goes for society as well as for the parties. A small cost incurred by the testator in observing formal requirements can avoid a large cost for the taxpayers when it comes time for probate proceedings by reducing the chances of a will contest. In the absence of formalities, the benefits of scrimping on will preparation accrue to testators and perhaps their devisees. The costs of scrimping on will preparation fall on society; they are externalities to the testator. The result of eliminating formalities would be that the testators would spend inefficiently little on will preparation. One way to examine the question is to ask how much society should be willing to pay to determine the intent of the decedent when the decedent did not consider it worth spending a few hundred dollars to make it clear that a document was intended to be his will. Should we allow decedents to charge taxpayers thousands to save themselves hundreds? Let's call this function enhancing judicial economy.

Keep these functions of formalities in mind as you read the requirements and the cases imposing or ignoring those requirements.

(b) A Writing

UPC § 2–502 requires a will to be "in writing", with any reasonably permanent record being sufficient. In *In re Estate of Horton*, 925 N.W.2d 207 (Mich.Ct.App. 2018), infra, the Court of Appeals of Michigan affirmed the admission to probate of a will that the decedent had, the court found, typed into his cell phone. Electronic documents might be made more reliable by the use of blockchain technology, but the court admitted the Horton will even though such technology had not been used. In *Matter of Estate of Reed*, 672 P.2d 829 (Wyo. 1983), the court held that an audio recording was not admissible as a will. An audio or video recording is not a writing, although one might ask whether it is not as reliable a record as a cell phone entry. The writing must usually meet a number of additional requirements.

(c) Expression of the Animus Testandi

As discussed above under the intent element, courts require that the decedents have intended a document to be their will for it to be admitted to probate. But there can be an additional intent requirement. This additional requirement is that the document itself must indicate that it is intended to be the will, the operative instrument.

> Example 4.08: Thinking that a written letter would suffice to operate as a will, O sends her lawyer a letter saying that she wants her house to go to her sister when she dies. Under the traditional rule, if that letter did not itself express the intent that it would be the instrument that would serve as her will, the letter cannot be probated even if the court is convinced that O intended the letter to be her will.

The traditional requirement that the document itself express the idea that it is the will has been abandoned by UPC § 2–502(c), which allows extrinsic evidence to establish that the testator intended the instrument be her will. Under the UPC, there is room to litigate the probate of the letter in the example above.

Consider the following excerpt from a law review article.

THE HERMENEUTICS FILE

Thomas C. Grey
58 S. Cal. L. Rev. 211, 1985

. . . handwritten on a single piece of paper . . .

    * * *

Draft #13 (Conning McGarr)

I, Conn, sound as age allows,

Bequeath to friends in reasonable shares

My money and my goods. As for the rest,

My hoard (imagined, literary *res*)

Shall be arranged with care, substance preserved,

And put out in due time, plain as can be.

All this shall be done by George McGarr,

My colleague, friend, conscience of afternoons,

Who also shall respect this final wish:

That my inchoacies may never come,

My Scottish breadman, to harsh scrutiny,

Those of my writings that are incomplete,

Destroy.

The stacks of pages wait for you;

Do not see in them matter wanting form,

Pebbles for a Japanese gardener's hand,

But mind's fixed intercept of lexicon.

You said, through all our restless afternoons,

"To interpret is to find intent in words;"

Now, exegete, now that the words are mine,

Now, grave George, draw from them what I mean—

Who knows my currents better than the shore

Against whose sea-wall they have spent their surge?

If you can judge which of my works are done

Not seeking shape where I let fracture be

(Old seconder of motions to adjourn!)

Nor forcing me unfinished into view

(The literate insist, and what's to hide?)

Nor claiming bold emender's privilege

(Conn says to mean, so mean away his say)

Then can your last word close our long jaw-jaw

Conformant to your sober principles.

But take care. Traps are here. Words mean.

I mean. You, reading, want

Does the writing express the intent that it be Conn's will? What should George do with this document? The executor has a duty to present the will for probate and to defend it and follow its instructions after it is admitted. But the executor must first make some determination that a court could find that the document was intended to be a will of the decedent.

(d) Signature

The means of assent to a contract are many. The means of assent to a will are few, as one might expect given the functions of formalities discussed above. UPC § 2–502 requires a formal (witnessed or notarized) will to be "signed by the testator or in the testator's name by some other individual in the testator's conscious presence and by the testator's direction". Some sort of mark intended to serve as a signature is required, but a signature need not be a full name. Courts have accepted signatures in the form of an "X" for a person who cannot write. Note, however, that eleven states have adopted the harmless error doctrine, discussed below, and a court in such a state might conceivably admit to probate a will without a signature. Note also that the Uniform Electronic Wills Act (E-Wills Act), recommended for adoption by the National Conference of Commissioners on Uniform State Laws in 2019, says that "sign" means "(A) to execute or adopt a tangible symbol; or (B) to affix to or logically associate with the record an electronic symbol or process."

IN RE ESTATE OF CHASTAIN
Supreme Court of Tennessee, 2012
401 S.W.3d 612

CLARK, J.

The issue in this appeal is whether the statutory requirements for execution of an attested will prescribed by Tennessee Code Annotated section 32–1–104(1) (2007) were satisfied when the decedent failed to sign the two-page will but signed a one-page affidavit of attesting witnesses. We conclude that the decedent's signature on the separate affidavit of attesting witnesses does not satisfy the statute requiring the testator's signature on the will. Accordingly, the judgment of the Court of Appeals is reversed, and the judgment of the trial court that the will was not properly executed is reinstated.

Factual and Procedural History

Thomas Grady Chastain ("Decedent") died on November 6, 2009. On April 30, 2010, Decedent's daughter, June Chastain Patterson, filed a petition for the administration of his estate. Ms. Patterson alleged that Decedent died intestate and that she was Decedent's "sole surviving heir." Ms. Patterson sought appointment as administrator of Decedent's estate as well as a waiver of bond and inventory. Ms. Patterson's requests were granted the day she filed the petition, and letters of administration issued.

On July 7, 2010, Trent and Adrian Chastain ("Chastains"), two of Decedent's grandchildren, filed a motion for bond, inventory, and an accounting of Decedent's estate. The Chastains alleged that Ms. Patterson had falsely sworn to being Decedent's sole heir, that Decedent had two predeceased sons, and that the six surviving issue of Decedent's predeceased sons are also his heirs and entitled to a share of his estate under the laws of intestacy.

Notwithstanding her prior petition alleging that Decedent died intestate, on August 24, 2010, the date of the hearing on the Chastains' motion, Ms. Patterson "deposited" with the trial court a consecutively numbered, two-page document dated September 4, 2004, and titled "Last Will and Testament" ("Will"). The first paragraph of the Will is reproduced below.

I, *Thomas Grady Chastain*   a resident of *Polk*

County, *Tennessee*   do hereby make, publish, and declare this to be my Last Will

and Testament, hereby revoking any and all Wills and Codicils heretofore made by me.

The Will named Decedent's grandchildren and great-grandchildren and bequeathed to them his knife collection and any insurance monies remaining after Decedent's bills had been paid. The Will bequeathed the remainder of Decedent's estate to Ms. Patterson and named her as executrix. Decedent's initials, the initials of three witnesses, and the date appear at the bottom of the first page of the Will as follows:

Initials: _____

     Testator   Witness   Witness   Witness   Date

Although the second page of the Will, reproduced below, includes the signatures of three witnesses and a blank line on which Decedent's name apparently should have been printed, the Will included no blank line for Decedent's signature, and Decedent's signature is not on this page of the Will.[2]

> IN WITNESS WHEREOF I declare this to be my Last Will and Testament and execute it willingly as my free and voluntary act for the purposes expressed herein and I am of legal age and sound mind and make this under no constraint or undue influence, this 4th day of September, 2004 at Ducktow State of TN
>
> The foregoing instrument was on said date subscribed at the end thereof by
>
> _____, the above named Testator who signed, published, and declared this instrument to be his/her Last Will and Testament in the presence of us and each of us, who thereupon at his/her request, in his/her presence, and in the presence of each other, have hereunto subscribed our names as witnesses thereto. We are of sound mind and proper age to witness a will and understand this to be his/her will, and to the best of our knowledge testator is of legal age to make a will, of sound mind, and under no constraint or undue influence.

Sammy J. Ware   residing at Ducktow TN 37326

Missy Taylor   residing at Copperhill, TN 37317

Aneer Curts   residing at Ducktown, TN 37326

However, Decedent and the attesting witnesses signed a separate one-page document titled "Self-Proved Will Affidavit" ("Affidavit") that Ms. Patterson submitted along with the Will. The Affidavit is reproduced in its entirety below.

---

[2] At a hearing in the trial court, Ms. Patterson's attorney stated that the Will was prepared from a form without the assistance of counsel. This case illustrates the problems that may arise when lay persons, unversed in the statutory requirements for executing a will, use generic forms.

Self-Proved Will Affidavit
(attach to Will)

STATE OF _____ *TN*

COUNTY OF _____ *Polk*

I, the undersigned, an officer authorized to administer oaths, certify that _Thomas Grady Chastain_, the testator and _Jimmy Ware, Mary Taylor_, and _Nion ____ Curtis_, the witnesses, whose names are signed to the attached or foregoing instrument and whose signatures appear below, having appeared before me and having been first been duly sworn, each then declared to me that: 1) the attached or foregoing instrument is the last will of the testator; 2) the testator willingly and voluntarily declared, signed, and executed the will in the presence of the witnesses; 3) the witnesses signed the will upon the request of the testator, in the presence and hearing of the testator and in the presence of each other; 4) to the best knowledge of each witness, the testator was, at the time of signing, of the age of majority (or otherwise legally competent to make a will), of sound mind and memory, and under no constraint or undue influence; and 5) each witness was and is competent and of proper age to witness a will.

Thomas G. Chastain (Testator)

Jimmy J. Ware (Witness)

Mary Taylor (Witness)

Subscribed and sworn to before me by _Thomas Grady Chastain_ the testator, who is (personally) known to me or who has produced _____ as identification, and by _Jimmy Ware, Mary Taylor, Nion Curtis_ a witness, who is personally known to me or who has produced _personally known_ as identification, and by _Jimmy Ware, Mary Taylor, Nion Curtis_ witness, who is personally known to me or who has produced _Mary McGee_ as identification, this _4th_ day of _Sept._, 20_02_.

Carol M. Shook

Notary or other officer

My Commission Expires July 10, 2005

* * *

* * *

Analysis

The Legislature has the authority to prescribe the conditions by which property may be transferred by will in this State. The General Assembly exercised this power in 1941 by enacting the Execution of

Wills Act.[5] This legislation prescribed uniform standards for the execution of attested wills. These statutory requirements have remained virtually unchanged in the ensuing seventy-one years and are currently codified in Tennessee Code Annotated section 32–1–104, which provides:

> The execution of a will, other than a holographic or noncupative will, must be by the signature[8] of the testator and of at least two (2) witnesses as follows:
>
> (1) The testator shall signify to the attesting witnesses that the instrument is the testator's will and either:
>
>> (A) The testator sign;
>>
>> (B) Acknowledge the testator's signature already made; or
>>
>> (C) At the testator's direction and in the testator's presence have someone else sign the testator's name; and
>>
>> (D) In any of the above cases the act must be done in the presence of two (2) or more attesting witnesses.
>
> (2) The attesting witnesses must sign:
>
>> (A) In the presence of the testator; and
>>
>> (B) In the presence of each other.

(footnote added). This statute gives a testator some latitude in the manner of signing an attested will.[9] The testator may either sign the will in the presence of the attesting witnesses, or acknowledge a signature already made in the presence of attesting witnesses, or direct someone else to sign the will in the presence of the testator and of the attesting witnesses. But the statute demands that the testator's signature be placed on the will by one of these means. The testator's signature is essential to the creation of a will.

Tennessee courts have consistently interpreted statutes prescribing the formalities for execution of an attested will as

---

[5] The 1941 Execution of Wills Act was "a verbatim enactment of the Model Execution of Wills Act approved in 1940 by the National Conference on Uniform State Laws." Tennessee is the only state that enacted this model law.

[8] " 'Signature' or 'signed' includes a mark, the name being written near the mark and witnessed, or any other symbol or methodology executed or adopted by a party with intention to authenticate a writing or record, regardless of being witnessed."

[9] In contrast, attesting witnesses have no latitude as to the manner of signing a will, but are required to sign "[i]n the presence of the testator" and "[i]n the presence of each other."

mandatory and have required strict compliance with these statutory mandates. *See, e.g., Fann v. Fann*, 186 Tenn. 127 (1948) (holding that the will had not been properly executed where the attesting witnesses failed to sign it in each other's presence); *In re Estate of Stringfield*, 283 S.W.3d at 832 (holding that the will was not properly executed where the attesting witnesses failed to sign the will but initialed the first two pages of the will and submitted an affidavit of attesting witnesses); *In re Estate of Wait*, 43 Tenn.App. 217 (1957) (holding that the will had not been properly executed where the testatrix failed to sign it at the same time and in the presence of the attesting witnesses); *Ball v. Miller*, 214 S.W.2d 446, 450 (1948) ("Certain acts required in the execution of wills we view as mandatory[,] and an instrument does not attain the character admissible to probate unless and until they are performed."); *Eslick*, 215 S.W.2d at 15 (holding that the will had not been properly executed where the attesting witnesses signed it separately and later acknowledged their signatures in the presence of the testator and each other); *see also Pritchard* § 4, at 10 ("[I]t is indispensable that every requirement of the Tennessee Execution of Wills Act be complied with in the execution of a will."). Statutes requiring the observance of formalities in the execution of wills are designed to prevent fraud, mistakes, and uncertainty in the testamentary dispositions of property. Enforcing strict compliance with such statutory formalities is intended to preserve "the inviolability" and "sanctity" of a testator's right to dispose of property by will. "While in some cases a relaxation in the enforcement of these statutory provisions, or a liberal construction thereof, might appear to be justified, in many instances such a practice would serve only to thwart the testator's purposes." Accordingly, Tennessee courts will sustain a will as legally executed only if it is possible to do so consistently with statutory requirements.

With these principles in mind, we turn to the undisputed facts of this case. The parties agree that Decedent failed to sign the Will.[10] The dispute focuses on the legal effect, if any, of Decedent's signature on the Affidavit. The Chastains argue that Decedent's signature on the Affidavit does not cure his failure to comply strictly with the statutory formalities for executing an attested will. The Chastains maintain that the Affidavit is a separate document from the Will and intended for use in a probate court only if a will is uncontested.

---

[10] Ms. Patterson has not challenged the Court of Appeals' holding that Decedent's initials on the bottom of the first page of the Will failed to satisfy the statutory signature requirement.

On the other hand, Ms. Patterson argues that Decedent's signature on the Affidavit satisfies the statutory formalities because: 1) Decedent and the attesting witnesses signed the Affidavit on the same day the witnesses signed the Will; 2) Tennessee law recognizes that a will may consist of multiple documents and the Affidavit was found with the Will; 3) the statute does not require a testator to sign a will in a particular location; and 4) Decedent intended to sign the Will when he signed the Affidavit.

We hold that Decedent's signature on the Affidavit does not cure his failure to comply strictly with the statutory formalities for executing an attested will. Despite Ms. Patterson's assertion to the contrary, the Affidavit is not part of the Will. The Affidavit was prepared pursuant to Tennessee Code Annotated section 32–2–110, which states:

> Any or all of the attesting witnesses to any will may, at the request of the testator or, after the testator's death, at the request of the executor or any person interested under the will, make and sign an affidavit before any officer authorized to administer oaths in or out of this state, stating the facts to which they would be required to testify in court to prove the will, which affidavit shall be written on the will or, if that is impracticable, on some paper attached to the will, and the sworn statement of any such witness so taken shall be accepted by the court of probate when the will is not contested as if it had been taken before the court.

This statute authorizes use of an affidavit of attesting witnesses in lieu of live testimony only if a will is uncontested. By requiring the affidavit to "be written on the will or, if that is impracticable, on some paper attached to the will," a clear distinction is drawn between an affidavit of attesting witnesses and a will.

This distinction is also apparent from the language of the Affidavit at issue in this appeal. The instructions—"(attach to Will)"—are printed on the Affidavit immediately below the title "Self-Proved Will Affidavit." The first paragraph of the Affidavit refers to the Will as "the attached or foregoing instrument." Simply put, both the statute and the Affidavit establish that the Affidavit is not a continuation of the Will. Accordingly, Decedent's signature on the Affidavit is not sufficient to satisfy the statutory requirement that he sign the Will by one of the means provided by statute.

Our holding should not be interpreted as requiring a testator to sign each page of a will that is written on several detached sheets of paper. Nor does our holding require a testator to sign in a particular location on the will because Tennessee Code Annotated section 32–1–104 is silent on this issue. We hold only that a testator must sign the will, not a wholly separate document. Here, Decedent failed to sign either of the two consecutively numbered pages that constituted the Will. Decedent's signature on the wholly separate Affidavit does not rectify his failure to sign the Will.

Ms. Patterson asserts that Decedent signed the Affidavit intending to sign the Will and believing he was signing the Will, so his signature on the Affidavit should be deemed sufficient. Decedent's signature on the separate Affidavit provides little, if any, insight about Decedent's beliefs and intentions concerning the unsigned two-page Will. Even assuming Ms. Patterson's assertion is correct, however, our conclusion remains the same. Courts endeavor to effectuate a testator's intent "unless prohibited by a rule of law or public policy," and courts will sustain a will as legally executed if it can be done consistently with statutory requirements, However, courts may not ignore statutory mandates in deference to a testator's intent. Irrespective of Decedent's intent, we have no authority to dispense with the statute mandating Decedent's signature on the Will, and Decedent's signature on the Affidavit simply is not sufficient to satisfy this requirement.

Ms. Patterson also asks us to adopt the doctrine of integration by which "a separate writing may be deemed an actual part of the testator's will, thereby merging the two documents into a single instrument." As Ms. Patterson recognizes, this doctrine has not been judicially adopted in Tennessee, and the General Assembly has not enacted Section 2–504(c) of the Uniform Probate Code, which provides that "[a] signature affixed to a self-proving affidavit attached to a will is considered a signature affixed to the will, if necessary to prove the will's due execution." Rather, Tennessee Code Annotated section 32–1–104 plainly and unambiguously requires a testator's signature to appear on the will. This statutory requirement has been in place and strictly enforced for seventy-one years. The Legislature has neither relaxed this requirement nor provided that it may be satisfied by the testator's signature on a document separate from the will. "[T]he [L]egislature's failure to 'express disapproval of a judicial construction of a statute is persuasive evidence of legislative adoption of the judicial construction.' " As already noted, the Legislature is the entity authorized to prescribe the conditions by which property may be transferred by will in this State, and courts have no authority to modify those conditions. Given the Legislature's adoption of statutes prescribing the manner of executing an attested will and its tacit approval of court decisions strictly enforcing those statutory mandates, we decline to adopt the doctrine of integration because doing so would amount to a relaxation of statutory requirements. Whether the doctrine of integration should be adopted is a matter for the Legislature.

Conclusion

We conclude that Decedent's signature on the Affidavit does not satisfy the statute requiring the testator's signature on a will. Accordingly, the judgment of the Court of Appeals is reversed, and the judgment of the trial court finding that the Will had not been properly executed is reinstated. This matter is remanded to the trial court for any further necessary proceedings consistent with this opinion. Costs of this appeal are taxed to Ms. Patterson and her surety, for which execution may issue if necessary.

There was little doubt that the testator wanted the instrument to be his will, but that did not matter to the court. The statute required a signature, and there was none on the will. The proponent argued that the affidavit was part of the will, but the court rejected that argument, pointing to language in the statute and in the affidavit that indicated that the affidavit and the will were intended to be different documents.

Tennessee did not require that the signature be at the end of the will, but some states do. In such states, if the signature is not at the end of the document the court could refuse probate to all of the will or refuse probate to just the part of the document below the testator's signature. Does a requirement that the signature be at the bottom decrease false positives enough to outweigh the increase in false negatives?

A writing today might include a digital file, but it is hard to put a wet signature on a digital document, especially since the signature needs to be on the document and not merely on something containing the document. If a digital signature were to qualify as a signature, how would we make sure that the digital signature was affixed by the testator and that the digital document was not changed after the signing? Perhaps, blockchain or some other technology could be used to satisfy the purposes of the formalities. If no such technology is used, should a digital signature qualify as a signature under the statute?

TAYLOR V. HOLT

Court of Appeals of Tennessee, Eastern Section, 2003
134 S.W.3d 830

SWINEY, J.

OPINION

Steve Godfrey prepared his last will and testament on his computer and affixed his computer generated signature at the end. He had two neighbors witness the will. Mr. Godfrey died approximately one week later. Doris Holt ("Defendant"), Mr. Godfrey's girlfriend, submitted the will for probate. Donna Godfrey Taylor ("Plaintiff"), Mr. Godfrey's sister, filed a complaint alleging, in part, that the will was not signed and claiming that Mr. Godfrey had died intestate. The Trial Court granted Defendant summary judgment holding there were no undisputed material facts and that all legal requirements concerning the execution and witnessing of a will had been met. Plaintiff appeals. We affirm.

Background

Steve Godfrey ("Deceased") prepared a document in January of 2002, purporting to be his last will and testament. The one page document was prepared by Deceased on his computer. Deceased asked two neighbors, Hershell Williams and Teresa Williams to act as witnesses to the will. Deceased affixed a computer generated version of his signature at the end of the document in the presence of both Hershell and Teresa Williams. Hershell and Teresa Williams then each signed their name below Deceased's and dated the document next to their respective signatures. In the document, Deceased devised everything he owned to a person identified only as Doris. Deceased died approximately one week after the will was witnessed.

Defendant, Deceased's girlfriend, who lived with Deceased at the time of his death, filed an Order of Probate attempting to admit the will to probate and requesting to be appointed the personal representative of the estate. Defendant also filed affidavits of both

Hershell and Teresa Williams attesting to the execution of the will. The affidavits each state that the affiant was a witness to Deceased's last will and testament and that each had signed at Deceased's request in the presence of both Deceased and the other witness. The affidavits both also state: "That the Testator, Steve Godfrey personally prepared the Last Will and Testament on his computer, and using the computer affixed his stylized cursive signature in my sight and presence and in the sight and presence of the other attesting witness. . . ." Further, each affidavit states that the affiant "was of the opinion that the Testator, Steve Godfrey, was of sound mind" at the time the will was witnessed.

Plaintiff, Deceased's sister, filed a complaint alleging, *inter alia,* that she is the only surviving heir of Deceased, that Deceased died intestate, that the document produced for probate was void because it did not contain Deceased's signature, and that Doris Holt has no blood relation or legal relation to the Deceased and should not have been appointed administratrix of Deceased's estate. Defendant filed a motion to dismiss or in the alternative for summary judgment claiming that all of the legal requirements concerning the execution and witnessing of a will under Tennessee law had been met and filed the supporting affidavits of Hershell and Teresa Williams.

The Trial Court entered an order on December 23, 2002, granting Defendant summary judgment. The December order held that all of the legal requirements concerning the execution and witnessing of a will under Tennessee law had been met and held that Defendant was entitled to summary judgment as a matter of law. Plaintiff appeals.

Discussion

Although not stated exactly as such, Plaintiff raises two issues on appeal: 1) whether the Trial Court erred in finding that the computer generated signature on the will complied with the legal requirements for the execution of a will, and, thus, erred in granting Defendant summary judgment; and, 2) whether an alleged beneficiary under a will should be allowed to receive benefits from the estate even though the will refers to the beneficiary only by her first name. We will address each issue in turn.

* * *

Tenn.Code Ann. § 32–1–104 addresses the requisite formalities for the execution and witnessing of a will in Tennessee and states:

The execution of a will, other than a holographic or nuncupative will, must be by the signature of the testator and of at least two (2) witnesses as follows:

(1) The testator shall signify to the attesting witnesses that the instrument is his will and either:

(A) Himself sign;

(B) Acknowledge his signature already made; or

(C) At his direction and in his presence have someone else sign his name for him; and

(D) In any of the above cases the act must be done in the presence of two (2) or more attesting witnesses.

(2) The attesting witnesses must sign:

(A) In the presence of the testator; and

(B) In the presence of each other.

The definition of "signature" as used in the statute is provided by Tenn.Code Ann. § 1–3–105, which states: "As used in this code, unless the context otherwise requires: . . . 'Signature' or 'signed' includes a mark, the name being written near the mark and witnessed, or any other symbol or methodology executed or adopted by a party with intention to authenticate a writing or record, regardless of being witnessed."

We begin by considering whether the Trial Court erred in finding that the computer generated signature on the will complied with the legal requirements for the execution of a will, and, thus, erred in granting Defendant summary judgment.

Plaintiff claims that the will was not signed. Plaintiff's brief argues "there is no indication of any type or nature that there was a mark of any type made by the testator." Plaintiff cites to *Sunderland v. Bailey (In Re: Estate of Wait)*, a 1957 case in which this Court found that "the testatrix may have made a mark of some sort, either an initial or one or more letters of her signature, on the will but she clearly indicated that she did not consider such mark or marks to constitute her signature." *Sunderland v. Bailey (In Re: Estate of Wait)*, 306 S.W.2d 345, 348 (1957). The witnesses in *Estate of Wait* testified that the testatrix had stated to them when the will was witnessed that she could not sign the will at that time, but would sign it later. The *Wait* testatrix actually signed the will a day or two after it was witnessed.

The *Wait* testatrix stated to the witnesses that she did not consider any mark to be her signature and this is borne out by the fact that she later signed the will. The *Wait* Court did not "find it necessary or proper . . . to rule whether or not a testator may legally sign a will by mark." Rather, the Court upheld the determination that the will was not entitled to probate based upon the fact that the will was not executed and witnessed in conformity with the statute.

The situation in *Estate of Wait* is dissimilar to the instant case. In the case at hand, Deceased did make a mark that was intended to operate as his signature. Deceased made a mark by using his computer to affix his computer generated signature, and, as indicated by the affidavits of both witnesses, this was done in the presence of the witnesses. The computer generated signature made by Deceased falls into the category of "any other symbol or methodology executed or adopted by a party with intention to authenticate a writing or record," and, if made in the presence of two attesting witnesses, as it was in this case, is sufficient to constitute proper execution of a will. Further, we note that Deceased simply used a computer rather than an ink pen as the tool to make his signature, and, therefore, complied with Tenn.Code Ann. § 32–1–104 by signing the will himself.

Defendant made a properly supported motion for summary judgment claiming there were no disputed issues of material fact and that Defendant was entitled to judgment as a matter of law. Defendant supported this assertion with the affidavits of Hershell and Teresa Williams, the witnesses to the will, attesting to the circumstances surrounding the execution of the will. As Defendant made a properly supported motion, the burden shifted to Plaintiff to set forth specific facts establishing the existence of disputed, material facts which must be resolved by the trier of fact. Plaintiff failed to do this. Plaintiff produced a letter that Plaintiff's appellate brief claims "set out a very different picture of [Deceased's] feelings towards [Defendant]." However, this letter has absolutely no relevance as to whether the will was properly executed and witnessed. Plaintiff failed to set forth specific facts establishing the existence of disputed, material facts regarding the execution of the will which must be resolved by the trier of fact.

    * * *

The other issue Plaintiff raises concerns whether an alleged beneficiary under a will should be allowed to receive benefits from the estate even though the will refers to the beneficiary by first name, but fails to state the beneficiary's last name. The will devises everything Deceased owned to someone named Doris, but fails to give a last name for Doris. Plaintiff apparently raises an issue regarding whether the Doris named in the will is the Defendant.

The Trial Court based its decision to grant summary judgment upon whether the will in question met the statutorily prescribed elements to be a valid last will and testament. The Trial Court did not consider or decide whether the Doris named in the will is the Defendant as this issue is not germane to whether the will was properly executed and witnessed in conformity with Tennessee law. We agree. Defendant was entitled to summary judgment because the will was properly executed and witnessed in conformity with Tennessee law. The identification of the beneficiary has no bearing on the dispositive issue before the Trial Court of whether this was Deceased's validly executed and witnessed last will and testament. We affirm the grant of summary judgment.

Conclusion

The judgment of the Trial Court is affirmed, and this cause is remanded to the Trial Court for such further proceedings as may be required, if any, consistent with this Opinion and for collection of the costs below. The costs on appeal are assessed against the Appellant, Donna Godfrey Taylor, and her surety.

Does this case increase the chances of malfeasance? If Hershell and Teresa Williams fabricated the will, how would we know it?

(e) Attestation

To qualify as an attested will, a document must be signed by witnesses who meet certain requirements and their signatures must meet certain requirements. Although the UPC requires only two witnesses, the state in which the decedent is domiciled at the time of death might require three witnesses. Because testators often migrate after they execute their wills, it is safer to have three witnesses.

In addition to the number of witnesses, the following are other possible requirements. 1) The witness must witness the testator sign the will, or witness the testator acknowledge the will, or witness the testator acknowledge the signature, or witness someone else sign for the testator. 2) The witness must sign after the testator. 3) The witness must sign within a reasonable time of the testator's signing. 4) The witness must witness the other witnesses sign the will or witness their acknowledgments that the signatures on the will are theirs. 5) The witness must subscribe the will in the presence of other witnesses. 6) The witness must subscribe the will in the presence of the testator.

When the witness or the testator must be "in the presence of" someone, there are two standards that might apply. Some courts apply a "line-of-sight" test, requiring that there be a line of sight between the parties. Other courts apply a somewhat looser "conscious-presence" test, requiring that one party be conscious of the presence of the other.

KIRKEBY V. COVENANT HOUSE

Court of Appeals of Oregon, 1998
970 P.2d 241

HASELTON, J.

This appeal and cross-appeal arise from an unusually convoluted probate dispute. The central issue on appeal is whether the trial court erred in determining that the testator's 1992 will was invalid because it was not acknowledged "in the presence" of witnesses. The primary, albeit not exclusive, issue on cross-appeal is whether the court erred in determining that a statutory election, signed by the testator's husband but not filed until after the husband had himself died, was ineffective. We conclude that the trial court correctly resolved those and other disputed matters. Accordingly, we affirm on both the appeal and the cross-appeal.

On *de novo* review, the material facts are as follows: The testator, Margaret Kirkeby (Margaret) and her husband, Orrin, were residents of the northeastern Oregon town of Wallowa. In May 1989, Margaret executed a will that provided that the proceeds of her estate be placed in trust, with "income earnings" to be distributed to Orrin during his life, then to other beneficiaries for a period not to exceed five years. The corpus was then to be distributed to a named charitable beneficiary, Mille Lacs Health System (Mille Lacs), one of the respondents on appeal.

In June 1992, Margaret decided to revise some of the provisions of the 1989 will. She drafted a handwritten codicil dated June 10, 1992, which, among other things, included a specific bequest of the Kirkebys' home, including five acres of land, to two neighbors, Don Curtis and Gayle Lyman, in exchange for them providing physical care for both Margaret and Orrin until their deaths. However, the codicil was not properly executed.

In July 1992, Margaret again decided to change her will. After marking through the 1989 will and codicil and adding notes, she asked Gayle Lyman to type up a new will with the indicated changes. On July 15, 1992, Lyman took the document to her house, typed it on two pages and delivered it to Margaret, who signed it that same day. That 1992 will, although still providing that the assets be placed in trust with income distributions to Orrin for life, and then to other named beneficiaries, provided that the trust corpus be distributed to a different named charitable beneficiary, Covenant House. It also incorporated the specific bequest of the Kirkebys' house and land to Curtis and Lyman, which had been originally set out in the ineffective June 1992 codicil.

On July 15, after signing the will, Margaret telephoned Patricia Horton, a local notary whom she knew. Horton returned Margaret's phone call later that day, and Margaret, whose voice Horton recognized, told Horton that she had signed a document, that she wanted Horton to notarize it, and that Lyman would be bringing it to Horton's office. Still later on July 15, Lyman delivered the document to Horton who recognized Margaret's handwriting and notarized the second page. Horton did not know that the document was a will, and she did not see the first page, because it was not attached. Lyman then returned the document to Margaret.

Although the dates are somewhat in dispute, it appears that 10 days later, on July 25, Margaret asked Lyman if she had had the will witnessed. Lyman replied that she had not and took the will to her house to type "witness" lines on the second page. Apparently while Lyman was gone, Margaret called Hazel Ortega, another neighbor. Margaret told Ortega that she had signed her will and that she wanted Ortega to witness it. Ortega arrived at Margaret's house, but Lyman had not yet returned with the will, so Ortega went home. When Lyman returned to Margaret's house, Margaret told her to take the will to Ortega's house. Lyman then took the second page of the document to Ortega, who signed as "witness." Another neighbor, James Pullen, also signed as a witness; unlike Ortega, he had not spoken to Margaret about the instrument or about signing as a witness. Once all the signatures were on the document, Lyman placed it in Margaret's satchel next to her bed.

Margaret died on September 2, 1992. In October 1992, Glenn Kirkeby (Glenn), Orrin's brother, filed a petition in probate alleging that the 1992 will was invalid as "not properly attested in that decedent did not sign her Will in the presence of the witnesses nor did she acknowledge to said witnesses that she had signed her Will," and that, consequently Margaret had therefore died intestate. Covenant House, Lyman, and Curtis, as named beneficiaries of the 1992 will (hereinafter, "objectors"), filed objections to Glenn's petition, alleging that the 1992 will was valid or, in the alternative, that Margaret's 1989 will and the June 10, 1992 codicil were valid.

In June 1993, the court issued a memorandum opinion and subsequent order, determining that (1) the July 1992 will and the June 1992 codicil to the 1989 will were both invalid as improperly executed; but (2) Margaret did not die intestate because, applying the doctrine of "dependent relative revocation,"[5] the 1989 will remained valid. The court's memorandum included the following pertinent findings and conclusions:

> "The 1989 will is marked up and provisions are crossed out, but it is still legible.
>
> " * * * * *
>
> "The 1989 will is valid unless it was revoked. It is also clear to the Court that is was Decedent's intent to revoke the 1989 will and replace it with the 1992 will.
>
> "Therefore, if the 1992 will is valid, there is no need to inquire further.
>
> "The 1992 Will:
>
> "Mrs. Horton's and Mr. Pullen's testimony and affidavits do not meet the requirements of the law to prove a will.
>
> "Mrs. Ortega's testimony and affidavit does meet the requirement to prove a will.

---

[5] Under the doctrine of dependent relative revocation, a court can probate a will that was revoked by a testator through the execution of a subsequent will where that subsequent will is later declared invalid. The applicable principle is that the court may declare the revoked will valid, if it determines that the testator did not intend to die intestate and would not have revoked the prior will if he or she had known that the subsequent will would prove to be invalid.

" * * * * *

"Under the facts as found above by the Court, the 1992 will is simply not provable as a valid will under the law.

"Deceased certainly intended her estate to pass under a will and would not have revoked her 1989 will if she had realized that the 1992 will was not valid. The essential dispositions of these two wills are the same.

"The doctrine of dependent relative revocation applies. * * *

"The 1989 will is the valid Last Will of Decedent and shall be admitted to probate."

On June 25, 1993, the court entered its order admitting the 1989 will to probate.

On June 29, 1993, Orrin signed an election as the surviving spouse to take against Margaret's will, but instructed attorney William Kirby to "hold" the document and not to file it.[7] On July 13, 1993, Orrin died. On August 30, 1993, at Glenn's direction, Kirby, who was both Glenn's attorney and the attorney for Margaret's estate at that time, filed the written election. That filing occurred within 90 days of the order admitting the 1989 will to probate.

In December 1997, after protracted additional proceedings, the probate court entered a comprehensive and detailed Decree of Final Distribution. That judgment reiterated that Margaret's 1989 will was "the valid will of the decedent" and also adjudicated three matters that underlie the cross-appeal: (1) The written election, signed by Orrin on June 29, 1993, but filed after his death, was not effective under ORS 114.105. (2) The so-called "Meleen note" was properly included as an asset of Margaret's estate. (3) The provision in the 1989 will for the distribution of "income earnings" to Orrin for life and then to other beneficiaries for five years was "net income" and thus subject to certain deductions and administrative expenses before distribution.

All parties appeal or cross appeal. The "objectors"-Covenant House, Curtis, and Lyman-as putative beneficiaries of the 1992 will, appeal, challenging the court's conclusion that that will was not properly acknowledged. Mille Lacs, a beneficiary under the 1989

---

[7] There is some dispute as to whether Orrin, who had limited ability to speak because of health problems, intended Kirby to "hold" the election temporarily or "hold" the election until Orrin instructed him to file it.

will, but not under the 1992 will, resists the appeal. Glenn Kirkeby, who is, nominally, a respondent on appeal, takes no position on the merits of that dispute. Conversely, Glenn, individually and as Orrin's personal representative, cross-appeals, challenging the three determinations described in the previous paragraph, and Mille Lacs, joining forces with Covenant House, Curtis, and Lyman, resists the cross-appeal. We deconstruct that tangle of issues and cross-cutting interests, strand by strand, beginning with the appeal.

Objectors argue that the 1992 will was properly executed because Horton, the notary, and Ortega, the neighbor, were both proper witnesses. In particular, objectors assert that Margaret properly acknowledged the 1992 will to both Ortega and Horton when she: (1) telephoned them, (2) told them that she had signed the will, and (3) told them that Lyman was bringing the instrument over for each to attest. Respondent Mille Lacs counters that the court properly declared the 1992 will invalid, even assuming that Horton's signature as a notary was sufficient to meet the witness requirements of ORS 112.235, because Margaret did not properly acknowledge her signature "in the presence" of either witness, as that term has been construed under Oregon law.

Assuming, without deciding, that Horton signed as a witness and not merely as a notary, we agree with respondents that the 1992 will was invalid and that the 1989 will was properly probated.[11] As amplified below, the execution of Margaret's 1992 will did not comply with ORS 112.235, because Margaret's "acknowledgment" of her signature via the telephone in the circumstances presented here, was not "in the presence" of either of the witnesses, much less both.

ORS 112.235 provides, in part:

"A will shall be in writing and shall be executed with the following formalities:

"(1) The testator, *in the presence of each of the witnesses,* shall:

" * * * * *

"(c) *Acknowledge the signature previously made* on the will by the testator * * *.

" * * * * *

---

[11] No party disputes the trial court's conclusion that, under the doctrine of "dependant relative revocation," *see supra* n. 5, if the 1992 will was invalid, the 1989 will is valid.

"(3) At least *two witnesses* shall each:

" * * * * *

"(b) *Hear the testator acknowledge the signature on the will; and*

"(c) Attest the will by signing the witness' name to it." (Emphasis added).

The "in the presence" requirement for acknowledgment by the testator was first codified in 1969,[12] and has never been explicitly construed in a reported Oregon decision. *Cf. Perry v. Adams*, 112 Or.App. 77, 82 (1992) ("The statute requires that witnesses be present when the testator signs the will or acknowledges the signature on the will."). However, before 1973, ORS 112.235 and its predecessor also included the requirement that attestation *by the witnesses* take place "in the presence of the testator and at his request."[13] In several cases, most notably, *Demaris' Estate,* the Supreme Court construed the meaning of "in the presence" in that context and concluded that attestation was valid so long as the witnesses were in the testator's "conscious presence."

In *Demaris' Estate,* the testator made out his will with the assistance of his doctor. The doctor and the doctor's wife were present when the testator signed the will. However, 20 to 30 minutes later, and in a room 20 feet from where the testator lay, the doctor and his wife, as attesting witnesses, signed the will. Because of the layout of the office, the testator could not physically see the doctor witness the will, but he could have seen the doctor's wife, had he adjusted his position slightly. A contestant of the will argued that, in those circumstances, the statutory requirement that the witness sign "in the presence" of the testator had not been satisfied. The court, after noting "it is essential, not only that the signatures be genuine and that they be found upon an instrument which all three

---

[12] Although the original statutes pertaining to execution of wills did not specifically require that the testator "acknowledge" the signature previously made, the Supreme Court, in 1890 looked to the general statute regarding the witnessing of an instrument when determining whether a witness properly attested a will and held:

"A subscribing witness to a will, therefore, must be something more than a person who subscribes his name as a witness to it. The testator must either sign the will in the presence of the witness, or must acknowledge to him by word or act that he had signed it. It is not necessary that the witness know the contents of the instrument subscribed by him, or its nature or character, but he must be able to testify that the principal in the affair put his name upon the identical piece of paper upon which he placed his own."

[13] That requirement was eliminated as part of an omnibus revision of the Probate Code in 1973.

persons intended to sign, but also that the attesters signed in the testator's presence," concluded:

> "We are, of course, satisfied that the attestation must occur in the presence of the testator and that no substitution for the statutory requirement is permissible. But we do not believe that sight is the only test of presence. We are convinced that any of the senses that a testator possesses, which enable him to know whether another is near at hand and what he is doing, may be employed by him in determining whether the attesters are in his presence as they sign his will. * * * It is unnecessary, we believe, that the attestation and execution occur in the same room. And, as we just stated, it is unnecessary that the attesters be within the range of vision of the testator when they sign. If they are so near at hand that they are within the range of any of his senses, so that he knows what is going on, the requirement has been met."

See also In re Estate of Shaff, 125 Or. 288, 296 (1928) (where the testator could have seen the witnesses, who were standing on the other side of a partition, affix their signatures had he "slightly exerted himself," the "presence" requirement was met).

Respondent Mille Lacs argues that the same "conscious presence" principle necessarily applies to the "in the presence" requirement with respect to testator's acknowledgment of a previously made signature. In particular, Mille Lacs suggests that the "in the presence" requirement is designed to avoid "bait and switch" tactics, *cf. In re Estate of Shaff,* 125 Or. at 295[14] and that that purpose is effectuated only if there is "concurrence in time and place" between (1) the testator's acknowledgment of the signature to each of the witnesses and (2) the presentation of the instrument to the witnesses. Thus, respondent reasons:

> "[T]he presence requirement of ORS 112.235 * * * requires not only the presence of the testator and witness, but also implicitly requires the presence of the will. To put it another way, a signature can't be acknowledged to a witness if the signature isn't available to be perceived by the

---

[14] In *In re Estate of Shaff,* the court observed:

"The reason of the rule * * * is to obviate any opportunity of the witnesses committing a fraud upon the testator, by changing or altering the document * * *."

witness. The will must be present for the witness to know what signature on what document is being acknowledged."

We agree with respondent that to satisfy the "in the presence" requirement of ORS 112.235(1)(c), the will, bearing the signature that the testator acknowledges, must be before the witness at the time of the acknowledgment. Even if we were to assume that telephonic acknowledgment would otherwise satisfy the "in the presence" requirement-a question we do not resolve today-an "acknowledgment" made to a witness who cannot perceive what is being "acknowledged" is meaningless. If the "in the presence" requirement is to have any context, it must require *at least* the "concurrence" of the testator's acknowledgment and the witnesses' "perception."

Applying that principle here, neither Horton nor Ortega validly witnessed Margaret's "acknowledgment." In neither instance did the witness have the 1992 will before her at the time Margaret spoke with her. Thus, neither Ortega nor Horton was close enough at hand to have known that the instrument, which was later presented to them, was, in fact, the instrument upon which Margaret had previously "acknowledged" her signature, or whether Margaret had actually signed that instrument at the time she stated her "acknowledgment."

Objectors argue, nevertheless, that we should resort to remedial principles of "substantial compliance" in this case because the validity of Margaret's signature is undisputed; because the 1992 will did, in fact, comport with Margaret's long-standing testamentary intent; and because "[n]o party has raised any question of fraud * * * or any question about [Margaret's] competence." Whatever the ultimate accuracy of those assertions,[15] "substantial compliance" does not mean noncompliance, and the fact that the testator's and witnesses' signatures may be genuine does not obviate other express statutory requirements. *See Demaris' Estate*, 166 Or. at 58–59 ("[I]t is essential, not only that the signatures be genuine and that they

---

[15] Respondent Mille Lacs does take issue with the second and third of those propositions and notes, with reference to the potential for fraud, that:

"No witness was ever given or shown the first page of the 1992 will being proposed by Covenant House, Curtis and Lyman. Moreover, the person in charge of the witnessing of the will, and who chose not to reveal the first page of it to the witnesses, was a beneficiary, i.e., Ms. Lyman. Her bequest in the 1992 will appears on that undisclosed first page.

" * * * * *

"If there was a switch of the first page of the 1992 will, it could go undetected because it was Ms. Lyman's typewriter that was used to type the will."

be found upon an instrument which all three persons intended to sign, but also that the attesters signed in the testator's presence."). The trial court did not err in admitting the 1989 will to probate.

* * *

Affirmed on appeal and cross-appeal.

———————

How hard would it have been for Margaret's neighbors to change her will so as to give themselves more of her estate? Also, remember *Kirkeby* when we reach the doctrines of substantial compliance and dependent relative revocation, below.

STEVENS V. CASDORPH

Supreme Court of Appeals of West Virginia, 1998
508 S.E.2d 610

PER CURIAM.

The plaintiffs below and appellants herein Janet Sue Lanham Stevens, Peggy Lanham Salisbury, Betty Jean Bayes, and Patricia Miller Moyers (hereinafter collectively referred to as the "Stevenses") appeal a summary judgment ruling for the defendants by the Circuit Court of Kanawha County. The Stevenses instituted this action against Patricia Eileen Casdorph and Paul Douglas Casdorph, individually and as executor of the estate of Homer Haskell Miller, defendants below and appellees herein (hereinafter referred to as "Casdorphs"), for the purpose of challenging the will of Homer Haskell Miller. The circuit court granted the Casdorphs' cross-motion for summary judgment. On appeal, this Court is asked to reverse the trial court's ruling. Following a review of the parties' arguments, the record, and the pertinent authorities, we reverse the decision of the Circuit Court of Kanawha County.

I.

FACTUAL BACKGROUND

On May 28, 1996, the Casdorphs took Mr. Homer Haskell Miller to Shawnee Bank in Dunbar, West Virginia, so that he could execute his will.[1] Once at the bank, Mr. Miller asked Debra Pauley, a bank employee and public notary, to witness the execution of his will. After Mr. Miller signed the will, Ms. Pauley took the will to two other

———————

[1]   Mr. Miller was elderly and confined to a wheelchair.

bank employees, Judith Waldron and Reba McGinn, for the purpose of having each of them sign the will as witnesses. Both Ms. Waldron and Ms. McGinn signed the will. However, Ms. Waldron and Ms. McGinn testified during their depositions that they did not actually see Mr. Miller place his signature on the will. Further, it is undisputed that Mr. Miller did not accompany Ms. Pauley to the separate work areas of Ms. Waldron and Ms. McGinn.

Mr. Miller died on July 28, 1996. The last will and testament of Mr. Miller, which named Mr. Paul Casdorph[2] as executor, left the bulk of his estate to the Casdorphs.[3] The Stevenses, nieces of Mr. Miller, filed the instant action to set aside the will. The Stevenses asserted in their complaint that Mr. Miller's will was not executed according to the requirements set forth in W.Va.Code § 41–1–3 (1995).[4] After some discovery, all parties moved for summary judgment. The circuit court denied the Stevenses' motion for summary judgment, but granted the Casdorphs' cross motion for summary judgment. From this ruling, the Stevenses appeal to this Court.

* * *

III.

DISCUSSION

The Stevenses' contention is simple. They argue that all evidence indicates that Mr. Miller's will was not properly executed. Therefore, the will should be voided. The procedural requirements at issue are contained in W.Va.Code § 41–1–3 (1997). The statute reads:

> No will shall be valid unless it be in writing and signed by the testator, or by some other person in his presence and by his direction, in such manner as to make it manifest that the name is intended as a signature; and moreover, unless it be wholly in the handwriting of the testator, *the signature shall be made or the will acknowledged by him in the presence of at least two competent witnesses, present at the same time; and such witnesses shall subscribe the will in the*

---

[2]   Paul Casdorph was a nephew of Mr. Miller.

[3]   Mr. Miller's probated estate exceeded $400,000.00. The will devised $80,000.00 to Frank Paul Smith, a nephew of Mr. Miller. The remainder of the estate was left to the Casdorphs.

[4]   As heirs, the Stevenses would be entitled to recover from Mr. Miller's estate under the intestate laws if his will is set aside as invalidly executed.

presence of the testator, and of each other, but no form of attestation shall be necessary. (Emphasis added.)

The relevant requirements of the above statute calls for a testator to sign his/her will or acknowledge such will in the presence of at least two witnesses at the same time, and such witnesses must sign the will in the presence of the testator and each other. In the instant proceeding the Stevenses assert, and the evidence supports, that Ms. McGinn and Ms. Waldron did not actually witness Mr. Miller signing his will. Mr. Miller made no acknowledgment of his signature on the will to either Ms. McGinn or Ms. Waldron. Likewise, Mr. Miller did not observe Ms. McGinn and Ms. Waldron sign his will as witnesses. Additionally, neither Ms. McGinn nor Ms. Waldron acknowledged to Mr. Miller that their signatures were on the will. It is also undisputed that Ms. McGinn and Ms. Waldron did not actually witness each other sign the will, nor did they acknowledge to each other that they had signed Mr. Miller's will. Despite the evidentiary lack of compliance with W.Va.Code § 41–1–3, the Casdorphs' argue that there was substantial compliance with the statute's requirements, insofar as everyone involved with the will knew what was occurring. The trial court found that there was substantial compliance with the statute because everyone knew why Mr. Miller was at the bank. The trial court further concluded there was no evidence of fraud, coercion or undue influence. Based upon the foregoing, the trial court concluded that the will should not be voided even though the technical aspects of W.Va.Code § 41–1–3 were not followed.

Our analysis begins by noting that "[t]he law favors testacy over intestacy." However, we clearly held in syllabus point 1 of *Black v. Maxwell,* 131 W.Va. 247 (1948), that "[t]estamentary intent and a written instrument, executed in the manner provided by [W.Va.Code § 41–1–3], existing concurrently, are essential to the creation of a valid will." *Black* establishes that mere intent by a testator to execute a written will is insufficient. The actual execution of a written will must also comply with the dictates of W.Va.Code § 41–1–3. The Casdorphs seek to have this Court establish an exception to the technical requirements of the statute. In *Wade v. Wade,* 119 W.Va. 596 (1938), this Court permitted a narrow exception to the stringent requirements of the W.Va.Code § 41–1–3. This narrow exception is embodied in syllabus point 1 of *Wade:*

Where a testator acknowledges a will and his signature thereto in the presence of two competent witnesses, one of whom then subscribes his name, the other or first witness, having already subscribed the will in the presence of the testator but out of the presence of the second witness, may acknowledge his signature in the presence of the testator and the second witness, and such acknowledgment, if there be no indicia of fraud or misunderstanding in the proceeding, will be deemed a signing by the first witness within the requirement of Code, 41–1–3, that the witnesses must subscribe their names in the presence of the testator and of each other.

See Brammer v. Taylor, 175 W.Va. 728, 730 n. 1 (1985), ("[T]he witnesses' acknowledgment of their signatures . . . in the presence of the testator [and in the presence of each other] is tantamount to and will be deemed a 'signing' or 'subscribing' in the presence of those persons").

Wade stands for the proposition that if a witness acknowledges his/her signature on a will in the physical presence of the other subscribing witness *and the testator,* then the will is properly witnessed within the terms of W.Va.Code § 41–1–3. In this case, none of the parties signed or acknowledged their signatures in the presence of each other. This case meets neither the narrow exception of *Wade* nor the specific provisions of W.Va.Code § 41–1–3.

IV.

CONCLUSION

In view of the foregoing, we grant the relief sought in this appeal and reverse the circuit court's order granting the Casdorphs' cross-motion for summary judgment.

Reversed.

WORKMAN, J., dissenting.

The majority once more takes a very technocratic approach to the law, slavishly worshiping form over substance. In so doing, they not only create a harsh and inequitable result wholly contrary to the indisputable intent of Mr. Homer Haskell Miller, but also a rule of law that is against the spirit and intent of our whole body of law relating to the making of wills.

* * *

I am authorized to state that JUSTICE MAYNARD joins in this dissent.

In the dissent, Justice Workman writes as if sensible people would come to his conclusion and admit the document to probate. What would the result have been under UPC § 2–502?

UPC § 2–502

SECTION 2–502. EXECUTION; WITNESSED OR NOTARIZED WILLS; HOLOGRAPHIC WILLS.

(a) [Witnessed or Notarized Wills.] Except as otherwise provided in subsection (b) and in Sections 2–503, 2–506, and 2–513, a will must be:

(1) in writing;

(2) signed by the testator or in the testator's name by some other individual in the testator's conscious presence and by the testator's direction; and

(3) either:

(A) signed by at least two individuals, each of whom signed within a reasonable time after the individual witnessed either the signing of the will as described in paragraph (2) or the testator's acknowledgment of that signature or acknowledgment of the will; or

(B) acknowledged by the testator before a notary public or other individual authorized by law to take acknowledgments.

(b) [Holographic Wills.] A will that does not comply with subsection (a) is valid as a holographic will, whether or not witnessed, if the signature and material portions of the document are in the testator's handwriting.

(c) [Extrinsic Evidence.] Intent that a document constitute the testator's will can be established by extrinsic evidence, including, for holographic wills, portions of the document that are not in the testator's handwriting.

Under the UPC, witnesses must sign within a reasonable time, but they need not sign at the same time as they witnessed the testator's signature or acknowledgment and need not sign in the presence of the testator or each other. Given that the witnesses often do not know the content of the will, how do they know that they are signing the same document that they witnessed being signed?

The possibility of electronic wills has increased the pressure on the issue of remote attestation. In what ways should the law allow a person to witness a will? In 2019, the National Conference of Commissioners on Uniform State Laws recommended for adoption the Uniform Electronic Wills Act (E-Wills Act), which allows witnessing to occur in the "electronic" presence of the testator. If it is adopted by a state, what will be the effect on false positives, false negatives, costs of execution, and litigation? COVID-19 increased the risks of acknowledgment in person. Some states responded by temporarily allowing remote witnessing by telecommunication.

There are numerous steps to be observed in executing a will, and the requirements vary across states. Practice manuals describe the process for each state. But it is not necessarily the case that the decedent will die domiciled in the state of execution. Although many states provide, as does UPC § 2–506, that a will may be probated if execution complies with the rules of the state of execution, a safer approach is to follow a procedure that will suffice in all states. You can find one in A. James Casner, ESTATE PLANNING, § 3.3.1 edited by Jeffrey E. Pennell.

To be a formal will, it must be signed by attesting witnesses. Some wills go further than merely providing a line for the witnesses to sign by including an attestation clause. Such a clause might look something like the following:

> We, the undersigned testator and the undersigned witnesses, respectively, whose names are signed to the attached or foregoing instrument declare:
>
> (1) that the testator executed the instrument as the testator's will;
>
> (2) that, in the presence of both witnesses, the testator signed or acknowledged the signature already made or directed another to sign for the testator in the testator's presence;
>
> (3) that the testator executed the will as a free and voluntary act for the purposes expressed in it;
>
> (4) that each of the witnesses, in the presence of the testator and of each other, signed the will as a witness;

(5) that the testator was of sound mind when the will was executed; and

(6) that to the best knowledge of each of the witnesses the testator was, at the time the will was executed, at least eighteen (18) years of age or was a member of the armed forces or of the merchant marine of the United States or its allies.

In a case taking the formalities perhaps to the limit, *In re Colling*, 1 W.L.R. 1440 (Cha. 1972), the will was denied probate because the testator acknowledged his signature after one of the witnesses had signed instead of before both witnesses signed.

(i) Witness Competence

To perform their legal role, witnesses must be competent. For a signature of an attesting witness to be effective, the witness had to be competent at the time she witnessed and attested; it does not matter if she became incompetent later. To be a witness to testify to prove execution of a will at a probate hearing, the witness had to be competent at the time of witnessing and attesting, and also must be competent at the time of probate. Competence requires mental competence of the same sort that is required of a witness at trial.

Under the Statute of Frauds, 1676, witnesses had to be credible, which courts construed to require that witnesses be disinterested. An interested person was not a competent witness. If the will made a gift to a witness, that witness was viewed as being untrustworthy, and for good reason. A witness might be less likely to blow the whistle on undue influence or fraud if he knew he would take under the will. Therefore, the signature of the interested witness did not count, with the effect sometimes that the will did not qualify for probate for lack of a sufficient number of competent witnesses. As a result, a document procured by undue influence by a witness who took a gift from it would be denied probate. This approach might be called the strike-the-witness method of dealing with interested witnesses. Being appointed an executor or trustee in a will was not, however, viewed as being interested.

Dissatisfaction with this approach led to reform, which shifted the focus from preventing wills procured by undue influence from being probated to reducing the incentives for undue influence by preventing witnesses from taking under wills they witnessed. These purging statutes were adopted in England and a majority of the states. The English statute struck gifts to witnesses, making them disinterested and therefore able to serve as witnesses. A subsequent statute made clear that a witness who was also a trustee or an executor designated in a will could receive a fee because it was earned and not a gift subject to purging. Some states still follow this strike-the-gift model, purging the entire gift to witnesses.

Most modern purging statutes take a more lenient, strike-the-gain approach, striking gifts to witnesses only to the extent the witness will gain from the will being probated. Many purging statutes do not strike gifts to witnesses that are supernumeraries, extra witnesses not necessary to probate the will.

The UPC has continued the drift of the law toward lenience, taking it all the way to the other end of the spectrum. Under UPC § 2–505, the signing of a will by an interested witness does not invalidate the witness or any provision of the will. The comment to that section says:

> This approach does not increase appreciably the opportunity for fraud or undue influence. A substantial devise by will to a person who is one of the witnesses to the execution of the will is itself a suspicious circumstance, and the devise might be challenged on grounds of undue influence. The requirement of disinterested witnesses has not succeeded in preventing fraud and undue influence; and in most cases of undue influence, the influencer is careful not to sign as a witness, but to procure disinterested witnesses.

Will all of the cases of undue influence prevented by the disinterest requirement be caught by an undue influence challenge and at an equally low cost? Does it matter whether the requirement of disinterested witnesses has not succeeded in preventing all fraud and undue influence? Maybe the strike-the-gift approach was too lenient to do that job. California law says that a gift to a witness creates a presumption of undue influence. Is that approach better?

(ii) Self-Proved Wills

As is indicated in *Chastain*, attestation clauses should not be confused with self-proving affidavits. Originally and technically, a self-proving affidavit was an additional document executed after the execution of the will. A self-proving affidavit is not part of the will but is sometimes attached to a will. This affidavit makes it possible in most states for the will be admitted to probate without the testimony of any witnesses, which is especially helpful if they are all dead. When a self-proving affidavit is added to a will, the will is often called a "self-proved will" or "self-proving will". However, despite that terminology, the self-proving affidavit is not necessarily part of the will and, if it is not part of the will, then the execution of the affidavit does not qualify as execution of the will, as can be seen in *In re Estate of Ricketts*, 773 P.2d 93 (Wash. Ct. App. 1989). The Washington statute in *Ricketts* has since been amended to allow the execution of the affidavit to serve as the execution of the will. UPC § 2–504 provides that a will may be simultaneously executed, attested, and made self-proved by duly acknowledging and executing a clause such as the model clause provided in that section.

(f) Notarization

Most jurisdictions require two witnesses. UPC § 2–502(a)(3)(B), added in 2008, allows the substitution of a notary public for the two witnesses. Compared to two witnesses, does one notary provide as much confidence that the will reflects the intent of the decedent? Notice also that the notary might not need to notarize at the time the testator signs or acknowledges. However, the E-Wills Act provides that notarization of a self-proving affidavit must be at the same time as the execution of an electronic will.

4. INFORMAL, HOLOGRAPHIC WILLS

Some states and civil law jurisdictions such as Germany and France allow admission to probate of wills that have not been witnessed, sometimes known as holographic or informal wills. Even those wills must, of course, meet other requirements. A couple of states require that holographic wills be dated. Holographic wills must be entirely in the hand of the testator. In some states, any words that are typed or pre-printed prevent admission to probate. Other states take a more relaxed approach, merely ignoring words not in the hand of the testator, although sometimes the result is that the document does not qualify for probate because the handwritten words do not contain any indication that the document is supposed to be a will. A printed or typed form, for example, might state at the top "Last Will and Testament". If the court ignores those and other words not in the testator's hand, the document might look like nothing more than a list of persons and things.

The UPC is, as usual, even more relaxed than earlier laws regarding requirements for holographic wills. UPC § 2–502(b) says that a will "is valid as a holographic will, whether or not witnessed, if the signature and material portions of the document are in the testator's handwriting." The comments indicate that all of the "material portions" need to be in the hand of the testator. However, the UPC comments imply that printed, typed, or stamped words such as "I give, devise, and bequeath to ___" are not material and do not disqualify the document if the blanks are filled in by hand.

Many states do not allow unattested wills at all. Should holographic wills be admitted to probate if they lack attestation? Which of the purposes or functions of the Wills Acts does the handwriting requirement satisfy? Are there opportunities for mistake, undue influence, or fraud? Do you want your own holographic will to be admitted? Do you want to pay for the litigation sometimes resulting from admitting the holographic wills of others?

5. NUNCUPATIVE WILLS

Going beyond the UPC, statutes in some states allow testators to pass property by an oral, "nuncupative", will. These statutes may limit oral wills to personalty and may limit the value of the personalty. In addition, the statutes may limit oral wills to specified circumstances, such as active military service or last illnesses, and require witnesses to memorialize the will within a certain period of time.

6. FURTHER RELAXING THE REQUIREMENTS

As seen above, the formal requirements for a will to be admitted to probate serve many goals. But the denial of probate to wills that were clearly intended to be wills has disturbed commentators, and there is pressure to relax the formalities in cases of clear intent. Relaxing the formalities sacrifices, to some degree, the goals summarized above. But it is especially ironic that, in some cases, relaxation of formalities will lead to results that are further from the intent of the decedent. Keep these false positives and the other goals of formalities in mind as you read on.

(a) Narrow Exceptions to the Statutory Formalities

One way to reduce false negatives is to carve narrow exceptions to the formalities in certain cases that are rare enough and are cabined easily enough that the exception will result in little erosion of the benefits of the formalities. One example of such a situation is when two spouses sign wills at a single ceremony, but both accidentally sign the wrong will. Under the standard analysis, the decedent did not intend the document he signed to be his will and the decedent did not sign the document he intended to be his will, so neither document is admissible to probate. A court could admit the unsigned will to probate on the ground that the purposes of the formalities are satisfied. Such a narrow exception to the formalities might allow justice to be done in a few more cases without creating any substantial opportunity for fraud or other false-positive error. In *Matter of Snide*, 418 N.E.2d 656 (N.Y. 1981), the majority reached such a result by allowing the document signed by the testator to be reformed to conform to the document the testator intended to sign. Judge Jones, dissenting, wrote:

> I agree with the Appellate Division that the Surrogate's Court had no authority to reform the decedent's will and am of the conviction that the willingness of the majority in an appealing case to depart from what has been consistent precedent in the courts of the United States and England will prove troublesome in the future. This is indeed an instance of the old adage that hard cases make bad law.

> Our analysis must start with the recognition that any statute of wills operates frequently to frustrate the identifiable dispositive intentions of the decedent. It is never sufficient under our law that the decedent's wishes be clearly established; our statute, like those of most other common-law jurisdictions, mandates with but a few specific exceptions that the wishes of the decedent be memorialized with prescribed formality. The statutes historically have been designed for the protection of testators, particularly against fraudulent changes in or additions to wills. "[W]hile often it may happen that a will truly expressing the intention of the testator is denied probate for failure of proper execution, it is better that this should happen under a proper construction of the statute than that the individual case should be permitted to weaken those provisions intended to protect testators generally from fraudulent alterations of their wills".

Should courts carve narrow exceptions to the formalities, or should the balancing of the costs and benefits of exceptions be left to the legislature?

(b) Broad Exceptions to the Statutory Formalities

(i) Substantial Compliance

In an influential article in 1975, Professor John Langbein argued against strict compliance with the formalities. He favored a lesser standard of "substantial compliance," which would allow admission of a document if it expressed the decedent's testamentary intent and "its form sufficiently approximate[d] Wills Act formality to enable the court to conclude that it serves the purposes of the Wills Act." John H. Langbein, Substantial Compliance with the Wills Act, 88 Harv. L. Rev. 489 (1975).

ESTATE OF BURTON V. DIDRICKSEN
Court of Appeals of Washington, Division 2, 2015
358 P.3d 1222

MAXA, P.J.

Victor White appeals the trial court's order declaring that Ray Burton died intestate. RCW 11.12.020(1) states that wills must be signed by the testator and attested by two witnesses to be valid. White submitted evidence that Burton drafted and signed a document leaving his entire estate to White. The document was signed by one witness, but subsequently was lost. Burton later drafted a second, purportedly similar, document leaving his entire estate to White. That document was signed by a different witness. Richard Didricksen, Burton's legal heir, challenges the validity of the document under RCW 11.12.020(1). White argues that because two witnesses attested to Burton's testamentary intent to leave his estate to White, the documents together constituted a validly executed will under both strict compliance and substantial compliance theories.

We hold that Burton's testamentary documents do not constitute a valid will because Burton did not strictly comply with the requirement in RCW 11.12.020(1) that two witnesses attest to a will. We also hold that even assuming the substantial compliance doctrine applies to RCW 11.12.020(1), Burton did not substantially comply with the attestation requirement. Accordingly, we affirm the trial court's order declaring that Burton died intestate.

FACTS

Burton was a successful businessman with substantial assets, including two gold mines and a number of collectible cars. He allegedly was estranged from his living relatives and considered himself without family. Beginning in 2011, White helped the elderly Burton with a variety of tasks around his home. At some point, Burton allegedly began to prepare White to take over his business dealings after he died. Burton was hospitalized for pneumonia in 2013, and after his release White became his caretaker. Burton also received home nurse visits, and later hospice care. Throughout this time, Burton apparently had no will.

Shortly before he died, Burton handwrote and signed a document in red ink that was witnessed and signed by Lisa Erickson, a nurse. Erickson stated in a declaration that the document was for the purpose of Burton leaving his property to White. However, Erickson provided no testimony regarding the actual language used in that document, and she does not know what happened to the document.

The day before he died, Burton handwrote another testamentary statement, again in red ink, on a blank portion of a preprinted healthcare directive form. He apparently needed some assistance from another nurse, Shirley Outson, to complete the writing. The final statement, which is difficult to read, appears to state:

> Thank[2] Victor White remain my caretaker till I go to sleep/die. The transfer of Gold Mines Montecarlo and Black Hawk One, all my collector cars and real estate located at 36619 Mountain Hwy E, Eatonville, WA 98320. I wish all my worldly possessions to go to Victor White.

Burton signed the form below the statement, as did Outson. But no other witness signed the document.

Burton died on January 25, 2014. White petitioned the trial court to recognize Burton's statement on the healthcare directive form as his will and to name White as personal representative of Burton's estate. Didricksen, Burton's cousin and legal heir, moved for an order declaring that Burton died intestate. The trial court granted Didricksen's motion, finding that Burton had not executed a valid will and therefore had died intestate. White moved for reconsideration, which the trial court denied. In denying White's motion for reconsideration, the trial court noted that White was free to pursue other legal remedies.

---

[2] The exact word Burton used is difficult to decipher. Didricksen interprets the writing as stating "*That* Victor White remain my caretaker," while White interprets the writing as stating "*Thank* Victor White remain my caretaker."

White appeals the trial court's order declaring that Burton died intestate and its denial of his motion to reconsider that order.

ANALYSIS

A. STRICT COMPLIANCE WITH TWO WITNESS REQUIREMENT

White argues that the trial court erred by concluding that Burton died intestate because Burton complied with the requirements of RCW 11.12.020(1) and executed a valid will by creating two equivalent documents, each witnessed by a different person. We disagree.

* * *

2. No Strict Compliance

RCW 11.12.020(1) requires that a will meet three basic formalities:

> Every will shall be [1] in writing [2] signed by the testator or by some other person under the testator's direction in the testator's presence, and shall be [3] *attested by two or more competent witnesses,* by subscribing their names to the will, or by signing an affidavit that complies with RCW 11.20.020(2), while in the presence of the testator and at the testator's direction or request.

(Emphasis added).[4] Attestation by two witnesses always is required, and Washington does not recognize "holographic" wills.

White argues that the healthcare directive document is a valid will that complies with the two witness requirement. But that document was signed by only one witness. Therefore, on its face the document does not comply with RCW 11.12.020(1).

However, White argues that two witnesses did attest to Burton's will. White claims that they attested to the will in counterparts, separately signing two counterpart documents describing the same testamentary gift. White notes that nothing in RCW 11.12.020(1) prohibits executing a will in counterparts and that no Washington cases address this situation.

Even if we assume that witnesses can attest to a will in counterparts, the facts here show that Burton's witnesses did not sign counterpart documents. A "counterpart" is "one of two

---

[4] Only nuncupative wills—restricted to members of the armed forces or merchant marine and testamentary gifts of personal property amounting to $1,000 or less—are exempt from some of these formality requirements.

corresponding copies of a legal instrument;" a synonym is "duplicate." WEBSTER'S THIRD NEW INT'L DICTIONARY, 520 (2002). Here, there is no evidence that Burton prepared duplicative copies of any testamentary document. The witnesses stated that the two handwritten testamentary documents both left Burton's entire estate to White, but neither witness stated that the documents were identical. Having one witness sign one testamentary document and having another witness sign a different testamentary document does not constitute signing one document in counterparts.

White also argues that the two documents must be viewed as a single integrated document that was signed by two witnesses. However, even if we assume that these documents somehow formed a single will, there were no witnesses that signed that will. Erickson and Outson each signed a portion of the will, but neither witnessed the "integrated" document.

Without evidence that two witnesses signed the same document, or at least identical duplicates of that document, White cannot show that Burton complied with RCW 11.12.020(1). Because only one witness signed the healthcare directive document—the only testamentary writing signed by Burton in the record—we hold that Burton did not strictly comply with the two witness requirement in RCW 11.12.020(1).

B.   SUBSTANTIAL COMPLIANCE

White argues that even if Burton did not strictly comply with the two witness requirement in RCW 11.12.020(1), we should conclude that he executed a valid will because he substantially complied with that requirement. We disagree.

1.   Legal Principles

Under the substantial compliance doctrine a party complies with statutory requirements by "satisfaction of the substance essential to the purpose of the statute." Courts may invoke the doctrine where a party has "substantially complied with the requirements crucial to the underlying design intended by the legislature." However, some statutes are not susceptible to substantial compliance.

2.   Substantial Compliance and RCW 11.12.020(1)

Washington courts have not applied the substantial compliance doctrine to the requirements of RCW 11.12.020(1). The only Washington case that even mentions substantial compliance with regard to RCW 11.12.020(1) is *In Re Estate of Ricketts*, 54 Wash.App.

221 (1989). In that case, the two witnesses to a will codicil did not subscribe their names to the codicil, but instead signed an affidavit that was stapled to it. It was undisputed that this procedure did not strictly conform with the requirements of the version of RCW 11.12.020(1) then in effect.[6] But the proponent of the will cited to a number of cases approving probate of wills despite irregularities in the placement of witnesses' signatures.

The court in *Ricketts* discussed an Oklahoma case in which a will was admitted to probate when the testator signed at the end of the will near the bottom of the page and the subscribing witnesses signed on the following page. The court stated that the record in that case "show[ed] much more substantial compliance with the requirements for execution than here present."

Ricketts could be interpreted as accepting the notion that a testator can comply with RCW 11.12.020(1) through substantial compliance. However, the court did not specifically address that issue and in fact did not find substantial compliance. Instead, the court applied the requirements of RCW 11.12.020(1) and reversed the trial court's decision to admit the codicil to probate.

Regardless of the significance of *Ricketts,* in order to assess the merits of the present case we assume without deciding that the substantial compliance doctrine applies to RCW 11.12.020(1).

3.   Substantial Compliance with Will Validity Provisions

Even assuming that substantial compliance is sufficient to satisfy the two witness requirement of RCW 11.12.020(1), Didricksen argues that there was no substantial compliance here. We agree.

The deficiency with Burton's testamentary documents was more than merely technical or procedural. The fundamental problem is that only Erickson saw and witnessed the first document and only Outson saw and witnessed the second, *different* document. If Erickson and Outson had seen an identical document but both signatures for some reason were not on that document, White's substantial compliance argument might be more compelling. But the fact that Erickson and Outson signed different documents precludes any finding of substantial compliance of the requirement in RCW 11.12.020(1) that two witnesses attest to the will.

---

[6]   The legislature subsequently amended RCW 11.12.020(1) to allow this procedure.

Applying substantial compliance here also would work against the purposes of RCW 11.12.020. The statutory purposes underlying the formality requirements of the statute are "to ensure that the testator has a definite and complete intention to dispose of his or her property and to prevent, as far as possible, fraud, perjury, mistake and the chance of one instrument being substituted for another." Here, the risk of mistake—if not fraud—would be high if we allowed probate of a testamentary document signed by only one witness when the second "witness" never saw that document.

We hold that under the facts of this case, Burton's healthcare directive document did not substantially comply with RCW 11.12.020(1).

* * *

We affirm the trial court's order declaring that Burton died intestate.

––––––––––––

The court did not decide whether Washington's general doctrine of substantial compliance could be applied to the statutory requirements for execution of a will. Should a court be open to arguments that a will may be admitted to probate when some of the statutory requirements have not been satisfied? Will such openness increase litigation? Can the court predict which requirements are needed to prevent fraud and mistake and which requirements are not?

(ii) The Australian Dispensing Power and Harmless Error

In 1975, about the same time that Langbein was arguing for the substantial compliance approach to replace strict compliance, the state of South Australia gave judges the power to dispense with the formalities in some situations. A court can dispense with the formalities, admitting the document to probate, if the court is satisfied that "the deceased intended the document to constitute his will." This dispensing power is also called the "harmless error" rule or doctrine and it has been adopted in § 2–503 of the UPC.

UPC § 2–503

SECTION 2–503. HARMLESS ERROR. Although a document or writing added upon a document was not executed in compliance with

Section 2–502, the document or writing is treated as if it had been executed in compliance with that section if the proponent of the document or writing establishes by clear and convincing evidence that the decedent intended the document or writing to constitute:

(1) the decedent's will,

(2) a partial or complete revocation of the will,

(3) an addition to or an alteration of the will, or

(4) a partial or complete revival of the decedent's formerly revoked will or of a formerly revoked portion of the will.

IN RE ESTATE OF HORTON

Court of Appeals of Michigan, 2018
925 N.W.2d 207

PER CURIAM.

Will contestant Lanora Jones appeals as of right the order of the Berrien Probate Court recognizing an electronic document as the valid will of her son, Duane Francis Horton II. Because the trial court did not err by concluding that Guardianship and Alternatives, Inc. (GAI) established by clear and convincing evidence that decedent intended his electronic note to constitute his will, we affirm.

The decedent, Duane Francis Horton II, committed suicide in December 2015, at the age of 21. Before he committed suicide, decedent left an undated, handwritten, journal entry. There is no dispute that the journal entry was in decedent's handwriting. The journal entry stated:

> I am truly sorry about this . . . My final note, my farewell is on my phone. The app should be open. If not look on evernote, "Last Note"[.]

The journal entry also provided an email address and password for "evernote."

The "farewell" or "last note" referred to in decedent's journal entry was a typed document that existed only in electronic form. Decedent's full name was typed at the end of the document. No portion of the document was in decedent's handwriting. The document contained apologies and personal sentiments directed to specific individuals, religious comments, requests relating to his funeral arrangements, and many self-deprecating comments. The document also contained one full paragraph regarding the distribution of decedent's property after his death:

> Have my uncle go through my stuff, pick out the stuff that belonged to my dad and/or grandma, and take it. If there is something he doesn't want, feel free to keep it and do with it what you will. My guns (aside from the shotgun that belonged to my dad) are your's to do with what you will. Make sure my car goes to Jody if at all possible. If at all possible, make sure that my trust fund goes to my half-sister Shella, and only her. Not my mother. All of my other stuff is you're do whatever you want with. I do ask that anything you well, you give 10% of the money to the church, 50% to my sister Shella, and the remaining 40% is your's to do whatever you want with.

In addition, in a paragraph addressed directly to decedent's uncle, the note contained the following statement: "Anything that I have that belonged to either Dad, or Grandma, is your's to claim and do whatever you want with. If there is anything that you don't want, please make sure Shane and Kara McLean get it." In a paragraph addressed to his half-sister, Shella, decedent also stated that "all" of his "money" was hers.

 * * *

 * * *

II. ANALYSIS

"The right to make a disposition of property by means of a will is entirely statutory." The Estates and Protected Individuals Code (EPIC), MCL 700.1101 et seq., governs wills in Michigan. The provisions in EPIC must "be liberally construed and applied to promote its purposes and policies," including to "discover and make effective a decedent's intent in distribution of the decedent's property."

In a contested will case, the proponent of a will bears "the burden of establishing prima facie proof of due execution." Generally, to be valid, a will must be executed in compliance with MCL 700.2502, which provides:

(1) Except as provided in subsection (2) and in sections 2503, 2506, and 2513, a will is valid only if it is all of the following:

(a) In writing.

(b) Signed by the testator or in the testator's name by some other individual in the testator's conscious presence and by the testator's direction.

(c) Signed by at least 2 individuals, each of whom signed within a reasonable time after he or she witnessed either the signing of the will as described in subdivision (b) or the testator's acknowledgment of that signature or acknowledgment of the will.

(2) A will that does not comply with subsection (1) is valid as a holographic will, whether or not witnessed, if it is dated, and if the testator's signature and the document's material portions are in the testator's handwriting.

(3) Intent that the document constitutes a testator's will can be established by extrinsic evidence, including, for a holographic will, portions of the document that are not in the testator's handwriting. [MCL 700.2502.]

As set forth in MCL 700.2502(1), there are specific formalities that are generally required to execute a valid will. However, as expressly stated in MCL 700.2502(1), there are several exceptions to these formalities, including less formal holographic wills allowed under MCL 700.2502(2) and the exception created by MCL 700.2503. MCL 700.2503 states:

Although a document or writing added upon a document was not executed in compliance with section 2502, the document or writing is treated as if it had been executed in compliance with that section if the proponent of the document or writing establishes by clear and convincing evidence that the decedent intended the document or writing to constitute any of the following:

(a) The decedent's will.

(b) A partial or complete revocation of the decedent's will.

(c) An addition to or an alteration of the decedent's will.

(d) A partial or complete revival of the decedent's formerly revoked will or of a formerly revoked portion of the decedent's will.

"The plain language of MCL 700.2503 establishes that it permits the probate of a will that does not meet the requirements of MCL 700.2502." Indeed, other than requiring "a document or writing added upon a document," there are no particular formalities necessary to create a valid will under MCL 700.2503. Essentially, under MCL 700.2503, any document or writing can constitute a valid will provided that "the proponent of the document or writing establishes by clear and convincing evidence that the decedent intended the document or writing to constitute . . . [t]he decedent's will." In considering the decedent's intent, "EPIC permits the admission of extrinsic evidence in order to determine whether the decedent intended a document to constitute his or her will."

In this case, it is undisputed that decedent's typed, electronic note, which was unwitnessed and undated, does not meet either the formal requirements for a will under MCL 700.2502(1) or the requirements of a holographic will under MCL 700.2502(2). Instead, the validity of the will in this case turns on the applicability of MCL 700.2503 and whether the trial court erred by concluding that GAI presented clear and convincing evidence that decedent intended the electronic document to constitute his will. To properly analyze this question, we must first briefly address Jones's characterization of decedent's note as a failed holographic will. In particular, contrary to Jones's attempt to conflate MCL 700.2503 and the holographic will provision, MCL 700.2503 is an independent exception to the formalities required under MCL 700.2502(1), which does not require a decedent to satisfy—or attempt to satisfy—any of the requirements for a holographic will under MCL 700.2502(2).[3] To require a testator to meet any specific formalities notwithstanding MCL 700.2503, "would render MCL 700.2503 inapplicable to the testamentary formalities in MCL 700.2502, which is contrary to the plain language of the statute." Instead, under MCL 700.2503, while the proposed will must be a document or writing, there are no specific formalities

---

[3]   Jones argues on appeal that the holographic will statute will be rendered meaningless if MCL 700.2503 can be used to circumvent the necessity of all requirements for a formal will under MCL 700.2502(1) as well as all requirements for a holographic will under MCL 700.2502(2). Contrary to this argument, the requirements for a holographic will under MCL 700.2502(2), like the more formal requirements for a will under MCL 700.2502(1), remain a viable—and perhaps more straightforward—means for expressing intent to create a will. MCL 700.2503 simply makes plain that other evidence clearly and convincingly demonstrating intent to adopt a will should not be ignored simply because the decedent failed to comply with formalities.

required for execution of the document, and any document or writing can constitute a will, provided that the proponent of the will presents clear and convincing evidence to establish that the decedent intended the document to constitute his or her will.

Turning to the facts of this case, we find no error in the trial court's determination that decedent intended for the electronic document in question to constitute his will. In basic terms, "[a] will is said to be a declaration of a man's mind as to the manner in which he would have his property or estate disposed of after his death." A will need not be written in a particular form or use any particular words; for example, a letter or other document, such as a deed, can constitute a will. However, in order for a document to be considered a will it must evince testamentary intent, meaning that it must operate to transfer property "only upon and by reason of the death of the maker." Moreover, the document must be final in nature; that is, "[m]ere drafts" or "a mere unexecuted intention to leave by will is of no effect." Ultimately, in deciding whether a person intends a document to constitute a "will," the question is whether the person intended the document to govern the posthumous distribution of his or her property. As noted, whether the decedent intended a document to constitute a will may be shown by extrinsic evidence.

In this case, to determine whether decedent intended his farewell note to constitute a will, the trial court considered the contents of the electronic document as well as extrinsic evidence relating to the circumstances surrounding decedent's death and the discovery of his suicide note as described by witnesses at the evidentiary hearing. After detailing the evidence presented and assessing witness credibility, the trial court concluded that the evidence "was unrebutted that the deceased hand wrote a note directing the reader to his cell phone with specific instructions as to how to access a document he had written electronically in anticipation of his imminent death by his own hands."[5] Regarding

---

[5] Jones argues that GAI did not present testimony that anyone saw decedent type the suicide note and that, because it was merely in electronic form, someone else could have typed or altered the suicide note. The trial court rejected Jones's argument that the document had been written or altered by someone other than decedent as mere speculation without supporting evidence. Jones does not dispute that the handwritten, journal entry was in decedent's handwriting. That journal entry directed its finder to decedent's cell phone. One of the individuals who found and read the electronic note on decedent's cell phone identified the contents of the note at the hearing. She indicated that she "know[s]" what the notes "says" and that she would "[a]bsolutely" recognize if the note had been changed. The probate court expressly found this witness's testimony to be credible. Deferring to the trial court assessment of credibility, the evidence shows that decedent wrote the electronic note and that it was not altered by anyone else.

the language of the document itself, the trial court determined that the document unequivocally set forth decedent's wishes regarding the disposition of his property. Finding that decedent clearly and unambiguous expressed his testamentary intent in the electronic document in anticipation of his impending death, the trial court concluded that decedent intended the electronic document to constitute his will.

Reviewing the language of the document de novo, we agree with the trial court's conclusion that the document expresses decedent's testamentary intent. On the face of the document, it is apparent that the document was written with decedent's death in mind; indeed, the document is clearly intended to be read after decedent's death. The note contains apologies and explanations for his suicide, comments relating to decedent's views on God and the afterlife, final farewells and advice to loved ones and friends, and it contains requests regarding his funeral. In what is clearly a final note to be read upon decedent's death, the document then clearly dictates the distribution of his property after his death. Specifically, decedent was clear that he did not want his mother to receive the remains of the trust fund. Decedent stated that the money in his trust fund was for his half-sister and he wanted his uncle to receive any of his personal belongings that came from his father and grandmother. He left his car to "Jody." All of decedent's "other stuff" was left to the couple with whom decedent had been living. In short, the note is "distinctly testamentary in character," and the document itself provides support for the conclusion that decedent intended for the note to constitute his will.[7]

Extrinsic evidence may also be used to discern a decedent's intent, and considering the evidence presented at the hearing, we see no clear err in the trial court's findings of fact regarding the circumstances surrounding decedent's death and decedent's intent for the electronic note to constitute his will. In this regard, as detailed by the trial court, the evidence showed that decedent's

---

Contrary to Jones's arguments, the trial court did not clearly err by concluding that the electronic note was written by decedent.

[7]   In disputing the note's validity as a will, Jones specifically emphasizes that the electronic note does not contain a handwritten signature and Jones asserts that the document should simply be viewed as an informal "note" rather than a "will." However, as discussed, the formalities of MCL 700.2502 are not required for a valid will under MCL 700.2503. Moreover, we note that, although the electronic note does not contain a handwritten signature, decedent ended the document with the more formal use of his full name—"Duane F. Horton II," which added an element of solemnity to the document, supporting the conclusion that the document was intended as more than a casual "note."

handwritten journal entry directed the reader to an electronic, final "farewell." Decedent left his journal and his phone containing the electronic note in his room; he then left the home and committed suicide. Given the surrounding circumstances, although the note was undated, the trial court reasonably concluded that the electronic note was written "in anticipation of [decedent's] imminent death by his own hands." The fact that decedent wrote a note providing for disposition of his property in anticipation of his impending death supports the conclusion that it was a final document to govern the disposition of decedent's property after his death. Moreover, the evidence showed that decedent had, at best, a strained relationship with his mother, and the trial court reasoned that Jones's testimony regarding her strained relationship with decedent "actually provides an understanding of the intent of [decedent] when he drafted the cell phone document." In other words, the nature of decedent's relationship with his mother, when read in conjunction with his clear directive that none of his money go to his mother, supports the conclusion that decedent intended for the electronic note to govern the posthumous distribution of his property to ensure that his mother, who would otherwise be his heir, did not inherit from him. We see no clear error in the trial court's factual findings, and the extrinsic evidence in this case strongly supports the conclusion that decedent intended the electronic note to constitute his will.

Overall, considering both the document itself and the extrinsic evidence submitted at the hearing, the trial court did not err by concluding that GAI presented clear and convincing evidence that decedent intended the electronic note to constitute his will, and thus the document constitutes a valid will under MCL 700.2503.

Affirmed. Having prevailed in full, GAI may tax costs pursuant to MCR 7.219.

(iii) Questioning and Reforming Harmless Error

Is "harmless error" harmless? The substantial compliance and harmless error doctrines raise questions regarding the functions served by Wills Acts. One function of the formalities is to hold down the costs of litigation borne by estates, families, and society generally. There are cases that would not be disputed under a strict compliance approach that would be disputed when a court has the option to say that the document's form serves the purposes of the

Wills Act or that an error was harmless. On the other hand, it is theoretically possible that some cases that would be litigated under the strict compliance standard would not be litigated under a more lenient standard of substantial compliance or harmless error. Considering all of the possibilities, it seems likely that strict compliance is a more determinate approach than substantial compliance or harmless error. Should the estate and society pay for litigation to admit some wills to probate when the decedent (or the decedent's lawyer) was unwilling to devote substantially fewer resources to assure that the will would be probated? The question here is how and whether to prevent the false negative of an intended document not being admitted to probate. The failure to spend resources in the execution of the will suggests that it is not worth it for society to spend substantially more resources in litigation at the time of probate.

Another function perhaps served by a strict compliance approach is that of preventing false positives. The point of the substantial compliance standard is to admit more wills to probate. But in that group of additional wills, some might not accomplish what the decedent wanted. Given that false positives do occur even under the criminal standard of beyond a reasonable doubt, it seems likely that false positives will also occur when a lesser standard of clear and convincing evidence is applied in probate cases.

A third function called into question is the function of reassuring the living that their estates will devolve as they intended. If false positives are possible, testators can be less confident that their well-planned wills will not be superseded by something that should not have been admitted to probate. Questions can be asked about some of the other functions of the formalities as well.

Setting aside the interests of society generally and focusing only on the interests of decedents, would you want a court to apply a substantial compliance standard or a harmless error rule to your will? Will you be confident in your plan and instruments if they can be replaced by a document that has not been executed in strict compliance with the formalities? Do you want your estate to pay for litigation regarding whether the document you sign or a fraudulent document is in substantial compliance? Might a testator reasonably conclude, as lawmakers did in the past, that the risks of the strict compliance approach are fewer than the risks associated with the harmless error rule?

One way to amend UPC § 2–503 is to make it optional, either opt in or opt out. Given that courts once required strict compliance and that the UPC now does not, perhaps both rules are plausible. If so, then private ordering, in the form of an option between the two, is appropriate. UPC § 2–503 might be improved by allowing testators to opt out of it with a valid will. In other words, in a properly executed will, the testator might opt out of UPC § 2–503 for subsequent wills, unless a subsequent will executed in strict compliance opted back into UPC § 2–503 for wills after that. A testator might include such a provision on the thought that it would reduce the costs of litigation for her estate, as well as allowing her more repose by reducing the risks of false positives in the future.

B. PARTS OF A WILL

Once a will has been admitted to probate, a court must determine what facts and documents are part of the will or should otherwise be given effect. This inquiry triggers the application, sometimes *sub silentio*, of a few different doctrines, explored here.

1. INTEGRATION OF WILLS

The integration of wills doctrine says that the will is all of the papers present at the time and place of execution and intended to be part of the will. Basically, this is just a doctrine that tells us what is part of the will and what is not. Of course, if a state requires a will to be signed at the bottom, then portions below that might not be considered to be part of the will, notwithstanding this integration doctrine. Indeed, if there are other papers to be included as part of the will, there could be some confusion as to what is the bottom. One application of the integration of wills doctrine was litigated in *Chastain*, above. In that case, the court was asked to apply the integration doctrine so that the signed affidavit would be considered to be part of the will, supplying a signature to the unsigned will. However, the court declined, leaving the adoption of the integration doctrine to the legislature.

2. INCORPORATION BY REFERENCE

Setting aside trusts and other will substitutes, discussed later, when can a writing that is not part of a will be given testamentary effect? In many states, a writing that is not duly executed can be given effect as if it were part of the decedent's will if it meets the requirements of the doctrine of incorporation by reference. In some jurisdictions, such a document is not technically admitted to probate, but it is part of the probate file, and recipients of gifts in it are called devisees.

UPC § 2–510

SECTION 2–510. INCORPORATION BY REFERENCE. A writing in existence when a will is executed may be incorporated by reference if the language of the will manifests this intent and describes the writing sufficiently to permit its identification.

_____

For the most part, the UPC adopts the common-law requirements for incorporating a writing by reference. The writing must be in existence at the time the will is executed. The will must show the decedent's intent to incorporate the document and of course must sufficiently identify the document.

Consistent with the UPC's general approach of reducing formalities, the UPC jettisons two requirements imposed by some states for incorporation by reference. One such requirement is that the incorporated document exist at the death of the decedent. One might think that it is impossible to incorporate a document that does not exist, but that is not true. A document could be destroyed, but its former physical existence and contents might still be proved by other evidence in probate court.

The other requirement in some states, but not in the UPC, is that the will must refer to the document as being in existence. In other words, some courts have required not only that the incorporated document be in existence at the time the will was executed, but also that the will say that the document exists. Certainly, that extra step generated false negatives. Might it have also reduced false positives?

By requiring that an incorporated document exist at the time the will is executed, the common law and the UPC prevent a person from executing a will that allows the testator to avoid the Wills Act requirements in the future. Without that requirement, a testator's will could simply say, follow my instructions on any future document that I label with "My Will". Allowing such wills to be effective would substantially increase the costs of probate administration as well as increasing possibilities of distributing assets in ways not intended by the testator, due to mistake, fraud, or undue influence.

For tangible personally, however, the UPC relaxes the requirements even more. UPC § 2–513, adopted by about half of the states, gives effect to gifts of non-cash tangible personalty made in writings referred to in a will without regard to whether the writing is in existence at the time the will is executed.

UPC § 2–513

SECTION 2–513. SEPARATE WRITING IDENTIFYING DEVISE OF CERTAIN TYPES OF TANGIBLE PERSONAL PROPERTY. Whether or not the provisions relating to holographic wills apply, a will may refer to a written statement or list to dispose of items of tangible personal property not otherwise specifically disposed of by the will, other than money. To be admissible under this section as evidence of the intended disposition, the writing must be signed by the testator and must describe the items and the devisees with reasonable certainty. The writing may be referred to as one to be in existence at the time of the testator's death; it may be prepared before or after the execution of the will; it may be altered by the testator after its preparation; and it may be a writing that has no significance apart from its effect on the dispositions made by the will.

———————

Incorporation by reference raises additional questions in jurisdictions that recognize holographic wills. Dispositive provisions of informal wills are supposed to be in the hand of the testator. A document incorporated by reference, on the other hand, need not be in the hand of the testator. Courts are split as to whether a holographic will can incorporate by reference a non-holographic document.

Incorporation by reference can be combined with republication by codicil in jurisdictions recognizing that doctrine.

> Example 4.09: In 2014, O executes a will which says, "I give $1,000 to each person listed on an existing list titled 'Grand Friends.' I intend that list to be incorporated into this will." In 2015, O types and signs a list titled "Grand Friends", which lists A and B. (Under UPC § 2–510, if O dies at this point, that list is not effective because it was not in existence when O executed the will.) In 2016, O executes a "Codicil to the will of 2014" which says that he gives his car to C. In 2017, O dies. The $1,000 gifts to A and B are effective because the codicil updates the will by republication,

making the effective date 2016, and at that time the typed list is in existence and can be incorporated.

3. ACTS OF INDEPENDENT SIGNIFICANCE

Because the formalities demanded by the Wills Acts serve many functions, it is important to block attempts to circumvent those formalities. But not all circumventions are prevented. One such method of circumvention, now allowed by the UPC to the degree discussed above, is the incorporation by reference of documents that do not qualify for probate on their own. Another potential method of circumvention is to include provisions in a will that reach different results depending on subsequent actions taken by the testator or someone else.

> Example 4.10: O executes a will which says, "I give the contents of my lockbox to my sister." O can then make testamentary transfers by adding items to the lockbox or revoke testamentary transfers by removing items from the lockbox. Unfortunately, of course, it is also possible for someone else to make testamentary transfers or revocations by changing the contents of the lockbox, before or after O's death and inconsistent with O's intent. O's brother might remove items from the lockbox, or O's sister might add items to it.

Enforcement or non-enforcement of such provisions in wills raises issues of both false positives and false negatives. Following the approach of many courts, UPC § 2–512 allows a decedent's acts to change testamentary dispositions if those acts have "significance apart from their effect upon the dispositions made by the will". This is sometimes known as the doctrine of nontestamentary acts or acts of independent significance. Applied to Example 4.10 above, the contents of the lockbox would go to the sister since the transfer of items to or from the lockbox has independent significance, serving the purpose of secure storage. On the other hand, a testator might fail in his attempt to circumvent the statutory formalities.

> Example 4.11: O executes a will which says, only, "I leave Blackacre to all persons in the class of persons to whom I give a gold star autographed by me." O gives autographed gold stars to X, Y, and Z. O dies. The gold stars do not comply with the statutory formalities. Without more information,

the gold stars do not have independent significance and would not be effective to transfer Blackacre.

Problem 4.12: O has two children, A and B. O executes a will which says only "I leave Blackacre to my children." Thereafter, O has another child, C. O does not make a new will. O dies. Does C take part interest in Blackacre?

C. REVOCATION OF A WILL

After proper execution with intent and capacity, a will remains ambulatory and can be amended and nullified. To prevent a will or a part of a will from becoming effective it must be revoked. How might that happen? A will can be revoked automatically by operation of law and can be revoked by revocatory action taken by a testator intending to revoke the will.

1. REVOCATION BY OPERATION OF LAW

Wills might be revoked in whole or in part in cases of divorce and sometimes marriage.

(a) Divorce

Under the common law, divorce automatically revoked the wills of the spouses. Under UPC § 2–804 and in a majority of states, divorce does not revoke the entire will, but does revoke gifts to the former spouse and spouse's kin. The former spouse and former in-laws are treated as if they disclaimed. This is only a default rule, which may be overcome by express provisions in the dispositive instrument. In addition, if the couple remarries or the divorce is nullified, the gifts are revived.

(b) Marriage

In some states, marriage revokes a person's will, unless the will contains provisions for the marriage. The UPC rejects this rule, leaving wills effective after marriage. There are other provisions, discussed later, that protect surviving spouses to varying degrees against wills executed before marriage that give the decedent's estate to persons other than the spouse.

2. VOLITIONAL REVOCATION

One point of a will is to make a gift that is effective at death, while being revocable before death. So, in addition to automatic revocations, the law allows volitional revocations of wills. For such revocations, the law imposes the same requirements of intent and capacity as it does for the execution of a will. The intent in this situation is referred to as the animus revocandi and, just as with the animus testandi, there is no such subjective intent if there is coercion, duress, undue influence, or fraud in the execution.

UPC § 2–507

SECTION 2–507. REVOCATION BY WRITING OR BY ACT.

(a) A will or any part thereof is revoked:

(1) by executing a subsequent will that revokes the previous will or part expressly or by inconsistency; or

(2) by performing a revocatory act on the will, if the testator performed the act with the intent and for the purpose of revoking the will or part or if another individual performed the act in the testator's conscious presence and by the testator's direction. For purposes of this paragraph, "revocatory act on the will" includes burning, tearing, canceling, obliterating, or destroying the will or any part of it. A burning, tearing, or canceling is a "revocatory act on the will," whether or not the burn, tear, or cancellation touched any of the words on the will.

(b) If a subsequent will does not expressly revoke a previous will, the execution of the subsequent will wholly revokes the previous will by inconsistency if the testator intended the subsequent will to replace rather than supplement the previous will.

(c) The testator is presumed to have intended a subsequent will to replace rather than supplement a previous will if the subsequent will makes a complete disposition of the testator's estate. If this presumption arises and is not rebutted by clear and convincing evidence, the previous will is revoked; only the subsequent will is operative on the testator's death.

(d) The testator is presumed to have intended a subsequent will to supplement rather than replace a previous will if the subsequent will does not make a complete disposition of the testator's estate. If this presumption arises and is not rebutted by clear and convincing evidence, the subsequent will revokes the previous will only to the extent the subsequent will is inconsistent with the previous will; each will is fully operative on the testator's death to the extent they are not inconsistent.

(a) Revocation by an Instrument

As was indicated above in the discussion of codicils, it is possible for a testator to execute an instrument that revokes a will in whole or in part, expressly or by implication. For an instrument to have that effect, it must be executed in compliance with the same formalities as apply to the execution of a will.

(b) Revocation by a Physical Act

The best practice, in nearly all if not all situations, is to revoke a will with another instrument, as just described. However, best practices are not always followed, and it is useful to know when other attempts are or are not effective in revoking a will. A will can be revoked by cancellation, destruction, obliteration, or similar act done to the will. For the act to have legal effect, the act must be done to the original will, not to a copy. However, a court of equity might be persuaded to impose a constructive trust on the devisees of a will where the testator attempted to revoke the will by a revocatory act on a copy if the testator thought it was the original will due to fraud or perhaps mistake.

In some cases, the original will cannot be found. That does not mean it cannot be admitted to probate; it may be admitted if its due execution is established, its contents are proved, and in some states, the reason for its nonproduction is shown. However, if the original is known to have been in the hands of the testator and it cannot be found at the testator's death, a rebuttable presumption arises that the will was destroyed by the testator with the intent to revoke it.

The revocatory act may be performed by the testator or by the testator's agent at the testator's direction. However, UPC § 2–507 requires that the revocatory act performed by an agent be done in the conscious presence of the testator. It is not enough for the lawyer to destroy the will after receiving instructions from the client to do so.

MILBOURNE V. MILBOURNE
Supreme Court of Georgia, 2017
799 S.E.2d 785

GRANT, J.

This case comes to us as a dispute between the daughter and sister of decedent Edison Jamal Milbourne ("Edison"). Daughter Janay Milbourne ("Janay") filed a caveat asserting that Edison's January 2013 Will was invalid because it had been procured by undue influence by sister and guardian Vashti Milbourne ("Vashti"); because it had been revoked by Edison; because it had been improperly executed; and because Edison lacked testamentary capacity to make the will in the first place. The Gwinnett County Probate Court rejected all of these contentions on summary judgment motions except the first; the court found that a question of fact remained on the issue of undue influence. Vashti disagrees with that decision, and this Court granted her application for an interlocutory appeal. Janay, meanwhile, filed a cross appeal of the probate court's grant of summary judgment to Vashti on the issue of revocation.* * *

I.

Viewed in the light most favorable to the non-movant, the facts show that in 1999, Edison suffered a work-related brain injury that impaired his ability to care for himself independently. He initially lived at home with his wife Janita and his infant child, Janay, but it soon became clear that his round-the-clock care requirements were more than Janita could handle (she worked two jobs and also cared for Janay). Edison then lived in rehabilitation facilities. His sister Vashti was appointed as guardian in 2009—approximately 10 years after Edison's brain injury and one month after his $726,000 workers compensation settlement was finalized. Up until the settlement, Vashti had not been Edison's caregiver.

Following Vashti's appointment, she came to Georgia and moved Edison out of his rehabilitation facility. Vashti began to make significant financial demands. "Because of the huge budget requested by [Edison's] guardian," the probate court appointed a guardian ad litem to advise the court on how best to manage Edison's budget and living arrangements. In that same order, the court provided that Edison would receive a monthly allotment of $1,000; as it turns out, that was the only money that Edison, Vashti, or Vashti's daughter Tiffany, who also lived with Edison, had to pay their living expenses; Vashti earned no income on her own. Guardian ad litem Janet Grayson explained that she had tried to make Edison and Vashti understand that the combination of Edison's medical needs and his likely lifespan of 26 more years meant that the settlement money could not be spent quickly. Nonetheless, Grayson recounted that Vashti repeatedly demanded a Cadillac Escalade (in spite of the fact that Edison himself had no prospect of being able to drive), about $300,000 for a four or five bedroom home, and $27,000 to furnish the home. Vashti also asked for $30,000 in advance for her services as care giver. According to Grayson, Vashti also told Edison "many times" that "[t]hey're going to put you in one of those homes." Grayson stated that she could see the fear in Edison's face when Vashti made these kinds of remarks, and added that in her view Vashti induced Edison's fear of long-term care facilities.

Grayson also recalled that Vashti repeatedly stated that "everybody else had gotten paid, and it was her turn to get paid." With respect to Edison's daughter Janay, on the other hand, Grayson testified that "he very strongly had a desire to reestablish a relationship with her and to include her in his financial bounty," but also that his expectation that Janay may come live with him was "very sweet but very unrealistic." There is evidence that Vashti hindered Edison's relationship with Janay. When Janay attempted to call Edison at his home, for instance, Vashti informed her that he was not there, or that he did not want to speak with her. When Janay visited Edison for one of his birthdays, which coincided with Christmas Eve, Vashti and Janay got into an argument and Vashti called the police. Grayson considered calling Adult Protective Services and recommending that Vashti be removed as Edison's guardian, but made the reluctant decision not to do so because he was "emotionally dependent" on her.

Edison did not have a will when Vashti became his guardian, but apparently began to seek one after Vashti arrived in Georgia. In her deposition, Vashti asserted that Edison's conservator, John Tomlinson, refused to write the will. Tomlinson, in contrast, testified that he wrote a will for Edison but when he called to let Edison know the draft was ready to review, Vashti relayed that she had hired a different lawyer, Charles Tingle, to write the will. When Tomlinson called Tingle to ask about paying the bill for Edison's will, Tomlinson was told that the bill had already been paid.

As it turns out, Vashti found Tingle "[i]n the Yellow Pages just randomly" and called to set up an appointment with him. Vashti drove Edison to visit Tingle between two and five times. During one visit, Vashti approached Tingle about the possibility of replacing Tomlinson as conservator of the estate, and shared relevant documents with him, but, after reviewing the papers, Tingle declined to do so. Vashti admitted that she filled out the client information sheet for Edison during the first visit with Tingle, but gave inconsistent testimony on whether she was present as Edison described his wishes to Tingle, ultimately claiming that she could not recall whether she was present or not. For his part, Tingle testified that Vashti had "probably" attended at least one of two meetings regarding the will. As noted above, there were several additional meetings between at least Vashti and Tingle; the record is not clear whether Edison attended any of those meetings. Vashti paid the bills for Tingle's work over the course of several visits, and, during one of the meetings, Edison executed the January Will.

Nine months later, in October 2013, Edison executed a second will ("October Will").[2] Following Edison's death in July 2014, Vashti submitted the October Will to probate. Janay filed a caveat alleging that the October Will was procured through undue influence. The jury returned a verdict denying probate of the October Will, concluding that it was invalid because Vashti had exercised undue influence and because Edison had failed to properly execute the document.

After the jury verdict on the October Will, Tiffany Wootson, Vashti's daughter, petitioned to probate the January Will. As she had done for the October Will, Janay filed a caveat to the probate of the January Will, this time arguing that lack of testamentary capacity, fraud, undue influence, and revocation barred probate. Subsequently, Vashti joined Tiffany's petition to probate the January Will.

Vashti and Tiffany filed a motion for summary judgment, contending that Janay's caveat was meritless and that they were entitled to probate the January Will as a matter of law. The probate court conducted a hearing on the motion for summary judgment on December 15, 2015. During a recess in the hearing, Janay filed a

---

[2] Although the Court need not determine the contents of either the January Will or the October Will, and does not do so in this decision, a brief review of each illustrates the way the two documents distributed Edison's estate. The January Will devised most of Edison's property, including the house he owned, to Vashti except for equal devises of $50,000 to Tiffany and Janay. Under the terms of the January Will, if Vashti predeceased Edison, Janay would take Vashti's place as devisee. The October Will devised all of Edison's property to Vashti. If Vashti predeceased Edison, Tiffany would take Vashti's place as devisee.

copy of former guardian ad litem Janet Grayson's testimony from the October Will trial, a proceeding that had been held before the same probate judge. On December 21, 2015, the probate court entered an order granting Vashti and Tiffany's motion for summary judgment on all but one ground, leaving the claim that the January Will was procured by undue influence for the jury to decide.

Vashti and Tiffany now appeal the probate court's order denying their motion for summary judgment on the undue influence claim, as well as the probate court's decision to consider Grayson's testimony and other evidence that they claim was untimely filed. Janay cross-appeals the probate court's order granting summary judgment against her claim that Edison revoked the January Will.

* * *

III.

* * * In short, because genuine issues of material fact relevant to the issue of undue influence exist, the probate court did not err in denying Vashti's motion for summary judgment on this point.

IV.

Having addressed Vashti's claim of error, we turn to Janay's. On cross-appeal, Janay argues that the probate court erred in concluding as a matter of law that Edison did not revoke the January Will. According to Janay, Edison explicitly told Vashti that he no longer wanted the January Will, and Vashti then breached the fiduciary duty that she owed to Edison as his legal guardian by failing to destroy the January Will. In Janay's telling, that statement served as an express revocation that Vashti had an obligation to carry out. Janay's primary legal argument seems to be that a guardian has a duty to destroy a ward's will upon the ward's request, even where that guardian has not been granted testamentary powers by the court, and even where the ward has testamentary capacity. There are several reasons this contention is incorrect.

First, to the extent that Janay contends that Edison's statement that he no longer wanted the January Will was a sufficient revocatory act in and of itself, we disagree. This Court has rejected such simplistic forms of revocation. See *Driver v. Sheffield*, 211 Ga. 316, 316 (4) (1955) ("[R]evocation of a will cannot be established by proof of parol declarations by the testator."); see also *Harper v. Harper*, 281 Ga. 25, 27 (2006) (use of parol evidence to prove the existence of a revocation clause in a subsequent will "cannot be tolerated because it puts us in danger of returning to the days of revocation by oral declaration.").

Rather, under Georgia law, there are only two ways to expressly revoke a will: by so stating in a subsequent will or legal document, or by "destruction or obliteration of the will done by the testator with an intent to revoke, or by another at the testator's direction." Neither party argues that the subsequent (and rejected) October Will had the legal effect of revoking the January Will. But the parties also agree that neither Edison nor Vashti destroyed the January Will or took any steps to obliterate the January Will. That kind of act is plainly required under Georgia law. See, e.g., *Lovell v. Anderson*, 272 Ga. 675, 676 (2) (2000) ("To effect a revocation of a will by obliteration, in addition to the requirement that the obliteration be material, there must be proof of a joint operation of act and intent."); *Wells v. Jackson*, 265 Ga. 181, 183 (1995) ("Revocation is not accomplished by the maker's unsuccessful attempt to destroy or obliterate."); *Payne v. Payne*, 213 Ga. 613, 615 (1957) (No revocation occurred where testator threw his will into a fire but his wife jerked it out of the fire before "a single word which the testator employed to express his testamentary wish [was] destroyed, obliterated or even so much as rendered obscure in the slightest degree."). Janay is correct that the law does not require that the testator in particular perform the act of destruction to validly revoke a will. But the law does require that *someone* perform the act of destruction.

Janay relies heavily on Vashti's status as guardian, but appointment of a guardian offers neither an exception to the physical destruction rule, nor a determination that the ward lacks testamentary capacity. Indeed, Janay's argument seems to hinge on the fact that Edison *retained* testamentary capacity; otherwise, any statement that he wished to revoke the January Will would be without legal effect. In any event, Georgia law specifically bars a guardian from disposing of a ward's property without the involvement of a conservator. And absent an order otherwise, Edison's conservator, and not his guardian, would have been responsible for estate planning matters if Edison lacked testamentary capacity. Again, there is no suggestion that Edison or his conservator destroyed or obliterated the January Will after it was executed.

For all of these reasons, even assuming that Edison stated that he no longer wanted the January Will to be in effect, that statement would be insufficient to revoke the will or to require his guardian to do so. Accordingly, the probate court did not err when it granted Vashti's motion for summary judgment on the revocation issue.

Judgment affirmed.

THOMPSON V. ROYALL

Supreme Court of Appeals of Virginia, 1934
175 S.E. 748

HUDGINS, J.

The only question presented by this record, is whether the will of Mrs. M. Lou Bowen Kroll had been revoked shortly before her death.

The uncontroverted facts are as follows: On the 4th day of September, 1932, Mrs. Kroll signed a will, typewritten on five sheets of legal cap paper; the signature appeared on the last page duly attested by three subscribing witnesses. H. P. Brittain, the executor named in the will, was given possession of the instrument for safe-keeping. A codicil typed on the top third of one sheet of paper dated September 15, 1932, was signed by the testatrix in the presence of two subscribing witnesses. Possession of this instrument was given to Judge S. M. B. Coulling, the attorney who prepared both documents.

On September 19, 1932, at the request of Mrs. Kroll, Judge Coulling, and Mr. Brittain took the will and the codicil to her home where she told her attorney, in the presence of Mr. Brittain and another, to destroy both. But instead of destroying the papers, at the suggestion of Judge Coulling, she decided to retain them as memoranda, to be used as such in the event she decided to execute a new will. Upon the back of the manuscript cover, which was fastened to the five sheets by metal clasps, in the handwriting of Judge Coulling, signed by Mrs. Kroll, there is the following notation: "This will null and void and to be only held by H. P. Brittain, instead of being destroyed, as a memorandum for another will if I desire to make same. This 19 Sept. 1932.

"M. Lou Bowen Kroll."

The same notation was made upon the back of the sheet on which the codicil was written, except that the name, S. M. B.

Coulling, was substituted for H. P. Brittain; this was likewise signed by Mrs. Kroll.

Mrs. Kroll died October 2, 1932, leaving numerous nephews and nieces, some of whom were not mentioned in her will, and an estate valued at approximately $200,000. On motion of some of the beneficiaries, the will and codicil were offered for probate. All the interested parties including the heirs at law were convened, and on the issue devisavit vel non the jury found that the instruments dated September 4th and 15, 1932, were the last will and testament of Mrs. M. Lou Bowen Kroll. From an order sustaining the verdict and probating the will this writ of error was allowed.

For more than one hundred years, the means by which a duly executed will may be revoked, have been prescribed by statute. These requirements are found in section 5233 of the 1919 Code, the pertinent parts of which read thus: "No will or codicil, or any part thereof, shall be revoked, unless * * * by a subsequent will or codicil, or by some writing declaring an intention to revoke the same, and executed in the manner in which a will is required to be executed, or by the testator, or some person in his presence and by his direction, cutting, tearing, burning, obliterating, canceling, or destroying the same, or the signature thereto, with the intent to revoke."

The notations, dated September 19, 1932, are not wholly in the handwriting of the testatrix, nor are her signatures thereto attached attested by subscribing witnesses; hence under the statute they are ineffectual as "some writing declaring an intention to revoke." The faces of the two instruments bear no physical evidence of any cutting, tearing, burning, obliterating, canceling, or destroying. The only contention made by appellants is, that the notation written in the presence, and with the approval, of Mrs. Kroll, on the back of the manuscript cover in the one instance, and on the back of the sheet containing the codicil in the other, constitute "canceling" within the meaning of the statute.

Both parties concede that to effect revocation of a duly executed will, in any of the methods prescribed by statute, two things are necessary: (1) The doing of one of the acts specified, (2) accompanied by the intent to revoke—the animo revocandi. Proof of either, without proof of the other, is insufficient.

The proof established the intention to revoke. The entire controversy is confined to the acts used in carrying out that purpose. The testatrix adopted the suggestion of her attorney to revoke her will by written memoranda, admittedly ineffectual as revocations by subsequent writings, but appellants contend the memoranda, in the handwriting of another, and testatrix's signatures, are sufficient to effect revocation by cancellation. To support this contention appellants cite a number of authorities which hold that the modern definition of cancellation includes, "any act which would destroy, revoke, recall, do away with, overrule, render null and void, the instrument."

Most of the authorities cited, that approve the above, or a similar meaning of the word, were dealing with the cancellation of simple contracts, or other instruments that require little or no formality in execution. However there is one line of cases which apply this extended meaning of "canceling" to the revocation of wills. The leading case so holding is Warner v. Warner's Estate, 37 Vt. 356. In this case proof of the intent and the act were a notation on the same page with, and below the signature of the testator, reading: "This will is hereby cancelled and annulled. In full this the 15th day of March in the year 1859," and written lengthwise on the back of the fourth page of the foolscap paper, upon which no part of the written will appeared, were these words, "Cancelled and is null and void. (Signed) I. Warner." It was held this was sufficient to revoke the will under a statute similar to the one here under consideration.

In Evans' Appeal, 58 Pa.St. 238, the Pennsylvania court approved the reasoning of the Vermont court in Warner v. Warner's Estate, supra, but the force of the opinion is weakened when the facts are considered. It seems that there were lines drawn through two of the three signatures of the testator appearing in the Evans will, and the paper on which material parts of the will were written was torn in four places. It therefore appeared on the face of the instrument, when offered for probate, that there was a sufficient defacement to bring it within the meaning of both obliteration and cancellation.

The construction of the statute in Warner v. Warner's Estate, supra, has been criticized by eminent textwriters on wills, and the courts in the majority of the states in construing similar statutes have refused to follow the reasoning in that case.

The above, and other authorities that might be cited, hold that revocation of a will by cancellation within the meaning of the statute, contemplates marks or lines across the written parts of the instrument, or a physical defacement, or some mutilation of the writing itself, with the intent to revoke. If written words are used for the purpose, they must be so placed as to physically affect the written portion of the will, not merely on blank parts of the paper on which the will is written. If the writing intended to be the act of cancelling, does not mutilate, or erase, or deface, or otherwise physically come in contact with any part of written words of the will, it cannot be given any greater weight than a similar writing on a separate sheet of paper, which identifies the will referred to, just as definitely, as does the writing on the back. If a will may be revoked by writing on the back, separable from the will, it may be done by a writing not on the will. This the statute forbids.

The learned trial judge, A. C. Buchanan, in his written opinion, pertinently said:

"The statute prescribes certain ways of executing a will, and it must be so executed in order to be valid, regardless of how clear and specific the intent. It also provides certain ways of revoking and it must be done so in order to a valid revocation, regardless of intent. As said in Will of Ladd, 60 Wis. 187:

" 'The difficulty with the rule contended for is that it gives to the words written in pencil, although not attested, witnessed, nor executed in the manner prescribed by statute, the same force as though they had been so attested, witnessed and executed, for the purpose of proving that the act of putting the words there was with the "intention" of revoking the will. It is the language, the expression by written words alone, which is thus sought to be made effectual; whereas the statute in effect declares that such written words shall have no force or effect as such unless executed, attested and subscribed as required.'

"The same reasoning led the Illinois court to the same conclusion in Dowling v. Gilliland, * * * where it is said:

" 'The great weight of authority is to the effect that the mere writing upon a will which does not in any wise physically obliterate or cancel the same is insufficient to work a destruction of a will by cancellation, even though the writing may express an intention to revoke and cancel. This appears to be the better rule. To hold otherwise would be to give to words written in pencil, and not attested to by witnesses nor executed in the manner provided by the statute, the same effect as if they had been so attested.'

"The same rule seems to prevail in New York, Massachusetts and North Carolina. The Georgia cases are to the same effect, although it does not appear that the Georgia statute is the same as ours.

"A different rule seems to be followed in Tennessee, as shown by Billington v. Jones, 108 Tenn. 234, but the court there points out that Tennessee has no statute on the subject, and says the same thing is true in Connecticut * * *"

The attempted revocation is ineffectual, because testatrix intended to revoke her will by subsequent writings not executed as required by statute, and because it does not in any wise physically obliterate, mutilate, deface, or cancel any written parts of the will.

For the reasons stated, the judgment of the trial court is affirmed.

Affirmed.

Would the same result obtain under the UPC?

IN RE WILL OF LITWACK

Surrogate's Court, New York County, 2006
827 N.Y.S.2d 582

ROTH, S.

Incident to this probate proceeding in the estate of Gloria Litwack, the court is required to construe two statutes governing the execution and revocation of wills (EPTL 3–2.1, 3–4.1) that appear to be in conflict. The circumstances which created the issue are as follows.

Testatrix's handwritten obliteration of a paragraph in the propounded instrument was witnessed by two friends who duly signed their names in her presence. Such obliteration and the signatures evidencing its due execution were, however, added to the instrument after the will itself had been executed. The statute governing revocation of wills (EPTL 3–4.1 [a] [1] [B]) is silent as to whether the executed will may be used as the required "writing." Furthermore, the statute governing execution of wills (EPTL 3–2.1 [a] [1] [B]) provides that "[n]o effect can be given to any matter . . . preceding [the testatrix's] signature which was added subsequently to the execution of the will." Accordingly, the question is whether part of a will can be revoked by markings added to the original instrument following its execution.

The propounded instrument was executed by testatrix on April 27, 1999, in the presence of two witnesses and under the supervision of an attorney. The validity of the instrument itself is not in dispute.

The first page of the instrument as executed contained an unnumbered paragraph entitled, "BEQUEST," which read as follows: "I give, devise and bequeath . . . my Cooperative apartment be sold and the net proceeds distributed to my son PETER LITWACK, of Corte Madera, CA." In the instrument offered for probate, the paragraph has been obliterated and immediately following it is the handwritten notation "delete 2/05/03" followed by testatrix's signature. At the foot of the same page are the signatures of John T. Witmer and Maria T. Kennedy, each followed by their addresses and the date, "2/05/03."

According to an affidavit submitted by Mr. Witmer, dated April 5, 2006, while he was having lunch with testatrix on February 5, 2003, she asked him to witness the deletion from her will of the bequest of the cooperative apartment. She showed him the executed instrument, then obliterated such paragraph, wrote the word "delete" following the obliteration, signed her name and entered the date. She then asked Mr. Witmer to sign his name as a witness, which he did, entering his signature, address and the date at the foot of the page.

The other witness, Marie T. Kennedy, also submitted an affidavit, dated April 3, 2006, which states that on February 5, 2003, testatrix asked her to witness the deletion of the bequest at issue. According to Ms. Kennedy, testatrix showed her the original will with the obliterated paragraph, acknowledged her signature next to such paragraph, and asked Ms. Kennedy to sign as witness.

Both of such affidavits contain statements to the effect that, at the time testatrix made the deletion, she was fully competent to make a will and under no restraint. Accordingly, petitioner asks that the instrument be admitted to probate without the obliterated paragraph.

Section 3–4.1 (a) (1) (B) of the EPTL provides that all or part of a will may be revoked or altered by "[a] writing of the testator clearly indicating an intention to effect such revocation . . . [and] executed with the formalities prescribed by this article for the execution and attestation of a will." It is silent as to whether the executed will itself may be used for such a writing, although it does not expressly disallow it. Thus, it is concluded that the revocation attempted in this case—by markings superimposed on the original instrument— is invalid only if section 3–2.1 (a) (1) (B) (as quoted above) in effect requires that an instrument separate from the executed instrument must be used for such purpose.

Sections 3–2.1 and 3–4.1 (commonly referred to as the statute of wills) share the same purpose, namely, to prevent the probate of fraudulent instruments. As its title indicates, EPTL 3–2.1 is intended to further such objective by requiring specified formalities for purposes of the "Execution and attestation of wills" and disallowing matter not executed in accordance with such safeguards. Section 3–4.1, entitled "Revocation of wills," in turn specifies its own apparently comprehensive safeguards against fraudulent revocations. There is nothing to suggest that the fraud-preventing purposes of these sections would be frustrated if effect is given to a revocatory "writing" added to the original, executed instrument so long as such addition is itself duly executed. In other words, there is no reason to conclude that the terms of section 3–2.1 (a) (1) (B) were intended to limit the terms of section 3–4.1 (a) (1) (B) .

Based upon the foregoing, it is concluded that the obliteration to the propounded instrument, executed with the formalities required for the execution of a will, effected a revocation of the obliterated paragraph.

Accordingly, a decree has been signed admitting the propounded instrument to probate without the obliterated paragraph.

(c) Partial Revocation by a Physical Act

All states allow partial revocation by instrument, of course. But states vary in their willingness to allow partial revocation by physical act. Some states do not allow it at all. On the other end of the spectrum, many states and UPC § 2–507 do allow partial revocation by revocatory act. And states also fall in between, allowing the partial revocation but with restrictions. One of the restrictions a court might apply is that the partial revocation by physical act cannot enlarge another gift in the will. Another possible restriction is that a revocation may not change the character of the will.

In states that prohibit or limit a partial revocation by physical act, the question arises as to what should be done when the testator attempted a partial revocation by revocatory act.

> Example 4.13: O's will says, "I give $5,000 to A and B. I give all my realty to C for life, remainder to R." After that, O crosses out "and B" and "for life, remainder to R".

On the facts of Example 4.13, in a jurisdiction that does not recognize partial revocations by physical act, the court must choose between total revocation and no revocation. In a jurisdiction allowing partial revocation with limits, a court might allow the revocation of the gift to B while ignoring the attempted revocation of the gift to R. Obviously, litigation might be necessary to resolve these issues.

The UPC honors attempts to revoke part of a will by physical act, and both excisions in Example 4.13 may be given effect as partial revocations. However, that approach does not entirely avoid litigation, either. Litigation could arise under the UPC as to whether a mark is an attempted partial revocation or just an accident. It is also possible for a partial destruction to raise the question of whether the destruction was intended to be partial or total revocation. And litigation is not the only cost of allowing partial revocations by physical act. The UPC approach might make it easier for someone such as R in the example to change the will when that was not intended by the decedent.

PATRICK V. PATRICK
Court of Special Appeals of Maryland, 1994
649 A.2d 1204

CATHELL, J.

Appellant, Daniel E. Patrick, Sr., personal representative of the estate of Edna Lorraine Patrick (the testatrix), appeals from the judgment of the Circuit Court for Baltimore County. The trial court found that the testatrix had attempted to revoke a $5,000 bequest to her granddaughter, Rachel, in trust, and a bequest of one-half of the residuary estate to her son, David, by drawing lines through portions of her will. * * *

THE FACTS

As relevant to this appeal, the testatrix's will provided (with the lined and emphasized portions representing the text she crossed out and the portions enclosed in brackets representing the text she added):

LAST WILL AND TESTAMENT OF
EDNA LORRAINE PATRICK

I, EDNA LORRAINE PATRICK of Baltimore County, Maryland, being of sound mind and memory, and not acting under duress, menace, fraud or undue influence of any person whatsoever, do make, publish and declare this to be my Last Will and Testament, and I revoke all previous Wills and Codicils made by me.

FIRST: I direct that all my just debts, expenses of my last illness and funeral, expenses of the administration of my estate, and estate and inheritance taxes on the whole of my estate be paid out of the first available funds as administrative expenses.

SECOND: I give, devise and bequeath the sum of One Hundred ($100.00) Dollars ~~to each of my grandchildren.~~ [Rick's and Dave's] I give, devise and bequeath the additional sum of ~~Five Thousand ($5,000.00)~~ Dollars to my ~~grandchild Rachel, in trust until her 18th birthday~~ at which time it is to be distributed to her along with any accumulated earnings.

THIRD: I give, devise and bequeath all the rest and residue of my property, after payment of debts, expenses and taxes provided for in the First Item above, whether such property be real, personal or mixed, of whatever kind or character or wheresoever situated to ~~my sons,~~ Daniel E. Patrick, Sr. and ~~David M. Patrick, Sr.,~~ equally, share and share alike.

The trial court held, and neither party disputes, that the testatrix had made the changes in the will and that she "had the intent to alter the Will as initially executed and thereby to strike provisions which would have benefitted her son, David, and his heirs." Specifically, the trial court found that she attempted to revoke the $5,000 bequest to her granddaughter, Rachel, apparently the daughter of David, in trust, and the bequest of one-half of her residuary estate to her son David M. Patrick, Sr.

LEGAL ANALYSIS

Appellant contends that the trial court erred by not following the literal language of Md.Code § 4–105 of the Estates and Trusts Article and by following the precedent of two Court of Appeals cases that interpreted an earlier statute that used the word, "clause," instead of the word, "part," which is currently used. As stated above, we believe that the trial court erred in its interpretation of those Court of Appeals cases, but we agree with the trial court in its holding that the legislature did not intend to change the meaning of § 4–105 when it substituted the word, "part," for the word, "clause."

Section 4–105 currently reads, in pertinent part:

> A will, *or any part of it*, may not be revoked in a manner other than as provided in this section.
>
> (1) *Subsequent will.*—By provision in a subsequent, validly executed will which (i) revokes any prior will or part of it either expressly or by necessary implication, or (ii) expressly republishes an earlier will that had been revoked by an intermediate will but is still in existence;
>
> (2) *Destruction.*—*By burning, cancelling, tearing, or obliterating the same,* by the testator himself, or by some other person in his presence and by his express direction and consent. . . . [Emphasis added.]

The 1991 replacement volume of the Estates and Trust Article does not contain any Revisor's Note or Comment. The 1974 volume, however, did. The Revisor's Note from that volume provided, "This section formerly appeared as Article 93, § 4–105. Changes are in style and language." The Comment to former Article 93, § 4–105 provided, in pertinent part:

> This section adopts, without change of substance, former § 351, which was recently reconsidered and amended by the General Assembly.

Article 93 § 351, in turn, provided:

> No will or codicil in writing, nor any clause thereof, shall be revoked otherwise than as provided herein:
>
> (a) By some other will, codicil, or other writing, executed as provided in § 350, altering or revoking said will or codicil.

(b) *By burning, cancelling, tearing or obliterating the same*, by the testator himself, or by some other person in his presence and by his express direction and consent. [Emphasis added.]

Appellant requests that we ignore the Comment to section 4–105, which would then permit us to ignore the Court of Appeals's decisions interpreting language very similar to that of Article 93 § 351. By examining the current language of section 4–105 of the Estates and Trust Article in this vacuum, appellant suggests that, under the plain meaning rule of statutory construction, the testatrix was allowed to strike certain portions of her will regardless of the effect this would have on the rest of her will. We disagree and explain.

In *Barr v. Barberry Bros., Inc.*, 99 Md.App. 33, 38–39 (1994), we quoted from *Mazor v. Dep't of Correction*, 279 Md. 355, 360–61 (1977), and *Subsequent Injury Fund v. Ehrman*, 89 Md.App. 741, 746–47 (1992), and stated:

[S]ix principal guidelines of statutory interpretation [are]:

"The cardinal rule of construction of a statute is to ascertain and carry out the real intention of the Legislature. . . .

The primary source from which we glean this intention is the language of the statute itself. . . .

And in construing a statute we accord the words their ordinary and natural signification. . . .

If reasonably possible, a statute is to be read so that no word, phrase, clause or sentence is rendered surplusage or meaningless. . . .

Similarly, wherever possible an interpretation should be given to statutory language which will not lead to absurd consequences. . . .

Moreover, if the statute is part of a general statutory scheme or system, the sections must be read together to ascertain the true intention of the Legislature."

While the language of the statute is the primary source from which to glean the legislative intent, we do not ignore other possible sources of that intent. The Court of Appeals, in *Kaczorowski v. City of Baltimore*, 309 Md. 505, 513–14 (1987), stated:

Of course, in our efforts to discover purpose, aim, or policy we look at the words of the statute. That is the thrust of the plain-meaning rule relied on by Kaczorowski, and the rule comports with common sense, because what the legislature has written in an effort to achieve a goal is a natural ingredient of analysis to determine that goal. But the plain-meaning rule is not rigid.

> We also recognize the rule that where a statute is plainly susceptible of more than one meaning and thus contains an ambiguity, courts consider not only the literal or usual meaning of the words, but their meaning and effect in light of the setting, the objectives and purpose of the enactment. In such circumstances, the court, in seeking to ascertain legislative intent, may consider the consequences resulting from one meaning rather than another, and adopt that construction which avoids an illogical or unreasonable result, or one which is inconsistent with common sense.

The Court added:

> When we pursue the context of statutory language, we are not limited to the words of the statute as they are printed in the Annotated Code. We may and often must consider other "external manifestations" or "persuasive evidence," including a bill's title and function paragraphs, amendments that occurred as it passed through the legislature, its relationship to earlier and subsequent legislation, and other material that fairly bears on the fundamental issue of legislative purpose or goal, which becomes the context within which we read the particular language before us in a given case.

> . . . Thus, in *State v. One 1983 Chevrolet Van*, 309 Md. 327 (1987), we held that when a motor vehicle is forfeited under Art. 27, § 297, and is then sold in a commercially reasonable manner, the person who owned it prior to forfeiture is not prohibited from purchasing it. Although we did not describe any of the statutes involved in that case as ambiguous or uncertain, we did search for legislative purpose or meaning—what Judge Orth, writing for the Court, described as "the legislative scheme." We identified that scheme or purpose after an extensive review of the

context of Ch. 549, Acts of 1984, which had effected major changes in Art. 27, § 297. That context included, among other things, a bill request form, prior legislation, a legislative committee report, a bill title, related statutes and amendments to the bill. *See also Ogrinz v. James*, 309 Md. 381 (1987), in which we considered legislative history (a committee report) to assist in construing legislation that we did not identify as ambiguous or of uncertain meaning.

Id. at 514–15.

In *Office & Professional Employees Int'l Union v. MTA*, 295 Md. 88, 100–01 (1982), the Court stated:

A change in the phraseology of a statute as part of a recodification will ordinarily not be deemed to modify the law unless the change is such that the intention of the Legislature to modify the law is unmistakable.

Moreover, the Revisor's Note to § 7–601 confirms that no substantive change was intended. The note states as follows:

"This section is new language derived without substantive change from the first paragraph of former Article 64B, § 37(b)."

The notes or reports of a revisor or revision commission are entitled to considerable weight in ascertaining legislative intent.

* * *

We additionally note that other authorities have not discerned any significant difference between the words, "clause" and "part," as they are used in this context.

* * *

We hold, therefore, that the legislature, by substituting the word "part" for "clause," did not intend that section 4–105 would have a different meaning from the earlier statute, Article 93 section 351. This, however, does not resolve the issue, as we must still determine whether the attempt to revoke the two provisions in the will were valid under Maryland law as expressed by the Court of Appeals in *Eschbach v. Collins, supra,* and *Home of the Aged v. Bantz, supra.*

In *Eschbach*, 61 Md. at 499–500, the Court interpreted essentially the same language from an earlier statute (the word, "clause," was used in that statute) and stated:

> It is not necessary that the words erased should be wholly illegible, but the act of the testator must be such as to clearly indicate an intention to expunge the whole clause, so that it shall no longer constitute a subdivision of the will. But when by the obliteration of certain words a different meaning is imparted, there is not a mere revocation. There is something more than the destruction of that which has been antecedently done. There is a transmutation by which a new clause is created. There is another and a distinct testamentary disposition which must be authenticated by the observance of the statutory requirements.

As we have indicated, in *Eschbach* the testator originally had his will drafted so as to divide his estate into ten equal parts, with two of his seven sons, whom he specifically named, taking a fee simple interest and the rest taking a life estate in a trust. The testator then attempted to change his will by crossing out the names of his two sons who were to take a fee simple interest, leaving the word "sons." The majority believed that to allow this, the court would have permitted all of the testator's sons to take a fee simple interest, thus increasing the share of those sons who were originally only given a life estate in the trust.

The attorney who was attempting to have the Court invalidate the attempted partial revocation provided an example which highlighted the Court's concern:

> As aptly illustrated by learned counsel in argument, if the words were "to my son William I give nothing, and give all my estate to my son John," the will could be made to read, without the insertion of any additional words, "to my son William I give all my estate."

In *Bantz*, 107 Md. at 555, the Court noted:

> In *Eschbach v. Collins*, 61 Md. 478, we distinctly recognized the right of a testator to revoke one or more clauses of his will without invalidating the rest of it, if such revocation *does not operate to enlarge the estate of any one who takes under the same will*, or to change the character of the remaining provisions of the instrument. [Emphasis added.]

In *Bantz*, the Court held that the testator revoked a clause in his will without invalidating the entire will. The effect of the revocation was to increase the amount of the estate that passed through intestacy.

In the case *sub judice*, the revocation of the $5,000 bequest to Rachel in trust enlarges the residuary estate and the revocation of one-half of the residuary estate going to David increases Daniel's share of the residuary estate. The trial judge stated that "there is no question but that the attempted cancellation by the Testatrix would run afoul of the *Eschbach/Bantz* limitation and be legally ineffective" because "[c]ancellation here would mean one son, David, and his heirs would get less and the other son, Daniel, and his heirs would receive an enlarged estate." We believe, however, that, when the Court of Appeals in *Eschbach* and *Bantz* prohibited a revocation of a clause that would "enlarge the estate of anyone taking under the will," it was not referring to a revocation that increases the value of a legatee's interest in the residuary estate.

Neither the *Eschbach* nor *Bantz* cases specifically addressed whether the revocation of a bequest or devise that merely increases the "residuary estate," such as the $5,000 bequest to Rachel in trust, "operate[s] to enlarge the estate of any one who takes under the same will, or to change the character of the remaining provisions of the instrument." In holding that it does not enlarge the estate of anyone taking under the will, we note that the word, "estate," is capable of more than one meaning. The court in *Fletcher Trust Co. v. Morse*, 97 N.E.2d 154, 162–63 (Ind.App. in banc 1951), stated:

> The varied meaning given to the word "estate" is cause for much of this conflict which seems to appear in the cases. For example, where the word "estate" is used as describing the character of the fee as from a life estate to a fee simple estate, revocation resulting in an increase thereof is not permitted. However, where the word "estate" is used in its larger sense as pertaining to "beneficial interest" or the "residuary estate"; such increases in remaining devisees are permitted.

Although that court was subsequently reversed on other grounds, we agree with its observation that the *Bantz* Court's use of the word, "estate," was in the narrow context of prohibiting an enlargement of the character of the legal estate, *i.e.*, life estate to fee simple.

Having determined that the revocations attempted in the case sub judice do not "enlarge the [type of] estate of any one who takes under the same will," we must now examine whether the revocations "change the character of the remaining provisions of the instrument." We shall first examine whether the revocation of the $5,000 bequest in trust to Rachel changes the character of the remaining provisions.

The revocation of the bequest to Rachel increases the residuary estate. Residuary clauses are very common in wills. Except in rare circumstances, any revocation of a clause or part of a will does increase the residuary estate.

We do not believe that the legislature or the Court of Appeals intended that every attempted partial revocation that merely increases the value of residuary estates must fail. We note that the Court in *Eschbach* cited with approval the Massachusetts case of *Bigelow v. Gillott*, 123 Mass. 102 (1877), stating:

> [T]here was an entire obliteration of the sixth and thirteenth clauses of the will by ink lines drawn through and across every word constituting those clauses. This was held to be a revocation of these two clauses; leaving intact the other clauses in the will.

Significantly, there was a residuary clause in *Bigelow*, and the effect of the revocation of the two clauses was to increase the value of the residuary estate.

The majority position taken by those states that have addressed the issue is that a partial revocation that increases the residuary estate is valid. * * *

We note that not every partial revocation that increases the value of the residuary estate changes the character of that provision. We also believe, however, that it is possible for a partial revocation of a will to increase the value of the residuary estate to such an extent that it would change the character of that provision. Thus, we believe that the approach that we observe the Washington courts have taken to be most appropriate. Specifically, if the $5,000 bequest to Rachel can be considered minor in respect to the testatrix's entire estate, then the revocation of that bequest should stand. As the value of the testatrix's estate was approximately $150,000, we conclude that it was minor. We hold, therefore, that the revocation of the

$5,000 specific bequest was valid and that, accordingly, that bequest passes under the residuary clause of the will.

We next address whether the revocation of the bequest of one-half of the residuary estate to David changes the character of the residuary clause. The effect of that revocation is to increase Daniel's share of the residuary estate from one-half of the estate to the entire estate. This, it appears to us, is not, under the circumstances of the case *sub judice*, a mere by-product of the alterations. Rather, the primary purpose of that revocation was to effect a major change in beneficiaries and a major change in the value of the estate devised and bequeathed. The change here altered the number of beneficiaries, *i.e.*, 2 to 1, in a significant manner. Unlike the revocation of the bequest to Rachel, which merely increased the residuary estate, this revocation alters the very meaning of the residuary clause. The entire scheme is changed, *i.e.*, the testatrix, who left half of her estate to a devisee under the original will, now leaves it all to that devisee after the change. We believe that this revocation changes the character of the will and, in order to be effective, must be accompanied by the necessary formalities. *See Appelton*, 2 P.2d 71 (Wash.1931), where the court declared that the testatrix's attempt to alter the residuary clause in such a manner as to increase the share of one taking under the residuary clause from one-half of the residuary estate to all of it was invalid because such alteration altered the testamentary disposition of the will.

JUDGMENT AS TO THE SPECIFIC BEQUEST OF $5,000 REVERSED; JUDGMENT OTHERWISE AFFIRMED; COSTS TO BE PAID BY APPELLANT.

If the gift of an asset in a will is revoked, someone else will take that asset. If the asset passes outside the will by intestate succession, perhaps that result does not offend the general rule that gifts effective at death must be executed in compliance with statutory formalities. However, if the asset in question passes under the will, the *Patrick* court is rightly troubled that the effect of the revocation is to make a gift to a devisee without observance of the formalities. The court affirms and refines previous Maryland cases that reduce the possibilities of fraud by imposing two restrictions on partial revocations by physical act. One limitation focuses on whether the revocation enlarges the quantum of estate for other devisees. The other limitation asks whether the revocation changes the character of the remaining provisions of the instrument. The court followed other states in holding that a mere increase in the value of the residuary estate would not be enough to invalidate the revocation. At some point, however, an increase in the residuary devise could be large enough to qualify as a change in the character of the will, which must be accompanied by the necessary formalities.

(d) Revocation of Codicils and Duplicate Wills

As noted above, a codicil is an instrument that amends an existing will, but does not completely replace it. Under the prevailing rule, the revocation of a will has the effect of revoking codicils to the will. On the other hand, the revocation of a codicil does not revoke the underlying will. If a will has been executed in multiple originals, the revocation of one original will revoke all originals.

3.   DEPENDENT RELATIVE REVOCATION

Revocation? What revocation? Sometimes what looks like a revocation will be ignored by a court, leaving the ostensibly revoked will effective in order to come closer to the intent of the decedent than would result by giving effect to the revocation. The courts accomplish this by applying the doctrine of dependent relative revocation (DRR). The *Kirkeby* decision, supra, provides an example. The court found that Margaret revoked her 1989, presumably by marking through provisions of that will when she executed her 1992 will. But Margaret's 1992 will was inadmissible because her telephonic acknowledgement was not in the presence of the attesting witnesses. Because the court was convinced that Margaret did not wish to die intestate, the court applied DRR to ignore the revocation of the 1989 will. The application of DRR in *Kirkeby* was straightforward. The application of DRR in other cases is not so easy.

IN RE ESTATE OF MURPHY

District Court of Appeal of Florida, Second District, 2016
184 So.3d 1221

LUCAS, J.

At the age of 107, Virginia E. Murphy passed away, leaving behind an estate worth nearly twelve million dollars, a series of wills, a phalanx of potential heirs, and extensive litigation. Following a trial, appeal, and remand from this court, the probate court entered an order in which it concluded that the vast majority of Mrs. Murphy's estate should pass through intestacy. For the reasons explained below, we are compelled to reverse the probate court's order following remand because it failed to apply the presumption of dependent relative revocation to Mrs. Murphy's last will.

I.

A.

Born in 1899, Virginia Murphy died on September 6, 2006, after more than a decade of declining health and acuity. Her parents and husband predeceased her, and she had no children or siblings. In the years before her passing, Mrs. Murphy executed a number of wills prepared by her longtime attorney, Jack S. Carey, including her last will and testament dated February 2, 1994 ("1994 will"). When Mrs. Murphy died, Mr. Carey filed a Petition for Administration submitting the 1994 will to probate. The 1994 will named Mr. Carey as personal representative of Mrs. Murphy's estate; and it purported to leave the bulk of that estate to Mr. Carey, Gloria DuBois (Mr. Carey's legal assistant), and George Tornwall (Mrs. Murphy's accountant, who died the year before Mrs. Murphy passed away).

Upon learning of the probate proceedings, Mrs. Murphy's second cousin, Jacqueline "Jackie" Rocke, a devisee under one of Mrs. Murphy's prior wills, filed an objection to the residuary devises in the 1994 will. In her objection, Ms. Rocke alleged undue influence on the part of Mr. Carey and Ms. DuBois over Mrs. Murphy. The case proceeded through discovery, motion hearings, and pleading amendments, all of which focused primarily on the litigants' competing claims as potential devisees of the estate.

The probate court held a multiday trial in February 2008 on Ms. Rocke's objection to the 1994 will. During the trial, several prior wills executed by Mrs. Murphy were discussed at length. We briefly summarize the testamentary schemes set forth in the last six of Mrs. Murphy's wills that were admitted into evidence below,[1] as they are all pertinent to this appeal:

---

[1] In the interest of brevity, these summaries do not include all of the wills' specific bequests to various charities and caregivers (which were numerous and relatively minor in proportion to the residuary of the estate) but only those germane to this appeal. It appears Mrs. Murphy executed other wills prior to these six, but none of them were made a part of the record in this appeal. None of Mrs. Murphy's last six wills contained a survivorship clause with respect to any beneficiary or devisee.

May 10, 1989, Will ("1989 Will")

This will, the earliest of the wills admitted into evidence, included a specific bequest to Ms. Rocke in the amount of $150,000 and specific bequests to Mr. Tornwall, Mr. Carey, and Ms. DuBois in the amount of $50,000 each and devised the entire residuary of the estate to Northwestern University's medical school.

June 11, 1991, Will ("1991 Will")

This will contained specific bequests to the Northwestern University medical school in the amount of $500,000, Ms. Rocke in the amount of $400,000, and Mr. Tornwall, Mr. Carey, and Ms. DuBois in the amount of $100,000 each, with the residuary of the estate divided in equal fourths between Ms. Rocke, Mr. Tornwall, Mr. Carey, and Ms. DuBois.

February 4, 1992, Will ("February 1992 Will")

This will, nearly identical to the 1991 will, also contained specific bequests to Northwestern University's medical school in the amount of $500,000, Ms. Rocke in the amount of $400,000, and Mr. Tornwall, Mr. Carey, and Ms. DuBois in the amount of $100,000 each, while the residuary of the estate was divided in equal fourths between Ms. Rocke, Mr. Tornwall, Mr. Carey, and Ms. DuBois. Ms. Rocke argued below and on appeal that this will's residuary devises (excluding Mr. Carey, Mr. Tornwall, and Ms. DuBois's devises) should have been the controlling testamentary scheme for probate of the residuary estate.

August 25, 1992, Will ("August 1992 Will")

This will included specific bequests to the medical school of Northwestern University in the amount of $500,000, Ms. Rocke in the amount of $400,000, and Mr. Tornwall, Mr. Carey, and Ms. DuBois in the amount of $100,000 each, but the residuary of the estate was now divided into equal thirds between Mr. Tornwall, Mr. Carey, and Ms. DuBois.

January 29, 1993, Will ("1993 Will")

The 1993 will contained specific bequests to Northwestern University's medical school in the amount of $500,000, Ms. Rocke in the amount of $400,000, Ms. DuBois in the amount of $150,000, and Mr. Tornwall and Mr. Carey in the amount of $100,000 each. The residuary of the estate was devised in equal thirds between Mr. Tornwall, Mr. Carey, and Ms. DuBois.

1994 Will

This will, like the 1993 will, included specific bequests to Northwestern University's medical school in the amount of $500,000, Ms. Rocke in the amount of $400,000, Ms. DuBois in the amount of $150,000, and Mr. Tornwall and Mr. Carey in the amount of $100,000 each. The residuary of the estate was again devised in equal thirds between Mr. Tornwall, Mr. Carey, and Ms. DuBois.

In addition to these testamentary documents, the probate court also considered the testimony of Mr. Carey, Ms. DuBois, Ms. Rocke, and other witnesses who had been involved with Mrs. Murphy's estate planning. By nearly all accounts, Mrs. Murphy maintained few personal relationships in the final decades of her life; she never knew anyone in her extended family other than Ms. Rocke, with whom she had enjoyed a close, social relationship since the early 1960s. Over time, Mr. Carey and Ms. DuBois built their own relationship with Mrs. Murphy (Ms. DuBois would eventually manage Mrs. Murphy's day-to-day finances for several years) founded upon Mr. Carey's service as her counsel. While Mrs. Murphy's health and mental awareness diminished, Mr. Carey and Ms. DuBois' share of the estate grew under the wills Mr. Carey drafted.

After the conclusion of the trial, on August 1, 2008, the probate court entered its Order on Objection to Petition for Administration and Order Admitting Will to Probate ("Order on Objection"). The Order on Objection included thorough and detailed findings that Mr. Carey and Ms. DuBois had, in fact, exerted undue influence through their confidential, fiduciary, and personal relationships with Ms. Murphy in order to become residuary devisees of her estate.[2] The probate court further concluded that the residuary devises in the 1994 will were void but that "[t]he remainder of the provisions of the will are valid and shall control the disposition of the assets specifically devised." The court then admitted the 1994 will to probate, excluding its residuary devises, and ordered that "the rest,

---

[2] We need not recount all of the probate court's findings of undue influence—which were quite extensive—but would echo the court's sense of puzzlement as to why Mr. Carey, an esteemed lawyer and a former city councilman, FBI agent, and Army Air Corps veteran, succumbed to the temptation to pursue a pecuniary windfall at the expense of a frail and susceptible client. Sadly, the pall of this case cast a long shadow over an otherwise exemplary professional reputation. *Cf.* Fla. R. Prof. Conduct 4–1.8(c) ("A lawyer shall not . . . prepare on behalf of a client an instrument giving the lawyer . . . any substantial gift unless the lawyer . . . is related to the client."). We make this observation not to impugn the memory of Mr. Carey, who passed away in 2014, but to state this simple point: the repercussions from a single ethical lapse may carry far beyond a lawyer's license to practice law.

residue and remainder [of the estate] shall pass by the laws of intestate succession" as a lapsed gift.

Implicit in the probate court's determination was that the 1994 will's revocation clause, revoking all of Mrs. Murphy's prior wills, remained valid, so that the vast majority of Mrs. Murphy's estate would now pass to her intestate heirs who were, as yet, still unknown. Suffice it to say, none of the litigants were particularly satisfied with that result.

B.

Mr. Carey and Ms. DuBois appealed the Order on Objection, and Ms. Rocke filed a cross-appeal, arguing that the probate court should have effectuated her residuary devise in the February 1992 will under the doctrine of dependent relative revocation. In *Carey v. Rocke*, 18 So.3d 1266 (Fla. 2d DCA 2009), this court affirmed the probate court's determinations in every regard, except its decision to administer the residue of Mrs. Murphy's estate through intestacy. As to the residuary disposition, we pointed the probate court's attention to the doctrine of dependent relative revocation, citing the Fifth District's decision in *Wehrheim v. Golden Pond Assisted Living Facility*, 905 So.2d 1002 (Fla. 5th DCA 2005). We noted that we could not determine whether the doctrine's presumption applied based on the record then before us and that "the decision as to whether the residuary clause in one of Mrs. Murphy's prior wills is enforceable necessarily requires factual determinations in this case." We then remanded the case to the probate court for further proceedings to make those factual determinations.

Unfortunately, the proceedings on remand appear to have taken a somewhat unusual turn. Rather than convene an evidentiary hearing, the probate court, apparently proceeding under the mistaken assumption that it had only been asked to clarify whether it had considered the doctrine of dependent relative revocation, entered an Order on Remand dated March 12, 2010. Relying solely on the wills that had been admitted at the prior trial, and without identifying the potential intestate heirs, the probate court concluded that the doctrine of dependent relative revocation did not apply.

In its order, the probate court briefly traced the history of the doctrine of dependent relative revocation and provided its view of various cases and law review articles interpreting the doctrine. But the court felt bound to discern Mrs. Murphy's intent solely from the testamentary instruments and without consideration of extrinsic evidence such as the testimony from the prior trial, a task which, it allowed, presented a difficult challenge. The probate court determined that the doctrine was not applicable because of what it deemed "dramatic" changes between the residuary devises throughout Mrs. Murphy's last six wills and the lack of evidence either that "the decedent's intent to revoke her preceding wills was equivocal or conditional" or that she intended to revive any prior will by republication. The probate court clarified its previous finding, concluding that the undue influence that permeated the residuary clause of the 1994 will had not tainted that will's revocation clause. It then observed that "the inference that decedent would have preferred probate of the residuary clause in the February 1992 Will over intestacy is purely speculative." Finally, the probate court opined that "to adopt any of the five residuary clauses [from the prior wills], all unreflective of the testator's intent, would require this court to speculatively re-draft [sic] the testatrix's will." The court again ordered that Mrs. Murphy's residuary estate should pass through intestacy.

It would take another four years before the probate court was able to effectuate that ruling and render a final order disposing of Mrs. Murphy's estate. The delay was likely attributable to the task of tracing all of Mrs. Murphy's ancestry. Eventually, an heir search firm identified and located forty-eight heirs through Mrs. Murphy's deceased grandparents. Most of these heirs were spread across the United States and, apparently, were completely unaware of their familial connection to Mrs. Murphy. With this information, but still without convening an evidentiary hearing, the probate court entered a Final Order Determining Beneficiaries and Respective Shares on July 28, 2014, implementing an intestate succession plan pursuant to section 732.103, Florida Statutes (2006). Ms. Rocke then initiated this appeal.

II.

The issues in this appeal present mixed questions of law and fact. The application of an evidentiary presumption such as the doctrine of dependent relative revocation is an issue of law subject to a de novo standard of review. Whether or to what extent the predicate facts giving rise to a legal presumption or its rebuttal were established is an issue of fact, which we review for competent, substantial evidence.

III.

We begin by examining the legal construct at the heart of this appeal, the doctrine of dependent relative revocation. Founded in the common law of early eighteenth century England, the doctrine was first adopted by the Florida Supreme Court, which explained:

> This doctrine has been stated and reiterated by many courts since it was first expounded in 1717, but stated simply it means that where [a] testator makes a new will revoking a former valid one, and it later appears that the new one is invalid, the old will may be re-established on the ground that the revocation was dependent upon the validity of the new one, [the] testator preferring the old will to intestacy.

Stewart v. Johnson, 194 So. 869, 870 (1940). Grounded in the axiom of probate law that intestacy should be avoided whenever possible, the doctrine of dependent relative revocation, our court has observed, is "a rule of presumed intention" that creates a rebuttable presumption that the testator would have preferred to have a prior will effectuated over statutory intestacy. The presumption's application hinges on whether "the provisions of the present invalid will are sufficiently similar to the former will." In cases of undue influence, if a prior will is sufficiently similar to an invalidated will then the presumption arises but may be rebutted by evidence that "the revocation clause was not invalidated by undue influence and that it was not intended by the decedent to be conditional on the validity of the testamentary provisions" of the will. *Wehrheim*, 905 So.2d at 1009–10; *cf.* § 732.5165 (stating any part of a will procured by fraud, duress, mistake or undue influence is void, "but the remainder of the will not so procured shall be valid if it is not invalid for other reasons").

With this framework, then, the proper analysis in this case on remand should have proceeded along the following sequence: (i) did Ms. Rocke establish sufficient similarity between Mrs. Murphy's wills that would have given rise to the doctrine of dependent relative revocation; (ii) if so, were there sufficient record facts to overcome that presumption so that the 1994 will's revocation clause could withstand; and (iii) if not, if the presumption remained intact, which, if any, will or residuary devise in Mrs. Murphy's prior wills reflected her true testamentary intention? It appears to us that the probate court focused too closely on this third analytical step to the point of conflating it with the first two. That was error. We must examine each step in its proper turn.

A.

In order to give rise to the presumption that the 1994 will's revocation clause was conditioned upon the validity of its testamentary devises, Ms. Rocke had to establish that Mrs. Murphy's prior, revoked wills were "sufficiently similar" to the 1994 will. Ms. Rocke argues that when viewed broadly and without regard to the devises to Mr. Carey and Ms. DuBois, the overall dispositional plan of the wills remained fairly constant. She also points to the execution of so many wills over the years, which, Ms. Rocke posits, was proof of Mrs. Murphy's preference to leave her property through testacy. Finally, Ms. Rocke contends that the extrinsic evidence presented to the probate court lent further proof that the revocation clause in the 1994 will was also the product of Mr. Carey and Ms. DuBois' undue influence and that Mrs. Murphy would have never intended to leave the bulk of her estate to a collection of individuals she had never met or known. The appellees disagree that there was any similarity between the wills, focusing on the fact that Ms. Rocke was only a residuary devisee in two of Mrs. Murphy's last six wills and that the bequests and devises to Ms. Rocke varied from will to will. Furthermore, according to the appellees, the probate court was precluded from considering any extrinsic evidence apart from the testamentary documents themselves in deciding whether Mrs. Murphy's wills were sufficiently similar to implicate the doctrine of dependent relative revocation.

The discrete point of contention here is one of measurement. Somewhere in the conceptual space between "identical" and "antithetical" resides "similar," and the parties disagree where its boundaries should be marked for this kind of case. One could draw the notion of sufficient similarity between wills broadly or narrowly. Florida courts have seldom expounded upon the issue, but in the context of undue influence we would incline toward a broader definition of similarity, one that takes into account the testamentary instruments themselves and any admissible evidence that may be relevant. We do so for several reasons.

1.

Unlike cases where a will has been invalidated for an impropriety with its execution, see *Lubbe*, 142 So.2d 130 (interested beneficiary acted as witness), or a legal impediment exists that precludes the execution of a testator's wishes—cases where there is no serious question about the testator's intent (only the legal efficacy of his or her testamentary documents)—in cases of undue influence, the decedent's intent has been impaired, destroyed, or overridden by someone else. The undue influence effectively grafts a different disposition or scheme into a testamentary instrument than would have otherwise been created. Keeping in mind that the requirement of sufficient similarity serves to ensure the indicia of the testator's intent, any construction of similarity must necessarily account for the intrusion of another's intentions in cases of undue influence. A broad construction of similarity does so.

We also find support for a broad construction of the doctrine's similarity requirement from the Fifth District's decision in *Wehrheim.* In *Wehrheim,* a decedent's last will submitted to probate named her assisted living facility as the primary beneficiary of her estate. The decedent's children initiated adversary proceedings, alleging undue influence on the part of the facility. In response, the facility argued that under the doctrine of dependent relative revocation the children would have no standing to challenge the will because none of them were named as beneficiaries within any of the decedent's prior three wills. While reversing the trial court's summary judgment in favor of the facility, the Fifth District rejected the children's argument that the doctrine of dependent relative revocation could not apply because the prior wills were not sufficiently similar to one another. The *Wehrheim* court offered this analysis of the similarity between the instruments:

> The Wehrheims contend that the 2002 will is not sufficiently similar to the prior wills because the decedent had never before made a charitable devise of her estate. . . . While the charitable devise may be a difference between the 2002 will and the prior wills, we discern a very significant similarity among all of the decedent's wills, which is her intention not to devise any portion of her estate to her children. Based on this similarity, we are unable to say that the presumed preference of the decedent for her prior dispositions and for testacy over intestacy has been rebutted.

In its comparison, the *Wehrheim* court gave passing consideration to the specific beneficiaries in any of the wills at issue. Rather, the court found sufficient similarity for the doctrine's application simply from noting who was *not* a beneficiary under any of the wills. The absence of the decedent's children was enough of a common thread to construe a similar testamentary intent between all of the decedent's wills. We agree with the Fifth District's broad conception of similarity for cases involving undue influence, as it furthers the doctrine of dependent relative revocation's underlying purpose of promoting testacy over intestacy whenever possible. Indeed, to hold otherwise, to apply an overly strict or narrow construction of similarity, would likely consign the doctrine of dependent relative revocation to a minute corner of irrelevance for cases of undue influence. We see no reason to corral the presumption for this class of cases.

2.

But we must part company with the Fifth District insofar as *Wehrheim* would preclude a probate court from considering extrinsic evidence when deciding the doctrine's applicability in claims involving undue influence. In determining whether testamentary instruments are sufficiently similar for purposes of the doctrine of dependent relative revocation, a court should always look first to the documents themselves. However, in cases of undue influence, its analysis cannot simply end there.

Extrinsic evidence may be essential in order to grasp the true testamentary intentions of a testator who has left multiple wills, some of which may or may not have been affected, to some degree, by another's undue influence. Without resort to extrinsic evidence, a proponent for the doctrine's presumption may have no viable means of showing sufficient similarity between the tainted and untainted portions of testamentary documents and an adverse party would never have a way to rebut the presumption.

* * *

We find no reason to erect a barrier between admissible evidence and the task of sifting similarities between wills that have been affected by undue influence. Rather, we join the courts of our sister states to hold that, in cases involving undue influence, a probate court is not confined to the testamentary documents when determining whether the doctrine of dependent relative revocation should apply. Upon a finding of undue influence, a probate court may consider any relevant, admissible evidence to decide if the testator intended a will's revocation clause to be conditional upon the will's efficacy.

3.

Comparing Mrs. Murphy's wills in the appropriately broad light, and in the light of all the evidence, we find there were sufficient similarities between Mrs. Murphy's 1994 will and her prior wills to support the application of the doctrine of dependent relative revocation to the 1994 will. We discern several contours of similarity that were unrefuted in the record.

First, Mrs. Murphy's execution of six wills over a period of five years evidences a sustained concern about the disposition of her property upon her death. Mrs. Murphy prized her right to dictate how her property should be divided, and she exercised that right, repeatedly, in the final years of her life. No one seriously disputes that she preferred testacy over intestacy. And that is, of course, the very foundation for the doctrine of dependent relative revocation's application.

Moreover, the testamentary documents themselves evince an overall pattern of similarity. Each of Mrs. Murphy's wills employed a similar testamentary scheme in which Mrs. Murphy made numerous specific bequests to charities and caregivers while limiting the division of the residuary of her estate to a few devisees. Although their respective proportions varied from will to will, the identities of the devisees and beneficiaries within the six wills, overall, remained fairly constant. Indeed, in its Order on Remand, the probate court observed, "Over the course of six wills, the changes in specific bequests were insubstantial." The variance the probate court fixed upon, the alteration of residuary devisees, is likewise modest once the effect of Mr. Carey and Ms. DuBois' undue influence is properly taken into account. When Mr. Carey and Ms. DuBois are removed from consideration, there is only one change between the six wills' residuary clauses that did not involve Mr. Carey or Ms. DuBois' illicit gain over the residuary estate: the change between the 1989 will and the 1991 will, which exchanged Northwestern University's medical school and Ms. Rocke's respective positions as a specific beneficiary and a residuary devisee. For her part, Ms. Rocke appeared repeatedly throughout Mrs. Murphy's wills, either as a residuary devisee, a designee of a specific bequest, or both.

Finally, the extrinsic evidence proffered before the probate court further demonstrated the appropriateness of applying the presumption in this case. With the exception of four individuals, including Ms. Rocke, none of the forty-eight intestate heirs ultimately identified in the Final Order Determining Beneficiaries and Respective Shares were mentioned within any of Mrs. Murphy's six wills. In contrast to the close relationship she had with Ms. Rocke, it appears Mrs. Murphy never knew her intestate heirs, and they never knew her. The intestate heirs' ancestral ties to Mrs. Murphy apparently remained forgotten until this litigation (and an heir search firm) brought them to light. Intestacy, in this case, would usurp the repeated testamentary dispositions of Mrs. Murphy's property throughout her wills, dispositions that were invariably tied to individuals she cared about or charities and institutions which she supported. We hold, as a matter of law, that Mrs. Murphy's six wills were sufficiently similar to give rise to the doctrine of dependent relative revocation's presumption.

B.

Having determined that the doctrine of dependent relative revocation should have been applied to the 1994 will, we next consider whether there were sufficient facts to rebut the doctrine's presumption.* * *

* * *

* * * Thus, the doctrine of dependent relative revocation, when applied in a case of undue influence, shifts the burden of proof to the parties opposing its application.

It was incumbent, then, upon any party opposing the presumption to prove that the 1994 will's revocation clause was untainted by the same undue influence that infected its residuary clause and that Mrs. Murphy held an independent, untainted intention to revoke all of her prior wills at the time she executed the 1994 will so that the bulk of her estate would pass by intestacy. *See Wehrheim*, 905 So.2d at 1009–10 (noting the "daunting task" of refuting the doctrine's presumption in a case where undue influence had been established). No such showing was ever made here. This will's revocation clause, an otherwise unremarkable example of boilerplate testamentary language, contains no statement of an intent to sever its application from the rest of the will. Nor did the probate court elucidate any independent, factual basis to support its conclusion that the undue influence that permeated the residuary clause of the 1994 will somehow left its revocation clause untouched. Our review of the record has found no evidence that would support such a counterintuitive conclusion. Quite the contrary, the presumption appears particularly apt in this case, as one of the individuals found to have unduly influenced Mrs. Murphy, Jack Carey, drafted both the residuary clause and the revocation clause of the 1994 will and stood to gain from both of those clauses' execution.

The presumption that arose from the doctrine of dependent relative revocation was never rebutted in the proceedings below. The revocation clause within the 1994 will should, therefore, have been deemed invalid, as it was dependent upon the effectiveness of that will's invalid residuary clause.

C.

Stripping the undue influence that spanned the residuary devises of Mrs. Murphy's last six wills leaves two alternative residuary devises that remained untainted: the medical school of Northwestern University or Ms. Rocke. Northwestern University would receive the entire residuary of Mrs. Murphy's estate under the express provision of the 1989 will. Ms. Rocke would stand to receive all of the residuary estate by operation of law under the February 1992 will as the only remaining residuary devisee in that will. *See* § 732.5165 (establishing that any part of a will procured by undue influence is void, "but the remainder of the will not so procured shall be valid if it is not invalid for other reasons"). The question then becomes which devise from which will should determine the disposition of the residuary estate.

From our review of the evidence proffered below,[6] the February 1992 will's residuary clause, which includes the last untainted residuary disposition Mrs. Murphy made, controls the disposition of her residuary estate. Although it is true Mr. Carey and Ms. DuBois procured part of the February 1992 will's residuary clause through their illicit efforts, the probate court made no finding—as, indeed, no one has ever argued—that Ms. Rocke was, in any way, associated with that exertion of undue influence over Mrs. Murphy. The February 1992 will would remain perfectly intelligible and true to Mrs. Murphy's repeated indications of preferring testacy over intestacy had the probate court excised Mr. Carey and Ms. DuBois'

---

[6] The parties have argued the issue of the doctrine of dependent relative revocation extensively and repeatedly before the probate court; and notwithstanding the court's refusal to consider it, they have proffered a substantial amount of testimony and evidence into the record below. Lest this lawsuit devolve into a Dickensian epic, we will not delay a final decision about Mrs. Murphy's estate any longer. *Cf. J. Sourini Painting, Inc. v. Johnson Paints, Inc.*, 809 So.2d 95, 98 (Fla. 2d DCA 2002) ("Litigants, and the public generally, have a right to expect that controversies between parties respecting their rights and liabilities should be expeditiously resolved in our judicial system.").

devises and left Ms. Rocke's to stand. The court must honor the last uninfluenced residuary devise Mrs. Murphy made: to her cousin, Jackie Rocke.

IV.

In conclusion, we hold that in cases of undue influence over a testator, the presumption from the doctrine of dependent relative revocation requires only a showing of broad similarity between a decedent's testamentary instruments. We further hold that a probate court may consider any admissible extrinsic evidence when measuring similarity for purposes of the doctrine's application. Consistent with sections 90.302(2) and 733.107(2), we hold that when the doctrine's presumption arises the burden of proof then shifts to the opponent of the presumption to show that the testator held an independent, unaffected intention to revoke the otherwise affected will.

Having clarified the doctrine's application, we find that the presumption under the doctrine was established here and was not rebutted. The probate court erred and should have admitted the February 1992 will to probate with Ms. Rocke receiving the residuary of the estate as the last remaining devisee. Accordingly, we reverse the order of the probate court and remand with directions to enter an order consistent with this opinion. We certify conflict with *Wehrheim v. Golden Pond Assisted Living Facility*, 905 So.2d 1002, 1008 (Fla. 5th DCA 2005), as discussed in section III(A)(2) of our opinion.

Reversed and remanded; conflict certified.

The case would have been easier if the court had felt free to invalidate entirely each of the wills that were procured by undue influence. But the court instead followed the statutory mandate to probate the provisions of the will that were not influenced by the influencers. That left the general devises but knocked out the residuary devises for the three more recent wills. Could this appellate court have reached the same result by finding that the revoking clauses in the wills were included in the instruments as a result of undue influence, allowing the court to ignore the revocations?

As the case indicates, courts are free to apply DDR but do not always do so. To put it another way, DDR only sets up a rebuttable presumption that the will was not revoked. The goal is to reach a result closer to what the decedent would have wanted than the result that would obtain if the revocation were recognized.

The doctrine of dependent relative revocation is sometimes said to employ a fiction. The fiction is that the testator's intent to revoke was dependent or conditional and the condition was not satisfied, so the will is not revoked. But conditional intent is not involved in most of the cases applying the doctrine. In *Murphy*, there was no such conditional intent; indeed, there was an absence of intent because of undue influence. Dependent relative revocation is also applied in cases of mistake. Sometimes the testator's mistake was that a new plan of disposition would be effective. Other times, the mistake was about some other fact that was recited in the revoking instrument. In some jurisdictions, the mistake need not be recited in the revoking instrument if it is proved by clear and convincing evidence. In many cases, the mistake was essentially a mistake in the inducement for revoking a will. Because of that mistake, the revocation is ignored. But a mistake in the inducement usually has no effect on the admission of a will to probate. Courts seem to think that a mistake in the inducement for a revocation of a will is different from a mistake in the inducement for execution of a will.

DDR allows courts to reach results they could not reach under statutes and other doctrines. Courts have applied the doctrine of dependent relative revocation for three centuries. Can deviation from the terms of the statutes be justified? Why don't legislatures stop courts from doing so?

4.   REVIVAL

Sometimes it is possible for a will that has been revoked to be brought back to life. And sometimes it is not. Under the UPC, it is not possible to revive a will that has been revoked by revocatory act. On the other hand, if a will was revoked by another instrument, a revocation of the revoking instrument might revive the earlier will, and the UPC establishes categorical presumptions. If Will 1 is partly revoked by Will 2 and Will 2 is revoked by a revocatory act, then the revoked parts of Will 1 are presumed revived. In all other cases, Will 1 is presumed not to be revived. What evidence can be used to overcome the presumptions depends on the situation.

UPC § 2–509

SECTION 2–509. REVIVAL OF REVOKED WILL.

(a) If a subsequent will that wholly revoked a previous will is thereafter revoked by a revocatory act under Section 2–507(a)(2), the previous will remains revoked unless it is revived. The previous will is revived if it is evident from the circumstances of the revocation of the subsequent will or from the testator's contemporary or subsequent declarations that the testator intended the previous will to take effect as executed.

(b) If a subsequent will that partly revoked a previous will is thereafter revoked by a revocatory act under Section 2–507(a)(2) , a revoked part of the previous will is revived unless it is evident from the circumstances of the revocation of the subsequent will or from the testator's contemporary or subsequent declarations that the testator did not intend the revoked part to take effect as executed.

(c) If a subsequent will that revoked a previous will in whole or in part is thereafter revoked by another, later will, the previous will remains revoked in whole or in part, unless it or its revoked part is revived. The previous will or its revoked part is revived to the extent it appears from the terms of the later will that the testator intended the previous will to take effect.

Example 4.14: O executes Will 1, which says, "I give everything to A." O executes Will 2, which says, "I give my ring to B." Will 2 is a codicil, which revokes by inconsistency the gift of the ring to A in Will 1 (UPC § 2–507(a)(1)), but not the rest of Will 1. O destroys Will 2, with intent to revoke it. O dies, leaving H as O's heir. The revocation of Will 2 by revocatory act is presumed to revive Will 1's gift of the ring to A (UPC § 2–509(b)). Since there is no evidence of intent not to revive that gift from the circumstances of revocation or O's declaration, the gift of the ring is revived and A takes everything.

Example 4.15: Assume the same facts as above except that O revokes Will 2 by executing Will 3, instead of by destruction. That triggers a different presumption under the UPC. The gift of the ring is not revived unless the intent to revive it appears in Will 3.

Problem 4.16: O executes Will 1, which says, "I give everything to A." O executes Will 2, which says, "Will 1 is revoked. I give everything to B." O revokes Will 2. O dies leaving H as his heir. In this case, the UPC presumes Will 1 is not revived. What evidence does it take to overcome that presumption?

Example 4.17: O executes Will 1, which says, "I give everything to A." O tears Will 1 into two pieces with intent to revoke it. O tapes Will 1 back together, intending for it to be effective. Will 1 is not revived.

To sum up these rules: Where Will 1 is revoked by revocatory act, Will 1 cannot be revived. Where Will 1 is revoked by Will 2, Will 1 can be revived by revoking Will 2. If Will 2 partially revokes Will 1 and Will 2 is then revoked by revocatory act, Will 1 is presumed revived. Otherwise, Will 1 is presumed not to be revived. If a third will, Will 3, is involved, the intent needed to overcome the presumption must appear in Will 3.

Not all states follow the UPC rules on revival. Some do not allow revival at all. In others, if the second will is revoked, the first will is "uncovered" and effective again.

5. REPUBLICATION BY CODICIL

In the states that accept the doctrine of republication by codicil, a will that has been revoked may become effective again if a codicil to that will is properly executed.

D. INTERPRETATION OR CONSTRUCTION OF A WILL

Once a court admits a will to probate, the court needs to decide what that will means. In the ideal case, of course, the meaning is clear and acceptable to all. But wills are drafted by humans, and humans, even lawyers who draft wills, are flawed. Sometimes flaws of drafting or of planning work their way into the will, and it is up to a court to decide what to do about those flaws. There are many issues that arise in the interpretation or construction of wills. Some of the default rules will be covered in the next sections. Others will be covered later in a section relating to the construction of both wills and trusts.

1. MISTAKES

There are various sorts of mistakes that arise in the context of wills. One sort of mistake, a mistake in the inducement, arises if a provision in a will was drafted on the basis of a mistake as to external facts. The traditional approach in such situations is to ignore the mistake and apply the terms of the will as written, without reformation. For example, if a testator wrongly believed his brother was dead and left everything to his sister, the mistaken belief of his brother's death would not allow the court to reform the instrument. However, UPC § 2–302 carves an exception: "If at the time of execution of the will the testator fails to provide in the will for a living child solely because the testator believes the child to be dead, the child is entitled to share in the estate . . .". The narrowness of the exception shows the breadth of the general rule.

Another sort of mistake is a mistake in the execution, where the testator is mistaken as to the contents of the document. Such mistakes are considered by courts in a couple of contexts. First, if extrinsic evidence shows that an entire document was not intended to be a will, a court can exclude it because the decedent lacked testamentary intent, even though the document looks like a properly executed will.

Second, if extrinsic evidence shows that the testator did not intend a portion of the will to be included in the will, testamentary intent is missing for that portion and those words can be denied probate, leaving only the words that were intended. *But see Breckner v. Prestwood*, infra. Mistakenly included clauses can be deleted. However, whether courts will add mistakenly excluded clauses is a quite different question.

KNUPP V. DISTRICT OF COLUMBIA
District of Columbia Court of Appeals, 1990
578 A.2d 702

NEWMAN, J.

This is an appeal from a judgment of the Superior Court construing a will. The problem at issue is that the will's sixth paragraph states that the residual estate is to pass to the person specified in the eighth paragraph of the will, but the eighth paragraph does not name a residual legatee. Appellant explains that the inconsistency is a result of an error on the part of the attorney who drafted the will: that although the testator allegedly instructed the attorney to name appellant as the beneficiary of the residual estate, the attorney forgot to insert such a clause in the will. Appellant argued in the construction proceeding in Superior Court that, based upon extrinsic evidence showing that the testator intended the appellant to be the beneficiary of the residual estate, the court should interpret the will to give Appellant the residual estate. The trial court held that it was without power to reform the will by inserting the name of a legatee alleged to have been omitted by mistake. As a consequence, the residue would go to the District of Columbia by escheat. We agree with the Superior Court's ruling and, thus, we affirm.

I

The facts of this case show that the testator, a District of Columbia resident, executed a will from his hospital bed in March 1986 and died approximately one month thereafter. Paragraph Six of the will states:

> I direct my Executor to sell or otherwise convert into cash such of the rest and remainder of my estate as, in his judgment, is or may be necessary to pay my just debts, expenses of administration, funeral expenses, expenses of last illness, estate and inheritance (and other) taxes, and the cash legacies specified in subparagraphs A through G, inclusive, of paragraph *SEVENTH* hereof. I request that the remaining assets of my estate that are not required to be sold in order to pay debts, expenses, taxes, and cash legacies as provided in the preceding sentence be retained in kind by said Executor and distributed in kind to the residual legatee as stipulated in paragraph *EIGHTH* hereof.

Paragraph eighth of the will states, in pertinent part:

> I hereby nominate and appoint RICHARD L. KNUPP, . . ., as Executor of this my last will and testament, and I direct that no bond or security be required of him. I ask that he retain MILTON W. SCHOBER, . . ., as attorney for my estate.

Nowhere does paragraph eighth name a residual beneficiary.

The will was drafted by Milton W. Schober, the attorney referred to in the eighth paragraph of the will and the drafter of the testator's two prior wills. In his two prior wills, the testator left significant bequests to his personal friend, Richard L. Knupp ("Knupp").

Appellant alleges that in this will testator also intended Knupp to benefit. Allegedly, approximately one month prior to his death, the testator told Schober to draft a new will which would leave specific dollar amounts to several named beneficiaries and which would leave the bulk of the estate to Knupp, as residual beneficiary. Schober drafted the new will and the testator signed it. The will, however, did not name the residual legatee. Schober submitted an affidavit to the trial court admitting that he mistakenly failed to designate a residual beneficiary in the will even though the testator had instructed him to name Knupp. Schober also provided the trial court with notes he took of his conversations with the testator to prove that the testator intended Knupp to be the residual legatee.

In an order dated November 16, Judge Barnes found that the will was ambiguous on its face and that the court should consider extrinsic evidence to determine the testator's intent. In a supplemental order, though, Judge Barnes ruled that as a matter of law, specific extrinsic evidence concerning the names of omitted legatees must be excluded.

II

A

The general rule in construing a will in the District of Columbia is that the testator's intent is the guiding principle. If the intent is clear from the language of the will, the inquiry ends there. However, "if the language 'upon its face and without explanation, is doubtful or meaningless' . . . a court may examine extrinsic evidence in order to understand the will."

While the intent of the testator is the "polestar in construction of a will," extrinsic facts are not always permitted into evidence in order to prove the testator's intent. Certain conditions must be present to warrant the introduction of extrinsic evidence. First, there must be some ambiguity in order for a court to consider extrinsic evidence. In addition, in all cases in which such evidence is received, it can be "utilized only for the purpose of interpreting something actually written in the will and never to add provisions to the will." As one treatise states:

> evidence of surrounding circumstances is admissible to enable the court to understand the meaning of the words which the testator has used in his will, it is not admissible to add to the will provisions which cannot fairly be inferred

from the language which is used therein, or to take from the will provisions which are clearly expressed therein.

When an ambiguity exists regarding the testator's intent, often a court will allow extrinsic facts into evidence to clear up the ambiguity. As the Supreme Court noted over a century ago:

> It is settled doctrine that, as a latent ambiguity is only disclosed by extrinsic evidence, it may be removed by extrinsic evidence. Such an ambiguity may arise upon a will, either when it names a person as the object of a gift, or a thing as the subject of it, and there are two persons or things that answer such name or description; or, secondly, it may arise when the will contains a misdescription of the object or subject: as where there is no such person or thing in existence, or, if in existence, the person is not the one intended, or the thing does not belong to the testator.

Patch v. White, 117 U.S. 210, 217 (1886). *See also 7th Ga. Regiment, supra*, 55 App.D.C. at 158 ("[A]mbiguity may arise when a will names a person as the object of a gift, or a thing as the subject of it, and there are two persons or things that equally well answer such name or description. In such a case, it is apparent that extrinsic evidence is not only useful, but indispensable to a proper interpretation of the will."); *Mitchell v. Merriam*, 88 U.S.App.D.C. 213 (1950) (where testatrix devised property to "my nephew Edward A. Mitchell" and testatrix had both a nephew and a grand nephew named Edward A. Mitchell, the court allowed in extrinsic evidence to show which of the two individuals the testatrix was referring to in her will); *In re Miller's Estate*, 127 F.Supp. 23 (D.D.C.1955) (where testatrix's will stated "I give and bequeath to my cousin, Sue McCook . . . any monies that are left after my just debts are paid," extrinsic evidence was allowed in order to determine whether testatrix intended the word "monies" to be restricted to cash and money on deposit in bank accounts or whether the word should be understood in the colloquial sense as meaning all personal property).

Any ambiguity in the will under consideration in this case is not of the sort that can be corrected by the consideration of extrinsic evidence. There is no language in the will that could lead a court to infer that the testator intended Knupp to be the recipient of the residual estate; thus, it was proper for the court not to admit the extrinsic evidence.

The United States Court of Appeals for this Circuit, in decisions binding on this court (decisions of the United States Court of Appeals for the District of Columbia Circuit decided prior to February 1, 1971 are binding on divisions of this Court; only the *en banc* Court can decline to follow such decisions), has held that the name of a legatee that was omitted from a will cannot subsequently be added to that will by a court. In the will at issue in *Hall v. Killingsworth*, 102 U.S.App.D.C. 307 (1958), the testatrix left to five named persons the right to live in the testatrix's building after her death. The will then gave four of the five named individuals the right to share any income the property produced. Extrinsic evidence showed that the *Hall* testatrix intended all five individuals to share in the income of the property, but due to the "almost incredible ineptitude of the lawyer" who drafted the will, the fifth person was mistakenly not mentioned. The *Hall* court stated:

> Of course we cannot accept, as is argued, that [the fifth person] should be read into the second group, no matter how clear is the proffered evidence that the testator intended this result. We may construe one name to mean another, but we can not supply a name where an unambiguous vacuum exists.

Id. at 310. In *In re Estate of Kerr, supra*, 139 U.S.App.D.C. at 332, the court held that extrinsic evidence can be used to clear up an ambiguity in a will "only for the purpose of interpreting something actually written in the will and never to add provisions to the will." As the court put it: "no matter how clearly a testator's wish to make a particular disposition may appear from sources outside the will, a court can not give it effect unless the words written into the will effect that disposition or are reasonably susceptible to the interpretation that they do."

For the aforementioned reasons, the decision is hereby

Affirmed.

Although mistakenly included clauses can be deleted, the converse is not always true. The doctrinal reason for this distinction is that the omitted words were not executed in compliance with the Wills Act formalities. One policy question raised by this distinction is whether the dangers of injustice and administrative costs are greater when courts can add words than when courts can subtract words. The persons who might benefit from deleting words from a will are probably limited to those identified, individually or by class, in the will plus those who would take in intestacy. The persons who might benefit from adding words include all of those same persons, plus any others who might get themselves added to a will. Thus, the number of malefactors who might benefit from deleting words from a will is probably smaller than the number who could benefit from adding words. Are there considerations on the other side of the balance that make additions less dangerous than subtractions?

UPC § 2–805

SECTION 2–805. REFORMATION TO CORRECT MISTAKES. The court may reform the terms of a governing instrument, even if unambiguous, to conform the terms to the transferor's intention if it is proved by clear and convincing evidence what the transferor's intention was and that the terms of the governing instrument were affected by a mistake of fact or law, whether in expression or inducement.

UPC § 2–805 would allow the court to consider extrinsic evidence that many states would reject. One benefit of doing so is that the court might come closer to accomplishing the intent of the testator. One cost of doing so is an increase in litigation, borne by the estate as well as society. The vast majority of wills do not get litigated. Opening up their construction to litigation could result in a large increase in the amount of will litigation. Another cost might be errors that would have been avoided if the evidence had been excluded, although this cost is reduced by the clear and convincing evidence standard. Given that a testator might see costs as well as benefits in the UPC's approach to reformation of wills, perhaps private ordering is in order. UPC § 2–805 could be amended to allow a testator to opt out of 2–805 by a specific provision in her will, leaving her with the rules traditionally applied in the jurisdiction before 2–805 was adopted. Should the testator be allowed to choose which rules apply to her will? In a jurisdiction following UPC § 2–805, what external costs would a testator impose on society by opting out? If UPC § 2–805 does apply to a given will and a party asks the court for reform, a court must determine both the intention of the decedent and whether terms of the will were affected by a mistake of fact or law.

2. PLAIN MEANING, AMBIGUITIES, AND EXTRINSIC EVIDENCE

"While the object of construction is to ascertain the intention of the testator, it must be an intention expressed in the will, and must be determined from the language used, and the will cannot be reformed to conform to any intention of the testator not expressed in it, no matter how clearly a different intention may be proved by extrinsic evidence. The reason is that, if the rule were otherwise, all wills would be subject to proof of mistake and of a different intention from that expressed, so that, in fact, property would pass without a will in a writing, which the law demands."

Appleton v. Rea, 58 N.E.2d 854 (Ill. 1945).

The policy expressed in the Wills Acts is that probate courts should not give effect to any evidence relating to intent except evidence contained in the documents that are part of the probate file. Consistent with that policy, courts enforcing the plain meaning rule exclude extrinsic evidence and limit evidence to the four corners of the probate documents, plus dictionaries and sources of legal authority. Some courts, when interpreting the will, say that "construction" is not allowed unless there is an ambiguity. This rule likely reduces litigation costs since, when there is no ambiguity, there is no point in trying to come up with evidence to bring before the fact finder, as it will be inadmissible. Moreover, in some cases there is no point in challenging the plain meaning because there will be no evidence that can be heard to support the challenge. The scope of disputation is limited. The plain meaning rule also makes it difficult for those who would benefit from creating false evidence to change the meaning of the will. The greater the degree of enforcement a jurisdiction gives the plain meaning rule, the more it discourages litigation and fraud. The easier it is for a court to say that a meaning is plain, the less often a court will need to hear evidence about the decedent's intent. To whom should the meaning be plain?

IN RE ESTATE OF HYMAN

Court of Appeals of South Carolina, 2004
606 S.E.2d 205

PER CURIAM.

M. Richardson Hyman, Jr. appeals a circuit court order affirming the special referee's decision that a vested remainder in certain stocks owned by Hyman's father passed to his wife through the residuary clause of his will and not through a direct devise to his children. We affirm.

FACTS

Following a lifetime of distinguished service to the people of this state as a highly respected member of the South Carolina Bar, Melvin Hyman passed away in 1973. He was survived by his wife, Maintzie R. Hyman, and two children, Melvin R. Hyman and Mary C. Hyman. In his last will and testament, Melvin Hyman granted a life estate in certain securities to his wife, with a remainder interest to his two children. Melvin Hyman expressly stated in his will that his children's remainder interest would "vest immediately upon [his] death, subject only to the life estate devised and bequeathed to my said wife."

In 1984, Melvin Hyman's son, Melvin R. Hyman ("Testator"), was diagnosed with a life threatening disease. Because his condition worsened over the years following this diagnosis, Testator decided to undergo an operation in September 1987. In contemplation of serious risks inherent in this particular kind of surgery, he executed a will shortly before the operation. A few weeks following the surgery, Testator passed away. Testator was survived by his mother, Maintzie; his second wife, Sara Hyman; and three children from his first marriage, M. Richardson Hyman, Jr. ("Appellant"), Benjamin F. Hyman, and M. Caroline Hyman.

Article three of Testator's will, which establishes a trust for the benefit of his children, states the following:

> I will, devise, and bequeath to my three children any and all property which I may receive by reason of inheritance from my mother's [Maintzie's] estate.

Testator also provided that the residue of his estate was to be distributed to his wife, Sara Hyman, outright and free of trust.

In January 1999, Maintzie R. Hyman, wife of Melvin Hyman and mother of Testator, passed away, terminating her life estate in the aforementioned securities at issue in this case. At this time, the remainder interests devised to Testator and Mary C. Hyman became possessory. Sara Hyman, Testator's wife, began receiving distributions and paying taxes on Testator's portion of the securities pursuant to the residuary clause of Testator's will.

In 2001, Appellant filed this action seeking to reopen Testator's estate and declare Testator's three children the lawful heirs of the securities pursuant to article three of Testator's will. The case was referred by consent of the parties to a special referee. At trial, Appellant offered testimony, over the respondents' objection, from Mary C. Hyman, sister of Testator, which evidenced Testator's intent that his remainder interest in the securities pass through his will to his children, notwithstanding the will's express language.[1] Although this testimony was allowed at trial, the referee later determined it was improperly admitted, as the will contained no ambiguity which would warrant the admission of extrinsic evidence. The referee found, by the plain and ordinary meaning of the will's language, that the remainder interest in the securities owned by Testator passed to his wife through the residuary clause of his will and not to his children by the direct devise of article three. The circuit court affirmed the referee's decision. This appeal follows.

STANDARD OF REVIEW

The standard of review applicable to cases originating in the probate court is controlled by whether the underlying cause of action is at law or in equity. This is an action at law. *NationsBank of South Carolina v. Greenwood*, 321 S.C. 386, 392 (Ct.App.1996) (holding an action to construe a will is an action at law). If a proceeding in the probate court is in the nature of an action at law, review by this court extends merely to the correction of legal errors.

LAW/ANALYSIS

Appellant argues the probate court erred in finding no ambiguity in Testator's will and refusing to consider extrinsic evidence to ascertain Testator's true intent. We disagree.

In construing a will, a court should give effect to the expressed intention of the testator. In ascertaining this intent, a court's first reference is always to the will's language itself. When construing this language, the reviewing tribunal must give the words contained

---

[1] Specifically, Testator's sister testified she and her brother both frequently referred to their vested remainder interests in their mother's life estate as property that would come to them from their mother, their "mother's estate," or "the Hyman estate."

in the document their ordinary and plain meaning. Where the testator's intent is ascertainable from the will and not counter to law, we will give it effect. Only when the will's terms or provisions are ambiguous may the court resort to extrinsic evidence to resolve the ambiguity.

In the case at bar, the Testator's remainder interest in the securities clearly does not pass through article three of the will to his children when the language of article three is given its plain and ordinary meaning. The provision states, "I will, devise, and bequeath to my three children any and all property which I may receive by reason of inheritance from my mother's estate." Testator owned his remainder interest in the securities at the time he executed his will. The remainder interest, though subject to his mother's life estate, was at no time part of his mother's actual estate and, thus, never passed to him through inheritance from his mother. Appellant contends, however, that the provision is ambiguous; therefore, the court should consider extrinsic evidence to ascertain Testator's true intent. We do not agree with this position.

There are two types of ambiguities found in the construction of wills:

> Ambiguities . . . are patent and latent; the distinction being that in the former case the uncertainty is one which arises upon the words of the . . . instrument as looked at in themselves, and before any attempt is made to apply them to the object which they describe, while in the latter case the uncertainty arises, not upon the words of the . . . instrument as looked at in themselves, but upon those words when applied to the object or subject which they describe.

It is undisputed that the will in the case before us contains no patent ambiguity arising from the will's own language. It is, however, argued that, when one considers Testator's property and the circumstances known to him at the execution of his will, a latent ambiguity arises and extrinsic evidence may be admitted to resolve it.

Appellant first contends the will is inconsistent when applied to Testator's property because, without the remainder interest, the children's trust is left unfunded. According to Appellant, Testator must have been aware of his mother's relative good health at the time of the will's execution and, thus, could not have intended to leave the trust barren in the probable circumstance that he predeceased his mother. Because a testator is presumed to have disposed of all property that he owned and the remainder interest was not specifically disposed, Appellant argues the will is ambiguous.

The presumption, arising from the law's disfavoring of partial intestacy, that a testator intends to dispose of his entire estate is, in fact, a longstanding rule in South Carolina. However, intestacy is not an issue in this matter. Testator disposed of his entire estate under the will's residuary clause. Furthermore, by Testator's language in article three, he acknowledges he does not own the property, which he "*may* receive by reason of inheritance" from his mother. These words clearly establish a contingency providing for Testator's children in the event their grandmother died before their father, no matter how unlikely. Where a testator employs language that is clear and definite, the function of the court is consigned to the interpretation of the will and the enforcement of its provisions without resorting to rules of construction. "Circumstances known to Testator at the time of execution are an admissible aid in construing doubtful provisions, but the main recourse must be to the language used in the will." Because the language of Article three is clear and definite, not doubtful, the referee was proper in upholding the provision's plain meaning.

Appellant also contends the will is ambiguous because extrinsic evidence in the form of Testator's sister's testimony shows Testator's intent to be different from the plain language of the will and the findings of the special referee. Again, we disagree.

A court may admit extrinsic evidence to determine whether a latent ambiguity exists.[2] In order to find an ambiguity, however, the extrinsic evidence must reflect that the words of the will, when applied to the object or subject which they describe, are "incapable of application as they stand." The mere showing that a testator may have intended a testamentary construction in direct contradiction to the plain meaning of the will's language is not enough. As the supreme court has stated, "[a] will must be read in the ordinary and grammatical sense of the words employed, unless some obvious absurdity, repugnancy or inconsistency with the declared intention of the testator" should follow.

---

[2] Once the court finds a latent ambiguity, extrinsic evidence is also permitted to help the court determine the testator's true intent and resolve the ambiguity.

The special referee correctly found that giving the language of this will its plain and ordinary meaning did not render it "incapable of application" or result in "an obvious absurdity, repugnancy, or inconsistency with Testator's declared intent." At the time Testator created his will, Maintzie Hyman had a considerable estate she conceivably could have left to Testator if the contingency of her death before his had been met, thereby fulfilling his primary goal of providing for the "reasonable comfort" and proper education of his three children. Accordingly, the evidence supports the trial court's findings that no latent ambiguity exists; therefore, the use of extrinsic evidence to determine Testator's intent is not appropriate.

CONCLUSION

For the reasons stated herein, the circuit court is

AFFIRMED.

The court gives priority to the "ordinary and plain" meaning of the words in the will. To whom was the court's meaning plain, lawyers or the decedent's family members? Whether words have a plain meaning is inversely correlated with whether they are ambiguous. To give broad application to the plain meaning rule, the court must find ambiguities rarely. What was the standard the court set for finding an ambiguity? Suppose O dies and O's will says, "I give my beach house to my sister." When the executor identifies O's assets, she learns that O has two beach houses. Does that situation meet the *Hyman* definition?

Courts sometimes make an exception to the plain meaning rule when the testator used a word in an idiosyncratic way. This personal usage exception might be used to allow evidence that the testator did not mean to refer to his actual mother when he made a devise to "mother", but instead meant to make the gift to his wife, the mother of his children, whom he always referred to as "mother". The court will allow extrinsic evidence to establish this idiosyncratic or personal usage.

Courts may admit extrinsic evidence when the meaning is not plain, in other words when there is an ambiguity. Courts traditionally admitted evidence when the ambiguity was latent and excluded evidence when the ambiguity was patent (possibly resulting in failure of a devise), but the doctrine applied is not always that simple. Consider the distinctions made in the next case.

BRECKNER V. PRESTWOOD

Missouri Court of Appeals, Eastern District, Division Four, 1980
600 S.W.2d 52

SATZ, J.

This case involves a construction of two provisions of the Last Will and Testament of Ruth Quinn, Deceased. Appellant, Ada S. Cain, and Respondents, Delmar Baptist Church, Missouri Baptist Children's Home, Home for Aged Baptists and The Salvation Army of St. Louis, are named beneficiaries in the will. The will was drafted by an attorney. The attorney and Mrs. Quinn had been employed by an insurance company for approximately 30 years, and, during 4 of those years, Mrs. Quinn was the attorney's secretary. She retired in 1971. The attorney left the insurance company, became affiliated with a law firm in 1972 and was working there when Mrs. Quinn asked him to draft her will. The attorney and a Kenneth Breckner were named as co-executors, and the attorney resigned as co-executor shortly after his appointment. As executor, Mr. Breckner filed a petition to construe the will which has conflicting clauses. As named beneficiaries, appellant and respondent charities are among the defendants in that action.

The two provisions of the Quinn will which are conflicting concern the disposition of Mrs. Quinn's intangible and tangible personal property. Item Second of the will provides:

> All articles of household furniture and furnishings, books, pictures, silverware, my automobiles, all of my clothing and jewelry, not otherwise disposed of, and all similar articles of household use and wearing apparel *and any and all personal property* which I may own at the time of my death, I give and bequeath unto my aunt, MRS. ADA STRAYHORN CAIN, . . ., or to her descendants, per stirpes, if my said aunt shall predecease me. [Emphasis Added.]

Item Eighth states:

> I give, devise and bequeath all the *rest, residue and remainder of my property, both real and personal, and of every kind and description*, wherever the same may be situated, in equal shares to DELMAR BAPTIST CHURCH, . . .; MISSOURI BAPTIST CHILDREN'S HOME, . . .; HOME FOR AGED BAPTISTS, . . .; and THE SALVATION ARMY OF ST. LOUIS, ... [Emphasis Added.]

As can be seen from the underlined portions, the will contains a patent ambiguity because both Item Second and Item Eighth of the will seemingly bequeath the same personal property to different beneficiaries.

To resolve this ambiguity, the entire probate file was admitted into evidence without objection. The probate inventory showed that Mrs. Quinn's estate contained stocks, bonds and cash valued at $199,295.00, in addition to furniture, household goods, wearing apparel, jewelry and real estate. The remaining evidence consisted primarily of the testimony of the scrivener, the attorney who drafted the will, and, apparently, by agreement between the parties, counsel for the respondent Baptist charities objected to the entire testimony of the scrivener. Although not explicitly stated, the court apparently reserved its ruling on this continuous objection, and, in its Findings of Facts and Conclusions of Law, the court excluded all of the scrivener's testimony from consideration, although it is not clear whether the court excluded this testimony because it was inadmissible, or, because it was admissible, but not credible. In addition, written correspondence between the scrivener and the beneficiaries was offered by appellant to corroborate the scrivener's testimony concerning his understanding of Mrs. Quinn's testamentary intent.[2] The respondent charities' objection to these letters was sustained and the appellant's offer of proof overruled.

The trial court entered judgment for the charities, ruling that personal effects similar to those specifically designated in Item Second passed to Appellant Cain and, other than certain cash bequests, the remainder of the testatrix's personal property passed to the charities under Item Eighth. We affirm.

Three of appellant's four points on appeal concern the admissibility of the scrivener's testimony about the testatrix's declaration of her testamentary intent. More specifically, appellant's principal argument is that evidence of the testatrix's declarations of intent was admissible and that the trial court erroneously concluded this evidence was inadmissible and rejected it. As noted, the particular ground used by the trial court to reject the scrivener's testimony is not clearly reflected in the record. However, that is not material here, for we find the scrivener's testimony concerning the

---

[2] This correspondence consisted of six letters. Three of the letters were written to Ella M. Alexander, the daughter of appellant Ada Cain, by the scrivener. The fourth was a letter from Ella M. Alexander to the scrivener. The fifth and sixth were letters from an attorney in the scrivener's law firm, one to appellant Cain and the other to respondent Salvation Army.

testatrix's declarations of her testamentary intent was inadmissible and, thus, the rejection of this testimony by the trial court was proper, regardless of the grounds used by the court.

The evidentiary rules which have been developed permitting or excluding extrinsic evidence to aid in the interpretation of a will depend, in large measure, on whether the interpretation is of a patent ambiguity or of a latent ambiguity. A patent ambiguity is one which is apparent on the face of the will. A latent ambiguity occurs when the will is unambiguous on its face but becomes open to more than one interpretation when applied to the particular factual situation before the court. Generally speaking, there are two types of wills that present latent ambiguities. One type explicitly describes a person or thing, and two or more persons or things fit exactly the description or condition in the will. The other type exists when no person or thing fits the description or condition in the will, but two or more persons or things do fit the description or condition, in part, and imperfectly.

Extrinsic evidence of circumstances in a testator's life are admissible to help resolve these latent ambiguities. The type of extrinsic evidence contemplated is evidence of objective, operative facts, which give precise and explicit meaning to the language used by the testator and, thus, compel a clear inference of the testator's exact intent. Thus, extrinsic evidence of the intimate and friendly relationship of the testator and his grandsons was admitted to show the testator intended a bequest to be made to his grandsons rather than his grandnephews, although the grandsons as well as the grandnephews carried the names of the legatees named in the will. This evidentiary rule may also be used to aid in the interpretation of a patent ambiguity in a will and, thus, where a patent ambiguity exists, extrinsic evidence is admissible to determine the amount, nature, extent and condition of a testator's property, his relation to or association with persons having an interest in his property, any motives which could have actuated the testator, and the persons who were the natural objects of his bounty.

However, this type of extrinsic evidence does not include evidence of the testatrix's declarations about her intent, and generally evidence of a testatrix's statements concerning her intentions, whether made before, at the time of, or subsequent to the execution of her will is not admissible to construe the will. The intentions of the testatrix must be gleaned from the will because those intentions were reduced to writing and she, being dead, could not dispute proffered evidence of intent. Moreover, such evidence violates the Statute of Wills and is susceptible to perjury. Nonetheless, in spite of these real and possible dangers, an exception has been developed for latent ambiguities, and a testatrix's declarations of intent are admissible to explain latent ambiguities. The rationale supporting this exception is that the designation in the will which gives rise to a latent ambiguity is itself an explicit name of a beneficiary or an explicit description of property, and evidence of the testator's declarations of intent does not add to or replace this explicit designation but merely gives the designation the precise meaning intended by the testator. Comparable reasoning has not been applied to patent ambiguities, and evidence of declarations of intent made by the testator are still inadmissible and cannot be used to resolve a patent ambiguity in a will.

As noted, it is clear that the Quinn will contains a patent ambiguity since, on its face, both Item Second and Item Eighth of the will bequeath the same personal property to different beneficiaries. Because the will contains a patent ambiguity, the testimony of the scrivener as to the declarations of the intention of the testatrix was properly rejected by the trial court. A small part of the scrivener's testimony did describe the relationship and feelings of the testatrix to appellant Cain. Our Supreme Court has held that "(t)estimony of the relationship of the parties and the testatrix's feelings toward them (is) not error" in resolving a patent ambiguity because, according to the Court, such testimony does not contain statements of the testatrix's intentions. *Obetz v. Boatmen's Nat'l Bank*, 234 S.W.2d 618, 625 (Mo.1950). But the scrivener's testimony here as to the testatrix's relationship and feelings, if admissible, was, as it was in the *Obetz* case, "of very little, if any, probative value".

The other extrinsic evidence rejected by the trial court was, as noted, letters written by the scrivener, by an attorney in his office, and one letter received by the scrivener. These letters merely reflected, in writing, opinions as to the testatrix's testamentary intent. The fact that the testatrix's declarations of her intent were interpreted and reflected in the scrivener's written correspondence made the declarations of intent in the letters no more admissible than the declarations would be if the scrivener had attempted to state his understanding of her intent at trial. Thus, the trial court properly excluded these letters.

Thus, under the present rules of evidence, we are constrained to affirm the trial court's rejection of extrinsic evidence of the testatrix's declarations of intent to resolve the patent ambiguity in question. However, the rationale for admitting a testatrix's declarations of intent to resolve a latent ambiguity applies with equal sense and force to the resolution of a patent ambiguity, and, conversely, the dangers of justifying the exclusion of a testatrix's declarations to resolve a patent ambiguity exist with equal force in the resolution of a latent ambiguity. Moreover, the categorization of an ambiguity as latent or patent is not exact, precise or explicit and the two categories, at times, seemingly overlap. Were we not constrained to follow the rules of evidence peculiar to patent ambiguities in a will, we would, as appellant urges, make admissible here the scrivener's testimony of the testatrix's intent.

Appellant also contends that the scrivener admitted that the word "personal" "slipped in" to Item Eighth and that, in hindsight, he would not have used it in Item Eighth and, because of this "admitted mistake", appellant argues, extrinsic evidence namely, the scrivener's testimony of the testatrix's declaration of intent was admissible to correct the mistake. As we read the present transcript, the scrivener's testimony about his "mistake" was subject to the respondent charities' continuous objection. However, if his testimony that he made a "mistake" were in evidence, appellant seeks to correct this mistake by changing the will to conform to the scrivener's description of the testatrix's intentions and instructions. We have ruled, albeit unwillingly, that evidence of the testatrix's declarations of her intent was not admissible, and such evidence is not admissible to show a scrivener's mistake or to correct it.

In addition, appellant contends that the trial court erred and ignored the unique facts of this case as revealed by the extrinsic evidence which was rejected. The unique facts to which appellant refers consisted of the testatrix's declarations, which were inadmissible.

Finally, appellant complains that the trial court erred in using the rule of ejusdem generis to construe the conflicting clauses of the will rather than relying on the evidence of the testatrix's statements of intent. We have determined that evidence of the testatrix's declarations was inadmissible and, thus, the only question which remains is whether the rule of ejusdem generis was properly applied by the court. We find the trial court made proper use of the rule.

Simply stated, the rule of ejusdem generis suggests that general words following the enumeration of words of specific meaning are not to be construed in their widest extent but only as applying to those things of the same kind, nature or class as those specifically enumerated. The rule is not absolute. It is simply an aid to construction. The issue which the trial court resolved by the use of this rule was, as noted, whether the phrase personal property, as used in Item Second of the will, included all of the testatrix's personal property, i.e., her stocks, bonds, certificates, bank accounts, cash and the like, remaining after her specific bequests of her personal effects, or, whether the remainder of this personal property passed under Item Eighth to the charities by the phrase "all the rest, residue and remainder of my property, both real and personal, and of every kind and description".

Item Second of the will provided for specific bequests to three different legatees in three different paragraphs. The first paragraph bequeathed a bracelet to Julia Alyson Prestwood. The second paragraph bequeathed two watches and two cocktail rings to Mrs. Virginia Priesmeyer, or to Mrs. Martha Lyngaas if the former be deceased. In the third paragraph, the testatrix bequeathed her household furniture and furnishings, books, pictures, silverware, automobiles, clothing, remaining jewelry, "and all similar articles of household use and wearing apparel and any and all personal property" which she owned at the time of her death to appellant. Item Third devised real property located in Tyler, Texas to Mrs. Ella Marie Cain Alexander, the daughter of appellant. Items Fourth, Fifth, Sixth and Seventh bequeathed $5,000 each to four different named legatees. Item Eighth was the residuary clause in question.

The specific bequests in the first two paragraphs of Item Second were valuable items of a personal nature worn by the testatrix. The enumerated articles in the third paragraph of Item Second, one of the paragraphs in question, were items surrounding testatrix in her home and used by her there. All three paragraphs include bequests of tangible property closely associated with testatrix in an intimate way. Thus, with this language immediately preceding the phrase "and any and all personal property", it is sensible to conclude the testatrix intended to use the phrase in Item Second as a residuary clause only for the remainder of her personal, tangible, intimate goods. Moreover, if the testatrix intended this phrase to bequeath to appellant not only all of her tangible personal effects, but also all of her intangible personal property remaining after her specific bequests in the first two paragraphs of Item Second, as appellant contends, then there was no need for the testatrix to make the specific bequests of personal property she made to appellant immediately preceding the phrase in question, for all of the specifically designated personal property would have passed to appellant under the phrase "and any and all personal property" owned at the time of the testatrix's death. Furthermore, the testatrix did follow Item Second with specific cash bequests in Items Fourth, Fifth, Sixth and Seventh. To accept appellant's argument that the term personal property in Item Second included the remainder of testatrix's tangible and intangible personal property, and thus included cash, would render Item Fourth through Seventh nugatory. Arguably the remaining real property could be sold in order to satisfy these cash bequests, but appellant does not suggest this strained construction to be testatrix's intent. Testatrix evidently had a scheme of specific bequests in mind which disposed of her personal, intimate items of adornment and household effects and cash in Items Second and Items Fourth through Seventh, and the remaining real and personal property was to pass, as the trial court found, to respondent charities. Finally, although legal precedents are of little value in will construction cases because two wills seldom contain identical language, our courts do construe the phrase personal property to mean tangible items of a personal nature, excluding intangible personal property of the type in issue here, particularly where the language in issue and the structure of the will is similar to the language in issue and structure here. Thus, the trial court's interpretation of the present will not only fits the specific language used in the context of the entire will, but that interpretation also fits comfortably within the import of the construction of wills which have used similar language.

We reach our decision based upon our understanding of the present status of law which makes the testatrix's declaration of her testamentary intent inadmissible to help resolve a patent ambiguity in a will. However, our courts have carved out an exception to this rule and permit evidence of the testator's declarations of intent in the case of latent ambiguities, and we see no real reason not to treat patent ambiguities in the same way. The dangers against and the benefits derived from the use of the testator's declarations of intent in resolving a latent ambiguity would exist to the same degree and effect if those declarations were used to resolve a patent ambiguity. Therefore, if the conclusion is first reached that, because of an ambiguity, extrinsic evidence is proper to aid in arriving at the testator's intentions, we find no real basis for excluding extrinsic evidence of the testator's intention, regardless of whether the ambiguity is latent or patent. However, as noted, we are constrained to follow the rules of evidence as they presently exist. Accordingly, we affirm the order and judgment of the trial court.

———————

Sometimes courts distinguish between direct and indirect extrinsic evidence of the testator's intention. Examples of direct extrinsic evidence include instructions he gave his lawyer in preparing the will and notes or statements of the testator as to his intention, whenever made. Examples of indirect extrinsic evidence include facts known to the testator at the time he made the will, such as the testator's property and his relationships with family and friends. What extrinsic evidence did the court determine was properly excluded and why? What evidence did the *Breckner* court say should have been admitted, but was not too helpful? Some courts have applied a rule that no extrinsic evidence may be admitted if an ambiguity is patent.

Notice the conflicting relationship between the rule noted above that allows a court to strike words not intended to be in the will and the rule in *Breckner* that direct extrinsic evidence of the testator's intent may not be admitted. To put it another way, if there is an intent requirement at all, does that not require a court to hear extrinsic evidence that the will was not intended by the testator to be his will? Or, when considering animus testandi, should courts be limited to admitting either the whole will or none of it, without the option of admitting just some portions? At least in hindsight, should the lawyer arguing for reform on the basis of mistake have argued for denial of probate to the following portion of Item Eighth: ", both real and personal, and" on the ground that it "slipped in" and was not intended by the testator to be part of the will?

Although the *Breckner* court does a good job of showing that the testator's intent was consistent with the will as construed without the help of extrinsic evidence, the court is unhappy with the doctrinal distinctions it applies, suggesting that the law should be changed to allow the court to admit evidence of the testator's declarations in cases of patent ambiguities. Does it make a convincing case for reform when the application of the existing rules reaches the result intended by the decedent? One reason given by the court for abolishing the distinction is that it is sometimes hard to distinguish patent from latent ambiguities. Is it hard to classify the ambiguity in *Breckner*? If a distinction has administrative costs, one issue is whether there are benefits that accrue from incurring those administrative costs. One benefit of excluding direct evidence of the testator's intent is that such evidence can be completely manufactured yet still be very convincing, perhaps outweighing other evidence and perhaps changing the terms of a will. Because of that combination, direct extrinsic evidence can lead to errors in favor of malefactors. Evidence of other facts about the testator's life might be both more difficult to make up and less likely to override other evidence. Thus, admission of indirect extrinsic evidence could be less likely to result in transfers to miscreants.

> Problem 4.18: O's will says, "I leave my estate to my nieces and nephews, to be divided equally." The facts reveal that O had substantial assets and one niece and one nephew; as those terms are usually construed they include only blood relatives. However, his wife had 19 nieces and nephews. Is there a latent ambiguity? Is there a patent ambiguity? (Note: 2019 UPC § 2–705(c) provides that a class gift excludes in-laws unless "the language or circumstances otherwise establish that in-laws were intended to be included." For this problem, assume that provision has not been adopted in the jurisdiction.)

In re Matter of Estate of Smith v. Flowers, 201 S.3d 1099 (Miss. Ct. App. 2016) shows how much litigation can be generated on the question of whether there is ambiguity in a will. James Oldrum Smith Jr. ("Big J.O.") owned the majority of stock in three businesses. Nine months before he died in 2006, without the help of a lawyer, Big J.O. drafted and executed codicil 3, which was admitted to probate. That codicil left "41% of the shares that I own in . . . Yazoo River Towing" to his son, "Little J.O.", and it left "29% of the stock of Yazoo River Towing, Inc. divided equally" to Patrick Smith and Lela Smith Flowers. Little J.O. argued that 29% of Yazoo stock was supposed to mean 29% of the Yazoo shares Big J.O. owned, not 29% of all Yazoo shares. The issue for the court of appeals was "whether the chancellor improperly excluded extrinsic evidence of Big J.O.'s intent in construing the codicil. Little J.O. and Patrick argue that the codicil contained a latent ambiguity. Lela argues there was no ambiguity." Supported by the fact that the decedent held enough Yazoo stock to make a gift of 29% of all Yazoo stock, the court agreed with the chancellor that there was no patent ambiguity. But the majority of the court found that there was a latent ambiguity. The court said that the "inconsistent" language made the whole codicil ambiguous. On the other hand, the dissent agreed with the chancellor that there was no ambiguity, finding that there was only one "reasonable interpretation," which was to add the words "that I own" into the gift to Flowers. The result was a remand for more litigation, including extrinsic evidence on the intent of Big J.O. Would he have wanted that delay and more of his estate to be used up in litigation? Was he aware that his self-drafted codicil might lead to that result? Note also that he might have meant exactly what he wrote because 29% of all Yazoo stock was about the same as 41% of his Yazoo stock.

The modern trend is to reject the distinction between patent and latent ambiguities in favor of allowing extrinsic evidence to clear up any sort of ambiguity. By providing that a finding of a contrary intention may override the rules of construction, UPC § 2–601 allows extrinsic evidence of intention on any issue of construction. The effect of allowing extrinsic evidence in all cases is essentially to reject the plain meaning rule. One hopes that the additional cases in which the testator's meaning will be followed will justify the additional litigation employed to get there.

3.   TYPES OF DEVISES

Devises are classified into various types. A specific devise, or specific bequest, is a gift of a particular item of property held by the decedent. A devise of "my car" is a specific devise. A devise of "my 100 shares of stock in X Corp." is also specific. A gift of "all my money in my savings account at the credit union" is specific, too. A general devise, by contrast, is a devise of something that has no specific source. If the testator has no stock in X Corp., and maybe even if she does, a devise of "100 shares of stock in X Corp." is a general devise. The executor can buy the stock from any source to give to the devisee. A demonstrative devise is somewhere in between a specific and general devise, where the source of the thing is specified for some or all of the gift. A gift of "$1,000 to be paid from my savings account at the credit union" is a demonstrative gift. To the extent the savings account has funds, up to $1,000 will be paid from those funds, and to that extent the gift is specific. But if the savings account is inadequate to supply the entire gift, then other assets will be used to complete the gift of the $1,000, and to that extent the gift is general. A residuary devise is a devise of the residue of the testator's estate, the probate assets not given away by other devises in the will. The residuary devise, although usually listed last, is often the largest part of the estate, sometimes all of it.

Devises can be made to specified persons, of course, and also groups of persons. Devises to groups of persons are often made by a class gift. A class gift is a gift in which the testator was "group minded," such as "to my children" or "to my brother's grandchildren". There are a number of special rules dealing with class gifts, which we will mention along the way.

4. BENEFICIARY DIES BEFORE TESTATOR

As the New York court pointed out in the case involving Marilyn Monroe's will, *Shaw Family Archives Ltd. v. CMG Worldwide, Inc.*, supra, a will takes effect at the death of the testator, not when it is executed. It sometimes happens that a devisee named in the will dies before the testator. What happens in such cases? Do the assets pass to the estate of the devisee? What does the next case tell us regarding the devolution of a specific devise or a general devise? What happens to a residuary devise?

(a) Lapse

ESTATE OF RHOADES
Court of Appeals of Texas, Fort Worth, 2016
502 S.W.3d 406

SUDDERTH, J.

I.   Introduction

In two issues, appellants Norma Anderson, Paula Gilleland, Gerald Don Marrs, Joann Dycus, and Vicki George appeal the trial court's judgment for appellee Elise Kinler, arguing that the trial court erred by denying their motion for summary judgment and by granting Kinler's motion for summary judgment. We reverse.

II. Factual and Procedural Background

Article III of Glenda Rhoades's will, which she signed on October 4, 2007, made [various bequests.] * * *

* * *

III. Discussion

* * *

B. Summary Judgment

* * *

As this court has previously stated with regard to will construction,

> The cardinal rule for construing a will is that the testator's intent must be ascertained by looking at the language and provisions of the instrument as a whole, as set forth within its four corners. The question is not what the testator intended to write, but the meaning of the words he actually used. Terms used are to be given their plain, ordinary, and generally accepted meanings unless the instrument itself shows them to have been used in a technical or different sense.

> If possible, all parts of the will must be harmonized, and every sentence, clause, and word must be considered in ascertaining the testator's intent. We must presume that the testator placed nothing meaningless or superfluous in the instrument. Where practicable, a latter clause in a will must be deemed to affirm, not to contradict, an earlier clause in the same will.

> Whether a will is ambiguous is a question of law for the court. A term is not ambiguous merely because of a simple lack of clarity or because the parties proffer different interpretations of a term. Rather, a will is ambiguous only when the application of established rules of construction leave its terms susceptible to more than one reasonable meaning. If the court can give a certain or definite legal meaning or interpretation to the words used, the will is unambiguous, and the court should construe it as a matter of law.

Steger v. Muenster Drilling Co., 134 S.W.3d 359, 372–73 (Tex.App.-Fort Worth 2003, pet. denied) (citations omitted).

Appellants contend that the trial court misconstrued article III of the will.

Article III of the will states as follows:

III.

DISPOSITION OF ESTATE

A. I give all of my interest in the real property and the improvements thereto which constitute my residential homestead at the time of my death to Glen Rhoades in equal shares.

B. I give, devise and bequeath all of my personal property to Glen Rhoades in equal shares.

C. I give, devise and bequeath all of the rest of my estate of whatsoever kind and wheresoever situated as follows to Glen Rhoades. In the event that Glen Rhoades should predecease me, his portion shall be distributed to ELISE KINLER for the benefit of Elise and Michael Kinler. In the event that Elise Kinler should predecease me, then said portion shall be distributed to Michael Kinler.

D. Any other property of mine that has not been disposed of under any other provision of this Will shall go and be distributed to my heirs-at-law. Their identity and respective shares shall be determined in all respects as if my death had occurred immediately following the happening of the event requiring such distribution, and according to the laws of Texas then in force governing the distribution of the estate of an intestate.

The parties agree that Glen Rhoades predeceased his daughter and that the will is unambiguous.

Kinler moved for summary judgment, arguing that "his portion" under Paragraph C meant Glen's entire "portion" under Article III because the entire estate could be categorized as either real or personal property under Paragraphs A and B and because in Article V, the testator again referenced Glen's "portion" to be used to create a trust for him if he was alive at the time of her death. In their competing motion for summary judgment, Appellants argued that all of Rhoades's property passed to them under the anti-lapse statute in estates code section 255.152 because there was no language in Paragraph A or B that stated what was to occur in the event that Glen predeceased his daughter. They further argued that under the estates code, the bequests in Paragraphs A, B, and C passed to the "residuary estate" in accordance with Paragraph D's plain meaning because the limiting language "as follows" in Paragraph C did not describe any property.

On appeal, however, Appellants offer an alternative argument that they argue harmonizes all four paragraphs in Article III:

> [t]he only logical interpretation . . . is that the bequests in paragraphs A and B lapse, causing those bequests (the Decedent's "residential homestead" and personal property) to fall into paragraph D—the residuary clause. Paragraph C would then pass all of Decedent's other real property to Appellee. No other interpretation of paragraph D satisfies the "harmony" requirement articulated in *Steger*.

In support of this argument, Appellants point out that, according to the Inventory filed in the probate proceeding, Rhoades's estate contains property that would fall under Paragraph C, a parcel of non-homestead real property that was not covered by Paragraph A or B. We agree with this interpretation of the will.

Estates code section 255.152, "Failure of Devise; Effect on Residuary Estate," provides in subsection (a), "Except as provided by Sections 255.153 and 255.154,[6] if a devise, other than a residuary devise, fails for any reason, the devise becomes a part of the residuary estate." This section applies unless the testator's will provides otherwise.

Paragraph A gave "equal shares" of Rhoades's residential homestead to her father. This clause lapsed because Glen predeceased her, and the residential homestead fell into the residuary per estates code section 255.152(a). Paragraph B gave "equal shares" of all of Rhoades's personal property to her father, and this clause lapsed too because of Glen's having predeceased her, dropping all of Rhoades's personal property into the residuary.

Paragraph C gave Rhoades's father "all of the rest of [her] estate of whatsoever kind and wheresoever situated as follows" unless he predeceased her. While the clause does not specify *what* property would pass under this paragraph, after subtracting the residential homestead real estate and all of her personal property, the only property remaining would be non-homestead real estate. Included in the summary judgment evidence was the inventory prepared by Kinler as temporary administrator, which shows a parcel of real

---

[6] Neither section 255.153, which governs a devisee who is a descendant of the testator or the testator's parent and who is deceased at the time the will is executed, nor section 255.154, which governs devisees under class gifts, applies here.

property designated as "Parcel #2." "Parcel #2" appears to be the only non-residential homestead real property and non-personal property remaining in Rhoades's estate, but to the extent that Rhoades owned other non-residential homestead real estate at the time of her death, that property would be conveyed pursuant to Paragraph C as well.

We hold that because Rhoades's father predeceased her, the gifts attempted under Paragraphs A and B failed and that property fell into the residuary clause in Paragraph D. However, since Paragraph C expressly provided that if Glen predeceased Rhoades, "his portion" should be distributed to Kinler, the property bequeathed under Paragraph C did not lapse, but rather passed to Kinler. To hold otherwise would require editing, deleting, modifying, or ignoring altogether some of the paragraphs at issue, which we may not do.[7] *See Steger*, 134 S.W.3d at 372–73 (setting out rules of will construction).

For these reasons, we sustain Appellants' first issue and part of their second issue regarding the denial of their motion for summary judgment.

IV. Conclusion

Having sustained Appellants' first issue and part of their second issue, we reverse the trial court's judgment and remand the case to the trial court to enter a declaratory judgment consistent this determination and our holding.

WALKER, J., filed a concurring and dissenting opinion.

Although devises may be made to an estate, the default is that devises are conditioned on the devisee surviving the testator. Under the common law, if the devisee dies after the will is executed but before the testator, the devise lapses. If the devisee dies before the will is executed, the gift is a void gift. In either case, the gift fails, and the gift is not made to the estate of the devisee. If the will does not specify an alternative taker and the devise was not a residuary devise, the assets pass under the residuary clause.

> Problem 4.19: O executes O's will which says, "I give my credit union savings account to Burt and Ida, share and share alike. I give the rest of my estate to Russ and Roxy."

---

[7] Characterizing Paragraph C as a residuary clause, as Kinler urges us to do, would force us to ignore Paragraph D entirely, rendering it meaningless.

Burt dies. O dies leaving a farm and $10,000 in the savings account. Henry is O's heir. Who takes what?

If the failed devise was a residuary devise, the common-law rule was that there could be no residue of a residue, and the gift passed outside the will by intestacy. The UPC and modern rule is that a failed residuary devise passes back through the residuary clause to the other residuary devisees; in other words, in such jurisdictions there can be a residue of a residue. However, the UPC rule is merely a default rule and may be overcome by evidence of the testator's intent.

> Problem 4.20a: O executes O's will which says, "I give the rest of my estate to Russ and Roxy, share and share alike." Roxy dies. O dies leaving a farm. Henry is O's heir. Who takes the farm under the common law?

> Problem 4.20b: Assume the same facts as above except that Roxy is a dog. Who takes the farm under the common law? What could O's lawyer do to prevent this problem from occurring?

> Problem 4.20c: Assume the same facts as just above. Who takes the farm under UPC § 2–604(b), which says "if the residue is devised to two or more persons, the share of a residuary devisee that fails for any reason passes to the other residuary devisee, or to other residuary devisees in proportion to the interest of each in the remaining part of the residue."? (UPC § 1–201(34) states that a "person" means an individual or an organization.)

> Problem 4.21: O and S have 2 minor children. O executes a will which says, "3/4 of the residue of my estate goes to S and 1/4 goes to the Red Cross." S dies. A week later, O dies. What do the children take under the UPC? What would O probably want?

Under the common law, the class-gift rules say that if one member of a class dies, the gift to that class is distributed to the remaining members of the class. The gift to the class member who dies before the testator does not lapse.

> Example 4.22: O executes O's will which says, "I give the rest of my estate to my friend Bill's children, share and share alike." Bill's children are A, B, and C. A dies. O dies leaving a farm as the residue of his estate. Henry is O's son

and heir. Who takes the farm under the common law? Because A died, the farm passes to B and C, the remaining members of the class. The class-gift rule applies before the no-residue-of-a-residue rule has a chance to apply. The class of Bill's children takes (without A because A predeceased O) the residue, and nothing passes by intestacy to the heir, Henry.

(b) Antilapse (or Lapse) Statutes

You might be wondering why we do not reallocate the lapsed gift to the descendants of the predeceased devisee. Well, sometimes we do, under "antilapse" or "lapse" statutes that have been adopted in nearly all states. Although these statutes are sometimes called antilapse statutes, they do not actually prevent the lapse of the gift to the deceased devisee, and many apply in non-lapse situations such as void devises. When they apply, the antilapse statutes make a substitute gift, unless there is evidence that the testator had a contrary intent. The substitute gift does not pass to or through the predeceased devisee's estate but instead passes from the testator's estate to the substitute taker. Whether the statutes do or do not make a substitute gift for the lapsed gift depends on two relationships. First, most statutes make a substitute gift only if the predeceased devisee left descendants surviving at the death of the decedent. Second, the UPC and many antilapse statutes require that the testator and the devisee be related. Under the UPC, the devisee must be a grandparent, or grandparent's descendant, or a stepchild, of the testator. Some statutes are narrower than the UPC, requiring the devisee to be a descendant of the testator. Other statutes are broader, not requiring a relationship between the testator and the devisee.

UPC § 2–603

SECTION 2–603. ANTILAPSE; DECEASED DEVISEE; CLASS GIFTS.

(a) [Definitions.] In this section:

(1) "Alternative devise" means a devise that is expressly created by the will and, under the terms of the will, can take effect instead of another devise on the happening of one or more events, including survival of the testator or failure to survive the testator, whether an event is expressed in condition-precedent,

condition-subsequent, or any other form. A residuary clause constitutes an alternative devise with respect to a nonresiduary devise only if the will specifically provides that, upon lapse or failure, the nonresiduary devise, or nonresiduary devises in general, pass under the residuary clause.

(2) "Class member" includes an individual who fails to survive the testator but who would have taken under a devise in the form of a class gift had the individual survived the testator.

(3) "Descendant of a grandparent", as used in subsection (b), means an individual who qualifies as a descendant of a grandparent of the testator or of the donor of a power of appointment under the (i) rules of construction applicable to a class gift created in the testator's will if the devise or exercise of the power is in the form of a class gift or (ii) rules for intestate succession if the devise or exercise of the power is not in the form of a class gift.

(4) "Descendants", as used in the phrase "surviving descendants" of a deceased devisee or class member in subsections (b)(1) and (2), mean the descendants of a deceased devisee or class member who would take under a class gift created in the testator's will.

(5) "Devise" includes an alternative devise, a devise in the form of a class gift, and an exercise of a power of appointment.

(6) "Devisee" includes (i) a class member if the devise is in the form of a class gift, (ii) an individual or class member who was deceased at the time the testator executed the will as well as an individual or class member who was then living but who failed to survive the testator, and (iii) an appointee under a power of appointment exercised by the testator's will.

(7) "Stepchild" means a child of the surviving, deceased, or former spouse of the testator or of the donor of a power of appointment, and not of the testator or donor.

(8) "Surviving", in the phrase "surviving devisees" or "surviving descendants", means devisees or descendants who neither predeceased the testator nor are deemed to have predeceased the testator under Section 2–702.

(9) "Testator" includes the donee of a power of appointment if the power is exercised in the testator's will.

(b) [Substitute Gift.] If a devisee fails to survive the testator and is a grandparent, a descendant of a grandparent, or a stepchild of either the testator or the donor of a power of appointment exercised by the testator's will, the following apply:

(1) Except as provided in paragraph (4), if the devise is not in the form of a class gift and the deceased devisee leaves surviving descendants, a substitute gift is created in the devisee's surviving descendants. They take by representation the property to which the devisee would have been entitled had the devisee survived the testator.

(2) Except as provided in paragraph (4), if the devise is in the form of a class gift, other than a devise to "issue," "descendants," "heirs of the body," "heirs," "next of kin," "relatives," or "family," or a class described by language of similar import, a substitute gift is created in the surviving descendants of any deceased devisee. The property to which the devisees would have been entitled had all of them survived the testator passes to the surviving devisees and the surviving descendants of the deceased devisees. Each surviving devisee takes the share to which the surviving devisee would have been entitled had the deceased devisees survived the testator. Each deceased devisee's surviving descendants who are substituted for the deceased devisee take by representation the share to which the deceased devisee would have been entitled had the deceased devisee survived the testator. For the purposes of this paragraph, "deceased devisee" means a class member who failed to survive the testator and left one or more surviving descendants.

(3) For the purposes of Section 2–601, words of survivorship, such as in a devise to an individual "if he [or she] survives me," or in a devise to "my surviving children," are not, in the absence of additional evidence, a sufficient indication of an intent contrary to the application of this section.

(4) If the will creates an alternative devise with respect to a devise for which a substitute gift is created by paragraph (1) or (2), the substitute gift is superseded by the alternative devise if:

(A) the alternative devise is in the form of a class gift and one or more members of the class is entitled to take under the will; or

(B) the alternative devise is not in the form of a class gift and the expressly designated devisee of the alternative devise is entitled to take under the will.

(5) Unless the language creating a power of appointment expressly excludes the substitution of the descendants of an appointee for the appointee, a surviving descendant of a deceased appointee of a power of appointment can be substituted for the appointee under this section, whether or not the descendant is an object of the power.

(c) [More Than One Substitute Gift; Which One Takes.] If, under subsection (b), substitute gifts are created and not superseded with respect to more than one devise and the devises are alternative devises, one to the other, the determination of which of the substitute gifts takes effect is resolved as follows:

(1) Except as provided in paragraph (2), the devised property passes under the primary substitute gift.

(2) If there is a younger-generation devise, the devised property passes under the younger-generation substitute gift and not under the primary substitute gift.

(3) In this subsection:

(A) "Primary devise" means the devise that would have taken effect had all the deceased devisees of the alternative devises who left surviving descendants survived the testator.

(B) "Primary substitute gift" means the substitute gift created with respect to the primary devise.

(C) "Younger-generation devise" means a devise that (i) is to a descendant of a devisee of the primary devise, (ii) is an alternative devise with respect to the primary devise, (iii) is a devise for which a substitute gift is created, and (iv) would have taken effect had all the deceased devisees who left surviving descendants survived the testator except the deceased devisee or devisees of the primary devise.

(D) "Younger-generation substitute gift" means the substitute gift created with respect to the younger-generation devise.

———————

Problem 4.23: O executes a will giving $1,000 to his brother B and leaving the residue to O's son S. B dies, survived by B's daughter N. O dies. Who takes the $1,000, B, N, or S? Would it make a difference if B had died before O executed the will? Would it make a difference if B died two days after O?

The antilapse statute can be overridden by a showing of the decedent's contrary intent. To put it another way, the decedent can opt out of the default rule supplied by the antilapse statute. Determining whether the testator did opt out has sometimes required litigation. In a majority of states, words such as "if B survives me" will prevent the antilapse statute from making a substitute gift if B does not survive the testator. Likewise, "to my surviving children" will often prevent the antilapse statute from applying. Under UPC § 2–603(b)(3), though, those words alone would not be enough to prevent the statute from making a substitute gift, leading to results that might surprise the testator, were he alive to witness them. It is your job as a lawyer to make sure that the instruments you draft send assets the way your client wishes them to go. You will need to be careful to opt out of the UPC antilapse provisions expressly if that is what is intended.

McGOWAN V. BOGLE
Court of Appeals of Kentucky, 2011
331 S.W.3d 642

THOMPSON, J.

This is a will construction dispute in which the sole question is whether the anti-lapse statutes require that the children of the predeceased beneficiaries inherit under the will. The Pulaski Circuit Court found that that the anti-lapse statutes were not applicable because the will unambiguously expressed the intention that the beneficiaries survive the testator in order to inherit under the will. We agree and affirm.

The facts are undisputed and brief. On August 9, 2006, testator, Mildred Bogle Hudson, executed a will. Item II of the will states:

I direct that my Executrix shall cause my entire estate both real, personal or mixed to liquidate and after payment of all charges against my estate as set forth above or otherwise legally chargeable to my estate, the residue of the proceeds shall be distributed equally among my living brothers and sister who survive me. Those living at the present time are Corine Bogle Tyree of Atlanta, Georgia, Al Jerry Bogle of Somerset, Kentucky, and Huston Bogle of Somerset, Kentucky.

When Mildred executed her will, seven of her siblings were deceased. At the time of Mildred's death in May 2009, the three remaining siblings designated as beneficiaries were also deceased.

The appellees are the children or grandchildren of the seven siblings who were deceased in 2006 when Mildred executed her will. The appellants are children of Huston Bogle, Al Jerry Bogle, and Corine Bogle Tyree and a granddaughter of Al Jerry Bogle.

The appellees filed an action in the Pulaski Circuit Court asserting that because the three named beneficiaries in the will predeceased Mildred, the bequeaths lapsed and the estate must pass under the Kentucky law of descent and distribution. The appellants countered that KRS 394.400 and KRS 394.410, the anti-lapse statutes, prevented lapse of the bequeath to the deceased siblings and the entire estate passed to them as the descendants of the three designated siblings alive when the will was executed.

Both parties moved for summary judgment. The circuit court found that the anti-lapse statutes did not apply because Mildred expressly intended that only the siblings that survived her inherit under the will.

We review a summary judgment *de novo* and will affirm the granting of a summary judgment only when it appears impossible for the non-movant to prove facts establishing a right to relief. In this case, the question presented is one of statutory interpretation.

Prior to the enactment of anti-lapse statutes, when a named beneficiary under a will predeceased the testator, the share of the deceased beneficiary "lapsed" and generally passed according to the residuary clause, if it existed, or the laws of intestacy. Because the common-law result was frequently not in conformity with the testator's intent, States, including Kentucky, enacted anti-lapse statutes. Kentucky's anti-lapse statutes are KRS 394.400 and KRS 394.410.

KRS 394.400 provides:

If a devisee or legatee dies before the testator, or is dead at the making of the will, leaving issue who survive the testator, such issue shall take the estate devised or bequeathed, as the devisee or legatee would have done if he had survived the testator, unless a different disposition thereof is made or required by the will.

KRS 394.410, which governs a devise that is made to several persons as a class and reiterates the provision of KRS 394.400, provides:

(1) When a devise is made to several as a class or as tenants in common, and one (1) or more of the devisees die before the testator, and another or others survive the testator, the share or shares of such as so die shall go to his or their descendants, if any; if none, to the surviving devisees, unless a different disposition is made by the devisor.

(2) A devise to children embraces grandchildren when there are no children, and no other construction will give effect to the devise.

(3) If a devise is made to several as joint tenants with right of survivorship and one (1) or more of the devisees dies before the testator and another or others survive the testator, the share or shares of such as so die shall go to such as so survive. Provided, however, in the event of the death of all the joint tenants before the death of the testator, the order of death of the joint tenants shall not affect the devolution of the property and, in this case, devolution shall be governed by subsection (1) hereof, as if the devise had been made to the deceased devisees as tenants in common.

Pursuant to the anti-lapse statutes, where a will beneficiary predeceases the testator and leaves issue who survives the testator, the statutes create "a rebuttable presumption that the surviving issue was meant to be substituted in the will for its ancestor." However, the statutes are not without a caveat: The presumption applies "unless a different disposition is made by the devisor." It is not the purpose of the anti-lapse statutes to restrict the testator's right to select the beneficiary but to "carry out the *presumed* intent of the testator, if he had thought of the possibility of a beneficiary predeceasing him." *Slattery v. Kelsch*, 734 S.W.2d 813, 814 (Ky.App.1987)(emphasis original). "Other rules of construction, including the anti-lapse statute itself, are to be invoked only when the testator's intent is otherwise unclear." *Blevins*, 12 S.W.3d at 701.

Slattery involved facts strikingly similar to those now presented. The testator executed a will that contained a residuary clause devising the residue of the estate to "my first cousins living at the time of my death." The children of the testator's deceased first cousin claimed an interest in the estate through the applicability of the anti-lapse statutes. The Court held the anti-lapse statute did not apply. Quoting *In Re Estate of Kerr*, 433 F.2d 479, 481 (D.C.Cir.1970), the Court reasoned:

> Where, . . ., the will reflects a countervailing intention with reasonable clarity, the statute does not save the gift from lapse.

> Such an intention is manifested, and plainly so, where the will articulates the gift in words effectively conditioning its efficacy upon the beneficiary's survival of the testator. If, in such a situation, the beneficiary predeceases the testator, the statutory bar to lapse and the concomitant substitution of issue in the beneficiary's stead are at war with the testator's purpose that the gift shall take effect only in the event that the beneficiary outlives the benefactor. Not at all surprisingly, then, the cases teach that antilapse legislation has no application to gifts limited to vest upon the beneficiary's survival of the testator and not otherwise.

Id. at 815.

The words used by the testator in *Slattery* and by Mildred are semantically consistent. Mildred unequivocally conditioned the bequest to "my living brothers and sister who survive me" and listed the brothers and sister living at the time she executed her will. Pursuant to the reasoning in *Slattery,* Mildred clearly expressed her intent that only those siblings who were living at the time of her death inherit under to the will.

Appellants point out that *Slattery* was decided before the 1990 revision of the Uniform Probate Code that expands its anti-lapse provision and suggests that the language used by Mildred under the current Code is insufficient to express an intent contrary to the anti-lapse statutes. In *Blevins,* the Court emphasized that Kentucky has not adopted the Uniform Probate Code and it is not the controlling authority. *Blevins,* 12 S.W.3d at 702. Thus, we are not persuaded that the revisions to the Code warrant a deviation from the law expressed in *Slattery.* We conclude that the use of language conditioning the gifts on the survival of the beneficiaries at the time of Mildred's death was sufficient to defeat the application of the anti-lapse statutes.

Despite the factual similarities, appellants distinguish *Slattery* where only one of the beneficiaries of the designated class died before the testator. They argue that a different result is compelled where, as here, all the beneficiaries intended to be "joint tenants with rights of survivorship" as used in KRS 394.410(3) die prior to the testator. We agree with the trial court that regardless of distinction, the result is the same. Under KRS 394.410(3), in instances when all joint tenants die prior to the testator, KRS 394.410(1) applies and the bequeath lapses if "a different disposition is made by the devisor." Mildred expressly stated that only her brothers and sister who survived her inherit under the terms of the will, thus, appellants' distinction is inconsequential.

In a further attempt to avoid the result mandated by *Slattery,* appellants argue that *Blevins* impliedly overruled *Slattery*. The *Blevins* opinion emphasized that the anti-lapse statutes create a rebuttable presumption that the surviving issue be substituted in the will for a deceased beneficiary and ultimately held that the testator did not intend to prevent the application of the anti-lapse statutes. However, the issue in *Blevins* substantially differed from the present question.

The testator in *Blevins* made four separate bequeaths to four separate beneficiaries all of whom predeceased the testator. Significantly, the bequeaths to the four deceased beneficiaries did not contain any language conditioning the gifts upon the survival of the beneficiaries. However, a residual clause provided:

> All the rest, residue and remainder of my estate, both real and personal, wherever situated and of whatever nature, kind and description that I own at my death, including legacies and devises, if any, which may lapse or fail for any reason, I give, devise and bequeath to my nephews, Donald W. Blevins and Barkley L. Blevins in fee simple in equal shares.

The Court held that the bequeaths of lapsed gifts to the residuary legatees did not defeat the application of the anti-lapse statutes to the bequeaths to the four beneficiaries who died with issue before the testator. The Court held:

In sum, although in other jurisdictions the result would perhaps be different, we are persuaded that the recital in a will's residuary clause that the residue is to include lapsed and failed gifts is not by itself sufficient evidence of a testator's contrary intent to overcome the strong presumption against lapse provided by KRS 394.400. Such clauses are to be construed, like all other will clauses, in light of the entire document, and are only to be given preclusive effect when such clearly was the testator's intent.

Id. at 700.

The *Blevins* holding is not applicable in this case because there was no residuary clause, only bequeaths to the brothers and sister who survived the testator. Certainly, had Mildred intended to avoid the laws of intestate distribution, she could have included a residuary clause designating her intended beneficiaries, including the appellants. Instead, the will reveals her express intent that only her brothers and sister who survived at the time of her death inherit her estate and, if all were deceased, that the estate pass intestate.

Because Mildred's will expressly and unambiguously stated her intention that her brothers and sister inherit pursuant to its terms only if surviving at the time of her death, the circuit court was not required to admit the extrinsic evidence sought to be introduced by appellants regarding their relationship with Mildred. The general rule is that if a will is unambiguous, no construction is called for, and extrinsic evidence may not be introduced as an aid to construction. *Dils v. Richey*, 431 S.W.2d 497, 498 (Ky.1968).

Based on the foregoing, the judgment of the Pulaski Circuit Court is affirmed.

(c) Class Gifts

As indicated by the court in *McGowan v. Bogle* and as can be seen in the UPC, the antilapse statutes may apply to class gifts as well as individual gifts.

> Example 4.24a: O has a nibling, N. ("Nibling", although not an established word, refers to a child of a sibling; the term is gender neutral, unlike "nephew" or "niece". Assume unless otherwise indicated that these terms refer to blood relatives, not in-laws.) N has 2 children, B and C. C has one

child, X. O executes a will bequeathing "$10,000 to be divided among the children of N." C dies. O dies. Under the common-law class-gift rule, C's gift lapses and B, the remaining member of the class, takes all $10,000. However, the antilapse statute in the UPC and most states would apply to the class gift in this situation. As a result, although C's gift lapses, a substitute gift of C's share is made to X, with the result that B and X split the $10,000.

Example 4.24b: Assume the same facts as above, except that C dies before O executes the will. In that case, C's gift is void rather than lapsed. The antilapse statute could apply, but some courts have refused to apply the antilapse statute to C's void gift on the theory that O would not have thought that C would take because C was already dead and that, if O wanted X to take, O would have named X.

5. CHANGES IN PROPERTY DEVISED IN WILL

(a) Ademption by Extinction

Sometimes a will specifically devises property that is not in the estate at the testator's death. Under the common law, the gift would be "adeemed by extinction", meaning that the gift would simply not be made.

> Example 4.25: O owns a car. O executes a will which devises "my car to X." At O's death, O owns no car. Because the estate does not include the car, the estate does not have the ability to transfer O's car to X. Under the common-law approach, X takes nothing in place of the car.

> Example 4.26: O executes a will which devises "my 100 shares of Z Corp. stock to X." At O's death, O holds only 44 shares of Z Corp. stock. Because O used the word "my", the gift is a specific devise. The devise is adeemed pro tanto and A receives only 44 shares.

IN RE ESTATE OF DONOVAN

Supreme Court of New Hampshire, 2011
20 A.3d 989

DALIANIS, C.J.

The petitioners, Brian, James, June, Laura and Robert Donovan (the Donovan Family), appeal the order of the Sullivan County

Probate Court (*Feeney,* J.) denying their summary judgment motion, granting the summary judgment motion filed by the respondent, Cathy C. Carter, and ruling that the Donovan Family is not entitled to a share of the proceeds from the sale of certain stock. We affirm.

The record reveals the following facts. The decedent, Timothy M. Donovan, died in June 2009. Article 4 of his will, executed on September 14, 2005, provided, in pertinent part: "All my intangible personal property, including but not limited to bank accounts, stocks, mutual funds, and the like, but *excluding shares in Optimum Manufacturing,* I devise and bequeath to [the respondent]." (Emphasis added.) Article 6 of the will provided:

> All the rest, residue and remainder of my estate, of every kind and description, and wheresoever situated, including but not limited to *my shares of stock and/or other interests in Optimum Manufacturing Corporation,* and the Optimum Real Estate, I give, devise and bequeath to that person or entity who is serving as my Trustee under a certain instrument or revocable trust heretofore executed by me and entitled the Timothy M. Donovan Revocable Trust of 2001 (the "Revocable Trust"), to be added to the property held in trust by him, and to be held and administered in accordance with the terms of said instrument as now provided and from time to time hereafter amended.

(Emphasis added.)

Also on September 14, 2005, the decedent executed the "THIRD AMENDED APPENDIX TO THE TIMOTHY M. DONOVAN REVOCABLE TRUST OF 2001" (Third Amended Appendix to Trust). Article 4 of the Third Amended Appendix to Trust, entitled *"DISPOSITIVE PROVISIONS: AFTER DEATH,"* instructed the trustee about distributing the trust estate upon the decedent's death. Article 4(C) provided, in pertinent part, that if, at the time of the decedent's death or incapacity, he owned or operated a business, either directly or by owning shares of stock, "including but not limited to the shares of Optimum Manufacturing Corporation" (Optimum Manufacturing), the trustee was authorized to "do all things related to the operation of the Business that [the decedent] could have done if living," including selling or liquidating the decedent's business interests "at such price and on such terms" as the trustee "may deem advisable."

Article 4(D) specifically authorized the trustee "[w]ithin a reasonable time after succeeding [the decedent] as Trustee," to "enter upon a process with respect to . . . selling" stock in Optimum Manufacturing to Optimum Manufacturing employees. If the trustee elected not to do this, then "the stock and/or assets of Optimum [Manufacturing] shall be operated and/or sold upon such terms" as the trustee deemed "prudent under the circumstances, in the sole discretion of [the] Trustee." Article 4(E) set forth a distribution scheme for the net proceeds from the sale of the assets of Optimum Manufacturing under which ten percent of the proceeds would go to the trustee, twenty-five percent of the proceeds would be distributed to the decedent's mother, petitioner June Donovan, if she survived him, forty-five percent would be distributed to the respondent, and twenty percent would be divided equally among his contingent remaindermen, petitioners Robert, Brian, Laura and James Donovan. Article 4(F) required the trustee to "apportion the balance of the principal and accumulated income of said trust estate, or the remaining principal and accumulated income of said trust estate, . . . to [the respondent]."

In August 2008, ten months before he died, the decedent sold all of his stock in Optimum Manufacturing and certain other Optimum Manufacturing assets to Optical Filter Corporation for $15 million. In November 2009, the Donovan Family filed the instant petition seeking a declaration that the proceeds from the sale of the decedent's Optimum Manufacturing stock passed to the trust upon his death, as set forth in article 6 of his will. The parties filed summary judgment motions on this issue. The respondent argued that the proceeds from the sale of the decedent's Optimum Manufacturing stock did not pass to the trust upon his death. The trial court ruled in the respondent's favor. This appeal followed.

Our standard for reviewing probate court decisions is set forth by statute. "The findings of fact of the judge of probate are final unless they are so plainly erroneous that such findings could not be reasonably made." "Consequently, we will not disturb the probate court's decree unless it is unsupported by the evidence or plainly erroneous as a matter of law."

The Donovan Family argues that the trial court erred by granting summary judgment to the respondent. In reviewing a trial court's grant of summary judgment, we consider the affidavits and other evidence, and all inferences properly drawn from them, in the light most favorable to the non-moving party. "If our review of that evidence discloses no genuine issue of material fact, and if the moving party is entitled to judgment as a matter of law, we will affirm the grant of summary judgment." When no material issue of fact is in dispute, we will determine only whether the prevailing party was entitled to judgment as a matter of law. We review the trial court's application of the law to the facts *de novo*.

On appeal, the Donovan Family asserts that the proceeds from the sale of the decedent's Optimum Manufacturing stock passed to the trust upon his death, and that they are entitled to a portion of them under the distribution scheme set forth in Article 4(E) of the trust. The respondent counters that "the Estate holds the proceeds" from the sale of the decedent's Optimum Manufacturing stock, and that she is entitled to them under Article 4 of the will. We agree with the respondent.

We first examine the terms of the will. Three well-settled rules govern our analysis of the matter at hand. First, the testator's intent is our principal guide in interpreting a will. Second, if no contrary intent appears in the will, words within the will are to be given their common meaning. Finally, the clauses in a will are not read in isolation; rather, their meaning is determined from the language of the will as a whole.

Under Article 4 of the will, all of the decedent's "intangible property," except his Optimum Manufacturing stock, passed to the respondent when he died. The rest of his estate, including his Optimum Manufacturing stock, passed to the trust under Article 6 of the will.

The Donovan Family argues that the proceeds from the decedent's sale of his Optimum Manufacturing stock passed to the trust under Article 6 of the will. We disagree. Under the will's plain terms, the *only* intangible property that did not pass to the respondent was the decedent's Optimum Manufacturing stock. Article 4 bequeathed to the respondent "[a]ll" of the decedent's "intangible personal property, including but not limited to bank accounts, stocks, mutual funds, and the like, *but excluding shares in Optimum Manufacturing*." (Emphasis added.)

As the trial court aptly ruled, any bequest of the decedent's Optimum Manufacturing stock was adeemed when he sold the stock before he died. Ademption applies when a decedent no longer owns property specifically devised at the time of death, or when the character of that property has so changed as to be no longer identifiable. *In re Estate of Reposa*, 121 N.H. 114, 115 (1981). "A mere change in the form of the gift is not an ademption, but a complete change in nature and character is." *Id*. In *Estate of Reposa*, for instance, we held that the testatrix's devise of her farm to her legatee was adeemed when, four years before her death, she sold the farm in exchange for cash, a mortgage and a promissory note for payment. We concluded that the farm's sale was a sufficiently radical change to constitute an ademption.

It is well-settled that if, after a testator has executed his will in which he makes a specific bequest of corporate stock, the testator sells the stock and does not acquire other stock, an ademption occurs, and a legatee has no valid claim on the proceeds of the sale. New Hampshire follows this general rule. *See Owen v. Busiel*, 83 N.H. 345, 348, 349 (1928).

The testator in *Owen* executed a codicil to his will directing his executors to transfer to his daughter, immediately upon his death, certain stocks. After the testator died, the executors, however, were unable to find the certificates for any of the stocks named in the will because the testator had apparently sold or transferred the stocks before he died. We held that "the subsequent transfer of the stocks operated as an ademption to nullify the specific legacy given by the codicil." Similarly here, because the decedent sold all of his shares of Optimum Manufacturing ten months before he died, his bequest to the trust of Optimum Manufacturing stock was adeemed.

Thus, when the decedent died, *neither* his Optimum Manufacturing stock *nor* the proceeds from the sale thereof passed to the trust. The bequest of the stock was adeemed by his sale of the stock before he died, and the proceeds passed to the respondent under Article 4 of the will.

In arguing for a contrary result, the Donovan Family relies upon the distribution set forth in Article 4(E) of the Third Amended Appendix to Trust. The Donovan Family contends that because the will incorporated the trust by reference, it is necessary to review the trust's terms, and that under the Third Amended Appendix to Trust, the proceeds from the sale of Optimum Manufacturing must be distributed to the family according to the schedule set forth therein. For the purposes of this discussion, we will assume, without deciding, that the trust documents are incorporated by reference into the will.

When interpreting an *inter vivos* trust evidenced by a written instrument, "the terms of the trust are determined by the provisions of the instrument as interpreted in the light of all the circumstances and other competent evidence of the intention of the settlor with respect to the trust." The "determination of the ultimate fact of the intent of the settlor rests with this court." To determine the settlor's intent, we first look to the language of the trust. "In searching for the proper interpretation of words used in a written instrument, we require that the words and phrases be given their common meaning." We examine the instrument as a whole, and look to extrinsic evidence of the settlor's intent only if the language used in the trust instrument is ambiguous.

Viewing the plain meaning of the trust, when examined as a whole, we conclude that the distribution to which Article 4(E) of the Third Amended Appendix to Trust refers applies *only* if, when he died, the decedent still owned shares of Optimum Manufacturing stock. Article 4(E) is part of Article 4, which specifically concerns the disposition of assets *after* the decedent's death. Article 4(E) is preceded by Article 4(D), which authorizes the trustee to sell the decedent's Optimum Manufacturing stock either to Optimum Manufacturing employees or "upon such terms" as the trustee deems "prudent under the circumstances, in the sole discretion of [the] Trustee." In context, then, the distribution set forth in Article 4(E) applies to the sale of stock that Article 4(D) authorized the trustee to make after the decedent's death. The plain meaning of these provisions evince the decedent's intent that the distribution of the proceeds from the sale of stock set forth in Article 4(E) applies only to a post-death sale of stock authorized by Article 4(D), and does not apply to the proceeds from any sale of stock that occurred before the decedent's death.

Therefore, even if the proceeds from the sale of Optimum Manufacturing stock had passed to the trust, because the sale occurred before the decedent died, the respondent would have been entitled to them under Article 4(F). For all of the above reasons, therefore, we uphold the trial court's decision.

We decline the parties' invitation to rule upon whether the Donovan Family is entitled to a share of the proceeds from the sale of the decedent's personal goodwill in Optimum Manufacturing. From the record submitted on appeal, it appears that this issue is not yet ripe for our review.

The record reveals that after the trial court issued its ruling, the executor filed a motion asking the court to clarify either that the decedent's personal goodwill was *not* the subject of that ruling or, "[i]f the court determines that the pleadings are ripe for decision with respect to [the decedent's personal goodwill], then amend its order to include specific direction" on that issue. The trial court denied the motion, stating: "The Executor has a job to perform, for which he charges a significant fee. The Court suggests that he needs to make the decisions that he has been empowered to make. Any party may then contest that decision." Under these circumstances, we decline to decide in the first instance whether any proceeds from the sale of the decedent's personal goodwill in Optimum Manufacturing should be distributed to the Donovan Family.

Affirmed.

Do you think Timothy Donovan thought he was making a $6 million change to his estate plans when he sold his shares in Optimum Manufacturing? As you can see from *Estate of Donovan*, when specifically devised property is not in the estate, the common law adeems the devise by extinction. The common-law approach is sometimes called the "identity theory". UPC § 2–606 rejects the common law's identity theory and applies an "intent theory" to these situations, supplying a rule of construction designed to achieve the intent of the decedent by making a substitute gift for the lapsed devise.

UPC § 2–606

SECTION 2–606. NONADEMPTION OF SPECIFIC DEVISES; UNPAID PROCEEDS OF SALE, CONDEMNATION, OR INSURANCE; SALE BY CONSERVATOR OR AGENT.

(a) A specific devisee has a right to specifically devised property in the testator's estate at the testator's death and to:

(1) any balance of the purchase price, together with any security agreement, owed by a purchaser at the testator's death by reason of sale of the property;

(2) any amount of a condemnation award for the taking of the property unpaid at death;

(3) any proceeds unpaid at death on fire or casualty insurance on or other recovery for injury to the property;

(4) any property owned by the testator at death and acquired as a result of foreclosure, or obtained in lieu of foreclosure, of the security interest for a specifically devised obligation;

(5) any real property or tangible personal property owned by the testator at death which the testator acquired as a replacement for specifically devised real property or tangible personal property; and

(6) if not covered by paragraphs (1) through (5), a pecuniary devise equal to the value as of its date of disposition of other specifically devised property disposed of during the testator's lifetime but only to the extent it is established that ademption would be inconsistent with the testator's manifested plan of distribution or that at the time the will was made, the date of disposition or otherwise, the testator did not intend ademption of the devise.

(b) If specifically devised property is sold or mortgaged by a conservator or by an agent acting within the authority of a durable power of attorney for an incapacitated principal, or a condemnation award, insurance proceeds, or recovery for injury to the property is paid to a conservator or to an agent acting within the authority of a durable power of attorney for an incapacitated principal, the specific devisee has the right to a general pecuniary devise equal to the net sale price, the amount of the unpaid loan, the condemnation award, the insurance proceeds, or the recovery.

(c) The right of a specific devisee under subsection (b) is reduced by any right the devisee has under subsection (a).

(d) For the purposes of the references in subsection (b) to a conservator, subsection (b) does not apply if, after the sale, mortgage, condemnation, casualty, or recovery, it was adjudicated that the testator's incapacity ceased and the testator survived the adjudication for at least one year.

(e) For the purposes of the references in subsection (b) to an agent acting within the authority of a durable power of attorney for an incapacitated principal, (i) "incapacitated principal" means a principal who is an incapacitated person, (ii) no adjudication of incapacity before death is necessary, and (iii) the acts of an agent within the authority of a durable power of attorney are presumed to be for an incapacitated principal.

———————

Would the UPC have reached the same result as the court did in *Estate of Donovan?*

> Problem 4.27a: O executes O's will which says, "I give my farm to my niece. I give the rest of my property to the homeless shelter." At the time of execution, O's farm is worth $900,000 and the rest of O's assets are tangible personal property worth $100,000. Later, O sells her farm and uses the cash to purchase a house in the city. O dies, leaving only the house and the tangible personalty. Which provision(s) of the UPC might apply?

> Problem 4.27b: Assume the same facts as above, except that O has become incompetent and needs nursing care. While competent, O had executed a durable power of attorney making A the agent to manage her property. A sells the house, putting the cash in the bank and using it to pay O's nursing home expenses. After A has spent $200,000 on O's care, O dies. Who takes what under the common law? Who takes under UPC § 2–606?

(b) Stock Splits

STRUNK V. LAWSON
Court of Appeals of Kentucky, 2013
447 S.W.3d 641

NICKELL, J.

These consolidated appeals challenge the McCreary Circuit Court's interpretation of the will of Mamie L. Strunk (Mamie).[1] * * *

———————

[1] Mamie died testate in 2003 at the age of eighty with an estate valued at about $2,500,000.00. Her estate contained realty, livestock, household furnishings, certificates of deposit, bank accounts, a vehicle, and a lien retained in a deed, but the largest asset was 10,000 shares of stock in McCreary Bancshares, Inc. (MBI) valued at about $2,200,000.00. Mamie had no children. At death, she was married to her third husband, Hobert Strunk (Hobert). Her will was filed for probate in McCreary District Court on October 15, 2003.

The will being interpreted was the second drafted for Mamie by attorney Hon. Ruben Hicks. He acknowledged drafting Mamie's first will (date unknown), but testified he did not retain a copy, nor did he recall any details. Family members speculated Hicks drew the first will when Mamie owned only 1,000 shares of bank stock, and claimed it made an identical distribution of stock as the will currently under review. The first will was not produced for comparison.

BACKGROUND

The rub in Mamie's will is a bequest of 970 shares of stock in the "Bank of McCreary County" (BMC) that were not owned by the estate when Mamie died in 2003, and 10,000 shares of stock in McCreary Bancshares, Inc. (MBI) that were owned by the estate but for which no specific provision was made in the will. Petitioners, primarily descendants of Mamie's second husband, W.Z. Lawson, through whom much of the bank stock originated, argued 9,700 of the 10,000 shares of stock in the estate should pass pursuant to Item II of the will which specified bequests of stock to 13 named individuals. Neal and Strunk, respondents below (now appellants), argued that only 970 shares of stock should pass under Item II of the will and the remaining 9,030 shares should pass under Item IV of the will, commonly referred to as a residual clause.

We begin with a recitation of relevant provisions of the will. Item II made specific bequests of stock. Item VI contained a residual clause directing the executrix and executor to sell all of Mamie's remaining realty and personalty ("including stock in the Bank of McCreary County not bequeathed in Item II") to pay debts and funeral expenses; to devise $11,000.00 in $1,000.00 increments pursuant to a schedule; and finally, "[t]o my husband, Hobert Strunk, and my dear friend, Peggy Neal, the balance of such proceeds, share and share alike." Item VII stated additional provision had been made for Hobert through survivorship accounts at BMC and title to other assets in their joint names with right of survivorship. Also deserving of mention is Item VIII, an *in terrorem* clause, directing:

> It is my desire that my property be divided as hereinabove set forth, and in keeping with that desire should any of my said devisees and legatees attempt to contest or otherwise pervert the orderly procedure and distribution as herein directed, then and in that event such recalcitrant devisee or legatee shall receive no part of my estate. None of the persons herein named, or anyone else, has any claim for services or otherwise against my estate.

Finally, Item IX designated Hobert and Neal to serve as executor and executrix without bond.

Following the denial of motions for summary judgment and a bench trial, on June 16, 2009, the trial court issued a 21-page opinion that closely followed pleadings filed by Robert on behalf of the estate.

The court found: BMC and MBI are separate legal entities; Mamie's MBI stock was directly attributable to her previously-owned BMC stock; Mamie was a competent, intelligent woman who was aware of her financial holdings, formation of MBI in 1982, and a 1995 stock split; Mamie dictated the desired language of her will to her attorney and he wrote it verbatim into the will that Mamie reviewed and executed in 1997; and finally, at death, Mamie owned no shares of BMC stock, but did own 10,000 shares of MBI stock.

From these facts, the court drew the following conclusions. The will's *in terrorem* clause was not triggered by the filing of the declaratory judgment action because requesting interpretation of a will's language is not a will contest. Under the polar star rule, the court must determine the testator's intent from what she said—not from what she might have said. So long as the testator's intent is clear from the four corners of the will, resort to rules of construction and extrinsic evidence is unnecessary.

Though Mamie did not own stock in BMC at the time of her death, the bequest of BMC stock did not fail (in other words, there was no ademption)[6], because the BMC stock she attempted to devise had been converted into the MBI stock she owned at death. Thus, the stock's change in form did not defeat the bequest contained in the will. The trial court found this view to be buttressed by KRS 394.550(3), Kentucky's anti-ademption statute, which, without reference to timing directs, "[a]ll shares of stock issued as a result of merger, consolidation, reorganization or other similar action, and attributable to the devised shares" are included in any legacy of stock. Thus, the fact that the stock was converted in 1983 and split in 1995, *before* the will was executed in 1997, was not fatal to the bequest.[8]

While the court found the bequest did not fail for attempting to devise an item that did not exist as named in the will, it did find the bequest was ambiguous due to the misidentification of the stock and therefore, an interpretation was necessary. The court stated that because it was converting the bequest of BMC stock into a bequest of MBI stock, it was also necessary to multiply the number of shares bequeathed by ten to reflect the ten-for-one stock split. (Thus, a

---

[6] Ademption is "[t]he destruction or extinction of a legacy or bequest by reason of a bequeathed asset's ceasing to be part of the estate at the time of the testator's death; a beneficiary's forfeiture of a legacy or bequest that is no longer operative."

[8] A codicil executed in 1999 rescinded a devise of 100 shares of BMC stock to a niece, Gail Stouse, who predeceased Mamie. The codicil was typed on BMC letterhead by a BMC employee.

bequest of 100 shares of BMC stock became a bequest of 1,000 shares of MBI stock). The court stated it would reach this conclusion whether it literally enforced the words of the will or relied upon rules of construction and extrinsic evidence to interpret the will. The court concluded this resolution was consistent with case law favoring distribution of one's estate to the natural objects of one's bounty, *Clarke, Trustee, et al. v. Kirk, et al.*, 795 S.W.2d 936 (1990), and a 1987 Shareholder Agreement restricting ownership of MBI stock to "parents, siblings, or lineal descendants."

Ultimately, the trial court adjudged the will to be valid and deemed each bequest of BMC stock to be a bequest of MBI stock. Furthermore, it multiplied the number of shares bequeathed under Item II of the will by ten to reflect the 1995 stock split. The court denied all other relief, awarded costs to the petitioners, and entered a final and appealable judgment.

The wrangling did not end. * * *

On September 4, 2009, the trial court entered an amended judgment that made only minor changes. * * *

     * * *

October 1, 2009, Neal and Strunk filed a joint notice of appeal challenging both the original judgment (entered June 2009) and the amended version (entered September 2009). On June 14, 2010, Neal filed another notice of appeal, this time challenging an order entered June 2, 2010, requiring tax returns to be reviewed and executed. Strunk filed a similar notice of appeal on June 22, 2010. On September 22, 2010, we consolidated all three appeals and now address the four issues raised on appeal.

I.   WAS THE WILL AMBIGUOUS?

The first question posed by Neal and Strunk is whether it was necessary for the trial court to interpret the will. Interpretation is required when a will is ambiguous. An ambiguity may be either patent or latent. If patent, there is doubt as to the testator's intention on the face of the will; if latent, the testator's intent is clear, but there is doubt about the object devised. Here, the trial court found a latent defect in the item devised since the estate contained no BMC stock.

The will Mamie executed in 1997 bequeathed 970 shares of BMC stock to thirteen heirs. This was a problem because Mamie had owned no BMC stock since 1983 when all shares of BMC were converted into shares of MBI, a closely-held bank holding company formed in 1982. Once MBI was created and all BMC stock converted into MBI stock, Mamie no longer owned any BMC stock and therefore, had none to bequeath in her will. There was no question Mamie's BMC stock of yesteryear existed as MBI stock in 1997 when she executed her will—thus, her consistent reference throughout the will (and in a codicil executed in 1999) to BMC stock was a mystery.

So long as the intention reflected in Mamie's will was legal, it controls distribution of her estate. *Clarke*, 795 S.W.2d at 938 (polar star rule). Based solely on the four corners of the will, the trial court had to determine what Mamie meant by what she said. Only if her intent was ambiguous, would the court apply extrinsic evidence and rules of construction.

Neal and Strunk acknowledge the trial court correctly converted the bequest of BMC stock into a bequest of MBI stock, but contend the judgment went too far in that it also multiplied the bequests mentioned in Item II by ten to account for a stock split that had occurred two years before Mamie's will was executed. In 1995, as the result of a ten-for-one stock split, the 1,000 shares of MBI stock Mamie had received via the exchange in 1983 increased to 10,000 shares of MBI stock. Both BMC and MBI legally exist today, but all BMC stock is owned by MBI and none is publicly traded. To account for the stock split, and to distribute Mamie's estate to the natural objects of her bounty as she intended, the trial court deemed it necessary to convert the BMC stock into MBI stock and then multiply it by ten. This meant that now 9,700 shares of MBI stock, as opposed to only the 970 shares specifically mentioned in the will, were to be distributed pursuant to Item II. Neal and Strunk disagreed with this interpretation, arguing that 9,030 shares should fall into the residual clause meaning Mamie's "dear friend" and her step-grandson by adoption, rather than her blood relatives, would share the bulk of her sizable estate.

Neal and Strunk argue the trial court's multiplication of the shares violates the polar star rule, especially since the stock split occurred in 1995, two years *before* the will was executed. However, Neal and Strunk minimize the fact that the stock conversion (which they agree was correctly applied) occurred in 1983, fourteen years *before* the will was executed. All agreed Mamie was bright, shrewd and well aware of the bank reorganization and the stock split as evidenced by her signature on documents and testimony about her business acumen. If it was permissible for the trial court to apply the

1983 stock conversion, it was equally permissible for the trial court to apply the 1995 stock split and multiply the shares.

Because there was no longer any BMC stock within the estate, and everyone agreed the will's reference to it was an attempt to devise the MBI stock, there was no ademption. Furthermore, KRS 394.550(1) and (3) specify a legacy of stock includes "[a]ll stock split shares attributable to the devised shares" and "[a]ll shares of stock issued as a result of merger, consolidation, reorganization or other similar action, and attributable to the devised shares[.]" Neal and Strunk would have us read this statute to apply only when a stock split or reorganization occurs *after* a will has been executed, but the legislature did not include a timing element in the statute and it is beyond our authority to add one in its absence. To determine the legislature's intent, we examine its precise statutory language without adding words that are not there or guessing what it might have intended to say but did not. Due to the will's latent ambiguity, interpretation was necessary. No error occurred.

II. *IN TERROREM* CLAUSE NOT TRIGGERED BY FILING OF DECLARATORY JUDGMENT ACTION

Neal and Strunk's second claim is that the filing of the declaratory judgment action required enforcement of Item VIII of the will—described as a "homegrown *in terrorem*" clause. In their view, no petitioner should inherit under the will.

As explained in *Commonwealth Bank & Trust Co. v. Young*, 361 S.W.3d 344, 352 (Ky.App.2012),

> [a] no-contest clause provision in a will or trust "is referred to as an 'in terrorem clause' because its purpose is to strike fear into the heart of a beneficiary who might wish to consider contesting the provisions of the trust." The reasons for such a clause include the deceased's attempt to avoid costly legal expenses to the estate or trust, antagonism between beneficiaries, and the public exposure of private matters. Although enforceable in Kentucky, no-contest provisions are strictly construed and are not extended beyond their express terms.

Here, the petition for declaratory judgment did not attempt to "annul or vacate any part of the will[.]" Its singular purpose was to interpret the will and establish how the estate should be distributed to carry out Mamie's intent. Such an action does not constitute a violation of a forfeiture clause.

Neal and Strunk argue actions other than petitioning for declaratory judgment perverted administration of the will and, therefore, violated the clause, such as Robert's moving the district court to appoint him as executor of the estate. In reviewing the motion to disqualify Neal as executrix, we noticed Robert did *not* ask to be named executor; he asked only that Neal be disqualified due to a conflict of interest and that she be replaced by a "disinterested third-party to serve with good and sufficient bond and corporate surety." It appears the district court *sua sponte* appointed Robert as co-executor. Thus, as the trial court correctly determined, enforcement of the *in terrorem* clause against the Lawson heirs, or against Robert specifically, was not required.

* * *

For the foregoing reasons, the amended findings of fact, conclusions of law and declaratory judgment, as well as the order and supplemental judgment, all entered by the McCreary Circuit Court on September 4, 2009, are affirmed.

Neal and Strunk conceded that the 970 shares of BMC stock devised in the will can be construed to refer to 970 shares of MBI stock. Under the statute quoted in *Strunk v. Lawson*, the 970 shares were increased to 9700 shares to account for the ten-for-one stock split. Would that ten-fold multiplication have been the result under UPC § 2–605, excerpted below?

UPC § 2–605

SECTION 2–605. INCREASE IN SECURITIES; ACCESSIONS.

(a) If a testator executes a will that devises securities and the testator then owned securities that meet the description in the will, the devise includes additional securities owned by the testator at death to the extent the additional securities were acquired by the testator after the will was executed as a result of the testator's ownership of the described securities and are securities of any of the following types:

(1) securities of the same organization acquired by reason of action initiated by the organization or any successor, related,

or acquiring organization, excluding any acquired by exercise of purchase options;

(2) securities of another organization acquired as a result of a merger, consolidation, reorganization, or other distribution by the organization or any successor, related, or acquiring organization; or

(3) securities of the same organization acquired as a result of a plan of reinvestment.

(b) Distributions in cash before death with respect to a described security are not part of the devise.

(c) Ademption by Satisfaction

Extinction is not the only way a devise might be adeemed. It can also be adeemed by satisfaction. The idea here is something like the advancements doctrine, which we saw during the discussion of intestate succession. Basically, a devise might be deemed to be prepaid by an inter vivos gift. The UPC deals with this situation in a narrow way, similar to its treatment of advancements.

UPC § 2–609

SECTION 2–609. ADEMPTION BY SATISFACTION.

(a) Property a testator gave in the testator's lifetime to a person is treated as a satisfaction of a devise in whole or in part, only if (i) the will provides for deduction of the gift, (ii) the testator declared in a contemporaneous writing that the gift is in satisfaction of the devise or that its value is to be deducted from the value of the devise, or (iii) the devisee acknowledged in writing that the gift is in satisfaction of the devise or that its value is to be deducted from the value of the devise.

(b) For purposes of partial satisfaction, property given during lifetime is valued as of the time the devisee came into possession or enjoyment of the property or at the testator's death, whichever occurs first.

(c) If the devisee fails to survive the testator, the gift is treated as a full or partial satisfaction of the devise, as appropriate, in applying Sections 2–603 and 2–604 , unless the testator's contemporaneous writing provides otherwise.

Problem 4.28: O executes a will devising $40,000 to A. O sends check to A for $14,000 and a check to A's spouse B for $14,000, with a letter to each saying that "this gift is in lieu of the devise to A in my will." O dies. How much of the $40,000 devise does A take from the estate under UPC § 2–609? Note that the 1969 UPC § 2–612 said, "Property which a testator gave in his lifetime to a person is treated as a satisfaction of a devise to that person in whole or in part only if . . .". What does the change in the 1990 code imply? Was that a good change?

In some jurisdictions, the ademption by satisfaction doctrine does not apply to specific devises.

(d) Exoneration

One thing to remember about exoneration is that the will should make it clear who should pay the mortgage if mortgaged property is devised separately from the residue of the estate. If your client wishes to devise her house to one brother and the rest of her estate to another, make it clear who pays off the mortgage on the house. In other words, make it clear whether specific devisees take their devises subject to security interests held by others. This problem, which has led to otherwise needless litigation, should be addressed in the will even if there is no mortgage at the time the will is executed because it is common for owners to re-mortgage their land after they have paid off their mortgage. The common law gave the specific devisee a right of exoneration, so a mortgage debt would have to be paid by the estate. UPC § 2–607 reverses the common-law rule, providing as a default that the specific devisee takes the property subject to the mortgage debt, even if the will instructs the executor to pay all debts.

(e) Abatement: Residuary, General, Specific

Once it has been decided who is supposed to take what under a will, after gifts have lapsed or been adeemed, there might still be a problem in accomplishing the result desired by the testator. Sometimes, there are not enough assets in the estate to make all of the devises described. If the will itself does not determine which gifts to reduce, the rules of abatement tell which devises are abated.

The common-law rules followed the difference in treatment between the title to realty, which passes directly to successors, and the title to personalty which passes to the personal representative first. Abatement rules in some states still follow the resulting common-law distinction by which all gifts of personal property abate before any gifts of realty. In other states, residuary devises of personalty abate before residuary devises of realty, and likewise within specific devises.

The UPC has eliminated this distinction between real and personal property. Under UPC § 3–902, the shares of the distributees abate in the following order: (i) property not disposed of by the will; (ii) residuary devises; (iii) general devises; (iv) specific devises, and within a class of gifts the gifts abate pro rata. To put it the other way around, first priority is given to the specific devises, then the general, and the residuary devise has the lowest priority. This can lead to a problem because the residuary devisee is often the person that the testator cares about most. Take care as a lawyer to plan and draft for the possibility that there are substantially fewer assets in the estate than is anticipated at the time the will is executed.

> Problem 4.29: O's will says, "I give $10,000 to my friend, F, and all my savings accounts to my grandchildren." At O's death, O has only $10,000 in a savings account. Who takes what?

6. SPOUSES OMITTED FROM WILLS EXECUTED BEFORE MARRIAGE

In various ways, the law protects a pretermitted spouse, a surviving spouse who was not included in the decedent spouse's will executed before their marriage. One protection is the statutory elective share and another protection is community property, both of which we will discuss infra. The old rule that marriage automatically revoked wills also served to protect surviving spouses. Under the UPC, marriage does not revoke a will, but the UPC sometimes provides a share of the estate for the pretermitted spouse.

UPC § 2–301

SECTION 2–301. ENTITLEMENT OF SPOUSE; PREMARITAL WILL.

(a) If a testator's surviving spouse married the testator after the testator executed the testator's will, the surviving spouse is entitled to receive, as an intestate share, no less than the value of the share of the estate the spouse would have received if the testator had died intestate as to that portion of the testator's estate, if any, that neither is devised to a child of the testator who was born before the testator married the surviving spouse and who is not a child of the surviving spouse nor is devised to a descendant of such a child or passes under Sections 2–603 or 2–604 to such a child or to a descendant of such a child, unless:

(1) it appears from the will or other evidence that the will was made in contemplation of the testator's marriage to the surviving spouse;

(2) the will expresses the intention that it is to be effective notwithstanding any subsequent marriage; or

(3) the testator provided for the spouse by transfer outside the will and the intent that the transfer be in lieu of a testamentary provision is shown by the testator's statements or is reasonably inferred from the amount of the transfer or other evidence.

(b) In satisfying the share provided by this section, devises made by the will to the testator's surviving spouse, if any, are applied first, and other devises, other than a devise to a child of the testator who was born before the testator married the surviving spouse and who is not a child of the surviving spouse or a devise or substitute gift under Sections 2–603 or 2–604 to a descendant of such a child, abate as provided in Section 3–902.

Problem 4.30: O has children, C1 and C2, by mother M. O executes a will devising $100,000 to Charity, $100,000 to S, and the residue to O's children. C1 has a child, GC. C1 dies. Ten years later, O marries S. O dies leaving an estate of $3,000,000 and $300,000 life insurance payable to S. Who takes what under the UPC (ignoring allowances and assuming S does not elect the elective share)?

7. CHILDREN OMITTED FROM WILLS

Sometimes, a testator executes a will, afterwards becomes a parent to a child, and then dies. If the decedent made a class gift to children, then that subsequent child is included. What happens if the will made gifts to individually named children instead? Consider the drafting that led to the following case.

ESPINOSA V. SPARBER, SHEVIN, SHAPO, ROSEN AND HEILBRONNER

Supreme Court of Florida, 1993
612 So.2d 1378

McDONALD, J.

We review *Espinosa v. Sparber, Shevin, Shapo, Rosen & Heilbronner,* 586 So.2d 1221 (Fla. 3d DCA 1991), which involves the following question of great public importance certified in an unpublished order dated September 17, 1991:

UNDER THE FACTS OF THIS CASE ... MAY A LAWSUIT ALLEGING PROFESSIONAL MALPRACTICE BE BROUGHT, ON BEHALF OF PATRICIA AZCUNCE, AGAINST THE DRAFTSMAN OF THE SECOND CODICIL?

We have jurisdiction pursuant to article V, section 3(b)(4) of the Florida Constitution. We answer the question in the negative and approve the decision of the district court.

Howard Roskin, a member of the Sparber, Shevin law firm, drafted a will for Rene Azcunce, the testator. At the time he signed his will, Rene and his wife, Marta, had three children, Lisette, Natalie, and Gabriel. Article Seventeenth of the Will specifically provided that:

(a) References in this, my Last Will and Testament, to my children, shall be construed to mean my daughters, LISSETE AZCUNCE and NATALIE AZCUNCE, and my son, GABRIEL AZCUNCE.

(b) References in this, my Last Will and Testament, to my "issue," shall be construed to mean my children [as defined in Paragraph (a), above] and their legitimate natural born and legally adopted lineal descendants.

Article Fourth of the will established a trust for the benefit of Marta and the three named children and also granted Marta a power of appointment to distribute all or a portion of the trust to the named children and their issue. In addition, the will provided that, upon Marta's death, the trust was to be divided into equal shares for each of the three named children.

Neither the will nor the first codicil to the will, executed on August 8, 1983, made any provisions for after-born children. On March 14, 1984, Patricia Azcunce was born as the fourth child of Rene and Marta. Rene contacted Roskin and communicated his desire to include Patricia in his will. In response, Roskin drafted a new will that provided for Patricia and also restructured the trust. However, due to a disagreement between Rene and Roskin on the amount of available assets, Rene never signed the second will. Instead, on June 25, 1986, he executed a second codicil drafted by Roskin that changed the identity of the co-trustee and co-personal representative, but did not provide for the after-born child, Patricia. When Rene died on December 30, 1986, he had never executed any document that provided for Patricia.[1]

Marta brought a malpractice action on behalf of Patricia and the estate against Roskin and his law firm. The trial court dismissed the complaint with prejudice for lack of privity and entered final summary judgment for Roskin and his firm. The Third District Court of Appeal reversed the dismissal with regard to the estate, affirmed it with regard to Patricia, and certified the question of whether Patricia has standing to bring a legal malpractice action under the facts of this case.

An attorney's liability for negligence in the performance of his or her professional duties is limited to clients with whom the attorney shares privity of contract. In a legal context, the term "privity" is a word of art derived from the common law of contracts and used to describe the relationship of persons who are parties to a contract. To bring a legal malpractice action, the plaintiff must either be in privity with the attorney, wherein one party has a direct obligation to another, or, alternatively, the plaintiff must be an intended third-party beneficiary. In the instant case, Patricia Azcunce does not fit into either category of proper plaintiffs.

---

[1]   Patricia brought suit in probate court to be classified as a pretermitted child, which would have entitled her to a share of Rene's estate. Her mother and adult sibling consented to Patricia's petition being granted. The probate court judge appointed a guardian ad litem for Patricia's two minor siblings, and the guardian opposed the petition. Subsequently, the court ruled that the second codicil destroyed Patricia's status as a pretermitted child, and the decision was upheld on appeal. *Azcunce v. Estate of Azcunce*, 586 So.2d 1216 (Fla. 3d DCA 1991).

We are not privy to the factors that the guardian ad litem considered in deciding not to consent to Patricia's classification as a pretermitted child, a decision that deprived Patricia of a share in the estate and ultimately led to costly litigation. We hope, however, that a guardian evaluating the facts of this case would not focus strictly on the financial consequences for the child, but would also consider such important factors as family harmony and stability.

In the area of will drafting, a limited exception to the strict privity requirement has been allowed where it can be demonstrated that the apparent intent of the client in engaging the services of the lawyer was to benefit a third party. Because the client is no longer alive and is unable to testify, the task of identifying those persons who are intended third-party beneficiaries causes an evidentiary problem closely akin to the problem of determining the client's general testamentary intent. To minimize such evidentiary problems, the will was designed as a legal document that affords people a clear opportunity to express the way in which they desire to have their property distributed upon death. To the greatest extent possible, courts and personal representatives are obligated to honor the testator's intent in conformity with the contents of the will.

If extrinsic evidence is admitted to explain testamentary intent, as recommended by the petitioners, the risk of misinterpreting the testator's intent increases dramatically. Furthermore, admitting extrinsic evidence heightens the tendency to manufacture false evidence that cannot be rebutted due to the unavailability of the testator. For these reasons, we adhere to the rule that standing in legal malpractice actions is limited to those who can show that the testator's intent *as expressed in the will* is frustrated by the negligence of the testator's attorney. Although Rene did not express in his will and codicils any intention to exclude Patricia, his will and codicils do not, unfortunately, express any affirmative intent to provide for her. Because Patricia cannot be described as one in privity with the attorney or as an intended third-party beneficiary, a lawsuit alleging professional malpractice cannot be brought on her behalf.

Rene's estate, however, stands in the shoes of the testator and clearly satisfies the privity requirement. Therefore, we agree with the district court's decision that the estate may maintain a legal malpractice action against Roskin for any acts of professional negligence committed by him during his representation of Rene. Because the alleged damages to the estate are an element of the liability claim and are not relevant to the standing question in this particular case, we do not address that issue.

For the reasons stated above, we answer the certified question in the negative and approve the decision of the district court.

It is so ordered.

————————————

Rene's will listed Patricia's older siblings by name. Why might the lawyer have drafted Rene's will to list his children instead of simply saying, "my children"? Notice the effect of the republication by codicil doctrine on the protection for omitted children under the Florida pretermitted child statute. (Rene's second codicil expressly republished the will and first codicil, both of which were executed before Patricia was born.) Is there a reason that the omitted child protection would not include children born before a will is written? Does that same rationale apply when the child was born between the execution of the will and the execution of a codicil? The court in the underlying dispute said, "Presumably, if the testator had wished to provide for Patricia, he would have done so in the second codicil as she had been born by that time; because he did not, Patricia was, in effect, disinherited which the testator clearly had the power to do." Is that your guess as to the intent of Rene? Suppose the protection was extended to include such children unless the codicil named other children. Can you think of situations in which that would be inconsistent with the intent of the testator? Because drafters are human, there will be errors of both inclusion and exclusion of children. Which error is worse? What could Rene's lawyer have done to prevent the disinheritance of Patricia? How burdensome would it be for lawyers to take such precautions? It is the job of the lawyer to plan for the unexpected.

IN RE GILMORE

Supreme Court, Appellate Division, Second Department, New York, 2011
925 N.Y.S.2d 567

LEVENTHAL, J.

A parent in New York State is under no obligation to leave any part of his or her estate to his or her children.[1] However, to address situations where a child is inadvertently left out of a parent's will because such child was born after the will's execution, the Legislature enacted EPTL 5–3.2. In this appeal, the petitioners Andrea Hofler and Malverick Hofler (hereinafter together the movants), who are nonparties in this probate proceeding, contend that they are the nonmarital, biological children of the deceased testator. They further contend that the testator only learned of their existence after he had executed his final will, and shortly before his death. On this appeal, we consider whether the Surrogate's Court

---

[1]   Louisiana is the only state that protects children from even intentional disinheritance by way of forced heirship.

properly determined that the biological children of a testator, born prior to the execution of a final will, are not entitled to be treated as adopted children under the caselaw-created exception to EPTL 5–3.2.

In June 1996, Roy Gilmore, the decedent, executed a last will. On January 13, 2007, the decedent died. Thereafter, Angela Manning, one of the decedent's children, as executor of the decedent's estate, offered the will for probate.

In a verified petition dated February 11, 2008, the movants asserted that they were born prior to the execution of the decedent's will and that the decedent did not know that they were his biological children. They alleged that, approximately 10 years after he executed his will, the decedent underwent DNA testing which revealed that he was their father. The movants further argued that the law and logic supported their application to be granted the rights of after-born children.

By notice of motion dated February 12, 2008, the movants, asserting that they were the decedent's nonmarital children, jointly moved, in effect, for summary judgment determining that they "are to be treated as afterborn children of the decedent pursuant to EPTL 5–3.2." In an affirmation, counsel for the movants noted that, although the decedent was survived by 11 children, his will left his entire estate to Manning. According to counsel, although the movants were born prior to the execution of the decedent's will, the decedent did not know that the movants were his biological children until after the subject will was executed in 1996.

In support of their motion, the movants submitted an affidavit from Mary Jane Martin, the decedent's sister. Martin averred that the decedent acknowledged in January or February 2006 that he had recently learned that the movants were his children. Martin added that in December 2006, the decedent had introduced the movants to her "as his two children, whom he had recently learned of."

In opposition, Manning acknowledged that the purpose of EPTL 5–3.2 was to guard against inadvertent or unintentional disinheritance. However, she argued that the recent amendments to that statute did not support the movants' contentions inasmuch as the Legislature chose to limit the definition of after-born children to just that, children born after the execution of a will.

In their reply papers, the movants reiterated their prior contentions that the term after-born, as employed by EPTL 5–3.2, can include children born prior to the execution of a will, but who are only established as children of a testator after the execution of a will, such as after-adopted children. The movants noted that a child adopted after the execution of a will, but born prior to the will's execution, is considered an after-born child under the pertinent case law.

In an order dated December 23, 2009, the Surrogate's Court found that the movants were not entitled to any rights under EPTL 5–3.2. The court noted that "the parties ha[d] consented to have the motion submitted assuming the truth of the movant[s'] allegations for a determination of whether as a matter of law those allegations state a cause of action entitling the claimants to after-born status." The Surrogate's Court acknowledged that a child is generally entitled to after-born rights only if born after the execution of a will. The Surrogate's Court further acknowledged that the only exception to that rule is for a child adopted after the execution of a will, even if born prior to its execution. With respect to EPTL 5–3.2, the Surrogate's Court stated that it was "not at liberty to conjecture about, add to or subtract from words having a definite and plain meaning," as such conduct would constitute "trespasses by a court upon the legislative domain." The movants appeal.

A review of nisi prius decisions is instructive. In *Matter of Wilkins* (180 Misc 2d 568 [1999]), the Surrogate's Court, New York County, was presented with a matter wherein the deceased testator's nonmarital son, Michael, sought to inherit as a child born after the execution of the decedent's will. In *Wilkins*, the decedent's will was executed in 1965, Michael was born in 1969, and the decedent died in 1988. At a hearing on the issue of paternity, the decedent's friend testified that the decedent often referred to Michael as his son, and Michael's mother testified that the decedent was aware that Michael was his son prior to Michael's birth. The Surrogate's Court determined that Michael was the decedent's son and that the decedent openly acknowledged his paternity for the purposes of EPTL 4–1.2. Construing a prior version of EPTL 5–3.2, the Surrogate's Court found that the term after-born included a nonmarital child. The instant case, however, is distinguishable from *Wilkins* because the movants were born prior to the execution of the subject will, whereas the child in *Wilkins* was born after the execution of that will.

In *Matter of Walsh* (NYLJ, May 13, 1998, at 31, col 6), a matter before the Surrogate's Court, Nassau County, the petitioner alleged that she was the nonmarital daughter of the decedent testator. The petitioner sought, inter alia, a declaration that she was entitled to inherit under the decedent's estate as if she was an after-born child pursuant to EPTL 5–3.2. The petitioner was born in 1964, the subject will was executed in 1984, and the decedent died in 1995. According to the petitioner, as a youth, her mother took her to see the decedent several times. In addition, the decedent was alleged to have visited the petitioner at school at least once, and had given her two cash gifts in 1991 to buy a home. Allegedly, the decedent also told various people throughout the petitioner's youth that she was the decedent's daughter. The petitioner sought to be classified as a nonmarital child pursuant to EPTL 4–1.2.

However, the Surrogate's Court found that "even assuming that Petitioner [was] in fact the non-marital child of decedent, petitioner cannot, as a matter of law, establish herself as an after born child under EPTL Sec. 5–3.2". Noting that the case was one of first impression, the Surrogate's Court stated the legislative intent of EPTL 5–3.2 and 4–1.2

> "might allow a non-marital child born and acknowledged as the child of decedent after the execution of a will to be treated as an after born child. In the case at bar, however, petitioner was born before decedent's 1984 will was executed and she alleges that he was aware that he was her father prior to the will's execution."

Furthermore, the court stated, "had petitioner been born after the execution of dec[e]dent's 1984 will, or perhaps even if dec[e]dent was unaware of petitioner's existence until after the execution of the will, she may have had a valid claim under Sec. 5–3.2 and Sec. 4–1.2" (id. [emphasis added]).

Relying upon the above-quoted language from *Walsh*, the movants contend that it is permissible for an "after-known" child to be treated as an after-born child. The movants concede that they are not, strictly speaking, "after-born" children as defined in EPTL 5–3.2, but they argue that because they were not known to the decedent, they are "after-knowns" and should be treated in the same manner as adopted children. The movants also cite to *Bourne v. Dorney* (184 App Div 476 [1918], affd 227 NY 641 [1919]). In *Bourne*, this Court considered the question of whether a child adopted by a testator subsequent to the making of his last will was an after-born child within the meaning of former Decedent Estate Law § 26 (the predecessor statute to EPTL 5–3.2). Section 26 of the Decedent Estate Law provided that where a child was born to a testator after the making of a will and the testator died leaving such child unprovided for and unmentioned in the will, that child will succeed to such part of the testator's estate as he would take if the parent died intestate. The testator in *Bourne* executed his will in 1886, and in 1897, the testator and his wife adopted the petitioner, who was born in 1892. As a result, the child was unprovided for in the will. Notwithstanding the fact that the operative statute required a child to be born of the testator in order to inherit, the Surrogate's Court found that the adopted child was born of the testator at the time of the adoption and, thus, eligible to inherit from the testator.

As a result of the decision in *Bourne*, children adopted in this State are considered born to a testator at the time of the adoption for the purposes of EPTL 5–3.2. The movants essentially seek the creation of an additional exception to the general rule that after-born children are limited to children born after the execution of a will. On appeal, the movants argue that EPTL 5–3.2 can be reasonably interpreted to protect so-called "after-known" children and that they should, therefore, be entitled to inherit as after-born children. The movants maintain that since an after-adopted child, born before the execution of a will, can inherit pursuant to EPTL 5–3.2, then so should they. They argue that the Court should interpret EPTL 5–3.2 to give effect to the intent of the Legislature, which, in this case, could not have been to preclude biological children discovered after the execution of a will from sharing in the decedent's estate while also allowing children adopted after the execution of a will to share in the decedent's estate.

The narrow issue presented for our review is whether the biological children of a testator,[2] born prior to the execution of a final will, are entitled to be treated as adopted children under the caselaw-created exception to EPTL 5–3.2. We answer this question in the negative.

When presented with a question of statutory interpretation, the Court's primary consideration "is to ascertain and give effect to the

---

[2] On this appeal, the issue has been framed in such a way that the Surrogate's Court decided the motion assuming that the movants had established paternity pursuant to EPTL 4–1.2, commonly referred to as the "paternity statute". Thus, for the purposes of this appeal, we also assume that the movants have established paternity.

intention of the Legislature". "The statutory text is the clearest indicator of legislative intent and courts should construe unambiguous language to give effect to its plain meaning".

EPTL 5–3.2, entitled "Revocatory effect of birth of child after execution of will," by its terms, only applies to after-born children who are unprovided for and unmentioned in a will. As discussed below, in certain situations, EPTL 5–3.2 can result in an after-born child inheriting from a testator as if the testator had died intestate. In that regard, it has been observed that "by effectively nullifying the will to the extent required to give the child his intestate share, the statute stands as a striking exception to the law's strong disposition to avoid intestacy whenever possible". Particularly relevant here is the statutory definition of the term "after-born" child.

EPTL 5–3.2(a) states as follows:

"Whenever a testator has a child born after the execution of a last will, and dies leaving the after-born child unprovided for by any settlement, and neither provided for nor in any way mentioned in the will, every such child shall succeed to a portion of the testator's estate as herein provided."

Further, EPTL 5–3.2(b) defines an after-born child as "a child of the testator born during the testator's lifetime or in gestation at the time of the testator's death and born thereafter." The manner in which, and whether, an after-born child succeeds to a parent's estate is contingent upon several factors. For example, if a testator had one or more children living when he or she executed a last will and no provision was made therein for any such child, an after-born child is not entitled to share in the testator's estate. If a testator had one or more children living when he or she executed a last will and a provision was made therein for one or more of such children, an after-born child is entitled to share in the testator's estate as limited to the disposition made to children under the will. For example, where, as here, a testator executes a last will when two or more of his children are alive and only leaves a disposition for one of those children (child A), and another child is born after the execution of the will (child B), the after-born child, child B, would be entitled to an equal share of the testamentary disposition to child A. Further, to the extent that it is feasible, the interest of the after-born child in the testator's estate shall be of the same character as the interest which the testator conferred upon his children under the will. Lastly, if a testator had no child living when he or she executed a last will, the after-born child succeeds to the portion of the testator's estate as would have passed to such child had the testator died intestate.

Applying the plain meaning of EPTL 5–3.2, the movants cannot be considered after-born children of the decedent because they were not "born after the execution of a last will". If the movants' arguments were to be accepted, the result would be that children born of a testator prior to the execution of a will, but unknown to such testator, could be entitled to be treated as an after-born child. This would lead to a result that would be contrary to the plain meaning of EPTL 5–3.2. " '[A] court cannot amend a statute by inserting words that are not there, nor will a court read into a statute a provision which the Legislature did not see fit to enact' ".

Assuming, as the movants contend, that EPTL 5–3.2 does not unambiguously preclude their contentions, a brief review of the legislative history of that statute with respect to the issue presented here is illuminative. Notably, nothing contained therein supports the movants' assertions. "[EPTL 5–3.2's] earliest forerunner, practically word for word identical, was enacted in 1830". The purpose of former Decedent Estate Law § 26 was "to guard against inadvertent or unintentional disinheritance". In 2006, EPTL 5–3.2 was amended to provide that an after-born child only includes a child born during the decedent's lifetime or at the time of his or her death. The memorandum in support of that amendment explained that developments in reproductive technology had made it possible that a child could be conceived long after a testator's death, whom the testator did not know or anticipate, and unfairly lessen the inheritance due to the children born during the testator's lifetime. EPTL 5–3.2 was most recently amended in 2007 to add the provision in subsection (b) which specifies that a nonmarital child, born after the execution of a will, is considered an after-born of the child's father when paternity is established pursuant to EPTL 4–1.2.

In view of the foregoing, there is no indication that the Legislature intended that nonmarital children, born prior to the execution of a will, are to be considered after-born children pursuant to EPTL 5–3.2 and, thus, are entitled to succeed to a portion of a testator's estate. A contrary holding would promote uncertainty in identifying persons interested in an estate and finality in its distribution, which are critical to the public interest in the orderly administration of estates.[3] The movants' reliance upon the *Walsh* decision is misplaced. The specific language in *Walsh* upon which the movants rely is merely dicta, as the facts before the Surrogate in that case demonstrated that the decedent was aware of the petitioner when that will was executed. Moreover, *Walsh* was decided prior to the 2007 amendment to EPTL 5–3.2 which specifically afforded nonmarital, after-born children the same rights as marital after-born children.

As Manning correctly contends, there is a significant difference between adopted children and so-called after-known children. Adopted children do not become the children of a person until after the adoption. On the other hand, after-known children are children of a person at the time of their birth. Further, by adopting a child, a parent makes an affirmative decision to incur legal obligations that are triggered by an adoption. By contrast, a child's birth prior to the execution of a will, and a testator's subsequent discovery of said child, involves no affirmative act. Here, the decedent's conduct prior to the execution of his will included activities which could have, and ostensibly did, result in the birth of nonmarital children. Thereafter, he executed a will which made no disposition to any unknown children that he may have fathered. This failure to address any potential offspring can be considered as an intent to preclude succession to the same.

In support of her contentions, Manning also cites to two somewhat similar court decisions from other jurisdictions in which analogous after-born statutes were construed (*see Lanier v. Rains*, 229 S.W.3d 656, 667 [Tenn Sup Ct 2007] [declining to treat "after-acknowledged" children in the same manner as after "after-adopted" children where petitioner was born out-of-wedlock, prior to execution of testator's will, despite claim that petitioner should be treated as after-born child because she was not known to testator until after execution of the will]; *Moyer v. Walker*, 771 S.W.2d 363 [Mo Ct App SD, Div. 1 1989] [rejecting petitioner's contention that he should be treated as after-born child, where petitioner was born out of wedlock prior to execution of testator's will, because he was not known to testator until after execution of will]). However, as the movants correctly note, those matters are distinguishable inasmuch as there was evidence suggesting that the testators in those cases

---

[3]   If an after-born child has not asserted a claim in the Surrogate's Court during the pendency of the estate administration, EPTL 5–3.4 provides that such a claim can be raised in the Supreme Court. The after-born child can then seek reimbursement from the beneficiaries.

might have known of the children at the time of the execution of their respective wills. On the other hand, the case of *Bailey v. Warren* (319 SW3d 185 [Tx Ct App 2010]), which interpreted a Texas statute similar to EPTL 5–3.2, is analogous. In *Bailey*, the petitioner was deemed not to be an after-born child of the decedent pursuant to Tex. Prob.Code § 67(c)[4] and, therefore, was not entitled to an intestate share of the decedent's estate, because he was born 12 years before the decedent executed his will.

We acknowledge that the movants' position is somewhat sympathetic considering that adopted children, even those born prior to the execution of a will, are considered after-born children pursuant to case law. Our review of the statutes of our sister states has revealed that in California, the legislature has enacted a statute which could have afforded the movants an opportunity to demonstrate that the sole reason the decedent did not provide for them in his will was because he was unaware of their birth. Pursuant to the California Probate Code, if a child can prove that a decedent failed to provide for him or her in a testamentary instrument "solely because . . . [the testator] was unaware of [his or her birth]," such a child may inherit from the decedent's estate as if the decedent had died intestate (Cal Probate Code § 21622 [entitled "Decedent's erroneous belief or lack of knowledge; child's share of estate"]).[5] This plainly demonstrates that if so-called after-known children are to inherit in New York in the same manner as after-born children to prevent an inadvertent disinheritance, such an intent must be expressed by the Legislature and not the courts.

Accordingly, the order is affirmed.

Why is the after-born child different from the after-known child? How confident are we regarding the testator's intent? If the testator did not address the situation and the legislature is not confident about what the testator wanted, can the legislature choose the

---

[4] Tex. Prob.Code § 67 provides that if a testator has a child or children at the time the testator makes a will and, upon the testator's death, leaves a child or children born or adopted after the making of the will and not provided for in the will, the after-born or after-adopted children, unless provided for by settlement, succeed to the same portion of the testator's estate as they would have been entitled to if the testator had died intestate (effective until January 1, 2014).

[5] Moreover, unlike New York, several states (*see e.g.* Ala. Code § 43–8–91; Conn. Gen. Stat. § 45a–257b[c]; Idaho Code § 15–2–302 [b]; 18–A Me Rev. Stat. Ann. § 2–302[b]; Mo Rev. Stat. § 474.240 [2]; Neb Rev. Stat. § 30–2321[b]; NJ Stat. Ann. 3B:5–16[c]; SC Code Ann. § 62–2–302), including California (*see* CA Probate Code § 21622), have enacted statutes providing that a child can inherit from a decedent as if the decedent died intestate, if that child can prove that he or she was not provided for in the will solely because the decedent believed that the child was dead.

default rule on the basis of fairness? Would the children in *Gilmore* have prevailed under the UPC?

UPC § 2–302

SECTION 2–302. OMITTED CHILD.

(a) [Parent-Child Relationship Established After Execution of Will.] Except as provided in subsection (b), if a testator becomes a parent of a child after the execution of the testator's will and fails to provide in the will for the child, the omitted child receives a share in the estate as follows:

(1) If the testator had no child living when the testator executed the will, the omitted child receives a share in the estate equal in value to that which the child would have received had the testator died intestate, unless the will devised all or substantially all of the estate to another parent of the omitted child and that parent survives the testator and is entitled to take under the will.

(2) If the testator had one or more children living when the testator executed the will, and the will devised property or an interest in property to one or more of the then-living children, the omitted child is entitled to share in the testator's estate as follows:

(A) The portion of the testator's estate in which the omitted child is entitled to share is limited to devises made to the testator's then-living children under the will.

(B) The omitted child is entitled to receive the share of the testator's estate, as limited in subparagraph (A), that the child would have received had the testator included all omitted children with the children to whom devises were made under the will and had given an equal share of the estate to each child.

(C) To the extent feasible, the interest granted the omitted child under this section must be of the same character, whether equitable or legal, present or future, as that devised to the testator's then-living children under the will.

(D) In the satisfaction of a share provided by this paragraph, devises to the testator's children who were living when the will was executed abate ratably. In abating the devises of the then-living children, the court shall preserve to the maximum extent possible the character of the testamentary plan adopted by the testator.

(b) [Intentional Omission of Child; Provision for Child Outside Will.] Neither subsection (a)(1) nor subsection (a)(2) applies if:

(1) it appears from the will that the omission was intentional; or

(2) the testator provided for the omitted child by transfer outside the will and the intent that the transfer be in lieu of a testamentary provision is shown by the testator's statements or is reasonably inferred from the amount of the transfer or other evidence.

(c) [Omission of Child Believed Dead.] If at the time of execution of the will the testator fails to provide in the will for a living child solely because the testator believes the child to be dead, the child is entitled to share in the estate as if the child were an omitted child.

(d) [Abatement.] In the satisfaction of a share provided by subsection (a)(1), devises made by the will abate under Section 3–902.

Problem 4.31: O executes a will giving substantially all of O's assets to X. O adopts C. O dies. X is C's other parent. Does C take an intestate share under UPC § 2–302?

Problem 4.32: O adopts A and B. O executes a will giving $30,000 to A and $15,000 in trust to B. O adopts C. O dies. Does C take an intestate share?

E. CONTRACTS RELATING TO WILLS

Contracts to make or revoke a will serve, or might serve, various purposes. Sometimes the contract is entered as a form of payment for services performed for the decedent. Other times the contract is designed by two parties, often spouses, to provide for a third party, who usually will have standing to enforce the contract. However, it might be harder to prove a contract relating to a will than it is to prove other contracts. Some jurisdictions require clear and convincing evidence to establish a contract relating to a will. One reason for this is that a will remains ambulatory, both revocable and amendable, until death. Enforcement of a contract relating to a will runs contrary to that traditional and important characteristic of a will.

UPC § 2–514

SECTION 2–514. CONTRACTS CONCERNING SUCCESSION. A contract to make a will or devise, or not to revoke a will or devise, or to die intestate, if executed after the effective date of this [article], may be established only by (i) provisions of a will stating material provisions of the contract, (ii) an express reference in a will to a contract and extrinsic evidence proving the terms of the contract, or (iii) a writing signed by the decedent evidencing the contract. The execution of a joint will or mutual wills does not create a presumption of a contract not to revoke the will or wills.

There are a couple of problems that arise when a survivor claims that the decedent breached a contract by failing to make a devise in the decedent's will.

> Example 4.33: In a writing signed by S, S promises spouse O that S will take care of O and O promises that O will devise Blackacre to S. O tells S that O agrees to the deal. S performs by taking care of O. O dies without having executed a will devising Blackacre to S. Without more, S cannot establish a contract under UPC § 2–514 because O did not sign the writing. However, the UPC does not prevent S from recovering in quantum meruit for the value of the services rendered.

The UPC does not recognize part-performance as a means of establishing the contract. Neither did the Statute of Frauds. However, courts engrafted that means of establishing a contract onto the Statute of Frauds. Perhaps some courts will do the same with the UPC in order to avoid unjust enrichment. But the writing requirement is not the only problem.

> Example 4.34: In a writing signed by S, S promises spouse O that S will take care of O and O promises O will devise Blackacre to S. O signs the agreement. S takes care of O. O dies without having executed a will devising Blackacre to S. Although this writing satisfies the signature requirement of UPC § 2–514, a court might refuse to enforce the terms of

the deal on the ground that S had a preexisting duty to care for O and, therefore, S offered O no consideration in return for Blackacre.

Similarly, services already rendered would not qualify as consideration for a promise to devise. And, in one case, a will leaving all property, which turned out to be nothing, was deemed no consideration for a promise to leave a large estate. *Levis v. Hammond*, 100 N.W.2d 638 (Iowa 1960). *But see Kitchen v. Estate of Blue*, 498 N.E.2d 41 (Ind. Ct. App. 1986) ($300 estate sufficient consideration for $130,000 estate). However, do not forget about other potential causes of action. If a person makes a promise that he does not intend to keep, he or his estate may be liable for fraud.

Under the UPC and in the majority of states, mutual (or reciprocal or mirror image) wills do not raise a presumption that they were executed pursuant to a contract not to revoke them. But, in some instances, courts have inferred contracts to not revoke a will when that will is a joint will, which is a will signed by two testators (often spouses).

> Example 4.35: A and B sign a joint will that leaves Blackacre to X after the death of both. A dies. B changes his mind and revokes the will. X sues to enforce an implicit contract not to revoke the will. X sometimes succeeds. However, consistent with UPC § 2–514's presumption, courts in most cases have refused to find a contract not to revoke from the mere execution of the joint will, leaving X with no recourse for being removed unilaterally from a joint testamentary plan. Indeed, in *In re Estate of Armijo*, 31 P.3d 372, 374 (N.M. 2001), the court did not find such a contract even where the joint will stated, "we agree that the provisions hereof shall not be changed." Joint wills are usually a bad idea and are not even allowed in France and Italy.

Remedies vary for a breach of contract relating to a will. Traditionally, although not always today, probate courts did not enforce contracts relating to wills. As a result, such agreements did not prevent the probate of a will, much less mandate the execution of a will. However, a remedy might be obtained in a different court. Some cases grant a cause of action against the estate, making the claimant a creditor of the estate, but with limited time to make a claim. Other cases impose a constructive trust against the recipients of the estate on behalf of the contract beneficiary. Courts have also varied in the ways they have treated conflicting claims of contract beneficiaries and spouses with rights in either community property or the statutory elective share (about which more later).

Even where courts will enforce contracts relating to wills, such contracts are rarely the best way to achieve the goals of the parties to the contract, as they generate a lot of litigation. In addition, they are often not flexible enough when circumstances, including tax rules, change. A trust is always a better vehicle for achieving the goals of the parties.

CHAPTER 5

AVOIDING THE DEFAULT RULES BY MEANS OTHER THAN A WILL

■ ■ ■

Execution of a will is one way to avoid the rules of descent and distribution, but not the only way. This chapter explores what are sometimes called will substitutes, mechanisms for transferring assets outside of probate. Note that these alternatives rarely obviate a client's need for a will. For comprehensive estate planning, they should be viewed as ways to reduce the assets transferred by will or intestacy rather than ways to avoid the execution of a will.

A. INTER VIVOS GIFTS

One obvious way to prevent assets from passing through probate is to donate the assets before death, in other words, to make a gift inter vivos. Making a gift requires, of course, that the donor be competent and the donee be capable of taking title. The law recognizes two kinds, ordinary inter vivos gifts and gifts causa mortis. Ordinary gifts require intent, delivery, and acceptance. Intent is the subjective intent to make a present transfer of title, an intent that the ownership changes immediately. Delivery is some act that evinces that intent. Delivery could be by delivery of the actual item or by delivery of a deed or symbol. Acceptance is presumed, but the presumption may be rebutted. Once an ordinary gift is made, it is irrevocable; title has transferred. Because it is not ambulatory, an ordinary inter vivos gift of complete legal title does not substitute well for a will.

A gift causa mortis has the same requirements, but adds a couple more. The gift causa mortis must be made in apprehension of imminent death and the donor must die of the anticipated cause. Unlike an ordinary gift, a gift causa mortis is revocable. It is automatically revoked if the donor survives the anticipated peril. And it can be volitionally revoked by the donor saying he revokes the gift. It does not serve well as a substitute for a will because it

495

requires the apprehension of imminent death, which is an unusual planning situation.

It should be noted that the other forms of will substitute discussed below often include a gift. For example, a gratuitous transfer of title from a donor into a joint tenancy or an irrevocable trust is at its heart a gift. And a gratuitous transfer of property into community property would also be a gift.

B. SHARED PROPERTY

1.   CONCURRENT INTERESTS WITH THE RIGHT OF SURVIVORSHIP

Two of the common law's concurrent interests, the joint tenancy and the tenancy by the entirety (or "entireties"), have as one of their attributes a right of survivorship. This right of survivorship means that such a concurrent interest holder's interest vanishes or evaporates at her death. The rights of the surviving holder, or holders, swell to absorb the whole. So, although the common law did not consider this shifting of ownership to be a transfer between owners, it does have the effect of transferring a part interest away from one cotenant when she dies. To a degree then, a concurrent interest with a right of survivorship can be used to accomplish a testamentary transfer.

> Example 5.01: O transfers Blackacre to X. X transfers Blackacre to O and O's spouse, S, as tenants by the entirety. If O dies, S becomes the owner, and vice versa. Suppose that before O dies, O changes his mind and does not want to transfer to S when O dies. In some states, O cannot unilaterally sever the tenancy by the entirety and eliminate S's right of survivorship other than by divorcing S. And even if O does divorce S, S still owns half of Blackacre, beyond the reach of O. So, the gift from O to S of one-half interest cannot be revoked, unlike a gift in a will.

> Example 5.02: O transfers Blackacre to X. X transfers Blackacre to O and J as joint tenants with the right of survivorship. If O dies, J becomes the owner, and vice versa. Suppose that before O dies, O changes his mind and does not want to transfer to J when O dies. O can unilaterally sever the joint tenancy, turning it into a tenancy in common and eliminating the right of survivorship. However, J still owns

half of Blackacre. So, although revocation of the right of survivorship in the joint tenancy is easy to accomplish, the transfer of one-half interest to J is a completed gift and is not revocable, unlike a gift in a will.

Example 5.03: O and J pay equal consideration to T for a transfer of Blackacre to O and J as joint tenants with the right of survivorship. In this situation, where the parties contribute equally and wish to make reciprocal gifts at death, the joint tenancy can act much like reciprocal wills. Suppose O changes his mind and does not want J to take all of Blackacre at O's death. O can unilaterally sever the joint tenancy, turning it into a tenancy in common and eliminating both of their rights of survivorship. O and J end up with equal halves held in tenancy in common. And if O needs to do so, O can petition for partition to separate their one-half interests entirely.

The joint tenancy is available in nearly all states. Traditionally, a joint tenancy was created if, at the moment of transfer to the parties, there were four "unities": time, title, interest, and possession. Unity of time means that the joint tenants got their interests at the same time. Unity of title means that they got their interests from the same transfer of title. Unity of interest means that they got the same interest, equal shares. And unity of possession means that the joint tenants have the same right to possession. The joint tenancy is unilaterally severable, so that any joint tenant can convert her interest into a tenancy in common and eliminate the right of survivorship.

The tenancy by the entirety is available in about half of the states that do not have community property. Some states allow it for both personalty and realty and some states allow it only for realty. Under the common law, the tenancy by the entirety was created if, at the time of transfer, there were five unities: the four listed above plus the unity of marriage. The unity of marriage means that only married couples can hold property as tenants by the entirety. The right of survivorship is the same as for the joint tenancy. The big difference between the tenancy by the entirety and the joint tenancy relates to severance. Traditionally, neither tenant by the entirety could unilaterally sever the tenancy by the entirety or in any other way eliminate the right of survivorship, other than by divorce. For that reason, one advantage of a tenancy by the entirety in some jurisdictions is that the property is not subject to the claims of creditors of either spouse alone, although it is subject to the claims of creditors of both spouses. This special protection from the claims of creditors of one spouse is an attractive feature of the tenancy by the entirety.

In some situations, the creation of legal concurrent interests will fit the needs of your client or clients. But if the parties do not contribute equally to the acquisition of the asset, one party will be making an irrevocable gift to the other. Another reason that a legal concurrent interest might not work well is that the parties will be tied up with each other in the use of the asset, which can lead to management conflicts along with holdout and free rider problems. This is especially troublesome when the asset being held is one that lasts forever, such as land.

2.   COMMUNITY PROPERTY

Concurrent interests should be distinguished from community property, which is a form of ownership that can be created in twelve states today. Community-property rules treat spouses as equal partners in the earnings of either. Community property includes income from work and earnings on community property accruing to either spouse during marriage. Depending on the state, community property can also include income from separate property during the marriage. Community property is automatic in nine states: Louisiana, Texas, New Mexico, Arizona, California, Nevada, Idaho, Washington, and Wisconsin. Spouses can choose to hold assets as community property in three more states: Alaska, Tennessee, and South Dakota.

Community property is owned by the marital community, with each spouse having rights in the property. When one spouse dies, she can devise one half of the community property along with her separate property. The surviving spouse keeps the other half of the community property. The net result is that one spouse might earn income during life, but half automatically belongs to her spouse and that half is beyond the earner's control when she dies.

Section 1014 of the Internal Revenue Code offers favorable income tax treatment to community property if it is sold between the deaths of the spouses. To see how, start by examining the tax treatment of a sole owner. When an owner sells an asset, the owner ordinarily pays taxes on the gains from that sale. If the owner bought a bond for $100, the "basis" in the bond is $100. If the owner sells the bond for $300, the owner subtracts the basis and pays tax on the $200 gain. If the owner dies before selling the bond, the basis of the bond is stepped up to $300, the value at death. If the owner's successor then sells the bond for $300, the successor pays no income tax on the sale. Now change the example to involve two spouses purchasing that same bond for $100 (but not held as community property). When one dies, that spouse's half of the basis is stepped up, with the result that one half of the basis would be $150 and the other half would remain $50. If the surviving spouse sells the bond, the survivor pays income tax on the $100 gain on the survivor's half, but no tax on the decedent's half of the bond. But if the bond is held as community property, then the entire basis is stepped up at the time one spouse dies. The surviving spouse can then sell the bond for $300 and pay no income tax on the sale. Do not advise clients to transmute community property into separate property unless you have considered the loss of this special tax treatment.

In some community-property states, there is a new form of ownership called community property with right of survivorship. This allows spouses to hold their community property in a way that will cause an automatic transfer to the other spouse at the death of one.

C. PAYMENT-ON-DEATH DESIGNATIONS

Pay-on-death (POD) designations can function much more like a will than can concurrent interests. They have the power to transfer title at death and are revocable before death. Because they have those two attributes, they are testamentary in nature. And because they are testamentary in nature, courts in the past found them to be ineffective unless they were executed in compliance with the formalities of Wills Acts. Now, they have been accepted by many courts and UPC § 6–101 as being valid without regard to compliance with statutory formalities for wills. The UPC accomplishes this by declaring them to be nontestamentary, which takes them out of the wills requirements and allows them to be effective without being executed as a will. Pay-on-death agreements raise various issues, such as whether they are revoked automatically by a change of status and whether a beneficiary can be changed in a will.

1. LIFE INSURANCE

Life insurance policies were the first pay-on-death instruments to be granted an exception to the usual rule that a testamentary instrument must comply with the Wills Act formalities. As a result, for many years, it was important to be able to distinguish insurance contracts from other agreements. The essence of insurance is that it has a contingent payoff that in effect shifts risks from a person who is averse to bearing the risk to another person who has less aversion to bearing the risk. The distinction between transferring risk and creating risk differentiates a policy of insurance from a gamble.

One issue that has arisen regarding life insurance is whether divorce automatically revokes beneficiary designations in favor of the former spouse and the former spouse's relatives. The UPC section dealing with divorce, UPC § 2–804, expands the automatic revocation of devises in wills to include automatic revocation of dispositions in other nonprobate transfers, including life insurance. An exception is made for private instruments and court orders expressly providing otherwise.

However, in some cases, federal law may preempt state law, with the result that the proceeds pass to the former spouse. In *Hillman v. Maretta*, 569 U.S. 483 (2013), the decedent had life insurance under the Federal Employees' Group Life Insurance Act of 1954. The decedent divorced, remarried, and died, all without changing the policy's designated beneficiary, his former wife. She claimed the proceeds of the policy. The decedent's widow then sued the former wife for those proceeds, bringing a cause of action established by a Virginia statute. The former wife defended on the ground that the Virginia statute was preempted by the federal law. The Supreme Court upheld that defense, yielding a result that seems contrary to the intent of the decedent.

Another of the issues that arise regarding insurance policies is whether the owner of the policy can change the designated beneficiary by a will.

COOK V. EQUITABLE LIFE ASSUR. SOC. OF U.S.
Court of Appeals of Indiana, First District, 1981
428 N.E.2d 110

RATLIFF, J.

* * *

FACTS

Douglas purchased a whole life insurance policy on March 13, 1953, from Equitable, naming his wife at that time, Doris, as the beneficiary. On March 5, 1965, Douglas and Doris were divorced. The divorce decree made no provision regarding the insurance policy, but did state the following: "It is further understood and agreed between the parties hereto that the provisions of this agreement shall be in full satisfaction of all claims by either of said parties against the other, including alimony, support and maintenance money."

After the divorce Douglas ceased paying the premiums on his life insurance policy, and Equitable notified him on July 2, 1965, that because the premium due on March 9, 1965, had not been paid, his whole life policy was automatically converted to a paid-up term policy with an expiration date of June 12, 1986. The policy contained the following provision with respect to beneficiaries:

> "BENEFICIARY. The Owner may change the beneficiary from time to time prior to the death of the Insured, by written notice to the Society, but any such change shall be effective only if it is endorsed on this policy by the Society, and, if there is a written assignment of this policy in force and on file with the Society (other than an assignment to the Society as security for an advance), such a change may be made only with the written consent of the assignee. The interest of a beneficiary shall be subject to the rights of any assignee of record with the Society.
>
> Upon endorsement of a change of beneficiary upon this policy by the Society, such change shall take effect as of the date the written notice thereof was signed, whether or not the Insured is living at the time of endorsement, but without further liability on the part of the Society with respect to any proceeds paid by the Society or applied under any option in this policy prior to such endorsement.
>
> If the executors or administrators of the Insured be not expressly designated as beneficiary, any part of the proceeds of this policy with respect to which there is no designated beneficiary living at the death of the Insured and no assignee entitled thereto, will be payable in a single sum to the children of the Insured who survive the Insured, in equal shares, or should none survive, then to the Insured's executors or administrators."

On December 24, 1965, Douglas married Margaret, and a son, Daniel, was born to them. On June 7, 1976, Douglas made a holographic will in which he bequeathed his insurance policy with Equitable Life to his wife and son, Margaret and Daniel:

"Last Will & Testimint [sic]

I Douglas D. Cook

Being of sound mind do Hereby leave all my Worldly posessions [sic] to my Wife and son, Margaret A. Cook & Daniel Joseph Cook. being my Bank Accounts at Irwin Union Bank & trust to their Welfair [sic] my Insurance policys [sic] with Common Welth of Ky. and Equitable Life. all my machinecal [sic] tools to be left to my son if He is Interested in Working with them If not to be sold and money used for their welfair [sic] all my Gun Collection Kept as long as they, my Wife & Son [sic] and then sold and money used for their welfair [sic]

I sighn [sic] this

June 7—1976

at Barth Conty

Hospital Room

1114 Bed 2

/s/ Douglas D. Cook

/s/ 6-7-76 Margaret A. Cook wife

/s/ Chas. W. Winkler

/s/ Mary A. Winkler"

This will was admitted to probate in Bartholomew Superior Court after Douglas's death on June 9, 1979. On August 24, 1979, Margaret filed a claim with Equitable for the proceeds of Douglas's policy, but Equitable deposited the proceeds, along with its complaint in interpleader, with the Bartholomew Circuit Court on March 14, 1980. Discovery was made; interrogatories and affidavits were filed; and all parties moved for summary judgment. The trial court found that there was no genuine issue as to any material fact respecting Doris's claim to the proceeds of the policy and entered judgment in her favor as to the amount of the proceeds plus interest, a total of $3,154.09. Margaret and Daniel appeal from this award.

ISSUE

Is the trial court's entry of summary judgment in this case contrary to Indiana law because the court entered judgment in favor of the named beneficiary of an insurance policy rather than in compliance with the insured testator's intent as expressed in his will?

DISCUSSION AND DECISION

Margaret and Daniel recognize that matters relating to summary judgment are controlled by Ind.Rules of Procedure, Trial Rule 56. Trial Rule 56(C) states, in pertinent part: "The judgment sought shall be rendered forthwith if the pleadings, depositions, answers to interrogatories, and admissions on file, together with the affidavits and testimony, if any, show that there is no genuine issue as to any material fact and that the moving party is entitled to a judgment as a matter of law." Margaret and Daniel do not dispute the facts in this case, yet they contend that the court's entry of summary judgment was erroneous because Indiana law does not require strict compliance with the terms of an insurance policy relative to a change of beneficiary in all cases. They argue, therefore, that strict compliance with policy provisions is not required for the protection of either the insurer or the insured once the proceeds have been paid by the insurer into court in an action for interpleader and that the court should shape its relief in this case upon the equitable principle "that the insured's express and unambiguous intent should be given effect." However, Margaret and Daniel cite no Indiana cases for this proposition stating that Indiana courts have never considered the precise factual combination giving rise to this appeal and citing instead cases from Minnesota and Arkansas. The latter jurisdiction they denominate as the leading proponent of the theory they espouse: "that the provisions of a Will, either alone or in conjunction with supporting circumstances, effectively change the beneficiary of a life insurance policy."

Doris agrees that less than strict compliance with policy change requirements may be adequate to change a beneficiary where circumstances show the insured has done everything within his power to effect the change. Nevertheless, Doris asserts that Indiana adheres to the majority rule finding an attempt to change the beneficiary of a life insurance policy by will, without more, to be ineffectual. We agree with Doris.

Margaret and Daniel are correct in asserting that there are no Indiana cases involving precisely the same set of facts as occur in this case. Nevertheless, there is ample case law in this jurisdiction to support the trial court's determination. Almost one hundred years ago our supreme court in *Holland v. Taylor*, (1887) 111 Ind. 121, 12 N.E. 116, enunciated the general rule still followed in Indiana: an attempt to change the beneficiary of a life insurance contract by will and in disregard of the methods prescribed under the contract will be unsuccessful. In *Holland*, the assured and testator, Charles D. Taylor, had been issued a benefit certificate by Royal Arcanum, a mutual benefit society, in which certificate Taylor's daughter, Anna Laura, was the named beneficiary. The certificate provided that Taylor could change the named beneficiary by following certain procedures. On the same day that Taylor applied for the certificate he made his will in which he acknowledged the certificate for his daughter's benefit, but also provided that the certificate benefits, under certain circumstances, were to inure to the benefit of his wife or estate rather than as provided in the certificate for the exclusive benefit of his daughter. After Taylor's death, Holland was appointed guardian of Anna Laura and brought an action requesting that the executors of Taylor's estate pay over to him the fund which they had collected from the Royal Arcanum. The trial court overruled a demurrer to the answer and held that the executors were entitled to dispose of the fund according to the will. On appeal, our supreme court reversed with instructions to the trial court to sustain appellant's demurrer to the answer. In doing so the court stated at 111 Ind. 130–31, 12 N.E. 116:

> "Taylor, the assured, neither changed, nor attempted to change, the beneficiary in the mode and manner provided in the by-laws. He could not accomplish that end, nor affect the ultimate rights of the beneficiary by a will. Upon his death, therefore, Anna Laura became entitled to the amount to be paid upon the certificate, as her absolute property; appellees' executors, having collected from the Royal Arcanum, hold the amount so collected in trust for her, but they have no right to control, manage, and dispose of the fund as directed by the will, because, as to that fund, the will is of no effect."

Indiana courts have recognized exceptions to the general rule that strict compliance with policy requirements is necessary to effect a change of beneficiary. Three exceptions were noted by this court in

Modern Brotherhood v. Matkovitch, (1914) 56 Ind.App. 8, 14, 104 N.E. 795, and reiterated in *Heinzman v. Whiteman*, (1923) 81 Ind.App. 29, 36, 139 N.E. 329, *trans. denied*:

> " '1. If the society has waived a strict compliance with its own rules, and in pursuance of a request of the insured to change the beneficiary, has issued a new certificate to him, the original beneficiary will not be heard to complain that the course indicated by the regulations was not pursued. 2. If it be beyond the power of the insured to comply literally with the regulations, a court of equity will treat the change as having been legally made. 3. If the insured has pursued the course pointed out by the laws of the association, and has done all in his power to change the beneficiary; but before the new certificate is actually issued, he dies, a court of equity will decree that to be done which ought to be done, and act as though the certificate had been issued.' "

In *Modern Brotherhood* the insured had attempted to change the beneficiary of a mutual benefit insurance certificate in accordance with the terms of the certificate, but was thwarted in her attempts to do so by wrongful acts of the original beneficiary. It was impossible, therefore, for the insured to comply literally with the bylaws and regulations of the society for changing beneficiaries even though she notified the society of her desires to change the beneficiary on her certificate and also indicated those desires in her will. The court on appeal held that the trial court had erred in sustaining a demurrer to paragraph three of the complaint which stated facts sufficient to constitute an action upon equitable principles, but had properly sustained a demurrer to paragraph four of the complaint which merely stated that the insured had changed the beneficiaries of her certificate by will. The court repeated the rule of *Holland* at 56 Ind.App. 16, 104 N.E. 795: "Our courts have indicated that the rule in this State is, that without some other fact or facts, in aid of the change the insured cannot change the beneficiary by the execution of a will."

The public policy considerations undergirding this rule and its limited exceptions involve protection of the rights of all the parties concerned and should not be viewed, as appellants advocate, for the exclusive protection of the insurer. Indiana, in fact, has specifically rejected this position. In *Stover v. Stover*, (1965) 137 Ind.App. 578, 204 N.E.2d 374, 380, *on rehearing* 205 N.E.2d 178, *trans. denied*, the court recognized an insured's right to rely on the provisions of the policy in regard to change of beneficiary:

> "We must reject appellant's contention that the provisions set forth in the certificate, as mentioned above, are for the exclusive benefit of the insurance company and may be waived at will. The deceased insured himself is entitled to rely upon such provisions that he may at all times know to whom the proceeds of the insurance shall be payable."

In *Holland* the court also recognized that the beneficiary had a right in the executed contract which was subject to defeat only by a change of beneficiary which had been executed in accord with the terms of the insurance contract: "In that contract Anna Laura, the beneficiary, had such an interest as that she had, and has, the right to insist that in order to cut her out, the change of beneficiary should be made in the manner provided in the contract." And in *Borgman v. Borgman*, (1981) Ind.App., 420 N.E.2d 1261, *trans. denied*, this court held that an interpleader action by a life insurance company does not affect the parties' rights.

Clearly it is in the interest of insurance companies to require and to follow certain specified procedures in the change of beneficiaries of its policies so that they may pay over benefits to persons properly entitled to them without subjection to claims by others of whose rights they had no notice or knowledge. Certainly it is also in the interest of beneficiaries themselves to be entitled to prompt payment of benefits by insurance companies which do not withhold payment until the will has been probated in the fear of later litigation which might result from having paid the wrong party. The legislature reflects this concern with certainty in the area of insurance beneficiaries in Ind.Code 27–1–12–14 by permitting changes of beneficiaries in insurance policies upon written notice to the insurance company when accompanied by the policy. Finally, society's interest in the conservation of judicial energy and expense will be served where the rule and its limited exceptions are clearly stated and rigorously applied.

Appellants argue that if, indeed, the will alone is not enough to effect the intended change, the added circumstance of divorce, "along with other supporting circumstances," which they fail to set forth, should be sufficient to substantiate the fact that Douglas intended Margaret and Daniel to receive his insurance money. To give effect to such intent they feel is a logical extension of *Modern Brotherhood* and would not abrogate existing Indiana law. We disagree.

It is a truism that in appeals from the granting of summary judgment we shall construe all materials on file in favor of appellants and resolve all doubts against the appellees to determine if a genuine issue of material fact exists. Nevertheless, unsupported allegations in a brief are not viewed as facts. And, even though a party against whom a motion for summary judgment is made need not present his entire case in a summary judgment proceeding, he must come forth with specific facts to show that there is a genuine issue as to the material facts. The rule in Indiana, as we have stated several times, recognizes substantial compliance with the requirements of the policy as sufficient to change a beneficiary so long as "the insured has done everything in his power to effect such a change."

Under the law of Indiana, therefore, in order for appellants to have defeated the motion for summary judgment in this case they must have made some showing that the insured had done all within his powers or all that reasonably could have been expected of him to comply with the policy provisions respecting a change of beneficiary, but that through no fault of his own he was unable to achieve his goal. Here there is no such indication or implication. Douglas was divorced in March of 1965 and remarried in December 1965. He was notified in July 1965 of the change in his policy, but took no action. A son was born of his second marriage. Eleven years after his divorce Douglas attempted to change the beneficiary of his insurance policy by a holographic will, but did not notify Equitable. He then lived three years after making that will. There is no indication that Douglas took any action in the fourteen years between his divorce from Doris and his death, other than the making of the will, to change the beneficiary of his life insurance policy from Doris to Margaret and Daniel. Surely, if Douglas had wanted to change the beneficiary he had ample time and opportunity to comply with the policy requirements. Nothing in the record suggests otherwise.

In *Hoess v. Continental Assurance Co., supra,* the court was presented with a situation in which a decedent likewise had failed to name his new wife as the beneficiary of his life insurance policy after his divorce. However, prior to his death, decedent orally requested his agent to change the beneficiary, but the change was not made. The policy required written notification. The court held:

"And where the policy or the contract of life insurance contains the right of the insured to change the beneficiary, such right must be exercised in the manner provided in such policy or contract. If the decedent knowing who was designated as beneficiary, desired to change, it was incumbent upon him to exercise his right to change the beneficiary as the master policy provided under Section 9 quoted above. A mere oral request in and of itself is not sufficient to comply with the terms of the policy governing a change of beneficiary.

This is not such a case where the insured has done all in his power which he can do to change the beneficiary, and then some intervening cause or his death before the change is effective has occurred preventing the effectuation of the change so that a court of equity will decree that to be done which ought to be done.

Nor does the fact that the appellee is designated as 'wife' alter the situation. The term 'wife' is merely descriptio personae.

'* * * and the fact that the one who otherwise answers the description does not, or did not at the inception of the insurance, have the legal status of wife of the insured does not prevent her from taking as beneficiary if it is otherwise clear that she is the person intended, assuming that she is eligible to designation as beneficiary and that the misdescription of her as "wife" does not amount to a breach of warranty or misrepresentation avoiding the insurance.'

And while the rights of a divorced beneficiary may be terminated by facts in addition to the divorce, in the absence of a policy provision to the contrary or regulation thereof by statute, the rights of a beneficiary under a policy of life insurance are not affected merely by the fact that the beneficiary named thereunder has been divorced from the assured subsequent to the issuance of the policy."

164 N.E.2d 129.

We may be sympathetic to the cause of the decedent's widow and son, and it might seem that a departure from the general rule in an attempt to do equity under these facts would be noble. Nevertheless, such a course is fraught with the dangers of eroding a solidly paved pathway of the law and leaving in its stead only a gaping hole of uncertainty. Public policy requires that the insurer, insured, and beneficiary alike should be able to rely on the certainty that policy provisions pertaining to the naming and changing of beneficiaries will control except in extreme situations. We, therefore, invoke a maxim equally as venerable as the one upon which appellants rely in the determination of this cause: Equity aids the vigilant, not those who slumber on their rights.

Judgment affirmed.

Most, but not all, courts have agreed with Cook on the issue of whether a will can change the designated beneficiary of a life insurance policy. This majority rule complicates your job as a lawyer. You should ask your clients whether they have life insurance and other assets for which the beneficiaries might be governed by contract and, if they do, you should warn them that they need to comply with the terms of those agreements if they wish to change the beneficiaries. Cook also shows the potential injustice of the majority rule. What are the countervailing benefits for the insurer, the insured, the beneficiaries, and society if designated insurance beneficiaries cannot be changed by will?

2. PAY-ON-DEATH ACCOUNTS

In addition to insurance companies, there are many other financial organizations that offer contracts that include pay-on-death (POD) provisions. There are POD brokerage accounts, POD mutual funds, POD stocks, individual retirement accounts (IRAs), and POD medical savings accounts, the last two of which have tax advantages. As noted above, many of these are now authorized by UPC § 6–101. And, as noted above, they raise issues as to whether and how the designation of a beneficiary can be revoked.

(a) Bank Accounts

One type of account that has proved quite troublesome is the ordinary bank account with more than one name on the account. It is often hard to tell what sort of legal arrangement was established by such a "joint account". There are at least four possibilities. One possibility is a true joint tenancy, which means that each account holder owns an equal share of the funds and a right of survivorship that increases the share if another joint tenant dies. A second possibility is a tenancy in common, which might have unequal ownership and does not have a right of survivorship. A third possibility is a convenience or agency account, which is owned by the depositor and includes no right of survivorship; this is an account set up to make it easier for others to help the depositor. And a fourth possibility is a POD account, where the depositor is the owner, but the other persons on the account take at the depositor's death.

Does the deposit of money in a "joint account" create a presumption of a present gift to the non-depositor? Many states would say yes, meaning that the account is held in some form of concurrent interest. The UPC says that parties to a joint and survivor account separately own values in the account in proportion to their net contributions, so a deposit in the account is not a gift to others on the account. Under the UPC, this presumption can be overcome by clear and convincing evidence of an intent to make a gift, which of course often requires litigation to resolve. Some states avoid that litigation by making their presumption irrebuttable.

(b) Individual Retirement Accounts

Another type of POD account generating some litigation is the individual retirement account or IRA. As with other POD accounts, one issue is whether a will can change the designation of the beneficiary. There are at least two questions involved, one being whether the terms of the IRA allow the beneficiary to be changed by will. The other issue is whether state law allows the beneficiary to be changed by will, and some states do.

Both traditional and Roth IRAs give taxpayers an income tax break for saving for retirement. The traditional IRA allows contributions to be deducted from income in the year of contribution and not taxed until the year of withdrawal. Taxes are deferred on both the contributions and the earnings in the account. The Roth IRA does not allow a deduction in the year of contribution, thus requiring taxes to be paid upfront. However, ordinary withdrawals are free of taxes, meaning that the earnings escape tax entirely. Which type is better depends in part on whether the taxpayer can put more money into one account than the other. Which type is better also depends on the taxpayer's present and anticipated tax brackets. If the taxpayer's tax bracket will be higher at the time of withdrawal, that favors the Roth IRA. If the taxpayer's tax bracket will be lower at the time of withdrawal, that fact favors the traditional IRA. Of course, there are two components of a taxpayer's tax bracket that must be predicted in order to make the required comparison. One is how the earnings of the taxpayer will change over time. The other is whether the tax rates for the taxpayer's brackets will increase or decrease over time, which calls for predicting acts of Congress. Good luck with that. Some advisors recommend reducing risk by splitting deposits, part going to each type of account.

The income tax benefits of IRAs (and 401(k)s and 403(b)s) do not necessarily terminate at the death of the owner of the account. After the owner dies, delaying distributions to the beneficiaries defers the payment of taxes on those distributions. During that distribution period, the gains on the amounts that would have been paid in taxes accrue for the benefit of the beneficiaries. It is as if the government made an interest-free loan in the amount of the deferred tax. If the beneficiaries of the account are individuals, the distributions can often be stretched out over a period long enough to generate a sizable tax advantage. The distribution period for individual beneficiaries is also available to a trust that meets the requirements of Treasury Regulation § 1.401(a)(9)–4, A–5(b). By employing such a "see-through trust", a planner may be able to achieve the tax benefits available to individual beneficiaries while also taking advantage of the protections of assets held in trust, discussed infra.

3. EMPLOYER PENSIONS

Currently the most popular form of pension is the "defined-contribution" plan, in which the employer puts money in the employee's account in the plan upfront, leaving investment decisions and the risk of loss or benefit of gain to the employee. However, still common are the traditional "defined-benefit" plans, which dominated during the post-WWII era. Under a defined-benefit plan, the employer promises to provide certain benefits when the employee reaches a certain age and length of service. Although the employee has a legal right to any vested benefits, it is the employer's obligation to make sufficient deposits, which are then invested by the plan's trustees, to ensure that the vested benefits can be paid when due. The employee generally has no say in the investment of the contributions, but also does not bear the risk of loss or enjoy the benefit of gain through investment of the principal, this risk and benefit being born by the employer. Kenneth Glenn Dau-Schmidt, Promises to Keep: Ensuring the Payment of Americans' Pension

Benefits in the Wake of the Great Recession, 52 Washburn L.J. 393, at 401 (2013).

Both types of pension plan allow the beneficiary to designate a successor if the employee should die. And here we see the recurring question of whether state laws revoking testamentary dispositions also change POD beneficiary designations. Moreover, because these pension plans are covered by the Employee Retirement Income Security Act of 1974 (ERISA), there is the additional question of whether state law is preempted by the federal law.

EGELHOFF V. EGELHOFF EX REL. BREINER

Supreme Court of the United States, 2001
532 U.S. 141

THOMAS, J.

A Washington statute provides that the designation of a spouse as the beneficiary of a nonprobate asset is revoked automatically upon divorce. We are asked to decide whether the Employee Retirement Income Security Act of 1974 (ERISA) pre-empts that statute to the extent it applies to ERISA plans. We hold that it does.

I

Petitioner Donna Rae Egelhoff was married to David A. Egelhoff. Mr. Egelhoff was employed by the Boeing Company, which provided him with a life insurance policy and a pension plan. Both plans were governed by ERISA, and Mr. Egelhoff designated his wife as the beneficiary under both. In April 1994, the Egelhoffs divorced. Just over two months later, Mr. Egelhoff died intestate following an automobile accident. At that time, Mrs. Egelhoff remained the listed beneficiary under both the life insurance policy and the pension plan. The life insurance proceeds, totaling $46,000, were paid to her.

Respondents Samantha and David Egelhoff, Mr. Egelhoff's children by a previous marriage, are his statutory heirs under state law. They sued petitioner in Washington state court to recover the life insurance proceeds. Respondents relied on a Washington statute that provides:

"If a marriage is dissolved or invalidated, a provision made prior to that event that relates to the payment or transfer at death of the decedent's interest in a nonprobate asset in favor of or granting an interest or power to the decedent's former spouse is revoked. A provision affected by this section must be interpreted, and the nonprobate asset affected passes, as if the former spouse failed to survive the decedent, having died at the time of entry of the decree of dissolution or declaration of invalidity."

That statute applies to "all nonprobate assets, wherever situated, held at the time of entry by a superior court of this state of a decree of dissolution of marriage or a declaration of invalidity." It defines "nonprobate asset" to include "a life insurance policy, employee benefit plan, annuity or similar contract, or individual retirement account."

Respondents argued that they were entitled to the life insurance proceeds because the Washington statute disqualified Mrs. Egelhoff as a beneficiary, and in the absence of a qualified named beneficiary, the proceeds would pass to them as Mr. Egelhoff's heirs. In a separate action, respondents also sued to recover the pension plan benefits. Respondents again argued that the Washington statute disqualified Mrs. Egelhoff as a beneficiary and they were thus entitled to the benefits under the plan.

The trial courts, concluding that both the insurance policy and the pension plan "should be administered in accordance" with ERISA, granted summary judgment to petitioner in both cases. The Washington Court of Appeals consolidated the cases and reversed. It concluded that the Washington statute was not pre-empted by ERISA. Applying the statute, it held that respondents were entitled to the proceeds of both the insurance policy and the pension plan.

The Supreme Court of Washington affirmed. It held that the state statute, although applicable to "employee benefit plan[s]," does not "refe[r] to" ERISA plans to an extent that would require pre-emption, because it "does not apply immediately and exclusively to an ERISA plan, nor is the existence of such a plan essential to operation of the statute." It also held that the statute lacks a "connection with" an ERISA plan that would compel pre-emption. It emphasized that the statute "does not alter the nature of the plan itself, the administrator's fiduciary duties, or the requirements for plan administration." Nor, the court concluded, does the statute conflict with any specific provision of ERISA, including the antialienation provision, because it "does not operate to divert benefit plan proceeds from distribution under terms of the plan documents," but merely alters "the underlying circumstances to which the distribution scheme of [the] plan must be applied."

Courts have disagreed about whether statutes like that of Washington are pre-empted by ERISA. To resolve the conflict, we granted certiorari.

II

Petitioner argues that the Washington statute falls within the terms of ERISA's express pre-emption provision and that it is pre-empted by ERISA under traditional principles of conflict pre-emption. Because we conclude that the statute is expressly pre-empted by ERISA, we address only the first argument.

ERISA's pre-emption section, 29 U.S.C. § 1144(a), states that ERISA "shall supersede any and all State laws insofar as they may now or hereafter relate to any employee benefit plan" covered by ERISA. We have observed repeatedly that this broadly worded provision is "clearly expansive." But at the same time, we have recognized that the term "relate to" cannot be taken "to extend to the furthest stretch of its indeterminacy," or else "for all practical purposes pre-emption would never run its course."

We have held that a state law relates to an ERISA plan "if it has a connection with or reference to such a plan." Petitioner focuses on the "connection with" part of this inquiry. Acknowledging that "connection with" is scarcely more restrictive than "relate to," we have cautioned against an "uncritical literalism" that would make pre-emption turn on "infinite connections." Instead, "to determine whether a state law has the forbidden connection, we look both to 'the objectives of the ERISA statute as a guide to the scope of the state law that Congress understood would survive,' as well as to the nature of the effect of the state law on ERISA plans."

Applying this framework, petitioner argues that the Washington statute has an impermissible connection with ERISA plans. We agree. The statute binds ERISA plan administrators to a particular choice of rules for determining beneficiary status. The administrators must pay benefits to the beneficiaries chosen by state law, rather than to those identified in the plan documents. The statute thus implicates an area of core ERISA concern. In particular, it runs counter to ERISA's commands that a plan shall "specify the basis on which payments are made to and from the plan," § 1102(b)(4), and that the fiduciary shall administer the plan "in accordance with the documents and instruments governing the plan," § 1104(a)(1)(D), making payments to a "beneficiary" who is "designated by a participant, or by the terms of [the] plan."

§ 1002(8).[1] In other words, unlike generally applicable laws regulating "areas where ERISA has nothing to say," which we have upheld notwithstanding their incidental effect on ERISA plans, this statute governs the payment of benefits, a central matter of plan administration.

The Washington statute also has a prohibited connection with ERISA plans because it interferes with nationally uniform plan administration. One of the principal goals of ERISA is to enable employers "to establish a uniform administrative scheme, which provides a set of standard procedures to guide processing of claims and disbursement of benefits." Uniformity is impossible, however, if plans are subject to different legal obligations in different States.

The Washington statute at issue here poses precisely that threat. Plan administrators cannot make payments simply by identifying the beneficiary specified by the plan documents. Instead they must familiarize themselves with state statutes so that they can determine whether the named beneficiary's status has been "revoked" by operation of law. And in this context the burden is exacerbated by the choice-of-law problems that may confront an administrator when the employer is located in one State, the plan participant lives in another, and the participant's former spouse lives in a third. In such a situation, administrators might find that plan payments are subject to conflicting legal obligations.

To be sure, the Washington statute protects administrators from liability for making payments to the named beneficiary unless they have "actual knowledge of the dissolution or other invalidation of marriage," and it permits administrators to refuse to make payments until any dispute among putative beneficiaries is resolved. But if administrators do pay benefits, they will face the risk that a court might later find that they had "actual knowledge" of a divorce.

---

[1]   One can of course escape the conflict between the plan documents (which require making payments to the named beneficiary) and the statute (which requires making payments to someone else) by calling the statute an "invalidation" of the designation of the named beneficiary, and by observing that the plan documents are silent on whether "invalidation" is to occur upon divorce. The dissent employs just such an approach. See *post*, at 1331–1332 (opinion of BREYER, J.). Reading a clear statement as an ambiguous metastatement enables one to avoid all kinds of conflicts between seemingly contradictory texts. Suppose, for example, that the statute required that all pension benefits be paid to the Governor of Washington. That seems inconsistent with the plan documents (and with ERISA), but the inconsistency disappears if one calls the statute an "invalidation" of the principal and alternate beneficiary designations. After all, neither the plan nor ERISA actually *says* that beneficiaries *cannot* be invalidated in favor of the Governor. This approach exploits the logical inability of any text to contain a complete set of instructions for its own interpretation. It has the vice-or perhaps the virtue, depending upon one's point of view-of draining all language of its meaning.

If they instead decide to await the results of litigation before paying benefits, they will simply transfer to the beneficiaries the costs of delay and uncertainty.[3] Requiring ERISA administrators to master the relevant laws of 50 States and to contend with litigation would undermine the congressional goal of "minimiz[ing] the administrative and financial burden[s]" on plan administrators-burdens ultimately borne by the beneficiaries.

We recognize that all state laws create some potential for a lack of uniformity. But differing state regulations affecting an ERISA plan's "system for processing claims and paying benefits" impose "precisely the burden that ERISA pre-emption was intended to avoid." And as we have noted, the statute at issue here directly conflicts with ERISA's requirements that plans be administered, and benefits be paid, in accordance with plan documents. We conclude that the Washington statute has a "connection with" ERISA plans and is therefore pre-empted.

III

Respondents suggest several reasons why ordinary ERISA pre-emption analysis should not apply here. First, they observe that the Washington statute allows employers to opt out. According to respondents, the statute neither regulates plan administration nor impairs uniformity because it does not apply when "[t]he instrument governing disposition of the nonprobate asset expressly provides otherwise." We do not believe that the statute is saved from pre-emption simply because it is, at least in a broad sense, a default rule.

Even though the Washington statute's cancellation of private choice may itself be trumped by specific language in the plan documents, the statute does "dictate the choice[s] facing ERISA plans" with respect to matters of plan administration. Plan administrators must either follow Washington's beneficiary designation scheme or alter the terms of their plan so as to indicate that they will not follow it. The statute is not any less of a regulation of the terms of ERISA plans simply because there are two ways of complying with it. Of course, simple noncompliance with the statute is not one of the options available to plan administrators. Their only choice is one of timing, *i.e.,* whether to bear the burden of compliance *ex post,* by paying benefits as the statute dictates (and in

---

[3] The dissent observes that the Washington statute permits a plan administrator to avoid resolving the dispute himself and to let courts or parties settle the matter. This observation only presents an example of how the costs of delay and uncertainty can be passed on to beneficiaries, thereby thwarting ERISA's objective of efficient plan administration.

contravention of the plan documents), or *ex ante,* by amending the plan.[4]

Respondents emphasize that the opt-out provision makes compliance with the statute less burdensome than if it were mandatory. That is true enough, but the burden that remains is hardly trivial. It is not enough for plan administrators to opt out of this particular statute. Instead, they must maintain a familiarity with the laws of all 50 States so that they can update their plans as necessary to satisfy the opt-out requirements of other, similar statutes. They also must be attentive to changes in the interpretations of those statutes by state courts. This "tailoring of plans and employer conduct to the peculiarities of the law of each jurisdiction" is exactly the burden ERISA seeks to eliminate.

Second, respondents emphasize that the Washington statute involves both family law and probate law, areas of traditional state regulation. There is indeed a presumption against pre-emption in areas of traditional state regulation such as family law. But that presumption can be overcome where, as here, Congress has made clear its desire for pre-emption. Accordingly, we have not hesitated to find state family law pre-empted when it conflicts with ERISA or relates to ERISA plans. See, *e.g., Boggs v. Boggs*, 520 U.S. 833, 117 S.Ct. 1754 (1997) (holding that ERISA pre-empts a state community property law permitting the testamentary transfer of an interest in a spouse's pension plan benefits).

Finally, respondents argue that if ERISA pre-empts this statute, then it also must pre-empt the various state statutes providing that a murdering heir is not entitled to receive property as a result of the killing. In the ERISA context, these "slayer" statutes could revoke the beneficiary status of someone who murdered a plan participant. Those statutes are not before us, so we do not decide the issue. We note, however, that the principle underlying the statutes—which have been adopted by nearly every State—is well established in the law and has a long historical pedigree predating ERISA. And because the statutes are more or less uniform nationwide, their interference with the aims of ERISA is at least debatable.

---

[4]   Contrary to the dissent's suggestion that the resolution of this case depends on one's view of federalism, we are called upon merely to interpret ERISA. And under the text of ERISA, the fiduciary "shall" administer the plan "in accordance with the documents and instruments governing the plan,". The Washington statute conflicts with this command because under this statute, the only way the fiduciary can administer the plan according to its terms is to change the very terms he is supposed to follow.

* * *

The judgment of the Supreme Court of Washington is reversed, and the case is remanded for further proceedings not inconsistent with this opinion.

It is so ordered.

SCALIA, J., with whom GINSBURG, J., joins, concurring.

I join the opinion of the Court, since I believe that the "relate to" pre-emptive provision of the Employee Retirement Income Security Act of 1974 (ERISA) is assuredly triggered by a state law that contradicts ERISA. As the Court notes, "the statute at issue here directly conflicts with ERISA's requirements that plans be administered, and benefits be paid, in accordance with plan documents." I remain unsure (as I think the lower courts and everyone else will be) as to what else triggers the "relate to" provision, which—if it is interpreted to be anything other than a reference to our established jurisprudence concerning conflict and field pre-emption—has no discernible content that would not pick up every ripple in the pond, producing a result "that no sensible person could have intended." *California Div. of Labor Standards Enforcement v. Dillingham Constr., N. A., Inc.,* 519 U.S. 316, 336, 117 S.Ct. 832 (1997) (SCALIA, J., concurring). I persist in the view that we can bring some coherence to this area, and can give the statute both a plausible and precise content, only by interpreting the "relate to" clause as a reference to our ordinary pre-emption jurisprudence.

BREYER, J., with whom STEVENS, J. joins, dissenting.

Like Justice SCALIA, I believe that we should apply normal conflict pre-emption and field pre-emption principles where, as here, a state statute covers ERISA and non-ERISA documents alike. Our more recent ERISA cases are consistent with this approach. See also *Boggs v. Boggs* (1997) (relying on conflict pre-emption principles instead of ERISA's pre-emption clause). And I fear that our failure to endorse this "new approach" explicitly, *Dillingham, supra,* at 336, 117 S.Ct. 832 (SCALIA, J., concurring), will continue to produce an "avalanche of litigation," *De Buono, supra,* at 809, n. 1, 117 S.Ct. 1747, as courts struggle to interpret a clause that lacks any "discernible content," (SCALIA, J., concurring), threatening results that Congress could not have intended.

I do not agree with Justice SCALIA or with the majority, however, that there is any plausible pre-emption principle that leads to a conclusion that ERISA pre-empts the statute at issue here. No one could claim that ERISA pre-empts the entire *field* of state law governing inheritance—though such matters "relate to" ERISA broadly speaking. Neither is there any direct conflict between the Washington statute and ERISA, for the one nowhere directly contradicts the other. Cf. *ante*, at 1329 (claiming a "direc[t] conflic[t]" between ERISA and the Washington statute). But cf. *ante*, at 1327 (relying upon the "relate to" language in ERISA's pre-emption clause).

The Court correctly points out that ERISA requires a fiduciary to make payments to a beneficiary "in accordance with the documents and instruments governing the plan." 29 U.S.C. § 1104(a)(1)(D). But nothing in the Washington statute requires the contrary. Rather, the state statute simply sets forth a default rule for interpreting documentary silence. The statute specifies that a nonprobate asset will pass at A's death "as if" A's "former spouse" had died first—*unless the "instrument governing disposition of the nonprobate asset expressly provides otherwise."* This state-law rule is a rule of interpretation, and it is designed to carry out, not to conflict with, the employee's likely intention as revealed in the plan documents.

There is no direct conflict or contradiction between the Washington statute and the terms of the plan documents here at issue. David Egelhoff's investment plan provides that when a "beneficiary designation" is "invalid," the "benefits will be paid" to a "surviving spouse," or "[i]f there is no surviving spouse," to the "children in equal shares." The life insurance plan is silent about what occurs when a beneficiary designation is invalid. The Washington statute fills in these gaps, *i.e.,* matters about which the documents themselves say nothing. Thus, the Washington statute specifies that a beneficiary designation—here "Donna R. Egelhoff wife" in the pension plan—is invalid where there is no longer any such person as Donna R. Egelhoff, wife. And the statute adds that in such instance the funds would be paid to the children, who themselves are potential pension plan beneficiaries.

The Court's "direct conflict" conclusion rests upon its claim that "administrators must pay benefits to the beneficiaries chosen by state law, rather than to those identified in the plan documents." But the Court cannot mean "identified *anywhere* in the plan documents," for the Egelhoff children were "identified" as recipients in the pension plan documents should the initial designation to "Donna R. Egelhoff wife" become invalid. And whether that initial designation became invalid upon divorce is a matter about which the plan documents are silent.

To refer to state law to determine whether a given name makes a designation that is, or has become, invalid makes sense where background property or inheritance law is at issue, say, for example, where a written name is potentially ambiguous, where it is set forth near, but not in, the correct space, where it refers to a missing person perhaps presumed dead, where the name was written at a time the employee was incompetent, or where the name refers to an individual or entity disqualified by other law, say, the rule against perpetuities or rules prohibiting a murderer from benefiting from his crime. Why would Congress want the courts to create an ERISA-related federal property law to deal with such problems? Regardless, to refer to background state law in such circumstances does not *directly* conflict with any explicit ERISA provision, for no provision of ERISA forbids reading an instrument or document in light of state property law principles. In any event, in this case the plan documents *explicitly* foresee that a beneficiary designation may become "invalid," but they do not specify the invalidating circumstances. To refer to state property law to fill in that blank cannot possibly create any direct conflict with the plan documents.

The majority simply denies that there is any blank to fill in and suggests that the plan documents require the plan to pay the designated beneficiary under all circumstances. But there is nonetheless an open question, namely, whether a designation that (here explicitly) refers to a wife remains valid after divorce. The question is genuine and important (unlike the imaginary example in the majority's footnote). The plan documents themselves do not answer the question any more than they describe what is to occur in a host of other special circumstances (*e.g.*, mental incompetence, intoxication, ambiguous names, etc.). To determine whether ERISA permits state law to answer such questions requires a careful examination of the particular state law in light of ERISA's basic policies. We should not short circuit that necessary inquiry simply by announcing a "direct conflict" where none exists.

The Court also complains that the Washington statute restricts the plan's choices to "two." But it is difficult to take this complaint seriously. After all, the two choices that Washington gives the plan are (1) to comply with Washington's rule or (2) not to comply with Washington's rule. What other choices could there be? A state statute that asks a plan to choose whether it intends to comply is not a statute that directly conflicts with a plan. Quite obviously, it is possible, not " 'impossible,' " to comply with both the Washington statute and federal law.

The more serious pre-emption question is whether this state statute " 'stands as an obstacle to the accomplishment and execution of the full purposes and objectives of Congress." In answering that question, we must remember that petitioner has to overcome a strong presumption *against* pre-emption. That is because the Washington statute governs family property law—a "fiel[d] of traditional state regulation," where courts will not find federal pre-emption unless such was the " 'clear and manifest purpose of Congress,' " or the state statute does " 'major damage' to 'clear and substantial' federal interests". No one can seriously argue that Congress has *clearly* resolved the question before us. And the only damage to federal interests that the Court identifies consists of the added administrative burden the state statute imposes upon ERISA plan administrators.

The Court claims that the Washington statute "interferes with nationally uniform plan administration" by requiring administrators to "familiarize themselves with state statutes." But administrators have to familiarize themselves with state law in any event when they answer such routine legal questions as whether amounts due are subject to garnishment, *Mackey v. Lanier Collection Agency & Service, Inc.*, 486 U.S. 825, 838, 108 S.Ct. 2182, 100 L.Ed.2d 836 (1988), who is a "spouse," who qualifies as a "child," or when an employee is legally dead. And were that "familiarizing burden" somehow overwhelming, the plan could easily avoid it by resolving the divorce revocation issue in the plan documents themselves, stating expressly that state law does not apply. The "burden" thus reduces to a one-time requirement that would fall primarily upon the few who draft model ERISA documents, not upon the many who administer them. So meager a burden cannot justify pre-empting a state law that enjoys a presumption against pre-emption.

The Court also fears that administrators would have to make difficult choice-of-law determinations when parties live in different States. Whether this problem is or is not "major" in practice, the Washington statute resolves it by expressly setting forth procedures whereby the parties or the courts, *not* the plan administrator, are responsible for resolving it.

The Court has previously made clear that the fact that state law "impose[s] some burde[n] on the administration of ERISA plans" does not necessarily require pre-emption. *De Buono*, 520 U.S., at 815, 117 S.Ct. 1747; *Mackey, supra*, at 831, 108 S.Ct. 2182 (upholding state garnishment law notwithstanding claim that "benefit plans subjected to garnishment will incur substantial administrative burdens"). Precisely, what is it about this statute's requirement that distinguishes it from the " 'myriad state laws' " that impose some kind of burden on ERISA plans?

Indeed, if one looks beyond administrative burden, one finds that Washington's statute poses no obstacle, but furthers ERISA's ultimate objective-developing a fair system for protecting employee benefits. The Washington statute transfers an employee's pension assets at death to those individuals whom the worker would likely have wanted to receive them. As many jurisdictions have concluded, divorced workers more often prefer that a child, rather than a divorced spouse, receive those assets. Of course, an employee can secure this result by changing a beneficiary form; but doing so requires awareness, understanding, and time. That is why Washington and many other jurisdictions have created a statutory assumption that divorce works a revocation of a designation in favor of an ex-spouse. That assumption is embodied in the Uniform Probate Code; it is consistent with human experience; and those with expertise in the matter have concluded that it "more often" serves the cause of "[j]ustice." Langbein, The Nonprobate Revolution and the Future of the Law of Succession (1984).

In forbidding Washington to apply that assumption here, the Court permits a divorced wife, who *already* acquired, during the divorce proceeding, her fair share of the couple's community property, to receive in addition the benefits that the divorce court awarded to her former husband. To be more specific, Donna Egelhoff already received a business, an IRA account, and stock; David received, among other things, 100% of his pension benefits. David did not change the beneficiary designation in the pension plan or life insurance plan during the 6-month period between his divorce and his death. As a result, Donna will now receive a windfall of approximately $80,000 at the expense of David's children. The State of Washington enacted a statute to prevent precisely this kind of unfair result. But the Court, relying on an inconsequential administrative burden, concludes that Congress required it.

Finally, the logic of the Court's decision does not stop at divorce revocation laws. The Washington statute is virtually indistinguishable from other traditional state-law rules, for example, rules using presumptions to transfer assets in the case of simultaneous deaths, and rules that prohibit a husband who kills a wife from receiving benefits as a result of the wrongful death. It is particularly difficult to believe that Congress wanted to pre-empt the latter kind of statute. But how do these statutes differ from the one before us? Slayer statutes-like this statute-"gover[n] the payment of benefits, a central matter of plan administration." And contrary to the Court's suggestion, slayer statutes vary from State to State in their details just like divorce revocation statutes. Compare Ariz.Rev.Stat. Ann. (requiring proof, in a civil proceeding, under preponderance of the evidence standard); Haw.Rev.Stat. (same), with Ga.Code Ann. (requiring proof under clear and convincing evidence standard); Me.Rev.Stat. Ann. (same); and Ala.Code (treating judgment of conviction as conclusive when it becomes final); Me.Rev.Stat. Ann., (same), with Ariz.Rev.Stat. Ann. (treating judgment of conviction as conclusive only after "all right to appeal has been exhausted"); Haw.Rev.Stat. (same). Indeed, the "slayer" conflict would seem more serious, not less serious, than the conflict before us, for few, if any, slayer statutes permit plans to opt out of the state property law rule.

"ERISA pre-emption analysis," the Court has said, must "respect" the "separate spher[e]" of state "authority." In so stating, the Court has recognized the practical importance of preserving local independence, at retail, *i.e.,* by applying pre-emption analysis with care, statute by statute, line by line, in order to determine how best to reconcile a federal statute's language and purpose with federalism's need to preserve state autonomy. Indeed, in today's world, filled with legal complexity, the true test of federalist principle may lie, not in the occasional constitutional effort to trim Congress' commerce power at its edges, *United States v. Morrison*, 529 U.S. 598, 120 S.Ct. 1740 (2000), or to protect a State's treasury from a private damages action, *Board of Trustees of Univ. of Ala. v. Garrett*, 531 U.S. 356, 121 S.Ct. 955 (2001), but rather in those many statutory cases where courts interpret the mass of technical detail that is the ordinary diet of the law, *AT & T Corp. v. Iowa Utilities*

Bd., 525 U.S. 366, 427, 119 S.Ct. 721, 142 L.Ed.2d 835 (1999) (BREYER, J., concurring in part and dissenting in part).

In this case, "field pre-emption" is not at issue. There is no "direct" conflict between state and federal statutes. The state statute poses no significant obstacle to the accomplishment of any federal objective. Any effort to squeeze some additional pre-emptive force from ERISA's words (*i.e.*, "relate to") is inconsistent with the Court's recent case law. And the state statute before us is one regarding family property-a "fiel[d] of traditional state regulation," where the interpretive presumption against pre-emption is particularly strong. For these reasons, I disagree with the Court's conclusion. And, consequently, I dissent.

The Court admits that it is difficult to get a firm grip on what "relate to" means. But that is not the only word that matters in the ERISA statute. Another such word is "supersede". There are at least two possible meanings of "supersede", "replace" and "displace". If supersede means displace, then ERISA displaces state laws that relate to the plan. If supersede means replace, then there is an argument that ERISA only replaces the portions of state law that deal with the same situations, leaving state law to deal with issues not covered by ERISA. Which would Congress have preferred? The Court said that Congress "made clear its desire for pre-emption." How clear did Congress make it that Congress would have wanted pre-emption in this case?

It might not be a good thing that defined-benefit pensions are going out of style. One of the advantages of defined-benefit pensions is that groups can annuitize at lower cost than individuals. An individual can buy an individual annuity, but adverse selection raises the cost compared to a group plan.

Another advantage of defined-benefit pensions is that most of the employees need not worry about management of the assets. Because of loss aversion, the unhappiness caused by bad investment decisions would be expected to be greater than the happiness caused by good decisions. In addition, we can expect a lot of bad decisions to be made by people who are not students of markets and finance.

4. TRANSFER-ON-DEATH DEEDS

Statutes have established the effectiveness of transfer-on-death (TOD) deeds of realty in about 30 states, and the UPC recognizes them, too. In such jurisdictions, O can execute and record a deed of Blackacre "to O, transfer on death to X" and X will become the owner at O's death. In that way, TOD deeds work like wills, although they have not been executed in strict compliance with the Wills Acts. Can you imagine any opportunities for undue influence or fraud?

D. TRUSTS

Trusts are used for many purposes. One purpose of the trusts we study in this course is to transfer wealth to others. Settlors settle trusts for the benefit of relatives and friends and for charitable purposes. Trusts are also used as a business form, established for the purpose of creating wealth through commercial deals. We will leave the discussion of business trusts to other courses. This chapter also excludes constructive trusts, which are quite different and were seen earlier.

1. TESTAMENTARY AND INTER VIVOS, REVOCABLE AND IRREVOCABLE

Trusts for private persons can be created in a will, testamentary trusts, or created during the settlor's life, inter vivos trusts. A settlor can choose to make an inter vivos trust revocable or irrevocable. A trust is revocable when the settlor has the power to terminate the trust and recover the trust property. The settlor of a revocable trust can revoke the entire trust or revoke the trust for just some of the assets in the trust. The revocable trust is an excellent will substitute in that, like a will, it can be used to make a transfer of wealth at the settlor's death while remaining revocable and amendable before the settlor's death. An irrevocable inter vivos trust does not operate as much like a will because it cannot be revoked, and a testamentary trust is not a substitute for a will at all because it is created in a will. All three are extremely useful in their own ways. In this course you have often heard that there are better ways to accomplish the client's goals than what was attempted by the lawyer. Trusts are almost always one of those better ways.

2. HISTORICAL BASIS

The modern trust is due in part to a lucky accident of English history. Kings and Queens of England maintained various courts, including the King's Bench or Queen's Bench, the Court of Common Pleas, and the Chancery. For a while, all three sat, at least sometimes, in Westminster Hall. One of the functions of the Chancellor was to do justice, acting as the King's conscience. In some cases, justice was at odds with the rulings of the law courts, the King's or Queen's Bench and the Court of Common Pleas, with the result that a person might be able to get relief from the Chancellor in equity even though he had no remedy at law. One of these situations was triggered by a transfer from O "to T for the use of B." This was called a *"use"*. The law recognized T as the legal owner, while equity recognized B as the equitable owner. As a result, T would hold legal title but would be forced by the Chancellor to use his legal ownership for the benefit of B. Thus, the trust divided ownership, with T as the trustee holding legal title and B as the beneficiary holding equitable title.

Uses were used to make transfers of land by will and to make transfers of land without livery of seisin (both of which were not possible at law in those early centuries). Another use of uses was to avoid feudal incidents. This avoidance of feudal incidents reduced the revenues of overlords and the King, and in 1535 Parliament put an end to it by passing the Statute of Uses, which became effective on May 1, 1536. The Statute of Uses eliminated legal title holders from the picture of dual ownership, leaving title wholly in the hands of the equitable title holders. However, this elimination of the use made transfer of land by will impossible, which Parliament remedied by passing the Statute of Wills in 1540. The courts recognized that uses were also legitimately useful when there was a need for someone to manage assets for the benefit of another person and so, in an assertion of judicial activism, they held that the Statute of Uses would not operate, and the legal title holder would not be eliminated, when the legal title holder had active duties to perform. Because of its usefulness, this ancient legal relationship survived the Statute of Uses and continues in the present time as the trust. The use of trusts is expanding in the U.S., and some foreign jurisdictions outside the common-law system have recently passed laws making trusts possible.

3. REQUIREMENTS

What does it take to create a trust?

Under the common law, a trust can be created only if certain requirements are met. But the requirements are not too onerous; indeed, they are in many ways easier to satisfy than the requirements for a will. Setting aside constructive trusts, the creation of a trust requires that there be some creator. When the trust is created in a will, the creator is often referred to as simply the testator. When the trust is created outside a will, the creator is often called the settlor. Creators of trusts also go by other names, including trustor, grantor, donor, settler, and founder.

The first requirement is that the creator must have the capacity to create a trust. If the trust is testamentary, the testator must have the capacity to make a will. If the trust is an irrevocable inter vivos trust, the settlor must have the capacity to make a gift, which might be slightly higher. Under the Uniform Trust Code, creating a revocable trust requires the same capacity as for a will.

The creator must also have the intent to create a trust and must manifest such intent by objective expression. As with wills, intent can be negated by mistake in the execution, coercion, undue influence, or fraud. No specific or magic words are required to create a trust; the word "trust" need not be used. Whether the alleged settlor had the intent to create a trust is a question made difficult by the fact that the settlor need not understand what a trust is. It can be enough that the settlor wished one person to hold property for the benefit of, and with duties to, another person. However, the intent to make a gift is not enough to satisfy the requirement that the settlor have the intent to create a trust. The settlor must have the intent that one person hold for the benefit of someone else. Because nothing formal is required, it sometimes takes litigation to determine whether the owner of the asset intended to create a trust. Did the decedent wish to create a trust in the following case?

IN RE ESTATE OF MALISZEWSKI

Supreme Court, Appellate Division, Third Department, New York, 2007
839 N.Y.S.2d 586

MERCURE, J.P.

Appeal from an order of the Surrogate's Court of Schenectady County (Kramer, S.), entered August 17, 2006, which construed paragraph four of decedent's last will and testament.

Petitioners commenced this proceeding to construe the fourth paragraph of decedent's last will and testament. That paragraph provided that if any part of decedent's estate vested "absolute ownership in a person under the age of [25]," then decedent's fiduciary was authorized "to hold the property so vested in a separate fund for the benefit of such person and to invest and reinvest the same." The fiduciary was also directed to apply so much of the net income or principal necessary for the "care, support, maintenance and education of said person" until he or she reached age 25, at which point the accumulated income, as well as the unexpended principal, would be paid to him or her. According to petitioners, the fourth paragraph was meant to establish trusts for the benefit of any beneficiaries who were under age 25 at the time of decedent's death. Surrogate's Court disagreed and concluded that this paragraph did not set up a valid trust, prompting this appeal.

At issue are the specific bequests of stocks in a separate paragraph of decedent's will that passed to individuals who were under the age of 25 at the time of decedent's death. Petitioners argue that it was decedent's intent that the stocks would be held in trust until the legatees attain the age of 25. We agree.

To constitute a valid trust, there must be a designated beneficiary, a designated trustee, an identifiable res and delivery with the intent of vesting legal title in a trustee. Surrogate's Court found that there was no showing of delivery with the intent of vesting legal title in the trustee; instead, the court determined that legal title was granted to the listed legatees by virtue of the language "vest in absolute ownership." The will also provided, however, that if the legatee was under age 25, the fiduciary was to hold the property "so vested" in a separate fund and to invest it and reinvest it as above set forth until the legatee reached 25 years of age. Thus, contrary to the findings of Surrogate's Court, even given the "so vested" language, the fiduciary did in fact gain legal title to the assets so as to be considered a trustee.

It is well settled that the "cardinal rule of construction of a will is to carry out the intent of the testator". The intent of the testator is not to be found "from a single word or phrase but from a sympathetic reading of the will as an entirety and in view of all the facts and circumstances under which [its] provisions ... were framed". While the "vested" language is suggestive of an absolute gift, the remainder of the language of the will demonstrates that decedent intended to establish a trust for each legatee. Specifically, by naming a "fiduciar[y]" for each legatee and directing him or her to hold the property in a separate fund and to invest it, as well as to apply the "net income ... or ... principal to the care, support, maintenance and education" of the legatee until the age of 25, decedent manifested his intent to create a trust for each legatee. Accordingly, this Court construes the fourth paragraph of the will as establishing trusts for the benefit of each legatee who was under 25 years of age at the time of decedent's death.

Ordered that the order is reversed, on the law, without costs, and matter remitted to the Surrogate's Court of Schenectady County for further proceedings not inconsistent with this Court's decision.

For there to be a split in ownership between equity and law, there must be some asset to be owned. Therefore, a trust cannot exist without a res, and the settlor must specify what the settlor intends to be that res. In *Brainard v. Commissioner of Internal Revenue*, 91 F.2d 880 (7th Cir. 1937), the settlor attempted to create a trust containing the profits from trading stocks. He did not put the stocks in the trust, just the profits. The court held that there was no trust because there were no profits from trading at the point in time when he supposedly created the trust. After he realized profits, he could have put them into a trust, but that would have been too late for his purposes of preventing the profits from being taxed as his income. *Brainard* is a classic citation for the proposition that the res of a trust must be some legally existing right, not some right that might come into existence in the future, not some mere expectancy. Brainard could have transferred his stocks into a trust and the gains from trading would have accrued to the trust, but he did not do that.

Brainard is sometimes compared to *Speelman v. Pascal*, 178 N.E.2d 723 (N.Y. 1961). In *Speelman*, Gabriel Pascal wrote a letter to Zaya Kingman (also known as Marianne Speelman) purporting to give her a share in his profits from a musical stage version of George Bernard Shaw's play, PYGMALION. MY FAIR LADY was that musical, and it was successful on Broadway, winning six Tony Awards, including Best Musical, before becoming a hit in London. The question was whether this letter made a gift to Kingman of a share of Pascal's profits, and the court held it did. The essential difference between the cases is that one can make a gift of future profits, just as one can make a contract about future profits. But a trust requires a res that is some previously existing legal right.

After the court decided *Speelman*, could Miss Kingman have created a trust with a res that was the right to the profits from *My Fair Lady*? An enforceable debt can be the res of a trust. And it is common for a trust to be funded with a life insurance policy. In *Gurnett v. Mutual Life Ins. Co. of New York*, 191 N.E. 250 (Ill. 1934) the court held that the res of such a trust is the contractual right to the proceeds of the life insurance policy conferred by naming the trustee the beneficiary of the policy.

In addition to intent and a res, another potential requirement for a voluntary trust is a definite beneficiary. Whether a trust must have a definite beneficiary depends on whether the trust is charitable. A beneficiary is not required for a charitable trust. A settlor may create a trust for the eradication of Alzheimer's disease without specifying which person will receive the funding, leaving that choice up to a trustee or, if necessary, a court. Charitable purposes were defined by Parliament in 1601 in the Statute of Charitable Uses, 43 Eliz. I, c.4. Today, charitable purposes include the relief of poverty, the advancement of education or religion, the promotion of health, the performance of governmental activities, and other purposes beneficial to the community. Suits to enforce the terms of a charitable trust may be brought by settlors, state attorneys general, and persons with special interests in the trust.

Noncharitable trusts must have at least one beneficiary. As a practical matter, the law needs someone to keep the trustee honest and to bring suit if he violates his fiduciary duties. For noncharitable trusts, that role is played by the beneficiary, the *cestui que trust*. The beneficiary must be definite, or at least definite enough. A trust for the benefit of the settlor's children has definite beneficiaries even if they have not yet been born. On the other hand, a trust for the benefit of the settlor's friends is not definite enough.

In addition to being definite, the beneficiaries must be capable of taking equitable title. Any person with capacity to hold title to property has capacity to be a beneficiary. If the beneficiaries are all humans, all is well.

The traditional rule is that a trust for the benefit of Roxy is no good if Roxy is a dog. Today, however, in some states, a noncharitable trust may be created even though the trust fails to specify a definite human beneficiary. UPC § 2–907 authorizes honorary trusts (limited to 21 years) and trusts for the care of pets (limited to the life of designated animals). Similarly, UTC § 408 allows trusts for the purpose of caring for animals that are alive during the life of the settlor and UTC § 409 allows trusts for the care of cemetery plots and general purposes such as distributing bequests to persons chosen by the trustee. These trusts should be distinguished from older "honorary trusts" that have been recognized by some courts. If the trustee of an honorary trust would not serve, the court would not appoint a new trustee and the trust would fail. In the UPC trusts referenced above, the court is authorized to appoint a trustee if one is needed.

Another limitation on beneficiaries is that they must not be exactly the same people as the trustees. If they are the same, i.e., the set of trustees and the set of beneficiaries are completely overlapping sets, and they hold legal and equitable title in the same way, a court may find that there is no trust because a traditional trust requires a division of legal title from equitable title.

There is another potential pitfall relating to beneficiaries. Although the settlor may certainly be a beneficiary of the trust she settles, if she has too large an interest in the trust it will be declared to be a "grantor trust". That can be a problem because the income to grantor trusts is taxed to the grantor. Tax liability might not bother some settlors, but others could be quite distressed to find that they must pay income taxes on assets they placed in a trust for the benefit of others. The Internal Revenue Code and regulations have specific tests for grantor trusts, but the basic idea is that a trust is a grantor trust if the assets in the trust could be used for the benefit of the grantor. For example, if stock in a trust might be voted in a way that benefits the settlor, the IRS may treat the trust as a grantor trust and tax the income to the settlor. The creation of such a trust could in some situations amount to malpractice. (On the other hand, the intentionally defective grantor trust (IDGT) can be an effective method of reducing tax liabilities. We leave the IDGT for other courses.)

Another requirement for a trust is that the trustee have some active duty to perform. As noted above, when one person held legal title to assets for the use of someone else, the Statute of Uses took title from that legal title holder and transferred it to the beneficiaries, leaving them with both equitable and legal title. But when the legal title holder had active duties to perform, the courts declared that the statute would not operate and the separation of legal and equitable titles would remain. As a result, a trust needs to be an active trust; it will fail if it is a passive trust, sometimes also known as a dry trust.

A trust needs a trustee. The trustee may be the settlor herself or may be another person who has the capacity to take legal title and perform the active duties, often including managing the property. One might think that it is essential for a trust instrument to designate a trustee. After all, someone must take legal title. But courts have held that a trust will not fail for want of a trustee. If the settlor does not designate a trustee that is both capable and willing to serve, the court will usually appoint one.

Whether a writing is required to create a trust depends on the trust. A testamentary trust obviously requires a writing, specifically a will. An inter vivos trust containing land requires a writing in order to comply with the Statute of Frauds, which requires transfers of land to be in a writing, such as a deed in trust. (However, UTC § 401 does not prohibit the creation of a trust of land by oral declaration.) Various forms of writing may be used to create an inter vivos trust. A settlor may sign a declaration of trust, creating a trust with himself as trustee. Or a settlor-trustee may pay for an asset, having the asset be transferred to him as trustee for the benefit of someone else. Or, as is often the case, a settlor may create a trust with a trust document and a transfer of assets to the trustee.

An inter vivos trust of personalty may be created orally in most states and under the Uniform Trust Code. That does not mean that oral declarations of trust are a good idea. The people of Maine had to pay the judicial costs of two appeals to the state supreme court to resolve issues raised by the oral trust in *In re Estate of Fournier*, 966 A.2d 885 (Me. 2009). Rules of law that lead to disputes in which the only winners seem to be lawyers impose litigation costs on society and undermine confidence in government. A requirement that trusts be in writing could reduce social costs and, perhaps, reduce the possibilities of false positives as well. On the other hand, of course, justice is advanced when we honor the settlor's intent despite his or her failure to execute a writing. Is that justice worth its costs?

ESTATE OF HEGGSTAD

Court of Appeal, First District, Division 2, California, 1993
20 Cal.Rptr.2d 433

PHELAN, J.

In response to respondent's petition for order instructing trustee, the probate court decreed that the decedent's undivided 34.78 percent interest in property identified as 100 Independence Drive, Menlo Park, San Mateo County, was vested in Glen P. Heggstad, as successor trustee of the Heggstad Family Trust, and was not part of the decedent's estate. We hold that the settlor's written declaration stating that he holds this property as trustee was sufficient to create a revocable living trust, and we affirm the probate court's order.

FACTS

On May 10, 1989, decedent Halvard L. Heggstad executed a will naming his son, respondent Glen P. Heggstad, as executor. Concurrently, the decedent executed a valid revocable living trust, naming himself as the trustee and his son Glen, the successor trustee (hereafter the Heggstad Family Trust). All the trust property was identified in a document titled schedule A, which was attached to the trust document. The property at issue was listed as item No. 5 on schedule A, and was mislabeled as "Partnership interest in 100 Independence Drive, Menlo Park, California."

In truth, decedent had an undivided 34.78 percent interest in that property as a tenant in common. There is no dispute as to the nature of the decedent's interest in this property. This property remained in decedent's name, as an unmarried man, and there was no grant deed reconveying this property to himself as trustee of the revocable living trust. Both sides agree that decedent had formally transferred by separate deeds, all the other real property listed in Schedule A to himself as trustee of the Heggstad Family Trust.

About one month after executing these documents, the decedent married appellant Nancy Rhodes Heggstad. She was not provided for in either the will or the trust documents, and all parties agree that she is entitled to one-third of the decedent's estate (her intestate share) as an omitted spouse pursuant to Probate Code section 6560.2 She takes nothing under the terms of the trust and makes no claim thereto.

Decedent died on October 20, 1990, and his son was duly appointed executor of his estate and became successor trustee under the terms of the Heggstad Family Trust. The trust documents were recorded following decedent's death on January 10, 1991.

During the probate of the will, Glen, the successor trustee, petitioned the court for instructions regarding the disposition of the 100 Independence Drive property. The trustee claimed that the trust language was sufficient to create a trust in the subject property and that the property was not part of his father's estate.

In pertinent part, article 1 of the trust provided: "HALVARD L. HEGGSTAD, called the settlor or the trustee, depending on the context, declares that he has set aside and transfers to HALVARD L. HEGGSTAD in trust, as trustee, the property described in schedule A attached to this instrument."

Appellant objected, arguing: the trustee is asking for a change of title, which is not available as a remedy in a petition for instructions; the property was not transferred to the trust by a properly executed document or by operation of law; and the trustee is also a beneficiary of the trust and should be removed because of this conflict of interest.

The probate court concluded that the trust document, specifically article 1, was sufficient to create a trust in the subject property.

DISCUSSION

Appellant contends that a written declaration of trust is insufficient, by itself, to create a revocable living trust in real property, and the decedent was required to have executed a grant deed transferring the property to himself as trustee of the Heggstad Family Trust. None of the authorities cited by appellant require a settlor, who also names himself as trustee of a revocable living trust, to convey his property to the trust by a separate deed. Our independent research has uncovered no decisional law to support this position. To the contrary, all the authorities we have consulted support the conclusion that a declaration by the settlor that he holds the property in trust for another, alone, is sufficient.

To create an express trust there must be a competent trustor, trust intent, trust property, trust purpose, and a beneficiary. The settlor can manifest his intention to create a trust in his property either by: (a) declaring himself trustee of the property or (b) by transferring the property to another as trustee for some other person, by deed or other inter vivos transfer or by will.

These two methods for creating a trust are codified in Probate Code section 15200: "(a) A declaration by the owner of property that the owner holds the property as trustee," and "(b) A transfer of property by the owner during the owner's lifetime to another person as trustee."

Where the trust property is real estate, the statute of frauds requires that the declaration of trust must be in writing signed by the trustee. Here, the written document declaring a trust in the property described in Schedule A was signed by the decedent at the time he made the declaration and constitutes a proper manifestation of his intent to create a trust. Contrary to appellant's assertion, there is no requirement that the settlor/trustee execute a separate writing conveying the property to the trust. A review of pertinent sections of the Restatement Second of Trusts, illustrates our point. This consideration is particularly appropriate, since the Law Revision Commission Comment to section 15200 indicates: "This section is drawn from section 17 of the Restatement (Second) of Trusts (1957)."

Section 17 of the Restatement provides that a trust may be created by "(a) a declaration by the owner of property that he holds it as trustee for another person; or (b) a transfer inter vivos by the owner of property to another person as trustee for the transferor or for a third person. . . ." The comment to clause (a) states: "If the owner of property declares himself trustee of the property, a trust may be created without a transfer of title to the property."

Illustration "1" of that same section is instructive. It reads: "A, the owner of a bond, declares himself trustee of the bond for designated beneficiaries. A is the trustee of the bond for the beneficiaries. So also, the owner of property can create a trust by executing an instrument conveying the property to himself as trustee. In such a case there is not in fact a transfer of legal title to the property, since he already has legal title to it, *but the instrument is as effective as if he had simply declared himself trustee."* (Emphasis added.)

Section 28 of the Restatement announces the rule that no consideration is necessary to create a trust by declaration. This rule applies both to personal and real property, and it also supports our conclusion that a declaration of trust does not require a grant deed transfer of real property to the trust. Illustration "6" provides: "A, the owner of Blackacre, in an instrument signed by him, gratuitously and without a recital of consideration declares that he holds Blackacre in trust for B and his heirs. B is not related to A by blood or marriage. A is trustee of Blackacre for B."

More directly, comment m to section 32 (Conveyance Inter Vivos in Trust for a Third Person) provides in pertinent part: *"Declaration of trust. If the owner of property declares himself trustee of the property a transfer of the property is neither necessary nor appropriate. . . ."* (Second emphasis added.)

Additionally, comment b to section 40 (statute of frauds) establishes that a written declaration of trust, by itself, is sufficient to create a trust in the property. Comment b states: *"Methods of creation of trust.* The Statute of Frauds is applicable whether a trust of an interest in land is created *by the owner's declaring himself trustee,* or by a transfer by him to another in trust." (Second emphasis added.)

Finally, Bogert, in his treatise on trusts and trustees observes: "Declaration of Trust [¶] It is sometimes stated that the transfer by the settlor of a legal title to the trustee is an essential to the creation of an express trust. The statement is inaccurate in one respect. Obviously, if the trust is to be created by declaration there is no real transfer of any property interest to a trustee. The settlor holds a property interest before the trust declaration, and after the declaration he holds a bare legal interest in the same property interest with the equitable or beneficial interest in the beneficiary. No new property interest has passed to the trustee. The settlor has merely remained the owner of part of what he formerly owned."

These authorities provide abundant support for our conclusion that a written declaration of trust by the owner of real property, in which he names himself trustee, is sufficient to create a trust in that property, and that the law does not require a separate deed transferring the property to the trust.

None of the practice guides relied upon by appellant state a contrary rule. In fact, as appellant concedes, these works only recommend that a deed be prepared conveying title to the settlor as trustee. The purpose is to provide solid evidence of the settlor's manifestation of intent to create a trust, should a question arise.

Moreover, the practice guide, Drafting California Revocable Living Trusts, supports our conclusion that a transfer of title is not necessary when the settlor declares himself trustee in his own property. Section 1.6 of that book states in part: "A trust always requires transfer of legal title to the trustee *or, if a settlor is also trustee, a declaration by the settlor that he or she holds legal title in trust for another*." (Emphasis added.) In fact, the very language recommended by that practice guide for declaring trusts is consistent with the decedent's trust document. Section 3.14–1 reads: "[Name of settlor] (called the settlor or the trustee, depending on the context) declares that [he/she] has set aside and holds in trust [e.g., the property described in Schedule A attached to this instrument]. . . ." Article One of the trust substantially tracks this language and constitutes a valid declaration of trust in the property identified in Schedule A. Decedent took all the necessary steps to create a valid revocable living trust.

Respondent/trustee errs when he argues that in order to uphold the trust, we must view the trust document as a valid conveyance of the property to the trust. This argument misses the point that a declaration of trust is sufficient to create a trust, without the need of a conveyance of title to the settlor as trustee.

* * *

The probate court's order declaring that the property identified as "100 Independence Way, Menlo Park, San Mateo County," is included in the living trust is affirmed.

---

4. REVOCABLE TRUSTS

Revocable trusts are like wills in that they can shift assets at death and can be changed and amended during the life of the settlor. Because trusts that the settlor can revoke are testamentary in nature and often not created in compliance with the Wills Act formalities, some courts in the past had difficulty holding them valid. The courts struggled to find a right that had passed from the settlor to a beneficiary and to find a duty that the settlor had imposed upon herself. The law has discarded those requirements today, recognizing revocable trusts whether or not they were created in compliance with the Wills Act formalities and in spite of the fact that the beneficiary has no vested or enforceable rights against the settlor. Indeed, UTC § 603(a) provides that while the settlor is alive and has capacity to revoke, the trustee of a revocable trust owes her duties to the settlor rather than the beneficiaries. Whether the law ought to require more formality for the creation of a revocable trust, given its testamentary nature, is not much of a policy debate today.

How a trust is made revocable depends on the jurisdiction. In some states and under UTC § 602, an inter vivos trust is revocable and amendable by default. But that is not the common-law rule, which requires that the settlor reserve the right to revoke or amend in order for the trust to be revocable or amendable.

The traditional rule is that a revocable trust can be revoked or amended only by following the procedure for revocation or amendment set out in the trust instrument. The modern and UPC rule is that a revocable trust can be revoked or amended by a clear manifestation of intent, unless the trust instrument specifies otherwise. Because the trust can specify how it is to be revoked and amended, you should not assume that a particular method will be effective. It is possible, for example, that a revocable trust cannot be revoked or amended by a provision in a will. If the settlor wishes to revoke or amend, it is important to review the terms of the trust to make sure that the revocation or amendment is done properly.

SCALFARO V. RUDLOFF
Supreme Court of Pennsylvania, 2007
934 A.2d 1254

CAPPY, C.J.

In this appeal, we consider whether a trust instrument gave a joint settlor, who was also a joint trustee, the authority to revoke an *inter vivos* trust when he became the sole trustee upon the death of his spouse. For the following reasons, we conclude that the trust instrument is clear and unambiguous in stating that the power of revocation was to be exercised by the settlors jointly and not by either one of them as sole trustee. Accordingly, the order of the Superior Court is reversed.

Robert C. Rudloff ("Mr.[ ]Rudloff") and Helen M. Rudloff ("Mrs. Rudloff") (collectively, the "Rudloffs") owned property ("Property") located in Bucks County, Pennsylvania as tenants by the entireties. On August 11, 1993, the Rudloffs executed a form-book Declaration of Trust, establishing an *inter vivos* trust (the "Trust"). The corpus of the Trust was the Property and the Rudloffs were the designated trustees. Under the terms of a quit claim deed, the Property was transferred to the Trust and into the Trust Estate.

Paragraph 1 of the Declaration of Trust named the Rudloffs' three children, Appellant Judith Scalfaro and Appellees Richard and James Rudloff, as equal one-third beneficiaries. In paragraphs 2 and 3, the responsibilities and interests of the beneficiaries were set forth. Paragraphs 4 and 5 specified the powers and rights the Rudloffs reserved, stating:

4. We reserve unto ourselves the power and right at any time during our lifetime (1) to place a mortgage or other lien upon the [P]roperty and (2) to collect any rental or other income that may accrue from the trust property. . . . .

5. We reserve unto ourselves the power and right at any time during our lifetime to amend or revoke in whole or in part the trust hereby created without the necessity of obtaining the consent of any beneficiary and without giving notice to any beneficiary. The sale or other disposition by us of the whole or any part of the [P]roperty held hereunder shall constitute as to such whole or part a revocation of the trust.

Paragraph 6 addressed the revocation of the beneficiary designation and termination of the Trust in the event that the beneficiaries predeceased the Rudloffs. Paragraph 7 addressed what role the survivor of the Rudloffs would assume, stating that "[i]n the event of the physical or mental incapacity or death of one of us, the survivor shall continue as sole Trustee."

Mrs. Rudloff died in October of 1996. On June 14, 2000, Mr. Rudloff executed and filed a deed conveying the Property to Appellees. Mr. Rudloff died on December 24, 2001. Appellees claimed ownership of the Property under the June 14, 2000 deed.

On June 19, 2003, Appellant filed a Complaint against Appellees in an Action to Quiet Title, alleging that given the terms of the

Declaration of Trust, Mr. Rudloff, as sole trustee, was not authorized to convey the Property. Appellant requested that the June 14, 2000 deed be voided and cancelled, and that the Property be administered under the Declaration of Trust. Appellee Richard Rudloff ("Appellee Rudloff") filed an Answer, New Matter and Counterclaim, alleging that the Trust was revocable by both or either one of the Rudloffs and that Mr. Rudloff's conveyance of the Property on June 14, 2000 served to revoke the Trust and extinguish Appellant's rights in the Property. Appellee Rudloff requested that Appellant's action be dismissed and that the court quiet title in the Property in Appellees.

A bench trial was held on March 1, 2004. The trial court decided in Appellant's favor, and entered an order dated March 2, 2004, voiding the June 14, 2000 deed, canceling the June 14, 2000 deed as matter of record, and directing that the Property be administered in accordance with terms and conditions of the Trust. Appellee Rudloff filed post-trial motions, which were denied. He then lodged a timely appeal in the Superior Court, raising whether the trial erred in not recognizing that under the Declaration of Trust, Mr. Rudloff as sole trustee, had the power to revoke the Trust and did so, by conveying the Property.

In its opinion, the trial court concluded that Appellee Rudloff's contention had no merit. The trial court recognized that a settlor may revoke or amend a revocable trust, provided that the power to revoke is reserved in the trust instrument's terms, and that the settlor's intent as to revocation is to be gathered from the language of the trust. Applying these principles to the Declaration of Trust, the trial court noted that paragraph 5 used plural words to describe the power of revocation that the Rudloffs reserved and included no words to indicate that either one of the Rudloffs were authorized to revoke the Trust alone, and that paragraph 7 did not state that the surviving and sole trustee was empowered to change the Trust. Thus, the trial court concluded that the Declaration of Trust clearly vested the power to revoke the Trust in the Rudloffs jointly, that the action taken by Mr. Rudloff as sole trustee on June 14, 2000 was unauthorized, and that the conveyance of the Property by deed to Appellees was void.

On appeal, in a published opinion, a divided panel of the Superior Court reached a different conclusion, and reversed the trial court's order. Relying heavily on a decision rendered by the Supreme Court of Utah in *Matter of Estate of West*, 948 P.2d 351 (Utah 1997), the Superior Court majority focused on the second sentence in paragraph 5, which stated that "the sale or other disposition by us of the whole or any part of the [P]roperty held hereunder shall constitute as to such whole or part a revocation of the trust" and the direction in paragraph 7 that upon the death of one of the Rudloffs, the survivor would continue as sole trustee. The majority repeated the observation made by the Utah Court in *Estate of West* that the sale of trust property can be accomplished only by a trustee who holds legal title, and reasoned that since Mr. Rudloff retained the powers of a trustee when Mrs. Rudloff died, the Declaration of Trust must be interpreted to mean that Mr. Rudloff was authorized to convey the Property on his own. Accordingly, the majority concluded that Mr. Rudloff had the right to convey the Property, and that the conveyance Mr. Rudloff made on June 14, 2000, to Appellees extinguished the Trust and Appellant's rights in the Property.

Judge Kelly dissented. Judge Kelly examined the language in the Declaration of Trust addressing the settlors' power to revoke and the context in which this power was set out, and concluded that the instrument gave the power to revoke to the Rudloffs jointly as settlors, and not to Mr. Rudloff as sole trustee. Accordingly, Judge Kelly would have determined that the trust became irrevocable upon Mrs. Rudloff's death, and would have affirmed the trial court.

This Court granted review to consider whether under the Declaration of Trust, Mr. Rudloff, acting as sole trustee, had the power to revoke the Trust.[2]

We begin with the principles that control in this area. Under Pennsylvania law, the power of revocation is a power that the settlor of the trust reserves. A settlor may revoke a trust, if and to the extent that power has been reserved in the trust instrument. A trustee does not decide whether or how the power of revocation will be exercised. The settlor's intent as to the power of revocation is to be determined from all the language within the four corners of the trust instrument, the scheme of distribution, and the circumstances surrounding the execution of the instrument. When a settlor of a trust reserves a power to revoke in a given manner and under certain conditions, revocation cannot be effected in another manner. A trust instrument that is unambiguous on a matter may not be superseded by extrinsic evidence of the settlor's intent.

---

[2]   This appeal raises a question of law. Our standard of review is de novo and our scope of review is plenary.

The parties' respective arguments applying these principles are straight forward. Appellant points to paragraph 5 of the Declaration of Trust and asserts that the plural words therein clearly demonstrate an intent on the settlors' part that the power of revocation was to be exercised jointly. According to Appellant, paragraph 7 does not change this result because it neither grants nor reserves any powers, but rather, authorizes the surviving trustee to continue administration of the Trust. Appellee Richard Rudloff counters that it never occurred to the Rudloffs that certain of the terms in the Declaration of Trust pertained to their powers as settlors and others related to their rights as trustees. Pointing to paragraph 7, Appellee argues that the Rudloffs must have meant that the survivor of them would have full and unlimited power over the Trust upon the death of the other, and intended for one or both of them to enjoy the power to revoke the Trust at any time and by any means, including by conveyance of the Property.

Our application of controlling principles leads us to Appellant's position. Turning to the Declaration of Trust, we see that the powers of the settlors were set forth in paragraphs 4 and 5, with the latter addressing the power to revoke. The first sentence of paragraph 5 stated that the settlors reserved the power to revoke; the second sentence stated that a particular action, the sale or disposition of the corpus of the trust by them, amounted to a revocation. In setting forth these provisions, paragraph 5 included only plural words and phrases, *i.e.*, "[w]e reserve unto ourselves," "during our lifetime," and "sale or disposition [of the Property] by us. . . ." There was no mention in paragraph 5 that the power of revocation could be exercised by either Mr. or Mrs. Rudloff alone or that either one of them could convey the Property on his or her own, either as sole trustee or surviving settlor. Indeed, no rights of survivorship were expressed in paragraph 5. The role the survivor of the Rudloffs would assume was covered in Paragraph 7. In this regard, Paragraph 7 contained only one authorization—that the survivor would continue as sole trustee—and made no reference to the power of revocation.

In our view, this language in the Declaration of Trust is clear and unambiguous in stating that the power of revocation was to be exercised by the Rudloffs jointly, and not by either one of them unilaterally as sole trustee.[5] Therefore, we hold that under the

---

[5]   Moreover, even if the terms of the Declaration of Trust were less than clear, as our respected colleague in the dissent would conclude, since paragraph 7 expressly provided that the

Declaration of Trust, Mr. Rudloff did not have the power to revoke the Trust as sole trustee, and accordingly, did not have the authority to convey the Property to Appellees in June of 2000.

For these reasons, the order of the Superior Court reversing the order of the trial court is reversed, and this matter is remanded to the Superior Court for remand to the trial court for reinstatement of the trial court's order and any necessary proceedings consistent with this opinion.

SAYLOR, J., dissenting.

In creating a trust for the ultimate benefit of their children, the Rudloffs used a form-book "living trust" document believed by the parties to have been obtained from a stationery store and executed without the benefit of legal advice. I respectfully differ with the majority's conclusion that the instrument is clear and definite; rather, I believe that the document is poorly drafted and materially ambiguous.

For purposes of this appeal, the critical portion of the declaration of trust is the revocation provision contained in its paragraph five, as follows:

> We reserve unto ourselves the power and right at any time *during our lifetime* to amend or revoke in whole or in part the trust hereby created without the necessity of obtaining the consent of any beneficiary and without giving notice to any beneficiary. The sale or other disposition by us of the whole or any part of the property held hereunder shall constitute as to such whole or part a revocation of this trust.

(emphasis added). I view the central question in this appeal as whether the Rudloffs believed that the phrase "during our lifetime," as well as other plural forms contained within this express reservation of a power to revoke, authorized revocation within the period of time representing the intersection of their individual lifetimes (in which case the power of revocation would not terminate upon the death of one spouse) or the broader period of time representing the union of their individual lifetimes (in which case the power of revocation would persist until the death of the survivor).

---

right of the trustees would continue in the survivor, but is silent as to the rights of the settlors, we would conclude that survivorship rights in the settlors were denied under the maxim *expressio unius est exclusion alterius* (the expression of one item serves to the exclusion of other, non-expressed, items of the same general character).

There are a number of suggestions within the declaration of trust that favor the latter interpretation. Significantly, the declaration of trust also employs the same and similar plural forms in other contexts in which it is reasonably clear that the intent was to refer to either or both of the settlors. For example, in paragraph one, the instrument provides for the appointment of a successor trustee upon physical or mental incapacity of the settlor/trustees "during our lifetime," and payment "to us" of income or principal "as may appear necessary or desirable for our comfort or welfare," with the trust property being transferred to the beneficiaries "[u]pon the death of the survivor of us." In paragraph four, the trust instrument reserves to the settlor/trustees the power and right "during our lifetime" to mortgage the premises and to collect rents and other income. Both of these paragraphs, in the context of the overall document, are reasonably read to convey a design to reserve the full benefit of the trust property to the surviving settlor, despite the use of the plural forms, as in the phrase "during our lifetime." This suggests that the use of identical phraseology in paragraph five, with reference to the power of revocation, also was intended to encompass either or both of the settlors.

As Appellee observes, the construction of the trust instrument that the majority adopts requires the Court to discern an intent that, should one of the settlors become incapacitated or die, the other would be deprived of the ability to revoke the trust and dispose of the property to address his or her life circumstances, such as infirmity caused by aging. As Appellee also notes, these sorts of form-book documents are frequently utilized by lay persons in an effort (albeit ineffectual) to avoid inheritance taxation, and it seems counterintuitive that such persons would wish to divest their survivor of the full use of significant assets which might be essential to their care.

According to the majority, the survivorship issue is covered in paragraph seven of the declaration of trust. Paragraph seven, however, is the trustee succession provision of the instrument. As Appellee stresses in his brief, trustees may terminate a trust, but only settlors have the power of revocation. Thus, I cannot agree with the majority that a provision explicitly addressed solely to trustee succession should also address itself to the power of revocation. Instead, paragraph five is explicitly the provision of the declaration of trust addressing the settlors' power of revocation, and I believe that the outcome of this case should be premised upon the resolution of the material ambiguity in that provision. *Cf.* Christian L. Barner, 17727 NBI-CLE 43, 95 (2004) ("Joint trusts are often poorly drafted, confusing the dispositive provisions of the respective settlors.").[1]

In the face of a material ambiguity within a trust document, parol or extrinsic evidence of the settlor's intent may be considered to resolve ambiguity. In the absence of a sufficient manifestation of intent, consistent with a majority of other jurisdictions, Pennsylvania's common law reflected a presumption of irrevocability.[2] Notably, however, such common-law default rules are to be resorted to only where the courts are unable to discern a sufficient manifestation of intent of the settlors.[3]

Here, I conclude that, although the trust declaration is poorly drafted and ambiguous, the reasonable inferences arising from language used throughout the document, as discussed above, are sufficient to overcome the common-law default presumption of irrevocability. Again, in light of the inadequate drafting of the

---

[1] For the same reason, I also differ with the majority's suggested application of the doctrine of *expressio unius est exclusio alterius* to paragraph seven of the declaration of trust. This canon of construction permits the exclusion of terms from an instrument by implication where other items of the same general character are expressed in the document, such that it would be reasonable to infer that the makers rejected the unmentioned terms. Again, however, the item addressed in paragraph seven (succession of trustees) is simply not of the same general character as that which the majority would exclude by implication (revocability by the settlors). Indeed, and again, the latter is actually addressed in another provision of the declaration of trust, namely, paragraph five, albeit in an ambiguous fashion. Therefore, it does not seem reasonable to infer that the makers would have addressed revocability within the inapposite content of paragraph seven. Rather, had the makers apprehended the ambiguity, it seems far more likely that they would have clarified their intent within the relevant provision (paragraph five).

I also have difficulty with implementing such a tenuous application of the *expressio unius* canon in a situation in which the instrument under review appears to be a generic, stationary-store document frequently purchased by lay persons with the single-minded purpose of attempting to avoid inheritance taxation. It does not appear to me to be reasonable to infer that persons in such circumstances intended to reject the prospect of a continuing power of revocation in their survivors merely because they acceded to a generic trustee succession provision.

[2] A contrary approach has emerged, which reverses the presumption in favor of revocability, as reflected in the Uniform Trust Code, approved and recommended by the National Conference of Commissioners on Uniform State Laws, and as adopted by the Pennsylvania General Assembly as Section 7752 of the Pennsylvania Uniform Trust Act. The Uniform Law Comment explains, however, that such reversal applies "only for trusts created after [the] effective date," which, in this case, is November 6, 2006, well after the creation of the trust in issue.

[3] As explained by a court of common pleas:

[S]tarting some years ago, our Supreme Court has progressively diminished the effect of artificial [judicial] canons of construction, or presumptions of intent, and has mandated our courts to determine, from the document itself and from other circumstances known to a testator, his intent as expressed by the most natural and reasonable meaning of the words used. The problem with [judicial] canons of construction and arbitrary presumptions was that one which led to one result could always be met by one which led to the opposite result[.]

Parenthetically, absent some constitutional infirmity, the courts are bound to apply statutory rules of construction concerning wills and trusts where they are implicated to the full extent intended by the Legislature.

declaration of trust, I reiterate that there remains a fair amount of uncertainty. My conclusion, to this point, is merely that the greater weight of the inferences concerning the Rudloffs' intentions that may reasonably be drawn from the document militate in favor of Appellees' position and, accordingly, the common-law presumption of irrevocability which would otherwise attach should not, in and of itself, control.

In light of the ambiguity, however, I believe that the common pleas court should have considered the extrinsic evidence offered by Appellant in its evaluation of Mr. and Mrs. Rudloff's intentions. In this regard, Appellant testified that her parents created the trust strictly to thwart any possibility that any of their children would be divested of his or her share of the trust property, since, according to Appellant, Mrs. Rudloff had been unfairly deprived of her own inheritance upon her mother's death. While this evidence was facially self-serving, the task of determining Appellant's credibility was initially for the common pleas court as fact finder. Additionally, although the testimony appears to have been hearsay, it was admitted into evidence without objection. Thus, the common pleas court should have assessed both the credibility and weight of the testimony in determining the Rudloffs' intentions concerning the potential for revocation of the trust by a surviving spouse. The court, however, circumvented this task by finding that the terms of the trust declaration were explicit in vesting the power to revoke only in the Rudloffs jointly. Since I differ with the common pleas court's (and the majority's) conclusion in this regard, I would return the matter to that court to complete the appropriate fact finding.

Finally, I recognize the policy indicated in *In re Solomon's Estate* (1938), and highlighted by Judge Kelly, that "[i]t should not be in the power of either party after the death of the other to destroy the trust both created and both intended to subsist." I do not read *Solomon's Estate*, however, as overturning the longstanding principle that settlors may reserve the power to revoke in the trust instrument under any such terms and conditions as they may desire, within the bounds of legality, to include a conferral of individual power. Rather, I believe that *Solomon's Estate* reflects a resolution of the particular controversy before the Court and an affirmation of the common-law presumption of irrevocability, in the absence of a sufficient manifestation of intent to the contrary.

How much did the settlors save by not employing a lawyer to draft their trust?

5. POUR-OVER WILLS, UPC § 2–511

Under the common law, a trust without a res was no trust at all. There could be no division of ownership if there was no asset to own. A testamentary trust could be created in a will, but an inter vivos trust could not be created without funding it with a res. If a will did not create a trust but included a devise to a trustee of a trust that had not been established before the testator's death, the devise failed. The law has moved beyond that conceptual difficulty and now allows the execution of a trust document that will become a trust when assets pass to the trust from a will. The Uniform Testamentary Additions to Trusts Act (UTATA) and UPC § 2–511 expressly allow a will to devise property to a trustee of a trust to be established at the testator's death by the devise to the trustee if the will identifies the trust and the terms of the trust are set forth in a writing other than the will. Unlike an instrument incorporated by reference, the trust instrument need not exist at the time the will is executed. Even in cases in which the devise from the will brings the trust to life at the moment the will is effective by providing a res, the trust is considered to be an inter vivos trust, which is not subject to the supervision of the probate court. One practical effect of allowing a will to pour over into a subsequently executed trust is that the testator-settlor may change the effect of the will by changing the terms of the trust. A person wishing to do so may avoid the Wills Act formalities for assets in her estate by making changes in the trust instrument instead of executing a new will.

6. RIGHTS IN TRUST ASSETS

(a) Revocable Trusts

A trust is revocable when the settlor has the power to terminate the trust and recover the trust property. When a settlor has the power to reach the assets in a trust, the creditors of the settlor can also reach the assets in the trust even though the settlor does not wish to revoke the trust. The assets are treated as belonging to the settlor and subject to the creditors' claims. Indeed, modern statutes and judicial decisions in most states allow the settlor's creditors to reach the assets in the revocable trust even after the settlor dies. On the flip side of that coin, the beneficiaries have no vested rights in the assets of the trust, and the creditors of the beneficiaries have no right to reach the assets of the trust to satisfy claims against the beneficiaries.

If a settlor makes himself the trustee of a revocable trust, beneficiaries cannot challenge the actions of the trustee as long as the trust remains revocable. As a matter of policy, this makes sense because the settlor-trustee, if asked, would usually not want to be subject to suit by beneficiaries. If the settlor had wanted beneficiaries to be able to sue to enforce the terms of the trust, the settlor could have made the trust irrevocable. However, if the settlor's decisions regarding trust assets are the result of undue influence, maybe the settlor would wish his actions to be subject to judicial review in order to catch or discourage those persons attempting to exercise unwanted influence. Perhaps the standing of the beneficiaries should depend on whether they are acting to protect the settlor. However, there is another way to bring undue influence to the attention of a court. UTC § 604 provides that the validity of a trust that was revocable at the settlor's death may be challenged for a limited period of time after the death of the settlor. Assuming that is the law, the policy question boils down to whether the beneficiaries should have to wait until after the settlor's death or should be allowed to bring their legal challenge before the settlor dies. On the side of allowing challenges during life, good evidence relating to undue influence or lack of capacity should be easier to marshal. On the other side, settlors might wish to be free of troublesome lawsuits. Would any settlor ever subject himself generally to suits in order to protect himself from undue influence?

(b) Irrevocable Trusts

If the settlor is not a beneficiary, the rights of the settlor and her creditors are simple. When a trust is irrevocable, neither the settlor nor her creditors have rights to reach the trust assets. By contrast, the rights of the beneficiaries of an irrevocable trust are not so simply summarized and depend on the terms of the trust. The trust instrument may impose on the trustee a wide variety of duties, including investment, management, administration, and distribution of assets, and these duties can be spelled out in detail or left quite general. Beneficiaries have standing to enforce these duties upon trustees. One of the most important rights held by beneficiaries, of course, is the right to force the trustee to make distributions of trust property. The scope of this right, like others, depends on the terms of the trust. Trusts are classified as being mandatory or discretionary, but there are also degrees in between.

(i) Mandatory Trusts

In a mandatory trust, the instrument tells the trustee what to do with the assets. For example, "pay the income to my spouse for life, and then pay the principal to my children outright." For mandatory trusts, the trustee has no discretion as to who takes or how much, and the beneficiaries have the right to bring an action against the trustee if the trustee fails to perform as instructed in the trust. The beneficiaries may be able to recover directly from the trustee and may be able to trace the property and recover via constructive trust from other parties to whom the trustee has wrongly transferred trust assets. If the trust is not a spendthrift trust, discussed below, the beneficiaries' creditors can reach the trust assets that the beneficiaries can reach. Upon proper application, a court can order the trustee to pay a creditor instead of making the distribution to a beneficiary.

(ii) Discretionary Trusts

In a discretionary trust with an ascertainable standard, the instrument gives the trustee discretion but also sets some standard for the trustee to apply in exercising that discretion. In other words, the trustee's discretion is limited by a standard in the instrument. It is common for the settlor to limit discretion by reference to the support of a beneficiary. For example, "the trustee may pay such of the income as it determines in its discretion for the comfortable support of my spouse for life." The trustee has a duty to provide enough for the beneficiary's comfort, and the beneficiary and court may hold the trustee to that duty. The support standard is often read to require that the trust assets be used to maintain the beneficiary in the standard of living to which he is accustomed. There are other standards for discretionary trusts in addition to the support standard. Obviously, these sorts of standards can lead to disputes and litigation between a beneficiary and the trustee. The value of leaving discretion in the trustee is high enough, however, that many settlors are willing to risk litigation to grant it. As above, if the trust is not a spendthrift trust, the beneficiaries' creditors can reach the trust assets that the beneficiaries can reach. However, support trusts are usually spendthrift trusts, which are described below.

Some trusts are pure discretionary trusts, also called extended discretion trusts. For example, "to my trustee to distribute so much of the income as she deems appropriate in her sole [or 'complete' or 'absolute' or 'uncontrolled' or 'unrestricted'] discretion to my children and grandchildren, and on the death of the last of my children to pay the principal to my grandchildren." Although it would appear that there are no constraints on the behavior of the trustee, courts have held otherwise. As Judge Learned Hand observed, even in a completely discretionary trust the court of equity has jurisdiction to protect the interests of the beneficiary. Were that not so, there would be no trust at all and the instructions would be merely precatory. Trustees have duties, even when the trust is completely discretionary, and courts will review trustee actions for good faith. Those duties are outlined infra. Since the beneficiaries of a completely discretionary trust cannot compel the trustee to make payments, the beneficiaries' creditors cannot reach the trust assets in most states. Indeed, if a beneficiary would not receive a distribution because of a creditor's claims, a trustee may have a duty to refrain from declaring the distribution. However, a creditor unable to attach funds can sometimes get a "Hamilton" order from the court requiring the trustee to pay the creditor before paying the beneficiary.

Uniform Trust Code § 504 provides generally that a creditor of a beneficiary may not compel a distribution from a discretionary trust. However, if a trustee has not complied with a standard of distribution or has abused discretion, UTC § 504(c) allows a court to order an equitable distribution to satisfy a judgment or court order against the beneficiary for support of exception creditors, including the beneficiary's child, spouse, or former spouse. Such a distribution is limited to the amount of the trustee's abuse or failure to comply with the standard of distribution.

In Problems 5.04 to 5.06, below, O settles a trust of $100,000 with T as the trustee for the benefit of B for life and then B's children as beneficiaries. After that, B negligently injures C with his car and C obtains a judgment against B. B has no assets, so C attempts to compel T to pay the judgment from the trust. Additional facts and trust language are supplied by the problems.

> Problem 5.04a: O transfers "to T to pay the income to B for life, then the corpus to B's children." Can C compel T to distribute principal to C to pay the judgment? What interest did B have?

Problem 5.04b: O transfers "to T to pay the income to B for life, then the corpus to B's children." Can C compel T to distribute income to C?

Problem 5.05: O transfers "to T to apply such income in his discretion for the reasonable comfort of B, then the corpus to B's children." Can C compel a distribution of income to C?

Problem 5.06: O transfers "to T to pay income or principal to B in T's complete discretion, then the corpus to B's children." Can C compel T to distribute trust assets to satisfy the judgment? Can B force T to pay B? Is it an abuse of discretion for T to pay B nothing?

Problem 5.07: O transfers "to T to pay income or principal to B in T's complete discretion, then the corpus to B's estate." X is B's child, spouse, or former spouse with a court order of support from B. Can X compel a distribution from the trust under the common law? Under the UTC?

Example 5.08: O transfers "to T. T shall pay the income to B every month, but if B's creditors attach B's interest, T has complete discretion as to whether to declare a distribution." This is an example of a protective trust, which switches from mandatory to completely discretionary when a creditor makes a claim. These are common in England, for reasons that will appear in a moment.

(iii) Spendthrift Trusts

If a trust is a spendthrift trust, a creditor's rights are often more limited than indicated above. A trust is made spendthrift by adding words that prevent the beneficiary from alienating her interest. Traditionally, to qualify for spendthrift protection, the terms of the trust had to prevent both intentional and unintentional alienation. For example: "The interest of B shall not be subject to the claims of any creditor or to legal process and may not be voluntarily or involuntarily alienated or encumbered."

Example 5.09: O devises "to T to pay the income to B until age 50, then the corpus to B, and B may not transfer her interest voluntarily or involuntarily" (creating a spendthrift trust). If B has no creditors, can B force T to make a distribution from the trust? Yes. Next, C becomes an ordinary, unsecured creditor of B. Can C compel a distribution from B's trust under the UTC or the law in most states? No.

Spendthrift protection offers the highly prized advantage of allowing the trustee to make distributions to beneficiaries without making those distributions available to the beneficiaries' creditors. The creditor cannot attach the assets, and a court will not order the trustee to pay the creditor instead of the beneficiary. Spendthrift trusts were originally quite controversial, and England still does not allow spendthrift protection, but they are now well accepted in American states. John Chipman Gray railed against them. They establish a legal divide between those who receive their income from trust assets and those who receive their income from labor. The law allows a settlor to protect a trust beneficiary's income from creditors while the law makes the laborer's income subject to attachment. Gray said that spendthrift trusts form a privileged class, "an aristocracy, though certainly the most contemptible aristocracy with which a country was ever cursed". This result is sometimes justified on the ground that the settlor could herself make gifts to a beneficiary without paying creditors. But that argument is true only for living donors, not for those who are dead. Once again, we see the issue that was raised at the start of the course: How much control should people have over assets after they die? The judgment of American lawmakers is that death should not stop donors from keeping their gifts out of the hands of their donees' ordinary creditors. Regarding spendthrift trusts, which is better, the English rule or the American rule?

Spendthrift clauses do not offer complete protection from the claims of creditors. There are exceptions that allow courts to pierce through the spendthrift protection on behalf of some kinds of creditors for some kinds of claims. Spouses seeking alimony payments can attach trust assets in some states. Minors seeking child support may also attach trust assets in some states. Usually, those two classes are treated the same, but not always. In Illinois, for example, a child seeking support may pierce through the spendthrift protection, whereas a divorced spouse seeking maintenance may not. Under the common law, a spendthrift clause is also unenforceable against those who have supplied necessary services or supplies to the beneficiary. The UTC does not include that exception, but it does include an exception for a judgment creditor who provided services for the protection of a beneficiary's interest in the trust, so you can get paid!

HURLEY V. HURLEY
Court of Appeals of Michigan, 1981
309 N.W.2d 225

ALLEN, J.

On March 31, 1980, Ingham County Circuit Court ordered garnishee-defendant, Michigan National Bank, to pay accrued and future income of a spendthrift trust to the court in satisfaction of an outstanding judgment for past due child support taken against defendant, James Hurley, former husband of plaintiff, Phyllis Hurley. Garnishee-defendant's motion for rehearing was denied on April 14, 1980. Garnishee-defendant appeals as of right.

The facts before this Court are undisputed. On September 26, 1966, Maybelle Hurley, defendant's mother and a resident of Missouri, executed a will in Missouri. The will devised the decedent's personalty and household goods and furnishings to defendant, her son James. The remainder of decedent's property was placed into four trusts. One-half of the property was placed in a spendthrift trust for James. He was to receive all income from the trust during his lifetime with the principal passing upon James' death into the trusts (described below) for James' two daughters, Linda Kay and Cherri Ann, the decedent's granddaughters. One-quarter of the property was placed into a spendthrift trust for the decedent's brother, Clifford E. Hemmer. He was to receive all income from the trust during his lifetime with $5,000 passing to decedent's niece, Florence Yoshimoto, if she should survive Clifford, and the remainder passing into James's trust, if he survived Clifford; otherwise the remainder would pass in the same manner as James's trust, i. e., to the decedent's granddaughters. The remaining one-quarter would be split equally between the decedent's two granddaughters. Until age 21, the granddaughters would receive only enough money for necessary maintenance, support, and education. From age 21 to age 28, the granddaughters would receive all income from the trusts. Upon reaching age 24, each granddaughter would receive one-half of the principal of the trust. Upon reaching age 28, each granddaughter would receive the remaining principal, and the trusts would terminate. The end result of the four interlocking trusts set up by the decedent is that each granddaughter or her issue would share the entire principal of all four trusts should they survive James. If neither granddaughter or her issue should so survive James, the entire principal of all four trusts would pass according to the statutes of descent and distributions of the State of Missouri as if the decedent had died intestate at the time of the termination of James's trust.

Plaintiff and defendant were divorced in Missouri approximately six years before the decedent executed her will in September 1966. The decedent did not provide for plaintiff in her will. In 1970, decedent moved from Missouri to Michigan where she remained until her death in 1978. Defendant, James Hurley, moved from Missouri and presently resides in California. He failed to maintain his child support payments. In 1977, plaintiff filed suit in Missouri for past due child support, and in 1979 obtained a Missouri judgment of $19,630 principal plus $5,728 interest. In 1978, Maybelle Hurley died in Michigan, and her will was admitted into probate in Ingham County, Michigan. Garnishee-defendant, Michigan National Bank, was appointed trustee under the will.

In 1979, plaintiff filed a complaint in the Ingham County Circuit Court against defendant and garnishee-defendant, seeking full faith and credit of the Missouri child support judgment. Plaintiff then moved to require the garnishee-defendant, as trustee, to pay plaintiff the past due and future income from defendant's trust to satisfy the outstanding Missouri child support judgment. Garnishee-defendant answered, claiming that the income from the spendthrift trust was not subject to process by the court. On March 31, 1980, the trial court granted plaintiff's motion and ordered garnishee-defendant to pay due and future income into the court to satisfy plaintiff's outstanding judgment. Only garnishee-defendant appeals as of right.

The sole issue before the Court is whether plaintiff, as defendant's former wife, can reach by judicial process the income from a spendthrift trust created in favor of defendant, her former husband, to obtain satisfaction of plaintiff's judgment against defendant for past due child support. The trust established under the terms of Maybelle Hurley's will meets the definition of a spendthrift trust set forth in *Rose v. Southern Michigan National Bank*, 255 Mich. 275, 281, 238 N.W. 284 (1931), and quoted with approval in *Preminger v. Union Bank & Trust Co., N. A.*, 54 Mich.App. 361, 365, 220 N.W.2d 795 (1974):

> " 'In order to create a spendthrift trust certain prerequisites must be observed, to-wit: first, the gift to the donee (footnote deleted) must be only of the income.* He

---

*   [Ed. This restriction to income was subsequently overruled.]

must take no estate whatever, have nothing to alienate, have no right to possession, have no beneficial interest in the land, but only a qualified right to support, and an equitable interest only in the income; second, the legal title must be vested in a trustee; third, the trust must be an active one.' "

Although the issue is one of first impression in Michigan,[1] it has been ruled upon in several other jurisdictions. The majority rule is that, in the absence of a specific state statute, the income of a spendthrift trust of which a former husband is the current income beneficiary may be reached to satisfy his former wife's claim for alimony, separate maintenance, or child support. Restatement, Trusts 2d, § 157, p. 328 provides:

> "Although a trust is a spendthrift trust or a trust for support, the interest of the beneficiary can be reached in satisfaction of an enforceable claim against the beneficiary,
>
> > (a) by the wife or child of the beneficiary for support, or by the wife for alimony * * *."[2]

Several reasons have been advanced in support of the rule. Some courts adhere to the rationale by finding an intention on behalf of the settlor of the trust to allow a wife to enforce a claim for alimony, maintenance, or child support. In *Keller v. Keller*, 284 Ill.App. 198, 1 N.E.2d 773 (1936), it was held that such an intention will be found unless the trust instrument discloses an intention that such a claim may not be enforced. Other courts have held that child support is not a "debt" contemplated by the spendthrift provision of a trust. Still other courts have held that it would be against public policy to hold that a wife may not enforce child support claims against a recalcitrant husband. In accord with holding a spendthrift provision contrary to public policy is *Shelley v. Shelley*, 223 Or. 328, 354 P.2d 282 (1960), which opines that if the beneficiary's interest cannot be reached to satisfy claims for alimony or child support, the state may

---

[1] *Gilkey v. Gilkey*, 162 Mich. 664, 127 N.W. 715 (1910), cited by garnishee-defendant, is not applicable to the present facts. *Gilkey* involved a discretionary trust, not a spendthrift trust, and a claim against the corpus of the trust, not the income of the trust. We also note that in the 70-plus years since Gilkey was decided it has not been cited as authoritative by any Michigan court.

[2] The special Comment on § 157(a) of the Restatement, Trusts 2d, is as follows: "Although a trust is a spendthrift trust or a trust for support, the interest of the beneficiary can be reached in satisfaction of an enforceable claim against him for support by his wife or children. In some cases a spendthrift clause is construed as not intended to exclude the beneficiary's dependents. Even if the clause is construed as applicable to claims of his dependents for support, it is against public policy to give full effect to the provision. The beneficiary should not be permitted to have the enjoyment of his interest under the trust while neglecting to support his dependents."

be called upon to support the wife and children. Further, *O'Connor v. O'Connor*, 3 Ohio Op.2d 186, 141 N.E.2d 691, 75 Ohio Law Abst. 420 (Oh.Com.Pl., 1957), holds that the husband has a legal duty to support his wife, that a father has a legal duty to support his minor children, and that these elements of public policy outweigh the public policy that an owner of property, such as the settlor of a trust, may dispose of it as he pleases and may impose spendthrift restraints on the disposition of income.

We find all of the above reasons persuasive and affirm, particularly in light of the existing law in Missouri at the time of the execution of the decedent's will and the creation of the present trusts. Missouri law provides:

> "All restraints upon the right of the cestui que trust to alienate or anticipate the income of any trust estate in the form of a spendthrift trust, or otherwise, and all attempts to withdraw said income of any trust estate from the claims of creditors of the cestui que trust, whether said restraints be by will or deed, now existing or in force, or, which may be hereafter executed in this state, be and the same are hereby declared null and void and of no effect, as against the claims of any wife, child or children, of said cestui que trust for support and maintenance, or, as against the claim of any said wife for alimony."

This law was in effect at the time of the creation of the present trusts. Therefore, the trusts as created, even though of a spendthrift nature, could not bar the recovery of the income from the trust for child support. We do not find that the settlor of these trusts intended to exclude such claims but rather intended the trusts to be administered in accordance with the laws of the state in which the trusts were created thereby allowing such claims.

The lower court order directing garnishee-defendant, Michigan National Bank, to pay the accrued and future income of defendant James Hurley's trust into the court in satisfaction of the outstanding child support judgment against defendant, James Hurley, in favor of plaintiff, Phyllis Hurley, was proper and is sustained.

Affirmed.

———————

The *Hurley* court endorses a few different rationales for exceptions from the spendthrift protection. But these rationales will not reach the same result in all cases. The rationale based on the settlor's intent would allow settlors to reject an exception, broadening the scope of the spendthrift clause, by language in the trust instrument. Rationales based on public policy would not allow settlors to reject the exception.

Uniform Trust Code § 502 generally protects spendthrift trusts against claims of creditors of the beneficiaries. However, UTC § 503 allows a court to order an appropriate distribution to satisfy a judgment or court order against the beneficiary for support of the beneficiary's child, spouse, or former spouse. UTC § 503 also pierces a spendthrift clause to pay for services for the protection of a beneficiary's interest, as noted above, and for claims of "this State or the United States" to the extent statutes so provide.

> Problem 5.10: O devises "to T to pay the income to B until age 50 then the corpus to B, and B may not transfer his interest voluntarily or involuntarily and the trustee shall not pay claims for child support, spouse support, alimony, or maintenance." X is a former spouse with a judgment against B for maintenance and C is a child with a judgment against B for support. Does *Hurley* decide whether X or C can compel a distribution from B's trust? Can X or C compel a distribution from B's trust under the UTC?

For an interesting case involving a trustee who breached his fiduciary duty and the unsuccessful attempt of his beneficiaries to satisfy the judgment against him by reaching the assets in a different spendthrift trust for his benefit, see *Mennen v. Wilmington Trust Company*, 2015 WL 1897828 (Del. Ch. 2015). Setting aside statutory exemptions, should courts ever allow persons harmed by spendthrift beneficiaries to pierce the spendthrift protection?

SCHEFFEL V. KRUEGER

Supreme Court of New Hampshire, 2001
782 A.2d 410

DUGGAN, J.

The plaintiff, Lorie Scheffel, individually and as mother and next friend of Cory C., appeals a Superior Court (*Hollman*, J.) order dismissing her trustee process action against Citizens Bank NH, the trustee defendant. We affirm.

In 1998, the plaintiff filed suit in superior court asserting tort claims against the defendant, Kyle Krueger. In her suit, the plaintiff alleged that the defendant sexually assaulted her minor child, videotaped the act and later broadcasted the videotape over the Internet. The same conduct that the plaintiff alleged in the tort claims also formed the basis for criminal charges against the defendant. The court entered a default judgment against the defendant and ordered him to pay $551,286.25 in damages. To satisfy the judgment against the defendant, the plaintiff sought an attachment of the defendant's beneficial interest in the Kyle Krueger Irrevocable Trust (trust).

The defendant's grandmother established the trust in 1985 for the defendant's benefit. Its terms direct the trustee to pay all of the net income from the trust to the beneficiary, at least quarterly, or more frequently if the beneficiary in writing so requests. The trustee is further authorized to pay any of the principal to the beneficiary if in the trustee's sole discretion the funds are necessary for the maintenance, support and education of the beneficiary. The beneficiary may not invade the principal until he reaches the age of fifty, which will not occur until April 6, 2016.

The beneficiary is prohibited from making any voluntary or involuntary transfers of his interest in the trust. Article VII of the trust instrument specifically provides:

> No principal or income payable or to become payable under any of the trusts created by this instrument shall be subject to anticipation or assignment by any beneficiary thereof, or to the interference or control of any creditors of such beneficiary or to be taken or reached by any legal or equitable process in satisfaction of any debt or liability of such beneficiary prior to its receipt by the beneficiary.

Asserting that this so-called spendthrift provision barred the plaintiff's claim against the trust, the trustee defendant moved to release the attachment and dismiss the trustee defendant. The trial court ruled that under RSA 564:23 (1997), this spendthrift provision is enforceable against the plaintiff's claim and dismissed the trustee process action.

In reviewing the trial court's ruling on a motion to dismiss, we determine whether the facts as alleged establish a basis for legal relief. "We will not disturb the findings of the trial court unless they lack evidentiary support or are erroneous as a matter of law."

We first address the plaintiff's argument that the legislature did not intend RSA 564:23 to shield the trust assets from tort creditors, especially when the beneficiary's conduct constituted a criminal act. The plaintiff's claim presents a question of law involving the interpretation of a statute, which we review de novo. "We interpret legislative intent from the statute as written, and therefore, we will not consider what the legislature might have said or add words that the legislature did not include."

We begin by examining the language found in the statute. RSA 564:23, I, provides:

> In the event the governing instrument so provides, a beneficiary of a trust shall not be able to transfer his or her right to future payments of income and principal, and a creditor of a beneficiary shall not be able to subject the beneficiary's interest to the payment of its claim.

The statute provides two exceptions to the enforceability of spendthrift provisions. The provisions "shall not apply to a beneficiary's interest in a trust to the extent that the beneficiary is the settlor and the trust is not a special needs trust established for a person with disabilities," RSA 564:23, II, and "shall not be construed to prevent the application of RSA 545–A or a similar law of another state [regarding fraudulent transfers]," RSA 564:23, III. Thus, under the plain language of the statute, a spendthrift provision is enforceable unless the beneficiary is also the settlor or the assets were fraudulently transferred to the trust. The plaintiff does not argue that either exception applies.

Faced with this language, the plaintiff argues that the legislature did not intend for the statute to shield the trust assets from tort creditors. The statute, however, plainly states that "a creditor of a beneficiary shall not be able to subject the beneficiary's interest to the payment of its claim." RSA 564:23, I. Nothing in this language suggests that the legislature intended that a tort creditor should be exempted from a spendthrift provision. Two exemptions are enumerated in sections II and III. Where the legislature has made specific exemptions, we must presume no others were intended. *See Brahmey v. Rollins*, 87 N.H. 290, 299, 179 A. 186 (1935). "If this is an omission, the courts cannot supply it. That is for the Legislature to do." The plaintiff argues public policy requires us to create a tort creditor exception to the statute. The cases the plaintiff relies upon, however, both involve judicially created spendthrift law. *See Sligh v. First Nat. Bank of Holmes County*, 704 So.2d 1020, 1024 (Miss.1997); *Elec. Workers v. IBEW-NECA Holiday Trust*, 583 S.W.2d 154, 162 (Mo.1979). In this State, the legislature has enacted a statute repudiating the public policy exception sought by the plaintiff. *Compare* RSA 564:23, I, *with Athorne v. Athorne*, 100 N.H. 413, 416, 128 A.2d 910 (1957). This statutory enactment cannot be overruled, because "[i]t is axiomatic that courts do not question the wisdom or expediency of a statute." Therefore, "[n]o rule of public policy is available to overcome [this] statutory rule."

The plaintiff next argues that the trust does not qualify as a spendthrift trust under RSA 564:23 because the trust document allows the beneficiary to determine the frequency of payments, to demand principal and interest after his fiftieth birthday, and to dispose of the trust assets by will. These rights, the plaintiff asserts, allow the beneficiary too much control over the trust to be recognized as a trust under RSA 564:23. Beyond the exclusion of trusts settled by the beneficiary, *see* RSA 564:23, II, the statute does not place any limitation on the rights a beneficiary is granted under the trust instrument. Rather, by its plain language the statute applies where a trust's "governing instrument . . . provides, a beneficiary . . . shall not be able to transfer his or her right to future payments of income and principal, and a creditor of a beneficiary shall not be able to subject the beneficiary's interest to the payment of its claim." RSA 564:23, I. In this case, the trust instrument contains such a provision. Because the settlor of this trust is not the beneficiary, the spendthrift provision is enforceable. The legislature did not see fit to pronounce further limitations and we will not presume others were intended.

Finally, the plaintiff asserts that the trial court erred in denying her request that the trust be terminated because the purpose of the trust can no longer be satisfied. The plaintiff argues that the trust's purpose to provide for the defendant's support, maintenance and education can no longer be fulfilled because the defendant will likely remain incarcerated for a period of years. The trial court, however, found that the trust's purpose "may still be fulfilled while the defendant is incarcerated and after he is released." The record before us supports this finding.

Affirmed.

Example 5.11: O devises "to T, income to B until age 50 then corpus to B, and B may not transfer his interest voluntarily or involuntarily" (creating a spendthrift trust). B molests minor child C, broadcasts it on the internet, and sits in prison for his crime. C sues B and wins a civil judgment of $500,000 for sexual assault. Can C compel a distribution from B's trust under the UTC? No. Under the Restatement (Third) of Trusts? Yes. Section 59 comment 'a' states the minority rule rather than the majority rule.

Example 5.12: O devises "to T to pay the income to B until age 50 then distribute the corpus to B, and B may not transfer his interest voluntarily or involuntarily" (creating a spendthrift trust). B fails to pay federal taxes. Can the IRS compel a distribution from B's trust? Yes. *U.S. v. Riggs Nat. Bank*, 636 F.Supp. 172 (D.D.C. 1986).

Exception creditors could include the IRS, spouses, children, those who provide necessities to beneficiaries, those who protect beneficiaries' interests in the trust, and underage victims of sexual assault. Which of them should be able to reach trust assets despite the spendthrift clause? Which creditors are more able to bear losses? Which creditors are in a better position to protect themselves in advance of becoming creditors?

Traditionally, spendthrift protection did not extend to the settlor of the trust; the settlor could not employ a spendthrift trust to protect himself from the claims of his creditors. That changed in the 1980s when the Cook Islands began to allow self-settled spendthrift trusts (SSSTs). Trusts properly settled in the Cook Islands are difficult for creditors to reach because the Cook Island banks will not repatriate funds to the United States. For that reason, offshore asset protection trusts (APTs) can protect settlors from their creditors, as long as the settlor puts the assets beyond his own control. If a court thinks the settlor can still exercise control, the court can jail the settlor for contempt for failing to order the trustee to make the res available to pay the settlor's creditors. It seems unjust to allow U.S. citizens to evade their obligations to pay creditors, especially involuntary creditors such as tort victims. Setting aside the question of morality, offshore APTs are of limited utility because the banks charge substantial fees and many people are unwilling to trust their money to banks beyond the reach of U.S. laws and to trustees beyond the control of the depositor. Moreover, the creditor may be able to bring suit in the foreign country, which would have jurisdiction over the trustee.

In 1997, Alaska started a new gold rush by passing a statute allowing settlors to settle spendthrift trusts for the benefit of themselves. The race to the bottom was on and a third of the states have followed suit by enacting laws allowing Domestic Asset Protection Trusts (DAPTs). However, these DAPTs will not always work to protect assets against the claims of creditors. A court may find that the transfer was a fraudulent transfer and bring the assets back into the hands of the debtor, making them available to satisfy the claims of the creditor. The common law allowed a court to reverse fraudulent transfers, but only when the transfer was made after the obligation was incurred. Under the Uniform Fraudulent Transfer Act, a transfer may be fraudulent even if it was made before the debt was incurred if it was made with the purpose to hinder creditors. In addition, bankruptcy law was amended in 2005 to allow the court to avoid transfers to SSSTs that were made within ten years before the filing of the bankruptcy petition if the purpose of the transfer was to hinder claims of creditors. Some lawyers are now recommending an asset protection trust called a bridge trust, which is a DAPT until the settlor is sued, at which point it becomes an offshore APT.

APTs put lawyers in a difficult position. It is unethical for a lawyer to facilitate a fraudulent transfer, but it might be malpractice to fail to alert a client to a legal method to protect legally acquired assets.

Another tricky professional problem for lawyers is negotiating the rules relating to Medicaid eligibility. The government counts the assets in some trusts as available to the beneficiary when determining Medicaid eligibility. As a starting point, if the trust is established by the beneficiary, the beneficiary's spouse, or a person acting for the beneficiary or spouse, and the beneficiary contributed all or part of the corpus of the trust, 1) if the trust is revocable by the beneficiary, Medicaid counts all the assets, or 2) if the trust is irrevocable, Medicaid counts the assets that could be distributed to the beneficiary. But there are exceptions that add more complexity. Medicaid usually does not count trust assets if the trust is a purely discretionary trust 1) created by the will of a spouse for the survivor or 2) for a disabled person to supplement state support with the remainder to reimburse the state for its payments on behalf of the beneficiary. If the trust is not established by the beneficiary or beneficiary's spouse or a person acting for either of them, Medicaid counts assets the beneficiary could force from the trustee, but not assets in a discretionary supplemental needs trust. Medicaid looks back 60 months for assets given away during life. Be careful and watch out for changing law.

7. DUTIES OF TRUSTEES

In addition to the duties made explicit in the trust instrument, trustees have fiduciary duties as a matter of law. These duties include the duty of loyalty, duty of care, duty to inquire, duty of impartiality, duty of prudence, duty to collect trust property and bring claims, duty to protect property and defend claims, duty to diversify (usually met if no more than 5% of the portfolio is invested in any single asset), duty to earmark trust property, duty to inform, and duty to keep and render accounts. The trustee must not commingle funds and must segregate and earmark the funds so they can always be identified. The trustee may not delegate his duties to others.

The duty of loyalty means that the trustee must always act for the benefit of the beneficiaries, never for his own benefit. No self-dealing is allowed. Under the no-further-inquiry rule, the fairness of the transaction and the benefit to the trust do not matter. The trustee may not sell assets to himself from the trust or sell his assets to the trust, no matter that the prices are fair or more than fair to the trust. A trustee is liable for any loss to the trust due to self-dealing and must disgorge any profits from self-dealing. The beneficiaries can recover the net value of the property as of the time the judgment is rendered. The trustee may not use the res of the trust to satisfy any of his own legal duties. *Jimenez v. Lee*, 547 P.2d 126 (Ore. 1976), held, for example, that the trustee could not spend money in his daughter's educational trust for her medical bills. The court also refused to allow the trustee to expand his powers beyond the purposes of the trust by transferring assets from the trust to a custodianship. The trustee, Jason Lee, was a judge on the Oregon Court of Appeals. Unfortunately, not all lawyers understand their duties as trustees.

MARSMAN V. NASCA

Appeals Court of Massachusetts, Norfolk, 1991
573 N.E.2d 1025

DREBEN, J.

This appeal raises the following questions: Does a trustee, holding a discretionary power to pay principal for the "comfortable support and maintenance" of a beneficiary, have a duty to inquire into the financial resources of that beneficiary so as to recognize his needs? If so, what is the remedy for such failure? A Probate Court judge held that the will involved in this case imposed a duty of inquiry upon the trustee. We agree with this conclusion but disagree with the remedy imposed and accordingly vacate the judgment and remand for further proceedings.

1. *Facts.* We take our facts from the findings of the Probate Court judge, supplemented on occasion by uncontroverted evidence. Except as indicated in note 8, *infra,* her findings are not clearly erroneous.

Sara Wirt Marsman died in September, 1971, survived by her second husband, T. Frederik Marsman (Cappy), and her daughter by her first marriage, Sally Marsman Marlette. Mr. James F. Farr, her lawyer for many years, drew her will and was the trustee thereunder.

Article IIA of Sara's will provided in relevant part:

"It is my desire that my husband, T. Fred Marsman, be provided with *reasonable maintenance, comfort and support* after my death. Accordingly, if my said husband is living at the time of my death, I give to my trustees, who shall set the same aside as a separate trust fund, one-third (1/3) of the rest, residue and remainder of my estate . . .; they shall pay the net income therefrom to my said husband at least quarterly during his life; and *after having considered the various available sources of support for him,* my trustees shall, if they deem it necessary or desirable from time to time, in their sole and uncontrolled discretion, pay over to him, or use, apply and/or expend for his direct or indirect benefit such amount or amounts of the principal thereof as they shall deem advisable for his *comfortable support and maintenance.*" (Emphasis supplied).

Article IIB provided:

> "Whatever remains of said separate trust fund, including any accumulated income thereon on the death of my husband, shall be added to the trust fund established under Article IIC. . . ."

Article IIC established a trust for the benefit of Sally and her family. Sally was given the right to withdraw principal and, on her death, the trust was to continue for the benefit of her issue and surviving husband.

The will also contained the following exculpatory clause:

> "No trustee hereunder shall ever be liable except for his own willful neglect or default."

During their marriage, Sara and Cappy lived well and entertained frequently. Cappy's main interest in life centered around horses. An expert horseman, he was riding director and instructor at the Dana Hall School in Wellesley until he was retired due to age in 1972. Sally, who was also a skilled rider, viewed Cappy as her mentor, and each had great affection for the other. Sara, wealthy from her prior marriage, managed the couple's financial affairs. She treated Cappy as "Lord of the Manor" and gave him money for his personal expenses, including an extensive wardrobe from one of the finest men's stores in Wellesley.

In 1956, Sara and Cappy purchased, as tenants by the entirety, the property in Wellesley which is the subject of this litigation. Although title to the property passed to Cappy by operation of law on Sara's death, Sara's will also indicated an intent to convey her interest in the property to Cappy. In the will, Cappy was also given a life estate in the household furnishings with remainder to Sally.

After Sara's death in 1971, Farr met with Cappy and Sally and held what he termed his "usual family conference" going over the provisions of the will. At the time of Sara's death, the Wellesley property was appraised at $29,000, and the principal of Cappy's trust was about $65,600.

Cappy continued to live in the Wellesley house but was forced by Sara's death and his loss of employment in 1972 to reduce his standard of living substantially. He married Margaret in March, 1972, and, shortly before their marriage, asked her to read Sara's will, but they never discussed it. In 1972, Cappy took out a mortgage for $4,000, the proceeds of which were used to pay bills. Farr was aware of the transaction, as he replied to an inquiry of the mortgagee bank concerning the appraised value of the Wellesley property and the income Cappy expected to receive from Sara's trust.

In 1973, Cappy retained Farr in connection with a new will. The latter drew what he described as a simple will which left most of Cappy's property, including the house, to Margaret. The will was executed on November 7, 1973.

In February, 1974, Cappy informed the trustee that business was at a standstill and that he really needed some funds, if possible. Farr replied in a letter in which he set forth the relevant portion of the will and wrote that he thought the language was "broad enough to permit a distribution of principal." Farr enclosed a check of $300. He asked Cappy to explain in writing the need for some support and why the need had arisen. The judge found that Farr, by his actions, discouraged Cappy from making any requests for principal.

Indeed, Cappy did not reduce his request to writing and never again requested principal. Farr made no investigation whatsoever of Cappy's needs or his "available sources of support" from the date of Sara's death until Cappy's admission to a nursing home in 1983 and, other than the $300 payment, made no additional distributions of principal until Cappy entered the nursing home.

By the fall of 1974, Cappy's difficulty in meeting expenses intensified.[6] Several of his checks were returned for insufficient funds, and in October, 1974, in order that he might remain in the house, Sally and he agreed that she would take over the mortgage payments, the real estate taxes, insurance, and major repairs. In return, she would get the house upon Cappy's death.

Cappy and Sally went to Farr to draw up a deed. Farr was the only lawyer involved, and he billed Sally for the work. He wrote to Sally, stating his understanding of the proposed transaction, and asking, among other things, whether Margaret would have a right to live in the house if Cappy should predecease her. The answer was no. No copy of the letter to Sally was sent to Cappy. A deed was executed by Cappy on November 7, 1974, transferring the property

---

[6] After Sara's death, Cappy's income was limited, particularly considering the station he had enjoyed while married to Sara. In 1973, including the income from Sara's trust of $2,116, his income was $3,441; in 1974 it was $3,549, including trust income of $2,254; in 1975, $6,624, including trust income of $2,490 and social security income of $2,576. Margaret's income was also minimal; $499 in 1974, $4,084 in 1975, including social security income of $1,686. Cappy's income in 1976 was $8,464; in 1977, $8,955; in 1978, $9,681; in 1979, $10,851; in 1980, $11,261; in 1981, $12,651; in 1982, $13,870; in 1983, $12,711; in 1984, $12,500; in 1985, $12,567; in 1986, $12,558. The largest portion from 1975 on came from social security benefits.

to Sally and her husband Richard T. Marlette (Marlette) as tenants by the entirety, reserving a life estate to Cappy. No writing set forth Sally's obligations to Cappy.

The judge found that there was no indication that Cappy did not understand the transaction, although, in response to a request for certain papers by Farr, Cappy sent a collection of irrelevant documents. The judge also found that Cappy clearly understood that he was preserving no rights for Margaret, and that neither Sally nor Richard nor Farr ever made any representation to Margaret that she would be able to stay in the house after Cappy's death.

Although Farr had read Sara's will to Cappy and had written to him that the will was "broad enough to permit a distribution of principal," the judge found that Farr failed to advise Cappy that the principal of his trust could be used for the expenses of the Wellesley home. The parsimonious distribution of $300 and Farr's knowledge that the purpose of the conveyance to Sally was to enable Cappy to remain in the house, provide support for this finding. After executing the deed, Cappy expressed to Farr that he was pleased and most appreciative. Margaret testified that Cappy thought Farr was "great" and that he considered him his lawyer.[7]

Sally and Marlette complied with their obligations under the agreement. Sally died in 1983, and Marlette became the sole owner of the property subject to Cappy's life estate. Although Margaret knew before Cappy's death that she did not have any interest in the Wellesley property, she believed that Sally would have allowed her to live in the house because of their friendship. After Cappy's death in 1987, Marlette inquired as to Margaret's plans, and, subsequently, through Farr, sent Margaret a notice to vacate the premises. Margaret brought this action in the Probate Court.

After a two-day trial, the judge held that the trustee was in breach of his duty to Cappy when he neglected to inquire as to the latter's finances. She concluded that, had Farr fulfilled his fiduciary duties, Cappy would not have conveyed the residence owned by him to Sally and Marlette. The judge ordered Marlette to convey the house to Margaret and also ordered Farr to reimburse Marlette from the remaining portion of Cappy's trust for the expenses paid by him and Sally for the upkeep of the property. If Cappy's trust proved

---

[7]   The judge noted that Farr, in response to an interrogatory filed by the plaintiff, stated that he rendered legal services to Sara from approximately 1948–1971; to Cappy from approximately 1951–1987; to Sally from 1974 until prior to her death; and to Marlette since 1983.

insufficient to make such payments, Farr was to be personally liable for such expenses. Both Farr and Marlette appealed from the judgment, from the denial of their motions to amend the findings, and from their motions for a new trial. Margaret appealed from the denial of her motion for attorney's fees. As indicated earlier, we agree with the judge that Sara's will imposed a duty of inquiry on the trustee, but we disagree with the remedy and, therefore, remand for further proceedings.

2. *Breach of trust by the trustee.* Contrary to Farr's contention that it was not incumbent upon him to become familiar with Cappy's finances, Article IIA of Sara's will clearly placed such a duty upon him. In his brief, Farr claims that the will gave Cappy the right to request principal "in extraordinary circumstances" and that the trustee, "was charged by Sara to be wary should Cappy request money beyond that which he quarterly received." Nothing in the will or the record supports this narrow construction. To the contrary, the direction to the trustees was to pay Cappy such amounts "as they shall deem advisable for his comfortable support and maintenance." This language has been interpreted to set an ascertainable standard, namely to maintain the life beneficiary "in accordance with the standard of living which was normal for him before he became a beneficiary of the trust."

Even where the only direction to the trustee is that he shall "in his discretion" pay such portion of the principal as he shall "deem advisable," the discretion is not absolute. "Prudence and reasonableness, not caprice or careless good nature, much less a desire on the part of the trustee to be relieved from trouble ... furnish the standard of conduct."

That there is a duty of inquiry into the needs of the beneficiary follows from the requirement that the trustee's power "must be exercised with that soundness of judgment which follows from a due appreciation of trust responsibility." In *Old Colony Trust Co. v. Rodd,* 356 Mass. 584, 586 (1970), the trustee sent a questionnaire to each potential beneficiary to determine which of them required assistance but failed to make further inquiry in cases where the answers were incomplete. The court agreed with the trial judge that the method employed by the trustee in determining the amount of assistance required in each case to attain "comfortable support and maintenance" was inadequate. There, as here, the trustee attempted to argue that it was appropriate to save for the beneficiaries' future medical needs. The court held that the "prospect of illness in old age does not warrant a persistent policy of niggardliness toward individuals for whose comfortable support in life the trust has been established. The payments made to the respondent and several other beneficiaries, viewed in light of their assets and needs, when measured against the assets of the trust show that little consideration has been given to the 'comfortable support' of the beneficiaries." See 3 Scott, Trusts § 187.3 (Fratcher 4th ed. 1988) (action of trustee is "arbitrary" where he "is authorized to make payments to a beneficiary if in his judgment he deems it wise and he refuses to inquire into the circumstances of the beneficiary").

Farr, in our view, did not meet his responsibilities either of inquiry or of distribution under the trust. The conclusion of the trial judge that, had he exercised "sound judgment," he would have made such payments to Cappy "as to allow him to continue to live in the home he had occupied for many years with the settlor" was warranted.

3. *Remedy against Marlette.* The judge, concluding that, had Farr not been in breach of trust, "[C]appy would have died owning the house and thus able to devise it to his widow, the plaintiff," ordered Marlette to convey the house to Margaret. This was an inappropriate remedy in view of the judge's findings. She found that, although the relationship between Cappy and Sally was "close and loving," there was "no fiduciary relation between them" and that Sally and Marlette "were not unjustly enriched by the conveyance." She also found that "Sally and Richard Marlette expended significant monies over a long period of time in maintaining their agreement with [C]appy."

Because the conveyance was supported by sufficient consideration (the agreement to pay the house expenses) and because Sally and Marlette had no notice of a breach of trust and were not themselves guilty of a breach of fiduciary duty, they cannot be charged as constructive trustees of the property. That portion of the judgment which orders Marlette to convey the property is vacated.

4. *Remainder of Cappy's trust.* The amounts that should have been expended for Cappy's benefit are, however, in a different category. More than $80,000 remained in the trust for Cappy at the time of his death. As we have indicated, the trial judge properly concluded that payments of principal should have been made to Cappy from that fund in sufficient amount to enable him to keep the

Wellesley property. There is no reason for the beneficiaries of the trust under Article IIC to obtain funds which they would not have received had Farr followed the testatrix's direction. The remedy in such circumstances is to impress a constructive trust on the amounts which should have been distributed to Cappy but were not because of the error of the trustee. Even in cases where beneficiaries have already been paid funds by mistake, the amounts may be collected from them unless the recipients were bona fide purchasers or unless they, without notice of the improper payments, had so changed their position that it would be inequitable to make them repay. Here, the remainder of Cappy's trust has not yet been distributed, and there is no reason to depart from the usual rule of impressing a constructive trust in favor of Cappy's estate on the amounts wrongfully withheld. There is also no problem as to the statute of limitations. The period of limitations with respect to those we hold to be constructive trustees (the beneficiaries of the trust under Article IIC) has not run as, at the earliest, their entitlement to funds occurred at Cappy's death in 1987.

That Cappy assented to the accounts is also no bar to recovery by his estate. The judge found that he was in the dark as to his rights to receive principal for the upkeep of the home. An assent may be withdrawn by a judge "if it is deemed improvident or not conducive to justice." The accounts were not allowed, and we need not consider the effect of G.L. c. 206, § 24,[8] which permits the impeachment of an account after a final decree has been entered only for "fraud or manifest error."

The amounts to be paid to Cappy's estate have not been determined. On remand, the Probate Court judge is to hold such hearings as are necessary to determine the amounts which should have been paid to Cappy to enable him to retain possession of the house.

5. *Personal liability of the trustee.* Farr raises a number of defenses against the imposition of personal liability, including the statute of limitations, the exculpatory clause in the will, and the fact that Cappy assented to the accounts of the trustee. The judge found that Farr's breach of his fiduciary duty to inquire as to Cappy's needs and his other actions in response to Cappy's request for principal,

---

[8] The docket shows that the judge was in error in finding that the accounts were allowed. They were assented to but not allowed. In Loring, A Trustee's Handbook § 62 (Farr rev.1962) the author states: "[P]reparing annual accounts, signed by the adult beneficiaries and allowing them to continue without adjudication is an unsafe procedure for the trustee."

including the involvement of Sally in distributions of principal despite Sara's provision that Cappy's trust be administered separately, led Cappy to be unaware of his right to receive principal for house expenses. The breach may also be viewed as a continuing one. In these circumstances we do not consider Cappy's assent. The judge also found that Margaret learned of Cappy's right to principal for house expenses only when she sought other counsel after his death.

The more difficult question is the effect of the exculpatory clause. As indicated in part 3 of this opinion, we consider the order to Marlette to reconvey the property an inappropriate remedy. In view of the judge's finding that, but for the trustee's breach, Cappy would have retained ownership of the house, the liability of the trustee could be considerable.

Although exculpatory clauses are not looked upon with favor and are strictly construed, such "provisions inserted in the trust instrument without any overreaching or abuse by the trustee of any fiduciary or confidential relationship to the settlor are generally held effective except as to breaches of trust 'committed in bad faith or intentionally or with reckless indifference to the interest of the beneficiary.' " The actions of Farr were not of this ilk and also do not fall within the meaning of the term used in the will, "willful neglect or default."

Farr testified that he discussed the exculpatory clause with Sara and that she wanted it included. Nevertheless, the judge, without finding that there was an overreaching or abuse of Farr's fiduciary relation with Sara, held the clause ineffective. Relying on the fact that Farr was Sara's attorney, she stated: "One cannot know at this point in time whether or not Farr specifically called this provision to Sara's attention. Given the total failure of Farr to use his judgment as to [C]appy's needs, it would be unjust and unreasonable to hold him harmless by reason of the exculpatory provisions he himself drafted and inserted in this instrument."

Assuming that the judge disbelieved Farr's testimony that he and Sara discussed the clause, although such disbelief on her part is by no means clear, the conclusion that it "would be unjust and unreasonable to hold [Farr] harmless" is not sufficient to find the overreaching or abuse of a fiduciary relation which is required to hold the provision ineffective. See Restatement (Second) of Trusts

§ 222, comment d (1959).[10] We note that the judge found that Sara managed all the finances of the couple, and from all that appears, was competent in financial matters.

There was no evidence about the preparation and execution of Sara's will except for the questions concerning the exculpatory clause addressed to Farr by his own counsel. No claim was made that the clause was the result of an abuse of confidence.

The fact that the trustee drew the instrument and suggested the insertion of the exculpatory clause does not necessarily make the provision ineffective. No rule of law requires that an exculpatory clause drawn by a prospective trustee be held ineffective unless the client is advised independently.

The judge used an incorrect legal standard in invalidating the clause. While recognizing the sensitivity of such clauses, we hold that, since there was no evidence that the insertion of the clause was an abuse of Farr's fiduciary relationship with Sara at the time of the drawing of her will, the clause is effective.

Except as provided herein, the motions of the defendants for a new trial and amended findings are denied. The plaintiff's claim of error as to legal fees fails to recognize that fees under G.L. c. 215, § 45, are a matter within the discretion of the trial judge. We find no abuse of discretion in the denial of fees.

The judgment is vacated, and the matter is remanded to the Probate Court for further proceedings to determine the amounts which, if paid, would have enabled Cappy to retain ownership of the residence. Such amounts shall be paid to Cappy's estate from the trust for his benefit prior to distributing the balance thereof to the trust under Article IIC of Sara's will.[11]

So ordered.

---

[10] The Restatement lists six factors which may be considered in determining whether a provision relieving the trustee from liability is ineffective on the ground that it was inserted in the trust instrument as a result of an abuse of a fiduciary relationship at the time of the trust's creation. The six factors are: "(1) whether the trustee prior to the creation of the trust had been in a fiduciary relationship to the settlor, as where the trustee had been guardian of the settlor; (2) whether the trust instrument was drawn by the trustee or by a person acting wholly or partially on his behalf; (3) whether the settlor has taken independent advice as to the provisions of the trust instrument; (4) whether the settlor is a person of experience and judgment or is a person who is unfamiliar with business affairs or is not a person of much judgment or understanding; (5) whether the insertion of the provision was due to undue influence or other improper conduct on the part of the trustee; (6) the extent and reasonableness of the provision."

[11] Since Cappy received the income on the "augmented" principal, interest should not be charged on the sums to be distributed to Cappy's estate for the period prior to his death.

Take another look at the authority cited in footnote 8 of the *Marsman* opinion. That is the same Farr as the trustee in the case. Nothing better illustrates the difficulty of satisfying the duties of a trustee than a case in which a court finds that an authority on trusts abused his "sole and uncontrolled" discretion as a trustee. As in *Marsman*, litigation often arises over the issue of whether the discretionary trustee should consider the other sources of income available to the beneficiary. The trust instrument should answer clearly the question whether the beneficiary's other sources of income are to be considered.

A trustee's failure to pay one beneficiary enough will often result in the unjust enrichment of some other beneficiary. The court can impose a constructive trust on those amounts for the benefit of the aggrieved beneficiary. It is also possible for a court to hold the trustee personally liable for breach of duty. If the settlor does not want the trustee to be personally liable, the trust instrument might include an exculpatory clause that protects the trustee. However, the drafter of the trust ought to be careful if she will be the trustee, as including such a clause could be an abuse of the drafter-trustee's fiduciary duty to the settlor. Suppose that a settlor attempts to limit the challenges to trustee decisions by including a mandatory arbitration clause. Should a court enforce the mandatory arbitration against the beneficiaries, or should the court, as a court of equity, refuse to give up jurisdiction of the dispute?

8. TERMINATION AND MODIFICATION OF TRUSTS

Both trustees and beneficiaries may initiate proceedings to terminate or modify a trust, and trusts terminate for various reasons. A trust may terminate or be modified according to its own terms. For example, a revocable trust terminates when the settlor revokes it as specified in the instrument. Or a trust may expire on its own when all beneficiaries have reached a certain age chosen by the settlor.

A trust may also terminate when its goals become illegal. For example, a trust for the purpose of reducing price competition in the sale of fossil fuels terminates for illegality. A court may terminate or modify a trust when no purpose remains possible to achieve. For example, a trust designed to take advantage of the marital deduction will terminate if the beneficiary has divorced and not remarried.

UTC § 414 adds another ground for termination or modification. A trustee may terminate or modify a trust if the trust property is worth less than $50,000 and the "trustee concludes that the value of the trust property is insufficient to justify the cost of administration." A court may do the same for any uneconomic trust, without regard to the value of the property. In this situation, the trustee is to distribute the property in a manner consistent with the purposes of the trust.

It is also possible to terminate, or *a fortiori* to modify, a trust if the settlor, the trustee, and all the beneficiaries agree. Moreover, the consent of the trustee is not required if the settlor and all the beneficiaries are of one mind. It might seem somewhat odd that the holder of legal title, the trustee, is protected less than the holders of beneficial rights, but that is probably consistent with what the settlor would have wanted when she settled the trust and is certainly consistent with the tenor of the Statute of Uses which, after all, vaporized legal rights.

What happens when some beneficiary does *not* agree to terminate the trust? In such a situation the common-law rule did not permit termination or modification. However, UTC § 411(e) loosens this rule and allows the change if the interests of the nonconsenting beneficiaries are protected, such as by continuation of part of the trust or by purchase of an annuity for those not consenting.

Sometimes, all of the beneficiaries of the trust wish to terminate the trust and the settlor is dead, but the trustee objects to termination. The attitude of American courts is indicated by the following case.

CLAFLIN V. CLAFLIN

Supreme Judicial Court of Massachusetts, Suffolk, 1889
20 N.E. 454

FIELD, J.

By the eleventh article of his will, as modified by a codicil, Wilbur F. Claflin gave all the residue of his personal estate to trustees, "to sell and dispose of the same, and to pay to my wife, Mary A. Claflin, one-third part of the proceeds thereof, and to pay to my son Clarence A. Claflin, one-third part of the proceeds thereof, and to pay the remaining one-third part thereof to my son Adelbert E. Claflin, in the manner following, viz.: Ten thousand dollars when he is of the age of twenty-one years, ten thousand dollars when he is of the age of twenty-five years, and the balance when he is of the age of thirty years." Apparently, Adelbert E. Claflin was not quite 21 years old when his father died, but he some time ago reached that age, and received $10,000 from the trust. He has not yet reached the age of 25 years, and he brings this bill to compel the trustees to pay to him the remainder of the trust fund. His contention is, in effect, that the provisions of the will postponing the payment of the money beyond the time when he is 21 years old are void. There is no doubt that his interest in the trust fund is vested and absolute, and that no other person has any interest in it; and the authority is undisputed that the provisions postponing payment to him until some time after he reaches the age of 21 years would be treated as void by those courts which hold that restrictions against the alienation of absolute interests in the income of trust property are void. There has indeed, been no decision of this question in England by the house of lords, and but one by a chancellor, but there are several decisions to this effect by masters of the rolls, and by vice-chancellors. The cases are collected in Gray, Rest.Alien. §§ 106–112, and appendix II. These decisions do not proceed on the ground that it was the intention of the testator that the property should be conveyed to the beneficiary on his reaching the age of 21 years, because in each case it was clear that such was not his intention, but on the ground that the direction to withhold the possession of the property from the beneficiary after he reached his majority was inconsistent with the absolute rights of property given him by the will. This court has ordered trust property conveyed by the trustee to the beneficiary when there was a dry trust, or when the purposes of the trust had been accomplished, or when no good reason was shown why the trust should continue, and all the persons interested in it were sui juris, and desired that it be terminated; but we have found no expression of any opinion in our reports that provisions requiring a trustee to hold and manage the trust property until the beneficiary reached an age beyond that of 21 years are void if the interest of the beneficiary is vested and absolute. See *Smith v. Harrington*, 4 Allen, 566; *Bowditch v. Andrew*, 8 Allen, 339; *Russell v. Grinnell*, 105 Mass. 425; *Inches v. Hill*, 106 Mass. 575; *Sears v. Choate*, 146 Mass. 395, 15 N.E.Rep. 786. This is not a dry trust, nor have the purposes of the trust been accomplished, if the intention of the testator is to be carried out.

In *Sears v. Choate* it is said: "Where property is given to certain persons for their benefit, and in such a manner that no other person has or can have any interest in it, they are in effect the absolute owners of it; and it is reasonable and just that they should have the control and disposal of it, unless some good cause appears to the contrary." In that case the plaintiff was the absolute owner of the whole property, subject to an annuity of $10,000, payable to himself. The whole of the principal of the trust fund, and all of the income not expressly made payable to the plaintiff, had become vested in him when he reached the age of 21 years by way of resulting trust as property undisposed of by the will. Apparently the testator had not contemplated such a result, and had made no provision for it, and the court saw no reason why the trust should not be terminated, and the property conveyed to the plaintiff. In *Inches v. Hill, supra,* the same person had become owner of the equitable life-estate and of the equitable remainder, and, "no reason appearing to the contrary," the court decreed a conveyance by the trustees to the owner. In the case at bar nothing has happened which the testator did not anticipate, and for which he has not made provision. It is plainly his will that neither the income nor any part of the principal should now be paid to the plaintiff. It is true that the plaintiff's interest is alienable by him, and can be taken by his creditors to pay his debts, but it does not follow because the testator has not imposed all possible restrictions that the restrictions which he has imposed should not be carried into effect. The decision in *Bank v. Adams,* 133 Mass. 170, rests upon the doctrine that a testator has a right to dispose of his own property with such restrictions and limitations, not repugnant to law, as he sees fit, and that his intentions ought to be carried out, unless they contravene some positive rule of law, or are against public policy. The rule contended for by the plaintiff in that case was founded upon the same considerations as that contended for by the plaintiff in this, and the grounds on which this court declined to follow the English rule in that case are applicable to this; and for the reasons there given we are unable to see that the directions of the testator to the trustees to pay the money to the plaintiff when he reached the ages of 25 and 30 years are against public policy, or are so far inconsistent with the rights of property given to the plaintiff, that they should not be carried into effect. It cannot be said that these restrictions upon the plaintiff's possession and control of the property are altogether useless, for there is not the same danger that he will spend the property while it is in the hands of the trustees as there would be if it were in his own.

In *Sanford v. Lackland,* 2 Dill. 6, a beneficiary who would have been entitled to a conveyance of trust property at the age of 26 became a bankrupt at the age of 24, and it was held that the trustees should convey his interest immediately to his assignee, as "the strict execution of the trusts of the will had been thus rendered impossible." But whether a creditor or a grantee of the plaintiff in this case would be entitled to the immediate possession of the property, or would only take the plaintiff's title *sub modo*, need not be decided. The existing situation is one which the testator manifestly had in mind, and made provision for. The strict execution of the trust has not become impossible; the restriction upon the plaintiff's possession and control is, we think, one that the testator had a right to make; other provisions for the plaintiff are contained in the will, apparently sufficient for his support; and we see no good reason why the intention of the testator should not be carried out.

Decree affirmed.

In cases dating back more than a century, trustees have opposed termination or modification even though all beneficiaries were in favor of the change. Courts in England have resolved these differences in favor of the beneficiaries on the ground that they hold all of the equitable interests in the trust. But American courts have taken the view that, without the consent of the settlor, even unanimous beneficiaries do not have the power to terminate the trust if there is a material purpose that the trust may yet achieve, and they do not have the power to modify the trust if that would be inconsistent with a material purpose of the trust. This judicial protection of the settlor's intent is called the *Claflin* rule. *Claflin* was a termination case, but it has been extended to modifications as well. *Claflin* protection is limited to the period of the Rule Against Perpetuities.

Claflin protects purposes that are material, which has included trusts that are designed to be discretionary, to provide lifelong income, to delay payment until the beneficiary is mature, and to be spendthrift, but might not include the purposes of providing successive gifts and preserving principal for remaindermen.

Suppose a testator creates a trust that has a material purpose but is not a spendthrift trust, then the beneficiaries sell their interests to a third party, and then the third party asks for termination? After the beneficiaries sell their interests, whatever material purposes the settlor had are probably impossible to achieve. Should a court allow termination for impossibility in such a situation? Courts could discourage circumvention of *Claflin* by refusing to allow termination in such cases. If the potential buyers knew the court would deny termination, beneficiaries would have a harder time selling their interests. However, if the relevant court cannot be counted on to refuse termination in such a situation, *Claflin* protection might be more reliable if the trust includes a spendthrift limitation.

Uniform Trust Code § 411(b) states that a "noncharitable irrevocable trust may be terminated upon consent of all of the beneficiaries if the court concludes that continuance of the trust is not necessary to achieve any material purpose of the trust." According to the Comments, UTC § 411(b) was not intended to change the *Claflin* rule, but the UTC wording could be read to lessen the *Claflin* protection by making it easier for the court to terminate the trust.

> Example 5.13: O transfers "$200,000 to T to provide funds for the education of B until B is 40 years of age." B is 35 and has $500,000 in assets. Despite B's wealth, the trust would qualify for traditional *Claflin* protection because there is a material purpose still to serve. But under the UTC, the trust might be terminated because it is not *necessary* for the trust to continue for the education of B to be funded.

If a state legislature adopts UTC § 411(b) without any comments, should the court read the words "necessary to achieve" to mean what they say or to mean something more like "helpful in achieving"?

The UTC also reduces *Claflin* protection by declaring that a spendthrift provision is not presumed to constitute a material purpose of the trust. By thus reducing *Claflin* protection, the UTC has moved a bit closer to the English rule, which does not provide *Claflin* protection to settlors at all. Which is the better approach? The arguments in favor of *Claflin* could include freedom of disposition, making settlors feel more secure that their intent will be followed, and reducing their efforts to make unchangeable trust provisions. On the other hand, the English approach is, perhaps ironically, more hostile to dynastic goals.

(a) Administrative Deviations

In addition to the situations described above, there are other cases in which a court may modify a trust, sometimes called equitable deviations, which come in two forms, administrative deviations and distributive deviations. An administrative deviation is a change in the way a trust is managed, without a change in who is to benefit from the change. One famous example is the change in the stocks held by the trust set up by Joseph Pulitzer to award prizes. The trustee was instructed to hold the stock in The New York World newspaper, but the trustee correctly thought that doing so would be unwise, so the stock was sold and replaced with other investments. Had that administrative action not been taken, the Pulitzer Prize might not be so well known today. The distributive purpose of Pulitzer's trust was served well by making an administrative deviation from the terms in the trust instrument. Courts generally consider the distributive purposes of the trust to be more important than the administrative purposes when the two are in conflict. However, courts might be reluctant to allow an administrative deviation if the trustee merely claims that a change would be better for the trust, increasing the expected income. Often the courts require some threat to the distributive purposes and allow an administrative deviation only to preserve the income stream expected by the settlor. UTC § 412 allows an administrative deviation if the terms are impracticable or wasteful or impair administration.

How much the courts should protect administrative purposes is open to question. The administrative provisions of a trust sometimes conflict with societal goals. When a settlor instructs a trustee not to sell an asset, the settlor has attempted to place a restraint on its alienation. For a fee simple interest in land, this runs contrary to the *Statute Quia Emptores*, which abolished restraints on the alienation of a legal fee simple with seisin. The policy that continues to support the *Statute Quia Emptores* also applies to other assets. It is efficient for assets to be able to flow to their highest use, and stopping them from doing so imposes costs on society.

(b) Distributive Deviations

A distributive deviation is a change in who is a beneficiary or what a beneficiary takes or when a beneficiary takes from the trust. Traditionally, courts have been quite hesitant to approve distributive deviations. In *In re Harrell*, 801 P.2d 852 (Ct. App. Or. 1990), for example, the court refused to allow a change that would have reduced the share of one beneficiary who could qualify for public assistance if not supported by the trust. The other beneficiaries wanted to change that child's portion to a supplemental needs trust, which could have been settled in the first instance. The court held that making the trust more advantageous to other beneficiaries was not enough reason to approve the change without the disabled child's approval.

Uniform Trust Code § 412 and some courts are more lenient than the traditional rule. This modern trend allows the court to modify the trust if there are circumstances not anticipated by the settlor and modification would further the purposes of the trust. For example, a court has allowed the trustee to change one beneficiary's interest to a supplemental needs trust, saving assets for the other beneficiaries, if that is what the settlor would have wanted. However, even though the UTC standard for a deviation is lower, it is not always met. It has been held, for example, that the fact that beneficiaries would prefer to have their money sooner rather than later is not an unanticipated circumstance justifying deviation. Many beneficiaries would like to accelerate possession of their interests, but that often runs counter to the settlor's intent.

A well-drafted supplemental needs trust can leave the beneficiary eligible for maximum support from the state while providing benefits that the state will not provide. But trusts are not always well drafted, and beneficiaries find out later that they could get more from the trust if it were modified. Should courts allow such modifications? An argument that they should is that settlors who hired bad trust drafters should get the same results as settlors who hired good drafters. Another argument is that the courts should do what the settlor would have wanted done. On the other hand, such modifications have the effect of transferring assets from some families to others. There are about 11 million trust beneficiaries in the United States. Odds are that they are wealthier than the median American. Distributive deviations might shift the costs of health care from wealthy families to the public, increasing taxes or reducing expenditures on programs. Is that desirable? Would a better approach be to deny the trust modification and allow a suit against the drafting lawyer?

The same basic question arises in the context of tax planning. Too often, trustees seek to change the terms of a trust to save taxes. Sometimes they are successful, sometimes not. In *Matter of Estate of Branigan*, 609 A.2d 431 (N.J. 1992), the court held that extrinsic evidence could be used to modify the trust to save taxes, but not where it might endanger the interests of some beneficiaries. It is possible that the failure to minimize taxes was a mistake by the lawyer, even malpractice, but it is also possible that it was intentional. Lawyers who draft estate plans that do not maximize tax savings because the client has other objectives should make this clear in the writing to avoid later claims that tax planning was overlooked. UTC § 417 allows courts to modify the terms of a trust to achieve the settlor's tax objectives. Does it serve the interests of the people of the nation for state legislatures to adopt that section?

(c) Trust Decanting

Decanting wine involves pouring wine from a bottle into another vessel, from which distributions of wine will eventually be made. Decanting a trust involves pouring assets from one trust into another trust. If a trustee has discretion to distribute trust property, the trustee can distribute the trust property to a new trust with terms that are different from the terms of the old vessel. Often the new trust will have the same beneficiaries but will have terms that save taxes or improve administration compared to the old trust. Decanting is now authorized in more than half of the states, in some by judicial decision and in many by legislation, starting with New York's statute in 1992.

It is one thing for a new law to allow a trustee to make deviations without court approval if the changes are ones a court would approve. It is another thing for a new law to allow a trustee to make changes to a trust that a court would not approve. If a trustee has power to distribute property outright, it seems reasonable to allow the trustee to distribute the property in further trust. But if the trustee lacks the power to make a particular distribution under the terms of a trust, should the trustee be given the power to make the same distribution by means of a new trust? To put the point another way, if the terms of the old trust could be amended, perhaps the same amendments may be accomplished by creating a new trust that combines the terms of the old trust with the new amendments. But if the old trust could not be amended with certain terms, should it be possible to decant into a new trust with those same terms?

(d) Removing a Trustee

If it is too easy for beneficiaries to remove a trustee, they can pressure the trustee into doing what they like rather than following the terms of the trust as the settlor would have wished. On the other hand, if it is too hard to remove a trustee, the trustee might devote too little attention to the needs of the beneficiaries. Under the common law, unless the trust instrument allowed it, beneficiaries could demand a change of trustee only for cause, meaning for dishonesty or a serious breach of trust. It is very important to pick a good trustee.

Once again, the UTC loosens the rules. UTC § 706(b) allows a court to remove a trustee if a trustee is unfit, or if trustees are substantially impairing the trust administration by not cooperating, or if there has been a substantial change in circumstances, or if all qualified beneficiaries request it. Notably, the UTC does not require the consent of all beneficiaries, only the qualified ones. One case has held that contingent remainderpersons are not "qualified beneficiaries". This is consistent with the virtual representation doctrine, which allows a beneficiary that cannot act to be represented by a beneficiary with substantially identical interests. The UTC rules are default rules and can be overridden by the terms of the trust. Which is the better default on trustee removal, the common law or the UTC?

The common law allowed a trustee to resign only with the permission of the court. UTC § 705 expands the methods of resignation by allowing a trustee to resign with the permission of the court or upon at least 30 days' notice to the qualified beneficiaries, the settlor, and all cotrustees.

(e) Trustee Compensation

Under UTC § 708, if the trust instrument does not set out compensation for the trustee, the trustee is entitled to compensation that is reasonable under the circumstances, which is obviously a standard that can lead to litigation. Even if a fee is specified in the trust instrument, it can be challenged as being unreasonably high or low. Litigation on trustee fees can also arise when a trust is terminated or transferred to a new trustee.

(f) Trust Protectors

Trust protectors are a cool tool in the trust lawyer's toolbox. They started with offshore trusts but now are used in domestic trusts as well. They are used to solve some of the problems of changed circumstances and bad planning mentioned above. A trust protector can be given the power to terminate the trust, approve deviations including changes to avoid taxes, remove the trustee, or anything else that the settlor chooses the trust protector to do. However, caution is necessary because there are situations in which a trust protector might interfere with the goals of the trust. For example, if the trust protector might operate the trust for the benefit of the settlor, there is a danger the trust will be considered a grantor trust for tax purposes. For another example, if the trust protector is within the control of the settlor and has enough power, a court might order the settlor to instruct the protector to bring assets back within the reach of the settlor's creditors.

In addition, trust protectors raise legal issues that are not yet solved in many jurisdictions. Are they fiduciaries and, if so, what are their duties? Can they last longer than the period of the Rule Against Perpetuities?

9. DIFFERENCES BETWEEN TRUSTS AND WILLS

One advantage of wills over trusts is that trusts are not protected by non-claim statutes that limit the time for creditors to bring claims against the estate. On the other hand, trusts are better at keeping secrets since wills are public and trust instruments need not be made public. In addition, a trust can specify that it is governed by the law of a particular jurisdiction that best fits the needs of the settlor; this is unlike a will, which is governed by the law of the decedent's domicile at death. An important advantage of trusts over wills is that a trust can set up its own standard for competence, shifting control over assets from the settlor to a new trustee without having to ask a court to declare the principal to be incompetent. The shift in control can come automatically at some point in time or can be decided by a single appointed person or group of persons.

(a) Formalities

The formalities are less onerous for executing a trust than for executing a will. In a way that is good because it lowers the costs of creating a trust. However, the reduction in formalities could increase opportunities for fraud and undue influence. How might a potential settlor protect herself against future overreaching? Could the law protect against unwanted behavior at lower cost than the settlor? Should we increase the requirements for a trust, to reduce the possibilities of overreaching? Some reformers argue that public demand for trusts shows that the formalities of wills should be reduced. Perhaps the lesson is the opposite, and the formalities of trusts should be increased. Or maybe it is a good idea to have two different degrees of formality, one for instruments that take effect during the life of the transferor and another for instruments that take effect when the transferor is dead and not available for questioning.

(b) Interpretation and Reform

The laws governing wills and trusts can differ in other ways. One difference, perhaps, relates to automatic revocation of trust provisions. By statute, divorce revokes a preexisting will's devises to the former spouse and family. Those statutes do not necessarily extend to gifts in trusts. In *Clymer v. Mayo*, 473 N.E.2d 1084 (Mass. 1985), the court decided that the automatic revocation did also apply to the gift to the former spouse in an inter vivos trust created by a pour-over will despite the absence of a statutory extension to trusts. Should the court have waited for the legislature to make that extension?

Another difference is in the provisions dealing with pretermitted children. An Arkansas decision refused to extend to a trust the statutory omitted child provisions that apply to wills.

As with wills, it is possible to petition the court to reform a trust. UPC § 2–805 and UTC § 415 allow reformation, even when the terms of a trust are unambiguous, if intent is proved by clear and convincing evidence and there was a mistake of fact or law, whether in expression or inducement. Although both wills and trusts can be reformed, a court might apply a different standard for reforming trusts than it does for reforming wills.

10. CHARITABLE TRUSTS

A HISTORY OF AMERICAN LAW
Lawrence M. Friedman (2019)
Excerpt from the Fourth Edition page 235

"One kind of dynastic trust is not rooted in family affairs: the long-term charitable trust. It has had a curiously checkered career in the United States. Charities, so goes the maxim, are favorites of the law. But charitable trusts were hardly favorites. In the early nineteenth century, this kind of trust was linked with the dead hand, especially the dead hand of established churches, and more especially, the Roman Catholic Church, suspected of holding massive wealth in land and other assets, and forever. This hardly fit American nineteenth century ideology."

The law today treats charities charitably. Charitable trusts can be created without definite beneficiaries, and they do not have to comply with the limits imposed by the Rule Against Perpetuities. And charities enjoy special tax status, their property often being exempted from property taxes, their income often being exempt from federal income taxes, and their contributors often receiving a deduction for contributions. As a tax expenditure, the deduction for contributions provides charitable organizations with more than $50,000,000,000 in federal support each year. Because there are no definite beneficiaries to monitor trustees of charitable trusts, the attorneys general of the states have the power to hold the trustees to account according to the provisions of the trusts. A person with a special interest in the enforcement of the trust might also have standing to enforce its terms. UTC § 405(c) allows a settlor of a charitable trust to enforce its terms.

Obviously, charitable trusts may be created only for charitable purposes.

UTC § 405

SECTION 405. CHARITABLE PURPOSES; ENFORCEMENT.

(a) A charitable trust may be created for the relief of poverty, the advancement of education or religion, the promotion of health, governmental or municipal purposes, or other purposes the achievement of which is beneficial to the community.

(b) If the terms of a charitable trust do not indicate a particular charitable purpose or beneficiary, the court may select one or more charitable purposes or beneficiaries. The selection must be consistent with the settlor's intention to the extent it can be ascertained.

(c) The settlor of a charitable trust, among others, may maintain a proceeding to enforce the trust.

A trust may be charitable even if the purpose has not been specified. In *In re Jordan's Estate*, 197 A. 150 (Pa. 1938), a devise to "charity" qualified as charitable. But do not assume that "charitable" has no limits.

ADYE V. SMITH

Supreme Court of Errors of Connecticut, 1876
1876 WL 1758

LOOMIS, J.

The testatrix by her last will appointed a trustee and attempted to dispose of the remainder of her estate in trust by the use of the following language: "It is my will that said trustee shall dispose of such remainder for any and all benevolent purposes that he may see fit, and at his option."

The question is, whether this language is sufficiently certain to uphold the trust, and divert the estate from the lawful heirs.

If this disposition is tested by the common law rules it is clearly invalid. By the common law there cannot be a valid bequest to an indefinite object, or a valid use without an ascertained cestui que trust. There must be a beneficiary, indicated in the will, capable of coming into court and claiming the benefit of the bequest. If the language is so indefinite that the court cannot ascertain who the cestui que trust is, it is the same thing as if there was none, and the property goes directly to the next of kin. And such a defect cannot be cured by any action on the part of the trustee, for the testator must for himself define the objects of his bounty and cannot delegate this power to another.

But while such are the established rules of the common law, it is conceded that in England a peculiar system of jurisprudence has grown up in disregard of these rules, whereby certain indefinite charitable gifts have been upheld by the exercise of chancery powers and the royal prerogative of the crown.

This system found its embodiment, if not its origin, in the statute of the 43d of Elizabeth, which specifically mentioned certain trusts to be upheld and executed by the Lord Chancellor, which trusts in the latter part of the act were referred to and characterized as "charitable and godly uses."

Ever since the enactment of this statute the word "charitable," when used in a will conveying property, has had a technical meaning, not only in England, but in this country as well, even in those states where the statute has never been re-enacted, or adopted by usage. And it may be remarked that in general the decisions of the English chancery upon trusts for charity have furnished the general rules of adjudication in the courts of the United States.

It will not therefore be amiss to inquire whether the trust now in question could stand if tested by the statute of Elizabeth and the decisions of the English courts.

Sir William Grant, the Master of the Rolls, in his opinion in *Morice v. The Bishop of Durham*, 9 Vesey, 399, said: "I am not aware of any case in which a bequest has been held charitable, where the testator has not used that word to denote his general purpose or specified some particular purpose which this court has determined to be charitable." In that case the testatrix by her will directed that the residue of her estate "should be applied to such objects of benevolence and liberality as the Bishop of Durham in his own discretion should most approve." It was held that this language was too indefinite to uphold the trust, upon the ground that benevolence and liberality could find numberless objects not included among the charities mentioned in the statute. This decision was affirmed by the Lord Chancellor on appeal, and is again reported in the 10th of Vesey, 521.

In *Vezey v. Jamson*, 1 Simons & Stuart, 69, where the estate was given to the executors in trust to dispose of at their discretion, either for charitable or public purposes, the trust was held too general and indefinite to be executed.

To the same effect was the decision in *Ellis v. Selby*, 1 Mylne & Craig, 286, where the fund was applied "to and for such charitable or other purposes as his trustees should think fit."

In *Williams v. Kershaw*, 5 Clark & Finnelly, 111, a direction by a testator to his trustees to apply the estate "to and for such benevolent, charitable and religious purposes as they in their discretion should think most advantageous and beneficial," was held void for uncertainty.

In *James v. Allen*, 3 Merivale, 15, it was held that a bequest in trust "for such benevolent purposes as the trustees may unanimously agree upon," could not be sustained, on the ground that there were benevolent purposes which the court could not construe to be charitable; and the trustees being directed to apply the property to benevolent purposes might select objects not charitable within the statute.

To the same effect is the reasoning in *Kenall v. Granger*, 5 Beavan, 300, and in other cases that might be cited, but the above will suffice to show that the trust in question must be held void in the light of the English decisions.

If now we pass to the decisions of the courts of last resort in the United States we shall find that such indefinite trusts as the testatrix here attempted to create have repeatedly been held void for uncertainty. An examination of the numerous cases cited in the brief for the plaintiff will abundantly sustain this position. We will only refer particularly to one of these cases, which is from an adjoining state whose system of jurisprudence relative to trusts for charity is similar to our own, and in which case the testator in attempting to create a trust used words almost literally identical with the language now under consideration. It is the recent case of *Chamberlain and others v. Stearns and others*, 111 Mass., 267. Gray, C. J., in delivering the opinion said: "The question presented by this case is, whether a devise in trust to be applied solely for benevolent purposes in the discretion of the trustees creates a public charity. And we are all of opinion that it does not. The word 'benevolent' of itself, without anything in the context to qualify or restrict its ordinary meaning, clearly includes not only purposes which are deemed charitable by a court of equity, but also any acts dictated by kindness, good will, or a disposition to do good, the objects of which have no relation to the promotion of education, learning or religion, the relief of the needy, the sick or the afflicted, the support of public works, or the relief of public burdens, and cannot be deemed charitable in the technical and legal sense. The only difference of opinion in the adjudged cases on this subject has been upon the question how far the word 'benevolent,' when used to describe the purposes of a trust, could be deemed limited in its meaning by being associated with other words more clearly pointing to a strictly charitable disposition of the fund."

Having shown that the trust in question would be held void upon the principles adopted in England and in our sister states, we will next inquire whether there is anything peculiar to our own system relative to trusts for charity that can save and enforce the bequest we are considering.

This state has never adopted the statute of Elizabeth. But we have a substitute statute of our own, first passed in 1684, but which did not appear in the printed statutes until 1702, and hence it has been generally called the "statute of 1702." The language of the act is as follows: "All estates that have been or shall be granted for the maintenance of the ministry of the gospel, or of schools of learning, or for the relief of the poor, or for any other public and charitable use, shall forever remain to the uses to which they have been or shall be granted, according to the true intent and meaning of the grantor, and to no other use whatever."

Our law is more strict than the English law in this, that it requires certainty in the persons to be benefited, or at least a certain and definite class of persons with an ascertained mode of selecting them. But the law of England in those cases where the statute applies, or where the doctrine of *cy pres* may be invoked, does not require any such certainty.

In *White v. Fisk*, 22 Conn., 31, the doctrine of *cy pres* was repudiated, as founded originally on kingly prerogative, and as inconsistent with the provisions of our statute. In that case a bequest in trust, "for the support of indigent pious young men preparing for the ministry in New Haven, Connecticut," was held void for uncertainty. Church, C. J., in giving the opinion of the court, after citing the closing part of the statute, which provides that the estates given to charitable uses "shall ever remain to the uses to which they have been or shall be given or granted, according to the *true intent and meaning* of the grantor, and to no other use whatever," says that "to carry out this provision of the law the intention of the donor must be certain, as well as the objects of his bounty reasonably definite, and the charity confined to the very use to which it was destined."

In the case under consideration the words used to express the trust lack every element of certainty heretofore required in this state. There is no certain beneficiary, no definite class, no ascertained mode of selection, and no certainty and no limitation in the purpose of the trust except as found in the world-wide field of benevolence; a realm as broad at least as the human race, and which may embrace even the domestic animals, for such even are now justly considered the legitimate objects of human kindness and protection.

It is conceded that there is nothing in the language of the bequest we are considering to bring the case within the provisions of our statute, unless the word "benevolent" as used in the will, is of the same import as the word "charitable" as used in the statute.

While it is true that there is no charitable purpose which is not also a benevolent purpose, yet the converse is not equally true, for there may be a benevolent purpose which is not charitable, in the legal sense of the term. We have already seen that the word "charitable," as used by the English courts and the courts of the United States, has a technical meaning. Our statute was passed nearly a century after the statute of Elizabeth and after the word "charitable" had received a definite meaning from a long line of the highest judicial opinions. When therefore our legislature, in framing an act on the same subject, deliberately used the same word to characterize the trusts they wished to protect and enforce, there can be no doubt that the word "charitable" was used in the same technical sense it had acquired under the famous act of the mother country.

This rule of construction was virtually adopted by this court in the case of *Hamden v. Rice*, 24 Conn., 350.

The foregoing considerations have led us to the conclusion that the apparent trust in the will, "for any and all benevolent purposes," is void for uncertainty, and that the estate in question, upon the death of the testatrix, vested in her heirs at law.

The finding shows that the trustee has made a statement of the purposes for which he intends to dispose of said funds, and if such purposes had been specified in the will it would have been valid. But no action or statement on the part of the trustee can avail in the least to cure a radical defect in the will. It is the will of the testatrix, not that of the trustee, which is to stand or fall. And to use the language of Sir William Grant in *Morice v. The Bishop of Durham*, "the question is not whether the trustee may apply the estate upon purposes strictly charitable, but whether he is bound so to apply it."

We advise that the property in dispute be distributed to the heirs at law of the testatrix.

Trusts for the relief of poverty are charitable. But if a trust also transfers wealth to persons not in poverty, it might be held not to be charitable. In *Marsh v. Frost National Bank*, 129 S.W.3d 174 (Tex. App. 2004), the testator attempted to transfer $1,000,000 in trust to the President, Vice President, and Speaker of the House, to be invested until the fund was sufficient to pay each and every U.S. citizen $1,000,000. While accepting that the gift was generous and benevolent, the court held that the trust would not necessarily benefit the public and did not qualify as a charitable trust.

Trusts to support education and public libraries are generally charitable. As the Supreme Court has written, "[w]e have repeatedly acknowledged the overriding importance of preparing students for work and citizenship, describing education as 'pivotal to sustaining our political and cultural heritage with a fundamental role in maintaining the fabric of society.'" *Grutter v. Bollinger*, 539 U.S. 306, 331 (2003). "[E]ducation provides the basic tools by which individuals might lead economically productive lives to the benefit of us all." *Plyler v. Doe*, 457 U.S. 202, 221 (1982).

However, not all trusts for education are charitable. Trusts for the education of one's relatives fail to qualify. In his will, George Griffin left the income of a trust for his widow, then for the education of his grandchildren in a Protestant Christian college, then for the education of deserving boys and girls at such a college who without financial assistance would be unable to attend. The state court held that the trust was charitable. But the Sixth Circuit held that for estate tax purposes the trust was only charitable after the death of the grandchildren even though substantial amounts had been used for support of non-relatives before that point in time, *Griffin v. United States*, 400 F.2d 612 (6th Cir. 1968). Trusts that might or might not be used for the benefit of education might also fail to qualify. In *Shenandoah Valley Nat. Bank of Winchester v. Taylor*, 63 S.E.2d 786, 788 (Va. 1951), the testator attempted to create a trust to pay the yearly income to first, second, and third graders of an elementary school "to be used by such child in the furtherance of his or her obtainment of an education." Because the trustee had no power to control what the students did with the money, the trust served no educational purpose. Similarly, the trustee did not have discretion to limit the payments to persons in "necessitous circumstances". As a result, the trust failed as a charitable trust, and the *cy pres* statutes were inapplicable.

To some extent charitable purposes overlap with the economist's concept of public goods. An economic public good has two characteristics: it is nonexcludable and nonrivalrous. Nonexcludable means that providing the good to one person will make it available to others. Nonrivalrous means that one person's use or enjoyment of the good does not prevent other persons from enjoying it. Examples of public goods include military defense, reduction of communicable disease, good laws, clean air, protection against wildfires, and informed voting. Public goods are goods that a market economy will not provide to an efficient level. Once the public good is provided to one person, it will be available to others and hard for the provider to make additional sales. Moreover, it would be undesirable to charge additional users of the good because their enjoyment does not interfere with the enjoyment by others. Since the market will not provide public goods to an efficient degree, it makes sense to encourage trusts that will provide such goods, and the provision of a public good should qualify as a charitable purpose. Should charitable purposes be limited to the provision of public goods? If the definition of charity is expanded beyond providing public goods to activities with large positive externalities, how should we determine when externalities are sufficient to qualify?

Charitable trusts are permitted to last forever. However, the Rule Against Perpetuities, infra, applies to split-interest trusts, where the charitable part of the trust is divided temporally from the part that is not charitable. And charitable trusts are subject to limitations on the accumulation of income, albeit with a more forgiving rule. For private trusts, accumulations of income beyond the perpetuity period are strictly forbidden. Charitable trusts fall under a rule of reasonableness.

A trust that fails as a charitable trust might be treated as an "honorary" trust, which the common law did not recognize as a true trust. The UTC expands permissible trusts by authorizing some sorts of noncharitable trusts that lack an ascertainable beneficiary and providing that they may be enforced by a person designated by the settlor or by a court. UTC § 408 authorizes trusts for the benefit of specific animals alive during the settlor's life; however, property not required for the intended use must be distributed to the settlor or the settlor's successor. UTC § 409 authorizes trusts for other, noncharitable purposes up to a limit of 21 years. A noncharitable trust to make gifts to school children each year could be enforced for 21 years under this provision. In some states, statutes also authorize trusts for the perpetual care of cemetery plots.

A trust for the support of a political party is not charitable. Why not? Do any political parties work for the benefit of the public generally, as opposed to the members? Should trusts for religious purposes lose their charitable status if the religious beneficiaries promote political ends? If a person makes a gift to a religious organization in order to increase the chances of getting to heaven, is that a charitable purpose?

Settlors of charitable trusts often fail to anticipate that the purposes of the trust might become unlawful, impracticable, or impossible to achieve. When that happens and the terms of the trust do not provide for that contingency, courts sometimes exercise their "*cy pres*" power to convert the trust to a trust for achievable charitable purposes. The goal of *cy pres* is to come as near as possible to the purposes stated by the settlor. A petition to *cy pres* may be brought by a settlor, co-trustee, state attorney general, or person with a special interest in the charitable disposition.

The traditional rule is that the court will exercise its *cy pres* power only if it finds that the settlor had a general charitable intent along with the particular, problematic, charitable purpose expressed in the trust. If the court finds such a general charitable purpose, it applies the trust property to that purpose. If not, the trust fails and the assets revert to the settlor or the settlor's successors. UTC § 413 increases the scope of the doctrine of *cy pres* by discarding the requirement that the court find a general charitable intent, which allows the court to *cy pres* more often, reduces the chances that charitable trusts will fail, and could reduce litigation.

In his influential text, ECONOMIC ANALYSIS OF LAW, Judge Richard Posner argues that charitable organizations do not have adequate incentives to use their assets efficiently. He proposes that they be required to distribute every gift within a specified period of years. Under such a rule, charities would have an incentive to spend efficiently so that potential donors would be inclined to give them more support. Would such a rule increase efficient administration of charitable trusts? Should legislatures adopt such a rule? Those who create charitable trusts could, presumably, include such a rule in their organizing documents, but often do not do so. Should they be prompted to consider the issue by a default rule implementing Posner's requirement unless the creators expressly opt out? Are there reasons that society would want such a rule but settlors would not?

CHAPTER 6

CONSTRUCTION OF WILLS AND TRUSTS

■ ■ ■

A. GIFTS TO CHILDREN OF OTHERS

Many gifts via wills and trusts include a devise to the children of a named person. Most of the time, the children can be identified without dispute. But there could be room for dispute when the parent adopted the child or when the parent did not raise the child.

Because adoptions are so common, the question often arises whether an adopted person qualifies as a child of that adopting parent. We saw above that the adopted child qualifies as a child under the instrument of that adopting parent. The question here is whether the adopted child qualifies under the will or trust of a person other than the adopting parent. In the past, the prevailing construction was that the adopted child did not qualify as the adopting parent's child in instruments executed by "strangers to the adoption". Most jurisdictions have by now abandoned the strangers-to-the-adoption rule, at least for ordinary adoptions of minors. A person adopted as an adult, however, will often not qualify as a child of the adopting parent. The UPC provides default rules of construction.

UPC § 2–705

SECTION 2–705. CLASS GIFTS CONSTRUED TO ACCORD WITH INTESTATE SUCCESSION; EXCEPTIONS.

(a) [Definitions.] In this section:

(1) "Assisted reproduction" has the meaning set forth in Section 2–115.

(2) "De facto parent" has the meaning set forth in Section 2–115.

(3) "Distribution date" means the time when an immediate or a postponed class gift is to take effect in possession or enjoyment.

(4) "Gestational period" has the meaning set forth in Section 2–104.

(5) "In-law" includes a stepchild.

(6) "Relative" has the meaning set forth in Section 2–115.

(b) [Terms of Relationship.] Except as otherwise provided in subsections (c) and (d), a class gift in a governing instrument which uses a term of relationship to identify the class members is construed in accordance with the rules for intestate succession.

(c) [In-Laws.] A class gift in a governing instrument excludes in-laws unless:

(1) when the governing instrument was executed, the class was then and foreseeably would be empty; or

(2) the language or circumstances otherwise establish that in-laws were intended to be included.

(d) [Transferor Not Parent.] In construing a governing instrument of a transferor who is not a parent of an individual, the individual is not considered the child of the parent unless:

(1) the parent, a relative of the parent, or the spouse or surviving spouse of the parent or of a relative of the parent performed functions customarily performed by a parent before the individual reached [18] years of age; or

(2) the parent intended to perform functions under paragraph (1) but was prevented from doing so by death or another reason, if the intent is proved by clear and convincing evidence.

(e) [Class-Closing Rules.] The following rules apply for purposes of the class-closing rules:

(1) If a particular time is during a gestational period that results in the birth of an individual who lives at least 120 hours after birth, the individual is deemed to be living at that time.

(2) If the start of a pregnancy resulting in the birth of an individual occurs after the death of the individual's parent and the distribution date is the death of the parent, the individual is deemed to be living on the distribution date if [the person with the power to appoint or distribute among the class members received notice or had actual knowledge, not later than [6] months after the parent's death, of an intent to use genetic

material in assisted reproduction and] the individual lives at least 120 hours after birth, and:

>(A) the embryo was in utero not later than [36] months after the deceased parent's death; or

>(B) the individual was born not later than [45] months after the deceased parent's death.

(3) An individual who is in the process of being adopted when the class closes is treated as adopted when the class closes if the adoption is subsequently granted.

(4) An individual who is in the process of being adjudicated a child of a de facto parent when the class closes is treated as a child of the de facto parent when the class closes, if the parentage is subsequently established.

Problem 6.01: O and S marry when they are both age 50. At the time, S has a child C, and O has no children. C becomes a parent of two minor children, F and G. O dies, devising "all my assets in trust, income to S for life, remainder in corpus to my grandchildren." Under UPC § 2–705, do F and G take anything?

Example 6.02a: O has a child, C. C has a child, GC1. C adopts 18-year-old GC2, with whom C had no relationship while GC2 was a minor. C dies. O dies. O's will devises "all my assets in trust, income to C for life, remainder in corpus to C's descendants who survive C by representation." Under UPC § 2–705(d), GC2 does not share in the corpus because C did not function as a parent of GC2 before GC2 reached the age of 18.

Question 6.02b: If the facts are the same as above except that O dies intestate instead of testate, GC2 shares in O's estate under UPC § 2–118. Do UPC § 2–118 and UPC § 2–705(d) provide the right default rules?

Problem 6.03: O has a son, C. O dies. O's will devises "all my assets in trust, income to C for life, then income to C's children until they reach 21, then remainder in corpus to C's children." C and M have a child, GC1, whom they raise together as a family. C and M decide to have another child, GC2, and M becomes pregnant again. Shortly afterward, C dies. M gives birth to GC2. M raises both GC1 and GC2 to the age of 21. Neither C nor any relative of C ever functions as a parent of GC2. Who has an interest in the trust under the UPC?

B. POWERS OF APPOINTMENT

The power of appointment is an essential tool in the estate planner's toolbox. It allows one person, the "donor," to transfer the power of disposition over specified property, the "appointive property," to another person, the "donee". This might be desirable for a variety of reasons.

First, the donor might wish the donee to enjoy the benefits of the power of disposition. Those benefits include the simple enjoyment of deciding who will end up with the appointive property and the friendly treatment the donee might receive from the potential recipients, the "objects of the power". (The objects are "permissible appointees"; the "non-objects" are everyone else.) In this way, the power of appointment is different from a trust because the purpose of the trust is usually not to benefit the trustee, and the trustee's actions should not be motivated by self-interest other than the self-interest involved in doing a job well. We see a corresponding difference in duties; the heavy fiduciary duties imposed on trustees are not automatically imposed on a donee of a power, and a donee's appointments are generally not subject to review by a court.

Second, a donor might wish to transfer the power of disposition to a person who has better information than the donor. The donee of the power might have better information because of his position or expertise, or because he will live longer and be able to observe unfolding events. In this way, a power is similar to a trust, but it is even more flexible than the discretionary trust because the donor need not constrain the future decision maker's choice of who will eventually take the property. While, under the traditional rule, a settlor of a noncharitable trust must specify definite beneficiaries, the donor of a power need not limit permissible appointees. That a power of appointment adds something to what can be accomplished by transfer to a trustee is confirmed by the fact that powers of appointment are created within trusts. Indeed, trust instruments often give to one person both the role of trustee and the role of donee of a power of appointment.

A power of appointment is not the same thing as ownership. Even if a donee can appoint to himself, he is not the owner until he has done so. If he fails to exercise the power of appointment, the appointive property goes to the "takers in default," if any are named in the instrument.

> Example 6.04: O transfers $1,000,000 "to T in trust, income to A for life, then principal to such person or persons as A shall appoint, and in default of appointment to B and C." This creates a trust in T and a power of appointment in A. O is the donor of the power of appointment; A is the donee of the power; the objects are everyone; B and C are the takers in default; and the appointive property is the $1,000,000 principal held by T at the end of A's life. A is not the owner of the property even though A could appoint it to himself. If A fails to appoint, B and C will become the owners as takers in default.

1. CREATION OF A POWER

The law gives the donor of a power of appointment great latitude in defining the scope of the power. In addition to limiting the permissible appointees, the donor can limit the time during which the donee can exercise, perhaps starting after the donor dies, and limit the means the donee must use in order to exercise the power, perhaps requiring the donee to file an instrument with the trustee or requiring the donee to make explicit reference to the power when exercising it. Donors often specify that the donee can appoint in trust and create further powers, which makes the power a flexible instrument for accomplishing the goals of the donee. By making the power "exclusive", donors allow the donee to exclude some objects; a "nonexclusive" power prevents the donee from excluding any object and can lead to litigation about how much must be appointed to each object.

IN RE ESTATE OF HOPE

Colorado Court of Appeals, Div. I, 2007
223 P.3d 119

DAILEY, J.

In this probate proceeding, claimant, Joanne C. Ehrlich, appeals the probate court's judgment dismissing her claims against Anita

Flowers and American National Bank, the co-personal representatives of the estate of decedent, Nancy R. Hope. We affirm.

I. Background

Claimant is decedent's sister, and both she and decedent are the children of Elsie Hope. Through a 1983 will and two codicils, Elsie established a "Family Trust," the assets of which were divided into two equal shares and held as separate trusts for each sister. Elsie provided the two sisters with special powers of appointment with respect to the assets in their respective trusts. She limited the objects of the powers of appointments, however, to (1) any descendant(s) of hers, other than the child (or her estate or creditors) for whom the particular trust was created; and (2) any charitable, scientific, or educational organization.

Elsie died in 1985, and, in 1989, the sisters had a falling-out with one another. Subsequently, decedent executed a Will and Codicil (collectively, the Will) and a Trust (the Nancy R. Hope Revocable Trust), the effect of which was to distribute, upon her death, her property and the trust property over which she held a power of appointment to parties other than claimant and her children.

Following decedent's death in 2005, claimant filed claims against decedent's estate for, among other things: * * * (3) half of the assets remaining in the Nancy R. Hope portion of the "Family Trust" that were due her under the limitations imposed by the terms of Elsie's power of appointment.

    * * *

II. Contentions on Appeal

Initially, we decline to consider claimant's contentions that are only perfunctorily asserted and for which no legal authority is cited.

We also decline to consider issues claimant raised for the first time in her reply brief.

    * * *

IV. Decedent's Exercise of the Power of Appointment

Claimant also contends that the probate court erred in determining that decedent exercised the power of appointment as allowed under Elsie Hope's will. We disagree.

Under § 15–2–102(1), C.R.S.2007, the donee of a power of appointment may appoint property covered by the appointment subject to such limits as the donor of the power may prescribe.

As summarized in the most recent draft of the Restatement of Property:

> A power of appointment whose permissible appointees are defined and limited is either exclusionary or nonexclusionary. An exclusionary power is one in which the donor has authorized the donee to appoint to any one or more of the permissible appointees, to the exclusion of the others. A nonexclusionary power is one in which the donor has specified that the donee cannot make an appointment that excludes any permissible appointee or one or more designated permissible appointees from a share of the appointive property.

Restatement (Third) of Property: Wills and Other Donative Transfers § 17.5 (Tentative Draft No. 5, 2006).

Here, the donor of the power, Elsie Hope, provided as follows in a section of her will, titled "Child's Power of Appointment by Will":

> My trustee shall distribute any amount of the principal of a child's trust and any accrued but undistributed income to, or for the benefit of, any descendant or descendants of mine other than my child for whom this trust is created, and any charitable, scientific or educational organizations as such child may appoint by a will which refers specifically to this provision of my will, provided that such appointment shall not include such child, her creditors, her estate or creditors of her estate.

In its written order, the probate court determined that, under this provision, "Decedent could appoint the assets contained in the trust received from Elsie Hope either to a charitable institution or to descendants of Elsie Hope."

On appeal, claimant contends that the probate court's interpretation erroneously substituted an "or" for the "and" which Elsie used to join the two categories (that is, family and charities) of objects of the appointment. In claimant's view, Elsie's use of the conjunctive word "and," rather than the disjunctive word "or," signaled an unequivocal intent that remaining trust assets be distributed equally between the two categories of objects for appointment. For the following reasons, we are not persuaded.

In construing a will, a court ascertains and gives effect to the testator's or testatrix's intent. In ascertaining that intent, we (1) give words and phrases their familiar, usual, and generally accepted meanings and (2) give effect to every word, rather than adopting a construction that renders any term superfluous. *Williams v. Stander*, 143 Colo. 469, 474 (1960) ("It is presumed that every word is intended by the testator to have some meaning; and no word or clause in a will is to be rejected to which a reasonable effect can be given. *Where two constructions are suggested, the one disregarding a word or clause of a will, and the other giving effect to the will as a whole, the latter must be adopted.*")

The interpretation of a will is a question of law subject to de novo appellate review.

Turning to claimant's contention, we note that "and" can be ambiguous:

> The word "and" is notoriously ambiguous and has been recognized as such since time immemorial. It has been described as having no "single meaning, for chameleonlike, it takes its color from its surroundings." Depending upon syntax and context, it can have either a conjunctive or disjunctive effect.

Here, claimant's contention ignores, in its entirety, that clause in the "Child's Power of Appointment by Will" allowing the distribution of "*any* amount of the principal . . . and *any* accrued but undistributed income" to the two categories of objects (family or charities) to which the assets could be appointed.

Because, in ordinary usage, the term "any" means "without limit or restriction," we, like the probate court, interpret Elsie's will as leaving to decedent the ultimate decision whether to give some, none, or all of the trust assets to individuals or entities falling in either of the designated categories of objects for appointment.

To otherwise interpret Elsie's will would, in our view, render the word "any" superfluous, a result we are unwilling to allow.

Our interpretation of Elsie's will is supported by authorities elsewhere. *See generally* John E. Howe, *Exclusive and Nonexclusive Powers and the Illusory Appointment*, 42 Mich. L.Rev. 649, 655

(1943–44) ("when the instrument states that the donee shall appoint . . . 'any part,' the power created thereby is an exclusive power").

Here, decedent exercised the power of appointment in favor of a charitable institution and to the exclusion of claimant or her children. Because decedent's exercise of the power fell within the limits of the power prescribed in Elsie's will, we uphold the probate court's ruling to this effect.

V. Attorney Fees

Finally, we reject the co-personal representatives' request for attorney fees incurred on appeal. Although claimant was unsuccessful on appeal, we do not consider her arguments to be so lacking in factual or legal justification as to warrant an award of fees under C.A.R. 38(d) or § 13–17–102, C.R.S.2007.

The judgment is affirmed.

Did the court correctly determine the intent of the testator? How much would it have cost for the lawyer to have avoided the litigation in this case? Should the lawyer be liable to the estate for those costs of litigation? If the appeal was reasonable, was the lawyer careless?

FERRELL-FRENCH V. FERRELL
District Court of Appeal of Florida, Fourth District, 1997
691 So.2d 500

KLEIN, J.

Mary Jane Ferrell, who died in 1974, gave her husband a power of appointment to be exercised by will, instructing him to divide trust assets "among my descendants in such manner and in such unequal proportions as he shall see fit." Mary's husband, Robert, who died in 1995, exercised the power of appointment and excluded one of their daughters. The daughter, Patricia, filed this suit, claiming she could not be excluded and that the exercise of the power was therefore invalid. We affirm the trial court's decision that Patricia could be excluded.

Both sides agree that this case involves a special power of appointment because the donor of the power designated a specific class, her descendants, as the objects of the power. What they disagree on, however, is whether the power is exclusive, i.e., whether the donee (Robert) could exclude persons in the class. The appellees, who are brother and sister of the appellant, persuaded the trial court that the power was exclusive, and that their father was therefore not required to include appellant in the distribution of the trust proceeds.

Although there is a dearth of authority in Florida on the question of whether a power of appointment is exclusive or non-exclusive, the modern trend is that unless the donor manifests a contrary intent, a special power of appointment is exclusive, allowing the donee to exercise it in favor of any of the objects, to the exclusion of others.

This trend developed as the result of the experience of the courts in having to deal with powers of appointment which were non-exclusive. As the leading case of *Moore v. Emery*, 137 Me. 259, 18 (1941), explains, the problem with a non-exclusive power is how much is the minimum amount that must be left to any member of the class in order for the appointment to be valid? Historically, at law, a nominal amount, for example, one dollar, would satisfy the requirement that all members of the class be included. Subsequently, equity intervened and held that the share given every member of a non-exclusive class must be "substantial and not illusory." That rule was unworkable because it put the burden on the donee of the power to try to figure out how little could be directed to a nonfavored member of the class. If a court later determined that amount to be illusory, the entire power of appointment would fail. England solved that problem by abolishing the equitable doctrine by statute, leaving the rule at law that a nominal amount would satisfy the requirement.

In *Moore*, the donor had empowered his daughters, by their wills, to dispose of the principal of trusts set up for their benefit by appointing the property to the donor's "descendants." The court concluded, after acknowledging that other courts had determined that similar language created a non-exclusive power, that this power was exclusive.

* * *

The Restatement (Second) of Property § 21.1 (1986) provides:

The donee of a power of appointment in exercising the power may exclude one or more of the objects from receiving an interest in the appointive assets unless the donor specifies the share of the appointive assets from which an object may not be excluded. If the donor does not specify any such share, the power is exclusive.

As comment "a" to the Restatement (Second) explains, the primary purpose of a power of appointment is to give flexibility to meet changing conditions, and the less the donee of the power is restricted in the selection of the objects who will benefit, the greater the flexibility.

We hold that a power of appointment is exclusive, unless the donor expressly manifests a contrary intent.[2] Applying that principle here, and finding no intent manifested by the language in the testator's will to restrict the power of appointment so that it is non-exclusive, we conclude that appellant could properly be excluded.

We have considered the other issues raised by appellant and find them to be without merit. Affirmed.

———

Are you convinced by both of the reasons the court offers for not adopting the Restatement position? One is that they can decide the case without deciding whether to adopt the Restatement. When would a court ever have to consider adopting the Restatement? Another reason given is that the legislature could adopt the Restatement position prospectively only. Could a court not do the same, at least in dictum?

Does comment 'a' provide a convincing justification for the position taken by the Restatement (Second)? Why does the law allow powers of appointment? Is it because, as a matter of policy, donees should have as much flexibility as possible to deal with changing circumstances? If so, why does the law allow a donor to limit the donee's flexibility, such as by making the power nonexclusive or specifying a small group of objects? The power of appointment seems better tailored to providing maximum flexibility to donors in choosing how much flexibility to give donees. If the donor's flexibility is the primary concern, how should the default rule be chosen? At least two considerations are relevant. One consideration is what rule

---

[2] We decline, at the present time, to adopt the Restatement (Second), which gives the donee even greater flexibility, not because we do not agree with it, but rather because it is unnecessary to consider it under these facts. One of our concerns regarding the adoption of that rule would be the fact that it would be applicable to powers of appointment drafted years before it was adopted. On the other hand, if the legislature adopted it as part of our probate code, it could do so prospectively.

would maximize the chances of construing the instrument as the donor would have wanted it construed. A second consideration is what rule would make it easiest for donors in the future to express their wishes. Does the Restatement (Second) approach give future donors maximum flexibility? A third consideration, important to both society and donors, is what rule would reduce the costs of litigation regarding powers of appointment. Which of these or other policies are served by the Restatement (Second) approach?

Powers of appointment are classified as either "special" or "general". If a donee cannot appoint to himself, his creditors, his estate, or his estate's creditors, the power is "special," a.k.a. "limited" or "nongeneral".

> Example 6.05: O transfers $1,000 "to T in trust, income to A for life and then principal to such person or persons as A appoints by deed or by will other than A, A's creditors, A's estate, or A's estate's creditors." This creates a special power of appointment.

Conversely, if a power allows the donee to appoint to himself, his creditors, his estate, or his estate's creditors, the power is classified as a "general" power of appointment. Was the *Ferrell-French* court right in calling the power a special power? Would the reason given by the court for calling the power a special power apply in all cases? The standard rule is that, if the instrument creating the power does not expressly limit the objects, the power is general. Donors of powers often wish to give their donees a large degree of discretion in choosing appointees, without giving them unlimited discretion. It will come as no surprise that donors of powers often limit the permissible appointees to persons in the donor's family.

Powers of appointment are divided into those that are exercisable during life and those that are exercisable at death. An instrument creates a lifetime or inter vivos power by making it exercisable "by deed."[1] An instrument creates a "testamentary" power by making it exercisable "by will". Many powers are exercisable both by deed and by will.

> Example 6.06: O devises "to T in trust, interest to A for life, then principal to one or more of A's issue as A appoints by deed or by will, and in default of appointment to A's issue

---

[1] Inter vivos powers are sometimes described as "presently exercisable". That usage is potentially confusing in that the word "presently" has two meanings; it means "now" and it means "soon".

per stirpes." The power is both inter vivos and testamentary. A's issue are both the objects and the takers in default.

HILLMAN V. HILLMAN

Supreme Judicial Court of Massachusetts, Suffolk, 2001
744 N.E.2d 1078

MARSHALL, C.J.

Howard B. Hillman filed a complaint for declaratory relief in the county court, seeking an interpretation of a power of appointment granted to him in a deed of trust executed by his mother in 1970. Specifically, he sought a declaration that the power of appointment does not authorize him to appoint the trust principal to himself, his estate, his creditors, or creditors of his estate. Because of the Federal tax implications, and because it is uncertain whether the Internal Revenue Service would abide by an interpretive decision on a matter of Massachusetts law other than a decision from this court, a single justice reserved and reported the case to the full court.

The defendants include ten individuals who are objects of Hillman's power of appointment, i.e., persons he may designate to receive trust principal either during his lifetime or through his will. Nine of these individuals also would become beneficiaries or contingent beneficiaries of the trust if Hillman were to die without exercising his power of appointment. Hillman himself, in his capacity as trustee of the trust, also is named as a defendant in the case.[2]

A guardian ad litem has been appointed to represent minors and unascertained persons who may have an interest in the trust. The guardian ad litem has filed a report indicating that he agrees with Hillman's interpretation concerning the limited scope of his power of appointment. Hillman further represents that the Internal Revenue Service, which is not named as a party, has been furnished with a copy of his complaint; however, the Internal Revenue Service has not sought to intervene or otherwise participate.

1. *Basic trust provisions.* On or about December 31, 1970, Hillman's mother, Dora B. Hillman (settlor), executed a deed of trust that created an irrevocable trust. Hillman is both the primary

---

[2] Hillman represents to us that all defendants have been served with process. None of them, other than Hillman himself in his capacity as trustee, has filed a responsive pleading or otherwise indicated any view as to the relief sought. As trustee, Hillman (through separate counsel) has filed an answer admitting the complaint's allegations and assenting to the relief sought.

beneficiary of the trust and its sole trustee. When the trust was created, the trust principal consisted of residential real property in the town of Chilmark. Subsequently other property was added: beach lots adjacent to the Chilmark property; residential properties in the town of Beverly and in Greenwich, Connecticut; and cash and securities.

Under the terms of the trust, Hillman is entitled to use and to occupy the trust properties free of rent, and to receive annually any net income derived from the principal. On his death, the properties may be used and occupied for the duration of the trust by his spouse, his issue, and his issue's spouses on terms and conditions prescribed in the deed of trust, and any net income is to be paid to the settlor's then living issue. The trust will terminate, at the latest, twenty-one years after the death of the last to survive from the group consisting of Hillman, his brother Tatnall L. Hillman, their spouses at the time the trust was created, and their children who were alive when the trust was created, and at that point the remaining principal is to be distributed to Hillman's then living issue. If all trust beneficiaries were to die before the scheduled termination of the trust, the trust will then terminate immediately, and the remaining principal is to be distributed to the settlor's living issue.

No discretion is given to any trustee under the deed of trust to make distributions of principal to any beneficiary of the trust while the trust remains in effect. However, paragraph G of Section First of the trust grants to Hillman, as trust beneficiary, the power to direct a trustee to distribute principal as follows:

> "Anything hereinbefore contained to the contrary notwithstanding, Trustees shall pay or distribute such amounts or proportions of the remaining principal (including the Properties) of the trust during the lifetime of my said son, Howard B. Hillman, to or in trust for such of the following (whether then living or thereafter born)-my said son's spouse, his issue, *my issue*, or the spouses of any of his issue or of any of my issue-on such terms and in such amounts and proportions as my said son may from time to time appoint by written instrument, duly executed, notarized and delivered to Trustees, or, following his death, as he may have appointed by Will containing specific reference to this power of appointment" (emphasis added).

2. *Discussion.* The difficulty for Hillman lies in the settlor's reference to "my issue" in the power of appointment. Read literally and in isolation, this language would permit Hillman to appoint trust principal to himself, for he is among the settlor's issue. However, the adverse tax consequences that might flow from such an interpretation could be considerable. If Hillman were authorized by the power of appointment to appoint trust principal to himself, the entire principal of the trust would be includible in his estate at the time of his death and be subject to Federal estate tax, regardless of whether he exercises the power; moreover, during Hillman's lifetime, any capital gains realized on a sale of trust assets might be treated as Hillman's for Federal income tax purposes.

When interpreting trust language, however, we do not read words in isolation and out of context. Rather we strive to discern the settlor's intent from the trust instrument as a whole and from the circumstances known to the settlor at the time the instrument was executed. If, read in the context of the entire document, a given word or phrase is ambiguous, we may accept and consider extrinsic evidence showing the circumstances known to the settlor when he or she executed the document. We tend to disfavor interpretations that would resolve ambiguities "by attributing to the [settlor] an intention which as a practical matter is likely to benefit the taxing authorities and no one else."

Viewing the deed of trust in this case as a whole, and giving due weight to all its language, we agree with Hillman that the settlor did not intend the words "my issue" in the power of appointment to include Hillman. We arrive at this conclusion for at least three reasons, which we shall outline.

First, as can readily be seen from the language creating the power of appointment, quoted above, the settlor not only referred to Hillman once by name, but also referred to him two additional times as "my said son." She further expressly referred to his spouse as "my said son's spouse," and to his issue as "his issue." If she had meant to authorize Hillman to appoint trust principal to himself under this power, we think it is most likely that she would have been consistent and employed the same convention, i.e., she would have referred to him either by name or as "my said son," to identify him along with the others as one of the objects of the power. We think it is highly improbable that, in the same paragraph in which she so clearly and specifically referred to Hillman by name and as "my said son," she would have intended to include him as one of the objects of the power solely by including him in the general, nonspecific phrase "my issue."

Second, if we were to construe the words "my issue" in the power of appointment to include Hillman, then the language identifying other persons who are objects of the power would become redundant and confusing. There would have been no need, for example, for the settlor specifically to have identified "my said son's spouse" (referring to Hillman's spouse at the time the deed of trust was executed) as one of the objects of the power of appointment, since Hillman's spouse also would have been included in the phrase "the spouses of any of . . . my issue." Likewise there would have been no need for the settlor to have referred separately to "his issue," referring to Hillman's issue, and "my issue," referring to the settlor's issue, since her issue necessarily would have included his issue. The only fair reading of the power is that the settlor intended the words "my issue" to refer only to her issue *other than Hillman and his issue.*

Third, as Hillman and the guardian ad litem point out, reading the power of appointment as a general power, one which permits Hillman to appoint principal to himself, would appear to be inconsistent with other provisions in the deed of trust that place restraints on Hillman's access to trust principal. For example, paragraph A.7 of Section First states that, during Hillman's lifetime, "[m]y said son or any of his issue designated by him may purchase all or any part of the Properties at fair market value determined by appraisal, even though he may then be serving as a Trustee hereunder." This provision would have little meaning if Hillman simply could appoint one or more of the properties to himself. Similarly, in Section Third, the deed of trust provides that "[t]he principal . . . and the income therefrom so long as the same are held by Trustees shall be free from the control, debts, liabilities and assignments of any beneficiary interested therein and shall not be subject to execution or process for the enforcement of judgments or claims of any sort against any beneficiary." This basic spendthrift provision clearly was intended to restrict Hillman's access to the trust principal, yet there would be no restriction whatsoever if his power of appointment were interpreted to be a general power.

3. *Conclusion.* We agree with Hillman that, when the deed of trust is properly interpreted under Massachusetts law, the words "my issue" appearing in paragraph G of Section First were not intended by the settlor to include Hillman or his estate.

So ordered.

The court says the words "my issue" do not mean what they usually mean. Is strict construction less important for wills than it is for statutes? Who gains from the result in *Hillman*? Who loses when the federal taxing authorities lose? Unless cutting estate taxes increases revenues, the government will have to raise other taxes, borrow more, or scale back its investments. Higher taxes or reduced investment would be borne by citizens across the United States. So, if the court finds that Hillman is not an object, the winners are those with trusts in the state of Massachusetts and the losers are scattered across the country. Is this decision a bailout for rich people and their lawyers? Will this decision increase or reduce litigation in Massachusetts in the future? Who pays for that litigation? Which of the parties represents the side of the taxpayers that would benefit from a decision against the donee of the trust? Should the court come to the rescue when a power of appointment is poorly drafted?

2.   FEDERAL TAX CONSEQUENCES

As *Hillman* shows, the distinction between general and special powers is important because the two types of powers are taxed differently. (The distinction can also be important in the context of creditors' rights, infra.) A special power, even though it can be very beneficial to the donee, is not ownership and is usually not taxed like ownership. However, when a grantor of a trust makes herself the donee of a power over assets in the trust, she may be taxed on the income to those trust assets. I.R.C. § 674(a).

A general power looks like ownership and is usually taxed like ownership under a variety of federal taxes. (State taxes do not necessarily follow the same rules.) Under I.R.C. § 678, the income from the appointive property is taxable as income to the donee. Under I.R.C. § 2514, the exercise of a general power during life is taxable as a gift from the donee to the appointee. Under I.R.C. § 2041, if the donee does not exercise a general power while alive, the appointive property is taxable as part of the donee's gross estate at death.

But there are exceptions that treat a general power like a special power in some situations. The donee's estate will not include the power of appointment if the donee's power to consume principal is "limited by an ascertainable standard relating to the health, education, support, or maintenance"[2] of the donee or if the power is held by an object along with an adverse party. Some powers created before 1942 are also grandfathered and treated like special powers. I.R.C. §§ 2041(b)(1) and 2514(c).

Often, the donor will prefer the tax treatment accorded a special power, i.e., that the appointive property be taxed as if not owned by the donee, while also wishing to give the donee maximum power to manage the property and maximum freedom to choose appointees.

> Example 6.07: O devises "to A in trust, interest to A for life, then principal to such person or persons as A appoints by deed or by will, except A may not appoint to A, A's creditors, A's estate, or A's estate's creditors, and in default of appointment to A's heirs per stirpes. A shall have the power to consume the property as needed to maintain the standard of living to which A is accustomed. In addition, A shall have the power to withdraw the greater of $5,000 or 5 percent of the property each year, which power is non-cumulative.[3] X shall also have the power to appoint the property to A." A has a special power of appointment, and the appointive property will not be taxed to A unless X appoints to A. However, at A's death, the greater of $5,000 or 5 percent of the property will be included in A's estate to the extent A has not exercised the power to withdraw such amount in the year of A's death.

In some cases, federal taxes will be lower if the donor chooses to create a general power of appointment. By making yearly transfers during life into a trust where the donee has a general power, a donor might take advantage of the $16,000 per year exclusion for gifts under I.R.C. § 2503(b). By creating a general power in her will, a donor might take advantage of the marital deduction for amounts given to the donor's surviving spouse. The donor's estate only qualifies for the marital deduction if the property will be taxable in the donee's estate.

> Example 6.08: O devises $20,000,000 "to T in trust, interest to spouse S for life, then principal to such person or persons as S appoints by deed or by will, and in default of appointment to my heirs per stirpes." S has a general power; the $20,000,000 will be taxed to S's estate at S's death; the

---

[2]   I.R.C. § 2041(b)(1)(A).

[3]   A has a "five-or-five" or "5 by 5" power.

trust qualifies for the marital deduction; and the $20,000,000 will not be taxed to O's estate. O has deferred estate taxation of the funds in the trust from O's death to S's death.

General powers of appointment are also used when the tax liability is lower under the estate tax than under the generation-skipping transfer (GST) tax. By making the asset taxable in the donee's estate, the donor can avoid the GST tax.

3.   CREDITORS' RIGHTS TO APPOINTIVE PROPERTY

When creditors are unable to satisfy their claims out of the assets owned by the debtor, they sometimes attempt to satisfy their claims from appointive property over which the debtor holds a power of appointment. Under the common law, donees were not considered to be owners of the property. The relation back doctrine held that, upon appointment, the asset passed from the donor to the appointee; it was never owned by the donee; the donee merely acted as agent for the donor. Thus, the appointive property under a special power of appointment is not subject to the claims of the donee's creditors, even in bankruptcy. 11 U.S.C. § 541(b)(1). But what about a general power? Can the donee's creditors reach property that a donee could appoint to himself?

IRWIN UNION BANK & TRUST CO. V. LONG
Court of Appeals of Indiana, First District, 1974
312 N.E.2d 908

LOWDERMILK, J.

On February 3, 1957, Victoria Long, appellee herein, obtained a judgment in the amount of $15,000 against Philip W. Long, which judgment emanated from a divorce decree. This action is the result of the filing by appellee of a petition in proceedings supplemental to execution on the prior judgment. Appellee sought satisfaction of that judgment by pursuing funds allegedly owed to Philip W. Long as a result of a trust set up by Laura Long, his mother.

Appellee alleged that the Irwin Union Bank and Trust Company (Union Bank) was indebted to Philip W. Long as the result of its position as trustee of the trust created by Laura Long. On April 24, 1969, the trial court ordered that any income, property, or profits, which were owed to Philip Long and not exempt from execution should be applied to the divorce judgment. Thereafter, on February

13, 1973, the trial court ordered that four percent (4%) of the trust corpus of the trust created by Laura Long which benefited Philip Long was not exempt from execution and could be levied upon by appellee and ordered a writ of execution. Union Bank, as trustee, filed its motion to set aside the writ of execution. Said motion was overruled by the trial court, whereupon Union Bank filed its motion to correct errors, which was by the court overruled.

The pertinent portion of the trust created by Laura Long is as follows, to-wit:

"ITEM V C

"Withdrawal of Principal.

When Philip W. Long, Jr. has attained the age of twenty-one (21) years and is not a full-time student at an educational institution as a candidate for a Bachelor of Arts or Bachelor of Sciences degree, Philip W. Long shall have the right to withdraw from principal once in any calendar year upon thirty (30) days written notice to the Trustee up to four percent (4%) of the market value of the entire trust principal on the date of such notice, which right shall not be cumulative; provided, however, that the amount distributable hereunder shall not be in excess of the market value of the assets of the trust on the date of such notice other than interests in real estate."

The primary issue raised on this appeal is whether the trial court erred in allowing execution on the 4% of the trust corpus.

* * *

* * *A summation of appellee's argument, as stated in her brief, is as follows: 'So it is with Philip-he can get it if he desires it, so why cannot Victoria get it even if Philip does not desire it?'

We have had no Indiana authority directly in point cited to us by either of the parties and a thorough research of this issue does not reveal any Indiana authority on point. Thus, this issue so far as we can determine is one of first impression in Indiana.

The distinction which appellee seeks to rely upon based on the Restatement of the Law of Property in regard to a power of augmentation is apparently such a distinction only in that authority. We have found no cases or treatises which follow the distinction made in the Restatement. We have found one treatise which expressly refutes the distinction between a power of appointment and a power of augmentation, as set out in the Restatement. Appleman, Basic Estate Planning, Ch. XVI, p. 696, discusses the Restatement distinction as follows:

> "The 'Definitions' section of the Restatement of the Law of Property says: 'The term power of appointment does not include * * * a power of revocation, a power to cause a gift of income to be augmented out of principal, * * * a discretionary trust * * *.' Today, for estate and gift tax purposes and consequently for estate planning purposes, this statement must be virtually disregarded."

* * *

The Supreme Court of Texas, in the case of Republic National Bank of Dallas v. Fredericks (1955), 155 Tex. 79, 88, 283 S.W.2d 39, 46, discussed and defined power of appointment and stated:

> "Subject to certain restrictions, the common law accords to the individual a right to delegate to another person the power of designating or selecting the takers of his property. The authority thus to control the disposition of the estate of the grantor or testator is referred to as a 'power of appointment.'
>
> * * *
>
> 'A power of appointment is a power of disposition given to a person over property not his own, by some one who directs the mode in which that power shall be exercised by a particular instrument. It is an authority to do an act which the owner granting the power might himself lawfully perform.' "

See, also, Commissioner of Internal Revenue v. Walston (4 Cir., 1948), 168 F.2d 211.

An examination of the pertinent parts of the trust created by Laura Long indicates that the power which was given to Philip Long in Item V C falls under the definition of power of appointment, as set out above. Philip Long may exercise the power which was delegated to him by Laura Long, that being to distribute property not his own. It is obvious that Laura Long would have had the same power to dispose of her property as that given to Philip Long, had Laura Long decided to dispose of her property in such a manner.

A reading of Item V C, *supra*, does not disclose any direct reference to a power of appointment. However, it is not necessary that the actual words "power of appointment" be used in order to create such a power.

In the case of Estate of Rosecrans (1971), 4 Cal.3d 34, 92 Cal.Rptr. 680, it was held that no particular form of words is necessary to create a power of appointment. In In Re Kuttler's Estate, *supra*, the court said: "No particular form of words is necessary to the creation of such a power." Thompson on Real Property, *supra*, § 2025, states:

> "No particular form or words is necessary for the creation of a power; any expression, however, informal, is sufficient if it clearly indicates an intention to give a power. Where the intention to create the power is plain, it should be given effect. All that is necessary is an indication of a clear intention to accomplish some proper purpose by the donor through the donee. It may be conferred by express words, or may be necessarily implied. . . ."

Appellee contends that the right of withdrawal of Philip Long is a vested property right rather than a power of appointment. However, it is our opinion that such is not the case. This problem was discussed in 62 Am.Jur.2d, Powers, § 107, p. 206, as follows:

> ". . . Creating a general power of appointment is virtually an offer to the donee of the estate or fund that he may receive or reject at will, and like any other offer to donate property to a person, no title can vest until he accepts the offer, nor can a court of equity compel him to accept the property or fund against his will, even for the benefit of creditors."

The leading case on this issue is Gilman v. Bell (1881), 99 Ill. 144, 150, 151, wherein the Illinois Supreme Court discussed powers of appointment and vesting as follows:

> ". . . No title or interest in the thing vests in the donee of the power until he exercises the power. It is virtually an offer to him of the estate or fund, that he may receive or reject at will, and like any other offer to donate property to a person, no title can vest until he accepts the offer, nor can a court of equity compel him to accept the property or fund against his will, even for the benefit of creditors. If it should, it would be to convert the property of the person offering to make the

donation to the payment of the debts of another person. Until accepted, the person to whom the offer is made has not, nor can he have, the slightest interest or title to the property. So the donee of the power only receives the naked power to make the property or fund his own. And when he exercises the power, he thereby consents to receive it, and the title thereby vests in him, although it may pass out of him *eo instanti*, to the appointee. . . ."

In the case of Shattuck v. Burrage (1918), 229 Mass. 449, it was held that:

". . . When a donor gives to another power of appointment over property, the donee of the power does not thereby become the owner of the property. The donee has no title whatever to the property. The power is simply a delegation to the donee of authority to act for the donor in the disposition of the latter's property. . . . The right to exercise the power is not property and cannot be reached by creditors. . . . On no theory of hard fact is the property appointed the property of the donee of the power. . . ."

Contrary to the contention of appellee, it is our opinion that Philip Long has no control over the trust corpus until he exercises his power of appointment and gives notice to the trustee that he wishes to receive his 4% of the trust corpus. Until such an exercise is made, the trustee has the absolute control and benefit of the trust corpus within the terms of the trust instrument.

* * *

The trust instrument was obviously carefully drawn with the tax consequences bearing an important place in the overall intent of the testator. The trust as a whole is set up to give the grandchildren of Laura Long the substantial portion of the assets involved. We note with interest that the percentage of corpus which Philip Long may receive is carefully limited to a percentage less than that which would be includable in the gross estate of Philip Long should he die within a year in which he had allowed his power of appointment to lapse.

It is elementary that courts will seek to ascertain the intention of the testator by giving a full consideration to the entire will. The trust created in the will of Laura Long, in our opinion, has the legal effect of creating a power of appointment in Philip Long under Item V C of the trust.

Philip Long has never exercised his power of appointment under the trust. Such a situation is discussed in II Scott on Trusts, § 147.3 as follows:

> ". . . Where the power is a special power, a power to appoint only among a group of persons, the power is not beneficial to the donee and cannot, of course, be reached by his creditors. Where the power is a general power, that is, a power to appoint to anyone including the donee himself or his estate, the power is beneficial to the donee. If the donee exercises the power by appointing to a volunteer, the property appointed can be reached by his creditors if his other assets are insufficient for the payment of his debts. But where the donee of a general power created by some person other than himself fails to exercise the power, his creditors cannot acquire the power or compel its exercise, nor can they reach the property covered by the power, unless it is otherwise provided by statute. . . ."

Indiana has no statute which would authorize a creditor to reach property covered by a power of appointment which is unexercised.

* * *

Appellee concedes that if we find that Philip Long had merely an unexercised power of appointment then creditors are in no position to either force the exercise of the power or to reach the trust corpus. Thus, it is clear that the trial court erred when it overruled appellant's motion to set aside the writ of execution.

Having found reversible error on the primary issue, it is unnecessary for this court to discuss other issues raised in this appeal.

Reversed and remanded.

Under the traditional rule, followed in *Long*, creditors could not reach appointive assets unless the power was a general power of appointment and the power had been exercised. Exceptions are eroding the traditional rule. Where the donor-settlor reserved himself a general power, although the power was not exercised, the Fourth Circuit held that the creditor could reach the appointive property. *United States v. Ritter*, 558 F.2d 1165 (4th Cir. 1977). A much larger hole in the protection from the donee's creditors has appeared in the law of some states. These states now follow a rule like that in UTC § 505(b)(1), which allows creditors of the donee to reach the appointive property under a general inter vivos power during the period the power may be exercised, whether or not the power has been exercised. In these states, creditors can reach what the debtor can reach.

The rule insulating special powers from creditors of the donee has also suffered a bit of erosion. The Illinois court in *In re Marriage of Chapman*, 297 Ill.App.3d 611 (1998), held that children of the donee who were objects of the power could reach the appointive property to satisfy a support order. Can that result be justified on the ground that the donor would have wanted them to reach the assets?

4. EXERCISE OF A POWER

Litigation sometimes arises over the question of whether a donee has exercised a power of appointment. One issue is capacity. An exercise of a power is a transfer of property and, therefore, it takes the same degree of capacity to exercise a power of appointment as it does to transfer property. Whatever standard applies for deeds will likely be applied to exercises by deed; whatever standard applies for wills (perhaps lower than for deeds) will likely be applied to exercises by will.

Another issue is whether the donee has observed the formalities stated in the instrument. In addition to requiring that the power be exercised by deed or by will, which have their own formalities, the donor may impose additional requirements, such as delivering an instrument to the trustee. If a power can be exercised "by will," what requirements should the will have to meet? Should a court be allowed to find that a will cannot be admitted to probate, but still find that the will exercises the power of appointment? Suppose a donee with a testamentary power leaves an instrument that qualifies as a will under the law of the donee's state, but not the donor's state. Should the court find that the power was exercised?

Many instruments creating powers require that the donee make specific reference to the power in order to exercise it. Does it satisfy that requirement for the donee to devise "all property over which I may have a power of appointment"? UPC § 2–704 presumes that the donor's intention behind the specific-reference requirement was to prevent inadvertent exercise of the power by the donee.

MATTER OF SHENKMAN

Supreme Court, Appellate Division, First Department, New York, 2002
290 A.D.2d 374

* * *

The subject trust instrument permits objectant's testator to exercise a general power of appointment over all remaining trust property "by a will specifically referring to this general power of appointment," and directs the trustees to distribute all such property "not effectively appointed" in a manner not here relevant. Objectant's testator's will gave objectant all of his tangible property, including "any trust . . . over which I may have a power of appointment, general or otherwise". The Surrogate correctly held that under EPTL § 10–6.1(b), the general reference in objectant's testator's will to powers of appointment was ineffective to exercise the specific power granted in the trust instrument. We reject objectant's argument that EPTL § 10–6.1(b) is not triggered unless the donor of the power of appointment expressly states not only that an instrument must specifically refer to the power but also that the appointment shall be ineffective absent such a reference. We also reject objectant's argument that a general reference is ineffective only when contained in a will's residuary clause, rather than, as here, a separate, pre-residuary clause. Assuming, arguendo, that the affidavit of the attorney drafter of objectant's testator's will is admissible, the testator's intent is irrelevant where, as here, the donor made clear that an exercise of the power of appointment would be effective only by specific reference thereto.

Draft your instruments to avoid such litigation by providing a determinate test for compliance.

Intent to exercise is a separate requirement for the exercise of a power, and it is not always clear whether the donee had the requisite intent, especially in the context of a possible exercise by will. Suppose a donee's will says, "the residue of my estate to my children," without referring to the power. Does that clause exercise a general testamentary power of appointment held by the donee? Unless overcome by other evidence, a default rule will decide the case. In most jurisdictions, a residuary clause does not exercise a power. In some jurisdictions, and under UPC § 2–608, such a residuary devise can exercise a power, but only a general power and only if the donor omitted takers in default. In a few jurisdictions, such a residuary devise exercises a power if the residuary devisees are objects. When you draft a will, try to find out what powers of appointment your client has and which of those your client wants to exercise, and then determine how to exercise them in a way that will not generate litigation.

Donees sometimes try to appoint to someone outside the group of permissible appointees. One scheme for accomplishing this is to appoint to an object who agrees to make a gift to a non-object. This is deemed to be "fraud on the power" or "fraud on a special power," and the appointee might take nothing. However, if the donee tries to appoint by will to a non-object, the court might be able to accomplish the donee's goals by "marshaling," using the appointive property to make gifts to persons who are objects and using the testator's other property to make gifts to those who are not objects.

> Example 6.09: O grants $100,000 "to T in trust, income to A for life, then to such issue of A as A shall appoint by will." A dies with $50,000 cash in his estate in addition to the power. A's will says, "I appoint half my trust to my friend X and the other half to my daughter, B. The remainder of my estate I leave to my son, C." A did not have the power to appoint to X but, using marshaling, the court can give $50,000 from the trust to B, $50,000 from the trust to C, and the $50,000 cash to X, accomplishing the goals of both O and A.

If the donee appoints by will to a person who is dead at the time of appointment, the appointment lapses, even if the power was created before the object died. Sometimes the lapse statute will apply, and sometimes not. The lapse provisions of UPC § 2–603 create a substitute gift if the appointee is a grandparent, or a descendant of a grandparent, or a stepchild of either the testator or the donor of the power. Unless the terms of the power expressly provide otherwise, the substitute gift may be made to a descendant of the appointee even though the descendant is not an object of the power. UPC § 2–603(b)(5).

5. FAILURE TO APPOINT

Failures to appoint can be both intentional, where the donee intends not to appoint, and unintentional, where the donee tries to appoint but fails to do so effectively. And failures to appoint can be total failures and partial failures. A well-advised donor will usually specify who takes appointive property that is not effectively appointed. If the donor does name takers in default, they hold a remainder. That remainder is vested if the takers in default are ascertainable and there is no unsatisfied condition precedent to their taking other than the donee's failure to appoint. If it is vested, it is subject to being divested by an effective appointment.

VETRICK V. KEATING

District Court of Appeal of Florida, Fourth District, 2004
877 So.2d 54

POLEN, J.

This appeal arises from a final order granting summary judgment in a matter that consolidated three complex probate and trust matters below. Initially there was an action seeking construction of Marjorie O'Hara's will, an action to terminate a testamentary trust, and an action for the construction of Vincent O'Hara's trust. All three matters were consolidated. The trial court ultimately concluded that Marjorie O'Hara's will exceeded a power of appointment. As a remedy, the trial court severed a portion of the disposition and enforced the remaining provisions. This remedy is the subject of this appeal. For the reasons explained below we affirm the order of the trial court.

Marjorie and Vincent O'Hara were married for many years. They had eight children and fourteen grandchildren. In 1992, Vincent created a revocable trust. In the trust, Vincent listed his eight children by name and specified that all references to "my children" in the trust document referred to the named children and no one else. Also within the trust, Vincent gave Marjorie a power of appointment. The power of appointment provided as follows: "My Spouse, Marjorie, shall have the limited power to appoint to my children, all or any part of the trust at the time of my spouse's death in a valid Will making specific reference to the power of appointment herein conferred upon my spouse."

Vincent died in 1995. Marjorie died in 2000. Jeffrey Keating, the trustee and personal representative, filed a petition for the administration of Marjorie's will. In the will, Marjorie exercised her power of appointment as follows:

> Upon my death, the remaining net trust assets of said Family Trust shall be divided into separate shares, per stirpes, with respect to my husband's then living descendants. Such shares shall be administered as follows:
>
> A. The share held for SUSAN, TIMOTHY, MICHAEL, KEVIN, and BRIAN or their then-living descendants per stirpes, shall be distributed outright, free of trust.
>
> B. The share held for JUDITH shall be held in further trust and administered by the trustees hereinafter named as follows:
>
> The trustees shall distribute to JUDITH all of the net income therefrom at least quarterly. In addition, the trustees may distribute all or any part of the trust principal to or for the benefit of JUDITH and her descendants as the trustee considers advisable for her or their health, education, maintenance and support, with no duty to equalize such payments among eligible beneficiaries. Any undistributed income shall be added to the principal.
>
> Any trust principal remaining at JUDITH's death shall be distributed outright, free of trust, to her then living descendants, per stirpes, or if none to my then living descendant per stirpes; provided, however, that any property thereby distributable to a person who is the income beneficiary or an eligible income beneficiary of a trust under this Agreement shall instead be added to the principal of such trust.
>
> I appoint my financial advisor, JEFFREY KEATING, and my daughter JUDITH as co-trustees of this trust. If JEFFREY is unable to serve for any reason, he shall have the power to appoint a disinterested trustee to serve in his place, or if he does not do so, my brother-in-law, TIMOTHY D. O'Hara of Chicago Illinois shall appoint a disinterested trustee. It is my express intent that at no time shall JUDITH serve as sole trustee of this trust.

Judith O'Hara Vetrick, one of the O'Hara children, filed a complaint challenging the validity of the testamentary trust on the basis that it failed to comply with the power of appointment created in the Vincent Trust. More specifically, Judith argued that by giving a remainder interest to her children, the testamentary trust failed to comply with the Vincent Trust and the power of appointment therein.

Judith argued that Marjorie did not comply with the power of appointment when she appointed successor donees to administer Judith's share and improperly broadened the class of beneficiaries by giving remainder shares to her children. The trial court concluded that Marjorie had improperly expanded the group of beneficiaries. The trial court found that Marjorie's creation of a trust for the benefit of Judith was proper, but that she exceeded the power of appointment by including Judith's children as beneficiaries. The trial court also determined that the inclusion of Judith's children was not an essential factor in Marjorie's scheme of disposition and could easily be severed and the scheme of disposition would best be maintained by severing the interests that were given to Judith's children. The trial court ordered that the appointment to Judith's children be severed and any remaining interest upon Judith's death, revert back to the Vincent Trust. Judith raises four arguments in this appeal. We are unpersuaded by any of them.

Judith first contends Marjorie's delegation of power over her trust to Keating was not a proper exercise of Marjorie's rights under the power of appointment. Rather Judith contends the assets should have been distributed to her outright not through a trust. Judith contends the power of appointment was specifically given to Marjorie. As such, according to Judith, Marjorie was the only person authorized to exercise the power, not a subsequent trustee. We disagree. "A summary judgment based on a review of documents, such as in this case, is reviewable by an appellate court de novo." *Rollins v. Alvarez,* 792 So.2d 695 (Fla. 5th DCA 2001) (review of summary judgment order based on trust documents).

Under the language of the power of appointment, there is nothing prohibiting Marjorie from giving a child assets from the Vincent trust via a new trust.

Judith also contends the trial court erred in concluding that Marjorie's intent could best be satisfied by giving effect to the Judith trust and severing the portion of the trust directed at Judith's children. Again, we disagree.

Section 23.1 of the Restatement (Second) of Properties, and the applicable comments, provide as follows:

> If one part of an appointment is ineffective and another part, if standing alone, would be effective, the effective part is given effect, except to the extent the donee's scheme of disposition is more closely approximated by allowing some or all of the effective part to pass in default of appointment.

Comment:

a. Rationale. Whenever part of a dispositive scheme fails, there always arises the question whether that part is so essential to the whole that its failure causes the failure of some or all of the remaining parts, of themselves effective. The answer to this question depends upon whether the general dispositive scheme disclosed in the instrument is more nearly approximated by treating as effective some or all of the remaining parts or by allowing some or all of the remaining parts to pass to those persons who would receive it if no disposition had been attempted; for it is assumed that the person making the disposition desires that some or all of the remaining parts stand only if thereby the purposes of the original disposition are advanced.

This general rule is applicable in cases where the donee of a power has made an appointment which is partially ineffective. The ineffective part will necessarily pass in default of appointment. If the general scheme of appointment shown in the donee's instrument would be better carried out by allowing some or all of the effective part of the appointment also to pass in default of appointment, some or all of the effective part of the appointment will pass in default of appointment.

. . .

d. Ascertaining the general scheme of the donee. The normal evidentiary rules apply in ascertaining the general scheme of the donee. This means that the entire language of the instrument of appointment must be considered along with the circumstances existing at the time the instrument of appointment was executed. The fact that the instrument of appointment describes the takers in default as taking "in default of appointment" or as taking "to the extent the appointive assets are not effectively appointed" is of no evidentiary value in ascertaining whether the general scheme of the donee is more clearly approximated by defeating all or some part of an otherwise effective appointment.

Restatement (Second) of Property § 23.1 cmt. a, d (1986).

The trial court properly relied on the above cited portions of the Restatement in reaching its conclusion.

Judith contends the trial court incorrectly determined how Marjorie and Vincent's intent could be best satisfied. Judith contended, at the trial court and in this appeal, that the scheme of disposition would be most satisfied if the entire power of appointment were to pass through the default provision of the Vincent trust.

The court concluded that Marjorie's general scheme of disposition, by giving assets in trust assets to three of the eight children, clearly intended to protect three of her children with the creation of protective trusts. This conclusion is supported by the record. On this basis, the court sought to protect Marjorie's intentions and solve the problem of the overextension of beneficiaries in the least disruptive way possible. This was clearly the appropriate analysis under the restatement.

The Restatement summarized, *inter alia, Old Colony Trust Co. v. Richardson*, 297 Mass. 147 (1937) as an example of a case where a partially invalid appointment was severed so that only the invalid portion failed and the rest was given full effect.

In *Old Colony Trust Co. v. Richardson*, 297 Mass. 147 (1937), the donor had given his wife a power of appointment over his estate, with the stipulation that she must appoint at least half the property in fee simple absolute to their adopted daughter Josephine. In default of appointment, Josephine was to receive all the property. Under this power, the wife appointed in trust, directing that the income be divided equally between Josephine and a granddaughter. While the appointment to the granddaughter was effective, the appointment to Josephine fell short of the fee simple absolute stipulated by the donor. As a result, Josephine claimed that the entire estate should pass to her in default. The court denied this request, noting that "the valid and invalid elements of the exercise of the power are not so interwoven that they cannot properly be separated." *Id.* at 152. As the donee intended for the granddaughter to receive half the property in trust, her intentions could be closely approximated by maintaining this appointment, and by allowing only half the property, comprising the ineffective part of the donee's appointment, to pass to Josephine in default.

Restatement (Second) of Property § 23.1, reporters note (1986).

In the case at bar, the trial court found that the portion of the disposition that gave trust assets to Judith's children was easily divisible from the portion of the disposition creating a trust for the benefit of Judith. The situation in the case at bar is akin to *Richardson* in that the apparent goal of the parties can be achieved by invalidating that portion of the trust that passed to Judith's children.

Further, it seems apparent that in severing the provisions, as the trial court did, the underlying goal of the Vincent trust and the power of appointment are realized. The assets would be divided among the eight children.

Judith also contends the trial court erred in holding that any remaining assets in the Judith trust at the time of Judith's death shall pass through the Vincent trust and be divided among the eight children. Her position is that if funds remain in the Judith trust at the time of her death and pass through the Vincent Trust her children would not take their equal share.

"In construing the provisions of a trust, the cardinal rule is to try to give effect to the grantor's intent, if possible." *Pounds v. Pounds*, 703 So.2d 487 (Fla. 5th DCA 1997). It is Judith's position that the intent of Marjorie and Vincent was to direct a per stirpes distribution of the trust assets to all eight children. However, under the solution the trial court created if there are trust assets left in the Judith trust they would be divided among all eight children, rather than pass directly to Judith's children.

While a per stirpes distribution is arguably one of the goals of Vincent and Marjorie, as evidenced in the various documents, the record makes clear that Marjorie and Vincent had other intentions as well. Most persuasively, it is clear that Marjorie intended some protections for the three children for whom she left assets in trust.

Certainly Marjorie's decision to leave three of the children's assets in trust, rather than give them outright distributions, indicated she had the intent to protect those trust assets in some way. In addition, as the trial court noted, it is evident that Judith is motivated to propose options that result in her receiving her distribution free of trust. We find it most compelling that the Vincent trust clearly prioritized that the assets go to his children and nobody else. Likewise, the children, rather than the grandchildren, were the focus of the disposition in Marjorie's will. As a result, although faced with a daunting task, the trial court appropriately focused on the assets being divided among the children when it ordered that any remaining trust assets in the trust for Judith pass through the Vincent trust.

In sum, we agree that the remedy selected by the trial court was the least disruptive and the most effective way to give effect to the grantor's intent. As a result, we affirm that order.

Judith's final argument is that the trial court improperly made factual findings in the final order in the absence of an evidentiary hearing. The record, and the final order in particular, make clear that the conclusions reached by the trial court, now challenged on appeal, would not be affected in the absence of these factual findings. As a result, this argument has no bearing on the issues resolved in this opinion, or the order of the trial court. We affirm the order of the trial court in all respects.

AFFIRMED.

Were the power and the appointment well drafted? The lawyer drafting the power might have explained to Vincent that his limitation to eight objects could prevent his wife from appointing remainders to his grandchildren. Do you think that Vincent would have said that Marjorie's appointment was outside the bounds of what he wanted done with the trust? If not, how might that power have been drafted to avoid that problem? What should the lawyer drafting Marjorie's appointment have done to achieve her goals? What would have happened if Judith had not sued?

What happens if a donor does not name takers in default of appointment?

LORING V. MARSHALL

Supreme Judicial Court of Massachusetts, Suffolk, 1985
484 N.E.2d 1315

WILKINS, J.

This complaint, here on a reservation and report by a single justice of this court, seeks instructions as to the disposition of the remainder of a trust created under the will of Marian Hovey.[3] In *Massachusetts Inst. of Technology v. Loring*, 327 Mass. 553 (1951), this court held that the President and Fellows of Harvard College, the Boston Museum of Fine Arts, and Massachusetts Institute of Technology (the charities) would not be entitled to the remainder of the trust on its termination. The court, however, did not decide, as we now must, what ultimate disposition should be made of the trust principal.

Marian Hovey died in 1898, survived by a brother, Henry S. Hovey, a sister, Fanny H. Morse, and two nephews, John Torrey Morse, Third, and Cabot Jackson Morse. By her will, Marian Hovey left the residue of her estate in trust, the income payable in equal shares to her brother and sister during their lives. Upon her brother's death in 1900, his share of the income passed to her sister, and, upon her sister's death in 1922, the income was paid in equal shares to her two nephews. John Torrey Morse, Third, died in 1928, unmarried and without issue. His share of the income then passed to his brother, Cabot Jackson Morse, who remained the sole income beneficiary until his death in 1946.

At that point, the death of the last surviving income beneficiary, Marian Hovey's will provided for the treatment of the trust assets in the following language:

"At the death of the last survivor of my said brother and sister and my two said nephews, or at my death, if none of them be then living, the trustees shall divide the trust fund in their hands into two equal parts, and shall transfer and pay over one of such parts to the use of the wife and issue of each of my said nephews as he may by will have appointed; provided, that if his wife was living at my death he shall appoint to her no larger interest in the property possessed by me than a right to the income during her life, and if she was living at the death of my father, he shall appoint to her no larger interest

---

[3] Questions involving the wills of Marian Hovey and her nephew, Cabot Jackson Morse, have been before this court on four prior occasions. See *Welch v. Morse*, 323 Mass. 233 (1948); *Massachusetts Inst. of Technology v. Loring*, 327 Mass. 553 (1951); *Frye v. Loring*, 330 Mass. 389 (1953); *Loring v. Morse*, 332 Mass. 57 (1954).

in the property over which I have a power of disposition under the will of my father than a right to the income during her life; and the same limitations shall apply to the appointment of income as aforesaid. If either of my said nephews shall leave no such appointees then living, the whole of the trust fund shall be paid to the appointees of his said brother as aforesaid. If neither of my said nephews leave such appointees then living the whole trust fund shall be paid over and transferred in in [sic] equal shares to the Boston Museum of Fine Arts, the Massachusetts Institute of Technology, and the President and Fellows of Harvard College for the benefit of the Medical School; provided, that if the said Medical School shall not then admit women to instruction on an equal footing with men, the said President and Fellows shall not receive any part of the trust property, but it shall be divided equally between the Boston Museum of Fine Arts and the Massachusetts Institute of Technology."[4]

The will thus gave Cabot Jackson Morse, the surviving nephew, a special power to appoint the trust principal to his "wife and issue" with the limitation that only income could be appointed to a widow who was living at Marian Hovey's death.[5] Cabot Jackson Morse was survived by his wife, Anna Braden Morse, who was living at Marian Hovey's death, and by his only child, Cabot Jackson Morse, Jr., a child of an earlier marriage, who died in 1948, two years after his father. Cabot Jackson Morse left a will which contained the following provisions:

"*Second*: I give to my son, Cabot Jackson Morse, Jr., the sum of one dollar ($1.00), as he is otherwise amply provided for.

"*Third*: The power of appointment which I have under the wills of my aunt, Marian Hovey, and my uncle, Henry S. Hovey, both late of Gloucester, Massachusetts, I exercise as follows: I appoint to my wife, Anna Braden Morse, the right to the income during her lifetime of all of the property to which my power of appointment applies under the will of Marian Hovey, and I appoint to my wife the right during her widowhood to the income to which I would be entitled under the will of Henry S. Hovey if I were living.

---

[4]   The parties have stipulated that at the relevant time the Harvard Medical School admitted women to instruction on an equal footing with men.

[5]   We are concerned here only with "property possessed" by the testatrix at her death and not property over which she had "a power of disposition under the will of [her] father." That property was given outright to his widow under the residuary clause of the will of Cabot Jackson Morse.

"*Fourth*: All the rest, residue and remainder of my estate, *wherever* situated, real or personal, in trust or otherwise, I leave outright and in fee simple to my wife, Anna Braden Morse."

In *Welch v. Morse*, 323 Mass. 233 (1948), we held that the appointment of a life interest to Anna Braden Morse was valid, notwithstanding Cabot Jackson Morse's failure fully to exercise the power by appointing the trust principal. Consequently, the trust income following Cabot Jackson Morse's death was paid to Anna Braden Morse until her death in 1983, when the principal became distributable. The trustees thereupon brought this complaint for instructions.

The complaint alleges that the trustees "are uncertain as to who is entitled to the remainder of the Marian Hovey Trust now that the trust is distributable and specifically whether the trust principal should be paid in any one of the following manners: (a) to the estate of Cabot Jackson Morse, Jr. as the only permissible appointee of the remainder of the trust living at the death of Cabot Jackson Morse; (b) in equal shares to the estates of Cabot Jackson Morse, Jr. and Anna Braden Morse as the only permissible appointees living at the death of Cabot Jackson Morse; (c) to the estate of Anna Braden Morse as the only actual appointee living at the death of Cabot Jackson Morse; (d) to the intestate takers of Marian Hovey's estate on the basis that Marian Hovey failed to make a complete disposition of her property by her will; (e) to Massachusetts Institute of Technology, Museum of Fine Arts and the President and Fellows of Harvard College in equal shares as remaindermen of the trust; or (f) some other disposition." Before us each named potential taker claims to be entitled to trust principal.

In our 1951 opinion, *Massachusetts Inst. of Technology v. Loring*, 327 Mass. at 555–556, we explained why in the circumstances the charities had no interest in the trust: "The rights of the petitioning charities as remaindermen depend upon the proposition that Cabot J. Morse, Senior, did not leave an 'appointee' although he appointed his wife Anna Braden Morse to receive the income during her life. The time when, if at all, the 'whole trust fund' was to be paid over and transferred to the petitioning charities is the time of the death of Cabot J. Morse, Senior. At that time the whole trust fund could not be paid over and transferred to the petitioning charities, because Anna Braden Morse still retained the income for her life. We think that the phrase no 'such appointees then living' is not the equivalent of an express gift in default of appointment, a phrase used by the testatrix in the preceding paragraph." In *Frye v. Loring*, 330 Mass. 389, 393 (1953), the court reiterated that the charities had no interest in the trust fund.

It is apparent that Marian Hovey knew how to refer to a disposition in default of appointment from her use of the terms elsewhere in her will. She did not use those words in describing the potential gift to the charities. A fair reading of the will's crucial language may rightly be that the charities were not to take the principal unless no class member who could receive principal was then living (i.e., if no possible appointee of principal was living at the death of the surviving donee). Regardless of how the words "no such appointees then living" are construed, the express circumstances under which the charities were to take did not occur. The question is what disposition should be made of the principal in the absence of any explicit direction in the will.

Although in its 1951 opinion this court disavowed making a determination of the "ultimate destination of the trust fund," the opinion cited the Restatement of Property § 367(2) (1940), and 1 A. Scott, Trusts § 27.1 (1st ed.1939)[6] to the effect that, when a special power of appointment is not exercised and absent specific language indicating an express gift in default of appointment, the property not appointed goes in equal shares to the members of the class to whom the property could have been appointed. For more recent authority, see 5 American Law of Property § 23.63, at 645 (A.J. Casner ed.1952 & Supp.1962) ("The fact that the donee has failed to apportion the property within the class should not defeat the donor's intent to benefit the class"); Restatement (Second) of Property § 24.2 (Tent.Draft No. 7, 1984).[7]

---

[6] "In Restatement: Property, § 367(2), it is said, with certain immaterial exceptions, that 'where there is a special power and no gift in default of appointment in specific language, property not effectively appointed passes to those living objects to whom the donee could have appointed at the time of expiration of the power, unless the donor has manifested an intent that the objects shall receive the property only so far as the donee elects to appoint it to them.' In Scott, Trusts, § 27.1, the author says, 'Where there is no express gift over in default of appointment the inference is that the donor intended the members of the class to take even though the donee should fail to exercise the power. The inference is that he did not intend that they should take only if the donee should choose to exercise the power. . . . The cases are numerous in which it has been held that the members of the class are entitled to the property in equal shares where the donee of a power to appoint among them fails to exercise the power.'"

[7] Section 24.4, concerning the disposition of unappointed property under a nongeneral power of appointment, states: "To the extent the donor of a non-general power has not specified in the instrument creating the power who is to take unappointed property, the unappointed property passes (1) In default of appointment to the objects of the power (including those who are substituted objects under an antilapse statute) living at the time of the expiration of the power as though they had been specified in the instrument creating the power to take unappointed property, if—(a) the objects are a defined limited class and (b) the donor has not manifested an intent that

Applying this rule of law, we find no specific language in the will which indicates a gift in default of appointment in the event Cabot Jackson Morse should fail to appoint the principal. The charities argue that the will's reference to them suggests that in default of appointment Marian Hovey intended them to take. On the other hand, in *Welch v. Morse*, 323 Mass. at 238, we commented that Marian Hovey's "will discloses an intent to keep her property in the family." The interests Marian Hovey gave to her sister and brother were life interests, as were the interests given to her nephews. The share of any nephew who died unmarried and without issue, as did one, was added to the share of the other nephew. Each nephew was limited to exercising his power of appointment only in favor of his issue and his widow.[8] We think the apparent intent to keep the assets within the family is sufficiently strong to overcome any claim that Marian Hovey's will "expressly" or "in specific language" provides for a gift to the charities in default of appointment.[9]

If we were to depart from the view taken thirty-four years ago in *Massachusetts Inst. of Technology v. Loring*, 327 Mass. 553, 99 N.E.2d 854 (1951), and now were to conclude that under the terms of Marian Hovey's will the charities were to receive the trust principal, we would face the problem that, under normal principles of res judicata, our earlier decision against the charities is binding on them. Any suggestion that our 1951 decision did not bind the charities because the Attorney General was not a party to that proceeding is not supported by authority. The charities themselves brought the earlier action and chose not to name the Attorney General as a party. * * * To conclude now that the Attorney General's involvement was indispensable to a valid determination in the 1951 action would cast a shadow over hundreds of pre-1954 decisions concerning charitable interests under wills and trusts.

The same arguments made by the charities and the Attorney General in this case were considered and rejected in 1951. Surely in

---

the objects shall receive the appointive property only so far as the donee elects to appoint it to them; or (2) To the donor or the donor's estate, if subsection (1) is not applicable."

[8] The gift to any widow was to be a life interest if she were living at Marian Hovey's death.

[9] The nominal distribution made to his son in the donee's will provides no proper guide to the resolution of the issues in this case. We are concerned here with the intention of Marian Hovey, the donor of the special power of appointment. The intentions of the donee of the power of appointment are irrelevant in construing the donor's intent. Similarly, those who rely on language in *Frye v. Loring*, 330 Mass. 389, 113 N.E.2d 595 (1953), as instructive in resolving questions in this case miss the point that Cabot Jackson Morse's intention with regard to his exercise of the power of appointment is irrelevant in determining his aunt's intention concerning the consequences of his partial failure to exercise that power.

a case such as this, at least in the absence of a statute to the contrary, the public interest in protecting the charities' rights was fully accommodated by the Justices of this court in its prior decision. The Attorney General does not suggest in his answer that, if the named charities could not take, other charities should take in their stead by application of the doctrine of cy-pres.

What we have said disposes of the claim that the trust principal should pass to Marian Hovey's heirs as intestate property, a result generally disfavored in the interpretation of testamentary dispositions. The claim of the executors of the estate of Anna Braden Morse that her estate should take as the class, or at least as a member of the class, must fail because Marian Hovey's will specifically limits such a widow's potential stake to a life interest.

A judgment shall be entered instructing the trustees under the will of Marian Hovey to distribute the trust principal to the executors of the estate of Cabot Jackson Morse, Jr. The allowance of counsel fees, costs, and expenses from the principal of the trust is to be in the discretion of the single justice.

So ordered.

O'CONNOR, J., dissenting, with whom HENNESSEY, C.J., joins.

As the Attorney General argues, the event specified in Marian Hovey's will as triggering the charities' right to the trust principal occurred—Marian Hovey's nephews died without leaving living appointees of the trust principal. Therefore, contrary to the court's holding, the trustees should not be instructed to pay the principal to the executors of Cabot Jackson Morse, Jr.'s, estate. Rather, they should be instructed that "the whole trust fund shall be paid over and transferred in equal shares to the Boston Museum of Fine Arts, the Massachusetts Institute of Technology, and the President and Fellows of Harvard College for the benefit of the medical school."

Our decision in *Massachusetts Inst. of Technology v. Loring*, 327 Mass. 553 (1951), does not bar a holding in the present case that the charities are entitled to the trust principal. * * *

It is well settled that "even where the technical requirements of *res judicata* have been established, a court may nonetheless refuse to apply the doctrine."* * *

* * *

Even if normal principles of res judicata are to be applied so as to bar the charities' claims, they do not bar the Attorney General's claim that the charities are entitled to the remainder of the trust fund. The Attorney General, the representative of the public, was not a party in the *Massachusetts Inst. of Technology v. Loring* case. Even if the decision in that case be deemed binding on the charities, it does not follow that the Attorney General is also bound. Inexplicably, the court gives virtually no attention to whether the Attorney General represents interests in the present case that are entitled to be heard and were not heard in the earlier case. Consideration of that question is highly relevant to a determination of whether the Attorney General has a right to be heard now.

The interest of the public in the proper application of funds given to public charities has been recognized by statute for well over 100 years.* * *

* * *

Marian Hovey's will clearly expresses her intent to dispose of the entire residue of her estate, in trust, for the benefit of several classes in accordance with expressed priorities; first, for the benefit of her brother, sister, and nephews; second, for the benefit of her nephews' wives (income only) and her nephews' issue to the extent the nephews, in their discretion, might determine; and, third, for the benefit of the charities to the extent that the trust fund is not exhausted for the benefit of the nephews' wives and issue. The provision that if neither nephew leaves "such appointees then living" the whole fund is to go to the charities obviously was designed to give to the charities those trust funds not appointed to issue who were living at the expected time of distribution. To express literally that manifest intent, a language modification is required, but the modification is minor and fits well within the principles of *Balcom v. Balcom, supra* at 602. As modified by insertion of the word "remaining," the relevant provision reads: "If neither of my said nephews leave such appointee then living the whole [remaining] trust fund shall be paid over" to the charities. The will, construed in any other manner even remotely justified by its language, fails to express a cohesive rational plan to dispose of Marian Hovey's property.

* * *

Adopting the result and the reasoning (indeed, the very language) of *Massachusetts Inst. of Technology v. Loring*, the court, erroneously in my view, concludes that the charities are not entitled to the trust principal. The court then proceeds, again erroneously, in my view, to the conclusion that the executors of the estate of Cabot Jackson Morse, Jr., are entitled to the fund. The court bases its conclusion on the rule, cited in numerous treatises, that "when a special power of appointment is not exercised and absent specific language indicating an express gift in default of appointment, the property not appointed goes in equal shares to the members of the class to whom the property could have been appointed." I do not quarrel with the rule, but I quarrel with the court's application of it. The rule includes the clause, "and absent specific language indicating an express gift in default of appointment." That is an important clause because the rule, like other rules of construction, is intended to aid in ascertaining the testatrix's intent, and should not be applied to defeat it. In the absence of such specific language, it is reasonable to infer that the testator intended that in default of appointment the property would go to the whole class of permissible appointees equally. Otherwise, distribution of the property would be controlled by the laws governing intestate succession, a result not likely to have been intended by one who makes a will. But here the critical language disclosing the testatrix's intent is present. There is no need for inference. Here, contrary to the court's holding, there is an express gift to the charities in default of appointment to living appointees, and it should be given effect. The "rule" does not say otherwise.

The doctrine of res judicata does not require that the court follow *Massachusetts Inst. of Technology v. Loring*, and, because the values in overruling that decision outweigh the values underlying stare decisis, I would overrule it, and I would instruct the plaintiff trustees to distribute the remainder of the trust fund in equal shares to the Massachusetts Institute of Technology, the Boston Museum of Fine Arts, and the President and Fellows of Harvard College.

––––––––––

For appointment of the principal after the death of his wife, what options were open to Cabot under the will of his aunt? Did he want to appoint to any permissible appointee? Which of the possibilities considered by the court do you think Marian would probably have wanted if she had known Cabot would die leaving a wife and a son and a will that failed to appoint the remainder? Would she have said, "Even if you do not want to appoint to your descendant, I want him (or his estate, as it turns out) to take"? What should Marian's lawyer have done?

Suppose that the donor did not specify any takers in default of appointment. Upon default of appointment of a special power, the appointive assets are usually divided equally among the objects if there are not too many of them. Some courts dress up this default rule by saying that there is an "implied gift in default of appointment" to the objects. Other authorities say that the donor created an "imperative" special power in the sense that it is imperative that the property pass to the donees even if the donee does not exercise the power. Upon default of appointment of a general power or a special power with too many objects, the unappointed property usually passes back to the donor or the donor's estate. There is a "capture" exception to this default rule: If the donee of a general power attempted to take full control but failed to do so, the appointive property passes in the donee's estate.

> Example 6.10: O devises "to T in trust for the benefit of A for life, then to such person or persons as A appoints by a will referring specifically and in these terms to the 'O trust power.' I give the residue of my estate to B." A dies, leaving a will which says, "I give any property over which I have a power of appointment to C. I leave the residue of my estate to R." A's will did not refer specifically to the "O trust power", so A's attempt to appoint is ineffective and C does not take. A's power was a general power, and under the general rule the property would revert to O's estate and pass to O's residuary devisee, B. But, instead, the capture exception passes the appointive property through A's residuary clause to R.

6.   RELEASE OF A POWER

The donee of a power is permitted to release the power, in whole or in part. A donee can release his power over some of the appointive property and can release his power to appoint to some of the permissible appointees. If the donee of a testamentary power wishes to assure the takers in default that they will take after the donee's death, a release can provide such assurance. A release can be accomplished by delivery of an instrument from the donee to the trustee.

It is possible for a donee to release his power without knowing he has released it. If a donee makes a contract to appoint to an object and then fails to appoint, a court may be persuaded to deem the contract to be a release of the donee's power to appoint to anyone but the object. The reason for recharacterizing the agreement is the difference between the contract and the release. A contract is not enforceable if it promises to exercise a power that is not exercisable at the time the contract is executed. To enforce such a contract would be directly contrary to the intent of the donor because it would allow the donee to exercise the power before the donor had allowed the donee to exercise. However, since a donee need not exercise and can release his power at any time, he can agree not to exercise his power. If, when the time comes, he then tries to exercise his power, the court can hold that the attempted exercise is ineffectual. The assets then pass as if the donee has released his power to exercise in favor of anyone else.

> Example 6.11: O devises "to T in trust for the benefit of A for life, then to such person or persons as A appoints by will and in default of appointment to B." A contracts to appoint to B. A dies, leaving a will which says, "I appoint to C." A's contract is unenforceable as a contract because A's power was not yet exercisable. But the court can declare the contract to be a release of A's power to appoint to anyone but B. A's appointment to C is then ineffective and the appointive property passes on default of appointment to B.

In recharacterizing the instrument, the courts do what better lawyers for the contract beneficiary could have done at the time of the contract. For obvious reasons of fairness, a court will deem a contract to be a release only if those who will gain under a release gain the same as, or less than, they would have gained under the contract. In *Seidel v. Werner*, 364 N.Y.S.2d 963, *aff'd,* 376 N.Y.S.2d 139 (N.Y. App. Div. 1975), the court refused to deem a separation agreement to be a release because the beneficiaries of the contract would not take the same amounts as they would take if the court found a release.

C. PRESENT AND FUTURE INTERESTS

We come now to the topic that evokes visceral memories of the first-year course in Property, the language and rules of present and future interests. For the most part, the rules of present and future interests apply to interests held both in law and in trust. However, good lawyers for good reasons usually use a trust if they wish to create future interests other than the reversion. The goal of this chapter is to develop your ability to manipulate the rules of future interests to achieve the goals of a client. These technical rules are like sharp knives; they have the precision to carve up estates in fine detail, but can cause serious economic bleeding if wielded carelessly. Handle with care.

Rights in things can be divided in many ways. In addition to the division by the trust into legal and equitable title, covered in an earlier chapter, rights may be divided temporally into present and future interests, the subject of this chapter. A person holding a present interest has the right to use an asset or to benefit from it at the present time; she need not wait to enjoy it. A person holding a future interest also owns an interest in the present, but so long as the interest remains a future interest, the holder has no right to possess or enjoy the underlying asset itself. We sometimes say that a present interest is vested in possession, whereas a future interest is not vested in possession. Keep in mind the distinction between vesting in possession and vesting in interest, as it will remain important. No future interest is vested in possession, but many are vested in interest. When the word "vested" is used alone, it usually refers to vesting in interest, which we will discuss later.

The complicated law of present and future interests has evolved over the course of a millennium, through both statutes enacted by legislatures and cases decided by courts. Much of the arcane language used centuries ago remains current, and many ancient rules created to solve feudal problems remain in effect, generating tricky puzzles today. It behooves you to learn this material well. This is one area of law in which *form is substance*; the form used in drafting will determine the legal substance of the instrument. You cannot master the substance without mastering the forms. Because there are many things that can go wrong and it is difficult to anticipate them all, many practitioners rely upon the templates that are published in books of forms.

1. BASIC ESTATES

All interests, whether they be present interests or future interests, have a maximum duration, and that duration is described by one of the basic estates. Those various estates are divided into freeholds and nonfreeholds. The freeholds are the fee simple, the fee tail, the life estate, and the estate *pur autre vie*, which can be viewed as a type of life estate. You will recall from your Property course that the nonfreeholds include the term of years, the periodic tenancy, the tenancy at will, and the tenancy at sufferance. It is primarily the freehold interests that interest us in this course.

(a) Freeholds and Seisin

Freeholds are separated from nonfreeholds by the concept of seisin. The holder of a legal freehold in land has seisin; the holder of a nonfreehold does not. Seisin is a somewhat mystical idea with very practical consequences. Seisin was how the law identified the key person for purposes of taxation. In the feudal world, the person seised of an interest was responsible for providing feudal services to the overlord. The services would flow up the feudal pyramid, eventually to the King. The services could be to provide knights for the King, religious services, personal services, food, or money. The person seised of an interest was also the person whose death triggered feudal incidents, the forerunners of today's estate taxes. These incidents included relief, wardship, marriage, homage, aids, and escheat. Because it was important that someone be responsible for paying taxes, it was necessary for someone who was seised at all times; there could be no gap in or abeyance of seisin. Because it was important to know who that someone was, highly determinate rules were established for identifying the holder of the seisin for every tract of land. Some modern statutes continue to attach responsibility for taxes to the person who is seised of land.

Seisin was and still is limited to legal interests in realty. Owners of personalty do not have seisin in the personalty. Holders of equitable interests (beneficial interests in trusts) do not have seisin. Nevertheless, the names of the freehold estates are used to describe interests in trusts as well as legal interests in land.

(i) The Fee Simple

The fee simple is an estate of potentially infinite duration; it can last forever. In the past it was created or transferred to humans by using the magic words, "and his heirs", "and her heirs", or "and their heirs". However, magic words were never required for transfer of a fee simple by will and are not required today in any context, no matter how often they continue to appear. Current law presumes that a transferor intends to transfer all her interest unless some other intent is indicated; in other words, the fee simple is the default estate. When they are used today, the words "and his heirs" are read as words of "limitation" rather than words of "purchase". That means that they describe the potential duration of the estate, rather than the persons who take the estate. So, when O transfers "Blackacre to A and his heirs," A takes a fee simple and A's heirs take nothing. The fee simple is inheritable and assignable. Indeed, attempts to restrain the alienation of a legal fee simple have been void since 1290, when the *Statute Quia Emptores* guaranteed that the estate in fee simple was freely alienable. Some scholars reserve the words "fee simple" for realty, describing a potentially infinite interest in personalty as absolute ownership; this book does not adhere to that distinction. (Note: for purposes of all hypotheticals, when a person is described by a name, even a short name such as "A", that person is presumed to be alive unless otherwise is indicated. Also presume, unless otherwise indicated, that the initial transferor starts with a fee simple absolute.)

(ii) The Fee Tail

The fee tail passes down from heir to lineal heir, and when the last of the lineal descendants dies, the estate in tail naturally terminates. The fee tail is created by the magic words, "to A and the heirs of his body", or one of a few variations on that theme. The fee tail was used to keep land in the family for generation after generation. Early on, the courts frustrated this intent by construing the "heirs of his body" language to create what is known as the "fee simple conditional," which might still be created in Iowa and South Carolina. The medieval dynasts responded by pushing Parliament to pass the *Statute De Donis Conditionalibus* (1285), which forced courts to respect the intent of the transferors, for a while. However, over time, the pressures in favor of alienation proved too strong and about two centuries later, in *Taltarum's Case*, Y.B. Mich. 12 Edw. IV, fo. 14b, pl. 16, fo. 19a, pl. 25 (1472), the judges allowed a tenant in tail to bar the entail, turning his estate into a fee simple by a collusive lawsuit called a common recovery. After that, the propertied class turned to other complex legal maneuvers for preventing heirs from transferring land outside the family, which led in turn to new judicial limitations on those settlements. In time, those limitations grew into the wonderful Rule Against Perpetuities.

It is still possible to create a fee tail in land in four states (Delaware, Maine, Massachusetts, and Rhode Island), but in all four the tenant can disentail the fee tail, turning it into a fee simple, by an inter vivos transfer. In the remaining states, the fee tail has been abolished and statutes prescribe some other construction for a transfer "to B and the heirs of his body, then to C." In some states, B takes a life estate and B's issue take a remainder in fee simple. In others, B takes a fee simple. In yet others, B takes a fee simple subject to an executory interest (discussed below) in fee simple in C, which vests if and only if B leaves no surviving issue at his death.

The tail of the fee tail tale is that the estate, long considered dead, might be making a comeback, albeit in a slightly different form. According to the Restatement, a settlor may transfer "to A for life, then to A's issue from time to time living forever." Restatement (Third) of Property, Wills and Other Donative Transfers § 24.4 comment 'c'. Except to the extent that it violates the Rule Against Perpetuities, such a transfer creates interests much like those of the fee tail. If this form is accepted by courts, perhaps some state legislatures will decide that the fee tail was not such a bad idea and that the state's trust companies would benefit if their customers were allowed to create accounts in fee tail. If legislatures do that, courts could eventually respond as they responded in the past, finding ways to allow fee tail tenants in possession to convert their interests into estates in fee simple. Will the Restatement (Twelfth?) of Property two centuries from now urge courts to put a stop to this version of the fee tail recommended by the Restatement (Third)? If courts do allow disentailment, will those decisions constitute a judicial taking of property from the more remote issue?

(iii) The Life Estate

The estate for life is exactly what it says it is. It is an estate that lasts during the life of some human being. At the end of that life, the estate ends too.

If the estate is measured by the life of the tenant in possession, it is an ordinary life estate. Words such as "to B for her life" create it. A life estate is also created by a grant "to B and C as long as they both shall live." Long, long ago, the life estate was the default estate, but today the default is the fee simple, and it takes some expression of intent to create a life estate. An ordinary life estate is alienable inter vivos, but it is not devisable or descendible at death because it terminates naturally with the death of the tenant. Thus, the life estate is relatively straightforward. But do not let the brevity of this paragraph mislead you; the life estate is an essential tool for a trusts and estates lawyer.

The estate *pur autre vie* is a special type of life estate, the maximum duration of which is measured by the life of someone other than the tenant or tenants. Such an estate is created when life tenant B transfers "to C, all of my rights whatever they may be." It is also created when O transfers "to C for the life of B." In both cases, C has an estate *pur autre vie*, which will terminate automatically upon the death of B.

(b) Nonfreeholds

The nonfreehold estates never carry seisin. The nonfreeholds include the term of years, the periodic tenancy, the tenancy at will, and the tenancy at sufferance. The term of years is defined by a maximum duration expressed by a single period of time or by a specific date, and it terminates automatically at the specified time. The periodic tenancy is an estate that runs from one period to the next, often monthly, until it is terminated by either party. A tenancy at will lasts as long as both parties have the will to continue it. And the tenancy at sufferance, which might not qualify as an estate, is the name given the relationship after a tenant holds over beyond the end of his estate and before the landlord makes an election as to the status of the tenant.

(c) Defeasibility

Any estate may be made defeasible, meaning it might terminate, or "determine", before it has reached its maximum duration. There are two basic ways to make an estate defeasible: by adding a special limitation, or by adding a condition subsequent. A transferor creates a special limitation when she includes durational language such as "during", "while", "as long as", "for so long as", or "until". A transferor creates a condition subsequent when she includes conditional language such as "if", "but if", "provided", or "on the condition that".

A fee simple that is not defeasible is called a fee simple absolute. In slight contrast, a life estate that is not defeasible is not called a life estate absolute but merely a life estate. Only a fee simple can be called absolute. The name we give a defeasible estate depends on the way in which it might come to an early termination. It will be easier to learn additional words describing defeasibility after we have learned the names for the various future interests, up next.

2. FUTURE INTERESTS

Owners of transferable interests have the power to subdivide their rights as they transfer them. They may retain packages of rights for themselves and may transfer packages of rights to others. Often, transferors divide their rights temporally, into a present interest and some number of future interests. All the estates, from the fee simple through the tenancies, can exist either as present estates (or present interests), where the holder has the right to possession at present, or as future estates (or future interests), where the holder does not have the right to possess at the present moment. As noted above, future interests are sets of rights that exist in the present but the holder will not take possession until sometime in the future, if ever. Holders of future interests can enjoy holding the rights, and often can transfer the rights, but they cannot make use of the underlying asset. The holder of a future interest has the power to prevent the present estate holder from committing waste to the asset and is sometimes entitled to compensation if the asset is taken by an exercise of the power of eminent domain. A future interest is described not only by one of the basic estates, e.g., life estate, but also by other characteristics that depend on how it is created and how it might end. The name we give a future interest depends on whether it was retained by the transferor or created in a transferee. The name we give the future interest is not changed by subsequent transfers of the interest, but can be changed by other events that occur after it is created.

(a) Future Interests in Transferors

Whenever there is some possibility that an asset transferred by a transferor might return to the transferor, the transferor has retained a future interest of some sort. The future interests that transferors might retain are the reversion, the possibility of reverter, and the right of entry for condition broken. Some authorities classify all three of those interests as reversionary interests. Other authorities classify only the reversion and the possibility of reverter as reversions, excluding the right of entry because it does not wait patiently for the expiration of the preceding estate.

(i) The Reversion (Including the Quantum of Estates)

If a transferor does not transfer a vested estate of at least the same quantum as she had immediately before the transfer, she retains a reversion (for herself or for her heir). In decreasing order of quantum, the estates are the fee simple, the fee tail, the life estate, the term of years, the periodic tenancy, the tenancy at will, and (maybe) the tenancy at sufferance.

> Example 6.12: B holds a life estate and transfers "to C for 200 years." B retains a reversion.

A reversion is fully transferable; it is alienable inter vivos and, at death, descendible and devisable.

> Example 6.13: B holds an estate for the life of X. B transfers "to C for 200 years." B dies leaving no will. B's heir inherits B's interest and it is still called a reversion in the hands of the heir even though the heir was not the original transferor.

> Example 6.14: O is alive and transfers Blackacre "to T to pay income to B for life." Does this transfer create a reversion? Yes. (Remember to assume that O starts with a fee simple absolute unless otherwise indicated.) If T will have duties after B dies, there is a resulting trust for O. Other ways to put it are that there is a reversion in equity in O, or O has an equitable reversion. If T will have no trustee duties to perform after B dies, T will be eliminated by the Statute of Uses, and O will have a reversion in law as well as equity (a reversion in fee simple).

> Example 6.15: O dies leaving a will which says, only, "I leave Blackacre to B for life." H is O's heir. Does this transfer create a reversion? Yes, this leaves a reversion in H. Although the answer is clear, this transfer is probably not well advised. It is almost always preferable to create equitable future interests rather than legal future interests following freehold estates.

(ii) The Possibility of Reverter

If an owner transfers an estate of the same quantum as she had but attaches a special limitation operating in her own favor, the future interest she retains is called a possibility of reverter.

> Example 6.16: O transfers Blackacre "to A as long as the premises are used for residential purposes." O retains a possibility of reverter. It does not matter that the transfer does not expressly state that the premises revert to O upon the divesting event.

> Problem 6.17: O transfers stocks "to T for the benefit of B and B's heirs until B and C divorce, then for the benefit of O." Has O retained a possibility of reverter?

If O transfers an estate of lesser quantum with a durational limitation, O's retained interest is called simply a reversion, and what would seem to be a possibility of reverter due to the durational limitation is left undescribed.

> Example 6.18: O transfers Blackacre "to B for life for so long as B and C remain married." O has kept a reversion, not a possibility of reverter. O takes upon B's death or divorce.

> Problem 6.19: O transfers Blackacre "to T for the benefit of B and B's heirs, but if B and C divorce then for the benefit of O." Has O retained a possibility of reverter?

At common law, the possibility of reverter was not alienable inter vivos except by release to the holder of the possessory estate. It has always been descendible and devisable, and it is fully alienable in most jurisdictions today.

(iii) The Right of Entry

The right of entry is also known as the right of entry for condition broken and also known as the power of termination. The transferor retains a right of entry when she attaches a condition subsequent that operates in her own favor.

> Example 6.20: O transfers Blackacre "to A, but if the land is not used for residential purposes then O shall have the right to re-enter and retake." O retains a right of entry.

For a right of entry to become possessory, the described condition must be satisfied *and* the grantor must exercise the right of entry. The right of entry is unique in this regard; all other future interests operate automatically, without an implicit requirement that the holder exercise her right after the triggering event. Until the grantor properly exercises her retained right of entry, the grantee retains the right to possession and his continued possession is not wrongful. One consequence of this is that the statute of limitations does not run against the grantor's cause of action. (By contrast, the right to possession under a possibility of reverter triggers the statute of limitations on the action to recover possession.) However, although the statute of limitations does not run until the exercise of the right of entry, a court could find that the grantor has waived her right to enter if she did not exercise her right of entry within a reasonable time after she could have done so. To exercise her right, the grantor need not take physical possession; she can exercise her right of entry by a lawsuit.

If O transfers an interest that is both of lesser quantum and subject to a condition subsequent, O's retained interest is called a right of entry incident to a reversion.

> Example 6.21: O transfers Blackacre "to B for life, but if B and C divorce then O can re-enter and retake possession." O has a right of entry incident to a reversion.

At common law, the right of entry incident to a reversion was fully transferable along with the reversion, but the bare right of entry was not alienable inter vivos except by release to the holder of the possessory estate. In some jurisdictions, an inter vivos attempt to transfer a bare right of entry resulted in the destruction of the right! It has always been descendible and devisable, and it is fully alienable in most jurisdictions today.

(b) Future Interests in Transferees

Before the Statute of Uses took effect in 1536, there was only one kind of future interest in a transferee that the courts of law would recognize, and that was the remainder. A future interest created in a transferee was a remainder or it was no legal interest at all. After the Statute of Uses, the courts of law recognized a new sort of legal future interest, the executory interest. Even though we are well past 1536, the first thing to do in interpreting a document creating a future interest in a stranger is to determine whether it is a remainder or an executory interest. It will be a remainder if it follows three rules. If it violates one of those rules, it will be an executory interest.

(i) The Remainder

To create any legal interest in a transferee before 1536, a transferor had to follow three rules, two of which grew directly out of the rules relating to seisin.

The first rule was that seisin could not spring out of the transferor to a transferee at some point in the future. This rule was sometimes summed up with the phrase "no freeholds to commence in futuro". Before 1536, a person holding legal title transferred seisin by a feoffment with livery of seisin, and the transfer of seisin from the transferor took place only at that moment. A transferor could not create a legal future interest that would require seisin to spring out of herself at some point in the future.

There were a couple of different contexts in which this rule might prevent the creation of a remainder.

> Example 6.22: B and C are not married. Otherwise observing the proper formalities, O attempts to give "my life estate in Blackacre to B effective as of the time when B marries C." At common law, B took nothing.

Note, however, that this rule does not prevent one transferee from carrying seisin for the benefit of a future transferee, as when O transfers "to A for life and then to B", because the seisin in such a case would not spring out of O at a point in time after the livery of seisin made to A.

Another context in which the rule against springing of seisin prevented the creation of a remainder arose because of the rule that there could not be an abeyance of seisin. Since seisin had to be somewhere at all times, seisin would in some cases return to O in the future and, if it did, it could not spring out to another transferee.

> Example 6.23: O transfers "to A for life, remainder to the first child of A to attain the age of 21 after A dies." At common law, the attempted remainder in the child was void from the start, and O held a reversion. Because O required that the child reach 21 after the death of A, seisin would have to pass back to O until that occurred. Once seisin was back in O, it could not spring out because that would occur after the livery of seisin.

Compare that with the following transfer.

> Example 6.24: O transfers "to A for life, remainder to the first child of A to attain the age of 21." This language creates a remainder. In this example, a child of A could reach the age of 21 before A dies. If so, then at A's death the seisin passes to that child immediately at A's death. The seisin does not return to O and does not spring out of O *in futuro*.

The second rule for legal future interests before 1536 was that seisin could not shift from one transferee to another transferee before the natural termination of the former's estate. This rule was sometimes summed up with the phrase "no conditions in strangers". Another way of putting this is that a transferor could not create a remainder that might "cut off" a preceding estate. A legal future interest that could take by causing seisin to shift prematurely from one transferee to another transferee was void. As a result of this rule, although a transferor could attach a condition subsequent that operated in her own favor, she could not attach a condition subsequent that operated in favor of a transferee. If the transferor used words that would seem to create a condition subsequent in a transferee, the intended transferee took no interest at all before 1536.

> Example 6.25: O transfers "to A for life, then to B either when A dies or when A drinks liquor on the land." Before 1536, B took nothing because B's future interest might cut off A's interest before its natural termination. This was true even though by the intent of the transfer B could also take possession at the natural expiration of A's estate at A's death. The possibility that a condition subsequent would cut short A's estate in favor of B prevented B's interest from being a remainder, and it was void *ab initio*.

One way to remember the rule is to imagine that the holder of seisin would not want to carry seisin to a person who might cut off his estate.

The third rule was that a transferor could not create a future interest in a transferee that would follow a vested interest in fee simple. In other words, a remainder cannot follow a vested fee simple.

> Example 6.26: O transfers "to A and his heirs until A drinks liquor, then to B and his heirs." B's interest did not violate the rule against conditions in strangers because A's estate would expire naturally, if at all, upon A's imbibing. Nevertheless, because a remainder could not follow a vested fee simple, at common law B took nothing from the transfer and O retained a possibility of reverter.

Before 1536, if a transferor followed the rules governing remainders, she could create a legal future interest in a transferee; if she violated a rule, the non-compliant attempt to create a legal remainder was void *ab initio*. Although we will see that it is possible today to create a legal future interest in a transferee without following these rules, these ancient English rules continue to govern the creation of remainders in the modern United States.

(A) Vested or Contingent

Remainders are further divided according to whether they are vested or contingent. A remainder is vested if a remainderperson can be identified and there is no unsatisfied condition precedent. If a remainder fails to satisfy either of these two requirements, it is not vested, it is contingent. Note that the natural expiration of the preceding estate is not considered to be an unsatisfied condition precedent; were it otherwise, all remainders would be contingent and the word "contingent" would lose all descriptive utility. The logical necessity that a remainderperson for life must survive until the time for possession is also not considered to be a condition precedent.

> Problem 6.27: O transfers "to T for the benefit of X for life, then Y for life, then Z." How many vested remainders did O create?

For a remainder to be vested, there must be an ascertainable taker.

> Example 6.28: B has no children. O transfers "to T for the benefit of B for life, then for B's children." The remainder in the children of B is contingent because there is no ascertainable taker until a child is born to B. There is a reversion in O.

Distinguish carefully between conditions precedent and conditions subsequent, for the former make a remainder contingent while the latter do not. How does one tell the difference? Is it a matter of the timing of the condition; does it depend on when the condition occurs? Or is it a matter of language, depending on where on the piece of paper the condition was written into the transfer? It is the latter; the position of the words in the sentence is the key. (Once again, form determines substance.) A condition is a condition precedent if the language of the condition precedes the language specifying the taker (the person who takes if that condition is satisfied) or if the conditional language is wrapped up in the description of that taker. A condition is subsequent if it comes after the description of the taker and is not wrapped up in the description of the taker.

> Example 6.29: O transfers "to E for life, then to J if J marries E before E dies, then to K if J does not marry E before E dies." Because the conditional words "if J marries E" are part of the language creating the interest in J, this language creates a condition precedent even though the words appear

after "to J". J's remainder in fee simple is contingent, and so is K's remainder. J and K have alternative contingent remainders. O has a reversion because O had a fee simple and did not transfer a vested estate in fee simple.

Example 6.30: O transfers "to E for life, then to J, but to K instead of J if J does not marry E before E dies." The conditional language here appears subsequent to the language creating an interest in J and not wrapped up with the description of J, so it creates a condition subsequent to J's interest, a divesting condition that will divest J's vested remainder in fee simple if E or J dies before they marry. O does not have a reversion because O transferred a vested remainder in fee simple to J.

There is no difference in the logic or timing of the key event in these two examples; in both, J must marry E before E dies before J can take. But the difference in the order of words creates a difference in legal result, with J's interest being contingent in the former case and vested in the latter. It is not uncommon to see statements to the effect that the timing of the condition is the key to whether it is precedent, but you can see that such statements are inconsistent with the traditional definition of a condition precedent.

GOODWINE STATE BANK v. MULLINS

Appellate Court of Illinois, Fourth District, 1993
625 N.E.2d 1056

KNECHT, J.

* * *

I.   FACTS

In 1966, James Mullins, the owner of a 120-acre farm, died. Through his will, James granted a life estate to his son, Harold Mullins, and provided that, upon Harold's death, the farm is granted outright to Harold's then-living descendents. Harold is still alive; thus, Jeffrey Mullins, Harold's only descendent, has a contingent remainder in the farm. In 1966, Harold, his wife Marjorie, and Jeffrey (then three years old) began living on the farm.

When Jeffrey was 14 or 15 years old, Harold and Marjorie told him about the terms of James' will. They did not tell Jeffrey he had an "interest" in the farm; rather, they told him when Harold died, Jeffrey would inherit the farm. At best, Jeffrey thought he had an "interest" in James' will and would someday inherit an interest in the farm.

Harold and Marjorie took out a series of loans from the Bank to finance their farming operation. In 1981 the Bank began to require Jeffrey to sign the notes and mortgages for his parents' loans. At this time Jeffrey was 18 years old and a senior in high school. After graduating from high school, Jeffrey was not involved in the farming operation, but became a welder.

In 1981 and 1982 Jeffrey signed the notes and mortgages for his parents' loans. The notes and mortgages were not explained to Jeffrey. His parents merely requested him to sign, and told him his signature was required because of the way James' will was written. In 1983 and 1984, Jeffrey was requested by his parents to sign only the mortgages, but not the notes. Again, he signed the mortgages, although they were not explained to him.

In April 1987, Harold was not actively involved in farming the land, and was no longer living at the farm. Harold and Marjorie were in the process of obtaining a dissolution. At this time Harold and Marjorie defaulted on the loan. Jeffrey went to the Bank to determine whether he could obtain a loan to pay off his parents' debt; however, since Jeffrey was not involved in the farming operation, he was ineligible for a loan.

In June 1987 the Bank prepared an agreement to settle debt (Agreement) and quitclaim deed. Under the terms of the Agreement, Harold, Marjorie, and Jeffrey would sign a quitclaim deed regarding the farm in exchange for the Bank's forgiveness of Harold and Marjorie's debt. The Agreement additionally provided if the farm was sold for an amount in excess of the debt, interest, and costs, the Bank would give the excess to Harold, Marjorie, and Jeffrey. One copy of the Agreement and deed was sent to either Marjorie or Gene Wright, the attorney handling her divorce. The Mullinses did not discuss the terms or implication of the Agreement; however, both Harold and Marjorie told Jeffrey it would be in the family's best interests to sign the Agreement.

Jeffrey accompanied his mother to Wright's office because she told him she needed him to sign some papers to help her get her divorce finalized. Wright advised Marjorie to sign the Agreement and deed, informing her she had no interest in the property as it was Harold's nonmarital property. Jeffrey was in the room when Wright advised Marjorie. Wright did not advise Jeffrey regarding whether he should sign the Agreement and the deed. Jeffrey signed the Agreement and deed. Separate copies of the Agreement and deed were signed by Harold. The quitclaim deed was in statutory form, and could not, as a matter of law, convey a contingent remainder.

In August 1987, the Bank sold the farm and Marjorie and Jeffrey were instructed to vacate the premises. The sales price was in excess of the debt, interests, and costs and in October 1987, checks totalling $10,384.03, made payable to Harold, Marjorie and Jeffrey jointly were sent to Harold's attorney. Due to a dispute with Harold regarding the distribution of the money, Jeffrey consulted with attorney Charles Hall in December 1987. In March 1988, Jeffrey filed a notice of contingent remainder.

The Bank filed this lawsuit. * * *

* * *

IV. THE CROSS-APPEAL

A. Declaratory Judgment Regarding the Nature of Jeffrey's Remainder Interest

In the original complaint and count I of the amended complaint, the Bank requested the court find Jeffrey had conveyed his interest in the farm by signing the quitclaim deed. The trial court granted Jeffrey's motion for summary judgment as he has a contingent remainder interest in the property, which cannot, as a matter of law, be conveyed by quitclaim deed unless words *specifically* conveying the contingent remainder are included in the quitclaim deed. Words conveying the contingent remainder were not included in the quitclaim deed drafted by the Bank. The Bank argues the trial court erred because Jeffrey's future interest in the farm is not a contingent, but a vested, remainder. The Bank's argument reflects a fundamental misunderstanding of the laws pertaining to future interests and a misunderstanding of the pertinent cases.

A vested remainder is a right to present or future enjoyment which is given to named or otherwise determinate persons ready to take possession at any time, and postponement of their estate is not for purposes personal to them. (*Danz v. Danz* (1940), 373 Ill. 482, 486.) In *Danz*, the court distinguished vested from contingent remainders, quoting from Gray's Rule Against Perpetuities, section 108, which states:

" 'Whether a remainder is vested or contingent depends upon the language employed. If the conditional element is incorporated into the description of, or into the gift to the remaindermen, then the remainder is contingent; but if, after words giving a vested interest, a clause is added divesting it, the remainder is vested. Thus, on a devise to A for life, remainder to his children, but if any child dies in the lifetime of A his share to go to those who survive, the share of each child is vested, subject to be divested by its death. But on a devise to A for life, remainder to such of his children as survive him, the remainder is contingent.' " *Danz*, 373 Ill. at 486–87, quoting J. Gray, The Rule Against Perpetuities § 108, at 86 (3d ed. 1915).

In *Danz*, the testator granted an estate to his wife, which was to terminate upon her death or remarriage. The will further provided " '[u]pon the death of my wife, or in the event of her marrying again, then all of said property herein before bequeathed to her shall be vested in my nephew Edward J. Danz and my niece Margaret Kathryn Williams, share and share alike.' " The will set forth contingent dispositions of the remainder interest in the property, should the niece or nephew die prior to the wife's death or remarriage. The court concluded the remainder described in the will was in named persons, the niece and nephew, who were ready to take possession at any time. The postponement of enjoyment of the estate was for reasons personal to the widow, not to the niece and nephew. Finally, the condition was not incorporated into the description of, nor into the gift to, the remaindermen, but rather was subsequently inserted as a clause divesting the estate. Thus the remainder was not contingent upon the niece and nephew surviving the wife but was a vested remainder, subject to divestment, if they did not survive her.

The will in the present case is unlike that in *Danz* as it does not provide a remainder interest in named or determinable persons, and the condition is included in the gift to the remaindermen. The provision in James Mullins' will is similar to the example given in *Danz* of one granting a contingent remainder. The will, in the present case, provides:

> "I give and devise all of my real estate to my son, Harold Wayne Mullins, for and during his natural life only. Upon the death of my son, Harold Wayne Mullins, I give and devise my real estate to the then[-]living descendants of my son, Harold Wayne Mullins, per stirpes and not per capita."

The remaindermen are not named in the will, rather, the remainder is to be divided among the "then[-]living descendants" of Harold. Since it cannot be determined, until Harold's death, who his "then[-]living descendants" will be, the remaindermen are not determinable. Moreover, the condition, "then living" is incorporated in the description of the remaindermen, it is not a subsequent insertion divesting the estate. Thus, the will in the present case is similar to the example of a contingent interest set forth in *Danz*, which states, " 'on a devise to A for life, remainder to such of his children as survive him, the remainder is contingent.' " *Danz*, quoting J. Gray, The Rule Against Perpetuities § 108, at 86 (3d ed. 1915).

The Bank argues the language "then living" in the will does not refer to the descendants of Harold who survive Harold, but those descendants who survive the testator. Thus, the Bank argues, since Jeffrey was the only descent of Harold surviving the testator, the remainder interest vested in Jeffrey at the time of the testator's death. In support of its position, plaintiff cites the Illinois public policy in favor of the vesting of a remainder at the earliest possible time. The supreme court, although acknowledging the public policy referred to by plaintiff, rejected a virtually identical argument in *Johnston v. Herrin* (1943), 383 Ill. 598.

In *Johnston*, the testator granted a life estate to his wife, and remainder interests to his descendants. His will provided:

> " 'At the death of my said wife, Fattima Herrin, it is my will that * * * my remaining estate * * * be equally divided among my surviving descendants in the same shares and proportions as they would be entitled to by the laws of descent of the State of Illinois in the event of my death intestate.' "

The testator died, survived by his wife, and his four children: John Herrin, Jeff S. Herrin, Mark Herrin, and Cora Dawson. After the testator's death, but prior to the wife's death, Jeff and Mark filed bankruptcy and were adjudicated bankrupts. Jeff and Mark did not list any interest in the testator's estate as an asset. After the death of the wife, the bankruptcy actions were reopened. Whether the remainder interest was part of the bankruptcy estate turned on whether the interest was a vested or contingent interest prior to the death of the wife. The trustees in bankruptcy alleged Jeff's and Mark's interests were vested remainder interests during the lifetime of the wife. The trustees argued that "surviving descendants" referred to the descendants surviving at the time of the testator's death, and not those surviving the life tenant. The trustees alleged the law favors the earliest possible vesting, and that since construing "surviving descendants" to mean the descendants surviving at the time of the testator's death would cause the remainders to vest upon the death of the testator, the earliest possible time, such a construction should be adopted by the court.

The supreme court noted the favoring of the earliest possible vesting will be applied unless the will shows an intent on the part of the testator forbidding its application. The court stated:

> "A gift to survivors, which is preceded by a particular estate at the expiration of which the gift is to take effect in possession, will take effect in favor of those, only, who survive the particular estate. Such a remainder is necessarily contingent since it cannot be known until the death of the life tenant who of the testator's surviving descendants will survive her to take the estate." (*Johnston*, 383 Ill. at 605.)

Concluding that the remainder interests were conditioned upon the survival of the life tenant, and therefore contingent, the court stated:

> "It is clear that the testator, by the use of the words 'surviving descendants,' had in contemplation the possible distribution of the remainder of his estate, after the termination of the life estate, to others than his children living at his death. Any other construction would render the use of the words 'surviving descendants' without meaning and useless. If it was the intention of the testator to vest the remainder of his estate subject to the life estate in his children, the use of the words 'surviving descendants' would be meaningless. Children are *eo nominee* descendants, but it by no means follows that descendants are necessarily children. When used in a will, 'descendants' means only lineal heirs,—those in the direct descending line from the person named,—unless there is a clear indication of intention to enlarge its meaning. 'Descendants' is good as a term of description in a will and includes all who proceed from the body of the person named to the remotest degree. * * * The word 'surviving' is a part of the description of those who are to take. * * * 'Surviving' is a word of survivorship

which describes the gift and the donees and precludes the vesting of the gift until it can be determined who such donees are." *Johnston*, 383 Ill. at 605–06.

Similarly, in the present case, the words "then living descendants" located in the sentence beginning with "[u]pon the death of my son" are words of survivorship. These words describe the remaindermen who are to receive the estate. If the testator had meant to vest the remainder of his estate, subject to Harold's life estate, in Harold's children, the use of the words "then [-]living descendants" would be meaningless. The testator's intent is even more clear in the present case than in *Johnston*, due to the testator's use of the word "then" before "living descendants." The word "then" references a time. The time referenced in the sentence is "[u]pon the death of my son, Harold." Thus, the remainder vests in the descendants of Harold who are alive at the time of Harold's death.

The Bank next argues the use of the words "per stirpes and not per capita" are words which contradict the requirement that the descendants survive Harold. *Per stirpes* and per capita are terms used to specify the method of distribution of property. A per capita distribution to a named person's descendants results in each descendant's receipt of an equal share of the property, regardless of whether the descendants are children, grandchildren, or great-grandchildren of the named person. A distribution *per stirpes* is the antithesis of a distribution per capita. The words *per stirpes* denote a taking by right of representation of that which an ancestor would take if living. Thus, in the present case, if Harold were to father another son, X, and X were to father two children, Y and Z, and X died prior to Harold's death, Harold's surviving descendants would be Jeff, Y, and Z. If the distribution were made per capita, Jeffrey, Y, and Z would each receive a one-third share of the property. However, under a *per stirpes* distribution, Y and Z would only be entitled to the share X would have taken had he survived Harold. Thus, Jeffrey would be entitled to a one-half share of the property, and Y and Z would each be entitled to a one-fourth share of the property (one-half each of X's one-half share).

Since *per stirpes* and per capita are merely terms used to designate the method of determining the shares to which the remaindermen are entitled, it does not contradict the requirement that in order to qualify as a remainderman under the will in the present case, an individual must (1) be a descendant of Harold and (2) survive Harold. Moreover, an argument that words of distribution were determinative of whether a remainder interest was vested or contingent was rejected by the supreme court in *Johnston*. The will in *Johnston* provided the remainder interest was to be divided among the testator's surviving descendants in the share they would receive under the State intestacy laws. The trustees argued this provision indicated an intent of the testator that the remainder interest vest at the time of the testator's death. The supreme court disagreed, finding the provision merely indicated the quantum of the estate to go to such descendants rather than those entitled to take under the will. Similarly, in the present case, the specification that distribution shall be made *per stirpes* rather than per capita is an instruction of the quantum of the estate which is to be given to each of Harold's surviving descendants. This is not inconsistent with the requirement that only the descendants of Harold who survive him may take under the will; rather, it is an instruction of how the estate shall be distributed to those descendants who do survive Harold.

Finally, the Bank argues this court's decision in *Jurgens v. Eads* (1978), 67 Ill.App.3d 52, requires a finding that Jeffrey's interest vested upon the death of the testator. Specifically, the Bank cites the following language:

> "A *contingent* remainder is either to a person not yet ascertained or not in being or depends upon an event which may never happen, while a *vested* remainder is to one ready to come into possession upon the termination of the prior estate. The distinction between vested and contingent is not the uncertainty whether the vested remainderman will live to enjoy his interests, but whether he will ever have a right to enjoyment. Thus, a gift is vested even if the right of enjoyment is deferred and neither a prior estate for life nor a condition subsequent will make it contingent." (Emphasis in original.)

In *Eads* the testator granted a life estate to his wife, and provided the remainder was to be distributed, after the wife's death, to six named individuals. The will further provided for contingent distributions in the event of the death of a named remainderman prior to the death of the wife. The will in *Eads* was similar to that in *Danz*. In both *Danz* and *Eads*, the interests of the named remaindermen were vested since the remaindermen were named, the postponement of the enjoyment of the estate was for reasons personal to the wife, rather than to the remaindermen, and the condition was not incorporated into the description of, nor into the gift to, the remaindermen, but was instead subsequently inserted as a clause divesting the estate if the remaindermen did not survive the life tenant. There is no discussion of the interests of "then[-]living descendants" in *Eads* simply because the testator in *Eads* did not grant a remainder to his "descendants," but to named individuals. Similarly, there is no discussion of a survivorship condition in the description of the remaindermen, simply because the testator in *Eads* did not include such a condition. However, in the present case, the testator did not name the remaindermen, and included a survivorship condition. Since the descendants surviving Harold are not determinable until Harold's death, and the survivorship condition was not a condition subsequent, but a condition on the ability of the descendants to take, the present case is unlike *Eads* and *Danz*, and Jeffrey's interest is not a vested, but a contingent, remainder.

A vested remainder may be conveyed by quitclaim deed. However a contingent remainder is not an estate, but merely the possibility of having an estate in the future, and it cannot be levied upon by legal process or voluntarily conveyed by deed, though a warranty deed may transfer the title by estoppel after the happening of the contingency. A quitclaim deed, executed in statutory form, will not convey a contingent remainder. A quitclaim deed may only convey contingent interests if appropriate words are employed in the deed to express such an intention. Since Jeffrey's future interest in the farm is a contingent remainder, the trial court correctly determined that, as a matter of law, Jeffrey could not convey his future interest in the farm by signing a quitclaim deed. Accordingly, the trial court correctly granted summary judgment regarding plaintiff's original complaint, and count I of its amended complaint.

* * *

Affirmed in part; reversed in part.

———————

Does *Goodwine* serve the interests of justice? Is it possible that the common-law rule preventing the casual transfer of contingent remainders served the interests of justice more often than the modern rule allowing their casual transfer by quitclaim deed? What are the consequences of making alienation more difficult?

Courts sometimes say that they favor the early vesting of interests or that they prefer vested interests. Coke said, "the law always delights in vesting of estates, and contingencies are odious in the law, and are the causes of troubles, and vesting and settling of estates, the cause of repose and certainty." *Roberts v. Roberts*, 80 E.R. 1002, 1009; (1611) 2 Bulst. 123; [1611] 1 WLUK 199 (K.B.). However, this preference is not so well established that you can depend upon it when you are drafting. *See Harris Trust and Savings Bank v. Beach*, 513 N.E.2d 833, 840 (Ill. 1987) ("the maxim favoring early vesting of remainders frequently ... frustrates what the ordinary settlor would have intended" and "should no longer be followed without question.").

The default of an appointment under a power is an exception to the usual rule that conditions located before the description of the taker make the remainder contingent.

> Example 6.31: O transfers "to T for the benefit of B for life, and then for the benefit of such person or persons as B appoints by will, and in default of appointment, to E." For E to take, B must fail to make the appointment. Even though the language appearing before and leading to E's interest contains a condition, that condition, B's default of appointment, is not considered to be a condition precedent. Therefore, E's remainder is vested subject to being divested by appointment.

However, that does not mean that all remainders in default of appointment are vested. If there are conditions other than the default of appointment written before the taker or if the remainder in default of appointment is not given to an ascertained person, the remainder in default of appointment is contingent.

Common-law courts gave vested remainders more respect than contingent remainders. As we just saw in *Goodwine*, the common law called a contingent remainder a mere "expectancy," not an interest, and said that it was not transferable inter vivos.

Why else might it matter whether an interest is vested or contingent? Another potential difference between vested and contingent remainders is that a court, perhaps a confused court, might assume that a contingent remainderperson must survive until distribution in order to take. In *Fletcher v. Hurdle*, 259 Ark. 640 (1976), the testator left land to his granddaughter for life, remainder to her issue if she had any, "and if not, then to Asbury Fletcher ...".

Asbury died. The granddaughter died without issue. The court held that Asbury's remainder was conditioned on his survival to the death of the life tenant, and that he did not satisfy that condition. That is not the traditional rule, but as you will see, a similar result might obtain today under a controversial provision of the Uniform Probate Code.

Another important difference between contingent and vested interests arises in the context of the Rule Against Perpetuities. Indeed, being able to figure out the last point in time at which a future interest might conceivably vest in interest is critical to understanding the Rule Against Perpetuities. It is therefore essential to know when vesting occurs in all jurisdictions where the Rule retains any force.

(B) Destructibility of Contingent Remainders

Yet another potential difference between vested and contingent remainders is that vested remainders are not destructible. Legal contingent remainders, under the common law, were destructible by merger, discussed later, or by failure to vest in time. A legal contingent remainder would be destroyed if it had not vested in interest by the time for vesting in possession.

> Example 6.32: O transfers Blackacre "to A for life, then to B if B has married C." A dies before B and C marry. When A dies, it is time for B's contingent remainder to vest in possession, but it cannot vest in possession because the condition precedent has not been satisfied. If contingent remainders are destructible, the contingent remainder is destroyed and it does not matter if B and C marry after that.

If contingent remainders are destructible and there is an unsatisfied condition precedent when it is time for the contingent remainderperson to take possession, the law will not wait for the condition to be satisfied. Similarly, if contingent remainders are destructible and the time has come for the contingent remainderperson to take possession but that remainderperson has not been identified, the law will not wait for the taker to be identified. Modern statutes have changed the rule of destructibility in almost all jurisdictions, and there is some support for the proposition that even under the common law contingent remainders in trusts were not destructible. A doctrinal reason to support the position that equitable contingent remainders are not destructible is that equitable interests were not subject to the rules governing the movement of seisin, which underpinned the destructibility doctrine. All that said, consider the following case.

MATTER OF GILBERT

Surrogate's Court, New York County, New York, 1992
592 N.Y.S.2d 224

ROTH, S.

The executor of the estate of Peter Gilbert asks the court to declare null and void a renunciation by Mr. Gilbert's son, Lester, of his interest in two wholly discretionary trusts under decedent's will.

Mr. Gilbert died on March 26, 1989, leaving an estate of over $40,000,000. He was survived by his wife and four children. Under his will, testator, after making certain pre-residuary legacies, created an elective share trust for the life income benefit of his wife. The amount of decedent's generation-skipping transfer (GST) tax exemption was divided into four discretionary trusts, one for the primary benefit of each of his children. The residue of Mr. Gilbert's estate was similarly divided. Upon the death of the widow, the remainder of her trust is to be added in equal shares to the residuary trusts for decedent's children. The trusts are wholly discretionary. Decedent's son, Lester, is therefore a discretionary income beneficiary of two testamentary trusts, one of which will be augmented at the widow's death. Decedent's issue, including Lester's sisters, nieces and nephews as well as Lester's issue (should he have any), are also discretionary beneficiaries of both of Lester's trusts.

Lester, who has no issue, timely served on the executor a notice of renunciation of his "dispositive share in the estate of Peter Gilbert".

The executor, supported by the guardian ad litem for decedent's minor grandchildren, takes the position that Lester's renunciation should be declared invalid. First, he states that permitting the renunciation would violate the testator's intention to provide for Lester. Second, the executor argues that Lester possesses no current property interest and therefore has nothing to renounce. The executor maintains that Lester's renunciation is premature and may be made only if, and at such time as, the trustees exercise their discretion to distribute income or principal to him.

The executor explains decedent's intention as follows:

Lester, who is approximately 32 years of age, . . . has left the religion of his birth and has for some time lived in Virginia with a small group of people who share a similar religious doctrine. Some months ago he phoned your petitioner and announced that he planned to renounce whatever bequest was left for him. When asked what he planned to do if he were ever taken seriously ill and needed expensive medical care, he responded "Jesus will provide for me".

The fact that Lester had chosen to alienate himself from his family did not stop the decedent from loving his son or worrying about his future needs. . . . [T]he decedent wanted to know that funds would be available if the Trustees, acting in the manner that they thought the decedent would have acted had he then been living, should ever decide, for example, to pay a medical bill for Lester.

In effect, the executor argues that if the beneficiary of a wholly discretionary trust is permitted to renounce his or her interest, then no trust can ever be created to protect someone who is now disdainful of financial assistance but may in the future be in dire need, or simply have a change of heart.

However, under these circumstances, decedent's intention is not controlling. With respect to every renunciation, the intent to make a transfer is thwarted by the beneficiary who refuses to accept it. But clearly, "the law does not compel a man to accept an estate, either beneficial or in trust, against his will".

The executor suggests in his memorandum that he might be forced "to inquire into the mental capacity of Lester, since there is no rational reason which explains Lester's conduct". However, the desire to renounce wealth is not necessarily irrational. Presumably, the executor would not argue that a nun who takes a vow of poverty is mentally incompetent. Here, the acceptance of a monetary benefit apparently conflicts with Lester's religious beliefs. It would not be appropriate for the court to determine the validity of those beliefs, even if requested to do so. Furthermore, even if Lester's renunciation were purely whimsical, this would not in itself be sufficient reason either to reject the renunciation or to find him incompetent. In any event, the question of Lester's mental capacity has not been raised. There is no allegation in the petition or in any affidavit that Lester is a person under disability. The court must therefore proceed on the assumption that Lester is competent to make an effective renunciation.

The executor's second argument is that Lester has no current property interest which he can renounce. Rather, the executor maintains that Lester must wait until the trustees exercise their discretion to distribute income or principal to him, at which time, the executor asserts, Lester can renounce the property subject to such exercise of discretion. There appears to be no decision in New York with respect to the renunciation of a discretionary interest.

Renunciations are governed by EPTL 2–1.11. Paragraph (b)(1) of such statute provides that "[a]ny beneficiary of a disposition may renounce all or part of his interest . . .". EPTL 1–2.4 defines "disposition" as "a transfer of property by a person during his lifetime or by will". "Property" is defined in EPTL 1–2.15 as "anything that may be the subject of ownership . . .". Therefore, under the statute, a renunciation may be made only with respect to a transfer of something which may be the subject of ownership. The statute, however, does not require that property be transferred *to* the beneficiary. Instead, the property may be transferred to a trustee *for the benefit of* a beneficiary. Furthermore, the statute does not require that the beneficiary renounce the disposition itself; rather, he may renounce "all or part of his *interest*" in the disposition (EPTL 2–1.11(b)(1) [emphasis added]).

In this case, decedent by his will transferred property to trusts of which Lester is a beneficiary, albeit a discretionary beneficiary. Similarly, the subject of Lester's renunciation is his interest in the trusts, although that interest is discretionary. The renunciation, therefore, appears to satisfy the terms of the statute.

The executor, however, contends that Lester's interest in the trusts does not rise to the level contemplated by the statute. He argues that for a renunciation to be effective, the renounced interest must be in the nature of property. Claiming that Lester's interest is not property, the executor cites *Hamilton v. Drogo* (241 NY 401), where the Court of Appeals held that a judgment creditor was not entitled to levy on the interest of one of the beneficiaries of a discretionary trust. Holding that the judgment creditor could attach the income if and when the trustee distributed it to the beneficiary, the court observed:

> In the present case no income may ever become due to the judgment debtor. We may not interfere with the discretion

which the testatrix has vested in the trustee any more than her son may do so. . . . But . . . if it is exercised in favor of the duke then . . . [a]t least for some appreciable time, however brief, the award must precede the delivery of the income he is to receive and during that time the lien of the execution attaches.

Similarly, in *Matter of Duncan* (80 Misc 2d 32), the court held that a beneficiary of a discretionary trust possesses no property reachable by creditors until distribution is made. The court observed that there was

no absolute right to receive income or principal from the trust and . . . therefore *there [was] no property or rights to property belonging to the beneficiaries*, specifically Thomas W. Doran, the subject of the levy. If, however, the trustee does at any time elect in his discretion to pay [the beneficiary] . . . the amount of said payment will be subject to the levy. . . . [emphasis added].

But the cases relied upon by the executor are clearly distinguishable from the instant case in that they deal with the rights of creditors and not with those of beneficiaries. More closely analogous are those decisions which determine the rights of beneficiaries to compel distribution by trustees. Although in this case Lester's creditors cannot reach the trusts, Lester may nonetheless have the right to force the trustees to distribute income or principal to him under certain circumstances.

Although our courts cannot ordinarily interfere with the exercise of a trustee's discretion, they can ensure that such discretion is exercised fairly and honestly. In the present case, the trustees' discretion is absolute and not limited by any standard. However, even in such a case, the trustees may be compelled to distribute funds to the beneficiary if they abuse their discretion in refusing to make distribution.

Thus, Lester may have the right to compel the trustees to distribute trust property to him under certain circumstances. Therefore, even if the court accepts the executor's interpretation of the statute, Lester arguably has a current interest which could be deemed "property" for the purpose of an effective renunciation. In such respect, the present case is distinguishable from *Matter of Heffner* (132 Misc 2d 361), where the disclaimants wished to renounce their interests as takers in default of the exercise of a power of appointment. In that case, the disclaimants had no rights whatsoever against the donee of the power since a court could not control such donee's exercise of the power in any respect.

Although Surrogate Radigan allowed the renunciation based on common law, he observed that there was no statutory right to renounce. Commenting that "[p]etitioners possess no present property interest which can be renounced" under the statute, he cited EPTL 2–1.11(a)(2), which provides that the "effective date" of a disposition created by the exercise or nonexercise of a testamentary power of appointment is the date of death of the powerholder. The Surrogate concluded that no property interest is created before the effective date.

It is noted, however, that no such effective date is specified for discretionary dispositions. Furthermore, this court approaches the question somewhat differently. As discussed earlier, a statutory renunciation need not relate to property. Instead, the statute merely requires the disclaimant to renounce his or her interest in a disposition. Even if the statute requires a property interest, this court does not conclude that the "effective date" of a disposition determines when such an interest is created. Rather, the sole purpose of EPTL 2–1.11(a)(2) is to provide a date from which the time to file a renunciation is measured.

Lester's renunciation also applies to his remainder interest in the elective share trust, which is contingent upon his surviving the widow. As discussed above, any interest, whether or not contingent, is within the scope of the statute. Even if the executor's interpretation is correct and a renunciation must relate to an interest in property, a contingent remainder has historically been recognized as a property interest.

Finally, the guardian ad litem argues that if Lester's renunciation is allowed, the remainder interests in his trusts should not be accelerated. The remainder of Lester's trusts would be payable to his issue. As mentioned earlier, Lester has no issue. If the interests are accelerated, Lester's unborn issue would be cut off and decedent's living grandchildren would lose certain present interests in these trusts. It is noted that acceleration of the trust remainders would have no direct tax consequences and any indirect effects would be relatively minor.

The question is whether under EPTL 2–1.11(d) this court has any discretion to suspend acceleration. Such statute, in relevant part, provides that:

> Unless the creator of the disposition has otherwise provided, the filing of a renunciation, as provided in this section, has the same effect with respect to the renounced interest as though the renouncing person had predeceased the creator or the decedent . . . and shall have the effect of accelerating the possession and enjoyment of subsequent interests. . . .

Thus, it appears that under the language of the statute, the remainder interests in Lester's trusts will be accelerated unless the decedent has "otherwise provided". There is no explicit "otherwise provision" in testator's will, but the guardian ad litem argues that the court should infer an "otherwise provision" from the general language of the will and the circumstances surrounding its execution.

* * *

When EPTL 2–1.11 was enacted in 1977, the language regarding acceleration was added to resolve the dispute reflected in a number of conflicting decisions. Those cases looked to testator's intent as the appropriate guideline and determined acceleration on a case-by-case basis, with unpredictable results. It is clear the addition of this language was intended to provide uniformity. To engage in the type of analysis suggested by the guardian ad litem would mean a return to the approach rejected by the Legislature.

Based upon the foregoing, it is concluded that Lester's renunciation is valid as to any and all interests in his father's estate. Lester is thus to be treated as if he predeceased his father without issue.

Gilbert indicates that, under the New York statutes governing acceleration of remainders, a contingent remainder might be destroyed when a vested remainder would not be. Vested remainders, being vested and ready to take possession, can "accelerate" into possession at the termination of the preceding estate. If the preceding estate terminates before a contingent remainder has vested, the contingent remainderperson cannot take possession, and the court in *Gilbert* accepts that the remainder is destroyed. The disclaimer statute gave Lester the power to destroy the interest in his children subsequently conceived. The result in *Pate v. Ford*, 297 S.C. 294 (1989), goes a sizable step further. A disclaimer by one son destroyed the interest of his brother's unborn children, enhancing the share of his own children.

(C) Indefeasibly Vested

Vested remainders are further classified into three groups. Those that can never be divested are called "indefeasibly vested".

> Example 6.33: O transfers "to A for life, then to B." B's remainder is indefeasibly vested. This does not mean that B is certain to take possession. B could die before A. In that event, B would leave his indefeasibly vested remainder to his heir or devisee.

Indefeasibly vested remainders have characteristics that might not appeal to clients. In many states, they are considered to be property that is subject to equitable division upon divorce. If your client does not want the remainderperson to have to share the value of the remainder with a former spouse, you should consider drafting the instrument so that the remainder is contingent on that remainderperson's survival until the time of possession or perhaps subject to divestment upon divorce. Other conditions precedent might also insulate the remainder from equitable division upon divorce in some jurisdictions. That raises this question: What sense does it make for courts to decide whether an interest is property for purposes of equitable division by looking to whether it is indefeasibly vested?

(D) Vested Subject to Open

Some remainders are vested in one person, but might vest in an additional person in the future. These remainders are called "vested subject to open".

> Example 6.34: O transfers "to A for life, then to all of A's children." B is born to A. B has a vested remainder subject to open.

Often vested remainders subject to open arise in the context of class gifts, which are governed by special rules discussed below. Be careful to note that a vested remainder remains subject to open as long as it remains possible for the remainder to vest in an additional person. Sometimes the phrase "vested subject to partial divestment" is used as an equivalent to "vested subject to open", but that can lead to confusion regarding the nature of the interest held by potential unborn members of a class, so this book avoids that usage.

(E) Vested Subject to Complete Divestment

A transferor can create a vested remainder that might be wholly divested by some event in the future.

> Example 6.35: O transfers "Blackacre to A for life, then to B, but if B drinks liquor before A dies then O has the right to re-enter and retake Blackacre." B has a vested remainder in fee simple subject to condition subsequent, or more generally, a vested remainder subject to complete divestment.

> A vested remainder may be both subject to open and subject to complete divestment.

> Example 6.36: O transfers "Blackacre to A for life, then to B's children, but if B drinks liquor before A dies then to D." B has one child, C, who has a vested remainder in fee simple subject to open and subject to complete divestment.

(F) Vested with Enjoyment Postponed

Finally, an instrument may contain conditions that determine when possession shall occur or a distribution shall be made, without creating conditions on whether possession or a distribution shall occur. In other words, an interest can be vested with enjoyment postponed.

CLOBBERIE'S CASE

Court of Chancery, England, 1677
86 Eng. Rep. 476; 2 Vent. 342; 1 WLUK 77

In one Clobberie's case it was held, that where one bequeathed a sum of money to a woman, at her age of 21 years, or day of marriage, to be paid unto her with interest, and she died before either, that the money should go to her executor; and was so decreed by my Lord Chancellor Finch.[4]

But he said, if money were bequeathed to one at his age of 21 years; if he dies before that age, the money is lost.

---

[4] Lord Chancellor Finch was later dubbed Lord Nottingham, and was the author of the decision in the Duke of Norfolk's Case, which grew into the Rule Against Perpetuities.

On the other side, if money be given to one, to be paid at the age of 21 years; there, if the party dies before, it shall go to the executors.

As *Clobberie's Case* held, a mere delay in the enjoyment of an interest does not prevent that interest from being vested, so do not assume that words postponing enjoyment make the interest contingent. Courts in the United States are split on whether to follow the second proposition in *Clobberie's Case*, but the first and third propositions in *Clobberie's Case* are still followed in many states today. Don't you love it?

> Problem 6.37: O transfers "$100,000 to T in trust, of which $20,000 is to be paid to A at the age of 25, remainder to B." A dies before reaching 25. Does A's estate receive anything and, if so, how much and when? Hint: Make sure that B is not unfairly treated.

> Problem 6.38: O devises "$100,000 to T in trust, with $20,000 for A at age 25, to be paid with interest." A dies before reaching 25. Does A's estate receive anything and, if so, how much and when?

(ii) *The Executory Interest*

The executory interest was created by the Statute of Uses. Before 1536, feudal owners could use "uses" to avoid feudal incidents because feudal incidents applied only to legal interests, not to uses. The Statute of Uses closed the revenue loophole by converting uses (equitable interests) into legal interests. When the statute operated, an equitable life estate became a legal life estate, an equitable remainder in fee simple became a legal remainder in fee simple, and so forth. Giving legal names to many of the converted uses was easy. But some kinds of uses did not have a legal equivalent. As we have seen, the courts of law did not allow legal interests that would require seisin to move in unpermitted ways. But equitable interests did not carry seisin, so uses did not have to follow the rules governing the movement of seisin. As a result, transferors could and did create future interests in equity that had no legal counterpart. When those equitable interests were converted to legal interests, there was no legal name to give them. So, they were given a new name, "executory interest", which referred to the fact that they were equitable interests that had been executed, i.e., made legal. After the Statute of Uses, future interests in transferees that failed to qualify as remainders could exist as executory interests. For a while, an executory interest created in an inter vivos transfer had to be created initially as a use to be executed by the statute, but that requirement no longer applies.

(A) The Springing Executory Interest

As we saw above, before 1536, a grantor could not create an interest that would require seisin to spring from the grantor to a grantee at some time in the future. Therefore, O could not transfer "to B starting when B marries." Nor could O transfer "to A for 5 years and then to B if B has married by then" because A's term of years (a nonfreehold) could not carry the seisin to B, and B could not take seisin immediately from O because B had not satisfied the condition precedent. However, O could accomplish O's goal by creating a "use".

> Example 6.39: O transfers "to T and his heirs to the use of O and his heirs, but when B marries then to the use of B and his heirs." Before 1536, T would hold legal title in fee simple and the rules of seisin would be satisfied. O and B would hold uses. B's use in fee simple would spring out of O's use when B married. After 1536, assuming T has no active duties to perform, the Statute of Uses executes both uses, making them legal interests and knocking the legal title holder T out of the picture, with the result that O has a legal fee simple subject to a springing executory interest in fee simple in B.

(B) The Shifting Executory Interest

Before 1536, a grantor could not create an interest that could require seisin to shift from one grantee to another grantee other than at the natural expiration of the former's estate. Hence, if O transferred "to A for life, then to B and her heirs, but if B does not survive A then to B's eldest daughter and her heirs", B's eldest daughter would take nothing because a condition cannot be reserved in a stranger. However, the technique of creating a use would work in this situation as well, allowing a grantor to transfer a similar interest that would be honored by the court of equity.

> Example 6.40: O transfers "to T and T's heirs for the use of A for life, then to the use of B for life, but if B does not survive A then to the use of B's eldest daughter for her life." Before 1536, T would hold legal title and the rules of seisin

would be satisfied. A, B, B's daughter, and O would hold equitable interests. The use would shift from B to her daughter if B died before A. After 1536, assuming T has no active duties to perform, the Statute of Uses executes the uses, making the uses into legal interests and eliminating T's interest. A has a legal life estate, B has a vested remainder for life subject to a shifting executory interest in B's eldest daughter for life, and O has a reversion.

(C) The Executory Interest Following a Fee Simple

Before 1536, a grantor could not create an interest in a grantee that would follow a fee simple. However, the technique of creating a use described above would work once again, allowing a grantor to transfer a similar interest that would be honored by the court of equity.

> Example 6.41: O transfers "to T and his heirs for the use of A and her heirs while A refrains from drinking alcohol, then to the use of B and her heirs." Before 1536, T would hold legal title and the rules of seisin would be satisfied. A and B would hold beneficial interests. The use would shift from A to B if A drank alcohol. After 1536, assuming T has no active duties to perform, the Statute of Uses executes the uses, making the uses into legal interests and eliminating T's interest. A has a legal fee simple; B has a shifting executory interest following A's fee simple.

(iii) Contingent Remainders Versus Executory Interests

What interest was created when a transferee was given an interest that looked like both a contingent remainder and an executory interest? You will not be surprised to learn that the name to apply to such a future interest was settled long ago. In *Purefoy v. Rogers*, 2 Wms. Saund. 380 (1670), the court decided that such an interest would be called a remainder.

> Example 6.42: O transfers "to A for life, then to A's first son to reach 21." A has one son S who is 14. S has a remainder. Clearly, it is possible for S's interest to take as a remainder. If A dies after S reaches 21, S takes without violating any of the rules of seisin. On the other hand, if A dies when S is 15 and S lives to age 21, S can take only if seisin springs from O to S when S reaches 21. Therefore, on those facts, S's

interest would have to be a springing executory interest. However, the courts did not allow both. S's interest is a remainder, not an executory interest. If A dies when S is 15 and contingent remainders are destructible, S has nothing.

Problem 6.43: How might you draft the transfer in Example 6.42 to avoid the common-law rule that contingent remainders are destructible, and thus to protect S's interest from being destroyed?

One other difference between contingent remainders and executory interests is the time at which they become vested. A contingent remainder vests in interest when the taker is identified and there is no unsatisfied condition precedent. Vesting for executory interests is simpler to state: an executory interest vests in interest when it becomes possessory (i.e., when the holder is entitled to possession, whether possession is actually taken or not).

Example 6.44: O transfers "to A and his heirs until A drinks liquor, then to B and her heirs." B is identified and there is no condition precedent (remember, the natural expiration of A's estate is not a condition precedent), but B's interest does not vest until A drinks liquor, giving B the right to possession.

3.   FURTHER DESCRIBING DEFEASIBLE INTERESTS

Now that you know the names for the various future interests, you can describe more completely the interests that precede those future interests. As we have seen, the name we give to an interest depends on whether it is a present or future interest and also how long it will last. With regard to maximum duration, quantum diminishes from the estate in fee simple, to the fee tail, to the life estate, to the term of years. In addition to words that describe the maximum duration, there are words to describe the possibility of early termination. We can tell which words to use to describe the possibility of early termination by looking at the subsequent interest.

If an interest might terminate early by virtue of a special limitation, we say the interest is determinable.

Example 6.45: O transfers "to A and A's heirs for so long as the land is used for residential purposes." O retains a possibility of reverter and A takes an estate in fee simple determinable. If the land is not used for residential purposes, the land reverts to O or whoever has succeeded to O's interest.

> Example 6.46: O transfers Blackacre "to A for life for so long as the land is used for residential purposes, then to B." B has a remainder in fee simple and A takes a life estate determinable. B will become entitled to possession automatically when either A dies or when the land ceases to be used for residential purposes.

A fee simple determinable is descendible, devisable, alienable inter vivos, and might last forever. Perhaps attempting to reduce litigation, some states have abolished the fee simple determinable, statutorily providing that language that would have created a determinable estate instead creates an estate subject to a condition subsequent, discussed next.

If the interest that might terminate early is followed by a right of entry for condition broken, we say the interest is subject to a condition subsequent.

> Example 6.47: O transfers "to A, but if the land is not used for residential purposes then O shall have the right to re-enter and retake." O has a right of entry and A takes a fee simple subject to condition subsequent. If the land is not used for residential purposes, O (or whoever has succeeded to O's interest)[5] may exercise the right of entry and retake the land. If A does not voluntarily relinquish the land to O, O can sue to recover possession, a process sometimes described as "declaring a forfeiture" of A's estate.

Unlike other future interests, the right of entry does not automatically become possessory when the specified condition is broken. One more step is required after the condition is broken; the grantor O must exercise the right of entry. When O exercises, O's interest becomes possessory. One way to exercise the right of entry is to bring suit to eject the possessor.

If the interest that might terminate early is followed by an executory interest, we say the interest that might terminate early is subject to an executory interest or with an executory limitation. In some situations, the following interest is an executory interest because it

---

[5] From here on, we may omit the "or whoever has succeeded to" parenthetical, but keep in mind that all future interests are at least descendible, except those measured by the life of the holder.

will cut short the preceding estate rather than waiting for its natural expiration.

> Example 6.48: O transfers "to A for life, but if the land is not used for residential purposes then to B." B has an executory interest in fee simple and A takes a life estate subject to an executory limitation. (Or, we can say that A takes a life estate subject to a shifting executory interest in B.) B will become entitled to possession automatically when either A dies or the land ceases to be used for residential purposes.

In other situations, the subsequent interest is an executory interest simply because it follows a fee simple.

> Example 6.49: O transfers "to A and his heirs for so long as A does not drink liquor, then to B and his heirs." B has an executory interest in fee simple, and A's interest is an estate in fee simple with an executory limitation in B.

Some people would say that an interest is "with an executory limitation" when it follows a durational limitation and "subject to an executory limitation" when it could be cut short by a conditional limitation, but it is probably not worth trying to maintain a distinction between "with" and "subject to" before "executory limitation" and we will not attempt to do so here. We can also say that A has a fee simple determinable, but that is not as descriptive as saying it is subject to an executory limitation because a determinable estate might also be followed by a possibility of reverter.

In yet other situations, the interest is an executory interest because it springs out of O in futuro.

> Example 6.50: O transfers "to A for life, reversion to O, but if B gives A a proper funeral then to B for the rest of O's life." B has a springing executory interest *pur autre vie*. O has a reversion subject to an executory limitation for life in B.

An interest can change from one type to another as events occur.

> Example 6.51: O devises "Blackacre to T for the benefit of A for life. After A dies, T shall manage as follows: If B married C before A died, for the benefit of B; and if B did not marry C before A died, for the benefit of C; however, if C dies without descendants surviving, then for the benefit of D." In equity, B, C, and D have contingent remainders, and O's heir has a reversion. Later, B marries C. In equity, B has a vested

remainder subject to a shifting executory interest in D. C and O's heir have nothing.

Problem 6.52: O transfers "to A for life, then to be divided among A's children, however, if A is not survived by issue, then to B." A has no children. Who has what? Is the interest in the children subject to open? Next, A has a child, C. What is the state of title? Later, C has a child, D. What does D have, if anything? C dies, devising all C's property to C's spouse S. Does S get anything? Finally, A dies. Who has what?

WEBB V. UNDERHILL

Court of Appeals of Oregon, 1994
882 P.2d 127

ROSSMAN, P.J.

In this action to partition real property, ORS 105.205, plaintiffs appeal from a summary judgment for defendant. We hold that the determinative issue in the case, whether the alternative beneficiaries' remainder interests are contingent or vested, is a question of law that is amenable to resolution on summary judgment, and that the trial court correctly held that those interests are contingent. Accordingly, we affirm.

Ernest Webb, owner of the Buck Hollow Ranch, died in 1972. His will devises all of his property to his wife Agnes for life, or until she remarries, with the remainder of the property to be divided equally among four of Ernest's six children upon Agnes' death or remarriage. If any one of the four named children is deceased at that time, that one-quarter share will go to his or her lineal descendants, if any. Specifically, the will provides:

> "For her use, benefit and enjoyment, for such period of her natural life as she shall remain unmarried, I give to my beloved wife, Agnes Webb, all of my property of every kind and nature, with the provision, however, that if my said wife shall remarry, that said property shall *at the date of the marriage* revert as follows: One Dollar ($1.00) each to Irene Barton and to Vivian Morse [two of Ernest's six children]. The remainder shall be divided equally between [the other four children]:
>
> "Delbert Webb

"Delores Rhodig

"La Velle Underhill

"Wayne L. Webb

"But if one or more of these shall be dead, their share shall go to their lineal descendants, if any. If one or more of the four who live in Oregon and are last mentioned, shall be dead leaving no lineal descendants, the share of the deceased one, dead without lineal descendants, shall go to the survivors of the four who live in Oregon (last mentioned) or to their lineal descendants. The said four being Delbert Webb, Delores Rhodig, La Velle Underhill, and Wayne L. Webb.

"*At the death of my said wife*, if she shall yet be in the use and enjoyment of said property, such as remains shall be divided as follows: One Dollar ($1.00) each to Irene Barton and to Vivian Morse. The remainder shall be divided equally between:

"Delbert Webb

"Delores Rhodig

"La Velle Underhill

"Wayne L. Webb

"But if one or more of these shall be dead, their share shall go to their lineal descendants, if any. If one or more of the four who live in Oregon and are last mentioned, shall be dead leaving no lineal descendants, the share of the deceased one, dead without lineal descendants, shall go to the survivors of the four who live in Oregon (last mentioned) or to their lineal descendants. The said four being Delbert Webb, Delores Rhodig, La Velle Underhill, and Wayne L. Webb." (Emphasis supplied.)

After Ernest's death, his son Delbert died. Delbert is survived by his wife Carol, who subleases a portion of the ranch, and their three adult children (the grandchildren).

Plaintiffs, who seek to sell the ranch as a single parcel and distribute the proceeds according to their respective interests, are Ernest's wife Agnes, two of Ernest's children (Wayne and Delores), Delbert's wife Carol and the grandchildren. Defendant is Ernest's daughter La Velle.

To maintain an action to partition property, a plaintiff must be a tenant in common, with a vested remainder in the property. ORS 105.205. Agnes, as the sole life estate holder, is not a tenant in common, and Carol is a mere lessee. Therefore, neither of those parties fits within the requirements of the partition statute. Below, plaintiffs argued that the grandchildren's interests vested indefeasibly at the time of Delbert's death. They conceded below that the children's interests are contingent, but, on appeal, their reply brief may be viewed as an attempt to withdraw that concession. Defendant argued that all of the remainder interests are contingent, in that the children or their lineal descendants must survive Agnes' death or remarriage to take under the will.

The trial court ruled that both the children's and grandchildren's interests are contingent and conditioned upon surviving to the date of Agnes' death or remarriage. Having concluded that none of the plaintiffs holds a vested remainder, the court held that they could not maintain this partition action. ORS 105.205. Accordingly, it granted defendant's motion for summary judgment and dismissed the case.

The issues on appeal are whether the children's and grandchildren's interests in the property are vested, and whether resolution of that question involves a factual determination that precludes summary judgment. * * *

We hold that, in this case, the question of whether the remainder interests are contingent or vested is a purely legal one. Although the trial court erroneously segmented its decision into factual "findings" regarding the testator's intent and legal "conclusions" regarding plaintiffs' ability to maintain this partition action, the dispositive legal question to be resolved was and is what type of future interests are possessed by Ernest's four named children and their lineal descendants under the terms of his will. In the emphasized portions of the will, set out above, the testator expressly provides that the triggering event by which all distributions are determined is the death or remarriage of the life tenant. When the language of a will is unambiguous, there is no basis for resorting to extrinsic evidence to ascertain the testator's intent.

We turn to trial court's legal conclusions, beginning with an analysis of the future interests of Ernest's four named children. Plaintiffs acknowledge that the will contains a survivorship requirement that the children must meet, in order for them to personally take, but contend that the children's interests are most aptly described as "vested remainders subject to divestment" should they fail to survive the life tenant. That is incorrect. The devise in this case created *alternative* remainder interests in both the children and the grandchildren. *Love v. Lindstedt*, 76 Or. 66 (1915).[5] When a life estate is followed by two alternative remainder interests, and "the vesting of the second depends upon the failure of the first, and the same contingency decides which one of the two alternative remainders shall take effect in possession," both interests are alternative contingent remainders. 76 Or. at 72, 147 P. 935. Here, surviving the death or remarriage of the life tenant is the contingency that decides whether and which of the alternative remainder interests will vest indefeasibly. If one of the children dies before the triggering event, his or her estate—and, accordingly, his or her spouse, if any—will take nothing under the will. Until the triggering event takes place, it cannot be known who will be entitled to take under Ernest's will.

Plaintiffs contend that the only contingency that conditioned the present three grandchildren's interests was to survive their father's death. They argue that, once Delbert died, his interest in the property indefeasibly vested in his children. It is true that, if Delbert's lineal descendants were taking by devise or by intestate succession from Delbert, those heirs would be determined at the moment of his death. However, the future interests of Delbert's children, if any, flow directly from their grandfather Ernest's will, not Delbert's. Their interests stem only from their membership in a class described as "lineal descendants." When a will includes a gift to a class of persons, the devise takes effect in favor of those who constitute the class at the death of the testator, unless the will shows a contrary intent. As noted above, Ernest's will unambiguously expresses a contrary intent. It states that upon *Agnes'* remarriage or death, Ernest's property is to be divided among his four named children or their lineal descendants. That language fixed Agnes' death or remarriage as the date on which a determination of the members of the "lineal descendants" class is to be made.[8] There may

---

[5]   There is support in the Restatement for plaintiffs' position that a remainder interest can be vested yet subject to a survivorship requirement, i.e., a survivorship requirement does not necessarily mean that the remainder interest is contingent. However, *Love v. Lindstedt, supra,* supports the view that a devise "to A for life, remainder to B, but if B predeceases A, then to C" creates alternative remainder interests in B and C. Under the facts of this case, "B and C" would represent Ernest's named children and their lineal descendants.

[8]   The *Restatement (Second) of Property*, "Donative Transfers," § 28.2 (1988), states that when a gift is made to a class described as the "descendants" of a named person, or by another

or may not be any lineal descendants of Delbert living at the date of Agnes' death or remarriage. If none are living, Delbert's share will be divided among his named siblings who live in Oregon or their lineal descendants.

Furthermore, before the life tenancy ends and the class closes, it will be impossible to determine the entire membership of the class of lineal descendants. Plaintiffs argue that once Delbert died, he could have no more lineal descendants and that, as a consequence, his portion of the class closed with Delbert's three children as its only members. That is incorrect. The term "lineal descendants" encompasses more than just children. The term includes all those who proceed from the body of the person named to the remotest degree, including grandchildren and great-grandchildren.

In sum, until Agnes' death or remarriage, all of the future interests in this case will remain contingent. There is presently no party who may maintain a partition action.

Affirmed.

––––––––––

The Oregon statute allowing partition requires, in this case, that there be concurrent vested remainders in the land. The first question is whether there are remainders in the named children. The testator devised to his beloved wife, Agnes, "for such period of her natural life as she shall remain unmarried". That language creates a life estate determinable. After that came remainders in his children. Two of those children received no interest in the land, and one child, Delbert, died before the case. That leaves three of the testator's children, Wayne, Delores, and La Velle, holding concurrent remainders in the land.

The next question is whether at least two of the three concurrent remainders are vested. The plaintiffs argue that their interests are vested subject to divestment. The court rejects that contention, stating in footnote 5 that "to A for life, remainder to B, but if B predeceases A, then to C" creates alternative remainders. Under the traditional rules, the court is wrong about that. The court quotes and cites to *Love v. Lindstedt*, but *Love* offers little support. A larger portion of that passage from the *Love* opinion reads, "where there

––––––––––

multigenerational term, "[a] class member must survive to the *date of distribution* in order to share in the gift." (Emphasis supplied). Under Oregon law, the "primary incidents of 'class gifts' * * * are survivorship and the admission of afterborn members."

are alternative remainders, and the vesting of the second depends upon the failure of the first, and the same contingency decides which one of the two alternative remainders shall take effect in possession, the rule that a remainder cannot be limited after a fee has no application." From this larger excerpt, we can see that the *Love* court assumed there were remainders (which there were in that case) and stated that alternative remainders are an exception to the rule that a remainder cannot follow a fee simple. If the *Webb* court had followed the traditional rules, it would have found that Wayne and Delores held vested remainders.

A policy argument could be made in favor of *Webb*'s deviation from the standard rules of construction. The Oregon statute allows only holders of vested remainders to demand a partition. Perhaps the point of that requirement was to prevent holders of interests that might never become possessory from forcing a partition on persons in possession. Since a vested remainder subject to divestment is like a contingent remainder in that it might not become possessory, its holder should be similarly disqualified from forcing a partition on others. Take Delbert for example. When he died, his interest was divested by the executory interest in his lineal descendants. Before he died, should he have been able to force a partition when, as it turns out, his interest would ultimately be divested?

Whatever the merits of that policy argument, that is not what the statute says. Moreover, look at how many of the interest holders in this case want to partition: decedent's wife, two of his children, and three of his grandchildren. The will created a bad situation, dividing the family and likely hindering optimal use of the land. A trust might have avoided those consequences.

4. SPECIAL RULES

There are additional special rules for you to keep in mind when working with present and future interests. Some are straightforward. Others get a bit tricky.

(a) Presumptions of Facts Regarding Fertility

The law of future interests usually presumes irrebuttably that people can conceive a child until their death, without regard to whether they actually have the physical capacity to conceive children. In the infamous Rule Against Perpetuities case of *Jee v. Audley*, 1 Cox 324 (Ch. 1787), Sir Lloyd Kenyon was unwilling to take into account the fact that a woman 70 years old was not going to give birth to any more daughters. The case gave rise to the pitfall known as the "fertile octogenarian". For a case overcoming the usual presumption, see *In re Bassett's Estate*, 104 N.H. 504 (1963), where the court was willing to terminate a trust based on medical evidence that neither spouse was able to conceive children. For future interest purposes, the law often presumes irrebuttably that a person cannot conceive a child after death, without regard to conception possibilities created by modern science. Without this presumption, some future interests that are now valid would be void under the Rule Against Perpetuities, which we will discuss in the chapter below.

(b) Merger

If one person holds a legal vested estate for life (or for a term of years) in land followed by a legal vested remainder or reversion in fee simple, the two estates merge together.

> Example 6.53: O transfers Blackacre "to A for life, then to B." A sells A's interest to B. B now holds the estate for the life of A followed by B's original remainder in fee simple and the two automatically merge into a present fee simple in B.

The merger rule includes two exceptions. First, and extremely important, the interests do not merge if they are separated by an indestructible interest. Note that this exception does not prevent merger when the interests are separated by a destructible contingent remainder. Second, and rarely relevant, the interests do not merge at the moment of creation if a destructible contingent remainder was created between them.

> Example 6.54a: At a time when and place where contingent remainders are destructible, O transfers "to A for life, then to B for life if B has married C before the death of A, then to A and A's heirs." Immediately thereafter, A has a life estate and a vested remainder, and A's interests do not merge at that moment because they are separated by the contingent remainder for life in B.

This second exception is quite limited. It does not prevent merger if either or both merging interests are transferred at some point in time after creation.

> Example 5.54b: Assume the same facts as above. Next, A transfers all of her interests to X. At that point, the

exception no longer protects B's destructible contingent remainder. X's interests merge, destroying B's contingent remainder, and X has a fee simple absolute. Of course, if a statute in the jurisdiction made contingent remainders indestructible, B would still have a contingent remainder and X would have what A had, a life estate for A's life and a vested remainder in fee simple.

(c) Survival as an Implied Condition Precedent

The common law usually did not require a person to survive until the time of distribution in order to take unless the transfer specifically required survival.

> Example 6.55: O transfers in trust "to A for life, then to B." B dies before A. According to the common law, B's vested remainder passes under B's will or by the laws of intestate succession.

The default is that survival is not required.

Keep in mind, however, that a transferor can require survival without using the word "survive". For instance, delaying payment could make the interest contingent on survival to the time of distribution.

> Example 6.56: O devises "$100,000 to T in trust, with $20,000 for A at the age of 25 years." In states that follow the second proposition in *Clobberie's Case*, A's interest is contingent on reaching 25; so, when A dies before that, the gift fails.

And some words, by definition, require survival in order to take. No one can qualify as an "heir of X" without surviving at least until the death of X. Another exception to the default rule, as you will see in a moment, occurs in the context of a class gift.

Who benefits when a court holds that a remainder is not subject to an implied condition of survivorship? Consider the following cases.

USRY v. FARR

Supreme Court of Georgia, 2001
553 S.E.2d 789

FLETCHER, C.J.

At issue in this appeal is when title to the remainder interest under the will of Watson Usry vested. On summary judgment, the trial court held that the remainder vested at the time of Usry's death and not at the death of the life tenant. Because Usry's will expressed the intention of providing for those who survive him and all five grandchildren survived him, we affirm.

Watson Usry died in 1967. The relevant clause of Usry's will provided successive life estates in his lands, first to his wife Lucille and then to their children, with the remainder to his grandchildren. Usry had three children, the last of whom died in 2000. There are five appellants: the four children of Usry's son Jack, and Jack's widow, Evelyn. Usry's fifth grandson, Hoyt, died in 1970 leaving three young children, all of whom were alive at the time of Usry's death. Hoyt's three children are the appellees. Appellants claim that the remainder vested upon the death of the last life tenant and not upon the death of Usry. Therefore, because they are the only grandchildren who survived the life tenants, they take all lands under the will. Appellees contend that the remainder vested upon Usry's death, and that Hoyt, who survived Usry, had a vested interest under the will, and therefore his children stand in his shoes and take under the will along with appellants.

1.   The construction of a will is a question of law for the court. The cardinal rule for construing wills is to ascertain and give effect to the testator's intent. Item Three of the will provided,

> I will, bequeath and devise all of the land, with improvements thereon, which I may own at my death to my Wife, LUCILLE, to be hers for and during her lifetime, and at her death same is to go to my children who may survive my wife, and to my grandchildren with restrictions as follows: Any of my children taking land under this Item shall have a life interest therein, share and share alike, with any grandchildren who take hereunder taking the part which their father or mother would have taken. Upon the death of my last surviving child title in fee simple to said lands shall vest in my grand-children, per stirpes and not per capita.

The first sentence of Item Three establishes a life estate first in Usry's wife Lucille and then in the children who survive Lucille. This sentence imposes a requirement that the children survive Lucille before taking under Item three. In contrast, no requirement that the grandchildren survive the life tenants is imposed. Therefore, at Usry's death, fee simple title vested in his five grandchildren, who were all alive at that time. The possessory interest vested when Usry's son Ned, the last life tenant, died in April 2000. At that time, the grandchildren were entitled to take possession, with the appellees taking the share that had vested in Hoyt.

The testator's intention that the only survivorship requirement apply to his life appears expressly in Item Eight of the will. In that provision, Usry declared that "my entire plan of disposition is the result of a conscientious effort to provide for the welfare of my loved ones who survive me, and to fairly divide and distribute the worldly goods for which I have worked so hard." Because we must construe the will as a whole, we must consider this clause in construing the remainder of the will. Usry's stated intention of providing for those who survive him is fatal to the claim of appellants who would defer vesting well beyond the death of Usry until the conclusion of the life estates.

The dissent's concern that this construction provides an anomalous result is not well-founded. The testator himself decided to leave successive life estates to his widow and children. Obviously, if his children were to enjoy a life estate that followed their mother's life estate, the children had to survive their mother. Because the testator decided that his children were to enjoy only a life estate, there is nothing unusual about his further providing for title to vest in his loved ones who survive him.

2.   Usry's express intention with regard to a survivorship requirement is consistent with the statutory rule in Georgia favoring vesting of title as of the time of the testator's death. Appellants contend that the last sentence of Item Three demonstrates an intention that the remainder vest, not at the testator's death, but at the conclusion of the life estates. However, this Court has repeatedly held that virtually identical language is not sufficient to divest the remainder share from one who survives the testator but predeceases the life tenant. In view of the strong preference in Georgia for early vesting, the language required to render a remainder contingent upon surviving the life tenant must be clear and unambiguous. The last sentence of Item Three fails to meet this standard when

considered along with Item Eight. To the extent that this sentence would permit a construction favoring a contingent remainder, it must give way to the construction favoring a vested remainder, where both constructions are possible.

We construe the final sentence of Item Three, and similar language in Item Five,[9] to refer to the time the grandchildren take possession in the land and become entitled to enjoy the title to the remainder, which had vested at Usry's death. This construction is consistent with our case law that recognizes that a vested remainder will have both a vesting of title and a vesting of possession.

3.   Appellants also rely on a deed of assent executed by Usry's widow as executrix in 1968. That deed refers to property devised in Usry's will as being left to "the living grandchildren of Watson Usry." The deed of assent, prepared after the testator's death, is irrelevant to determining the testator's intent.

Judgment affirmed.

CARLEY, J., dissenting.

[The dissent argued that the interest in the grandchildren was supposed to vest in interest at the death of the children, which would mean that it could not be vested before that, and therefore they had to survive until that point in time to be eligible to take.]

IN RE WILL OF UCHTORFF
Supreme Court of Iowa, 2005
693 N.W.2d 790

STREIT, J.

H.L. Mencken once said the capacity of human beings to bore one another seems vastly greater than that of any other animal. The subject-matter of this appeal—a medieval interest known as a remainder—proves Mencken's point, although we shall do our best to bring matters to resolution as painlessly and interestingly as possible. Much is at stake.

At issue is a trust fund. After the family patriarch who controlled the trust fund died, his only child, a son, followed him to

---

[9]   "If my daughter-in-law, EVELYN, has not married again by the time the title to my land vests in my grand-children, as per Item Three of this Will, then I desire that she take a child's part. . . ."

the grave. Years later the patriarch's wife passed away. The district court ruled the son was not entitled to the trust fund unless he survived his mother. The son's widow appeals. She claims her late husband's interest vested upon his father's death, and therefore she should receive the trust fund because the son left everything to her. We agree with the widow and reverse.

I.   Facts and Prior Proceedings

The facts are not disputed. Alfred Uchtorff died in 1979. Alfred's will is a hairy beast almost twenty pages in length. Fortunately, the parties only dispute "Item VI" of the will. In Item VI, Alfred exercised his power of appointment over "Trust A," a trust fund his father established before a majority of the members of this court were born. In relevant part, Item VI provided:

B.   I appoint [the trust fund] property to [a bank] and to my wife Pearl E. Uchtorff, in trust, nevertheless, and to hold as a trust fund for the following uses and purposes, to wit:

1.   During the lifetime of my wife Pearl E. Uchtorff . . . the trustees shall pay to her . . . the net income from the trust fund.

     . . . .

3.   The provisions of this subdivision 3 shall be effective in any of the following stated events: (i) the event of the death of my said wife before my death; (ii) the event of remarriage of my said wife after my death without renunciation by her; (iii) *the event of the death of my said wife after my death, without renunciation by her and without remarriage by her;* or (iv) the event of incompleteness or insufficiency or failure for any reason of the appointment hereinbefore made for the benefit of my said wife. . . .

In any of the stated events . . ., I appoint said [trust fund] . . ., in the manner in this subdivision 3 . . . provided.

(a) *In the event that my son, Richard E. Uchtorff shall survive me, I appoint the [trust fund] to the said Richard E. Uchtorff, as an indefeasibly vested interest in fee.*

(b) In the event that my son, Richard E. Uchtorff shall not survive me, I appoint the same to [a bank], and to Carolyn Uchtorff, . . ., in trust nevertheless and to hold as a trust fund for [a class composed of the representative issue of the marriage of Richard and Carolyn, subject to divestment under certain circumstances.]

(Emphasis added.)

When Alfred died, he was survived by his wife, Pearl Uchtorff, and their son and only child, Richard Uchtorff. Richard was married to Carolyn Uchtorff. Richard and Carolyn had three children, Sally Hanson, Taylor Armstrong-Lucas, and Julie Kurt ("the children"). Richard and Carolyn eventually divorced, and Richard later married Christa Uchtorff.

Richard died in 1988. Richard disinherited his three children in his will, writing:

I make no provisions in this will for my children for several reasons which I consider sufficient, and generally because of their longstanding and continuous disrespectful conduct to me.

Richard left everything to Christa instead.

Pearl enjoyed the income from the trust fund until her death in 2003. She never renunciated her beneficiary interest in the trust fund, nor did she ever remarry. Today the trust fund contains hundreds of thousands of dollars.

After Pearl's death, the bank, as surviving co-trustee of the trust fund, petitioned the district court for construction of Alfred's will. Two factions claimed the trust fund as their own. Christa argued Richard's remainder interest in the trust fund vested upon Alfred's death and should now pass, like the rest of Richard's assets, through Richard's will to her. The children rejoined, asserting Christa's claim must fail because Richard did not survive Pearl. The district court ruled Alfred's will was ambiguous and did not specifically state what should happen if Richard predeceased Pearl. The court held Iowa's new trust code therefore mandated the children receive the trust fund. Christa appealed.

II. Principles of Review

A declaratory judgment action to construe a will is tried in equity. Our review is de novo.

III. The Merits

A. Vested or Contingent Remainder

The first question presented in this appeal is whether Richard had a vested or a contingent remainder in the trust fund once he survived Alfred.[1] Contrary to the district court, we think the plain and unambiguous language of Alfred's will indicates Richard's remainder interest in the trust fund vested at Alfred's death.

1. General Principles

This appeal involves a remainder interest, long one of the law professor's favorite instruments of torture. Stated in its most general terms, a remainder

> is a future interest created in someone other than the transferor that, according to the terms of its creation, will become a present estate (if ever) immediately upon, and no sooner than, the expiration of all prior particular estates created simultaneously with it.

Alfred's will clearly gave Richard a remainder interest in the trust fund. Richard's interest was a future interest that could become a present estate immediately upon and no sooner than when Pearl's prior interest expired, i.e., when Pearl died, remarried, or renounced her life interest, but only if Richard survived Alfred.

A remainder is either vested or contingent.

> A vested remainder, whereby the estate passes by the conveyance, but the possession and enjoyment are postponed until the particular estate is determined, is where the estate is invariably fixed to remain to certain determinate persons. Contingent remainders are where the estate in remainder is limited to take effect either to a dubious or uncertain person or upon a dubious or uncertain event, so that the particular estate may be determined and the remainder never take effect.

A remainder may be vested even when enjoyment is postponed until the happening of some future condition; it is contingent only if the remainder interest is "dependent on some *dubious circumstance,*

---

[1] As an aside, we point out Iowa's anti-lapse statute is not involved in this appeal. Lapse only occurs when a beneficiary fails to survive the testator. Nor does the statute apply, in any event, to a will such as this one, which expressly makes survival of the testator a condition of taking under the will.

through which it may be defeated. . . ." Vested remainders are devisable and alienable.

To determine whether a remainder is vested or contingent, our well-settled canons of will interpretation apply. We need not repeat all of those familiar maxims here. It will suffice to simply remark that

> whether a testamentary remainder is vested or contingent must be determined by the intent of the testator as expressed by the language of the will, if it is plain and unambiguous, and nothing else, considering the will as a whole, and giving effect to every provision thereof if it is reasonably possible.

Whether a remainder is contingent or vested must also be constantly reassessed as time passes, events happen, and contingencies are fulfilled.

2.   The Terms of the Will: Richard's Remainder Vested Upon Alfred's Death

To decide the nature of Richard's remainder, the parties direct our attention to Item VI, paragraph 3(a) of the will. That provision states:

> (a) In the event that my son, Richard E. Uchtorff shall survive me, I appoint the [trust fund] to the said Richard E. Uchtorff, as an indefeasibly vested interest in fee.

This provision of the will initially rendered Richard's remainder interest contingent, because appointment of the trust fund to Richard was expressly conditioned upon one uncertain event, i.e., that Richard survive Alfred. Once Richard survived Alfred, this condition, the only uncertain event upon which appointment of the trust fund to Richard was predicated, was fulfilled. Richard's interest in the trust fund vested when Alfred died and needed only to wait until Pearl's interest ended to become an estate in possession.

Survival to Time of Possession Not Required

It could be argued the express terms of the will state Richard's remainder remained contingent until Pearl's death. The will indicates appointment of the trust fund to Richard in the manner set forth in paragraph 3(a) would occur in "in the event" Pearl renounced the trust fund, remarried, or died. Although it is true this part of Alfred's will places a *condition* upon Richard's *possession* of the trust fund, this *condition* does not make Richard's *interest* a *contingent remainder*. Expiration of Pearl's estate was inevitable. Although Pearl's interest might end earlier through renunciation or remarriage, it was certain to cease at the very latest at her death.

Only when a condition serves to make it dubious or uncertain that the remainder interest will ever pass does the condition make the remainder contingent. It does not matter that Richard did not survive Pearl, or even that it could not have been known at any time prior to Richard's death whether Richard would survive Pearl and gain possession of the trust fund. "It is not the certainty of possession or enjoyment which distinguishes the vested remainder, but the certainty of the right to future enjoyment if the remainderman lives until the life tenancy terminates." *Lingo v. Smith*, 174 Iowa 461, 468 (1916); *accord Dickerson*, 200 Iowa at 118; *cf. Houts*, 201 N.W.2d at 470–71 (noting an estate is not rendered contingent because the portion, quantity, or amount of property beneficiary will receive remains uncertain until a future date). This is because

> [a] vested remainder confers a present fixed right to the future enjoyment. . . . . [T]he fact that the devisee is not to have the enjoyment of possession until the termination of the intermediate estate does not prevent the vesting of the remainder immediately upon the death of the testator. . . . *No uncertainty of enjoyment will render the remainder contingent.*

Moore, 246 Iowa at 745–46 (emphasis added, citations omitted); *see Callison v. Morris*, 123 Iowa 297, 300–01 (1904) (expressing same principle and holding son need not survive mother for remainder to vest); *see also* 28 Am. Jur. 2d Estates § 265, at 281 (2000). Subdivision three of the will was certain to take effect *sometime*; if Richard had lived long enough, he would have had the right to enjoy the trust fund when Pearl died. Put another way, Richard's remainder vested *in interest* upon Alfred's death, even if it was not secured in enjoyment or possession. "Death of the life tenant merely fixed the time for enjoyment." *Clarken v. Brown*, 258 Iowa 18, 24 (1965). In this case Pearl's death simply came too late for Richard.

To rule otherwise would have absurd results. "[T]here could be no such thing as a vested remainder" because the very definition of a remainder assumes the existence of a prior estate. Bergin & Haskell at 69. As we stated in *Katz*,

> Of course [a remainderman] may predecease the termination of the trust. But this does not make the remainder . . . contingent for it is an uncertainty which may attach to all remainders, vested or contingent. Certainty of possession and enjoyment by the remainderman is not essential to a vested remainder.

242 Iowa at 652–53 (citations omitted); see also *Dickerson*, 200 Iowa at 118 ("He may die before coming into the actual possession of the remainder, but that is a contingency attaching to all remainders.").

At the time of Alfred's death it was clear that whatever happened in the future, it was certain Pearl's interest would terminate, and Richard was next in line. Because the trust fund was certain to pass at some time, "[t]he remainder then vested and only the right of possession and enjoyment await[ed] termination of the trust." *Katz*, 242 Iowa at 654. The text of the will states as much: Richard, upon surviving his father, took the trust fund "as an indefeasibly vested interest in fee." This phrase plainly and specifically indicates Richard's interest in the trust fund vested at the moment of his father's death and was not subject to defeasance upon the happening of any subsequent event. Richard was free to devise his vested remainder as he saw fit.[2]

Other Evidence of a Vested Remainder

The structure of the devise in Article VI bears the telltale signs of a vested remainder. First, the remainder was invariably fixed to a determinate person, Richard, whose only impediment to taking possession and enjoyment of the trust corpus was based upon a certain event, at the very latest his mother's death. Second, nothing in Article VI states that Richard's interest was contingent upon surviving his mother. *Dickerson* presents similar facts in this respect. We stated:

> The devise is not to the son in case he survives his mother, or is living at her remarriage, or at the termination of the trust. The devise of the remainder after the termination of the particular estate is to the son, to be his "sole and absolute property," subject to the trust. No disposition is made of the estate in case of his death before the termination of the trust.

---

[2]   Likewise Richard was free to convey his vested remainder during his life or borrow against it, as many do. To hold otherwise would wreak havoc upon the settled expectations of many parties to such transactions.

Third, the will does not explicitly provide any alternate beneficiaries who should take on the condition that Richard failed to survive his mother. The failure to do so is evidence of a vested remainder. Fourth, an alternative arrangement was provided in the will only for the circumstance in which Richard did not survive his father, which, as we have shown previously, was the only uncertain event upon which Richard's interest was predicated. Fifth, Article VI is different than another part of the will. Article IV of Alfred's will stated Richard was entitled to other assets "[i]n the event [he] shall outlive the survivor of myself *and my said wife*." (Emphasis added.) Article VI, on the other hand, simply says "[i]n the event that my son, Richard E. Uchtorff shall survive *me*." (Emphasis added.) Unlike Article VI, Article IV also provided for the disposition of the Article IV property in equal shares to Richard's children should Richard predecease Pearl. Divining testator intent is never an easy task, but looking at the whole of the will in this case it is clear Alfred knew how to make Richard's interest contingent upon Richard surviving Pearl but did not do so with respect to the trust fund.

No Latent Ambiguity

The children nonetheless contend Alfred's will contains a latent ambiguity because it does not in so many words indicate who should take under the trust if Richard did not survive his mother. There is no latent ambiguity. Alfred plainly stated what sort of interest Richard had and made clear it was a vested interest once Richard survived Alfred. The children themselves admit there is a "certain lock-tight quality" about the phrase "indefeasibly vested interest in fee"; we agree and furthermore hold there is no room for any other interpretation. To rule otherwise would require us to rewrite the will, judicially superinscribing a new condition of survival. We will not do so.

In re Trust of Cross

The Iowa Court of Appeals arrived at the same conclusion as we do on similar facts. In *In re Trust of Cross*, the testator bequeathed her property in trust to a trustee, directing that necessary amounts from the income and corpus of the trust be used to care for her daughter. The testator also directed that a portion of the remaining trust assets be given to the testator's brother "to be his absolutely and in his own right" upon her daughter's death. The brother predeceased the daughter. The court of appeals, principally relying upon the above quoted phrase, held the plain language of the will indicated the brother's rights vested at the time of the testator's death, and therefore it did not matter that he predeceased the daughter. For similar reasons, the court also held the will was not latently ambiguous. The court ruled the terms of the will were clear and plain, and by its terms the will "did not place a survivorship contingency upon [the brother's] interest." The same reasoning applies with equal, if not greater force in this case, given the utterly unambiguous phrase "indefeasibly vested interest in fee."

B.   The Iowa Trust Code

1.   Iowa Code § 633.4701

The children also maintain a provision of the new Iowa Trust Code supersedes our reasoning and that of the court of appeals in *Cross*. That provision provides:

> *Unless otherwise specifically stated by the terms of the trust,* the interest of each beneficiary is contingent on the beneficiary surviving until the date on which the beneficiary becomes entitled to possession or enjoyment of the beneficiary's interest in the trust.

Iowa Code § 633.4701(1) (emphasis added). The children contend Alfred's will is insufficiently specific concerning the nature of Richard's interest in the trust fund. Christa rejoins that the trust code does not apply in this case, and, to the extent it purports to apply retroactively to this case and divest Roger's estate of a vested property right, it is unconstitutional. Although the legislature enacted the trust code in 1999, see 1999 Iowa Acts ch. 125, and it did not become effective until 2000, see 1999 Iowa Acts ch. 125, § 109, it purports to apply to all trusts past, present, and future, as well as all proceedings concerning trusts commenced on or after July 1, 2000.

2.   Alfred's Will Specifically States Richard's Interest Vested

Alfred's will states with sufficient specificity that Richard's interest vested upon his mother's death. By its terms it states Richard took "an indefeasibly vested interest in fee." It is true Alfred's will does not mimic the statute and state "the interest of each beneficiary is *not* contingent on the beneficiary surviving until the date on which the beneficiary becomes entitled to possession or enjoyment of the beneficiary's interest in the trust." This is not surprising, however, since Alfred's will was written decades before the new trust code was a glimmer in the legislature's eye. We do not think the statute requires magic words. "We must think things not words, or at least we must constantly translate our words into the facts for which they stand, if we are to keep to the real and the true." Oliver Wendell Holmes, Jr., *Law in Science and Science in Law,* 12 Harv. L. Rev. 443, 460 (1899). This is not so much a matter of interpretation than it is of translation. Translating the old-fashioned phrase "indefeasibly vested interest in fee" into post-trust code language, we find a specific statement that Richard need not survive Pearl. This reading of the statute is consistent with the overall framework of the trust code. "The provisions of a trust shall always control and take precedence over any section of this trust code to the contrary." The provisions of Alfred's will that granted Richard a vested interest therefore trump any provisions in the trust code that would, by default, mandate a different result. Notwithstanding the enactment of the new trust code, the intent of the testator still reigns supreme in this instance.

3.   A Little History Helps

Some history will also illuminate matters. As indicated, Alfred referred to Richard's interest as an "indefeasibly vested interest in fee." Given the history of the law in the area, Alfred's use of this phrase is telling. The question has often arisen in the courts as to whether, *in the absence of such a phrase,* one should *imply* a condition of survival of the possessor of the precedent estate. Historically, courts did not do so; for various reasons, remainder interests were usually construed as vested rather than contingent whenever possible. In the context of the case at bar, there was

> a pervasive constructional preference in the property law for vested future interests over contingent future interests and for early vesting over vesting at a later time; this means, in this context, *that there is a constructional preference for there being no condition of survivorship of the life tenant.*

Bergin & Haskell at 127 (emphasis added). Thus in 1916 in *Lingo* we stated:

> *[A]ll estates will be regarded as vested unless a condition precedent thereto is so clearly expressed that it cannot be regarded as vested without doing violence to the language of the will.* To effectuate this rule, words of seeming condition are, if possible, to be construed as postponing the time of enjoyment. . . .

> *The law presumes that words of postponement relate to the enjoyment of the remainder rather than the vesting thereof, and the intent to postpone the vesting of the estate must be clear and manifest.*

Lingo, 174 Iowa at 467, 468 (emphasis added). For example, we held the mere grant of a life estate to one does not render a beneficiary's interest contingent on the life tenant's survival. Over time, however, this preference waned so that it was unsettled by the time Alfred wrote his will in 1972. Viewed in this historical context, Alfred's use of the phrase "indefeasibly vested interest in fee" is evidence Alfred intended to forestall any implied inference that Richard's interest was contingent upon Richard surviving his mother. Although the new Iowa Trust Code completely reverses the common law preference for vested interests and deems all interests contingent upon survival to the time of possession unless specifically stated otherwise, it is also clear the provisions of the trust must govern. In this case we are constrained to follow the intent of the testator, determined at the time the will is made and based upon the facts then existing, that specifically granted a vested remainder to Richard, which is a specific statement he need not survive Pearl.

4. Constitutional Claim

Because we find the Iowa Trust Code does not apply retroactively to divest Roger's estate of a vested property right, we need not address Christa's constitutional claim in this case.

IV. Disposition

Upon the death of his father, Richard had a vested remainder in the trust fund. He was therefore free to devise it to his wife Christa instead of his children. The district court must be reversed.

REVERSED.

Because the court found strong enough evidence of Alfred's intent, the Iowa statute passed after Alfred's death did not change the effect of Alfred's will. Suppose the evidence on Alfred's intent had been sufficient to satisfy a preponderance standard, but no more. What goals would have been served if the court had allowed the statute to change the effect of Alfred's will?

UPC § 2–707

SECTION 2–707. SURVIVORSHIP WITH RESPECT TO FUTURE INTERESTS UNDER TERMS OF TRUST; SUBSTITUTE TAKERS.

(a) [Definitions.] In this section:

(1) "Alternative future interest" means an expressly created future interest that can take effect in possession or enjoyment instead of another future interest on the happening of one or more events, including survival of an event or failure to survive an event, whether an event is expressed in condition-precedent, condition-subsequent, or any other form. A residuary clause in a will does not create an alternative future interest with respect to a future interest created in a nonresiduary devise in the will, whether or not the will specifically provides that lapsed or failed devises are to pass under the residuary clause.

(2) "Beneficiary" means the beneficiary of a future interest and includes a class member if the future interest is in the form of a class gift.

(3) "Class member" includes an individual who fails to survive the distribution date but who would have taken under a future interest in the form of a class gift had the individual survived the distribution date.

(4) "Descendants", in the phrase "surviving descendants" of a deceased beneficiary or class member in subsection (b)(1) and (2), mean the descendants of a deceased beneficiary or class member who would take under a class gift created in the trust.

(5) "Distribution date," with respect to a future interest, means the time when the future interest is to take effect in possession or enjoyment. The distribution date need not occur at the beginning or end of a calendar day, but can occur at a time during the course of a day.

(6) "Future interest" includes an alternative future interest and a future interest in the form of a class gift.

(7) "Future interest under the terms of a trust" means a future interest that was created by a transfer creating a trust or to an existing trust or by an exercise of a power of appointment to an existing trust, directing the continuance of an existing trust, designating a beneficiary of an existing trust, or creating a trust.

(8) Surviving", in the phrase "surviving beneficiaries" or "surviving descendants", means beneficiaries or descendants who neither predeceased the distribution date nor are deemed to have predeceased the distribution date under Section 2–702.

(b) [Survivorship Required; Substitute Gift.] A future interest under the terms of a trust is contingent on the beneficiary's surviving the distribution date. If a beneficiary of a future interest under the terms of a trust fails to survive the distribution date, the following apply:

(1) Except as provided in paragraph (4), if the future interest is not in the form of a class gift and the deceased beneficiary leaves surviving descendants, a substitute gift is created in the beneficiary's surviving descendants. They take by representation the property to which the beneficiary would have been entitled had the beneficiary survived the distribution date.

(2) Except as provided in paragraph (4), if the future interest is in the form of a class gift, other than a future interest to "issue," "descendants," "heirs of the body," "heirs," "next of kin," "relatives," or "family," or a class described by language of similar import, a substitute gift is created in the surviving descendants of any deceased beneficiary. The property to which the beneficiaries would have been entitled had all of them survived the distribution date passes to the surviving beneficiaries and the surviving descendants of the deceased beneficiaries. Each surviving beneficiary takes the share to which the surviving beneficiary would have been entitled had the deceased beneficiaries survived the distribution date. Each deceased beneficiary's surviving descendants who are substituted for the deceased beneficiary take by representation the share to which the deceased beneficiary would have been entitled had the deceased beneficiary survived the distribution date. For the purposes of this paragraph, "deceased beneficiary" means a class member who failed to survive the distribution date and left one or more surviving descendants.

(3) For the purposes of Section 2–701, words of survivorship attached to a future interest are not, in the absence of additional evidence, a sufficient indication of an intent contrary to the application of this section. Words of survivorship include words of survivorship that relate to the distribution date or to an earlier or an unspecified time, whether those words of

survivorship are expressed in condition-precedent, condition-subsequent, or any other form.

(4) If the governing instrument creates an alternative future interest with respect to a future interest for which a substitute gift is created by paragraph (1) or (2), the substitute gift is superseded by the alternative future interest if:

(A) the alternative future interest is in the form of a class gift and one or more members of the class is entitled to take in possession or enjoyment; or

(B) the alternative future interest is not in the form of a class gift and the expressly designated beneficiary of the alternative future interest is entitled to take in possession or enjoyment.

(c) [More Than One Substitute Gift; Which One Takes.] If, under subsection (b), substitute gifts are created and not superseded with respect to more than one future interest and the future interests are alternative future interests, one to the other, the determination of which of the substitute gifts takes effect is resolved as follows:

(1) Except as provided in paragraph (2), the property passes under the primary substitute gift.

(2) If there is a younger-generation future interest, the property passes under the younger-generation substitute gift and not under the primary substitute gift.

(3) In this subsection:

(A) "Primary future interest" means the future interest that would have taken effect had all the deceased beneficiaries of the alternative future interests who left surviving descendants survived the distribution date.

(B) "Primary substitute gift" means the substitute gift created with respect to the primary future interest.

(C) "Younger-generation future interest" means a future interest that (i) is to a descendant of a beneficiary of the primary future interest, (ii) is an alternative future interest with respect to the primary future interest, (iii) is a future interest for which a substitute gift is created, and (iv) would have taken effect had all the deceased beneficiaries who left surviving descendants survived the distribution date except the deceased beneficiary or beneficiaries of the primary future interest.

(D) "Younger-generation substitute gift" means the substitute gift created with respect to the younger-generation future interest.

(d) [If No Other Takers, Property Passes Under Residuary Clause or to Transferor's Heirs.] Except as provided in subsection (e), if, after the application of subsections (b) and (c), there is no surviving taker, the property passes in the following order:

(1) if the trust was created in a nonresiduary devise in the transferor's will or in a codicil to the transferor's will, the property passes under the residuary clause in the transferor's will; for purposes of this section, the residuary clause is treated as creating a future interest under the terms of a trust.

(2) if no taker is produced by the application of paragraph (1), the property passes to the transferor's heirs under Section 2–711.

(e) [If No Other Takers and If Future Interest Created by Exercise of Power of Appointment.] If, after the application of subsections (b) and (c), there is no surviving taker and if the future interest was created by the exercise of a power of appointment:

(1) the property passes under the donor's gift-in-default clause, if any, which clause is treated as creating a future interest under the terms of a trust; and

(2) if no taker is produced by the application of paragraph (1), the property passes as provided in subsection (d). For purposes of subsection (d), "transferor" means the donor if the power was a nongeneral power and means the donee if the power was a general power.

UPC § 2–707 departs radically from the common-law rule. Under UPC § 2–707, as under the Iowa statute in *Uchtorff*, the default construction is that a future interest in trust is contingent on survival to the date of distribution. If a beneficiary fails to survive until the date of distribution, a substitute gift is sometimes made.

Example 6.57: O and O's spouse have two children, A and B. A has three children, C, D, and E. O settles a trust with "income to myself for life, then to my spouse for life, remainder in corpus to my children." O's spouse dies. A dies, devising all A's property to A's spouse, S. O dies. Under the common law, B takes half, and A's half passes to S under A's will. A's interest is taxable under the estate tax. Under UPC § 2–707, B takes half, A's gift fails, and substitute gifts are made to C, D, and E, which are taxable under the generation-skipping transfer tax.

When a substitute gift is not made, the assets might pass under the residuary clause of the will that created the trust.

Example 6.58: O executes a will which says, "I bequeath my stock in trust for my spouse during her life and for the support of my children after that. I give the residue of my estate to the City for the creation of a park." At the time of execution, O has one child, A, O's stock is worth $2,000,000, and the residue is worth $300,000. A marries S. O and S have a warm relationship. O dies. A dies, leaving a will leaving everything to S. O's spouse dies. Under the common law, S takes the remainder in trust. Under UPC § 2–707, the City takes the remainder along with the $300,000.

In Example 6.58, O might have preferred that the $2,000,000 support S instead of passing to the City. The example shows what can go wrong when the residue is devised to a relatively minor beneficiary. Whether UPC § 2–707 is the law or not, well-drafted wills reach whatever legally permissible results are desired by the testator under the events that transpire. Therefore, whether UPC § 2–707 improves the law depends on its effects when instruments are not drafted well. In Example 6.58, if O preferred S to the City, UPC § 2–707 would not reach the intended result.

Question 6.59: O has three children, A, B, and C. O devises land in trust, "for the benefit of my spouse for life, then the remainder in halves for the benefit of A and B." A dies without descendants, leaving a will devising everything to B. O's spouse dies. Under the common law, A's remainder goes to B, who ends up with all of the trust. Under UPC § 2–707, A fails to satisfy the condition of survival until the date of distribution, so A's remainder passes to O's heirs, B and C. UPC § 2–701 prevents the application of § 2–707 if there is a finding of contrary intention. Will § 2–707 increase the frequency of reaching results intended by transferors? Will § 2–707 increase litigation?

> Problem 6.60: O is married with one child, C. O devises "in trust for the benefit of my spouse for life, then for the benefit of C." C marries S and they have three children, J, K, and L. Before the children have reached adulthood, C dies, devising all of C's estate in trust "to S, for the support of my children in the compete discretion of S." O's spouse dies. Who takes under the common law? Who is presumed to take under UPC § 2–707? Would O have wanted C's will to control?

Often settlors and testators want to give trust beneficiaries the power to direct assets. As you can see from the examples above, UPC § 2–707 prevents beneficiaries who die too soon from directing their interests in the trust. Does UPC § 2–707 reach just results more often than the common-law rule? One indication of whether the UPC accomplishes the goals of testators is whether attentive drafters will let it apply in instruments they draft. Professor David Becker has argued that skilled practitioners will usually avoid the operation of UPC § 2–707. David M. Becker, Uniform Probate Code Section 2–707 and the Experienced Estate Planner: Unexpected Disasters and How to Avoid Them, 47 UCLA L. Rev. 339 (1999). *See also* Laura E. Cunningham, The Hazards of Tinkering with the Common Law of Future Interests: The California Experience, 48 Hastings L. J. 667 (1997). *But see*, Lawrence W. Waggoner, The Uniform Probate Code Extends Antilapse-Type Protection to Poorly Drafted Trusts, 94 Mich. L. Rev. 2309 (1996).

As a matter of policy, efficiency also matters. On that, the effect of UPC § 2–707 is unclear. There is no doubt that it prevents litigation on the issue of whether a remainder in trust is subject to a requirement of survival to the time of distribution, although it does not prevent litigation on the issue of whether the remainderperson must survive longer than that. But there are other situations in which § 2–707 will generate litigation.

> Problem 6.61: O devises "to X in trust, and then to Y if Y survives X." Y dies intestate, leaving child J as heir. Under the common law, Y's contingent remainder would fail because of the survival requirement. Under UPC § 2–707, a substitute gift might be made to J because § 2–707(b)(3) says that the words of survivorship have no effect unless there is additional evidence of intent contrary to § 2–707. The UPC thus calls for litigation in this situation.

Jesse Dukeminier predicted that UPC § 2–707 will likely increase litigation. Jesse Dukeminier, The Uniform Probate Code Upends the Law of Remainders, 94 Mich. L. Rev. 148, 151 (1995). If he is correct, should society be willing to pay those increased costs of litigation to solve problems the settlor was unwilling to pay to avoid?

Over time, caselaw can clarify the meaning of statutes, reducing litigation. However, UPC § 2–701 and UPC § 2–707 focus on intent and allow extrinsic evidence. It remains to be seen how often that will open the doors for parties to litigate, as they did in *Uchtorff*.

So far, about one-third of the states have adopted UPC § 2–707 or something like it. Whether a jurisdiction has adopted UPC § 2–707 or not, a drafter should make it clear whether beneficiaries must survive to take and, if so, to what point in time they must survive.

(d) Class Gifts

A class gift is a gift to a group of persons described by a single phrase, such as "my grandchildren". Of course, it is not always clear whether a class gift has been created and that has led to litigation. If a will alternates between group language and a list of the members of the group, a court can find that the will did not make a class gift. On the other hand, if a transferor was "group minded" when she made a transfer, a court can find a class gift even though the transfer named individuals and not the group. In this book, however, examples will assume that a gift to a group is a class gift and that a gift to a list of individuals is not a class gift.

Be careful to distinguish between the class and conditions precedent that must be satisfied by members of the class. A gift "to the children of B who attain the age of 21" is a class gift with a condition precedent attached to it. The class is the children of B and the condition precedent is the attainment of the age of 21. The class remains physiologically open while B is alive. It is possible that some members of the class will not qualify to take. Similarly, do not confuse a class being open with a vested remainder being subject to open. A class gift may be vested subject to open even though the class has closed.

> Problem 6.62: O transfers "to A for life, then to the children of B who reach 21 by A's death." B has two children, C and D. C is 22 and D is 19. What is the state of title? B dies. What is the state of title?

Many questions involving class gifts are resolved by the rules of construction in UPC § 2–705, excerpted above, which under UPC § 2–701 are controlling "[i]n the absence of a finding of contrary intention". Below are additional issues that arise in the context of class gifts.

(i) "Heirs"

The use of the word "heirs" can cause problems. Some of them arise because clients, and some lawyers too, do not know the meaning of the term. Under traditional and narrower usage, heirs were people who inherited realty under the laws of intestate succession. Modern usage often expands the term to include those who take personalty in intestate succession, and lay usage today expands it even further to include those who take under a will. Those varied definitions can lead to disputes about the meaning of wills and trusts. The use of the word "heirs" in an instrument can also generate unintended results because the shares of heirs change when statutes of descent and distribution are changed after the execution of the instrument. For example, "heirs" today include a surviving spouse of the designated individual.

Another problem with the word "heirs" is that it sometimes raises issues regarding the date to which the heir must survive. By definition, the heirs of a designated individual are determined as of the time that such individual dies. By definition, then, a person must survive the designated individual to be an heir. Until A dies, A has no heirs, only "heirs apparent". However, the existence of a standard definition has not prevented parties from arguing that heirs are to be determined as of a date later than the death of the designated decedent. That argument was presented in *Estate of Woodworth*, 22 Cal. Rptr. 2d 676 (Cal. Ct. App. 1993). The *Woodworth* court rejected it and applied the orthodox construction, holding that the heirs were determined at the death of the designated individual rather than later.

> Problem 6.63: O devises in trust, "the income to A, then the corpus to the heirs of B." At the time of O's death, B is married to S and B has four children, C and D by previous spouse P, and E and F by S. F dies. E dies, survived by E's child G. B dies. C dies, survived by C's child, H. S remarries. A dies. Who takes the corpus under the orthodox construction of "heirs"?

Some drafters define heirs using the intestacy statute but change the time for determining the heirs to the date of distribution instead of the date of death of the designated individual. UPC § 2–711 adopts this approach for the default definition of "heirs", "next of kin", "relatives", "family", and so forth. As a result, a person qualifies if and only if the person would qualify as a member of the class if the designated individual died at the time of distribution of the gift. If a spouse that was an heir at the death of the decedent is remarried at the time of distribution, the spouse does not qualify as an heir.

> Problem 6.64: What would be the result in Problem 6.63 under UPC § 2–711?

UPC § 2–711 also specifies that the law of the designated individual's domicile is used to determine heirs, not the jurisdiction of the donor. The law of intestate succession of the domicile of the designated individual determines not only the heirs but also the shares they take.

> Problem 6.65: O, a domiciliary of a jurisdiction following the 2019 UPC, devises $2,100,000 in trust "income to A, and one half of the corpus to the heirs of B and one-half of the corpus to the heirs of C." B is domiciled in the same jurisdiction as O. C is domiciled in a jurisdiction following the 1969 UPC. B and C die, each leaving a surviving spouse and child by that spouse (and the surviving spouses have no other children). A dies. C's surviving spouse would take $550,000. Would B's surviving spouse take the same amount?

(A) The Rule in Shelley's Case

Not only is the word "heirs" often ambiguous, it triggers special rules which can lead a court to deviate from the intent of the decedent. The Rule in *Shelley's Case*, 1 Co. Rep. 93b (1531), oddly enough, dates back at least another two centuries to *Abel's Case*, Y.B. 18 Edw. 2, 577 (1324). It says: if one instrument creates a life estate in land in A and a remainder in the heirs of A (or the heirs of A's body), and the life estate and remainder are either both legal or both equitable, then the remainder is in A rather than A's heirs. This is a rule of law, not a rule of construction, so it cannot be avoided by proof of contrary intent. The original purpose of the Rule in *Shelley's Case* was probably to protect the overlords' feudal incidents (the estate taxes of the day) against avoidance schemes.

Example 6.66: O devises "Blackacre to A for life, and then to A's heirs." Without the Rule in *Shelley's Case*, when A dies, A's heirs take nothing from A and therefore owe no feudal incidents (relief, wardship, marriage, homage, aids) to the overlord. The Rule in *Shelley's Case* transmogrifies the contingent remainder in A's heir into a vested remainder in A. The merger doctrine then applies, merging A's life estate into that remainder in fee, resulting in complete ownership by A. Unless A transfers A's interest, A's heir still takes when A dies, but the heir must pay relief to the overlord upon A's death.

The original rationale for the rule was long ago swept into the dustbin of history, but the rule continues to serve a useful purpose today. To see it, simply add the following fact to the example above. X places a higher value on Blackacre than anyone else in the world, but only if he can purchase a fee simple absolute. Without the Rule in *Shelley's Case*, X has a difficult time purchasing Blackacre because the heirs of A are uncertain. With the rule, X can buy a fee simple from A. Whether those benefits are adequate to justify the rule is open to debate. England and most states have eliminated the Rule in *Shelley's Case*. Because the rule is easy to circumnavigate, it has been criticized as being a trap for clients with bad lawyers. Don't let those be your clients.

(B) The Doctrine of Worthier Title

The Doctrine of Worthier Title is another rule that might have derived from attempts to prevent the avoidance of feudal incidents. If O transferred a future interest to the "heirs of O", the heirs got nothing and O kept a reversion. If O died intestate, the reversion passed to O's heirs, but the heirs were subject to feudal incidents. This rule of law has been abolished in some jurisdictions, including those following the UPC, and has been changed into a rule of construction in others, potentially generating litigation. In some states, the doctrine might apply to personalty as well as realty.

(ii) "Children"

"Children" is a simple word and might be the right word to describe a decedent's intent, but it deserves careful usage in drafting. We often use the word "children" to refer to minors, but a court will usually read the word to include the first generation of offspring regardless of age. A common mistake in drafting is to forget about the possibility that a parent's child might die before the parent, leaving grandchildren as the survivors of the parent. Because the word "children" does not include grandchildren, those grandchildren are excluded even though the testator or settlor might have wished them to take.

> Problem 6.67: O devises "to A for life, then to the children of A." At the time, A has two children, B and C. B dies, leaving two children, D and E, and a will which devises all B's property to S. A dies. Do D and E take?

When drafting, think carefully about whether the word "descendants" or "issue" will better describe the intent of your client.

(iii) "Issue" or "Descendants"

A gift to "issue of X" or "descendants of X" would literally be read to include all issue of X, but that is not the result. The descendants of X who take are usually the living issue of nearest degree, the same descendants as would take under statutes of intestate succession. The determination of who qualifies is often made as of the time of distribution, limiting the takers to persons who are alive at that time.

(iv) When the Class Shrinks

The potential problem of unintentionally omitting some lines of descent arises in various contexts, some having to do with gifts of principal and others having to do with gifts of income.

TRUST AGREEMENT OF WESTERVELT v. FIRST INTERSTATE BANK OF NORTHERN INDIANA

Fourth District Court of Appeals, Indiana, 1990
551 N.E.2d 1180

MILLER, J.

* * *

FACTS

In 1926, Edmund C. Westervelt created an inter vivos trust consisting of certain securities[1] which contained the following relevant provisions:

---

[1] The estimated market value of the trust is $5,658,136.28.

The [Trustee] shall collect and receive all income paid by the present securities taken from and after this date and from securities taken instead of the securities this day turned over to said [Trustee]. Out of the proceeds of such income, said Trustee contracts and agrees to pay unto Nellie B. Vaughn, daughter of said [Settlor], the net income derived, therefrom quarterly, for and during the period of the life of said Nellie B. Vaughn. Upon the death of said Nellie B. Vaughn, if she leaves, surviving her, a child or children, then said net income is to be paid unto said child or children, during their lives, share and share alike. Upon the death of said child or children of said Nellie B. Vaughn then the principal of said fund held by second party shall be paid to the issue of said child or children, share and share alike.

In the event of the death of said Nellie B. Vaughn, leaving no child or children, or no children, the issue of her said children, then the principal of said fund shall be paid to the Trustees of Oberlin College, at Oberlin, Ohio, in trust to be invested by said trustees and the income therefrom to be used by said trustees in the aid of boys and girls taking a course, preferably of Vocational Training at Said College.

In the event of the death of the child or children of said Nellie B. Vaughn leaving no issue, then said principal of said fund shall be paid to the trustees of Oberlin College, Oberlin, Ohio, to be invested and the income used as stated in the paragraph above.

At her death, daughter Nellie B. Vaughn [Nellie] had two surviving daughters, Florence W. Vaughn Carroll [Florence] and Marian Vaughn Williams Swortzel [Marian]. After Nellie's death the trustee paid the income to Florence and Marian. Florence died on May 20, 1988 leaving no surviving children or grandchildren. Marian is living and has three children and three grandchildren. The trustee petitioned the probate court for instructions on the disposition of Florence's interest in the trust. The probate court instructed the trustee "to retain all of the corpus in trust for the benefit of the life income interest of Marian Vaughn Williams, a/k/a Marian Williams Swortzel, and to pay to her all of the net income of the Trust after May 20, 1988, for the rest of her life."

DECISION

* * *

With this caution in mind, we note that the primary consideration in construing trusts is to determine the intent of the settlor. As this court explained in *Hauck v. Second National Bank of Richmond* (1972), 153 Ind.App. 245, 259–60.

> "The primary rule in construing trust instruments is that the court must ascertain the intention of the settlor and carry out this intention unless it is in violation of some positive rule of law or against public policy."
>
> * * * * * *
>
> "The plain and unambiguous purpose and intention of the settlor must be determined only from the terms of the instrument itself without taking individual clauses out of context and considering same without reference to the whole instrument. . . ." (citations omitted)

quoted in *Matter of Walz* (1981), Ind.App., 423 N.E.2d 729, 733.

Oberlin claims that when Florence died without surviving issue, it was entitled to Florence's interest in the trust. Oberlin bases its argument on the following trust provisions:

> Upon the death of said child or children of said Nellie B. Vaughn then the principal of said fund held by [Trustee] shall be paid to the issue of said child or children, share and share alike.
>
> * * * * * *
>
> In the event of the death of the child or children of said Nellie B. Vaughn leaving no issue, then said principal of said fund shall be paid to the trustees of Oberlin College, Oberlin, Ohio, to be invested and the income used as stated in the paragraph above.

* * *

* * *

Reading the instrument as a whole, the intent of the settlor is clear. The income from the trust was to be paid to Nellie during her life, then to her surviving children during their lives, and then the principal was to be divided among the issue of Nellie's surviving children, whether such issue were the issue of one, or more than one of Nellie's children.[5] Oberlin is entitled to the principal only if *no* child of Nellie has surviving issue.

We reach this conclusion from a careful reading of the trust provisions. The gift to Oberlin in the event Nellie should die without issue reads as follows:

> In the event of the death of said Nellie B. Vaughn, leaving no child or children, *or no children, the issue of her said children,* then the principal of said fund shall be paid to the trustees of Oberlin College. . . .[6]

(Our emphasis). This language indicates that the settlor intended Oberlin to receive the principal only if neither Nellie nor her children had surviving issue at the time of her death. In addition the use of the term "the issue of her said children" indicates that the settlor considered Nellie's children and their issue to be two distinct classes—his grandchildren and the issue of his grandchildren. As this court stated in *Laisure, supra,* 56 Ind.App. at 310–11:

> "A gift to a class is a gift of an aggregate sum to a body of persons uncertain in number at the time of the gift, to be ascertained at a future time, and who are all to take in equal or in some other definite proportions, the share of each being dependent for its amount upon the ultimate number of persons".

Further indication of a class gift may be found when the recipients are designated by their relationship to the settlor, rather than individually named.

The trust also provides:

> Upon the death of said child or children of said Nellie B. Vaughn then the principal . . . shall be paid to the issue of said child or children, *share and share alike.*" (Our emphasis).

Generally, when a gift is to a group of individuals sharing the same relationship to the settlor, the use of the words "share and share alike" denotes a *per capita* distribution rather than a *per stirpes* distribution. *Per capita* is defined as denoting that "an equal share

---

[5] We note this provision may run afoul of the rule against perpetuities. However this issue is not before us and we need not consider it.

[6] We note this provision appears to leave a gap in the trust provisions. If Nellie's children had predeceased her leaving issue, Oberlin would not receive the principal, but there is no gift over.

is given to each of a number of persons, all of whom stand in equal degree to the decedent, without reference to their stocks or the right of representation." BLACK's LAW DICTIONARY 1292 (Rev. 4th ed. 1968). In contrast, as this court explained in *Matter of Estate of Walters*, (1988), Ind.App., 519 N.E.2d 1270, 1272:

> Per stirpes means literally by roots or stocks; by representation. It denotes that method of dividing an intestate estate where a class or group of distributees take the share which their ancestor would have been entitled to, taking it by their right of representing such ancestor, and not as so many individuals, or as the expression is used, per capita.

In *Laisure, supra*, 56 Ind.App. at 310, the court stated:

> The foundation of the *per capita* rule of distribution rests in a large measure on the presumption that when the beneficiaries are in equal degrees of relationship to the testator his affection for each is equal, and therefore he will desire to benefit each equally.

Here, the issue of Nellie's children all stand in the same relationship to the settlor. We find nothing in the trust provisions to indicate that the settlor intended the issue of Nellie's children to take *per stirpes*. On the contrary, he intended that the issue, his great-grandchildren, should take equal shares. This indicates that the settlor intended the issue of Nellie's children to take equal shares of the principal without regard to the identity of their parents.

This conclusion is also supported by the settlor's repeated use of the term "child or children", when referring to Nellie's children. At the time the trust was created, the settlor could not have known how many, if any, of Nellie's children would survive her, or how many, if any, of her children would have issue.[7] This language indicates the settlor considered two possible circumstances—either one child or more than one child would survive Nellie. Thus, the income of the trust was to be paid to Nellie's surviving children whether there was only one child or several children. The language merely reflects the settlor's uncertainty concerning the number of Nellie's surviving children. In addition, the trust provisions indicate the settlor considered two other possible circumstances: (1) At her death, Nellie would have no surviving children or grandchildren, in which case

---

[7] The record does not reveal if Nellie had any children at the time the trust was created.

the principal would be paid to Oberlin; or (2) At her death, Nellie would have no surviving children, but would have surviving grandchildren. As we noted, in this latter event—which has not occurred—there is no clear direction as to the disposition of the principal. However, it is clear that Oberlin was not to be paid the principal in preference to Nellie's grandchildren (the settlor's great-grandchildren). Therefore, we conclude that Oberlin is not entitled to any portion of the corpus, as long as Nellie has surviving issue.

However, this conclusion does not answer the question of the proper disposition of Florence's interest in the trust. For clarification we restate the issue as follows:

> What is the proper disposition of an income beneficiary's interest in a trust, where the settlor gives an income interest to two or more beneficiaries and provides for the distribution of the principal after the termination of all the life interests, but makes no provision for the disposition of one of the beneficiaries' shares during the time between that beneficiary's death and the death of all the life beneficiaries.

Here, the settlor gave the income to his grandchildren and the principal to his great-grandchildren after the death of his grandchildren. However, he made no specific provision for the disposition of a deceased grandchild's (Florence's) interest during the period of time between her death and the death of the last surviving grandchild (Marian).

When faced with this problem, courts in other jurisdictions have reached a variety of solutions. Some courts have ordered the income to be paid to the surviving income beneficiaries under the doctrine of implication of cross remainders, as a gift to a class, or as an implied joint tenancy. Other courts have ordered the income to be paid to the deceased beneficiary's estate until the death of the last income beneficiary. Other courts have ordered the income to be paid to the remaindermen. Finally, some courts have ordered the income to be accumulated until the death of the last income beneficiary.

We have examined the cases cited in *Annot.* 71 A.L.R.2d 1332 (1960) and other cases cited by the parties. Once again we are struck by the difficulty encountered in applying seemingly analogous cases to a case of this kind. Because of the great variety of language used in trusts and similar documents it is difficult, if not impossible, to find any authority which is directly on point. Therefore, we will not engage in a lengthy discussion of such cases. Instead, we will return to the primary consideration in construing a trust—the determination of the intent of the settlor.

We conclude that the settlor intended the gift of the income to Nellie's children to be a gift to a class and that all the income was to be paid to the members of such class, regardless of their number. We further conclude that although Marian and Florence, the members of this class, were tenants in common, in order to effectuate the intent of the settlor, the total net income must be paid to Marian for the rest of her life under the implication of cross remainders.

Cross remainders are defined as:

> Where land is devised or conveyed to two or more persons as tenants in common, or where different parts of the same land are given to such persons in severalty, with such limitations that, upon the determination of the particular estate of either, his share is to pass to the other, to the entire exclusion of the ultimate remainder-man or reversioner until all the particular estates shall be exhausted, the remainders so limited are called "cross-remainders."

BLACK'S LAW DICTIONARY, 1456 (Rev. 4th ed. 1968). Cross remainders may also be created in personal property, and may arise by implication in wills or *inter vivos* trusts.

The controlling factor in determining whether cross remainders will be implied is whether the settlor intended the whole estate to go over at one time.

Here, the trust states:

> Upon the death of said Nellie B. Vaughn, if she leaves, surviving her, a child or children, then said net income is to be paid unto said child or children *during their lives*, share and share alike. Upon the death of said child or children of said Nellie B. Vaughn then the principal . . . shall be paid to the issue of said child or children, *share and share alike*.

(Our emphasis). The emphasized language indicates that the settlor intended the principal to be distributed at one time—upon the death of the last income beneficiary. As we noted, the use of the term "child or children" merely denotes the settlor's uncertainty concerning who would survive Nellie. The addition of the words "during *their* lives" indicates the settlor intended the income to be paid to Nellie's children as long as any such children were living. This conclusion is further supported by the use of the term "share and share alike" in reference to the portion of the principal to be taken by Nellie's grandchildren. As we explained, this language indicates a *per capita* distribution of the principal to a class—Nellie's grandchildren. As the Illinois Supreme Court explained in *Kiesling, supra*:

> "a determination in favor of a *per capita* division to a class in remainder requires the ambiguous words to be interpreted in favor of a single point of division upon the termination of the last of the preceding limited interests with the consequent implication of cross-interests to the takers of preceding estates in the property. On the other hand, a determination that remaindermen take *per stirpes* impels no such result."

We conclude that the settlor intended the principal to be distributed as a whole upon the death of the last of Nellie's children. Therefore, cross-remainders will be implied and Marian is entitled, as the trial court held, to the total net income from the trust for the rest of her life.

Oberlin contends that Ind.Ann.Stat. § 12174 which, as we explained, requires Marian and Florence to be deemed tenants in common, compels a different result.[8] We disagree. Cross-remainders are implied when the income beneficiaries hold their interests as tenants in common. In addition, IND. CODE § 30–4–1–3 states:

> "The rules of law contained in this article shall be interpreted and applied to the terms of the trust so as to implement the intent of the settlor and the purposes of the trust. If the rules of law and the terms of the trust conflict, the terms of the trust shall control unless the rules of law clearly prohibit or restrict the article which the terms of the trust purport to authorize."

We find nothing in Ind.Ann.Stat. § 12174 to clearly prohibit or restrict an implication of cross remainders.[9]

Affirmed.

---

[8] We note that, even if this statute did compel a different result, Oberlin would not be entitled to the income, because, when read as a whole, the trust clearly indicates Oberlin receives nothing so long as there are surviving issue of Nellie's children.

[9] The Trustee and Oberlin have cited a number of cases involving the application of such a statute. All of the cases cited are distinguishable on a wide variety of grounds. It is unnecessary to add to this opinion a lengthy discussion of these cases. However, we note none of the cases involved a gift of income to a class. . . . Our research has revealed no case in which such a statute was applied so as to deprive an income beneficiary of the deceased beneficiary's income interest, when the gift of income was to a class.

In some ways, *Westervelt* was easy because the first child to die did not leave surviving children.

> Example 6.68: O has two children, B and C. O devises in trust, "income to my children for their lives, and when the last child has died, principal to my grandchildren." B has a child, X. C has a child, Y. C dies. Under the common-law presumption, B takes all the income until B dies.

The common law presumed, rebuttably, that only the surviving members of the class would take the income while they remained alive even when the deceased members of the class left surviving descendants. This leaves some branches of the family tree without income or principal for a time. In some opinions, this result was given a doctrinal justification by finding that the members of the class share as joint tenants. Does the common-law presumption reach the result the transferor would want in Example 6.68 or 6.69?

> Example 6.69: T devises in trust "income to my housekeepers for life, then to my descendants, *per stirpes*." Under the common-law presumption, each housekeeper's income would terminate with death.

In cases like the Example 6.68, some courts have found sufficient evidence to overcome the common-law presumption so that all lines of descent continue to share the income. *See Dewire v. Haveles*, 404 Mass. 274 (1989) (reasoning that the testator's final gift over to all lines of descendants indicated that the testator intended for all lines of descendants to continue receiving income after the death of a life tenant).

(v) When the Class Might Expand (the "Rule of Convenience")

Sometimes, a gift is made to a class that has not yet closed physiologically. This is not a problem while no one is entitled to possession or enjoyment. But a problem arises if some members of the class become entitled to possession while more members could be conceived or adopted into the class. A distribution to class members who have qualified might not leave enough for those who enter the class later. To allow members of a class to benefit from a class gift as soon as they individually qualify for a distribution, without waiting to see how many others will also qualify, the "rule of convenience" closes the class as soon as one member of the class becomes entitled to a distribution of a share, i.e., some sort of possession or enjoyment of the gift. Once the class is closed, the maximum size of the class is known and a portion may be distributed to each of those entitled to possession. The size of the distribution is determined by the maximum number of takers, vested and unvested together, at a given point in time. Members of the class with contingent interests must wait until they have satisfied all conditions, of course, before they can take. When the interest of a member vests, that member is entitled to possession of a portion. If it becomes clear that a class member cannot qualify, that member's share will be divided according to the recalculated maximum number of takers, with those entitled to possession taking their shares immediately.

> Problem 6.70: O bequeaths "$15,000 in trust to the children of B who reach 21, in equal shares." At O's death, B has two children, C1 (age 7) and C2 (age 4). Three years later, C3 is born to B. Does C3 take an interest in the trust? Eleven years later, C1 reaches 21. Is C1 entitled to anything? One year later, C4 is born to B. Does C4 take an interest in the trust? Later, C3 reaches 21. Is C3 entitled to a distribution?

The rule of convenience closes the class when one member is entitled to a distribution. Sometimes, due to poor drafting, it is not clear when the distribution to the class is to be made.

> Example 6.71: O devises as follows: "Distribute the assets in the trust when my youngest grandchild reaches 21." As long as O's children are alive, more grandchildren can be born. Do the grandchildren have to wait until all of O's children are dead? In *Lux v. Lux*, 109 R.I. 592 (1972), the court closed the class of grandchildren when the youngest living grandchild reached the age of 21, despite the fact that this would close out any grandchildren conceived later.

The rule of convenience is a rule of construction. Courts usually adhere to it, but it can be overcome by sufficient evidence of contrary intent.

(vi) Division of the Class Gift

Sometimes it is unclear from the instrument whether members of a class are to take equally (*per capita*) or by right of representation (*per stirpes*).

Example 6.72: O devises "to my spouse for life, then to my grandchildren." O has three grandchildren, A from O's son and B and C from O's daughter. After O's spouse dies, do all three take a third, or does A take half while B and C take quarters?

It is the lawyer's job to avoid contention and litigation by making this clear. Unfortunately, the use of the words "per stirpes" is not sufficient to prevent litigation. In *In re Estate of Damon*, 109 Hawai'i 502 (2006) the distribution of $120,000,000 depended on whether donor meant English or modern per stirpes.

(e) Federal Estate Tax Treatment

Federal estate tax treatment of an interest turns on whether the interest is "transmissible" at death. If the interest disappears at death, it is not transmissible and not taxable to the estate of the decedent. In ordinary circumstances, be careful to avoid creating a taxable interest unless your client wants to create an interest that is taxable at the donee's death.

Problem 6.73: O devises property in trust "with income to A for life, then principal to B, but if B dies before A dies then principal to C." Consider two separate sets of facts:

a) B dies during A's lifetime. Is the value of B's future interest includible in B's taxable gross estate under the federal estate tax?

b) C dies before A and B. Is the value of C's future interest includible in C's taxable gross estate?

(f) Valuation of Future Interests

Tax reporting, division of assets in a trust, and other situations call for determining the value of present and future interests. Here is one way to value a future interest. Determine 1) what the future interest holder is supposed to receive, 2) when she is supposed to receive it, 3) what its value will be at that time, which will depend on the character of the corpus of the trust, and 4) how much the future interest holder would have to receive now in order for that amount to grow into the correct amount at the time of possession or enjoyment of the future interest. Complications arise when one must calculate the likelihood of satisfying conditions or estimate the time it will take for events to occur. It is important to get expert financial help if you need it.

Problem 6.74: Your client owns a remainder interest following a life estate in a trust holding land as its res. The trustee proposes to sell land and deposit the proceeds in a bank account and pay the interest to the life tenant. Do you advise your client to object or to keep quiet?

CHAPTER 7

SHACKLING THE DEAD HAND

■ ■ ■

It is clear from the preceding materials that the law places great importance on the goals expressed by decedents in their wills and trusts. But that does not mean that the law will honor all instructions no matter what preferences they express. The law sets boundaries and refuses to enforce instructions that offend social policy in one way or another.

A. THE RULE AGAINST PERPETUITIES

For hundreds of years, decedents have attempted to control the use and ownership of assets long after their death. And for hundreds of years, owners in the grip of a dead hand of the past have gone to lawyers and court to free themselves from the dead hand. The *Statute De Donis Conditionalibus* enacted in 1285 reflected the wishes of owners to control future ownership via the fee tail estate. By the time of *Taltarum's Case*, supra, in 1472, the courts were willing to allow the "common recovery" to bar the entail. This battle back and forth eventually resulted in the Rule Against Perpetuities (the RAP or "the Rule"). Your course in Property might have mentioned this rule. If so, great! If not, you are in for a treat. The Rule limits the temporal reach of the dead hand. The Rule did not start as a clear rule against remote limitations. It could be said to have started with the decision in *The Duke of Norfolk's Case* 3 Ch. Cas. 1 (Chancery 1682), which allowed a decedent to control his assets during the life of another person whose life overlapped the decedent's. About 150 years later, in *Cadell v. Palmer*, 6 Eng. Rep. 956, 1 Cl. & F. 372, 1 WLUK 17 (H.L. 1833), the House of Lords decided that the limit for vesting of interests would be lives in being plus twenty-one years plus periods of gestation. We will spend some time and effort learning what that means before briefly discussing modern reforms.

1. THE COMMON-LAW (WHAT-MIGHT-HAPPEN) RULE AGAINST PERPETUITIES

In his classic treatise, John Chipman Gray presented his enduring formulation of the Rule Against Perpetuities: "No interest is good unless it must vest, if at all, not later than twenty-one years after some life in being at the creation of the interest." (You'll need to memorize that for cocktail party conversation.) This is one of the hardest rules to master in all of the common law. If you do a Westlaw search for "Rule Against Perpetuities" in case opinions, you might find that there are more opinions referring to the rule as a standard of difficulty than there are cases actually involving an application of the Rule. However, the paucity of cases does not mean the Rule is unimportant. The Rule is important, but there are few cases because the Rule, though difficult, is determinate. Lawyers do not need to go to court to work out the answer to a perpetuities question. Under the common-law RAP, an interest is either good or bad, and whichever it is can be proved.

(a) An Interest Is Void if It Might Vest Too Late

To learn the Rule, it may be helpful to start with a simpler statement than Gray's. Under the common-law Rule Against Perpetuities, *an interest is void if it might vest too late*. After we parse that sentence, you will be a long way down the road to mastery of the Rule. We will take it a word or phrase at a time.

"An interest" means remainders, executory interests, powers of appointment, options, and perhaps rights of first refusal. The Rule applies to legal interests and beneficial interests alike, but only to those types of interest just listed. It does not apply to reversions, possibilities of reverter, and rights of entry for condition broken. (However, be aware that the duration of such interests retained by grantors is sometimes limited by statutes.) There is one narrow but important exception that should be noted here; an interest in a charity following an interest in a charity is immune to the RAP. Some authorities expand this exception by saying that all interests in charities are immune to the RAP.

The traditional approach is to start by construing the instrument to determine which interests were purportedly created and then, when construction is done, apply the Rule "remorselessly" to each of those interests. In other words, construe first, then apply the Rule. This traditional approach stands in contrast to a common approach to construing statutes, under which a court may construe a statute in a way that avoids constitutional difficulties. So, do not be surprised if a court refuses to construe an instrument so as to avoid RAP difficulties. However, other courts will in some situations construe the instrument to avoid perpetuities violations.

"Is void" means the interest is void *ab initio*. If an interest is void, it is void from the moment the instrument becomes effective. The offending language is simply stricken from the instrument. Ordinarily, the Rule does not invalidate any other interests, much less the entire instrument,[1] only the language creating the interests that might vest too late.

Be careful on this point. Striking the offending language from the instrument means that all takers of that interest lose their interest. If an interest might vest in one person too late, it is void as to all persons who take under that interest, even those for whom the interest is already vested. Bad as to one, bad as to all. That rule is commonly known as the class-gift rule or the all-or-nothing rule. However, there are exceptions, of sorts, that limit the scope of this all-or-nothing rule. First, separate gifts to members of a class are treated separately. In other words, if there are separate gifts, then it is not a class gift. A "gift over" of each child's interest to each child's eldest child might not be a class gift to all such eldest children, but rather a series of separate gifts to each of the eldest children. Second, specific amounts or shares (as opposed to "equal shares") given to each of the members of a class are viewed as separate gifts to each member rather than one class gift to all members. Third, if a court decides to apply it, the rule of convenience might close a class, and the effect of closing the class could be to eliminate the possibility of an interest vesting too late.

In addition to the rules above that narrow the application of the Rule, there is an exception that expands the scope of the Rule. Under the doctrine of infectious invalidity, a court may invalidate other

---

[1] The movie BODY HEAT does not explain why the estate's lawyer concludes that the decedent's entire will is invalid. It would be highly unusual for the will to have created nothing but future interests that might vest too late. It would seem that at least one of the devises would be a present interest which would not be invalidated. It is possible to invalidate the entire will by applying the "infectious invalidity" doctrine, but neither that doctrine nor a reason for applying it is suggested in the movie. The movie also seems to err in holding that once the will fails there is no other will. If the last will is wholly invalid, the previous will remains in effect unless it was separately revoked. If the last will is partly invalid, perhaps the valid portion revoked the previous will, but that is not suggested either. And, even if the previous will was revoked, that revocation could be ignored under the doctrine of dependent relative revocation. Finally, the gift that had the potential to vest remotely might have been saved if the court was willing to apply the wait-and-see variation of the Rule.

provisions of a will or trust, along with the interest that violates the Rule. A court might do this if it thinks the transferor intended those other provisions to be effective only if the invalidated interest was effective. (This might remind you of the *cy pres* power, under which the court can modify a charitable trust to come as close as possible to what the settlor intended.)

"Might" means might. "Might" refers to what might happen in the future, when analyzed at the point of time when the interest is created. For a will, that point in time is the death of the testator. For an inter vivos gift of a legal interest, that point in time is the completion of the gift, usually at delivery. For an inter vivos transfer in trust, that point in time is when the trust becomes irrevocable. It does not matter what actually happens after the start of the perpetuities period. When the period of the Rule begins to run, if the interest in question might vest remotely, it is void. It does not matter how fanciful the scenario is that results in remote vesting, one single scenario is enough to invalidate the interest. For that reason, the common-law rule is sometimes known as the "what-might-happen" Rule. (Note that the rule in this paragraph does not always apply when a power of appointment is involved, as we will see below.)

However, there are some exceptions. In other words, there are some things that actually might happen in the world that would lead to remote vesting that are not considered to be possibilities under the Rule and are not taken into account when determining "what might happen". First, the Rule is applied without considering events made possible (or foreclosed) by modern medical science. The common-law Rule presumes, irrebuttably, that people can have children while they are alive (even if they cannot) and cannot have children more than a period of gestation after their deaths (even though they now can). In particular, given modern fertility assistance, people can conceive children long after death; such possibilities are not considered when applying the Rule. Second, the Rule is applied without considering events made possible by a change in the law. It is possible that a change in the law would lead to the remote vesting of an interest that could not have vested too late under the old law, but that possibility does not matter to the Rule unless it happens. The effect of these two limitations could be to save an interest by ruling out the scenarios in which the interest would vest remotely.

"Vest" means vest in interest. For remainders and executory interests, "vest" means what it meant when we studied those interests. An executory interest vests in interest when it vests in possession. A remainder vests in interest when a taker is identified and all conditions precedent are satisfied for that taker.

"Too late" means more than twenty-one years plus relevant periods of gestation after the death of all people alive when the perpetuities period starts to run. For most interests created in a will, the perpetuities period starts to run when the testator dies. For an interest in a trust, the perpetuities period starts when the trust becomes irrevocable. For an interest created by the exercise of a general inter vivos power of appointment, the perpetuities period starts when that power is exercised. For an interest created by the exercise of any other power of appointment, the perpetuities period starts when that power is created.

Once again, an interest is void if it might vest too late. To put it another way, an interest is valid under the Rule Against Perpetuities if it cannot vest too late.

> Problem 7.01: O transfers "Blackacre to A for life, then to B if B walks on Mars." Is it possible that B's interest will never vest? Is B's interest valid or void?

> Problem 7.02a: O transfers "Blackacre to A for life, then to B if any person walks on Mars." Is B's interest valid or is it void in a jurisdiction in which contingent remainders are indestructible?

> Problem 7.02b: O transfers "Blackacre to A for life, then to B if any person walks on Mars." Was B's interest valid in a jurisdiction in which contingent remainders were destructible? (Hint: What might happen when A dies?) This is an example of the point, mentioned above, that a change in the law in the future (here, retroactive indestructibility) might allow an interest to vest too late.

> Problem 7.03: O devises Blackacre "to A for life, then for life to A's eldest child who survives A, then to the eldest child of that child for life, then to B." (The "eldest child who survives A" is construed to mean the eldest of the children living at the death of A.) A, B, and A's first child, S, survive O. Are the future interests valid or void?

> Example 7.04: O devises in trust, "income to my children for life, then to my grandchildren for their lives, then corpus to Z. No person may alienate his or her interest voluntarily or involuntarily." O is survived by Z and O's children, A and B.

The interests in A, B, and Z are vested and the class of O's children closed physiologically when O died. Next, O's grandchildren, X and Y, are born to A and B respectively, and the contingent remainder vests in them, subject to open. Z dies and H inherits Z's remainder. A and B die, preventing any more grandchildren from being conceived, closing the class physiologically. Twenty-one years and a period of gestation pass. That is the end of the perpetuities period. Can X, Y, and H terminate the trust if they all agree? Yes. *Claflin* protection terminated at the end of the perpetuities period.

Problem 7.05: B has a child, C1, and grandchild, GC1. O devises "to B for life, then remainder to B's grandchildren for their lives, then to X." Is GC1's vested remainder void or valid? (Does the answer depend on whether the court construes O's will to incorporate the rule of convenience?)

Example 7.06: O devises "to A for life, then to the children of A for life, then to the grandchildren of A then living." A is a woman 80 years of age. At O's death, A has a grandchild GC. The interest in the grandchildren is void, so GC's interest is void. This is "the case of the fertile octogenarian".

Example 7.07: O devises in trust "to A for life, then to A's widow for life, then to the issue of A then living." The interest in the issue is void. This is "the case of the unborn widow".

Example 7.08: O devises in trust "to my grandchildren alive when my estate has been probated." O is survived by children. The interest in the grandchildren is void. This is "the case of the slothful executor".

Other scenarios in this parade of horrors include "the case of the precocious toddler" and "the case of the magic gravel pit". Learn to avoid assuming that unlikely things cannot happen because many things are possible in the imaginary world of the what-might-happen Rule Against Perpetuities.

(b) The Split Contingencies Doctrine

For more than a century, courts have recognized the split contingencies doctrine, also known as the alternative contingencies doctrine. This doctrine says that if an interest might vest in two or more ways identified separately in the instrument, then the different ways of vesting will be separated for purposes of the Rule. If an interest might vest under one alternative too late, then that alternative is void. But if the same interest will definitely not vest too late under another alternative, that alternative is valid. For this doctrine to apply, the different alternatives for vesting must be set out in the instrument. As put by Sir George Jessel, Master of the Rolls, in *Miles v. Harford*, 12 Ch.D. 691 (Ch. 1879), "that is what [the courts] mean by splitting, they will not split the expression by dividing the two events, but when they find two expressions they give effect to both of them as if you had struck the other out of the will."

> Example 7.09: O devises property in trust "to Earl, but if Earl ever drinks alcohol or if anyone ever walks on Mars, then to Nelle." The contingency of walking on Mars is void, but the contingency of Earl drinking is valid, so Nelle's executory interest is not entirely void.

(c) The Application of the RAP to Powers of Appointment

As noted above, the starting point for the Rule Against Perpetuities period is ordinarily the date the interest is created and what might happen is determined as of that same point in time. But there are special rules for applying the Rule to powers of appointment and the interests created by powers of appointment. There are two questions to ask when applying the Rule in the context of powers of appointment. First, is the power valid? Second, are the interests created by the exercise of the power valid? We will take up general inter vivos powers of appointment first, then other powers.

A general inter vivos power of appointment is void if it might *become exercisable* (i.e., might *be acquired*) too late. The idea is that as soon as the power becomes exercisable, whether it is exercised or not, the donee could exercise the power. At that point, the assets are not inalienable, not tied up by the dead hand. So, the power is good if it is a sure thing that the power will become exercisable (i.e., be acquired) within the period of the Rule. The measuring period begins at the time the power is created.

> Example 7.10: O devises property in trust "to A for life, then to A's eldest child living at A's death, with a general power in such child to appoint his or her share of the corpus at age 25." The power is void. Here is an invalidating scenario: O dies. Two years later, A has a child, B. A year after that, A

dies along with all others who were alive at the time that the power was created. B's general power becomes exercisable 24 years later, which is more than 21 years after the death of A and all the other lives in being at O's death.

An interest created by the exercise of a general inter vivos power of appointment is void if it might vest too late. The period of the Rule runs from the time the power is exercised. Since that exercise is what creates the interest, this application of the Rule is no different from the usual Rule.

> Example 7.11: O devises property in trust "to A for life, then to A's eldest child living at A's death, with a general power in such child to appoint his or her share of the corpus at age 18." A gives birth to B. A dies. B gives birth to C. B exercises at age 50, appointing to "C for life, then to C's eldest child then living." Even though vesting of those interests occurs long after the deaths of O and A, the interests created by the appointment are good because they are measured from the time of the appointment, B's exercise of the power, not from the time the power was created.

For any power other than a general inter vivos power of appointment, the power is void if it might *be exercised* too late. The idea here is that the appointive property is tied up by the dead hand (neither belonging to the donee nor to the objects) until the power is actually exercised, so it is crucial that the donee not be able to exercise too late. If the donee cannot exercise the power too late, the property will not be tied up too long. Just as any possibility that an interest vests too late invalidates the interest, any possibility of a power being exercised too late invalidates the power. The period runs from the time the power is created.

> Example 7.12: B has two children, X and Y. O devises property in trust "to B for life, remainder to be appointed by B's eldest surviving child by deed or by will." The power is void. Here is an invalidating scenario: O dies. B has a child Z. B, X, Y, and all lives in being die. Twenty-five years later, Z exercises.

An interest created by the exercise of a power other than a general inter vivos power of appointment is, as usual, void if it might vest too late. But in this situation there are a couple of special rules. The period runs from the time that the power is created, not when the interest is created by the exercise of the power. However, when we look at what might happen, we consider only the possibilities that still exist as of the time that the power is exercised. This is called the second-look doctrine.

> Example 7.13: B has two children, X and Y. O devises property in trust "to pay the income to B for life, then to distribute the principal to such descendants of B as B shall appoint by will." B dies, appointing in trust "the income to my children for their lives, then after the death of all my children to my grandchildren." The power itself is valid because it cannot be exercised later than B's life, and B was alive at O's death. For the interests created by the power, they are read back into the will of O and the perpetuities period starts to run when the power was created, at O's death. B's appointment to B's children is good because they will be conceived within B's life and B was alive at O's death. The appointment to B's grandchildren vests in them when they are conceived, which must be within the lives of B's children. If we consider what might happen as of the death of O, B might have another child, Z, and that child might conceive a grandchild of B long after the death of all persons alive at O's death. However, the second-look doctrine says that we consider the facts known at the time of B's appointment by will. At that time, we know that B did not have another child, Z, after O's death. Therefore, the interest in the grandchildren of B must vest if ever during the lives of X and Y, who were alive at the time the power was created. So, the interests created by the exercise of the power are good. If, however, B had been able to exercise the power by deed and had exercised during life to the same persons, we would not know at the time of exercise that B will not have another child and the interest in the grandchildren of B would have been void.

The application of the Rule to powers of appointment raises another planning problem. The problem is sometimes called the Delaware Tax Trap, which can be a trap for the unwary or can be a useful option in the hands of a careful estate planner. Under § 2041(a)(3)(B) of the Internal Revenue Code, the estate of the donee of a nongeneral power is sometimes taxed on the appointive property. The donee's estate includes the appointive property if the donee exercises "by creating another power of appointment which under the applicable local law can be validly exercised so as to postpone the vesting of any estate or interest in such property, . . . for a period ascertainable without regard to the date of the creation of the first power." By this provision, the Code offers the donee a choice between subjecting the appointive property to the estate tax or to the generation-skipping transfer (GST) tax. Which tax would be lower depends on exemptions and rates.

(d) Malpractice and Saving Clauses

Although *Lucas v. Hamm*, 56 Cal.2d 583 (1961), stated that it was not malpractice to violate the Rule in that case, you cannot rely on it, *see Wright v. Williams*, 121 Cal. Rptr. 194 (1975) (questioning the validity of *Lucas*). To make sure you are not violating the Rule, include a saving clause in the instrument. Such a clause saves the interests and saves your assets and perhaps your career. The basic idea is to name a reasonable number of living persons in the instrument and to specify that twenty-one years after the last of those persons dies all interests that might yet vest shall terminate and the property associated with those terminated interests shall vest in other takers. There are examples of saving clauses in form books.

(e) Interests in Charities

Another point to remember is that interests in charities following interests in charities do not violate the Rule. Because charities benefit the public, the law encourages giving to charities by providing a way for the donor to make sure that the gift is used as intended. One way to do that is to allow the donor to create an interest in a second charity that will divest the first charity if the first charity fails to follow the terms of the gift. Because the divesting gift is insulated from the RAP, the divesting condition can remain effective forever. However, it is not clear whether it ultimately benefits society to allow owners to assert their control forever. The Hershey candy company trust has an endowment of more than $12,000,000,000 which it spends to support a boarding school for a couple thousand low-income children a year.

(f) Statutes Imposing Limits Somewhat Similar to the RAP

Be aware that there are rules in some states that prevent income from accumulating in trusts for too long. These rules are not the RAP, but they may define temporal limits by reference to the Rule.

The Rule does not apply to possibilities of reverter and rights of entry for condition broken, which makes it possible for grantors to retain contingent interests that might vest far in the future. Concerned about the abuse of such interests, some legislatures have enacted statutes that limit those two interests to periods such as thirty years.

Four states, Kentucky, Wisconsin, South Dakota, and Idaho, replaced the common-law Rule Against Perpetuities with a different rule, a rule against the suspension of the power of alienation. This rule prevents the power of alienation from being suspended for more than lives in being plus twenty-five or thirty years. The first state to pass an anti-suspension rule, New York, now has both an anti-suspension rule and the Rule Against Perpetuities. The anti-suspension rule serves some, but not all, of the purposes of the RAP, and has been viewed as a mistaken reform.

The following case illustrates many of the points made above.

HOCHBERG V. PROCTOR

Supreme Judicial Court of Massachusetts, Suffolk, 2004
805 N.E.2d 979

GREANEY, J.

This is a complaint for instructions by the trustees under the will of Thomas E. Proctor, Jr. (Thomas, Jr.), as to the distribution of the principal of three trusts created by the will. A judge in the Probate and Family Court appointed guardians ad litem to represent minors and unascertained and unborn issue, and, following argument, entered an amended judgment directing distribution of two of the trusts and reforming the third, in a manner that will be discussed later in this opinion. Respondents Mattina Proctor (Mattina) and James Proctor Morss and Nicholas Emerson Proctor King, by their guardian ad litem, appealed. We granted their application for direct appellate review. For reasons that follow, we now vacate portions of the amended judgment and direct that the principal of the trusts created by the THIRD and FIFTH paragraphs of the will be added to the residuary trust created by the FIFTEENTH paragraph, to be distributed, as directed in the amended judgment, on the expiration of Mattina's life estate, to Thomas, Jr.'s, heirs at law. The amended judgment as so modified is to be effective as of May 31, 1999.

The case was submitted on a statement of agreed facts and legal issues, which may be summarized as follows. Thomas E. Proctor, Sr.

(Thomas, Sr.), died on December 7, 1894, leaving in his will a power of appointment over specified property to his son (Thomas, Jr.). Thomas, Jr., died on March 21, 1949, unmarried and without issue. In his will, dated August 19, 1936 (as amended by two codicils in 1937 and 1947), Thomas, Jr., distributed his own property and exercised the power of appointment granted to him under the will of his father. The three trusts here at issue, the trusts under paragraphs THIRD, FIFTH, and FIFTEENTH, are the only trusts presently in existence under the will of Thomas, Jr. All three are funded solely with property appointed by Thomas, Jr., by exercise of the power of appointment granted to him under his father's will. Paragraph FIFTEENTH is the residuary clause of the will.[5]

Mattina was the life income beneficiary of the trusts created by paragraphs THIRD[6] and FIFTH[7] of the will, as of May 31, 1999. On that date, those trusts terminated by operation of the following language contained in paragraph ELEVENTH of the will:

> "If any of the foregoing trusts shall not have theretofore terminated under the provisions of this my will applicable thereto, then such trust shall terminate at the expiration of twenty-one (21) years from the date of the decease of the last survivor of the descendants of my father and mother [Thomas, Sr., and Emma H. Proctor] who were living at the date of the decease of my father [December 7, 1894]."[8]

---

[5] The paragraph FIFTEENTH trust originally contained no appointive property. In 1947, Thomas, Jr., executed a second codicil to his will (the first is not here involved), amending paragraph EIGHTEENTH to state that he intended by paragraph FIFTEENTH (the residuary clause) completely to exercise all powers of appointment that he had under the will of his father.

[6] The relevant portion of paragraph THIRD established a trust with one quarter of the appointive property for the benefit of Thomas, Jr.'s, nephew, Thomas E. Proctor, Second (Thomas 2d), for life, with remainder in trust to his then living issue. In the event that Thomas 2d died without issue, the trust provided that remainder would go, in trust with income for life, to Thomas, Jr.'s, grandniece, Mattina, and his grandnephew, James Howe Proctor, Second (James 2d), remainder to their issue. Both Thomas 2d and James 2d died without issue. Accordingly, Mattina became the sole life beneficiary of the paragraph THIRD trust. Its terms provide that, if both James 2d and Mattina died without issue, the remainder passes in equal shares "to and among the then living male descendants of [Thomas, Sr.], bearing the name of Proctor."

[7] The relevant portion of paragraph FIFTH established a trust with one-quarter of the appointive property for the benefit of Thomas, Jr.'s, other nephew, John Riker Proctor (John) for life, with remainder in trust to Mattina (John's daughter), and then to her issue, and, in default of her issue, to James 2d (John's son) for life and his issue. The trust provided that, if James 2d had no issue, the remainder shall go "in equal share to and among the then living male descendants of [Thomas, Sr.], bearing the name of Proctor."

[8] Paragraph ELEVENTH was inserted to avoid a conflict with the rule against perpetuities. That rule is classically defined as the rule that "[n]o interest is good unless it must vest, if at all, not later than twenty-one years after some life in being at the creation of the interest." J.C. Gray, Rule Against Perpetuities § 201 (4th ed.1942). See Leach, Perpetuities in a Nutshell, 51 Harv. L.Rev. 638, 639 (1938) ("Gray's formulation would be more realistic if it were preceded by the words *Generally speaking* and if the word *vest* were put in quotation marks"). In the context of trusts, the

Because the last survivor of the descendants of Thomas, Sr., and Emma H. Proctor living at the date of Thomas, Sr.'s, death, was Thomas E.P. Rice, who died May 31, 1978, the termination date specified under paragraph ELEVENTH for the trusts under paragraphs THIRD and FIFTH is May 31, 1999, exactly twenty-one years after the death of Thomas E.P. Rice. Paragraph ELEVENTH specifies that, on such termination, the trust property under the THIRD and FIFTH paragraphs shall be paid "to and among those persons who would have been entitled to take the same if such trust had terminated at such date and pursuant to its terms upon the decease of a specified life beneficiary."

The provision for distribution of the remainder of the paragraph THIRD and FIFTH trusts on their termination is "in equal shares to and among the then living male descendants of [Thomas, Sr.], bearing the name of Proctor." As of May 31, 1999, there were no male descendants of Thomas, Sr., bearing the last name of Proctor. There was one living female descendant (Mattina) bearing the last name of Proctor. There were three living male descendants and six living female descendants bearing the middle name of Proctor.

Paragraph FIFTEENTH established a trust for Thomas, Jr.'s, nephew, John Riker Proctor (John) for life and, after his death, in equal shares to John's two children, James Howe Proctor, Second (James 2d), and Mattina, and all to the survivor for life. If either James 2d or Mattina were deceased, their respective shares of the life estate were to go to their issue, if any. On the death of the last survivor of Thomas, Jr.; John; James 2d; and Mattina, the trust provided that the principal be distributed equally to the then living issue of James 2d and Mattina. John having died in 1969, and James 2d in 1942 (with no issue), the income of the paragraph FIFTEENTH trust currently is distributable to Mattina for her lifetime. Mattina is seventy-four years of age and has no issue. Following her death, in default of any of her issue, the provision for distribution of the remainder of the paragraph FIFTEENTH trust (as under the paragraph THIRD and FIFTH trusts) is "in equal shares to and among the then living male descendants of [Thomas, Sr.], bearing the name of Proctor."

---

rule governs how long equitable contingent interests may remain unresolved before they must extinguish or be converted into vested interests. In this case, the terms of paragraph ELEVENTH ensured that all interests in Thomas, Sr.'s, appointive property contained in the paragraph THIRD and FIFTH trusts terminated within the perpetuities time limit.

The judge determined, with respect to the paragraph THIRD and FIFTH trusts, that, because there were no male descendants of Thomas, Sr., bearing the last name of Proctor as of the trusts' termination date of May 31, 1999, the remainder interests in the trusts' property lapsed. Accordingly, she ordered the property to be distributed to the heirs of Thomas, Jr., as of May 31, 1999.[9] With respect to the paragraph FIFTEENTH trust, the judge determined that, when Thomas, Jr., died in 1949, Mattina had only a contingent interest in the trust property that was not certain to vest within the perpetuities period. The judge concluded, therefore, that Mattina's life estate in the paragraph FIFTEENTH trust was invalid under the rule against perpetuities.[10] Pursuant to her authority under G.L. c. 184A, § 6 (b),[11] the judge ordered reformation of that trust to comport with Thomas, Jr.'s, intended distribution. Accordingly, she ordered that Mattina's life estate be continued in effect until her death, and, on her death, the remainder interest to be distributed outright to the heirs of Thomas, Jr., as of May 31, 1999.

Three sets of claimants have filed briefs in this appeal. They may be identified, and their respective contentions summarized, as follows:

(1) Mattina is the grandniece of Thomas, Jr., and, as stated above, the only living descendant of Thomas, Sr. (she is his great-granddaughter), who bears the last name of Proctor. She contends that, in the absence of any male descendants bearing that last name, it is she who is entitled to the property in the paragraph THIRD and FIFTH trusts, outright and free of trust. Alternatively, she suggests that, if Thomas, Jr., intended distribution only to males "bearing the name of Proctor," the above trusts fail for lack of a specified beneficiary, and the trusts' property, under the doctrine of capture, passes into the residue of his estate, contained in the paragraph

---

[9]   No party has challenged on appeal the judge's determination that the paragraph THIRD and FIFTH trust funds should be distributed to Thomas, Jr.'s, heirs determined as of May 31, 1999, as opposed to his heirs as of the date of his death.

[10]   Because the power of appointment over the property in the trusts at issue was created well before statutory modifications were enacted to ease the harshness of the traditional rule against perpetuities, the judge properly applied the common-law rule, which was in force until 1954. G.L. c. 184A, inserted by St.1954, c. 641, § 1. The current rule against perpetuities statute, G.L. c. 184A, as appearing in St.1989, c. 668, § 1, applies only to property interests created on or after June 30, 1990. St.1989, c. 668, § 2.

[11]   Judicial reformation of a power of appointment created before G.L. c. 184A's effective date is authorized under G.L. c. 184A, § 6 (b), if done in "the manner that most closely approximates the transferor's manifested plan of distribution and is within the limits of the rule against perpetuities applicable when the nonvested property interest or power of appointment was created."

FIFTEENTH trust. Her life estate in the latter, Mattina argues, was vested at the time of Thomas, Jr.'s, death, and thus, contrary to the judge's conclusion, does not invoke the rule against perpetuities at all. According to Mattina, her life estate in the paragraph FIFTEENTH trust is valid and, as of May 31, 1999, that trust should include all property from the paragraph THIRD and FIFTH trusts;

(2) James Proctor Morss and Nicholas Emerson Proctor King are two of three living males with the middle name Proctor. They present arguments (through their guardian ad litem) that Thomas, Jr., intended the designation "bearing the name of Proctor" to include male descendants of Thomas, Sr., with the middle name of Proctor. Further, they argue that the perpetuities savings clause in paragraph ELEVENTH should be construed to apply to the appointed property contained in the paragraph FIFTEENTH trust. They urge this court to resolve this case by ordering that the property in all three trusts (in which they claim a one-third interest) be distributed outright to the three living male descendants of Thomas, Sr., whose middle name is Proctor;

(3) Emery Van Daell Rice; Thomas Emerson Proctor Rice, Jr.; and Jane Patricia Rice (Rices) are among the living heirs of Thomas, Jr., as of May 31, 1999. They assert that the judge properly construed the words "bearing the name of Proctor" to apply only to male descendants and, on appeal, agree that the judge properly reformed the paragraph FIFTEENTH trust "in the manner that most closely approximates the transferor's manifested plan of distribution."

From the rather complex fact pattern emerges four distinct legal issues to be resolved before the trustees may be instructed regarding the proper distribution of the principal of the trusts. They are: (1) whether the words "male descendants ... bearing the name of Proctor" refer solely to males whose surname is Proctor; (2) whether the terms of paragraph ELEVENTH operate to terminate the paragraph FIFTEENTH trust as of May 31, 1999; (3) if not, whether Mattina's life estate in the paragraph FIFTEENTH trust property is valid under the rule against perpetuities or, alternatively, whether that trust should be reformed in order to continue Mattina's life estate; and (4) whether the property in the paragraph THIRD and FIFTH trusts must be distributed outright or whether it may it be added to the residue of Thomas, Jr.'s, estate, contained in the paragraph FIFTEENTH trust. Because the case was submitted on the basis of a fully stipulated record, we consider the legal issues presented on appeal de novo.

1. We have no difficulty concluding that the bequest to "male descendants of [Thomas, Sr.], bearing the name of Proctor" is limited to males whose surname is Proctor. Our conclusion is based on an examination of the plain meaning of the words "bearing the name," as well as on our determination that Thomas, Jr., intended to describe a class of male beneficiaries who would carry out his father's wish to perpetuate the family name. We keep in mind that, in construing language in a will, "[t]he fundamental object . . . is to ascertain the testator's intention from the whole instrument, attributing due weight to all its language, considered in light of the circumstances known to the testator at the time of its execution, and to give effect to that intent unless some positive rule of law forbids."

(a) There appear to be no cases in Massachusetts that conclusively define the phrase "bearing the name" in the context of a will or trust instrument.[12] Guidance may be found, however, in decisions of this court using that language to refer to circumstances where a testator clearly has sought to perpetuate a family name. Thus, in *Rogers v. Attorney Gen., supra*, this court characterized a requirement in a charitable trust provision that an institution be called "The Johnson Home for Aged Women" as a requirement that the home "bear the family name," in reflection of the testatrix's desire "to have the family name perpetuated." Similarly, in *Norris v. Loomis*, 215 Mass. 344 (1913), the testatrix left her home in trust for establishment as a home for the aged "to be called The Tabor Home." This court stated, "[t]he testatrix's desire that the Home should bear her name may be accomplished by perpetuating the name 'Tabor' in connection with the framing of a scheme for the administration of the trust."[13]

Decisions from other jurisdictions, cited by the parties, also demonstrate that the use of "bearing the name" in a will or a trust instrument generally carries an expectation that the family name will be perpetuated by its use as a last name. Considering a bequest

---

[12] The current version of Black's Law Dictionary 147 (7th ed.1999) defines the word "bear" as "to support or carry." Definitions contained in The New Webster Encyclopedic Dictionary of the English Language 70 (1952), an edition more closely approximating the age of the language at issue, include "to carry," "to bring forth," and "[to] convey."

[13] This court's use of that language in other contexts is also helpful. For example, in *Rusconi, petitioner*, 341 Mass. 167 (1960), some members of the Rusconi family objected to a petition by other family members to change their surname to Bryan. While concluding that the change of name must be permitted, this court nevertheless stated that "[w]e believe that most persons are entirely content, indeed proud, to bear the names which they acquired at birth."

to "each and every male child of my sons who shall by birth inherit and bear the name of Earle," the Supreme Court of Pennsylvania stated that the testator was influenced by his "pride in the family name and desire to have that name perpetuated by as many lineal male descendants of the blood and name as possible." *Earle Estate*, 369 Pa. 52, 54, 57 (1951). The Superior Court of the City of New York, in *Dominick v. Sayre*, 3 Sand. Ch. 555, 5 N.Y.Super.Ct. 555 (1850), construed the words "male descendants of my family of the name of Dominick" to mean male descendants of the testator's children "bearing the surname of Dominick." *Id.* at 569–570, 5 N.Y.Super.Ct. 555. See *Walker v. Brown*, 36 Ohio App. 463, 468 (1930) ("patent" that nephew must be willing to bear the name of "Charles Dexter" alone); *National Bank of Commerce v. Greenberg*, 195 Tenn. 217, 220 (1953) (condition imposed by testator that child's name not be changed violated when name changed from Eleanor Cohen to Eleanor Cohen Greenberg).[14]

(b) The entire will demonstrates Thomas, Jr.'s, intent to concentrate the family wealth in the male bloodlines.[15] In the trusts created by paragraphs THIRD, FOURTH, and FIFTH of his will, Thomas, Jr. (who had no issue), executed the power of appointment over three-fourths of the principal in his father's estate entirely in favor of his only brother's sons' branches of the family. One-fourth of the appointive property passed to his brother's daughter's branch, but in default of issue, passed back under the paragraph THIRD trust. It is significant that, although, at the time his will was executed in 1936, three males in the family had Proctor as a middle name, Thomas, Jr., made no mention of these persons in his will.

We conclude that the words "bearing the name of Proctor" connote Thomas, Jr.'s, desire that, in the event that his specific bequests in those trusts failed, the Proctor wealth should be carried on in the family name. The dearth of possible takers at the time of

---

[14] The decision of *Matter of Gardiner*, 69 N.Y.2d 66 (1986), has been cited as support for the proposition that the bequest was intended for males with Proctor as any part of their name. The Appellate Division had construed the words in a power of appointment "bearing the name Gardiner" to mean "bearing the surname of Gardiner." The Court of Appeals reasoned that the testator himself had used the words "bearing the surname Gardiner" in another part of his will. Because Thomas, Jr., made no separate reference in his will to "the surname of Proctor" or "the last name of Proctor," from which to discern a plain intent that "the name of Proctor" could include a first or middle name, we find the reasoning of that case to be unpersuasive.

[15] The record indicates that the will of Thomas, Sr., also demonstrated concern that the family name be perpetuated. His will left a substantial amount of money to Massachusetts General Hospital for construction of an "asylum for the insane" and provided that "one or more of said buildings shall be known as the 'Proctor Building.'" His will also provided that any property vesting in either Massachusetts General Hospital or Harvard College by virtue of any of its provisions "shall be known as the 'Thomas E. Proctor Fund.'"

his death in 1949 (the only living male descendants of Thomas, Sr., being his two nephews, Thomas 2d and John, both of whom were without issue), does not persuade us otherwise. At the time Thomas, Jr., executed his will in 1936, he had no reason to doubt that the name of Proctor would carry on. Although Thomas, Jr., himself had no son, his brother, James, had two. Of the two, Thomas 2d, was thirty-eight years of age and John, only thirty-six, already had an eight year old son (James 2d). It is true that, by the time Thomas, Jr., executed his second codicil in 1947, James and James 2d already had died, and so the potential for "male descendants of [Thomas, Sr.], bearing the [last] name of Proctor," theoretically, had been significantly reduced. Thomas, Jr., however, left that language unchanged. There is no evidence in the record, beyond language in his will, to discern his intentions at this point in time with respect to the remainder bequests at issue. We do not find it unreasonable, however, for Thomas, Jr., to have hoped that John (forty-six years of age) or Thomas 2d (forty-eight years of age and married) would yet beget a male heir.[16]

We reject Mattina's claim that, as the only living descendant of Thomas, Sr., with the last name of Proctor, she is entitled to the principal of the paragraph THIRD and FIFTH trusts.[17] The word "male" is unambiguous. In the face of this clear language, there is no basis to read into the will an implied intent that a female descendant should take the remainder in the absence of male descendants. Doing so would go beyond permissible limits. "While intent is the lodestar of testamentary construction, it cannot be used to displace what a will has said. Likewise, it cannot be used to supply a missing clause or to permit speculation as to what the testatrix might have intended had she foreseen or contemplated events as they actually turned out, but for which she made no provision."

2. By its express terms, paragraph ELEVENTH applies to the "foregoing trusts" in the will (including the paragraph THIRD and FIFTH trusts), but not to subsequent trusts such as the paragraph FIFTEENTH trust. It cannot, thus, operate to terminate the latter as of May 31, 1999. The judge properly rejected the argument that the use of the word "foregoing" was a scrivener's error. She reasoned

---

[16] It is conceivable that Thomas, Jr., wished to encourage males in his sisters' branches of the family to change their last names to Proctor. See *Goodwin v. New England Trust Co.*, 321 Mass. 502, 503 (1947) (testator with no sons conditioned bequests to daughters' sons on their changing their last name to his last name).

[17] The Equal Rights Amendment, suggested to favor the inclusion of female descendants of Thomas, Jr., within the designated category of male descendants, has no applicability here.

that, under the will as originally written in 1936, the paragraph FIFTEENTH trust contained no appointive assets, see note 4, supra, and, so, the testator had good reason to treat that trust differently from the trusts under paragraphs THIRD and FIFTH. The judge inferred, correctly in our view, that Thomas, Jr., plainly did not focus on the rule against perpetuities as it related to the paragraph FIFTEENTH trust.[18]

3. We next consider the operation of the rule against perpetuities on Mattina's life interest in the income of the paragraph FIFTEENTH trust. Under the terms of that trust, Mattina's life estate (and that of her brother, James 2d) was to come into effect on the death of their father, John. At the time the trust was created in 1949, Mattina was ascertained.[19] James 2d had died, leaving no issue. During John's lifetime, there was no event that would extinguish Msttina's life interest in the trust; on John's death, the only condition that would prevent her taking was her own death.

As has been discussed, the rule against perpetuities places a limit on how long certain types of trusts may continue. The rule, however, only applies to contingent interests that are not certain to vest within the perpetuities period. Further, the rule is against only the remoteness of vesting of an interest and not the remoteness of vesting in possession. See G.G. Bogert, Trusts and Trustees (rule is "concerned with vesting in interest or ownership, and not with vesting in possession [the right to occupy or enjoy the subject-matter of the transfer]"). In our view, that condition is not the type that would render her interest in the life estate contingent. Although the terms of paragraph FIFTEENTH describing the life estate appear to be conditional (e.g., "all to the survivor;" "if either . . . shall be deceased"), this language adds nothing to the nature of her interest; it merely states the obvious—one may not enjoy possession of a life interest unless one is living. See L.M. Simes & A.F. Smith, Future

---

[18] In considering the disposal of property subject to a power of appointment, the remoteness limitation of the rule against perpetuities is measured from the time the power is created and not when it is exercised by the donee. Thomas, Jr., thus, would have known that the perpetuities period with respect to the disposition of the appointive assets contained in the paragraph THIRD and FIFTH trusts would be measured by a life in being at the time of the creation of the power at Thomas, Sr.'s, death in 1894, and not the exercise of the power at his own death. Because the paragraph FIFTEENTH trust was intended to pass only his own nonappointive property, Thomas, Jr., would have expected that trust's termination date, for purposes of the rule against perpetuities, would be measured by his own death and not his father's.

[19] As stated in note 17, *supra*, the requirements of the rule are satisfied if it appears from the facts and circumstances existent when the appointment is exercised that the required vesting will take effect within the applicable perpetuities period, "although this may not have been certain at the death of the donor of the power." *Minot v. Paine, supra* at 522, 120 N.E. 167, citing J.C. Gray, Rule Against Perpetuities §§ 523, 524 (3d ed.).

Interests ("If the remainder is for life, the remainderman will enjoy the possession only if he survives the termination of the preceding life estate. Nevertheless the death of the remainderman is not regarded as a condition, but as a limitation of the remainderman's estate. Hence, there being no words of condition, the remainder for life . . . in an ascertained person is vested").[20] We conclude that Mattina's life estate in the paragraph FIFTEENTH trust vested in interest, although not in possession, when the trust was created in 1949. Because vesting in interest is what matters for purposes of the rule against perpetuities, the rule is not violated by Mattina's life estate.[21]

We reach this conclusion after consideration of past cases and numerous authorities on the subject of trusts. In *Minot v. Paine* (1918), the testatrix, Hannah F. Lee, died in 1865, by her will creating a trust to pay the income for life to her granddaughter, Julia Bryant, "and on her death to transfer and convey the same in fee to such persons and on such terms as [Julia] may direct and appoint." Julia, in her will, left property (a combination of her own and appointive) in trust for her husband for life, and, on his death, a certain share to be set aside and income to be paid to her son, Sumner, for life. On Sumner's death, Julia's will provided that a portion of the income be paid to his adopted daughter, Margaret. We find relevant the following statement by this court: "The gift of income to Sumner and to [ ] Margaret was vested, although the enjoyment of the latter was postponed until his decease. This appointment was good, since the rule against perpetuities does not apply to such vested gifts." *Id.* at 524. Similarly, the testator in *Seaver v. Fitzgerald*, 141 Mass. 401 (1886), bequeathed a lifetime interest in property to his daughter, Annie, and to her children, if

---

[20] The reasoning of this court in *Doggett v. New England Trust Co.*, 327 Mass. 167 (1951), illustrates the import of true conditional language: The will of Stephen H. Williams provided for the distribution of the remainder of his property, on the termination of successive life estates to his wife and children, to his living children or their issue and, in default of any then living children or issue, to his cousins, Alice A. Hobbs and Edith M. Hobbs, if living. Recognizing that no absolute gift of property was made to either cousin unless (1) there were no living child or issue of the testator and (2) each cousin herself was living, the Doggett court concluded that the cousins' interests were contingent only. The court distinguished cases "where there are no words importing survivorship or where there are simply interests in remainder preceded by interests of life beneficiaries." Here, had the gift to Mattina been outright and absolute, instead of a life estate, but only "if living," we indeed would agree that no vesting of her interest could take place until her father's death.

[21] Because we agree with Mattina that her life estate was vested at the time of its creation, we need not respond to her contention that we should reconsider this court's holding in *Fiduciary Trust Co. v. Mishou, supra,* that the perpetuities time limit for property interests created by the exercise of a power of appointment runs from the creation of the appointment power, and not from its exercise.

any. After Annie's death (or after the death of any child), the property was to pass to the Augustinian Society of Lawrence. This court held that the case presented no perpetuities problem. It reasoned that the "interest vested in the Augustinian Society . . . upon the testator's death, subject to the preceding life estates. All that is required by the rule against perpetuities is, that the estate or interest shall vest within the prescribed period. The right of possession may be postponed longer."

As explained by the author of one treatise, "if a fee owner dies leaving a will by which he creates a trust for A and his successors to last for twenty-five years, remainder to B (a person living at that time), the rule is not involved because the interest of B is vested at once as far as ownership is concerned, and the fact that he will not come into the enjoyment of the property until the lapse of twenty-five years is immaterial. There is no contingent interest involved." G.G. Bogert, Trusts and Trustees. See L.M. Simes & A.F. Smith, Future Interests ("it is not the certainty of the taking effect in possession which makes [an interest] vested but the certainty of the right to possession"); A.W. Scott & W.F. Fratcher, Trusts ("the rule against perpetuities deals with remoteness of vesting and not with the duration of vested interests").

Even assuming a measure of ambiguity in the matter, our preference for avoiding a perpetuities problem by construing an interest, where possible, as vested rather than contingent, resolves any uncertainty. The general doctrine of favoring construction to avoid the rule against perpetuities was well established at the time of Thomas, Jr.'s, death. Indeed, almost one century ago, in the case of *Gray v. Whittemore*, 192 Mass. 367 (1906), this court concluded that certain remainders vested "at the decease of [each of the testator's children], though the right of present possession was postponed in each case until the expiration of an intervening life estate [of the children's surviving spouses]." The *Gray* court stated: "Not only is this construction in accord with the manifest intent of the testator and effectual to accomplish the object which he had in view, but the opposite construction 'would defeat that purpose, by creating a perpetuity which the law would not sustain. In such a case, the court is bound to adopt that construction which will sustain the will and effectuate the objects of the testator.' "

In any case, there is no disagreement that the remainder interest stated in paragraph FIFTEENTH is void under the rule against perpetuities. Under the terms of the trust at the time it was created, potential beneficiaries of the remainder interest, to be identified at the death of the last survivor of Thomas, Jr.; John; James 2d; and Mattina, were living issue of Mattina, living issue of James 2d, or, alternatively, living male descendants of Thomas, Sr., bearing the name of Proctor. Because there was no way to predict in 1949, nor was it certain to be known, within the applicable perpetuities period, which of the above contingent beneficiaries, if indeed any at all, would ultimately qualify to take the principal of the paragraph FIFTEENTH trust, that remainder interest violates the rule against perpetuities. This determination, however, does nothing to alter the validity of Mattina's life estate.

4.   The parties agree that, if Thomas, Jr.'s, appointment of his father's property under the paragraph THIRD and FIFTH trusts is incomplete for lack of a beneficiary (as it is), the trusts lapse and the principal therein passes by resulting trust into the estate of Thomas, Jr. Under the doctrine of capture, "where the donee of a general power attempts to make an appointment that fails, but where, nevertheless, the donee has manifested an intent wholly to withdraw the appointive property from the operation of the instrument creating the power for all purposes and not merely for the purposes of the invalid appointment, the attempted appointment will commonly be effective to the extent of causing the appointive property to be taken out of the original instrument and to become in effect part of the estate of the donee of the power." The application of this doctrine "captures" the property that is the subject of the power and makes it part of the donee's estate. In this case, the rule directs that, on termination of the paragraph THIRD and FIFTH trusts, the trust principal passes, by way of a resulting trust, into the residue of Thomas, Jr.'s, estate and becomes part of the res of the paragraph FIFTEENTH trust.

Contrary to what the judge concluded in her memorandum of decision on the trustees' complaint, there is no perpetuities infirmity that would make this result impermissible. The origin of our disagreement is the judge's determination that Mattina's interest in the paragraph FIFTEENTH trust was contingent and, because it was not certain to vest within the perpetuities period, her current life estate in that trust was invalid. On that basis, the judge concluded (incorrectly) that the assets of the paragraph THIRD and FIFTH trusts could not pass into the paragraph FIFTEENTH trust. The judge reasoned, that to augment property in a life estate (in her view) void for remoteness under the rule against perpetuities, by the addition of assets from trusts terminated expressly to avoid the operation of the rule, would itself be impermissible under the rule. Because we reach a different conclusion with respect to the nature of Mattina's life estate in the paragraph FIFTEENTH trust, we see no obstacle presented by the rule against perpetuities, or otherwise, to prevent the assets of the paragraph THIRD and FIFTH trusts from passing, by way of resulting trust, into the residue of Thomas, Jr.'s, estate contained in the paragraph FIFTEENTH trust.

5. The judge's reformation of the paragraph FIFTEENTH trust, as reflected in part 3 and 4 of the amended judgment entered in the Probate and Family Court, to continue Mattina's life estate in effect until her death, and, on her death, to distribute the remainder of the paragraph FIFTEENTH trust outright to the heirs of Thomas, Jr., is entirely consistent with the result we reach. There appears to be agreement among the parties that the amended judgment accurately directs distribution of the paragraph FIFTEENTH trust to Thomas, Jr.'s, heirs, as of May 31, 1999, and sets forth the correct proportional interests of each.

Part 2 of the amended judgment is vacated, and part 1 of the amended judgment is vacated and replaced by the following: the life estates in the paragraph THIRD and FIFTH trusts, having terminated under the terms of paragraph ELEVENTH on May 31, 1999, the remainders of said trusts are added, as of that date, to the residuary trust of Thomas, Jr.'s, estate created by paragraph FIFTEENTH. Parts 3, 4, and 5 of the amended judgment are affirmed.[22]

So ordered.

---

2. REFORMS OF THE RULE

Various proposals have been made to end the RAP's "reign of terror".

(a) Specific Exceptions

Some states have enacted statutory exceptions to the Rule by preventing specific invalidating scenarios from being considered. Some statutes eliminate the unborn-widow problem by specifying that the word "widow" refers to a person alive when the interest is created. Some statutes eliminate the fertile-octogenarian problem by

---

[22] Costs and expenses on appeal are in the discretion of the Probate and Family Court.

specifying that only persons between certain ages can have a child. It is also possible for the courts of a state to allow a party to rebut the presumption that a given person can have a child. The Rule Against Perpetuities was originally a common-law rule. If it has not been codified, courts have the power to amend it. Even where the RAP has been codified, courts can avoid perpetuities problems by changing the way they construe instruments.

(b) *Cy Pres*

Another reform allows courts to apply their *cy pres* power to modify the terms of an instrument so that the interests do not violate the RAP. The goal, as with charitable trusts, is to come as close as possible to the intent of the transferor. One way to do that would be for the court to insert a saving clause. Another way is to modify the terms of each interest that violates the rule in a way that eliminates the possibility of vesting too late. One problem with *cy pres* is that it takes a judicial decision to accomplish it in each case, and the process of getting to that decision requires litigation when different changes benefit different parties.

(c) Wait and See for the Common-Law Period

Another group of reforms replace the what-might-happen approach with a wait-and-see approach to the Rule. The wait-and-see Rule might be summarized as follows: "An interest is void if it does vest too late." One problem with this approach is that it keeps some contingent interests alive longer, resulting in more uncertainty of ownership. In addition, the court must figure out which lives to wait out. Statutes can solve that latter problem by specifying the measuring lives to be followed, or the lives to wait out might be limited to those that might affect vesting of the interest. There are perhaps ten jurisdictions that wait and see for the common-law period.

(d) Wait and See for 90 Years, USRAP

The UPC has adopted a different variation on the wait-and-see approach, the Uniform Statutory Rule Against Perpetuities (USRAP). Under the USRAP, an interest is valid if it vests within 90 years. In some cases, this saves the administrative costs of following lives. However, this variation of wait and see still increases uncertainty compared to the what-might-happen approach of the common law. It also fails to save students from having to understand the concept of lives in being because the USRAP says that an interest is good if it vests in 90 years *or* if it is valid under the what-might-happen approach. The USRAP approach might also generate some litigation because it calls for the *cy pres* power to be applied to those interests that are void. The USRAP has been adopted in more than a third of the states.

Yet another problem with the USRAP is that it creates a tax trap, the USRAP tax trap. When the generation-skipping-transfer (GST) tax was enacted, old trusts were grandfathered so that they would not be taxed under the new tax. A trust can lose its grandfathering and become subject to the GST tax if the donee of a nongeneral power exercises the power in the wrong way. To retain the grandfather status under the GST tax, the donee of a special power should either turn the trust into a 90-year trust, not allowing any interest to vest after that, or make sure not to violate the common-law RAP when exercising the power. Which is better for your client in a particular case requires you to understand both versions of the RAP as well as the tax consequences.

(e) Abolition

A recently popular reform of the RAP is to partly abolish it. In more than half of the states, interests in personalty in trust are not subject to the RAP. In some of these states, the change is an option; a transferor may choose whether the Rule applies or not.

One effect of abolishing the RAP as applied to trusts is to create the possibility of trusts that last forever, sometimes called perpetual trusts or dynasty trusts. A settlor can place assets into a trust for the benefit of a child for life, with a special power in the child to appoint the corpus of the trust in further trust to the settlor's descendants. At the child's death, the child can appoint in further trust in the same manner. This can continue forever, with appointments being made that would violate the Rule Against Perpetuities if it had not been abolished. The generation-skipping transfer (GST) tax currently allows a couple to place more than $24,000,000 in a generation-skipping trust without incurring the GST tax. However, the GST tax exemption is scheduled to drop by about half in 2025. If the current exemption is not extended, we might see an increase in $24,000,000 perpetual trusts shortly before the expiration.

3. RAP POLICY

There are many considerations that are relevant to the question of whether and how to reform the RAP.

(a) Benefits of the RAP

The Rule Against Perpetuities increases social welfare in at least seven ways, with different benefits in different contexts.

The Rule increases alienability.

> Example 7.14: O devises Blackacre "to A for life, then to A's grandchildren." A has no children or grandchildren at O's death. The RAP invalidates the remainder in A's grandchildren, leaving a reversion in O's heir.

Alienability is beneficial in two ways. First, A and O's heir together can pledge Blackacre as security for a loan for improvements to make Blackacre more productive. Second, A and O's heir together can transfer Blackacre to a person who would derive more benefit from owning Blackacre.

The Rule reduces dead hand control of the behavior of the living.

> Example 7.15: O devises in spendthrift trust "to T to pay the income to A and A's heirs, but if the beneficiary ever drinks alcohol then to B's eldest heir living at the time." The Rule strikes the clause following the comma, freeing A and subsequent beneficiaries to drink alcohol.

The Rule reduces uncertainty.

> Example 7.16: O devises in trust "to T to manage the assets and pay the income to A and A's heirs, but if Indiana University ever wins another NCAA basketball championship, then to B and her heirs." The RAP strikes the clause after the comma. Unlike the example above, the problem is not that the trust will influence the behavior of A. The problem with this transfer is that, but for the RAP, A and A's heirs worry about losing income. Because of loss aversion, that possibility of loss likely generates more costs to A than the possibility of gain generates in benefits for B.

The Rule adds enjoyment from ownership of future interests.

> Example 7.17: In a jurisdiction where contingent remainders are indestructible, O devises in trust "to T for A for life, then for A's grandchildren." A is five years old. The

RAP strikes the interest in the grandchildren, leaving a reversion in O's heir, H. By shifting rights from the unborn to the living, the RAP increases the enjoyment from ownership of the rights. Until they are born, the grandchildren cannot possibly enjoy their interest. But H can enjoy the rights. While A is alive, H can enjoy holding or transferring the reversion. When A dies, H can enjoy possession.

The Rule avoids the problem of first-generation monopoly.

Example 7.18: Imagine 26 generations, from A to Z, and a trust with substantial assets in it. Consider two possible allocations of rights to income from the trust.

1) A1 (one person in generation A) decides who takes the income for all 25 generations B through Z, and decides that B1 followed by C1, and so forth to Z1, will take the income. The RAP prevents this possibility.

2) A1 decides that B3 takes, and so forth, M60 decides that N80 takes, and so forth until Y155 decides that Z2 takes.

We might prefer possibility (2) for a few reasons. First, A1 might get less enjoyment out of deciding that N1 takes in the N generation than M60 would get out of deciding that N80 takes in the N generation. M60 knows some of the people in the N generation and A1 knows none of the people in that generation. In addition, perhaps the allocating remainders for life has a marginal utility that declines like other experiences. (Been there, done that.) If so, A1 does not enjoy making A1's twentieth gift as much as M60 enjoys making M60's first gift. Second, Z2 might enjoy the rights more than Z1. Y155 would almost certainly have a better idea of the needs of the Z generation than A1 had. Moreover, Z2 might enjoy the gift more than Z1 because Z2 knows Y155 and Z1 has never heard of A1. Third, perhaps it is simply more fair to divide up control rather than to concentrate control in older generations.

The Rule reduces the problem of accumulations.

Example 7.19: In a state without a rule against accumulations of income, O devises "$1,000,000 in trust to accumulate for 500 years and then to distribute the corpus among my descendants then alive and under the age of 16." The Rule invalidates this trust and O's heir takes.

In this instance, the Rule allows the nearer descendants to decide between current consumption and future consumption. From a family point of view, perhaps some generation of descendants needs to consume simply to create a next generation. From a social point of view, some consumption during the 500 years might increase welfare. It seems unlikely that people of 500 years ago should have forgone consumption so that we would have more to consume today.

The Rule reduces the problem of multiplication of beneficiaries. If there are many, the administrative costs of finding them could be high. The Rule reduces those costs. See the example just above.

(b) Costs of the RAP

What are the costs of the Rule Against Perpetuities?

There is injustice if some people take when the transferor intended others to take. Few people will know of the injustice, but it could qualify as an injustice nevertheless.

The Rule makes some transferors less happy by preventing them from controlling the future. Is this a major source of discontent? According to Professor Leach, lawyers can accomplish their client's goals in most cases. Moreover, sometimes the client goes to the grave unaware of the RAP's constraint because the lawyer is unaware that an interest violates the Rule.

Another cost of the Rule is that some grantees will learn that they have lost their gifts. How often this happens is unclear. Have you ever heard of it? Most of the time, the error will be discovered by the lawyer or trustee and sometimes there will be no point in telling the would-be beneficiary that she lost her interest. It would be helpful to have empirical data on how often this occurs.

Sometimes transferors become unhappy when they learn that the Rule has upset their plans. If they are still alive, they might be able to redirect the voided interests, mitigating their unhappiness. Other times, they are dead, and it is too late to do anything about the interests voided by the Rule. The diminution in their happiness is questionable, however, because they are, as just mentioned, dead.

All told, the benefits of the Rule outweigh its costs. If the Rule is abolished, is there much chance a legislature will bring it back to life? Perhaps we should be cautious in eliminating a potentially beneficial rule that would be hard to resurrect or re-create when the need for it becomes more obvious.

B. PROTECTION OF FAMILY MEMBERS

Over the centuries, the law in American states has offered various forms of protection for family members.

1. FAMILY ACCESS TO BENEFICIAL INTERESTS IN TRUSTS

We saw one form of family protection above in the discussion of trusts. When a beneficiary of a trust is past due in payment of support to a child or spouse or maintenance to a former spouse, that child, spouse, or former spouse might seek payment from the beneficiary's trust. These family creditors sometimes have the power to reach trust assets in a spendthrift or discretionary trust that would be shielded from the claims of ordinary creditors. Whether family creditors can compel payment from the trust depends on their status and the type of trust held for the debtor. UTC § 503 and UTC § 504, discussed above, treat all three groups as exception creditors, but some states do not give them equal treatment. Moreover, even when exception creditors can pierce spendthrift protection, they do not necessarily have the power to compel a distribution from a discretionary trust.

When courts allow family members to reach trust assets, they sometimes justify this result by saying that the duties to the children, spouse, and former spouse, like the duty to pay taxes to the government, are not mere debts to a creditor, but reflect some deeper duty. But, whatever the doctrinal reasoning, the law reflects a policy that exception creditors should be given better treatment than other sorts of claimants to the assets in the trust. The bottom line is that the intent of the trust's creator, whether the dead hand of the past or a living settlor, is outweighed by the interest in allowing these creditors to reach the beneficiary's interest.

2. SURVIVING CHILDREN OF THE DECEDENT

Another way that the law protects family members is by giving them a right to some of a decedent's assets, sometimes in spite of the intent of the decedent. Children of employees have a right to Social Security in some situations. Along with surviving spouses, children may also be protected under the homestead allowance, exempt property, and family allowance, which provide a basket of assets before the decedent's unsecured creditors take any of the decedent's estate. In some states, the homestead right of children is substantially greater than it is under the UPC. Other than that, however, American law (except in Louisiana) offers little to children whose dead parents decided to exclude them from the family assets, even in situations where the children would have a right of support if the parent were alive. Indeed, under the UPC rules of intestate succession, children take nothing when the decedent is survived by a spouse whose children are the same as the decedent's children. By forced heirship under the civil law and by family maintenance under the common law, the laws of succession in some countries abroad do more to protect children from the financial and psychological harms that flow from disinheritance.

3.   SURVIVING SPOUSES

Protections for surviving spouses exceed those for children. The homestead allowance and exempt property provisions give the spouse priority. Social Security supports not only surviving spouses but some former spouses as well. Pension plans covered by ERISA must provide an annuity for a surviving spouse of the covered employee. Other important protections for surviving spouses vary across the states.

(a) Community Property

Community property forces spouses to share income during their marriage, with the result that some of that income might, it is to be hoped, still be available for support after the death of one spouse. As discussed earlier, community-property rules treat spouses as partners in the earning of income. Income to one spouse, from labor during the marriage and from community property, is shared by both spouses. As a result, in the nine states where community property is automatic, there may be some protection for the surviving spouse no matter what the decedent wanted.

Two types of spousal support, an ERISA pension and community property, came into conflict in *Boggs v. Boggs*, 520 U.S. 833 (1997). Interpreting ERISA to preempt state law, the majority held that a surviving subsequent spouse's rights in a decedent's pension overrode a former spouse's community-property rights in that pension, which the former spouse had devised to the couple's children. The employee's children lost to the employee's surviving subsequent spouse. Should the federal pension law override the state law allocation of half of the community property (in the pension) to each spouse?

(b) Common-Law Rights of Surviving Spouses

In the past, when land was the primary form of wealth, dower and curtesy provided important support after one spouse died. A surviving spouse's dower right is a life estate in one-third of the lands of which the decedent was seised of an inheritable interest during the marriage. A transfer of the realty by the owner did not eliminate the spouse's inchoate dower right, and that right became possessory upon the death of the spouse. As a result, the protection for surviving spouses tended to clog up transfers of land. And because dower does not apply to personalty, which makes up relatively more of today's wealth, it provides less protection now than it once did. For these reasons, dower has been eliminated in all but a few states, following curtesy to the graveyard for common-law spousal interests.

By contrast, the tenancy by the entirety remains vigorous in about one-half of the states that do not have mandatory community property. Tenancies by the entirety protect surviving spouses by means of the right of survivorship. Under the common law and still today in some states, the tenancy by the entirety cannot be severed unilaterally (except by divorce). As a result, one spouse cannot prevent the other spouse from succeeding to the assets held in tenancy by the entirety.

(c) The Statutory Elective Share

The elective share is the primary protection for surviving spouses in all non-community-property states except Georgia. In those states, the elective share (also called the forced share) is probably the greatest constraint on freedom of disposition today.

One reason legislatures have enacted elective-share statutes is to give surviving spouses a fair share of the decedent's estate. Another reason is to prevent spouses from being left with no means of support other than the state. The elective-share statutes give the surviving spouse an opportunity to take a share of the decedent's net probate estate despite the decedent's intent to provide less or nothing to the surviving spouse. (The first half of the following opinion was presented in the materials on attestation and dependent relative revocation.)

KIRKEBY V. COVENANT HOUSE

Court of Appeals of Oregon, 1998
970 P.2d 241

HASELTON, J.

* * *

We proceed to the cross-appeal by Glenn Kirkeby, individually and as Orrin's personal representative. The cross-appeal raises three assignments of error: (1) The trial court erred in failing to give effect to the written election pursuant to ORS 114.105 that Orrin signed before his death but that was filed after his death. (2) The court erred in probating the "Meleen note" as the property of Margaret's estate, rather than determining the note to be joint tenancy property not subject to probate. (3) The court erred in treating the distribution of "interest earnings" under Margaret's will to be a distribution of net, rather than gross, income.

For the reasons described in the cross-respondents' briefs, including certain representations and admissions by Orrin as to the ownership of the "Meleen note," we reject the second assignment of error without further elaboration. We proceed to the other two.

The disposition of the first assignment of error turns on the proper construction of ORS 114.105 and ORS 114.145. ORS 114.105 provides, in part:

> "(1) If a decedent is domiciled in this state at the time of death and dies testate, the *surviving spouse* of the decedent has a right to elect to take [against the will] the share provided by this section." (Emphasis added.)

Here, it is undisputed that Margaret was domiciled in Oregon at the time of her death and, as determined above, that she died testate. Thus, Orrin, as the surviving spouse, could elect to take against Margaret's will.

ORS 114.145 provides that the "surviving spouse is considered to have elected to take under the will" unless,

> "within 90 days after the date of the admission of the will to probate or 30 days after the date of the filing of the inventory, whichever is later, *the surviving spouse serves* on the personal representative or the attorney of the personal representative *and files* in the estate proceeding a statement that the surviving spouse elects to take under ORS 114.105 instead of under the will. The *surviving spouse* may bar any

right to take under ORS 114.105 by filing in the estate proceeding a writing, signed by the spouse, electing to take under the will." (Emphasis added.)

Cross-appellant argues that a surviving spouse's right to elect against the will of the deceased spouse, ORS 114.105, is a "property right" that, upon Orrin's death, passed to his estate, which, in turn, could file the election, ORS 114.145. Cross-respondents respond, *inter alia*, that "an election to take against a will is a right personal to the surviving spouse that expires if not exercised during his or her life."[16]

The text of ORS 114.105 and ORS 114.145 specifically provides that the "surviving spouse" may make, serve, and file the election. There is nothing in those provisions that suggests that the election can be served or filed by any other person, including the heirs of the surviving spouse. *See* ORS 174.010 (court is not to "insert what has been omitted, or to omit what has been inserted").

The statutory context confirms that construction. ORS 114.155 provides:

"An election under ORS 114.105 may be filed on behalf of a financially incapable surviving spouse by a court acting under ORS 125.650 [exercising any power that could be exercised by guardian or conservator to enter protective order] or by the conservator of the estate of the spouse. The court or conservator may elect against the will only if additional assets are needed for the reasonable support of the surviving spouse, taking into account the probable needs of the spouse, the provisions of the will, any nonprobate property arrangements made by the decedent for the support of the spouse and any other assets, whether or not owned by the spouse, available for such support. The election is subject to the approval of the court, with or without notice to other interested persons."

Implicit in that provision are two operative principles. First, to the extent the legislature intends to permit any exceptions to the general requirement that the election must be served and filed by the surviving spouse, it does so explicitly. ORS 114.155 is the only such statute. Second, and in all events, the election is ultimately for

---

[16] Cross-respondents also emphasize that Orrin told Kirby, the attorney, to "hold" the election and not to file it.

the surviving spouse's financial benefit and, thus, must be filed during the surviving spouse's lifetime.

We note, finally, that, to permit the personal representative of the surviving spouse to exercise the statutory election could-as it would here-permit the heirs of that spouse to frustrate the testamentary scheme of the decedent spouse. ORS 112.227 provides:

> "The intention of a testator as expressed in the will of the testator controls the legal effect of the dispositions of the testator. The rules of construction expressed in this section, ORS 112.230 and 112.410 apply unless a contrary intention is indicated by the will."

Obviously, the statutory election mechanism of ORS 114.105 qualifies ORS 112.227 by permitting a surviving spouse to at least partially modify or defeat the decedent's testamentary scheme. Nevertheless, nothing in ORS 114.105, or in the Probate Code generally, suggests that that statute can be employed as a device for one spouse's heirs to profit at the expense of the others, subverting ORS 112.227.

We thus conclude that the right of election was personal to Orrin and could only be exercised during Orrin's lifetime. *Cf. Varner et al. v. Portland Trust Bank,* 210 Or. 658, 664 (1957) ("[A] probate homestead itself and its enjoyment are creatures of claim and unless exercised by those entitled to do so and at the time and in the manner provided by statute, the probate homestead and its incident of ownership, possession and enjoyment are lost."). Accordingly, the trial court did not err in refusing to give effect to the purported election.[17]

* * *

Affirmed on appeal and cross-appeal.

The elective-share rules vary widely across the states on a number of important dimensions: What is the share allowed under the election? To what assets does the elective share apply? Does the statute consider the assets held by or passing to the survivor in determining the share that the survivor can take? Under what circumstances should waivers of the elective share be effective?

---

[17] Our conclusion in that regard comports with decisions from many other jurisdictions.

JOHNSON V. LA GRANGE STATE BANK

Supreme Court of Illinois, 1978
383 N.E.2d 185

RYAN, J.

These consolidated cases involve the validity of *inter vivos* transfers of property by one spouse against the marital rights of the surviving spouse in the property transferred.

Johnson v. La Grange State Bank, cause Nos. 49875 and 49876, concerns an *inter vivos* trust created by Eleanor Johnson for the ultimate benefit of several relatives and various charities. The second case, *Havey v. Patton*, involves savings accounts created by Myra Havey in which she named her sister-in-law as joint tenant. The plaintiff in each case is the surviving husband. Each has claimed his respective statutory share in the assets transferred.

In the *Johnson* case, plaintiff, H. Franklin Johnson, and Eleanor Johnson had been married in 1937 and for more than 36 years enjoyed a happy marriage. The plaintiff, who had accumulated an estate in excess of $2,000,000, was very generous towards his wife and quite frequently gave her substantial gifts of money and securities. Mrs. Johnson relied on her husband's business acumen and followed his advice in making investments, as well as in managing the accumulated gifts which he gave her. The trial court found, and it is not disputed, that there was no estrangement or feeling of antipathy of one spouse toward the other.

In 1966, Mrs. Johnson learned that she had cancer; she later learned that her life expectancy was less than five years. Prior to 1969 the Johnsons, who had no children, had simple reciprocal wills which provided that in the event of the death of either of them, the survivor would receive the decedent's entire estate. On February 5, 1969, the Johnsons executed new wills in which Johnson provided that his wife's relatives would receive 20% of his estate if his wife did not survive him, and Mrs. Johnson provided that her entire estate was left to her family if Johnson did not survive her.

In the summer of 1970, Mrs. Johnson executed a new will and again in February of 1972, seven months before her death, she executed another will and simultaneously executed a revocable *inter vivos* trust in which she placed in trust substantially all of her assets. The will, by the residuary clause, poured the balance of her estate into the *inter vivos* trust. By the terms of the trust, Mrs. Johnson named herself trustee of certain properties (stocks, bonds, etc.). The entire income of the trust was to be paid to her during her lifetime, and she reserved the power to invade the principal of the trust, as she in her discretion saw fit. She retained broad powers to invest, reinvest, divide, and distribute the trust property and likewise retained the power to alter, amend or modify the trust provisions in any manner. The La Grange State Bank was designated as successor trustee to act upon her death or disability. The trust instrument provided the method of determining when she would be considered disabled. Upon her death, the successor trustee was to distribute assets of the trust to Mrs. Johnson's mother, sister, niece, and certain named charities. The trust document included a provision whereby her husband, plaintiff, was to receive so much of the income and principal to meet any emergency situation for his reasonable support, medical, and burial expenses. The trustee, however, was advised to consider other sources available to him and the needs of Mrs. Johnson's mother and sister before making any such emergency payments.

In 1972, Mrs. Johnson moved to Florida, where she lived until her death in September 1972. Her will was admitted to probate in Florida on October 19, 1973. During the pendency of the Florida proceeding, the plaintiff instituted an action in the circuit court of Cook County against the trustee and the trust beneficiaries to set aside the *inter vivos* trust established by his wife, insofar as it deprived him of his marital rights in the property held in trust. Plaintiff sought to impose a constructive trust on the trust assets to the extent of his claim. In count I of his three-count amended complaint he alleged that, as the surviving spouse, the trust was illusory and fraudulent as to him and that he was therefore entitled to receive a statutory one-half share of the original corpus of the trust. Count II alleged that the decedent established the trust with the intention of defeating plaintiff's marital interest in the settlor's personal estate. Count III alleged that the decedent acted in an intentional, deliberate, and fraudulent manner for the purpose of denying plaintiff his statutory share of the decedent's estate. The court allowed defendants' motion to dismiss counts I and II of the amended complaint, but allowed count III to stand. Trial was held without a jury. At the conclusion of the plaintiff's case, judgment was entered for the defendants. The trial court also found no support for the plaintiff's contentions that decedent's actions were fraudulent and held that the plaintiff's allegations were made in bad faith and without reasonable cause, and assessed attorney's fees and costs against the plaintiff. Plaintiff appealed from both orders.

The First District Appellate Court reversed the trial court, holding that an *inter vivos* trust may not defeat the marital rights of a settlor's surviving spouse where the settlor effectively retains ultimate control of the trust assets. Also, since the appellate court sustained the plaintiff's cause of action, the trial court's judgment assessing attorney's fees and expenses against the plaintiff as a sanction under section 41 of the Civil Practice Act was accordingly reversed.

The second case in this appeal, *Havey v. Patton* involves certain joint accounts created by the decedent, Myra Havey. Myra Havey and Paul Havey were married for more than 35 years at the time of Mrs. Havey's death in 1972. They had been living apart and had experienced marital difficulties. In July 1972, she converted a savings account standing in her name at a bank to a joint account with defendant Frances B. Patton, her sister-in-law, and likewise opened a joint savings account with this defendant at a savings and loan association and purchased a jointly held certificate of deposit in another savings association. She also created a joint tenancy in some real estate which is not involved in this appeal. Defendant Patton never contributed any funds to the accounts, nor did she have the power to withdraw from the accounts except to pay Mrs. Havey's bills. The record discloses, moreover, that Mrs. Havey created the accounts at a time when she knew she was terminally ill, and that the accounts were intended by Mrs. Havey to give her property to defendant Patton and keep it from her husband after her death.

Mrs. Havey executed her will in 1972. She named defendant Patton as executor and ordered her estate to be divided between defendant Patton and Paul Havey. The fourth paragraph of her will provided as follows:

> "I have set up certain accounts in joint tenancy with the right of survivorship which are to pass by operation of law and are not to be made part of my estate in probate."

Mrs. Havey's probate estate totaled approximately $4,000, which was not enough to cover the expenses incurred by the last illness, funeral expenses, and cost of administration. The joint accounts held with defendant Patton, however, contained $47,509.77.

Paul Havey renounced his wife's will. He died during the administration of the estate; subsequently his executor, John F. Havey, filed this action for declaratory judgment alleging that the aforementioned creation of joint accounts by Mrs. Havey fraudulently deprived Paul Havey of his marital rights in the property. The trial court rejected this contention and entered judgment for defendant Patton.

The Fourth District Appellate Court, with one justice dissenting, affirmed the decision of the trial court, holding that there was sufficient donative intent on behalf of the decedent to sustain a gift of the joint accounts to defendant Patton. The court noted that the fact that the accounts were created for the express purpose of depriving Paul Havey of his interest in the property did not support his contention that as to him the decedent's intent was fraudulent.

* * *

Plaintiffs in both of these cases rely on this court's opinion in *Montgomery v. Michaels* (1973), 54 Ill.2d 532. In *Montgomery*, the issue was whether certain savings account trusts ("Totten trusts") created by the decedent for the benefit of her children by a former marriage defrauded the surviving spouse of his marital rights. The decedent had provided that the accounts were to be paid to the named beneficiaries upon her death, but during her lifetime she retained complete control over the accounts and made deposits in and withdrawals from them. This court held that while Totten trusts were not invalid *per se*, such trusts were ineffective to defeat a surviving spouse's statutory or forced share in the estate of his deceased spouse. The opinion stated:

> "In the case at bar the settlor was also the trustee. During her lifetime she retained absolute, unqualified control over the bank accounts, and possessed and exercised all incidents of complete ownership, including the right to receive interest payable thereon and withdraw the principal thereof. The enjoyment of the proceeds of the accounts by the beneficiary or beneficiaries named therein would arise only upon the death of the settlor-trustee with the accounts remaining intact.
>
> Under these circumstances, the expressed statutory policy of protecting a surviving spouse's statutory share in the estate should prevail, regardless of the intent of the deceased spouse in creating the savings-account trust."

* * *

The "retention of ownership" test of *Montgomery* was limited on its facts to Totten trusts. A Totten trust, in effect, purports to change ownership of the deposited funds to the designated beneficiaries upon the death of the settlor. The requirements for their establishment are very informal. The enjoyment of the beneficiaries is provisional and tentative, since there are no limitations or qualifications on the ability of the settlor to withdraw funds from the account. Inevitably, a great deal of control and ownership is reserved to the settlor over the funds. These are valid reasons for invalidating such trusts *per se* insofar as they relate to the claims of the surviving spouse. Because the degree of ownership by the trustee is customarily so great, public policy in favor of protecting surviving spouses permits the categorical conclusion that such arrangements are testamentary in character and are ineffective to deprive surviving spouses of their lawful claims.

The courts of this State have readily upheld *inter vivos* trust arrangements where the settlor has named himself trustee and retained indicia of ownership and control. (*Farkas v. Williams* (1955), 5 Ill.2d 417.) There is no contention in this case that the trust was not a valid *inter vivos* trust. It is only contended that it is invalid to the extent that it deprived the plaintiff of his marital rights in the property. With the exception of *Montgomery v. Michaels* and the rules therein concerning the validity of Totten trusts, no general principles have emerged invalidating such other *inter vivos* transfers *per se* in respect to the marital rights of surviving spouses. Rather, whether the transfer of property in trust is vulnerable to attack depends on whether the trust employed is colorable and illusory and a fraud on marital rights. This determination necessarily turns on the facts of each individual case. We therefore reject the reasoning of the appellate court that our decision in *Montgomery* is controlling in this case.

In *Montgomery*, the court acknowledged that, in some instances, whether the trust is invalid as to a surviving spouse is determined by a consideration of all the facts and circumstances which might be indicative of an intent to defraud the surviving spouse of his statutory share and cited *Rose v. St. Louis Union Trust Co.* (1969), 43 Ill.2d 312. The defendants in this court likewise urge that *Rose* adopted the "intent to defraud" test in determining if an *inter vivos* trust is invalid as to the surviving spouse. *Rose* did in fact apply the "intent to defraud" test; however, it is important to note that *Rose* was applying Missouri law, and under the Missouri statute and decisions a voluntary conveyance which a surviving spouse may set aside as fraudulent is one that is executed with the intent and purpose of defeating the marital rights of the spouse in the property conveyed. In Illinois, however, and by the weight of authority in other jurisdictions, the owner of property has an absolute right to dispose of his property during his lifetime in any manner he sees fit, and he may do so even though the transfer is for the precise purpose of minimizing or defeating the statutory marital interests of the spouse in the property conveyed. Such a gift or transfer is not vulnerable or subject to attack by the surviving spouse unless the transaction is a sham and is "colorable" or "illusory" and is tantamount to a fraud. *Holmes v. Mims* (1953), 1 Ill.2d 274.

The general rule stated by this court in *Holmes* is widely accepted and has been generally applied by the courts of this State. The difficulty arises, as is so often the case, in the application of the general rule. The use of the phrase "intent to defraud" is confusing and carries a connotation not relevant to the question to be resolved. When the cases discuss fraud on the marital rights of the surviving spouse, they are not considering fraud in the traditional sense. Also, a minority view, in considering whether there has been a fraud on the marital property rights, has held that any conveyance made with the intent to minimize or defeat the marital rights of the surviving spouse in the property conveyed is presumed fraudulent. As noted above, this is the rule followed in Missouri, and the rule that was followed by this court in *Rose*, applying Missouri law. In Illinois and in a majority of jurisdictions, however, as previously noted, such a conveyance is not presumptively a fraud on the surviving spouse.

Although not applicable to this case, Public Act 80 737, approved and effective September 16, 1977, provides:

"Sec. 1. An otherwise valid transfer of property, in trust or otherwise, by a decedent during his or her lifetime, shall not, in the absence of an *intent to defraud*, be invalid, in whole or in part, on the ground that it is *illusory* because the deceased retained any power or right with respect to the property.

Sec. 2. This Act takes effect upon becoming a law and applies to savings account trusts established on or after its effective date, and as to all other transfers this Act is *declaratory of existing law*." (Emphasis added.)

This enactment has thus retained "intent to defraud" as necessary to be established in proving the invalidity of a transfer on the ground that it was illusory. The Act also states that except as to savings account trusts (Totten trusts) its requirement is declaratory of existing law. What effect the amendment had on our holding in *Montgomery* is not before us.

Since "intent to defraud" in the context of these cases does not carry the traditional meaning of fraud, and since a property owner may convey his property for the precise purpose of defeating his spouses's [*sic*] marital property rights, the meaning of "intent to defraud" must be construed in connection with the words "illusory" and "colorable" with which it is usually associated in the cases cited. It has been suggested that the intent by which a transfer is to be tested should not be stated in the confusing terms of "intent to defraud," but it should be tested by the intent of the donor either to retain or to part with the ownership of property.

The cases do not always differentiate between the terms "illusory" and "colorable." However, it is acknowledged, within the sphere of the subject that we are now discussing, that an illusory transfer is one which takes back all that it gives, while a colorable transfer is one which appears absolute on its face but due to some secret or tacit understanding between the transferor and the transferee the transfer is, in fact, not a transfer because the parties intended that ownership be retained by the transferor.

The intent to defraud is found in the nature of the transfer, whether it be illusory or colorable. In either event the transfer is a fraud on the marital rights because the transferor in reality had no intent to convey any present interest in the property but, in fact, intended to retain complete ownership. Although the spouse's marital rights can be defeated by an actual transfer, a purported transfer whereby the owner does not intend to convey a present interest, but intends to retain ownership, is evidence of an intent to defraud. See *Newman v. Dore* (1937), 275 N.Y. 371.

* * *

We conclude that an *inter vivos* transfer of property is valid as against the marital rights of the surviving spouse unless the transaction is tantamount to a fraud as manifested by the absence of donative intent to make a conveyance of a present interest in the property conveyed. Without such an intent the transfer would simply be a sham or merely a colorable or illusory transfer of legal title.

    * * *

With these considerations in mind, we now turn our attention to whether the transfers in question are vulnerable to attack by the surviving spouses, first in *Johnson v. La Grange State Bank*, and then in *Havey v. Patton*.

We are satisfied that the *inter vivos* trust created by Eleanor Johnson was not colorable, illusory, or tantamount to fraud. The fact cannot be denied that as trustee of a revocable trust she retained a significant degree of control over the trust assets. However, the form of control which the donor retains over the trust does not make it invalid. In addition, it is well established that the retention by the settlor of the power to revoke, even when coupled with the reservation of a life interest in the trust property, does not render the trust inoperative.

Nevertheless, the facts of a particular case may show that the trust in question, while ostensibly valid, is in actuality a sham transaction, essentially testamentary in character, and therefore invalid. In this case, the facts do not support such a conclusion. Mrs. Johnson was certainly well aware of the fact that her husband had a net worth of over $2,000,000, and was, and would most likely continue to be, well provided for. She was concerned, however, with the welfare of certain of her relatives, particularly her mother, who was dependent on her. She formalized a declaration of trust, with advice of counsel, for the benefit of her relatives. The declaration of trust immediately created an equitable interest in the beneficiaries, although the enjoyment of the interest was postponed until Mrs. Johnson's death and subject to her power of revocation. This, however, did not make the transfer illusory. And the power of control that she had as trustee was not an irresponsible power; she was charged with a fiduciary duty in respect to the beneficiaries' interest, and her management and administration of the assets in trust could only be exercised in accordance with the terms of the trust.

The conclusion of the appellate court that Mrs. Johnson parted with nothing during her life is incorrect. The trust directed that the trustee, in event of the grantor's disability, was to use the income and principal of the trust estate for the grantor's benefit and for the benefit of any person dependent on her. The trust instrument provided that the successor trustee was to assume the office of trustee during her lifetime should she become disabled, and the instrument set forth the means of determining her disability. There is no evidence that Mrs. Johnson made any withdrawals from the principal or otherwise exercised any of her reserved powers to deplete the trust assets. These facts tend to show that she intended to make a valid and effective transfer at the time her declaration of trust was executed. We find that a valid transfer was effected under the trust.

We have yet to address two additional points raised by the appeal in *Johnson v. La Grange State Bank*. The plaintiff argues that a constructive trust should be imposed on the trust property because the assets were fraudulently obtained from the plaintiff. In this regard, he argues that he parted with the assets in the expectation that they would be returned to him upon his wife's death.

The allegations of the amended complaint, which would support the imposition of a constructive trust, were found to be not supported by the evidence both in the trial court and in the appellate court. We agree with this determination. The Johnsons had a warm and loving marriage, and the evidence shows that Johnson's frequent gifts to his wife were out of his concern for her welfare. They were made with no strings attached. He had some knowledge of his wife's contact with her attorneys for the purpose of preparing a trust instrument and a will, and the plaintiff elected not to involve himself in the matter. These facts, along with other evidentiary matter in the record, show that there was an absence of fraud in this case. The plaintiff's attempt to impose a constructive trust on the assets in question must fail.

* * *

The principles set forth above relevant to the validity of the transfer under scrutiny in *La Grange State Bank v. Johnson* apply in *Havey v. Patton*. The dispositive inquiry is whether the deposit of funds in the joint accounts created by Myra Havey in which she named her sister-in-law joint tenant qualify as complete and effective *inter vivos* transfers, or whether the establishment of the accounts was illusory or colorable and in the nature of a sham transaction. The appellate court affirmed the trial court's finding that there was sufficient donative intent to sustain the gift inherent in the joint account. We affirm the appellate court.

The fact that Mrs. Havey contributed all the funds to the accounts and retained the right to withdraw them does not negate the existence of donative intent required to validate a gift. Thus, as far as the present case is concerned, we do not believe that Mrs. Havey's right to use the funds, or her direction that her sister-in-law have no immediate use of the funds, demonstrates a lack of donative intent. Rather, where joint accounts are concerned, the creation of the joint tenancy accounts is evidence of donative intent and is sufficient to establish ownership in the survivor upon the death of the original owner, in absence of evidence to the contrary.

The joint account agreements were made pursuant to the provisions of "An Act to revise the law in relation to joint rights and obligations.", and by their very terms indicated the existence of a valid gift. Mrs. Havey was terminally ill at the time she created the accounts, and intended for her sister-in-law, rather than her husband, from whom she had separated, to receive the funds therein. As we have indicated, the fact that the donor executes a valid gift for the express purpose of defeating the rights of the surviving spouse does not make the transfer vulnerable to attack by such spouse. She needed money enough to sustain herself through the period of her terminal illness, a period of about four months, and then intended for her sister-in-law to have enjoyment of the funds. Under these circumstances, it cannot be said that the accounts were made solely for the depositor's convenience. Mrs. Havey accomplished her goal of intending to create a valid present interest for her sister-in-law in the funds.

In summation, the holding of the appellate court in *Johnson v. La Grange State Bank* is reversed except insofar as it reverses the order of the circuit court of Cook County which assessed attorney's fees and costs under section 41 of the Civil Practice Act, and in that regard, the appellate court is affirmed. The holding of the appellate court in *Havey v. Patton* is affirmed.

The first wave of elective-share statutes, some of which are still in effect, applied only to the net probate estate. This left decedents with the option to avoid the elective share by making inter vivos transfers that would keep the assets out of the probate estate. Courts in many jurisdictions closed some of the loopholes by adopting doctrines that declared some transfers to be illusory or to be a fraud on the spouse's interest, allowing the transfers to be reversed and the assets to be brought back into the probate estate and thus within the elective share. Courts have varied in their application of these doctrines, some being more aggressive than others in preventing the decedent from avoiding the elective share. What transfers did *Johnson v. La Grange State Bank* allow spouses to employ for circumvention the elective-share statute?

Spouses that do not work for pecuniary income often contribute mightily to the pecuniary income produced by the other spouse. In addition, there are many forms of income and wealth, only some of which are pecuniary. If one spouse raises children and the other brings in a paycheck, the spouses have implicitly, if not explicitly, said by their choices that the raising of the children and other in-kind contributions to family welfare are more valuable than that spouse's paycheck would have been. Keep in mind the principle of comparative advantage, which says that it is entirely possible that the in-kind contributor might be better at earning money but is not doing so because that same spouse is much better at taking care of children. If the in-kind contributor to household production were to die first, the paycheck contributor would still be left with many of the in-kind benefits that were generated by the decedent. The in-kind provider cannot devise the children and family harmony to someone outside the family unit. In the opposite case, unless there is a legal limitation, the paycheck contributor can direct assets away from the survivor. Would that be fair?

Keep both fairness in dividing family wealth and financial security in mind. They are related in that both are about financial assets, but they are not the same thing. Do we have enough facts in either of the two Illinois matters above to determine whether the outcomes leave the survivor with a fair share of the family wealth? Do we have enough facts to tell whether the survivors are left with sufficient support for financial security?

In 1969, the UPC employed the concept of the "augmented estate" to prevent many sorts of circumventions of the surviving spouse's elective share. The UPC augmented the probate estate by adding specified forms of transfers during the marriage, such as substantial gifts, revocable trusts, and other will substitutes, but not insurance payable to persons other than the surviving spouse. The UPC also took into account many of the survivor's assets received from the decedent, including insurance proceeds, but not other independent wealth of the survivor.

The elective share of the surviving spouse has undergone important revisions since the 1969 UPC, further expanding the assets that are included in the augmented estate. The assets held by the surviving spouse at the death of the decedent are now included whether derived from the decedent or not. And life insurance payable to others has lost its loophole and is now included within the UPC's augmented estate, although that loophole persists in many states. Today, there is huge variation in the ambit of the elective share. As always, it is essential to check your local code and judicial decisions.

Below is an excerpt from Part 2 (Elective Share of the Surviving Spouse) of UPC Article II (Intestacy, Wills, and Donative Transfers). The excerpt discusses the rationales for the UPC elective-share provisions and changes from earlier versions.

UPC ELECTIVE SHARE OF SURVIVING SPOUSE

General Comment

The elective share of the surviving spouse was fundamentally revised in 1990 and was reorganized and clarified in 1993 and 2008. The main purpose of the revisions is to bring elective-share law into line with the contemporary view of marriage as an economic partnership. The economic partnership theory of marriage is already implemented under the equitable-distribution system applied in both the common-law and community-property states when a marriage ends in divorce. When a marriage ends in death, that theory is also already implemented under the community-property system and under the system promulgated in the Model Marital Property Act. In the common-law states, however, elective-share law has not caught up to the partnership theory of marriage.

The general effect of implementing the partnership theory in elective-share law is to increase the entitlement of a surviving spouse in a long-term marriage in cases in which the marital assets were disproportionately titled in the decedent's name; and to decrease or even eliminate the entitlement of a surviving spouse in a long-term marriage in cases in which the marital assets were more or less equally titled or disproportionately titled in the surviving spouse's name. A further general effect is to decrease or even eliminate the entitlement of a surviving spouse in a short-term, later-in-life marriage (typically a post-widowhood remarriage) in which neither spouse contributed much, if anything, to the acquisition of the other's wealth, except that a special supplemental elective-share amount is provided in cases in which the surviving spouse would otherwise be left without sufficient funds for support.

The Partnership Theory of Marriage

The partnership theory of marriage, sometimes also called the marital-sharing theory, is stated in various ways. Sometimes it is thought of "as an expression of the presumed intent of husbands and wives to pool their fortunes on an equal basis, share and share alike." M. Glendon, The Transformation of Family Law 131 (1989). Under this approach, the economic rights of each spouse are seen as deriving from an unspoken marital bargain under which the partners agree that each is to enjoy a half interest in the fruits of the marriage, i.e., in the property nominally acquired by and titled in the sole name of either partner during the marriage (other than in property acquired by gift or inheritance). A decedent who disinherits his or her surviving spouse is seen as having reneged on the bargain. Sometimes the theory is expressed in restitutionary terms, a return-of-contribution notion. Under this approach, the law grants each spouse an entitlement to compensation for non-monetary contributions to the marital enterprise, as "a recognition of the activity of one spouse in the home and to compensate not only for this activity but for opportunities lost." Id. See also American Law Institute, Principles of Family Dissolution § 4.09 Comment c (2002).

No matter how the rationale is expressed, the community-property system, including that version of community law promulgated in the Model Marital Property Act, recognizes the partnership theory, but it is sometimes thought that the common-law system denies it. In the ongoing marriage, it is true that the basic principle in the common-law (title-based) states is that marital status does not affect the ownership of property. The regime is one of separate property. Each spouse owns all that he or she earns. By contrast, in the community-property states, each spouse acquires an ownership interest in half the property the other earns during the marriage. By granting each spouse upon acquisition an immediate half interest in the earnings of the other, the community-property regimes directly recognize that the couple's enterprise is in essence collaborative.

The common-law states, however, also give effect or purport to give effect to the partnership theory when a marriage is dissolved by divorce. If the marriage ends in divorce, a spouse who sacrificed his or her financial-earning opportunities to contribute so-called domestic services to the marital enterprise (such as child-rearing and homemaking) stands to be recompensed. All states now follow the equitable-distribution system upon divorce, under which "broad discretion [is given to] trial courts to assign to either spouse property acquired during the marriage, irrespective of title, taking into account the circumstances of the particular case and recognizing the value of the contributions of a nonworking spouse or homemaker to the acquisition of that property. Simply stated, the system of equitable distribution views marriage as essentially a shared enterprise or joint undertaking in the nature of a partnership to which both spouses contribute—directly and indirectly, financially and nonfinancially—the fruits of which are distributable at divorce." J. Gregory, The Law of Equitable Distribution ¶ 1.03, at p. 1–6 (1989).

The other situation in which spousal property rights figure prominently is disinheritance at death. The original (pre-1990) Uniform Probate Code, along with almost all other non-UPC common-law states, treats this as one of the few instances in American law where the decedent's testamentary freedom with respect to his or her title-based ownership interests must be curtailed. No matter what the decedent's intent, the original Uniform Probate Code and almost all of the non-UPC common-law states recognize that the surviving spouse does have some claim to a portion of the decedent's estate. These statutes provide the spouse a so-called forced share. The forced share is expressed as an option that the survivor can elect or let lapse during the administration of the decedent's estate, hence in the UPC the forced share is termed the "elective" share.

Elective-share law in the common-law states, however, has not caught up to the partnership theory of marriage. Under typical American elective-share law, including the elective share provided by the original Uniform Probate Code, a surviving spouse may claim a one-third share of the decedent's estate—not the 50 percent share of the couple's combined assets that the partnership theory would imply.

Long-term Marriages. To illustrate the discrepancy between the partnership theory and conventional elective-share law, consider first a long-term marriage, in which the couple's combined assets were accumulated mostly during the course of the marriage. The original elective-share fraction of one-third of the decedent's estate plainly does not implement a partnership principle. The actual result depends on which spouse happens to die first and on how the property accumulated during the marriage was nominally titled.

Example 1—Long-term Marriage under Conventional Forced-share Law. Consider A and B, who were married in their twenties or early thirties; they never divorced, and A died at age, say, 70, survived by B. For whatever reason, A left a will entirely disinheriting B.

Throughout their long life together, the couple managed to accumulate assets worth $600,000, marking them as a somewhat affluent but hardly wealthy couple.

Under conventional elective-share law, B's ultimate entitlement depends on the manner in which these $600,000 in assets were nominally titled as between them. B could end up much poorer or much richer than a 50/50 partnership principle would suggest. The reason is that under conventional elective-share law, B has a claim to one-third of A's "estate."

Marital Assets Disproportionately Titled in Decedent's Name; Conventional Elective-share Law Frequently Entitles Survivor to Less Than Equal Share of Marital Assets. If all the marital assets were titled in A's name, B's claim against A's estate would only be for $200,000—well below B's $300,000 entitlement produced by the partnership/marital-sharing principle.

If $500,000 of the marital assets were titled in A's name, B's claim against A's estate would still only be for $166,667 (1/3 of $500,000), which when combined with B's "own" $100,000 yields a $266,667 cut for B—still below the $300,000 figure produced by the partnership/ marital-sharing principle.

Marital Assets Equally Titled; Conventional Elective-share Law Entitles Survivor to Disproportionately Large Share. If $300,000 of the marital assets were titled in A's name, B would still have a claim against A's estate for $100,000, which when combined with B's "own" $300,000 yields a $400,000 cut for B—well above the $300,000 amount to which the partnership/marital-sharing principle would lead.

Marital Assets Disproportionately Titled in Survivor's Name; Conventional Elective-share Law Entitles Survivor to Magnify the Disproportion. If only $200,000 were titled in A's name, B would still have a claim against A's estate for $66,667 (1/3 of $200,000), even though B was already overcompensated as judged by the partnership/marital-sharing theory.

Short-term, Later-in-Life Marriages. Short-term marriages, particularly the post-widowhood remarriage occurring later in life, present different considerations. Because each spouse in this type of marriage typically comes into the marriage owning assets derived from a former marriage, the one-third fraction of the decedent's estate far exceeds a 50/50 division of assets acquired during the marriage.

Example 2—Short-term, Later-in-Life Marriage under Conventional Elective-share Law. Consider B and C. A year or so after A's death, B married C. Both B and C are in their seventies, and after five years of marriage, B dies survived by C. Both B and C have adult children and a few grandchildren by their prior marriages, and each naturally would prefer to leave most or all of his or her property to those children.

The value of the couple's combined assets is $600,000, $300,000 of which is titled in B's name (the decedent) and $300,000 of which is titled in C's name (the survivor).

For reasons that are not immediately apparent, conventional elective-share law gives the survivor, C, a right to claim one-third of B's estate, thereby shrinking B's estate (and hence the share of B's children by B's prior marriage to A) by $100,000 (reducing it to $200,000) while supplementing C's assets (which will likely go to C's children by C's prior marriage) by $100,000 (increasing their value to $400,000).

Conventional elective-share law, in other words, basically rewards the children of the remarried spouse who manages to outlive the other, arranging for those children a windfall share of one-third of the "loser's" estate. The "winning" spouse who chanced to survive gains a windfall, for this "winner" is unlikely to have made a contribution, monetary or otherwise, to the "loser's" wealth remotely worth one-third.

The Redesigned Elective Share

The redesigned elective share is intended to bring elective-share law into line with the partnership theory of marriage.

In the long-term marriage illustrated in Example 1, the effect of implementing a partnership theory is to increase the entitlement of the surviving spouse when the marital assets were disproportionately titled in the decedent's name; and to decrease or even eliminate the entitlement of the surviving spouse when the marital assets were more or less equally titled or disproportionately titled in the surviving spouse's name. Put differently, the effect is both to reward the surviving spouse who sacrificed his or her financial-earning opportunities in order to contribute so-called domestic services to the marital enterprise and to deny an additional windfall to the surviving spouse in whose name the fruits of a long-term marriage were mostly titled.

In the short-term, later-in-life marriage illustrated in Example 2, the effect of implementing a partnership theory is to decrease or even eliminate the entitlement of the surviving spouse because in such a marriage neither spouse is likely to have contributed much, if anything, to the acquisition of the other's wealth. Put differently, the effect is to deny a windfall to the survivor who contributed little to the decedent's wealth, and ultimately to deny a windfall to the survivor's children by a prior marriage at the expense of the decedent's children by a prior marriage. Bear in mind that in such a marriage, which produces no children, a decedent who disinherits or largely disinherits the surviving spouse may not be acting so much from malice or spite toward the surviving spouse, but from a natural instinct to want to leave most or all of his or her property to the children of his or her former, long-term marriage. In hardship cases, however, as explained later, a special supplemental elective-share amount is provided when the surviving spouse would otherwise be left without sufficient funds for support.

2008 Revisions. When first promulgated in the early 1990s, the statute provided that the "elective-share percentage" increased annually according to a graduated schedule. The "elective-share percentage" ranged from a low of 0 percent for a marriage of less than one year to a high of 50 percent for a marriage of 15 years or more. The "elective-share percentage" did double duty. The system equated the "elective-share percentage" of the couple's combined assets with 50 percent of the marital-property portion of the couple's assets—the assets that are subject to equalization under the partnership theory of marriage. Consequently, the elective share effected the partnership theory rather indirectly. Although the schedule was designed to represent by approximation a constant fifty percent of the marital-property portion of the couple's assets (the augmented estate), it did not say so explicitly.

The 2008 revisions are designed to present the system in a more direct form, one that makes the system more transparent and therefore more understandable. The 2008 revisions disentangle the elective-share percentage from the system that approximates the marital-property portion of the augmented estate. As revised, the statute provides that the "elective-share percentage" is always 50 percent, but it is not 50 percent of the augmented estate but 50 percent of the "marital-property portion" of the augmented estate. The marital-property portion of the augmented estate is computed by approximation—by applying the percentages set forth in a graduated schedule that increases annually with the length of the marriage (each "marital-portion percentage" being double the percentage previously set forth in the "elective-share percentage" schedule). Thus, for example, under the former system, the elective-share amount in a marriage of 10 years was 30 percent of the augmented estate. Under the revised system, the elective-share amount is 50 percent of the marital-property portion of the augmented estate, the marital-property portion of the augmented estate being 60 percent of the augmented estate.

The primary benefit of these changes is that the statute, as revised, presents the elective-share's implementation of the partnership theory of marriage in a direct rather than indirect form, adding clarity and transparency to the system. An important byproduct of the revision is that it facilitates the inclusion of an alternative provision for enacting states that want to implement the partnership theory of marriage but prefer not to define the marital-property portion by approximation but by classification. Under the deferred marital-property approach, the marital-property portion consists of the value of the couple's property that was acquired during the marriage other than by gift or inheritance. (See below.)

The 2008 revisions are based on a proposal presented in Waggoner, "The Uniform Probate Code's Elective Share: Time for a Reassessment," 37 U. Mich. J. L. Reform 1 (2003), an article that gives a more extensive explanation of the rationale of the 2008 revisions.

Specific Features of the Redesigned Elective Share

Because ease of administration and predictability of result are prized features of the probate system, the redesigned elective share implements the marital-partnership theory by means of a mechanically determined approximation system. Under the redesigned elective share, there is no need to identify which of the couple's property was earned during the marriage and which was acquired prior to the marriage or acquired during the marriage by gift or inheritance. For further discussion of the reasons for choosing this method, see Waggoner, "Spousal Rights in Our Multiple-Marriage Society: The Revised Uniform Probate Code," 26 Real Prop. Prob. & Tr. J. 683 (1992).

Section 2–202(a)—The "Elective-share Amount." Under Section 2–202(a), the elective-share amount is equal to 50 percent of the value of the "marital-property portion of the augmented estate." The marital-property portion of the augmented estate, which is determined under Section 2–203(b), increases with the length of the marriage. The longer the marriage, the larger the "marital-property portion of the augmented estate." The sliding scale adjusts for the correspondingly greater contribution to the acquisition of the couple's marital property in a marriage of 15 years than in a marriage of 15 days. Specifically, the "marital-property portion of the augmented estate" starts low and increases annually according to a graduated schedule until it reaches 100 percent. After one year of marriage, the marital-property portion of the augmented estate is six percent of the augmented estate and it increases with each additional year of marriage until it reaches the maximum 100 percent level after 15 years of marriage.

Section 2–203(a)—the "Augmented Estate." The elective-share percentage of 50 percent is applied to the value of the "marital-property portion of the augmented estate." As defined in Section 2–203, the "augmented estate" equals the value of the couple's combined assets, not merely the value of the assets nominally titled in the decedent's name.

More specifically, the "augmented estate" is composed of the sum of four elements:

  Section 2–204—the value of the decedent's net probate estate;

  Section 2–205—the value of the decedent's nonprobate transfers to others, consisting of will-substitute-type inter-vivos transfers made by the decedent to others than the surviving spouse;

  Section 2–206—the value of the decedent's nonprobate transfers to the surviving spouse, consisting of will-substitute-type inter-vivos transfers made by the decedent to the surviving spouse; and

Section 2–207—the value of the surviving spouse's net assets at the decedent's death, plus any property that would have been in the surviving spouse's nonprobate transfers to others under Section 2–205 had the surviving spouse been the decedent.

Section 2–203(b)—the "Marital-property portion" of the Augmented Estate. Section 2–203(b) defines the marital-property portion of the augmented estate.

Section 2–202(a)—the "Elective-share Amount." Section 2–202(a) requires the elective-share percentage of 50 percent to be applied to the value of the marital-property portion of the augmented estate. This calculation yields the "elective-share amount"—the amount to which the surviving spouse is entitled. If the elective-share percentage were to be applied only to the marital-property portion of the decedent's assets, a surviving spouse who has already been overcompensated in terms of the way the marital-property portion of the couple's assets have been nominally titled would receive a further windfall under the elective-share system. The marital-property portion of the couple's assets, in other words, would not be equalized. By applying the elective-share percentage of 50 percent to the marital-property portion of the augmented estate (the couple's combined assets), the redesigned system denies any significance to how the spouses took title to particular assets.

Section 2–209—Satisfying the Elective-share Amount. Section 2–209 determines how the elective-share amount is to be satisfied. Under Section 2–209, the decedent's net probate estate and nonprobate transfers to others are liable to contribute to the satisfaction of the elective-share amount only to the extent the elective-share amount is not fully satisfied by the sum of the following amounts:

Subsection (a)(1)—amounts that pass or have passed from the decedent to the surviving spouse by testate or intestate succession and amounts included in the augmented estate under Section 2–206, i.e. the value of the decedent's nonprobate transfers to the surviving spouse; and

Subsection (a)(2)—the marital-property portion of amounts included in the augmented estate under Section 2–207.

If the combined value of these amounts equals or exceeds the elective-share amount, the surviving spouse is not entitled to any further amount from recipients of the decedent's net probate estate or nonprobate transfers to others, unless the surviving spouse is entitled to a supplemental elective-share amount under Section 2–202(b).

Example 3—15-Year or Longer Marriage under Redesigned Elective Share; Marital Assets Disproportionately Titled in Decedent's Name. A and B were married to each other more than 15 years. A died, survived by B. A's will left nothing to B, and A made no nonprobate transfers to B. A made nonprobate transfers to others in the amount of $100,000 as defined in Section 2–205.

	Augmented Estate	Marital-Property Portion (100%)
A's net probate estate	$300,000	$300,000
A's nonprobate transfers to others	$100,000	$100,000
A's nonprobate transfers to B	$0	$0
B's assets and nonprobate transfers to others	$200,000	$200,000
Augmented Estate	$600,000	$600,000
Elective-Share Amount (50% of Marital-property portion) $300,000		
Less amount already Satisfied $200,000		
Unsatisfied Balance $100,000		

Under Section 2–209(a)(2), the full value of B's assets ($200,000) counts first toward satisfying B's entitlement. B, therefore, is treated as already having received $200,000 of B's ultimate entitlement of $300,000. Section 2–209(c) makes A's net probate estate and nonprobate transfers to others liable for the unsatisfied balance of the elective-share amount, $100,000, which is the amount needed to bring B's own $200,000 up to $300,000.

Example 4—15-Year or Longer Marriage under Redesigned Elective Share; Marital Assets Disproportionately Titled in Survivor's Name. As in Example 3, A and B were married to each other more than 15 years. A died, survived by B. A's will left nothing to B, and A made no nonprobate transfers to B. A made nonprobate transfers to others in the amount of $50,000 as defined in Section 2–205.

	Augmented Estate	Marital-Property Portion (100%)
A's net probate estate	$150,000	$150,000
A's nonprobate transfers to others	$50,000	$50,000
A's nonprobate transfers to B	$0	$0
B's assets and nonprobate transfers to others	$400,000	$400,000
Augmented Estate	$600,000	$600,000

Elective-Share Amount (50% of Marital-property portion) $300,000

Less amount already Satisfied $400,000

Unsatisfied Balance $0

Under Section 2–209(a)(2), the full value of B's assets ($400,000) counts first toward satisfying B's entitlement. B, therefore, is treated as already having received more than B's ultimate entitlement of $300,000. B has no claim on A's net probate estate or nonprobate transfers to others.

In a marriage that has lasted less than 15 years, only a portion of the survivor's assets—not all—count toward making up the elective-share amount. This is because, in these shorter-term marriages, the marital-property portion of the survivor's assets under Section 2–203(b) is less than 100% and, under Section 2–209(a)(2), the portion of the survivor's assets that count toward making up the elective-share amount is limited to the marital-property portion of those assets.

To explain why this is appropriate requires further elaboration of the underlying theory of the redesigned system. The system avoids the classification and tracing-to-source problems in determining the marital-property portion of the couple's assets. This is accomplished under Section 2–203(b) by applying an ever-increasing percentage, as the length of the marriage increases, to the couple's combined assets without regard to when or how those assets were acquired. By approximation, the redesigned system equates the marital-property portion of the couple's combined assets with the couple's marital assets—assets subject to equalization under the partnership/marital-sharing theory. Thus, in a marriage that has endured long enough for the marital-property portion of their assets to be 60% under Section 2–203(b), 60% of each spouse's assets are treated as marital assets. Section 2–209(a)(2) therefore counts only 60% of the survivor's assets toward making up the elective share amount.

Example 5—Under 15-Year Marriage under the Redesigned Elective Share; Marital Assets Disproportionately Titled in Decedent's Name. A and B were married to each other more than 5 but less than 6 years. A died, survived by B. A's will left nothing to B, and A made no nonprobate transfers to B. A made nonprobate transfers to others in the amount of $100,000 as defined in Section 2–205.

	Augmented Estate	Marital-Property Portion (30%)
A's net probate estate	$300,000	$90,000
A's nonprobate transfers to others	$100,000	$30,000
A's nonprobate transfers to B	$0	$0
B's assets and nonprobate transfers to others	$200,000	$60,000
Augmented Estate	$600,000	$180,000
Elective-Share Amount (50% of Marital-property portion) $90,000		
Less amount already Satisfied $60,000		
Unsatisfied Balance $30,000		

Under Section 2–209(a)(2), the marital-property portion of B's assets (30% of $200,000, or $60,000) counts first toward satisfying B's entitlement. B, therefore, is treated as already having received $60,000 of B's ultimate entitlement of $90,000. Under Section 2–209(c), B has a claim on A's net probate estate and nonprobate transfers to others of $30,000.

Deferred Marital-Property Alternative

By making the elective share percentage a flat 50 percent of the marital-property portion of the augmented estate, the 2008 revision disentangles the elective share percentage from the approximation schedule, thus allowing the marital-property portion of the augmented estate to be defined either by the approximation schedule or by the deferred-marital-property approach. Although one of the benefits of the 2008 revision is added clarity, an important byproduct of the revision is that it facilitates the inclusion of an alternative provision for enacting states that prefer a deferred-marital-property approach. See Alan Newman, Incorporating the Partnership Theory of Marriage into Elective-Share Law: the Approximation System of the Uniform Probate Code and the

Deferred-Community-Property Alternative, 49 Emory L.J. 487 (2000).

The Support Theory

The partnership/marital-sharing theory is not the only driving force behind elective-share law. Another theoretical basis for elective-share law is that the spouses' mutual duties of support during their joint lifetimes should be continued in some form after death in favor of the survivor, as a claim on the decedent's estate. Current elective-share law implements this theory poorly. The fixed fraction, whether it is the typical one-third or some other fraction, disregards the survivor's actual need. A one-third share may be inadequate to the surviving spouse's needs, especially in a modest estate. On the other hand, in a very large estate, it may go far beyond the survivor's needs. In either a modest or a large estate, the survivor may or may not have ample independent means, and this factor, too, is disregarded in conventional elective-share law. The redesigned elective share system implements the support theory by granting the survivor a supplemental elective-share amount related to the survivor's actual needs. In implementing a support rationale, the length of the marriage is quite irrelevant. Because the duty of support is founded upon status, it arises at the time of the marriage.

Section 2–202(b)—the "Supplemental Elective-share Amount." Section 2–202(b) is the provision that implements the support theory by providing a supplemental elective-share amount of $75,000. The $75,000 figure is bracketed to indicate that individual states may wish to select a higher or lower amount.

In satisfying this $75,000 amount, the surviving spouse's own titled-based ownership interests count first toward making up this supplemental amount; included in the survivor's assets for this purpose are amounts shifting to the survivor at the decedent's death and amounts owing to the survivor from the decedent's estate under the accrual-type elective-share apparatus discussed above, but excluded are (1) amounts going to the survivor under the Code's probate exemptions and allowances and (2) the survivor's Social Security benefits (and other governmental benefits, such as Medicare insurance coverage). If the survivor's assets are less than the $75,000 minimum, then the survivor is entitled to whatever additional portion of the decedent's estate is necessary, up to 100 percent of it, to bring the survivor's assets up to that minimum level. In the case of a late marriage, in which the survivor is perhaps aged in the mid-seventies, the minimum figure plus the probate exemptions and allowances (which under the Code amount to a minimum of another $64,500) is pretty much on target—in conjunction with Social Security payments and other governmental benefits—to provide the survivor with a fairly adequate means of support.

Example 6—Supplemental Elective-share Amount. After A's death in Example 1, B married C. Five years later, B died, survived by C. B's will left nothing to C, and B made no nonprobate transfers to C. B made no nonprobate transfers to others as defined in Section 2–205.

	Augmented Estate	Marital-Property Portion (30%)
B's net probate estate	$90,000	$27,000
B's nonprobate transfers to others	$0	$0
B's nonprobate transfers to C	$0	$0
C's assets and nonprobate transfers to others	$10,000	$3,000
Augmented Estate	$100,000	$30,000

Elective-Share Amount (50% of Marital-property portion) $15,000

Less amount already Satisfied $3,000

Unsatisfied Balance $12,000

Solution under Redesigned Elective Share. Under Section 2–209(a)(2), $3,000 (30%) of C's assets count first toward making up C's elective-share amount; under Section 2–209(c), the remaining $12,000 elective-share amount would come from B's net probate estate.

Application of Section 2–202(b) shows that C is entitled to a supplemental elective-share amount. The calculation of C's supplemental elective-share amount begins by determining the sum of the amounts described in sections:

2–207 .... $10,000

2–209(a)(1) 0

Elective-share amount payable from decedent's probate
estate under Section 2–209(c) $12,000

Total $22,000

The above calculation shows that C is entitled to a supplemental elective-share amount under Section 2–202(b) of $53,000 ($75,000 minus $22,000). The supplemental elective-share amount is payable entirely from B's net probate estate, as prescribed in Section 2–209(c).

The end result is that C is entitled to $65,000 ($12,000 + $53,000) by way of elective share from B's net probate estate (and nonprobate transfers to others, had there been any). Sixty-five thousand dollars is the amount necessary to bring C's $10,000 in assets up to $75,000.

Decedent's Nonprobate Transfers to Others

The pre-1990 Code made great strides toward preventing "fraud on the spouse's share." The problem of "fraud on the spouse's share" arises when the decedent seeks to evade the spouse's elective share by engaging in various kinds of nominal inter-vivos transfers. To render that type of behavior ineffective, the original Code adopted the augmented-estate concept, which extended the elective-share entitlement to property that was the subject of specified types of inter-vivos transfer, such as revocable inter-vivos trusts.

In the redesign of the elective share, the augmented-estate concept has been strengthened. The pre-1990 Code left several loopholes ajar in the augmented estate—a notable one being life insurance the decedent buys, naming someone other than his or her surviving spouse as the beneficiary. With appropriate protection for the insurance company that pays off before receiving notice of an elective-share claim, the redesigned elective-share system includes these types of insurance policies in the augmented estate as part of the decedent's nonprobate transfers to others under Section 2–205.

To a degree, the UPC implements a partnership theory of marriage. But to what degree? Does the community-property system do a better job of implementing the partnership theory?

> Problem 7.20: The community-property system excludes property earned before marriage or acquired by gift. Does the UPC elective share apply to assets the decedent earned before marriage or acquired by gift? Does the UPC follow the partnership theory of marriage?

> Example 7.21: O earns $1,000,000 during the marriage to S, all of which sits in an account in O's name. S has no financial assets. O dies. O devises all her property to her brother, Y. A week later, S dies. S devises all her property to her sister, X. Can S's executor make an election on behalf of S so that sister X takes from O's estate? No. Under UPC § 2–212, the right of election may not be exercised after the survivor dies. This limitation does not follow the partnership theory of marriage because partners would be able to pass their share of rights at death. However, if S is alive but lacks capacity to make the election, others can make the election for S.

> Problem 7.22: O has $2,000,000 in a bank account. O marries S. O earns $1,000,000 during marriage to S, all of which was deposited O's account. S has no financial assets. S dies. S devises all her property to her sister, X. Under S's will, how much does X take from O's bank account? Does the elective share follow the partnership theory of marriage?

The UPC portion of the decedent's estate available to the survivor by election has changed over time. Under the 1969 UPC, there was no minimum dollar amount; now there is a fixed-dollar, supplemental elective-share amount designed to implement the support theory of the elective share. Under the 1969 UPC, the percentage share was one-third. In 1990, the UPC revised the percentage to come closer to implementing a partnership theory of marriage by increasing the survivor's share with the length of marriage. In 2008, the UPC changed the method of calculation to increase transparency. The current UPC share is fixed at one-half, but that applies to the marital-property portion of the augmented estate which increases with the length of marriage. The marital property portion of the augmented estate is set out in the following table, with the length of marriage on the left and the percentage of the augmented estate on the right.

Less than 1 year 3%

1 year but less than 2 years 6%

2 years but less than 3 years 12%

3 years but less than 4 years 18%

4 years but less than 5 years 24%

5 years but less than 6 years 30%

6 years but less than 7 years 36%

7 years but less than 8 years 42%

8 years but less than 9 years 48%

9 years but less than 10 years 54%

10 years but less than 11 years 60%

11 years but less than 12 years 68%

12 years but less than 13 years 76%

13 years but less than 14 years 84%

14 years but less than 15 years 92%

15 years or more 100%

(Keep in mind that the sliding scale above determines the marital-property portion of the augmented estate. The elective-share amount is one-half of that. For example, for a marriage of 10 years, the marital-property portion is 60% of the augmented estate and, since the survivor's share is one-half, the survivor ends up with an elective-share amount that is 30% of the qualifying assets.)

Question 7.23: What is the rationale for a sliding scale?

Question 7.24: Older O marries younger S, saying "From this day forward we are one. With all my worldly goods I thee endow." They decide to have three children, and S gives up a promising law career to raise their young children. O dies after four years. O's will devises O's $1,000,000 estate to O's brother. They have no other assets. Which percentage do you think is fairer for S to receive under the election, 33% (1969 UPC) or 12% (1990 UPC)?

Question 7.25: Should the sliding scale depend on the number of minor children and the other provisions made for them?

Question 7.26: Considering all possible situations, which approach is the best?

A= 1/3 of the augmented estate.

B= a sliding percentage of the augmented estate.

C= 1/2 of the assets acquired during the marriage except for gifts and inheritances.

The elective share may be waived, but the waiver is not valid under the UPC if it is not in writing, not voluntary, or if it was unconscionable and there was inadequate disclosure.

(d) The Elective Share in Community-Property States

One problem with the elective share is that it does not protect surviving spouses in community-property states. Of course, those spouses might have community property. But they might not have substantial community property if they moved late in life to the community-property state from an elective-share state. Some community-property states have solved this problem with quasi-community property, which subjects some of the decedent's estate to the community-property rules. But a few states have not adopted such reforms, and it is possible for the surviving spouse to end up with little protection from a decedent who wishes to provide nothing.

C. RELIGIOUS RESTRICTIONS

IN RE ESTATE OF FEINBERG
Supreme Court of Illinois, 2009
919 N.E.2d 888

GARMAN, J.

This case involves a dispute among the surviving children and grandchildren of Max and Erla Feinberg regarding the validity of a trust provision. The circuit court of Cook County found the trust provision unenforceable on the basis that it is contrary to the public policy of the state of Illinois. The appellate court affirmed.* * *

For the reasons that follow, we reverse.

BACKGROUND

Max Feinberg died in 1986. He was survived by his wife, Erla, their adult children, Michael and Leila, and five grandchildren.

Prior to his death, Max executed a will and created a trust. Max's will provided that upon his death, all of his assets were to "pour over" into the trust, which was to be further divided for tax reasons into two trusts, "Trust A" and "Trust B." If she survived him, Erla was to be the lifetime beneficiary of both trusts, first receiving income from Trust A, with a limited right to withdraw principal. If Trust A were exhausted, Erla would then receive income from Trust B, again with a limited right to withdraw principal.

Upon Erla's death, any assets remaining in Trust A after the payment of estate taxes were to be combined with the assets of Trust B. The assets of Trust B were then to be distributed to Max's descendants in accordance with a provision we shall call the "beneficiary restriction clause." This clause directed that 50% of the assets be held in trust for the benefit of the then-living descendants of Michael and Leila during their lifetimes. The division was to be on a *per stirpes* basis, with Michael's two children as lifetime beneficiaries of one quarter of the trust and Leila's three children as lifetime beneficiaries of the other one quarter of the trust. However, any such descendant who married outside the Jewish faith or whose non-Jewish spouse did not convert to Judaism within one year of marriage would be "deemed deceased for all purposes of this instrument as of the date of such marriage" and that descendant's share of the trust would revert to Michael or Leila.

In addition, the trust instrument gave Erla a limited testamentary power of appointment over the distribution of the assets of both trusts and a limited lifetime power of appointment over the assets of Trust B. Under the limiting provision, Erla was allowed to exercise her power of appointment only in favor of Max's descendants. Thus, she could not name as remaindermen individuals who were not Max's descendants or appoint to a charity. The parties dispute whether Erla's power of appointment was limited to those descendants not deemed deceased under the beneficiary restriction clause. The trial court did not make a finding on this question and the appellate court did not discuss it.

Erla exercised her lifetime power of appointment over Trust B in 1997, directing that, upon her death, each of her two children and any of her grandchildren who were not deemed deceased under Max's beneficiary restriction clause receive $250,000. In keeping with Max's original plan, if any grandchild was deemed deceased under the beneficiary restriction clause, Erla directed that his or her share be paid to Michael or Leila.

By exercising her power of appointment in this manner, Erla revoked the original distribution provision and replaced it with a plan that differs from Max's plan in two significant respects. First, Erla altered the distribution scheme from *per stirpes* to *per capita*, permitting each of the grandchildren to take an equal share, rather than favoring Michael's two children over Leila's three children. Second, Erla designated a fixed sum to be distributed to each eligible descendant at the time of her death, replacing Max's plan for a lifetime trust for such descendants. The record suggests that Erla's gifts will deplete the corpus of the trust, leaving no trust assets subject to distribution under Max's original plan. Thus, while Erla retained Max's beneficiary restriction clause, his distribution provision never became operative.

All five grandchildren married between 1990 and 2001. By the time of Erla's death in 2003, all five grandchildren had been married for more than one year. Only Leila's son, Jon, met the conditions of the beneficiary restriction clause and was entitled to receive $250,000 of the trust assets as directed by Erla.

This litigation followed, pitting Michael's daughter, Michele, against Michael, coexecutor of the estates of both Max and Erla.

The trial court invalidated the beneficiary restriction clause on public policy grounds. A divided appellate court affirmed, holding that "under Illinois law and under the Restatement (Third) of Trusts, the provision in the case before us is invalid because it seriously interferes with and limits the right of individuals to marry a person of their own choosing." In reaching this conclusion, the appellate court relied on decisions of this court dating back as far as 1898 and, as noted, on the Restatement (Third) of Trusts.

ISSUE PRESENTED

As a threshold matter, we must clarify the issue presented. We need not consider whether Max's original testamentary scheme is void as a matter of public policy because Erla altered his scheme in 1997. Indeed, she could have done so again at any time before her death in 2003, exercising her lifetime or testamentary powers of appointment in any number of ways. For example, she could have named her grandson, Jon, as the sole beneficiary of the entire trust, or excluded the grandchildren entirely, appointing the entire corpus of the trust to Michael and Leila.

Indeed, counsel for Michele acknowledged at oral argument that Max and Erla could have accomplished the goal of benefitting only those grandchildren who married within their religious tradition by individually naming those grandchildren as beneficiaries of the will or the trust, without implicating public policy. Counsel argued that the violation of public policy occurred when Max used a religious description to define a class or category of descendants he wished to benefit, rather than mention them by name.

Of course, at the time Max prepared his estate plan, his grandchildren were too young to marry and it was possible that more grandchildren might have been born before the trust provisions took effect. As a result, Max could not have accomplished his purpose in the manner suggested by Michele. Even by the time Erla exercised her power of appointment, not all of the grandchildren had married.

Thus, the question we must answer is whether the holder of a power of appointment over the assets of a trust may, without violating the public policy of the state of Illinois, direct that the assets be distributed at the time of her death to then-living descendants of the settlor, deeming deceased any descendant who has married outside the settlor's religious tradition. In effect, we are not called upon to consider the validity of Max's estate plan as a whole, which would have continued to hold the assets in trust for the benefit of the grandchildren only so long as they complied with the restriction. Rather, we must assess Max's beneficiary restriction clause in conjunction with Erla's directions for distribution.

When the issue is clarified in this way, it becomes apparent that many of the arguments raised by Michele are not relevant. For example, under Max's plan, an unmarried grandson would have begun to receive distributions from Trust B upon Erla's death, only to forfeit further such payments if he were to marry a non-Jewish woman who did not convert to Judaism within one year. We need not decide if such a provision would violate public policy because no such provision is implicated in the present case.

Michele also suggests that a granddaughter who was married to a non-Jewish man at the time of Erla's death might subsequently divorce and remarry, this time to a Jewish spouse, and make a claim upon the trust. This circumstance would raise the issue of whether such a descendant, previously deemed deceased, would be "resurrected." Such an occurrence would require construction of the language of the trust document. Under Erla's plan, however, this circumstance cannot arise because a fixed amount became distributable upon her death only to those grandchildren who then met the requirements previously set by Max.

Similarly, Michele's argument that the beneficiary restriction clause is invalid because a court might be called upon to determine whether the spouse of a particular descendant is or is not Jewish is not well taken. It is undisputed in the present case that only one of the five grandchildren meets the requirements established by Max.

STANDARD OF REVIEW

This court has not had occasion to identify the applicable standard of review on the question of whether a provision in a trust document or will is void as a matter of public policy. It is clear, however, that such findings are subject to de novo review, because public policy is necessarily a question of law. This conclusion is consistent with the well-established principle that whether a provision in a contract, insurance policy, or other agreement is invalid because it violates public policy is a question of law, which we review *de novo*.

ANALYSIS

Michael argues before this court that the beneficiary restriction clause in his father's trust was intended "to encourage and support Judaism and preservation of Jewish culture in his own family," and that it was not binding upon Erla, who exercised her power of appointment consistently with the provision because it expressed her intent as well as Max's. Michael argues, further, that even if Max's beneficiary restriction was not revocable by Erla, the provision does not violate the public policy of this state when it is given effect via his mother's distribution scheme. He asserts that the distribution scheme is a valid partial restraint on marriage of a type that has long been enforced in Illinois and elsewhere. According to Michael, the beneficiary restriction clause has no prospective effect that might subsequently influence a descendant's decisions regarding marriage or divorce because, upon Erla's death, no contingencies remained. He distinguishes the cases relied upon by the appellate court and urges this court to reject the cited Restatement provision as not accurately stating Illinois law.

Michele defends the Restatement provision and argues that this case comes within a line of cases dating back to 1898 in which this court invalidated testamentary provisions that operated to discourage the subsequent lawful marriage by a legatee or to encourage a legatee to obtain a divorce. Specifically, she argues that under *Ransdell v. Boston*, 172 Ill. 439 (1898), testamentary restrictions on marriage are valid only if they operate to benefit the intended beneficiary. Further, she argues that enforcement of the clause would violate both state and federal constitutions and that it violates public policy by offering a financial inducement to embrace a particular religion.

We note that this case involves more than a grandfather's desire that his descendants continue to follow his religious tradition after he is gone. This case reveals a broader tension between the competing values of freedom of testation on one hand and resistance to "dead hand" control on the other. This tension is clearly demonstrated by the three opinions of the appellate court. The authoring justice rejected the argument that the distribution scheme is enforceable because it operated at the time of Erla's death and could not affect future behavior, stating that its "clear intent was to influence the marriage decisions of Max's grandchildren based on a religions criterion." The concurring justice opined that while such restrictions might once have been considered reasonable, they are no longer reasonable. The dissenting justice noted that under the facts of this case, grandchildren who had complied with the restrictions would "immediately receive their legacy" upon Erla's death, and that the weight of authority is that a testator has a right to make the distribution of his bounty conditional on the beneficiary's adherence to a particular religious faith.

We, therefore, begin our analysis with the public policy surrounding testamentary freedom and then consider public policy pertaining to testamentary or trust provisions concerning marriage.

When we determine that our answer to a question of law must be based on public policy, it is not our role to make such policy. Rather, we must discern the public policy of the state of Illinois as expressed in the constitution, statutes, and long-standing case law. We will find a contract provision against public policy only "if it is injurious to the interests of the public, contravenes some established interest of society, violates some public statute, is against good morals, tends to interfere with the public welfare or safety, or is at war with the interests of society or is in conflict with the morals of the time." Thus,

"In deciding whether an agreement violates public policy, courts determine whether the agreement is so capable of producing harm that its enforcement would be contrary to the public interest. The courts apply a strict test in determining when an agreement violates public policy. The power to invalidate part or all of an agreement on the basis of public policy is used sparingly because private parties should not be needlessly hampered in their freedom to contract between themselves. Whether an agreement is contrary to public policy depends on the particular facts and circumstances of the case."

Because, as will be discussed below, the public policy of this state values freedom of testation as well as freedom of contract, these same principles guide our analysis in the present case.

Public Policy Regarding Freedom of Testation

Neither the Constitution of the United States nor the Constitution of the State of Illinois speaks to the question of testamentary freedom. However, our statutes clearly reveal a public policy in support of testamentary freedom.

The Probate Act places only two limits on the ability of a testator to choose the objects of his bounty. First, the Act permits a spouse to renounce a testator's will, "whether or not the will contains any provision for the benefit of the surviving spouse." Thus, absent a valid prenuptial or postnuptial agreement (see, *e.g.*, *Golden v. Golden*, 393 Ill. 536 (1946) (wife can effectively bind herself to accept provisions of husband's will, thereby estopping her from renouncing the will after his death)), the wishes of a surviving spouse can trump a testator's intentions. Second, a child born to a testator after the making of a will is "entitled to receive the portion of the estate to which he would be entitled if the testator died intestate," unless provision is made in the will for the child or the will reveals the testator's intent to disinherit the child.

The public policy of the state of Illinois as expressed in the Probate Act is, thus, one of broad testamentary freedom, constrained only by the rights granted to a surviving spouse and the need to expressly disinherit a child born after execution of the will if that is the testator's desire.

Under the Probate Act, Max and Erla had no obligation to make any provision at all for their grandchildren. Indeed, if Max had died intestate, Erla, Michael, and Leila would have shared his estate, and if Erla had died intestate, only Michael and Leila would have taken. Surely, the grandchildren have no greater claim on their grandparents' testate estates than they would have had on intestate estates.

Similarly, under the Trusts and Trustees Act, "[a] person establishing a trust may specify in the instrument the rights, powers, duties, limitations and immunities applicable to the trustee, beneficiary and others and those provisions where not otherwise contrary to law shall control, notwithstanding this Act." Thus, the legislature intended that the settlor of a trust have the freedom to direct his bounty as he sees fit, even to the point of giving effect to a provision regarding the rights of beneficiaries that might depart from the standard provisions of the Act, unless "otherwise contrary to law."

Another legislative enactment that reveals a strong public policy of freedom of testation was the adoption, in 1969, of the Statute Concerning Perpetuities for the purpose of modifying the common law rule that a will or trust provision that violated the rule against perpetuities was void *ab initio*. The statute permits the settlor of a trust to create a "qualified perpetual trust" by including in the instrument a provision that the rule against perpetuities does not apply and by granting certain specified powers to the trustee. The statute also specifies other circumstances under which the rule shall not apply. In addition, the statute adopts a set of rules to be applied when determining whether an interest violates the rule against perpetuities. With regard to trusts, the statute provides that a trust containing a provision that would violate the rule against perpetuities, as modified by the statute, shall terminate 21 years after the death of the last surviving beneficiary who was living at the beginning of the perpetuities period or else at the end of the 21-year perpetuities period if no beneficiary was living when the period began to run. Thus, the trust is not rendered void *ab initio*, but is merely terminated by operation of law at the conclusion of the perpetuities period.

Also, in 1953, the legislature adopted the Rule in Shelley's Case Abolishment Act to abolish the common law rule that a life estate to A, with a remainder to A's heirs, shall pass to A in fee simple.

As demonstrated by the Probate Act, the Trusts Act, the Statute Concerning Perpetuities, and the Rule in Shelley's Case

Abolishment Act, the public policy of the state of Illinois protects the ability of an individual to distribute his property, even after his death, as he chooses, with minimal restrictions under state law.

Our case law also demonstrates the existence of a public policy favoring testamentary freedom, reflected in the many cases in which a court strives to discover and to give effect to the intent of a deceased testator or settlor of a trust.

The record, via the testimony of Michael and Leila, reveals that Max's intent in restricting the distribution of his estate was to benefit those descendants who opted to honor and further his commitment to Judaism by marrying within the faith. Max had expressed his concern about the potential extinction of the Jewish people, not only by holocaust, but by gradual dilution as a result of intermarriage with non-Jews. While he was willing to share his bounty with a grandchild whose spouse converted to Judaism, this was apparently as far as he was willing to go.

There is no question that a grandparent in Max's situation is entirely free during his lifetime to attempt to influence his grandchildren to marry within his family's religious tradition, even by offering financial incentives to do so. The question is, given our public policy of testamentary freedom, did Max's beneficiary restriction clause as given effect by Erla's appointment violate any other public policy of the state of Illinois, thus rendering it void?

Public Policy Regarding Terms
Affecting Marriage or Divorce

The contrary law relied upon by the appellate court to invalidate Max's beneficiary restriction clause is found in three decisions of this court: *Ransdell*, 172 Ill. 439, *Winterland v. Winterland*, 389 Ill. 384 (1945), and *Estate of Gerbing*, 61 Ill.2d 503 (1975) (which overruled Winterland in part). The appellate court concluded that the "language and circumstances" of the testamentary provisions in these cases, "which Illinois courts have found to be against public policy, are strikingly similar to the instant case." Specifically, the appellate court invoked the "principle that testamentary provisions are invalid if they discourage marriage or encourage divorce."

In *Ransdell*, the testator's will included provisions for his wife, his son, and his daughter. At the time the will was executed, the son and his wife were separated and cross-suits for divorce were pending. The father's bequest to the son provided that the property be held in trust, giving him use and income of the land for life, or "until such time as he * * * shall become sole and unmarried," at which time the trustee was to convey title to the land to him in fee simple. If the son died childless while still married to the wife, the land was to go to other devisees. Several years after the father's death, the son, who was still married but living apart from his wife, challenged the provision on public policy grounds. The circuit court granted judgment for the defendants and this court affirmed.

This court acknowledged the long-standing rule that conditions annexed to a gift that have the tendency to induce spouses to divorce or to live separately are void on grounds of public policy. However, the testator's purpose in this case "was simply to secure the gift to his son in the manner which, in his judgment, would render it of the greatest benefit to him in view of the relations then existing between him and his wife", which were strained, to say the least. "Certainly," this court noted, "it cannot be said that the condition tended to encourage either the separation or the bringing of a divorce suit, both having taken place long prior to the execution of the will."

This court weighed two potentially competing public policies, stating that it was "of the first importance to society that contract and testamentary gifts which are calculated to prevent lawful marriages or to bring about the separation or divorcement of husbands and wives should not be upheld." On the other hand, "it is no less important that persons of sound mind and memory, free from restraint and undue influence, should be allowed to dispose of their property by will, with such limitations and conditions as they believe for the best interest of their donees." Because the testator had not disinherited his son if he remained married, but made one provision for him in case he remained married (a life estate) and a different provision if he divorced (taking title in fee simple), the condition was not contrary to public policy.

Finally, this court distinguished between a condition subsequent (for example, if the will devised property to the beneficiary in trust for life, subject to divestment if he married), and a condition precedent, which directs that upon the fulfillment of the condition, ownership of the property is to vest in the beneficiary. The condition subsequent, such as one that would prohibit marriage generally, would be void and the donee would retain the property, unaffected by the violation of the condition. A condition precedent would be given effect, because until the condition was met, the beneficiary's interest was a mere expectancy.

The appellate court cited *Ransdell* for the "general rule that testamentary provisions which act as a restraint upon marriage or which encourage divorce are void as against public policy" and distinguished *Ransdell* from the present case on the basis that the Ransdells' marriage was "already in disrepair" at the time the will was executed. The appellate court noted that subsequent Illinois cases, however, have "reaffirmed the underlying principle."

One such case was *Winterland*, in which the testator created a trust for his wife that, upon her death, was to be distributed equally to their 11 children. However, in a later codicil, the testator directed that the share intended for their son, George, was to be held in trust for him "so long as he may live or until his present wife shall have died or been separated from him by absolute divorce." George predeceased his wife and she and their son challenged the codicil as promoting divorce, contrary to good morals, and against public policy. This court distinguished *Ransdell* on the basis that the couple's separation was "already an accomplished fact and a divorce suit was then pending" at the time the testator made his will. But where no separation was contemplated, the "natural tendency of the provision" was "to encourage divorce." For that reason, the provision was void. This court announced that it is "the public policy of this state to safeguard and protect the marriage relation, and this court will hold as contrary to that policy and void any testamentary provision tending to disturb or destroy an existing marriage."

This court further found that the codicil established two separate and divisible conditions upon which the trust would be distributed to George. First, George's life estate was to continue until the death of his wife; second, his life estate would terminate upon their absolute divorce. This court rejected the argument that the life estate itself failed and that title to the property vested in George upon his father's death. Rather, while the second condition was void, the first condition was not and, thus, could be given effect. *Winterland*, 389 Ill. at 388.

In *Gerbing*, this court considered the validity of a provision in a testamentary trust that would have terminated the trust and distributed the corpus to the testator's son in the event that his wife predeceased him or the couple divorced and remained divorced for two years. *Gerbing*, 61 Ill.2d at 505. This court restated the general principle that "a devise or bequest, the tendency of which is to encourage divorce or bring about a separation of husband and wife is against public policy." However, if the "dominant motive of the testator is to provide support in the event of such separation or divorce the condition is valid." Further, unless the couple was separated or a divorce was pending at the time the will was executed, the "exception to the general rule announced in *Ransdell*" was not applicable. This court found the provision void, but declined to sever the two conditions, as it had done in *Winterland*. Finding that it was the testator's general intent to benefit her son and that she would have preferred that he take the corpus of the trust, even if he remained married, rather than have him take nothing, this court found the entire provision void, overruling *Winterland* to the extent it held otherwise. *Gerbing*, 61 Ill.2d at 512.

In the present case, the appellate court found the "language and circumstances" of these three cases "strikingly similar" to the present case and saw "no reason to depart from this well-established principle" of these cases. We disagree with the appellate court's conclusion regarding the similarity of the present case to the cited cases. The beneficiary restriction clause as given effect by Erla's distribution scheme does not implicate the principle that trust provisions that encourage divorce violate public policy. That is, the present case does not involve a testamentary or trust provision that is "capable of exerting * * * a disruptive influence upon an otherwise normally harmonious marriage" by causing the beneficiary to choose between his or her spouse and the distribution. The challenged provision in the present case involves the decision to marry, not an incentive to divorce. This court has considered the validity of restrictions affecting marriage in cases going back as far as 1857.

In *Shackelford v. Hall*, 19 Ill. 212 (1857), the testator, Hall, left his estate to his wife for life or until she remarried, with the remainder to his four children, subject to the condition that they not marry before the age of 21. Any child who married before his or her twenty-first birthday was to receive one dollar only. The only daughter, Eliza, married four months before her twenty-first birthday, with the approval of her eldest brother, the executor of their father's estate. This court described the provision as a "devise with a condition subsequent," because the remainder interest vested in the four children immediately upon the death of the testator, "subject to be defeated by their marriage before they should attain that age." *Shackelford*, 19 Ill. at 213. This court noted that:

> "whoever will take the trouble to examine this branch of the law attentively, will find that the testator may impose reasonable and prudent restraints upon the marriage of the

objects of his bounty, by means of conditions precedent, or subsequent, or by limitations, while he may not, with one single exception, impose perpetual celibacy upon the objects of his bounty, by means of conditions subsequent or limitations. That exception is in the case of a husband in making bequests or legacies to his own wife. He may rightfully impose the condition of forfeiture upon her subsequent marriage." *Shackelford*, 19 Ill. at 214–15.

As for other conditions affecting marriage that might be imposed by a testator, this court said that:

[a]n examination of the subject, will show that the courts have very rarely held such condition void, although it might appear harsh, arbitrary and unreasonable, so as it did not absolutely prohibit the marriage of the party, within the period wherein issue of the marriage might be expected. It is enough for our present purpose, and we will go no further now, for it is not necessary, that it has been nowhere held, or pretended, that an absolute prohibition of marriage till twenty-one years of age is not reasonable and lawful, and must not be upheld, as a good condition, the violation of which may defeat a vested estate. The condition, then, annexed to this devise, was proper, reasonable and lawful, and its violation must be held to have forfeited the estate devised, unless it can be saved by some other equally well settled principle of law." *Shackelford*, 19 Ill. at 215.

Further:

"The facts of the case show, that all of the devisees of the estate in remainder, now in controversy, were the children and heirs at law of the testator, *and as such heirs at law, had expectations of this estate.* In the absence of the will, each would have been entitled to his or her respective proportions of it, according to our statute of descent. *When such is the case,* the condition subsequent, the breach of which shall divest the estate *which has become vested in the devisee by the will,* must be shown to have been brought home to the knowledge of the devisee, before the breach, in order to mark the forfeiture." (Emphases added.) *Shackelford*, 19 Ill. at 215–16.

In the end, this court found that the marriage of Hall's daughter prior to her twenty-first birthday did not divest her of the remainder interest conveyed to her upon her father's death. The basis for this decision was not that her father's partial restraint upon marriage was invalid, but that her remainder interest vested upon his death and could not be divested by a subsequent act on her part, absent a showing that she had notice of the condition subsequent. Other factors supporting this result were that she would have been one of her father's heirs at law should he have died intestate and that her brother, the executor, had unclean hands:

> "And this rule is in harmony with the general principles of law, which always lean hard against a forfeiture of estates once vested, and that it will not allow such forfeiture, where there has been no laches or misconduct. In the case before us, we must assume that the *defendant did not know of the existence of the will, and much less of the condition which it contained, that she should not marry till she was twenty-one years of age, under the penalty of forfeiting her interest in her father's estate.* In ignorance of the will, she supposed she was entitled to take as heir without any condition. When we look at this case as it is presented by the record, we see it would be a monstrous piece of injustice to enforce this forfeiture against her. Here was her elder brother, who was an executor named in the will, knowing of the condition of forfeiture, had an interest in keeping it from her, that she might, by doing the prohibited act, incur the forfeiture, that her portion might go to himself and the other heirs of the testator. Under the influence of this direct interest, he suffers her to go on in ignorance of the will, and marry only four months before she attained the age of twenty-one years, and now he comes forward and claims the benefit of the forfeiture, and insists upon depriving her of the portion devised to her by the will. To sustain this claim, would be to offer a premium for the commission of the most heartless frauds. * * * We have not the least doubt that, upon the soundest principles of law and morality, she must take the estate devised, discharged of the condition." (Emphasis added.) *Shackelford*, 19 Ill. at 217–18.

In the present case, Michael argues that the beneficiary restriction clause is a similar "reasonable and prudent restraint" that does not operate as a complete restraint upon marriage. Rather, the clause disqualifies from receipt of a share of the trust assets any grandchild who has chosen to marry outside the religious tradition their grandparents valued so highly.

More importantly, we note that, unlike Eliza Hall, the grandchildren did not receive a vested interest in the trust upon Max's death. By creating a power of appointment in Erla, Max created a situation in which the interests of the grandchildren were contingent on whether and in what manner she would exercise her lifetime and testamentary powers of appointment. Thus, the grandchildren had a mere expectancy that they might receive some portion of the remainder at the conclusion of Erla's life estate. No one had a vested interest in the remainder of the trust assets until Erla's death resolved all contingencies. Further, unlike Hall's daughter, the grandchildren in the present case were not Max's or Erla's heirs at law. Finally, while the record is unclear whether any or all of the grandchildren were aware of the existence of the beneficiary restriction clause, because they had no vested interest to protect, they were not entitled to notice of the condition.

More recently, the appellate court upheld the validity of a testamentary provision regarding the marriage of the intended legatee. In *In re Estate of Gehrt*, 134 Ill.App.3d 308 (1985), the testator, Forrest Gehrt, originally left a portion of his estate to six named individuals who were the children of Edna Bocock, apparently his deceased sister. Upon the death of one of these individuals, Harold Bocock, he executed a codicil leaving the portion originally intended for Harold to his widow, Betty, provided that at the time of Forrest's death, she remained unmarried. If, at the time of Forrest's death, it was determined that Betty had remarried, the share was to go to Harold's five siblings.

Betty remarried and, upon Forrest's death, sought Harold's share of the estate. The parties agreed that the condition operated as a condition precedent. Betty argued that it constituted an invalid restraint on marriage and asked that it be declared void as against public policy. The executor argued that the condition did not operate as a restraint because the interest "either vests or not at the date of the death of the testator depending on [Betty's] marital status at the time, not at some later time." *Estate of Gehrt*, 134 Ill.App.3d at 309.

The appellate court invoked a rule of reasonableness, quoting a case from the state of Louisiana in support of such a rule:

" '[C]onceding, without deciding, that a legacy conditioned upon the legatee remaining unmarried is against the public policy of this State, it is apt to observe here that the provision under consideration is not one forbidding the donee to marry during her lifetime or even for a fixed period of time, nor one that directs the legacy shall lapse in case the legatee should marry in the future, but rather one that is conditioned upon her status at the time of the testator's death. Certainly, such a provision is not against good morals, and we know of no law prohibiting the same.' " *Estate of Gehrt*, 134 Ill.App.3d at 311, quoting *Succession of Ruxton*, 226 La. 1088, 1091 (1955).

Applying this principle to the *Gehrt* estate, the appellate court noted the well-established principle that a will speaks as of the date of death of the testator. Thus, the court observed:

"[T]he testator, Forrest L. Gehrt, could have, for any reason, changed his codicil at any time prior to his death. He could have, at the time of plaintiff's remarriage, immediately executed another codicil cancelling the gift to the plaintiff, and could have given that portion of property to others. He can validly accomplish the same result by using the language that he did in the codicil in this case." *Estate of Gehrt*, 134 Ill.App.3d at 311.

The appellate court then quoted this court's opinion in *Ransdell*:

"While it is of the first importance to society that contract and testamentary gifts which are calculated to prevent lawful marriages or to bring about the separation or divorcement of husbands and wives should not be upheld, it is no less important that persons of sound mind and memory, free from restraint and undue influence, should be allowed to dispose of their property by will, with such limitations and conditions as they believe for the best interest of their donees." *Ransdell*, 172 Ill. at 446.

We conclude, reading *Ransdell*, *Shackelford*, *Gerbing*, and *Gehrt* together, that no interest vested in the Feinbergs' grandchildren at the time of Max's death because the terms of his testamentary trust were subject to change until Erla's death. Because they had no vested interest that could be divested by their noncompliance with the condition precedent, they were not entitled to notice of the existence of the beneficiary restriction clause. Further, because they were not the Feinbergs' heirs at law, the grandchildren had, at most, a mere expectancy that failed to materialize for four of them when, at the time of Erla's death, they did not meet the condition established by Max.

Applicability of Restatement (Third) of Trusts

In reaching its decision, the appellate court also relied on section 29 of the Restatement (Third) of Trusts, and the explanatory notes and comments thereto.

Since the Restatement (Second) of Trusts was adopted in 1959, this court has, on several occasions, cited various sections with approval. We have not yet had reason to consider whether any section of the Restatement (Third) of Trusts, which was adopted in 2003, is an accurate expression of Illinois law and we need not do so in this case.

The validity of a trust provision is not at issue, as the distribution provision of Max's trust was revoked when Erla exercised her power of appointment. Her distribution scheme was in the nature of a testamentary provision, which operated at the time of her death to determine who would be entitled to a $250,000 distribution.

The appellate court mistakenly compared the present case to an illustration accompanying Comment *j* to section 29 of the Restatement (Third) of Trusts. The illustration concerns a trust created by an aunt to benefit her nephew, who was to receive discretionary payments until age 18, and all income and discretionary payments until age 30, at which time he would receive an outright distribution of all trust property. However, all of his rights under the trust would end if, before the trust terminated on his thirtieth birthday, he married "a person who is not of R Religion." If he violated this condition, the remainder of the trust would be given to a college. The drafters of the Restatement called this an "invalid restraint on marriage," and stated that the invalid condition and the gift over to the college should not be given effect.

This illustration is similar to Max's original trust provision. Under his plan, the grandchildren who were not "deemed deceased" at the time of Erla's death would receive distributions from the trust for life, subject to termination if they should violate the marriage restriction. Erla's scheme, however, does not operate prospectively to encourage the grandchildren to make certain choices regarding marriage. It operated on the date of her death to determine which, if any, of the grandchildren qualified for distribution on that date. The condition was either met or it was not met. There was nothing any of the grandchildren could have done at that time to make themselves eligible or ineligible for the distribution.

As this court noted in *Ransdell*, a condition precedent, even if a "complete restraint" on marriage, "will, if broken, be operative and prevent the devise from taking effect." However, "[w]hen the condition is subsequent and void it is entirely inoperative, and the donee retains the property unaffected by its breach." *Ransdell*, 172 Ill. at 447, quoting 2 Pomeroy, Equity Jurisprudence § 933B (1881).

Max's will and trust created no vested interests in the children or grandchildren because Erla retained a power of appointment until her death. No vested interests were created in 1997 by Erla's exercise of her power of appointment. Her actions created a mere expectancy, contingent on her dying without further amending the distribution scheme. Because no interest vested in any of the grandchildren until Erla's death, her appointment created a condition precedent. As we noted in Ransdell, under these circumstances, even a complete restraint on marriage (*i.e.*, distribution only to unmarried grandchildren) would be operative.

Thus, this is not a case in which a donee, like the nephew in the illustration, will retain benefits under a trust only so long as he continues to comply with the wishes of a deceased donor. As such, there is no "dead hand" control or attempt to control the future conduct of the potential beneficiaries. Whatever the effect of Max's original trust provision might have been, Erla did not impose a condition intended to control future decisions of their grandchildren regarding marriage or the practice of Judaism; rather, she made a bequest to reward, at the time of her death, those grandchildren whose lives most closely embraced the values she and Max cherished.

The trial court and the appellate court erred by finding a violation of public policy in this case. While the beneficiary restriction clause, when given effect via Erla's distribution provision, has resulted in family strife, it is not "so capable of producing harm that its enforcement would be contrary to the public interest." *Kleinwort Benson*, 181 Ill.2d at 226.

Other Issues

The several other arguments made by Michele do not alter our conclusion.

First, Michele argues that even a partial restriction on marriage is void unless the "dominant motive for the restriction was to provide a benefit to the donee." She cites *Ransdell* and *Gerbing*, neither of which involved a restraint upon marriage, in support of this assertion. We concluded above, however, that the beneficiary restriction clause does not operate as a restriction on marriage because it operated only upon Erla's death to determine which grandchildren, if any, would share in the proceeds of the trust. Until that time, none of Max's heirs had a vested interest in the proceeds of the trust, over which Erla held a limited power of appointment. Michele's choices regarding when to marry and whom to marry were entirely unrestricted, even though, as it turns out, those choices did have consequences for her.

In any event, the cases cited do not condition the validity of a condition precedent regarding marriage solely on the settlor's "dominant motive" in creating it. The provision that this court upheld in *Ransdell* gave the testator's son a life estate in certain property, but provided that title would be conveyed to him upon the death of his wife or their subsequent divorce. Although a conditional gift that has the tendency to induce divorce is generally considered void, this court noted that "certain facts and circumstances" in the particular case could save such a condition. Specifically, the testator's "purpose was simply to secure the gift to his son in the manner which, in his judgment, would render it of the greatest benefit to him in view of the relations then existing between him and his wife," including a separation of several years' duration and a pending divorce suit. Thus, while *Ransdell* makes the testator's intent to provide a benefit to the donee a proper consideration, it does not elevate it to an absolute requirement. Hence, there is nothing illegitimate about a testator's preference for supporting a particular cause, value, or personal interest over the interests of potential beneficiaries, so long as the condition stated in the will or trust does not, at the relevant time, violate public policy.

The result in *Gerbing* differed because the provision that tended to induce divorce, in violation of public policy, was not within the "exception to the general rule announced in *Ransdell*." That is, the couple was not already separated and a divorce suit was not pending. After noting that a condition that might tend to induce divorce is valid "if the dominant motive of the testator is to provide support in the event of such separation or divorce", this court concluded that the testator's intent was to "deprive her son of the ownership of this property as long as he remained married to his wife," not to provide for his support in the event of divorce. Therefore, this court found the provision to be a "void condition precedent to the vesting of title to the property" in the son.

Gerbing is readily distinguishable from the present case. The son in that case had a vested interest in the trust, from which he was receiving income for life. Title to the trust property was withheld from him, however, so long as he remained married to the wife of whom his late mother had disapproved. The provision had a tendency to exert "a disruptive influence upon an otherwise normally harmonious marriage" and was, therefore, void as against public policy. *Gerbing*, 61 Ill.2d at 508. It could not be saved by reliance on the so-called *Ransdell* "exception."

Michele is mistaken when she asserts that a provision that tends to promote divorce or to restrain marriage is valid *only if* its dominant purpose is to benefit the potential donee. While such a dominant purpose may save such a provision, we have never stated that it is the only consideration. In any event, Michele had no interest in the trust whatsoever. Her taking title to trust property was not subject to a condition subsequent nor did she have an interest that would be divested by her marriage to a non-Jew. Her grandfather's purpose is, therefore, not implicated.

Second, Michele argues that the beneficiary restriction clause discourages lawful marriage and interferes with the fundamental right to marry, which is protected by the constitution. She also invokes the constitution in support of her assertion that issues of race, religion, and marriage have special status because of their constitutional dimensions, particularly in light of the constitutional values of personal autonomy and privacy.

Because a testator or the settlor of a trust is not a state actor, there are no constitutional dimensions to his choice of beneficiaries. Equal protection does not require that all children be treated equally; due process does not require notice of conditions precedent to potential beneficiaries; and the free exercise clause does not require a grandparent to treat grandchildren who reject his religious beliefs and customs in the same manner as he treats those who conform to his traditions.

Thus, Michele's reliance on *Shelley v. Kraemer*, 334 U.S. 1 (1948), is entirely misplaced. In Shelley, the Supreme Court held that the use of the state's judicial process to obtain enforcement of a racially restrictive covenant was state action, violating the equal protection clause of the fourteenth amendment. This court, however, has been reluctant to base a finding of state action "on the mere fact that a state court is the forum for the dispute." Indeed, *Shelley* has been widely criticized for a finding of state action that was not "supported by any reasoning which would suggest that "state action" is a meaningful requirement rather than a nearly empty or at least extraordinarily malleable formality."

Third, Michele argues that the beneficiary restriction clause is capable of exerting an ongoing "disruptive influence" upon marriage and is, therefore, void. She is mistaken. The provision cannot "disrupt" an existing marriage because once the beneficiary determination was made at the time of Erla's death, it created no incentive to divorce.

Finally, it has been suggested that Michael and Leila have litigated this matter rather than concede to Michele's demands because they wish to deprive the grandchildren of their inheritance. The grandchildren, however, are not the heirs at law of Max and Erla and had no expectancy of an inheritance, so long as their parents were living, even if Max and Erla had died intestate. In addition, Michael and Leila are the coexecutors of their parents' estates and, as such, are duty-bound to defend their parents' estate plans. *Hurd v. Reed*, 260 Ill. 154, 160 (1913) ("It is the duty of an executor to defend the will"), citing *Pingree v. Jones*, 80 Ill. 177, 181 (1875) (executor is "bound, on every principle of honor, justice and right" to defend the will, he "owes this, at least, to the memory of the dead who placed this confidence in him"). Although those plans might be offensive to individual family members or to outside observers, Max and Erla were free to distribute their bounty as they saw fit and to favor grandchildren of whose life choices they approved over other grandchildren who made choices of which they disapproved, so long as they did not convey a vested interest that was subject to divestment by a condition subsequent that tended to unreasonably restrict marriage or encourage divorce.

CONCLUSION

It is impossible to determine whether Erla's distribution plan was the product of her own wisdom, good legal advice, or mere fortuity. In any case, her direction that $250,000 of the assets of Trust B be distributed upon her death to each of the then-living grandchildren of Max who were not "deemed deceased" under the beneficiary restriction clause of Max's trust revoked his plan for prospective application of the clause via a lifetime trust. Because no grandchild had a vested interest in the trust assets and because the distribution plan adopted by Erla has no prospective application, we hold that the beneficiary restriction clause does not violate public policy.

Therefore, we reverse the judgment of the appellate court and remand to the circuit court for further proceedings.

Reversed and remanded.

Notice the facts that help the religious-marriage restriction in *Feinberg* to survive the public policy challenge. First, at the time that Erla died, each of the grandchildren either qualified or did not. Their behavior after the death of Erla would make no difference to their gifts. For that reason, future behaviors of the living would not be controlled or influenced by the dead hand of the past.

Second, the court states that the grandchildren did not have vested interests. As you know by now, the distinction between vested and contingent interests is a technical and formal one. Some conditions can be worded in one way to make an interest vested or in another way to make the interest contingent. And whether a condition is worded as a condition precedent or a condition subsequent is not necessarily related to the likelihood that the condition will be satisfied, i.e., to the chances that the interest holder will eventually take possession. As a matter of public policy, which is the challenge in *Feinberg*, does it serve any purpose to invest vestedness with importance in this context?

> Question 7.27: O devises into two trusts as follows: "In Trust A, the income is to accumulate until A reaches age 25. At that time, the trust assets shall be paid to the State of Israel, but if A is married to a Jew the trust assets shall be paid instead to A. In Trust B, the income is to accumulate until B reaches age 25. At that time, the trust assets shall be paid to B, but if B is not married to a Jew, the trust assets shall be paid to the State of Israel." At the time of O's death, A is 19 and B is 20. A and B both challenge the religious condition. As a matter of public policy, should A win? Should B win?

Courts often use the term "restraint" to refer to a condition that relates to the behavior of a devisee even when the condition merely creates incentives to behave one way or another without totally restraining the devisee. Courts have applied various tests to such restraints. Sometimes, the Constitution is in play. However, courts often find that there is no state action. Moreover, courts hesitate to get involved in deciding religious questions, such as whether a person observes a given religion or its principles.

Whether or not constitutional tests apply, a restraint must pass public policy tests. As indicated in *Feinberg*, conditions that encourage divorce are usually frowned upon. When restraints on marriage are at issue, some courts distinguish between total restraints and partial restraints. Total restraints on first marriage are usually unreasonable or contrary to public policy and are therefore void and unenforceable. Total restraints on remarriage can also be unreasonable, but have sometimes been held to be reasonable if the purpose is providing support until remarriage instead of discouraging remarriage. Partial restraints on marriage are valid if and only if they are reasonable. The factors within this reasonableness analysis include the likelihood that a marriage of the permitted sort will occur, the time given for thoughtful compliance, the degree to which the restriction will constrain religious expression and practice, and whether the restriction stops ongoing payments or prevents the start of distributions. A restriction that requires a devisee to marry a certain person is usually held to be unreasonable and contrary to public policy.

Other restrictions in wills and trusts that may be found to be contrary to public policy include provisions that disrupt family harmony, provisions that encourage harmful acts, and under the Restatement (Third) of Trusts, provisions that are "unreasonably intrusive into significant personal decisions or interests".

D. SEX AND RACE RESTRICTIONS

Daily discriminations on the basis of sex and race are uncountable. Many are illegal under federal, state, or local laws, while many others are beyond the scope of legal proscriptions. However, discriminations that would be outside legal constraints might run into trouble when attempted by means of a charitable trust. Questions arise, including the following: Is a trust that discriminates on the basis of sex or race permissible if only private actors are involved in its administration? If a government actor is a trustee of a trust that discriminates, may a court replace the trustee with a non-government actor? If the terms of a trust involve the government in some way other than as trustee, may a court strike those administrative provisions? When the terms of a trust eliminate some potential beneficiaries on the basis of sex or race, may a court strike the offending discriminatory terms? May a court strike the discriminatory terms when the instrument provides an alternative gift to take effect if the discriminatory provisions are illegal?

MATTER OF ESTATE OF WILSON
Court of Appeals of New York, 1983
452 N.E.2d 1228

COOKE, C.J.

These appeals present the question whether the equal protection clause of the Fourteenth Amendment is violated when a court permits the administration of private charitable trusts according to the testators' intent to finance the education of male students and not female students. When a court applies trust law that neither encourages, nor affirmatively promotes, nor compels private discrimination but allows parties to engage in private selection in the devise or bequest of their property, that choice will not be attributable to the State and subjected to the Fourteenth Amendment's strictures.

I

The factual patterns in each of these matters are different, but the underlying legal issues are the same. In each there is imposed a decedent's intention to create a testamentary trust under which the class of beneficiaries are members of one sex.

In Matter of Wilson, article ELEVENTH of Clark W. Wilson's will provided that the residuary of his estate be held in trust (Wilson Trust) and that the income "be applied to defraying the education and other expenses of the first year at college of five (5) young men who shall have graduated from the Canastota High School, three (3) of whom shall have attained the highest grades in the study of science and two (2) of whom shall have attained the highest grades in the study of chemistry, as may be certified to by the then Superintendent of Schools for the Canastota Central School

District." Wilson died in June, 1969 and for the next 11 years the Wilson Trust was administered according to its terms.

In early 1981, the Civil Rights Office of the United States Department of Education received a complaint alleging that the superintendent's acts in connection with the Wilson Trust violated title IX of the Education Amendments of 1972 (US Code, tit 20, § 1681 et. seq.), which prohibits gender discrimination in Federally financed education programs. The Department of Education informed the Canastota Central School District that the complaint would be investigated. Before the investigation was completed, the school district agreed to refrain from again providing names of students to the trustee. The trustee, Key Bank of Central New York, initiated this proceeding for a determination of the effect and validity of the trust provision of the will.

The Surrogate's Court held that the school superintendent's co-operation with the trustee violated no Federal statute or regulation prohibiting sexual discrimination, nor did it implicate the equal protection clause of the Fourteenth Amendment. The court ordered the trustee to continue administering the trust.

A unanimous Appellate Division, Third Department, modified the Surrogate's decree. The court affirmed the Surrogate's finding that the testator intended the trust to benefit male students only and, noting that the school was under no legal obligation to provide the names of qualified male candidates, found "administration of the trust according to its literal terms is impossible." The court then exercised its cy pres power to reform the trust by striking the clause in the will providing for the school superintendent's certification of the names of qualified candidates for the scholarships. The candidates were permitted to apply directly to the trustee.

Matter of Johnson also involves a call for judicial construction of a testamentary trust created for the exclusive benefit of male students. By a will dated December 13, 1975, Edwin Irving Johnson left his residuary estate in trust (Johnson Trust). Article SIXTH of the will provided that the income of the trust was to "be used and applied, each year to the extent available, for scholarships or grants for bright and deserving young men who have graduated from the High School of [the Croton-Harmon Union Free] School District, and whose parents are financially unable to send them to college, and who shall be selected by the Board of Education of such School District with the assistance of the Principal of such High School."

Johnson died in 1978. In accordance with the terms of the trust, the board of education, acting as trustee, announced that applications from male students would be accepted on or before May 1, 1979. Before any scholarships were awarded, however, the National Organization for Women, filed a complaint with the Civil Rights Office of the United States Department of Education. This complaint alleged that the school district's involvement in the Johnson Trust constituted illegal gender-based discrimination.

During the pendency of the Department of Education's investigation, a stipulation was entered into between the executrix of the will, the president of the board of education, and the Attorney-General. The parties sought "to avoid administering the educational bequest set forth in Article Sixth in a manner which is in conflict with the law and public policy prohibiting discrimination based on sex". The stipulation provided that "all interested parties agree to the deletion of the word 'men' in Article Sixth of the Will and the insertion of the word 'persons' in its place." The Attorney-General then brought this proceeding by petition to the Surrogate's Court to construe article SIXTH of the will.

The Surrogate found that the trustee's unwillingness to administer the trust according to its terms rendered administration of the trust impossible. The court, however, declined to reform the trust by giving effect to the stipulation. Rather, it reasoned that the testator's primary intent to benefit "deserving young men" would be most closely effected by replacing the school district with a private trustee.

A divided Appellate Division, Second Department, reversed, holding that under the equal protection clause of the Fourteenth Amendment, a court cannot reform a trust that, by its own terms, would deny equal protection of law. The court reasoned that inasmuch as an agent of the State had been appointed trustee, the trust, if administered, would violate the equal protection clause. Judicial reformation of the trust by substituting trustees would, in that court's view, itself constitute State action in violation of the Fourteenth Amendment. The court determined that administration of the trust was impossible and, in an exercise of its cy pres power, reformed the trust by eliminating the gender restriction.

II

On these appeals, this court is called upon to consider the testators' intent in establishing these trusts, evaluate the public policy implications of gender restrictive trusts generally, and determine whether the judicial reformation of these trusts violates the equal protection clause of the Fourteenth Amendment.

There can be no question that these trusts, established for the promotion of education, are for a charitable purpose within the meaning of the law. Charitable trusts are encouraged and favored by the law, and may serve any of a variety of benevolent purposes. Among the advantages the law extends to charitable trusts are their exemption from the rules against perpetuities and accumulations and their favorable tax treatment. Moreover, unlike other trusts, a charitable trust will not necessarily fail when the settlor's specific charitable purpose or direction can no longer be accomplished.

When a court determines that changed circumstances have rendered the administration of a charitable trust according to its literal terms either "impracticable or impossible", the court may exercise its cy pres power to reform the trust in a matter that "will most effectively accomplish its general purposes". In reforming trusts pursuant to this power, care must be taken to evaluate the precise purpose or direction of the testator, so that when the court directs the trust towards another charitable end, it will "give effect insofar as practicable to the full design of the testator as manifested by his will and codicil".

The court, of course, cannot invoke its cy pres power without first determining that the testator's specific charitable purpose is no longer capable of being performed by the trust. In establishing these trusts, the testators expressly and unequivocally intended that they provide for the educational expenses of male students. It cannot be said that the accomplishment of the testators' specific expression of charitable intent is "impossible or impracticable." So long as the subject high schools graduate boys with the requisite qualifications, the testators' specific charitable intent can be fulfilled.

Nor are the trusts' particular limitation of beneficiaries by gender invalid and incapable of being accomplished as violative of public policy. It is true that the eradication in this State of gender-based discrimination is an important public policy. Indeed, the Legislature has barred gender-based discrimination in education, employment, housing, credit, and many other areas. As a result, women, once viewed as able to assume only restricted roles in our society (see *Bradwell v. State*, 16 Wall [83 US] 130, 141), now project significant numbers "in business, in the professions, in government and, indeed, in all walks of life where education is a desirable, if not always a necessary, antecedent" (*Stanton v. Stanton*, 421 U.S. 7, 15). The restrictions in these trusts run contrary to this policy favoring equal opportunity and treatment of men and women. A provision in a charitable trust, however, that is central to the testator's or settlor's charitable purpose, and is not illegal, should not be invalidated on public policy grounds unless that provision, if given effect, would substantially mitigate the general charitable effect of the gift.

Proscribing the enforcement of gender restrictions in private charitable trusts would operate with equal force towards trusts whose benefits are bestowed exclusively on women. "Reduction of the disparity in economic condition between men and women caused by the long history of discrimination against women has been recognized as * * * an important governmental objective" (*Califano v. Webster*, 430 U.S. 313, 317). There can be little doubt that important efforts in effecting this type of social change can be and are performed through private philanthropy. And, the private funding of programs for the advancement of women is substantial and growing. Indeed, one compilation of financial assistance offered primarily or exclusively to women lists 854 sources of funding. Current thinking in private philanthropic institutions advocates that funding offered by such institutions and the opportunities within the institutions themselves be directly responsive to the needs of particular groups. It is evident, therefore, that the focusing of private philanthropy on certain classes within society may be consistent with public policy. Consequently, that the restrictions in the trusts before this court may run contrary to public efforts promoting equality of opportunity for women does not justify imposing a *per se* rule that gender restrictions in private charitable trusts violate public policy.

Finally, this is not an instance in which the restriction of the trusts serves to frustrate a paramount charitable purpose. In *Howard Sav. Inst. V. Peep*, 34 NJ 494, for example, the testator made a charitable bequest to Amherst College to be placed in trust and to provide scholarships for "deserving American born, Protestant, Gentile boys of good moral repute, not given to gambling, smoking, drinking or similar acts." Due to the religious restrictions, the college declined to accept the bequest as contrary to its charter. The court found that the college was the principal beneficiary of the trust, so that removing the religious restriction and thereby allowing the college to accept the gift would permit administration of the trust in a manner most closely effectuating the testator's intent.

In contrast, the trusts subject to these appeals were not intended to directly benefit the school districts. Although the testators sought the school districts' participation, this was incidental to their primary intent of financing part of the college education of boys who attended the schools. Consequently, severance of the school districts' role in the trusts' administration will not frustrate any part of the testators' charitable purposes. Inasmuch as the specific charitable intent of the testators is not inherently "impossible or impracticable" of being achieved by the trusts, there is no occasion to exercise cy pres power.

Although not inherently so, these trusts are currently incapable of being administered as originally intended because of the school districts' unwillingness to co-operate. These impediments, however, may be remedied by an exercise of a court's general equitable power over all trusts to permit a deviation from the administrative terms of a trust and to appoint a successor trustee.

A testamentary trust will not fail for want of a trustee and, in the event a trustee is unwilling or unable to act, a court may replace the trustee with another. Accordingly, the proper means of continuing the Johnson Trust would be to replace the school district with someone able and willing to administer the trust according to its terms.

When an impasse is reached in the administration of a trust due to an incidental requirement of its terms, a court may effect, or permit the trustee to effect, a deviation from the trust's literal terms. This power differs from a court's cy pres power in that "[t]hrough exercise of its deviation power the court alters or amends administrative provisions in the trust instrument but does not alter the purpose of the charitable trust or change its dispositive provisions". The Wilson Trust provision that the school district certify a list of students is an incidental part of the trust's administrative requirements, which no longer can be satisfied in light of the district's refusal to co-operate. The same result intended by the testator may be accomplished by permitting the students to apply directly to the trustee. Therefore, a deviation from the Wilson Trust's administrative terms by eliminating the certification requirement would be the appropriate method of continuing that trust's administration.

III

It is argued before this court that the judicial facilitation of the continued administration of gender-restrictive charitable trusts violates the equal protection clause of the Fourteenth Amendment. The strictures of the equal protection clause are invoked when the State engages in invidious discrimination. Indeed, the State itself cannot, consistent with the Fourteenth Amendment, award scholarships that are gender restrictive.

The Fourteenth Amendment, however, "erects no shield against merely private conduct, however discriminatory or wrongful." (*Shelley v. Kraemer*, 334 U.S. 1, 13; see *Blum v. Yaretski*, 457 U.S. 991, 1002; *Jackson v. Metropolitan Edison Co.*, 419 U.S. 345, 349; *Moose Lodge No. 107 v. Irvis*, 407 U.S. 163, 171–179, *supra.*; *Evans v. Abney*, 396 U.S. 435, 445). Private discrimination may violate equal protection of the law when accompanied by State participation in, facilitation of, and, in some cases, acquiescence in the discrimination. Although there is no conclusive test to determine when State involvement in private discrimination will violate the Fourteenth Amendment, the general standard that has evolved is whether "the conduct allegedly causing the deprivation of a federal right [is] fairly attributable to the state". Therefore, it is a question of "state responsibility" and "[o]nly by sifting facts and weighing circumstances can the * * * involvement of the State in private conduct be attributed its true significance".

The Supreme Court has identified various situations in which the State may be deemed responsible for discriminatory conduct with private origins. For example, one such instance appears when the State delegates one of its inherent functions to private parties and those parties engage in discrimination. Another arises when the State does not directly enforce or abet the private discrimination, but substantially facilitates and profits from it.

"The Court has never held, of course, that discrimination by an otherwise private entity would be violative of the Equal Protection Clause if the private entity receives any sort of benefit of service at all from the State, or if it is subject to State regulation in any degree whatever" (*Moose Lodge No. 107 v. Irvis*, 407 U.S. 163, 173, *supra*). Rather, "the State must have 'significantly involved itself with invidious discriminations' * * * in order for the discriminatory action to fall within the ambit of the constitutional prohibition".

The State generally may not be held responsible for private discrimination solely on the basis that it permits the discrimination to occur. Nor is the State under an affirmative obligation to prevent purely private discrimination. Therefore, when the State regulates private dealings it may be responsible for private discrimination occurring in the regulated field only when enforcement of its regulation has the effect of compelling the private discrimination.

In *Shelley v. Kraemer (supra)*, for example, the Supreme Court held that the equal protection clause was violated by judicial enforcement of a private covenant that prohibited the sale of affected properties to "people of Negro or Mongolian Race." When one of the properties was sold to a black family, the other property owners sought to enforce the covenant in State court and the family was ordered to move from the property. The Supreme Court noted "that the restrictive agreements standing alone cannot be regarded as violative of any rights guaranteed to petitioners by the Fourteenth Amendment. So long as the purposes of those agreements are effectuated by voluntary adherence to their terms, it would appear clear that there has been no action by the State and the provisions of the Amendment have not been violated". The court held, however, that it did have before it cases "in which the States have merely abstained from action leaving private individuals free to impose such discriminations as they see fit. Rather, these are cases in which the States have made available to such individuals the full coercive power of the government to deny petitioners, on the grounds of race or color, the enjoyment of property rights". It was not the neutral regulation of contracts permitting parties to enter discriminatory agreements that caused the discrimination to be attributable to the State. Instead, it was that the State court's exercise of its judicial power directly effected a discriminatory act.

In *Barrows v. Jackson*, 346 U.S. 249, *supra*, the court applied the same reasoning when it held that a court's awarding damages against a party who has breached a racially restrictive covenant also violates the equal protection clause. The court reiterated that "voluntary adherence [to the covenant] would constitute individual action only". But, "[t]o compel respondent to respond in damages would be for the State to punish her for failure to perform her covenant to continue to discriminate against non-Caucasians in the use of her property * * * Thus, it becomes not respondent's voluntary choice but the State's choice that she observe her covenant or suffer damages".

More recently, the Supreme Court considered whether a State's regulation of private clubs licensed to serve liquor caused a club's restrictive membership policy to be attributable to the State (see *Moose Lodge No. 107 v. Irvis*, 407 U.S. 163, *supra*). The court held that although the State extensively regulated these private clubs, it was not responsible for the private discrimination simply because the regulation permitted the discrimination to occur. The court stated that "[h]owever detailed this type of regulation may be in some particulars, it cannot be said to in any way foster or encourage * * * discrimination". The court distinguished the regulatory scheme's general neutral effect on the discrimination from a situation in which that scheme could be used to compel discrimination. One of the regulations provided that " '[e]very club licensee shall adhere to all of the provisions of its Constitution and By-Laws' ". The court acknowledged that if this regulation were used "to place state sanctions behind [the licensee's] discriminatory membership rules," the Fourteenth Amendment would be implicated. Accordingly, the court enjoined enforcement of the regulation.

A court's application of its equitable power to permit the continued administration of the trusts involved in these appeals falls outside the ambit of the Fourteenth Amendment. Although the field of trusts is regulated by the State, the Legislature's failure to forbid private discriminatory trusts does not cause such trusts, when they arise, to be attributable to the State. It naturally follows that, when a court applies this trust law and determines that it permits the continued existence of private discriminatory trusts, the Fourteenth Amendment is not implicated.

In the present appeals, the coercive power of the State has never been enlisted to enforce private discrimination. Upon finding that requisite formalities of creating a trust had been met, the courts below determined the testator's intent, and applied the relevant law permitting those intentions to be privately carried out. The court's power compelled no discrimination. That discrimination had been sealed in the private execution of the wills. Recourse to the courts was had here only for the purpose of facilitating the administration of the trusts, not for enforcement of their discriminatory dispositive provisions.

This is not to say that a court's exercise of its power over trusts can never invoke the scrutiny of the Fourteenth Amendment. This court holds only that a trust's discriminatory terms are not fairly attributable to the State when a court applies trust principles that permit private discrimination but do not encourage, affirmatively promote, or compel it.

The testators' intention to involve the State in the administration of these trusts does not alter this result, notwithstanding that the effect of the courts' action respecting the trusts was to eliminate this involvement. The courts' power to replace a trustee who is unwilling to act as in Johnson or to permit a deviation from an incidental administrative term in the trust as in Wilson is a part of the law permitting this private conduct and extends to all trusts regardless of their purposes. It compels no discrimination. Moreover, the minimal State participation in the trusts' administration prior to the time that they reached the courts for the constructions under review did not cause the trusts to take on an indelible public character.

In sum, the Fourteenth Amendment does not require the State to exercise the full extent of its power to eradicate private discrimination. It is only when the State itself discriminates, compels another to discriminate, or allows another to assume one of its functions and discriminate that such discrimination will implicate the amendment.

Accordingly, in Matter of Wilson, the order of the Appellate Division should be affirmed, with costs payable out of the estate to all parties appearing separately and filing separate briefs.

In Matter of Johnson, the order of the Appellate Division should be reversed, with costs payable out of the estate to all parties appearing separately and filing separate briefs and the decree of the Surrogate's Court, Westchester County, reinstated.

MEYER, J. (Concurring in Matter of Wilson and dissenting in Matter of Johnson).

I would affirm in both cases. Although the Constitution does not proscribe private bias, it does proscribe affirmative State action in furtherance of bias.

In Matter of Wilson the trust is private and the only involvement of a public official (the superintendent of schools) is his certification of a student's class standing, information which is, in any event, available to any student applying to the trustee for a scholarship. There is, therefore, no State action.

In Matter of Johnson, however, the trustee is the board of education, a public body. The establishment of a public trust for a discriminatory purpose is constitutionally improper, as Presiding Justice Mollen has fully spelled out in his opinion. For the State to legitimize that impropriety by replacement of the trustee is unconstitutional State action. The only permissible corrective court action is, as the Appellate Division held, excision of the discriminatory limitation.

Would the result in *Wilson* be the same if the court had applied the Restatement (Third) of Trusts § 28? Comment '*f*' states,

> Like other trusts, charitable trusts are subject to the rule of § 29 that trust purposes and provisions must not be unlawful or contrary to public policy. It is particularly common [to limit benefits] to persons of a particular national origin, religion, gender, sexual orientation, age group, political affiliation, ... Provisions of these types in charitable trusts are not valid if they involve *invidious* discrimination ...

In *In re Certain Scholarship Funds*, 133 N.H. 227 (1990), the New Hampshire court declined to follow *Wilson*:

> * * * Having concluded that the State's participation in the beneficiary selection process, management, and miscellaneous administration of these trusts is constitutionally impermissible, we now turn to the issue of whether the trial court erred in employing the *cy pres* doctrine to reform these trusts, replacing the terms "boy" and "protestant boy" with the term "student."
>
> * * *
>
> * * * we hold that the trial court properly invoked the doctrine of *cy pres* to strike the terms "boy" and "protestant boy" and to replace them with the term "student."
>
> * * *
>
> The two leading cases that have dealt with this issue are *Commonwealth of Pennsylvania v. Brown*, 392 F.2d 120 (3d Cir.), *cert. denied*, 391 U.S. 921 (1968), and *Matter of Estate of Wilson supra*. In *Commonwealth of Pennsylvania v. Brown*, the United States Court of Appeals for the Third

Circuit ruled on the constitutionality of the actions taken by the Orphan's Court in substituting a private trustee for a public trustee to administer a discriminatory trust established by Stephen Girard. The court held that the substitution and selection of trustees by the Commonwealth, in an effort to uphold the discriminatory purposes of the trust, did "significantly encourage and involve the Commonwealth in private discriminations" and was therefore unconstitutional "State action." * * *

* * *

* * * As we said above, we believe that the appropriate source of values for our judgment is the constitution, which forbids the agencies of the State to act in a manner that would preserve the constitutionally impermissible desires of the testator. We therefore reach the same result ordered in *Commonwealth of Pennsylvania v. Brown supra.* Furthermore, we hold that the use of the court's powers to appoint or reappoint a trustee in those cases where the trust involved is, and has been from its inception, a privately administered lawful discriminatory trust, does not rise to the same level of State involvement so as to be considered significant.

The lengthy dissent argued for following *Wilson.*

> Question 7.28: Your law office is in New Hampshire and a client asks you to set up a trust for scholarships for boys in a New Hampshire school. Should you tell your client that such a trust is contrary to New Hampshire public policy? Should you draft the trust to be governed by the law of New York or another state following *Wilson*? Should you advise the client to move the trust assets to a New York bank?

A settlor who includes a purpose that is illegal or contrary to public policy might fail to create a charitable trust or perhaps might fail to create a trust at all. When that happens, courts sometimes *cy pres* the instrument, striking the illegal terms or otherwise converting the purposes to legal purposes. There could be a boot-strapping problem with this solution. The *cy pres* power is limited to charitable trusts and one might argue that a trust cannot be charitable if it violates a statute or otherwise offends public policy. Nevertheless, courts have invoked their *cy pres* power, changing the terms to create a charitable trust.

For a trust to be a charitable trust, it must have a charitable purpose. Many charitable purposes overlap with the functions of government, including the provision of public goods. Providing services that are provided by governments increases the chances that constitutional and other prohibitions on discrimination will apply. Georgia Senator Augustus O. Bacon died in 1914, devising land to the City of Macon for recreation grounds to be called Baconsfield for "white women, white girls, white boys and white children of the City of Macon". The trustees were also given discretion to admit Macon's white men and white persons of other communities. Upon challenge, the City resigned as trustee and the probate court appointed private trustees. In *Evans v. Newton*, 382 U.S. 296 (1966), the Supreme Court found that the park had been in the public sector and the change of trustees was not enough to transfer the park to the private sector, making the race limitation unconstitutional. After that, a Georgia court found that *cy pres* was inappropriate because Bacon would have preferred termination to integration. In *Evans v. Abney*, 396 U.S. 435 (1970), the Supreme Court affirmed (7–2).

> Question 7.29: O devises "$10,000,000 to T in trust, the income to be paid to the Sierra Club Foundation (while it remains a charity) to support the hiring of white employees. If this limitation to white employees is unacceptable to the Sierra Club Foundation or declared noncharitable by a court, the income is to be paid to the Pacific Legal Foundation (while it remains a charity)." Since one of the original goals of the Pacific Legal Foundation was to fight against the environmental protections promoted by the Sierra Club, the Sierra Club Foundation convinces T to ask a court to apply its *cy pres* power to the trust and strike the "white" limitation. The Pacific Legal Foundation opposes the application of *cy pres*, claiming that the trust income should be paid instead to it. What should the court do?

HOME FOR INCURABLES OF BALTIMORE CITY v. UNIVERSITY OF MARYLAND MEDICAL SYSTEM CORP.

Court of Appeals of Maryland, 2002
797 A.2d 746

ELDRIDGE, J.

The controversy in this case concerns a paragraph in a will which makes a charitable bequest to a private nonprofit hospital known as the "Home for Incurables of Baltimore City" or the "Keswick Home." The purpose of the bequest, as stated in the will, was for the Keswick Home to construct a new building for "white patients who need physical rehabilitation." The racially discriminatory "white" patient limitation on the use of the building is clearly illegal.[1] The will further provides that if the bequest is "not acceptable to the Keswick Home, then this bequest shall go to the University of Maryland Hospital to be used for physical rehabilitation." The University of Maryland Hospital is part of the University of Maryland Medical System Corporation.

The Keswick Home will not and cannot comply with the racially discriminatory condition, but otherwise the bequest is fully acceptable to the Home. The alternative disposition to the University of Maryland Hospital does not contain the unlawful racially discriminatory condition.

The broad question before us is whether, under Maryland law, a court will enforce the illegal racially discriminatory condition by ordering that the proceeds be paid to the alternative beneficiary, the University of Maryland Hospital. Our answer to this question shall be "No." Instead, the provisions of the will should be applied without giving any effect to the word "white."

I.

* * *

Dr. Jesse C. Coggins executed six wills, with multiple codicils, over the course of his lifetime. Beginning with his original will prepared in January 1944, and in every will thereafter, Dr. Coggins left the residue of his estate in trust and provided that, upon termination of the trust, the corpus was to be distributed to the "Keswick Home, formerly Home for Incurables of Baltimore City, with the request that said Home use the estate and property thus passing to it for the acquisition or construction of a new building to provide additional housing accommodations to be known as the 'Coggins Building. . . .' " Throughout the years, Dr. Coggins and his wife were closely associated with the Keswick Home. Thus, Dr. Coggins operated the Laurel Sanitarium from which he regularly transferred patients to Keswick because of its rehabilitative

---

[1] Among other legal provisions, Maryland Code (1982, 2000 Repl.Vol.), § 19–355 of the Health General Article, flatly states: "A hospital or related institution may not discriminate in providing personal care for an individual because of the race, color, or national origin of the individual."

capabilities. Mrs. Coggins became a nurse at the Sanitarium in 1940, and she and her husband continued to operate the sanitarium for the next 23 years. Mrs. Coggins served actively on Keswick's Board of Directors, and, toward the end of her life, Mrs. Coggins was a resident in Keswick's integrated Coggins Building. According to a memorandum by the Trustee, Mercantile Safe Deposit & Trust Company, in 1986 Mrs. Coggins requested that the Trustee change some of the securities in the trust, "despite the fact that her . . . income would decline. . . ." The memorandum stated that "[h]er feeling is that her personal assets are also pledged to Keswick and that this gesture will enlarge the ultimate gifts which Keswick will receive."

Dr. Coggins died on January 21, 1963. In his last will, dated December 27, 1962, after making a bequest of tangible personal property and a number of other bequests, Dr. Coggins gave the residue of his estate to the Mercantile Safe Deposit & Trust Company ("Mercantile") to be held by it as Trustee under "ITEM 5" of the will. The trust provided for monthly payments to four income beneficiaries until the death of the last of them. The last of these annuitants was Dr. Coggins's widow who died on September 10, 1998.

Paragraph (f) of ITEM 5 of the will stated that, upon the death of the survivor of the four annuitants,

> "the trust shall terminate and the assets thereof as then constituted together with all unpaid income shall be paid over free of trust unto the KESWICK HOME, formerly Home for Incurables of Baltimore City, with the request that said Home use the estate and property thus passing to it for the acquisition or construction of a new building to provide additional housing accommodations to be known as the 'Coggins Building,' to house white patients who need physical rehabilitation. If not acceptable to the Keswick Home, then this bequest shall go to the University of Maryland Hospital to be used for physical rehabilitation."

The clause "to house white patients who need physical rehabilitation," and the alternative gift over to University Hospital, appeared for the first time in Dr. Coggins's final will executed less than one month before his death.

On February 7, 1963, about two weeks after Dr. Coggins's death, John T. Kenny, Vice President of Mercantile, provided a copy of the will to Keswick and stated in an accompanying letter:

"On the death of the last survivor of the four annuitants, the trust terminates, and the estate passes free of trust to the Keswick Home as directed in Item 5(f) of the Will."

In 1964, Keswick's Board of Directors began to discuss a plan, prepared by Keswick's "New Building Committee," for the construction of a new building. Keswick's Board of Directors in 1969 designated the new building that was to be constructed as the "Coggins" building, "in honor of the late Dr. Jesse C. Coggins and in appreciation of his great generosity to 'Keswick.'" Construction of the building began in 1970 and was financed by a loan from Mercantile, gifts, and a grant under the federal Hill Burton Act, 42 U.S.C. § 291 *et seq.* Construction was completed in 1974, and the building was dedicated as the "Coggins Building" in 1975.

During the next twenty years, Keswick made renovations and constructed a major addition to the Coggins Building. These were paid for by donations and bank loans. As of the date the trust terminated, Keswick had expended nearly $11 million in construction costs and capitalized repairs for the Coggins Building, which was being used to house approximately 160 residents, all of whom were or had been receiving physical rehabilitation services. After operating the Coggins building for many years, Keswick presented Mercantile with future plans that outlined a program for the expenditure of an additional $15.5 million, to be taken from the Coggins Trust, in construction costs for more additions and renovations to the Coggins Building.

Upon the death of Mrs. Coggins in September 1998, a Mercantile memorandum stated:

"The last beneficiary of this trust died recently. Therefore, the trust now terminates and the balance transfers to Keswick Home. According to the will, the money is for construction of the Coggins Building. Keswick actually built the Coggins Building with their own money ($10 million) . . . because they needed the building at that time and because we agreed to reimburse them from the trust when it terminated."

Nevertheless, Mercantile did not turn over the trust proceeds to Keswick. Instead, in 1999 Mercantile filed the present interpleader action pursuant to Maryland Rule 2–221, asserting that, depending upon the will's construction, the trust assets were to be "distribut[ed] to one of two . . . named, competing, and alternative beneficiaries." Mercantile stated that, in order to fulfill its obligation to distribute the trust assets properly, and being concerned that an improper distribution might subject Mercantile to liability, an order of interpleader was necessary.

The Circuit Court for Baltimore City entered an order of interpleader whereby Keswick was designated as the plaintiff and University Hospital was designated as the defendant. As earlier mentioned, both parties filed motions for summary judgment, and the case was presented to the Circuit Court on a stipulation of facts and several documents.

Keswick argued that Dr. Coggins did not intend the racial restriction to be a binding condition for Keswick to receive the bequest, and that he did not intend for the gift to fail if it became legally impossible for Keswick to comply with the racial restriction. Keswick also argued that it had "accepted" the bequest within the meaning of the will's language. In addition, Keswick contended that, as a matter of public policy and Maryland law, the illegal racial restriction should be excised. Keswick maintained that Maryland law does not "present Keswick with a Hobson's choice: either violate the law or forfeit a bequest that would significantly assist Keswick in pursuing its charitable endeavors." Keswick also relied upon the federal Civil Rights Act of 1866, 42 U.S.C. §§ 1981 and 1982, upon the Fourteenth Amendment, upon the Maryland Constitution, upon Maryland anti-discrimination statutes, and upon Maryland cases declining to enforce conditions in wills which are impossible to perform, illegal, or contrary to public policy.

University Hospital argued that the controlling factor in the case was Dr. Coggins's intention and that, based on the language of the will as well as the surrounding circumstances, it was clear that Dr. Coggins intended for the Coggins building to "house only white patients." University Hospital argued that, if Keswick would not comply with this racial restriction, Dr. Coggins clearly intended that the trust pass to the alternative beneficiary, University Hospital. University Hospital further contended "that the racial restriction" was not "so heinous that it should simply be read out of the will," and that the cases under the Fourteenth Amendment's Equal

Protection Clause did not require that the racial restriction " 'be treated as absolutely void.' " University Hospital claimed that judicial enforcement of the racially discriminatory restriction would not constitute state action in violation of equal protection principles. University Hospital maintained that, because the will involved a charitable bequest, the issue was controlled by the *cy pres* doctrine under state law. Moreover, according to University Hospital, the *cy pres* doctrine would not permit the striking of the illegal racial restriction because of the presence of the gift over to an alternative beneficiary. University Hospital argued that cases striking out illegal or impossible conditions in non-charitable trusts, such as *Fleishman v. Bregel, supra,* 174 Md. 87, were inapplicable to charitable trusts because the latter were controlled by the Maryland Uniform Charitable Trusts Administration Act, known as the *cy pres* statute, Code § 14–302 of the Estates and Trusts Article. University Hospital's position was that, even though it would be "illegal for Keswick to accept the bequest on Dr. Coggins' terms," nevertheless "the principle of freedom of testation entitled Dr. Coggins to impose the racial condition. . . ."

The Circuit Court filed a written opinion which essentially adopted the arguments by University Hospital. The court entered a judgment granting University Hospital's motion for summary judgment and ordering "that the proceeds of the bequest in question, . . . in the amount of $28,834,000.00, plus any additional interest earned minus costs of the proceeding shall be paid to University of Maryland Medical System Corporation." Keswick appealed, and this Court issued a writ of certiorari prior to any proceedings in the Court of Special Appeals.

II.

The issues raised and the arguments made by the parties in this Court are basically the same as those advanced in the Circuit Court. We find it unnecessary, however, to address every argument made by the parties. Instead, we shall assume, *arguendo*, that Dr. Coggins intended the racial restriction to be a condition for Keswick to have the bequest, that Keswick's inability to comply with the illegal condition means that Keswick has not "accepted" the gift within the meaning of the will, and that judicial enforcement of the racially discriminatory condition, by awarding the proceeds to University Hospital, will not violate the United States Constitution, federal statutes, or the Maryland Constitution. Nonetheless, we shall hold that, under our cases dealing with illegal conditions in wills as well as the *cy pres* doctrine, the bequest should be awarded to Keswick.

This Court has long held that where a bequest is conditioned upon the commission of an illegal act or an act which is legally impossible of fulfillment, the condition is invalid on the ground of public policy. Under these circumstances, the condition will not be enforced by awarding the bequest to an alternative beneficiary; instead, the illegal condition will be excised.

Thus, in *Fleishman v. Bregel, supra,* 174 Md. 87, the testator left her estate in trust, with directions that the trustee pay one-half of the net income to her older son William and one-half of the net income to her younger son Calvin. The will further provided that, when the younger son reached the age of 30, at which time, "if William . . . shall be no longer married to his present wife," the trust would terminate and the corpus would become the property of both sons "equally, as tenants in common." If, however, when Calvin became 30, William "shall be living with his present wife," the trust would continue as to him. He would receive a share of the income but would never receive any of the corpus which would pass under an alternative disposition. After the testator's death, William brought a declaratory judgment action challenging the viability of the condition that he divorce or cease living with his wife. In holding that the condition was unenforceable, and that William was entitled to one-half of the corpus of the trust upon Calvin's reaching the age of 30, this Court initially stated:

> "But under the conditions of that item, he must divorce his wife or in any event cease to live with her in order to have the corpus. He is thus afforded a financial reward for securing a divorce or ceasing to live with his wife. Since he has no valid reason for not living with her, he can secure a divorce only through fraud or collusion, and in either case the conditions which induce him to take such action for reward are against public policy. To enforce them by compliance would tend to disrupt appellant's family relations, and it is inconceivable that a more improper motive for terminating such relations could be held out to him than by the provisions in question."

The Court then concluded (174 Md. at 99–100):

> "[T]he conditions of that item relating to appellant's marital status, both in regard to no longer living with his wife and

with reference to securing a divorce from her, are void as against public policy, and . . . the bequest is consequently unaffected by such conditions. These conclusions concerning those conditions are in no way affected by the expression used by testatrix in the second paragraph of that item requiring their performance by the time of her decease, for since during the twenty-three days which elapsed between the date of executing the will and death of testatrix there existed no cause entitling appellant to a divorce from his wife, it must be assumed that he could not have procured one. That requirement must, therefore, be regarded as impossible of fulfillment."

The principle applied in *Fleishman v. Bregel* has also been applied by this Court to charitable bequests. In *Keyser v. Calvary Brethren Church, supra,* 192 Md. at 522, the testator left a sum of money to the Calvary Brethren Church "for the building of a Church to be held in trust for five years[;] if they do not build within five years then this returns to my estate." The testator died on May 14, 1942. The United States Government had restricted the use of building materials on April 9, 1942, because of the Second World War, and did not lift the restrictions until June 1947. In July 1947, more than five years from the testator's death, the Church began construction of the building. The executor and the residuary legatees appealed from a trial court order directing distribution of the bequest to the Calvary Brethren Church, relying on the noncompliance with the condition that the building be constructed within five years. Viewing the five-year building requirement as a "condition subsequent," this Court affirmed the decree on two grounds. The Court expressed the view that "[w]e cannot suppose that the testatrix intended that such a condition should defeat her express desire that the appellee build a church. It started to build such a church as soon as it could, and has now constructed one . . . ." Alternatively, the Court pointed out that the federal law restrictions made the condition legally impossible to comply with, and that " '[a] condition which is legally impossible of performance without violation of law may ordinarily be regarded as invalid by reason of illegality rather than of impossibility.' " The Court then summarized (192 Md. at 525):

"We conclude that, from either of these points of view, the church is relieved from compliance with the condition subsequent. The testatrix could not have intended to require performance in the contingency that arose, and the church could not have performed without a violation of law. Indeed, it may be doubted if it could have performed at all, because, had it attempted to proceed without a permit, and had it been able to get the materials needed without priorities, the construction undoubtedly would have been promptly stopped by action of the authorities."

In addition to the *Fleishman* and *Keyser* opinions, *see, e.g., Loats Asylum v. Essom*, 220 Md. 11, 22 (1959) (reiterating the holding of the Keyser case); *Ellicott v. Ellicott, supra*, 90 Md. at 331–332 ("The performance [of the condition] becoming impossible . . ., it is dispensed with and the estate vested absolutely"); *Hammond v. Hammond*, 55 Md. 575, 582–583 (1881) ("the condition annexed to this bequest is . . . so clearly posterior to the vesting of the legacy, that we have no difficulty in declaring it a condition subsequent, and its performance becoming impossible . . ., the legatee takes unconditionally"); *Martin v. Young, supra*, 55 Md.App. at 406–407 ("For centuries courts have recognized that impossibility of performance may modify the legal effect of the breach of a condition in a will. * * * The appellees herein insist that we follow the rule . . . that, before a devise of real property made upon a condition precedent could take effect, the condition had to be performed even though performance was rendered impossible through no fault of the devisee. We decline to do so").[3]

University Hospital distinguishes *Fleishman v. Bregel, supra*, 174 Md. 87, on the ground that *Fleishman* did not involve a charitable trust. University argues that the principle regarding illegal conditions in bequests, applied in *Fleishman*, has no application to charitable trust bequests, and that illegal conditions attached to charitable trust bequests are governed entirely by the *cy pres* doctrine, embodied in the Maryland Uniform Charitable Trusts

---

[3] The *Keyser, Ellicott,* and *Hammond* opinions in this Court distinguished between "conditions precedent" and "conditions subsequent" attached to bequests. The Court in *Keyser*, 192 Md. at 523–524, pointed out that "if a gift is first given and then a condition is added by later words, such condition is generally held to be" a condition subsequent, "that the law favors the early vesting of estates," and that when a " 'condition subsequent becomes impossible, the general rule is that an estate granted upon such condition becomes absolute,' ". The cases in this Court which have discussed "conditions precedent" and "conditions subsequent" in the context of wills and of illegal conditions or conditions which are impossible of performance, have all categorized them as "conditions subsequent" and have refused to enforce them. * * *

    * * *

In our view, the illegal racial condition in Dr. Coggins's will should be excised regardless of the distinction between conditions precedent and conditions subsequent. Consequently, we need not and shall not consider whether the distinction, as applied to bequests, has any viability today.

Administration Act, otherwise know as the *cy pres* statute, Code (1974, 2001 Repl.Vol.), § 14–302 of the Estates and Trusts Article.[4] University Hospital asserts that "the Maryland *cy pres* statute controls this case." University also argues that *Keyser v. Calvary Brethren Church, supra,* 192 Md. 520, although involving a charitable bequest, is similarly distinguishable because the will in that case was written prior to the adoption of the *cy pres* statute, and that, under Maryland cases, the *cy pres* statute has no application to wills written prior to its enactment.[5]

The *cy pres* statute directs a Maryland court to salvage a bequest for charity and administer the bequest as nearly as possible in accordance with the testator's intent if, at the time it becomes effective, the bequest "is illegal, or impossible or impracticable of enforcement," as long as "the settlor or testator manifested a general intention to devote the property to charity . . . ." Seizing upon the statutory language that the testator have a *general intention* to devote the property to charity, University Hospital contends that, in light of the gift over to the alternative beneficiary, Dr. Coggins did not have such a general charitable intent. University Hospital, citing some cases from other states, argues for an absolute rule

"that a 'general charitable intention' is not present where a testator has expressly provided a 'gift over' in the event that

---

[4]   Section 14–302 provides as follows:

"§ 14–302.   Uniform Charitable Trusts Administration Act.

   (a)   General rule.—If a trust for charity is or becomes illegal, or impossible or impracticable of enforcement or if a devise or bequest for charity, at the time it was intended to become effective, is illegal, or impossible or impracticable of enforcement, and if the settlor or testator manifested a general intention to devote the property to charity, a court of equity, on application of any trustee, or any interested person, or the Attorney General of the State, may order an administration of the trust, devise or bequest as nearly as possible to fulfill the general charitable intention of the settlor or testator.

   (b)   Uniformity of construction.—This section shall be interpreted and construed to effectuate its general purpose to make uniform the law of those states which enact it.

   (c)   Short title.—This section may be cited as the Maryland Uniform Charitable Trust Administration Act."

[5]   University Hospital also distinguishes *Keyser v. Calvary Brethren Church* on the basis of this Court's conclusion in the *Keyser* opinion that "[w]e cannot suppose that the testatrix intended that such a condition should defeat her express desire that the appellee build a church." 192 Md. at 524. As previously discussed, however, this was an alternative reason set forth in the *Keyser* opinion. Moreover, the statement was not based upon any extrinsic evidence, but was an inference drawn by this Court from the will itself. The same could be said about Dr. Coggins's last will. In December 1962, when the will was drawn, Dr. Coggins or the scrivener were undoubtedly aware that a publicly owned and operated hospital, like University, could not legally discriminate on the basis of race or color, and thus the racially discriminatory condition was not part of the gift over. Presumably, if Dr. Coggins had known that it would in the future become a violation of Maryland statutes for a private hospital to discriminate based on race or color, he would not have attached the racially discriminatory condition to the primary bequest to Keswick.

the initial charitable bequest fails for illegality, impossibility, or any other reason."

Furthermore, University's argument continues, there is no legal "support for Keswick's argument that a charitable bequest can be reformed or modified on some basis other than *cy pres*." As previously mentioned, University maintains that opinions of this Court such as *Fleishman v. Bregel, supra*, and *Keyser v. Calvary Brethren Church, supra*, which would support the excising of an illegal condition attached to a bequest, have no application to charitable bequests in wills written after the enactment of the *cy pres* statute.

Consequently, under University Hospital's theory, the *cy pres* statute, which was intended to save charitable bequests, should be used as a sword to strike down the charitable bequest to Keswick even though, under Maryland law prior to the *cy pres* statute, the bequest to Keswick would not have failed. We decline to adopt University Hospital's construction of the *cy pres* statute. It is not supported by the language of the statute, by the statutory purpose, by reason, or by any Maryland appellate case.

There are a few cases elsewhere which do support University Hospital's position regarding cy pres statutes. They hold that, where there is an illegal discriminatory condition attached to a charitable bequest, and a reversionary clause or provision for a gift over if the condition is not complied with, there is no general charitable intention and the *cy pres* doctrine does not permit a court to save the primary bequest by excising the illegal condition. Instead, under this view, a court should enforce the testator's discriminatory purpose by awarding the bequest to the alternative beneficiary. A leading case to this effect, and the case primarily relied on by University Hospital, is the 1972 opinion of the Superior Court of Connecticut in *Connecticut Bank and Trust Co. v. Johnson Memorial Hospital, supra*, 30 Conn.Supp. 1. *See also Smyth v. Anderson*, 238 Ga. 343, 348–349 (1977).

Most of the cases relied on by University Hospital, however, do not involve illegal conditions attached to charitable bequests; instead, they involve conditions which could not be complied with for other reasons. *See also*, Wilner, *The Cy Pres Doctrine Explored*, 22 Md. L.Rev. 340, 348 (1962) (citing a Pennsylvania lower court case and an Illinois case for the general proposition "that *cy pres* . . . will not be applied where the trust or will provides for a specific alternate distribution effective on the failure of the primary charitable gift").

On the other hand, the position taken in the Connecticut case has been criticized, and there are decisions to the contrary. As pointed out in IVA Scott and Fratcher, *Scott On Trusts*, § 399.4A (4th ed.1987),

> "it has been held that if it is expressly provided by the terms of the trust that if the restriction is illegal the property should go to a different charity, the doctrine of cy pres is not applicable and the gift over takes effect. In *Connecticut Bank & Trust Co. v. Johnson* a testatrix left money in trust to be used in a particular hospital for the care of patients of the caucasian race. She provided that if the terms of the trust should be illegal or ineffective, the money should go to other designated charities. It was held that the racial restriction was illegal, and that because there was a gift over, the doctrine of cy pres was not applicable.

> "On the other hand, it has been held in several cases that where the restriction was illegal, the doctrine of cy pres was applicable, and that the trust should be carried on free of the restriction."

For cases applying the *cy pres* doctrine and declining to invoke the absolute rule advocated by University Hospital, some of which involve wills containing gifts over or reversionary clauses and some of which do not, *see, e.g.,* [citing cases from eight jurisdictions].

As previously pointed out, the purpose of the *cy pres* statute was to save some charitable bequests which would have failed under prior law, and not to strike down bequests which would have been saved under cases like *Fleishman v. Bregel, supra,* 174 Md. 87, and *Keyser v. Calvary Brethren Church, supra,* 192 Md. 520. Moreover, nothing in the language of the *cy pres* statute mandates a rule that a court cannot excise an illegal condition attached to a charitable bequest whenever the will contains an express gift over or a reversionary clause. Furthermore, where the gift over is also to a charity, it would seem that the testator's general charitable intent is confirmed.

As acknowledged by University Hospital, no Maryland appellate case has held that a charitable bequest with an illegal condition will not be saved under the *cy pres* doctrine when the will contains an express reversionary clause or gift over. The Maryland cases dealing with the *cy pres* doctrine have not involved *illegal* bequests. Rather, they have involved charitable bequests which could not be carried out for other reasons. Even in this situation, however, where the testator's intent is not contrary to law and public policy, the Maryland cases have not adopted the absolute rule contended for by University Hospital. Instead, the presence or absence of a gift over is merely one factor among many in determining whether the testator had a general charitable intent and whether the *cy pres* doctrine should be applied to save the charitable bequest at issue.

Today in Maryland, there are few if any public policies stronger than the policy against discrimination based on race or color.

We continue to adhere to the holding in *Fleishman v. Bregel*, *supra*, 174 Md. 87, that where a condition attached to a bequest is clearly illegal and violates a strong public policy, the illegal portion of the condition should be excised and the bequest enforced without regard for the illegal condition. Moreover, this principle is consistent with the purpose of the *cy pres* statute, and, therefore, is fully applicable to illegal conditions attached to charitable bequests.

The illegal racially discriminatory condition in Dr. Coggins's will violates Maryland public policy to as great an extent as the illegal condition involved in the *Fleishman* case. Consequently the provisions of the will should be administered as if the word "white" was not contained in the bequest to the Keswick Home.

JUDGMENT OF THE CIRCUIT COURT FOR BALTIMORE CITY REVERSED, AND THE CASE IS REMANDED TO THAT COURT FOR FURTHER PROCEEDINGS CONSISTENT WITH THIS OPINION. COSTS TO BE PAID BY THE APPELLEE, UNIVERSITY OF MARYLAND MEDICAL SYSTEM CORPORATION.

E. DESTRUCTION OF PROPERTY

EYERMAN V. MERCANTILE TRUST CO., N.A.
Missouri Court of Appeals, St. Louis District, Division One, 1975
524 S.W.2d 210

RENDLEN, J.

Plaintiffs appeal from denial of their petition seeking injunction to prevent demolition of a house at #4 Kingsbury Place in the City of St. Louis. The action is brought by individual neighboring property owners and certain trustees for the Kingsbury Place Subdivision. We reverse.

Louise Woodruff Johnston, owner of the property in question, died January 14, 1973, and by her will directed the executor "... to cause our home at 4 Kingsbury Place ... to be razed and to sell the land upon which it is located ... and to transfer the proceeds of the sale ... to the residue of my estate." Plaintiffs assert that razing the home will adversely affect their property rights, violate the terms of the subdivision trust indenture for Kingsbury Place, produce an actionable private nuisance and is contrary to public policy.

The area involved is a "private place" established in 1902 by trust indenture which provides that Kingsbury Place and Kingsbury Terrace will be so maintained, improved, protected and managed as to be desirable for private residences. The trustees are empowered to protect and preserve "Kingsbury Place" from encroachment, trespass, nuisance or injury, and it is "the intention of these presents, forming a general scheme of improving and maintaining said property as desirable residence property of the highest class." The covenants run with the land and the indenture empowers lot owners or the trustees to bring suit to enforce them.

Except for one vacant lot, the subdivision is occupied by handsome, spacious two and three-story homes, and all must be used exclusively as private residences. The indenture generally regulates location, costs and similar features for any structures in the subdivision, and limits construction of subsidiary structures except those that may beautify the property, for example, private stables, flower houses, conservatories, play houses or buildings of similar character.

On trial the temporary restraining order was dissolved and all issues found against the plaintiffs.

Defendants question plaintiffs' standing to bring this suit, arguing that plaintiffs are not parties in interest who may invoke the rights of beneficiaries of the will against a trustee to enforce a trust or enjoin its breach. This is not such a suit. Plaintiffs' action is not to invoke the rights of beneficiaries of the will for enforcement of a trust or to enjoin its breach; instead, they seek protection of competing interests shared by themselves and the general community against a capricious condition of a will directing the defendant-executor to destroy estate property. If appellants are successful, important rights personal to plaintiffs and the public will be vindicated and it is only incidental that the effect on decedent's estate will increase funds available for distribution to the beneficiaries. Here the gift is not a devise of particular land to specific beneficiaries, but instead testatrix's house is to be razed and the lot converted to cash. From this we find no intent to preserve the land for a settled purpose or the use of any person or group; instead, it becomes a gift of money, indefinite as to amount, for the residual estate.

The issues, simply stated, involve: (1) Private nuisance; (2) enforcement of restrictive covenants and (3) public policy.

Plaintiffs clearly have standing to raise the issues of nuisance abatement and enforcement of the restrictive covenants in the subdivision indenture. Persons threatened with wrongful interference of property rights may seek injunction against a threatened nuisance and the trust indenture regulating Kingsbury Place empowers the trustees or any property owner to bring suit to enforce the covenants. * * *

* * *

Whether #4 Kingsbury Place should be razed is an issue of public policy involving individual property rights and the community at large. The plaintiffs have pleaded and proved facts sufficient to show a personal, legally protectible interest.

Demolition of the dwelling will result in an unwarranted loss to this estate, the plaintiffs and the public. The uncontradicted testimony was that the current value of the house and land is $40,000.00; yet the estate could expect no more than $5,000.00 for the empty lot, less the cost of demolition at $4,350.00, making a grand loss of $39,350.33 if the unexplained and capricious direction to the executor is effected. Only $650.00 of the $40,000.00 asset would remain.

Kingsbury Place is an area of high architectural significance, representing excellence in urban space utilization. Razing the home will depreciate adjoining property values by an estimated $10,000.00 and effect corresponding losses for other neighborhood homes. The cost of constructing a house of comparable size and architectural exquisiteness would approach $200,000.00.

The importance of this house to its neighborhood and the community is reflected in the action of the St. Louis Commission on Landmarks and Urban Design designating Kingsbury Place as a landmark of the City of St. Louis. This designation, under consideration prior to the institution of this suit, points up the aesthetic and historical qualities of the area and assists in stabilizing Central West End St. Louis. It was testified by the Landmarks Commission chairman that the private place concept, once unique to St. Louis, fosters higher home maintenance standards and is among the most effective methods for stabilizing otherwise deteriorating neighborhoods. The executive director of Heritage St. Louis, an organization operating to preserve the architecture of the city, testified to the importance of preserving Kingsbury Place intact:

> "The reasons (sic) for making Kingsbury Place a landmark is that it is a definite piece of urban design and architecture. It starts out with monumental gates on Union. There is a long corridor of space, furnished with a parkway in the center, with houses on either side of the street, ... The existence of this piece of architecture depends on the continuity of the (sic) both sides. Breaks in this continuity would be as holes in this wall, and would detract from the urban design qualities of the streets. And the richness of the street is this belt of green lot on either side, with rich tapestry of the individual houses along the sides. Many of these houses are landmarks in themselves, but they add up to much more ... I would say Kingsbury Place, as a whole, with its design, with its important houses ... is a most significant piece of urban design by any standard."

To remove #4 Kingsbury from the street was described as having the effect of a missing front tooth. The space created would permit direct access to Kingsbury Place from the adjacent alley, increasing the likelihood the lot will be subject to uses detrimental to the health, safety and beauty of the neighborhood. The mere possibility that a future owner might build a new home with the inherent architectural significance of the present dwelling offers little support to sustain the condition for destruction.

We are constrained to take judicial notice of the pressing need of the community for dwelling units as demonstrated by recent U.S. Census Bureau figures showing a decrease of more than 14% in St. Louis City housing units during the decade of the 60's. This decrease occurs in the face of housing growth in the remainder of the metropolitan area. It becomes apparent that no individual, group of individuals nor the community generally benefits from the senseless destruction of the house; instead, all are harmed and only the caprice of the dead testatrix is served. Destruction of the house harms the neighbors, detrimentally affects the community, causes monetary loss in excess of $39,000.00 to the estate and is without benefit to the dead woman. No reason, good or bad, is suggested by the will or record for the eccentric condition. This is not a living person who seeks to exercise a right to reshape or dispose of her property; instead, it is an attempt by will to confer the power to destroy upon an executor who is given no other interest in the property. To allow an executor to exercise such power stemming from apparent whim and caprice of the testatrix contravenes public policy.

The Missouri Supreme Court held in State ex rel. McClintock v. Guinotte, 204 S.W. 806, 808 (banc 1918), that the taking of property by inheritance or will is not an absolute or natural right but one created by the laws of the sovereign power. The court points out the state "may foreclose the right absolutely, or it may grant the right upon conditions precedent, which conditions, if not otherwise violative of our Constitution, will have to be complied with before the right of descent and distribution (whether under the law or by will) can exist." Further, this power of the state is one of inherent sovereignty which allows the state to "say what becomes of the property of a person, when death forecloses his right to control it." McClintock v. Guinotte, *supra* at 808, 809. While living, a person may manage, use or dispose of his money or property with fewer restraints than a decedent by will. One is generally restrained from wasteful expenditure or destructive inclinations by the natural desire to enjoy his property or to accumulate it during his lifetime. Such considerations however have not tempered the extravagance or eccentricity of the testamentary disposition here on which there is no check except the courts.

In the early English case of Egerton v. Brownlow, 10 Eng. Rep. 359, 417 (H.L.C. 1853) it is stated: "The owner of an estate may himself do many things which he could not (by a condition) compel his successor to do. One example is sufficient. He may leave his land uncultivated, but he cannot by a condition compel his successor to do so. The law does not interfere with the owner and compel him to cultivate his land, (though it may be for the public good that land should be cultivated) so far the law respects ownership; but when, by a condition, he attempts to compel his successor to do what is against the public good, the law steps in and pronounces the condition void and allows the devisee to enjoy the estate free from the condition." A more recent application of this principle is found in M'Caig's Trustees v. Kirk-Session of the United Free Church of Lismore, et al., 1915 Sess.Cas. 426 (Scot.). There, by codicil to her will, testatrix ordered certain statues erected to honor her family in a tower built in the form of an amphitheater on a hill. Balustrades were to be erected so that even the public would have no access inside the tower. Special provision was made for keeping out the public and the ground enclosed was expressly declared to be a private enclosure. There were no living descendants of any member of the family who might, if so permitted, take pleasure in contemplating the proposed statutes. The court states at 434: "If a bequest such as in Miss M'Ciag's codicil were held good, money would require to be expended in perpetuity merely gratifying an absurd whim which has neither reason nor public sentiment in its favor." In striking down the provisions of the codicil, the court further notes that there is indeed a "difference between what a man, uncognosed, may do at his own hand, and what the law will support under the provisions of his will . . . therefore, without being illegal in the sense of being contrary to any express rule of the common law or contrary to any statute, the principle of public policy will prevent such post-mortem expenditure. Whether the act is sufficiently contrary to public policy to warrant the court's interference must depend on the degree to which it is against public policy." The court further observed that the erection of the eleven statues "would be of no benefit to anyone except those connected with the carrying out of the work, for whose interest she expresses no concern." M'Caig's Trustees v. Kirk-Session of the United Free Church of Lismore, et al., supra at 438. In the case sub judice, testatrix similarly expressed no such concern; nothing in the will or record indicates an intent to benefit any razing company called upon to destroy her beautiful home.

In the case of In re Scott's Will, Board of Commissioners of Rice County v. Scott et al., 88 Minn. 386 (1903), the Supreme Court of Minnesota stated, when considering the provision of a will directing the executor to destroy money belonging to the estate: "We assume, for purpose of this decision, that the direction in the codicil to the executor to destroy all of the residue of the money or cash or evidences of credit belonging to the estate was void." See also Restatement, Second, Trusts § 124, at 267: "Although a person may deal capriciously with his own property, his self interest ordinarily will restrain him from doing so. Where an attempt is made to confer such a power upon a person who is given no other interest in the property, there is no such restraint and it is against public policy to allow him to exercise the power if the purpose is merely capricious." The text is followed by this illustration: "A bequeaths $1,000.00 to B in trust to throw the money into the sea. B holds the money upon a resulting trust for the estate of A and is liable to the estate of A if he throws the money into the sea." Restatement, supra at 267.

In Brown v. Burdett, 21 Chan.Div. 667 (Eng.1882), the testatrix devised her house with directions that the doors and windows be boarded, shuttered, bricked and sealed, to be held by the trustees in this wasteful manner for twenty years and thereafter to the named beneficiaries as tenants in common. This provision was stricken by the court at 673: "I think I must 'unseal' this useless, undisposed of property." The provision of the will was void and found to be a nullity and the court declared that the house and premises were undisposed of by will for a term of twenty years from the testatrix's death.

In Restatement, Second, Trusts § 124(g), at 267, the writers suggest this hypothesis as an illustration of the principle involved in Brown v. Burdett, *supra*:

> "A devises a house and lot to B 'in trust' to block up the windows and doors and leave the house vacant for 20 years. B holds the house and lot upon a resulting trust for the estate of A and is liable to the estate of A if he blocks up the windows and doors."

It is important to note that the purposes of testatrix's trust will not be defeated by injunction instead, the proceeds from the sale of the property will pass into the residual estate and thence to the trust estate as intended, and only the capricious destructive condition will be enjoined.

In Colonial Trust Co. v. Brown et al., 105 Conn. 261 (1926) the court invalidated, as against public policy, the provisions of a will restricting erection of buildings more than three stories in height and forbidding leases of more than one year on property known as "The Exchange Place" in the heart of the City of Waterbury. The court stated:

> " 'As a general rule, a testator has the right to impose such conditions as he pleases upon a beneficiary as conditions precedent to the vesting of an estate in him, or to the enjoyment of a trust estate by him as cestui que trust. He may not, however, impose one that is uncertain, unlawful or opposed to public policy.'

*   *   *   *   *   *

In the instant case, the length of time during which the testator directed that the property should remain in the trust, and the complete uncertainty as to the individuals to whom it would ultimately go, preclude any thought of an intent on his part to forbid the cumbering of the property by long leases or the burdening of it with large buildings, lest the beneficiaries be embarrassed in the development of it along such lines as they might themselves prefer. The only other purpose which can be reasonably attributed to him is to compel the trustee to follow his own peculiar ideas as to the proper and advantageous way to manage such properties. That the restrictions are opposed to the interests of the beneficiaries of the trust and that they are imprudent and unwise is made clear by the statement of agreed facts, but that is not all, for their effect is not confined to the beneficiaries. The Exchange Place property is located at a corner of the public square in the very center of the city of Waterbury, in the heart of the financial and retail business district, is as valuable as any land in the city, and is most favorably adapted for a large building containing stores and offices, and the homestead is located in the region of changing character, so that its most available use cannot now be determined. To impress the restrictions in question upon these properties, as the statement of agreed facts makes clear, makes it impossible to obtain from them a proper income return or to secure the most desirable and stable class of tenants, requires for the maintenance of the buildings a proportion of income greatly in excess of that usual in the case of such properties, and will be likely to preclude their proper development and natural use. The effect of such conditions cannot but react disadvantageously upon neighboring properties, and to continue them, as the testator intended, for perhaps 75 years or even more, would carry a serious threat against the proper growth and development of the parts of the city in which the lands in question are situated. *The restrictions militate too strongly against the interests of the beneficiaries and the public welfare to be sustained, particularly when it is remembered that they are designed to benefit no one, and are harmful to all persons interested, and we hold them invalid as against public policy.*" l.c. 564. (Emphasis ours.)

The term "public policy" cannot be comprehensively defined in specific terms but the phrase "against public policy" has been characterized as that which conflicts with the morals of the time and contravenes any established interest of society. Acts are said to be against public policy "when the law refuses to enforce or recognize them, on the ground that they have a mischievous tendency, so as to be injurious to the interests of the state, apart from illegality or immorality.'" Dille v. St. Luke's Hospital, 196 S.W.2d 615, 620 (1946); Brawner v. Brawner, 327 S.W.2d 808, 812 (Mo. banc 1959).

Public policy may be found in the Constitution, statutes and judicial decisions of this state or the nation. But in a case of first impression where there are no guiding statutes, judicial decisions or constitutional provisions, "a judicial determination of the question becomes an expression of public policy provided it is so plainly right as to be supported by the general will." In the absence of guidance from authorities in its own jurisdiction, courts may look to the judicial decisions of sister states for assistance in discovering expressions of public policy.

Although public policy may evade precise, objective definition, it is evident from the authorities cited that this senseless destruction serving no apparent good purpose is to be held in disfavor. A well-ordered society cannot tolerate the waste and destruction of resources when such acts directly affect important interests of other members of that society. It is clear that property owners in the neighborhood of #4 Kingsbury, the St. Louis Community as a whole and the beneficiaries of testatrix's estate will be severely injured should the provisions of the will be followed. No benefits are present to balance against this injury and we hold that to allow the condition in the will would be in violation of the public policy of this state.

Having thus decided, we do not reach the plaintiffs' contentions regarding enforcement of the restrictions in the Kingsbury Place trust indenture and actionable private nuisance, though these contentions may have merit.[5]

The judgment is reversed and the cause remanded to the Circuit Court to enter judgment as prayed.

CLEMENS, J., dissenting.

I dissent.

* * *

The leading Missouri case on public policy as that doctrine applies to a testator's right to dispose of property is In re Rahn's Estate, 291 S.W. 120(1, 2) (banc 1927), cert. den. 274 U.S. 745. There, an executor refused to pay a bequest on the ground the beneficiary was an enemy alien, and the bequest was therefore against public policy. The court denied that contention: "We may say, at the outset, that the policy of the law favors freedom in the testamentary disposition of property and that it is the duty of the courts to give effect to the intention of the testator, as expressed in his will, provided such intention does not contravene an established rule of law." * * * In resting its decision on public-policy grounds, the majority opinion has transgressed the limitations declared by our Supreme Court in Rahn's Estate.

The right of these plaintiffs to injunctive relief is by no means clear and injunction is "a harsh remedy, granted only in clear cases." American Pamcor, Inc., v. Klote, 438 S.W.2d 287[1] (Mo.App.1969). It requires judicial imagination to hold, as the majority does, that the mere presence of a second vacant lot on Kingsbury Place violates public policy.

---

[5]   The dissenting opinion suggests this case be decided under the general rule that an owner has exclusive control and the right to untrammeled use of real property. Although Maxims of this sort are attractive in their simplicity, standing alone they seldom suffice in a complex case. None of the cited cases pertains to the qualified right of testatrix to impose, post mortem, a condition upon her executor requiring an unexplained destruction of estate property; instead, they involve, respectively, surface water, use of property for commercial purposes and restrictive covenants as to subdivision lot sizes. Each acknowledges the principle of an owner's "free use" as the starting point but all recognize competing interests of the community and other owners of great importance. Accordingly, the general principle of "free and untrammeled" use is markedly narrowed, supporting in each case a result opposite that urged by the dissent in the case at bar.

As much as our aesthetic sympathies might lie with neighbors near a house to be razed, those sympathies should not so interfere with our considered legal judgment as to create a questionable legal precedent. Mrs. Johnston had the right during her lifetime to have her house razed, and I find nothing which precludes her right to order her executor to raze the house upon her death. It is clear that "the law favors the free and untrammeled use of real property." Gibbs v. Cass, 431 S.W.2d 662[2] (Mo.App.1968). This applies to testamentary dispositions. Mississippi Valley Trust Co. v. Ruhland, 222 S.W.2d 750[2] (1949). An owner has exclusive control over the use of his property subject only to the limitation that such use may not *substantially impair another's right to peaceably enjoy his property*. City of Fredericktown v. Osborn, 429 S.W.2d 17[2, 3] (Mo.App.1968), Reutner v. Vouga, 367 S.W.2d 34(11–13) (Mo.App.1963). Plaintiffs have not shown that such impairment will arise from the mere presence of another vacant lot on Kingsbury Place.

I find no plain error in the trial court's denial of injunctive relief, and on the merits I would affirm the trial court's judgment. Because of plaintiffs' defective brief, however, I would dismiss the appeal.

Franz Kafka, who died from tuberculosis in 1924 at the age of 40, left his manuscripts to his former fellow law student, subsequent friend and editor, Max Brod. (Recall the testator writing, "my Scottish breadman" in The Hermeneutics File by Thomas C. Grey, quoted above.) In what has been called a will, Kafka left instructions to Brod. He set out some stories "that can stand" which included THE JUDGMENT and THE METAMORPHOSIS. As for the rest, his literary res, everything else was to be burned. But Brod, also a writer, ignored those instructions. In 1939, before the Nazis closed the Czech border, Brod left Prague and made his way to Palestine with Kafka's papers. Brod edited and published works such as THE TRIAL, THE CASTLE, and AMERIKA. Brod died in 1968, leaving instructions for his secretary Esther Hoffe to transfer the Kafka papers to an academic institution. But dying wishes were again defied; Hoffe kept some of the papers. She sold the manuscript for THE TRIAL at auction for £1,000,000 and passed other manuscripts to her daughters when she died in 2007 at age 101. Israel demanded that Hoffe's heirs surrender the documents, arguing that Brod's will should be honored. After a Kafkaesque series of judicial proceedings, the

National Library of Israel won the rights to the archives in 2016 and, in 2019, a court in Zurich upheld the Israeli decision and allowed safe-deposit boxes to be opened and their contents to be shipped from Switzerland to the Library. In 2021, the Library announced that it had published its entire collection online. Should Brod have followed Kafka's instructions rather than preserving the works that would transform Kafka into one of the most celebrated authors of the twentieth century? Should a court order Brod to follow Kafka's instructions?

In the United States, the laws of succession give substantial authority to transferors, even while they are dead. But their control is not unfettered. The law imposes limits on the dead hand, sometimes freeing assets and successors from its grasp. The legal struggle between the desires of transferors to control the future and the yearning of transferees to be free of the past has persisted for centuries. That conflict will continue. In it, there is much human happiness at stake, and there is no guarantee that current law strikes the optimal balance for today, much less for tomorrow.

INDEX

References are to Pages